EXPERIENCING POWER
GENERATING AUTHORITY

Penn Museum International Research Conferences
Holly Pittman, Series Editor, Conference Publications

Volume 6: Proceedings of "Experiencing Power—Generating Authority: Cosmos and Politics in the Ideology of Kingship in Ancient Egypt and Mesopotamia," Philadelphia, November 5–11, 2007.

PMIRC volumes

1. *Landscapes of Movement: Trails, Paths, and Roads in Anthropological Perspective,* edited by James E. Snead, Clark L. Erickson, and J. Andrew Darling, 2009
2. *Mapping Mongolia: Situating Mongolia in the World from Geologic Time to the Present,* edited by Paula L.W. Sabloff, 2011
3. *Sustainable Lifeways: Cultural Persistence in an Ever-changing Environment,* edited by Naomi F. Miller, Katherine M. Moore, and Kathleen Ryan, 2011
4. *Literacy in the Persianate World. Writing and the Social Order,* edited by Brian Spooner and William L. Hanaway, 2012
5. *Evolution of Mind, Brain, and Culture,* edited by Gary Hatfield and Holly Pittman, 2013

EXPERIENCING POWER, GENERATING AUTHORITY

Cosmos, Politics, and the Ideology of Kingship in Ancient Egypt and Mesopotamia

EDITED BY

Jane A. Hill, Philip Jones, and Antonio J. Morales

University of Pennsylvania Museum of Archaeology and Anthropology
Philadelphia

Library of Congress Cataloging-in-Publication Data

ISBN-13: 978-1-934536-64-3
ISBN-10: 1-934536-64-4

© 2013 by the University of Pennsylvania Museum of Archaeology and Anthropology
Philadelphia, PA
All rights reserved. Published 2013

Published for the University of Pennsylvania Museum of Archaeology and Anthropology
by the University of Pennsylvania Press.

Printed in the United States of America on acid-free paper.

Contents

List of Figures	vii
List of Tables	xi
Abbreviations	xiii
Glossary	xvii
Contributors	xxiii
Acknowledgments	xxvii
Foreword	xxix

INTRODUCTION

Comparing Kingship in Ancient Egypt and Mesopotamia: Cosmos, Politics and Landscape   3
Jane A. Hill, Philip Jones, and Antonio J. Morales

I. COSMOS

1 *Propaganda and Performance at the Dawn of the State*   33
 Ellen Morris

2 *"I Am the Sun of Babylon": Solar Aspects of Royal Power in Old Babylonian Mesopotamia*   65
 Dominique Charpin

3 *Rising Suns and Falling Stars: Assyrian Kings and the Cosmos*   97
 Eckart Frahm

4 *Texts before Writing: Reading (Proto-)Egyptian Poetics of Power*   121
 Ludwig D. Morenz

5 *Images of Tammuz: The Intersection of Death, Divinity, and Royal Authority in Ancient Mesopotamia*   151
 JoAnn Scurlock

II. POLITICS

6 *Building the Pharaonic State: Territory, Elite and Power in Ancient Egypt in the 3rd Millennium BCE* — 185
Juan Carlos Moreno García

7 *The Management of the Royal Treasure: Palace Archives and Palatial Economy in the Ancient Near East* — 219
Walther Sallaberger

8 *Egyptian Kingship during the Old Kingdom* — 257
Miroslav Bárta

9 *All the King's Men: Authority, Kingship and the Rise of the Elites in Assyria* — 285
Beate Pongratz-Leisten

10 *Kingship as Racketeering: The Royal Tombs and Death Pits at Ur, Mesopotamia Reinterpreted from the Standpoint of Conflict Theory* — 311
D. Bruce Dickson

III. LANDSCAPE

11 *Mesopotamian Kings and the Built Environment* — 331
Michael Roaf

12 *Expeditions to the Wadi Hammamat: Context and Concept* — 361
Alan B. Lloyd

13 *"Imaginal" Landscapes in Assyrian Imperial Monuments* — 383
Mehmet-Ali Ataç

Appendix 1: *Chronologies for Ancient Egypt and the Near East* — 427
Appendix 2: *Map of Major Egyptian Sites* — 429
Appendix 3: *Map of Major Mesopotamian Sites* — 431

Index — 433

Figures

1.1	The Scorpion macehead; Oxford, Ashmolean Museum E.3632	36
1.2	The Narmer macehead; Ashmolean E. 3631	36
1.3	The Narmer palette; Cairo J.E. 14716, C.G. 32169	37
1.4	Narmer's label from Abydos	38
1.5	Narmer's ivory cylinder seal from Hierakonpolis	42
1.6	Reconstruction of Min colossi	47
4.1	Ceremonial palette; Oxford, Ashmolean E.3924	123
4.2	Development of semiophores	124
4.3	Development of semiophores in the 4th millennium	125
4.4	Davis comb (MMA 30.8.224); rows of animals = iconographic list	126
4.5	Knife-handle from Abu-Zeidan; Brooklyn Museum 09.889.118	127
4.6	Pitt-Rivers knife-handle; British Museum EA 68512	129
4.7	Jackal-human hybrid playing the flute, detail of ceremonial palette; Ashmolean E.3924	130
4.8	Kokopelli (hunchbacked flute-player); Southwestern Puebloan rock art	130
4.9	"Marvels of the East", detail of ceremonial palette; Ashmolean E.3924	131
4.10	Giraffe, detail of ceremonial palette; Ashmolean E.3924	132
4.11	Distribution of animals on ceremonial palette; Ashmolean E.3924	134
4.12	Knife-handle from Gebel el-Tarif	136
4.13	Reading the Davis comb; MMA 30.8.224	136
4.14	Detail of ostrich on the ceremonial palette; Oxford, Ashmolean E.3924	140
4.15	Detail of ibis on the ceremonial palette; Louvre E 11052	140
4.16	Pictorial "text" on a cylinder seal impression from Uruk; iconic narrative of offering	141

4.17	Cylinder seal from Uruk; symmetrical composition in boustrophedon	142
4.18	Cultic vessel from Uruk; Baghdad Museum 19606	143
4.19	Cultic vessel from Maikop culture; Hermitage Museum	144
6.1	Map of Egypt and the Western Desert	186
6.2	Map of Egypt in the 3rd millennium BC	191
6.3	Provincial administration in 19 Upper Egyptian nomes	197
8.1	Volume of the Old Kingdom pyramids	263
8.2	Comparison of the built area of individual funerary temples of the Old Kingdom kings and the areas of the storerooms within them	265
12.1	The Eastern Desert	361
12.2	Greywacke quarries in the Wadi Hammamat	362
12.3	One of many representations in the Wadi of the resident deities. Pharaoh makes offerings to Min	364
13.1	Ashurnasirpal II flanked by bird-headed *apkallus*, Northwest Palace of Ashurnasirpal II at Nimrud; British Museum, ANE 124584-5	384
13.2	Babylonian Map of the World, probably from Sippar, ca. 700–500 BCE; British Museum, ANE 92687	386
13.3	Detail of marine scene with transport of wood showing a winged human-headed bull (*lamassu*), Palace of Sargon II in Khorsabad; Paris, Louvre	399
13.4	Detail of marine scene with transport of wood showing a winged bull (Bull of Heaven?), Palace of Sargon II in Khorsabad; Paris, Louvre	399
13.5	Relief decorations in the Botanical Room of the Festival Hall (Akhmenu) of Thutmose III, Temple of Amun, Karnak, Thebes, Egypt	402
13.6	Drawing of the ivory pyxis found in Assur Tomb 45	404
13.7	The Assyrian "sacred tree" flanked by two bird-headed *apkallus*, Northwest Palace of Ashurnasirpal II at Nimrud; British Museum, ANE 124583.	405
13.8	One side of the Black Obelisk of Shalmaneser III found at Nimrud; British Museum, ANE 118885	406
13.9	Detail of Figure 8	407

13.10	Detail of one side of the Black Obelisk of Shalmaneser III; British Museum, ANE 118885	408
13.11	Detail of Figure 10	409
13.12	One side of the Black Obelisk of Shalmaneser III; British Museum, ANE 118885	410
13.13	Detail of Figure 12	411
13.14	One side of the Black Obelisk of Shalmaneser III; British Museum, ANE 118885	412
13.15	Relief panel showing royal gardens, North Palace of Ashurbanipal at Nineveh; British Museum, ANE 124939	414
13.16	Detail of the "Garden Scene" of Ashurbanipal showing the king banqueting with his queen, North Palace of Ashurbanipal at Nineveh; British Museum, ANE 124920	415

Tables

7.1	Overview of the main archive (L.2769) from Palace G at Ebla (24th c. BC)	221
7.2	Luxury goods in the archives of Ebla, Puzrish-Dagan (Ur III), and Mari	224
7.3	Silver at Ur III Umma: the situation in the province (amounts given in minas, shekels, and grains)	229
7.4	Royal gift of silver rings converted to everyday values	234
7.5	Number of personnel in the palace at Ebla, here listed in decreasing order of the average number of persons	236
7.6	Specified income of silver in the Drehem treasure archive; amounts given in talents, minas, and shekels	238
7.7	Amounts of silver expended for trade by the palace of Ebla during the years Ibbi-zikir 5 and 10	239
7.8	Expenditure of silver for purchases for one year according to the selected annual accounts of Ebla:	
	(a) MEE 10, 29, Ibbi-zikir 5: 108 minas spent for purchase, i.e., 24% of total expenditures	240
	(b) MEE 12, 36, Ibbi-zikir 10: 66,16.8 minas spent for purchase, i.e. 19% of total expenditures	241
7.9	Silver "expended" (E_3) and "stored/present" ($AL_6.\hat{G}AL_2$) in the palace of Ebla (amounts per year in minas); MEE 10 29 and MEE 12 36 added	243
11.1	Selected major new foundations or centers extensively rebuilt by rulers of Mesopotamia	345
11.2	Assyrian kings and their building inscriptions from the 11th–9th centuries BC	349

Abbreviations

AA = *American Antiquity*
AbB = *Altbabylonische Briefe in Umschrift und Übersetzung*
ABL = *Assyrian and Babylonian Letters*
AfO = *Archiv für Orientforschung*
AnOr = *Analecta Orientalia*, Rome
AOAT = *Alter Orient und Altes Testament*
ARET = *Archivi reali di Ebla, testi*. Rome: Missione Archeologica Italiana in Siria
ARM = *Archives Royales de Mari* (= Textes Cuneiformes, Musées du Louvre, 22–31)
Asb A = Assurbanipal's Prisma A
Ash. = Ashmolean Museum of Art and Archaeology, University of Oxford
AUCT = Andrews University Cuneiform Texts. Berrien Springs, MI: Andrews University Press
AVDAIK = Archäologische Veröffentlichungen des Deutschen Archäologischen Instituts, Abteilung Kairo
BACE = *Bulletin of the Australian Center of Egyptology*
BAfO = *Beihefte zum Archiv für Orientforschung*
BaM = *Baghdader Mitteilungen*
BAR = British Archaeological Reports
BIN = *Babylonian Inscriptions in the Collection of James B. Nies*. New Haven: Yale University Press
CA = *Current Anthropology*
CAD = Chicago *Assyrian Dictionary*
CAJ = *Cambridge Archaeological Journal*
CBS = Catalogue of the Babylonian Section, UPenn Museum, Philadelphia
CdE = *Chronique d'Égypte*
CDOG = *Colloquium der Deutschen Orient-Gesellschaft*
CF = Cairo fragment of the Palermo Stone
CM = Cuneiform Monographs, Groningen

CNI = Carsten Niebuhr Institute
CRIPEL = Cahiers de Recherches de l'Institut de Papyrologie et d'Égyptologie de Lille
CRRAI = Comptes Rendus de la Rencontre Assyriologique Internationale
CT = Cuneiform Texts from Babylonian Tablets in the British Museum. London: British Museum
CTN = Cuneiform Texts from Nimrud. London: British School of Archaeology in Iraq.
DP = *Documents présargoniques.* Paris: Leroux
EA = *Egyptian Archaeology*
FM = *Florilegium marianum*
GM = *Göttinger Miszellen*
HdOr = *Handbuch der Orientalistik*
HWP = *Historisches Wörterbuch der Philosophie*
IFAO = Institut Français d'Archaologie Orientale du Caire, Cairo
JANER = *Journal of Ancient Near Eastern Religions*
JAOS = *Journal of the American Oriental Society*
JARCE = *Journal of the American Research Center in Egypt*
JCS = *Journal of Cuneiform Studies*
JEA = *Journal of Egyptian Archaeology*
JEOL = *Jaarbericht van het vooraziatisch-egyptisch Genootschap Ex Oriente Lux*
JESHO = *Journal of the Economic and Social History of the Orient*
JNES = *Journal of Near Eastern Studies*
JSOT = *Journal for the Study of the Old Testament*
JSS = *Journal of Semitic Studies*
JWP = *Journal of World Prehistory*
KAR = *Keilschrifttexte aus Assur religiösen Inhalts*
LÄ = *Lexikon der Ägyptologie*
LAS = Parpola, Simo. *Letters from Assyrian Scholars to the Kings Esarhaddon and Assurbanipal,* I (= AOAT 5/1, 1970); II (= AOAT 5/2, 1983)
LAPO = Littératures anciennnes du Proche-Orient
LingAeg = *Lingua Aegyptia*
LKA = *Literarische Keilschrifttexte aus Assur*
MARI = *Mari, Annales de Recherches Interdisciplinaires*
MDAIK = *Mitteilungen des Deutschen Archäologischen Instituts,* Abteilung Kairo
MEE = Materiali epigrafici di Ebla. Naples: Istituto Universitario Orientale

MMA = The Metropolitan Museum of Art, New York
MOS = Midden-Oosten Studies, Leiden
MVN = Materiali per il Vocabolario Neosumerico. Rome: Multigrafia Editrice
NABU = *Nouvelles Assyriologiques Brèves et Utilitaires*
Nik 1 = Nikol'skij, Michail Vasil'evič. 1908. *Dokumenty chozjajstvennoj otčetnostj drevnejšej ėpochi Chaldei iz sobranija N.P. Lichačeva*. St. Petersburg: Gateuk
NIN = *Journal of Gender Studies in Antiquity*
OBO = Orbis Biblicus et Orientalis
OECT = *Oxford Editions of Cuneiform Texts*
OIP = Oriental Institute Publications, Chicago
OLA = Orientalia Lovaniensia Analecta
OLZ = *Orientalistische Literaturzeitung*
OrNS = *Orientalia,* Nova Series
PBS = Publications of the Babylonian Section, Penn Museum, Philadelphia
PdÄ = Probleme der Ägyptologie
PNA = *Prosopography of the Neo-Assyrian Empire*
PS = Palermo Stone (translations used from Wilkinson 2000; see bibliography in Morris's chapter)
PT = Pyramid Texts (translations used from Faulkner, R.O. 1969. *The Ancient Egyptian Pyramid Texts.* Oxford: Clarendon Press
RA = *Revue d'Assyriologie et d'Archéologie Orientale*
RdE = *Revue d'Égyptologie*
RIMA = Royal Inscriptions of Mesopotamia. Assyrian Periods. Toronto
RTC = *Recueil de tablettes chaldéennes.* Paris: Leroux
SAA = State Archives of Assyria
SAAB = *State Archives of Assyria Bulletin*
SAAS = State Archives of Assyria, Helsinki
SAALT = State Archives of Assyria Literary Texts
SAGA = Studien zur Archäologie und Geschichte altägyptens, Heidelberg
SAK = *Studien zur Altägyptischen Kultur*
Santag 6 = Koslova, Natalia. 2000. *Ur III–Texte der St. Petersburger Eremitage.* Santag 6. Wiesbaden: Harrassowitz
SAOC = Studies in Ancient Oriental Civilizations. Chicago
StP SM = Studia Pohl, Series Maior
TCL = *Textes cunéiformes.* Musée du Louvre. Paris: Geuthner.

TCNY = Sauren, Herbert. 1978. *Les tablettes cunéiformes de l'époque d'Ur des collections de la New York Public Library.* Leuven: Peeters
TM = Registration number of objects (tablets) from Tell Mardikh/Ebla
TrDr = Genouillac, Henri de. 1911. *La trouvaille de Dréhem. Étude avec un choix de textes de Constantinople et Bruxelles.* Paris: Geuthner
UET = Ur Excavations. Texts
UF = *Ugarit Forschungen*
Urk. I = *Urkunden des Alten Reichs* I
VAB = Vorderasiatische Bibliothek
VS = *Vorderasiatische Schriftdenkmäler der königlichen/staatlichen Museen zu Berlin*
VT = *Vetus Testamentum*
WdO = *Die Welt des Orients*
WVDOG = Wissenschaftliche Veröffentlichungen der Deutschen Orient-Gesellschaft
WZKM = *Wiener Zeitschrift für die Kunde des Morgenlandes*
YOS = Yale Oriental Series
ZA = *Zeitschrift für Assyriologie und Vorderasiatische Archäologie*
ZÄS = *Zeitschrift für ägyptische Sprache und Altertumskunde*
ZAW = *Zeitschrift für die Alttestamentliche Wissenschaft*

Glossary

1.1 AKKADIAN

abum – father
adê – covenant
andurârum – remission
awīlum – (a legal category of person)
barû – to watch over
bārû – haruspex (religious official who inspects the entrails of sacrificial animals for omens)
bêl purussī – "master of decisions" (epithet)
birbirru – radiance
dayyānu – judge
elûtum – highness
^{lú}*EME.SAG*^{meš} – important message or carrier of important messages
ešēru – to direct oneself steadily
eṭem kimti – a type of ghost
eṭemmu – ghost
gamlum – a divine weapon
haṭṭu – rod
ilku – corvée (unpaid labor owed in return for the right to hold a particular piece of land)
ilûtum – divinity
ina saparrim – "through/with a net," a description of a type of oath
izuzzum – to stand, to be present
kakkabī – "my star" (royal epithet)
kakkubu – star
kânu – to be stable
kayyamānu – "the steady one," an epithet of the planet Saturn
kimtu – family
kippatu – ring
kispum – ancestor cult
kittu u mīšaru – truth and justice
lisānu rēštu – important message

LÚ.ŠAMÁN.LÁ TUR – junior student
lumāšē – astral constellations
MAŠ.MAŠ É Aššur – chief exorcist of the Temple of Ashur
MAŠ.MAŠ TUR – junior exorcist
maṭlat, maṭṭaltu – mirror
meḫret, meḫru – counterpart
melammu – radiance
mîšarum – justice, redress
mu-ša-lum, mušālu – mirror
muškēnum – a social status
muštēširu – royal epithet, "he who guides aright, securer of justice"
muššulu – likeness; mirror
nadîtum – a type of priestess
namrirûtum – luminosity
nišēšu – people
nišūtu – kin
nûrum – light
pagrum – body
pisan šarrim – the king's treasure chest
rê'ûm – shepherd
salātu – kin
ṣalmu – image
ṣalmu Enlil dārû – an eternal image of Enlil
šalummatu – radiance
šamšum – the sun; a solar disk
šangû – a type of priest
šar mîšarim – "king of justice," a royal epithet
šarru – king
šarrûtum – kingship
šewerru – ring
šibirru – ring
šīr ilī/ilāni – "flesh of the gods," an epithet
šiṭir burūmê – "celestial writing"
šiṭir šamê – "celestial writing"
šubarûtum – exemption
šubtu, šubat – dwelling
šūrubtum – delivery
tamšīlu – equivalent
tarāku – to be dark
tāwītum – oracle query

terhatum – bride price
têmtum – sea
tupšarru – scribe
tupšikku – basket
ummânu – expert
wardum – servant
zaqiqu – spirit

1.2 HEBREW
gillul – idolatry
hêlēl ben šāḥar – "Bright Star son of Dawn," epithet of a heavenly body
ṣlm – graven image

1.3 PROPER NAMES
Bēl – DN
^{mul}lugal – (= "star of the king"; Regulus)
māt Aššur^{KI} – Land of Assur
MUL.APIN – an astronomical series
^{d}ṣalam-šarri – DN
^{d}šamšu Bābilim
^{d}utu – DN

1.4 SUMERIAN
al$_6$.ĝal$_2$ – stored, present
é-dub-lá-mah – a building name
é-eš-bar-zi-da – a temple name
e$_2$-gal – palace
e$_2$-mi$_2$ – "Female Quarter," a building name
e$_3$ – expended
ensi$_2$ – ruler, governor
giĝ$_4$ – shekel
ĝuruš – worker
^{tu9}guz-za – a type of cloth
kunga$_2$ – an equid
lugal – king
ma-na – mina – (a unit of measurement)
maš a-ša$_3$-ga – irrigation tax on fields
mu.du – delivered, delivery
nì-gi-na – order

nì-si-sá – redress
niĝ₂.ba – gift
nig₂.kaskal – a type of gift
niĝ₂-lim₄ – a type of cloth
niĝ₂.sam₂ – purchase
NIN – queen
sipa – shepherd
ugula mu-ús-si-rù-meš – a type of foreman

1.5 EGYPTIAN

3bḏw – sacred site of Abydos
3ḥt – horizon
Jbj – magnate, dignitary
jmj-r wpt jdw – overseer of missions of the young men
jmj-r pr n ḥwt-ᶜ3t – administrator of a great administrative center
jmj-r mšᶜ – military leader
jmj-r nwwt m3wt – overseer of the new localities
jmj-r ḥm(w)-nṯr – overseer of prophets
jmj-r z3w Šmᶜw – overseer of the phyles of Upper Egypt
jmj-r Šmᶜw – overseer of Upper Egypt
jmj-r k3t nt nzwt – overseer of the works of the king
ikr – superb, excellent
wᶜb – pure, clean
wᶜrt – regional circumscription
w3ḥ(w) – enduring
Wp-w3.wt – Opener of the Ways (jackal deity)
wr – chief
wr 10 Šmᶜw – greatest of the ten of Upper Egypt
b3w – effective power
bi3 – wonder, marvel
bi3yt – miracle, wonder
bity – King of Lower Egypt
p3ty – primeval
pr – house, home; representative local center
pr-ᶜ3 – lit. great house; pharaoh, the house the king inhabited
pr nzwt – house of the king, i.e., palace
pr-šnᶜ – production center
pr-ḏt – domain
pḥr ḥ3 inb – to circle the wall (in a ritual direction)
pzn – bread

mꜥꜣt – moral and physical order of the universe
mnḫw – efficient power
mrt – worker
mst – birth, (to be) born
nswt – king of Upper Egypt
nw – western Delta (toponym)
nwt mꜣwt – the new localities; royal agricultural domains
nfr – youthful vigor and creative force
nḥḥ – eternal
Nḫn – Hierakonpolis (location); placenta
nṯr ꜥꜣ – great god
rmnjjt – domain of a private individual
rḫ nzwt – king's acquaintance
ḥꜣtj-ꜥ – chief of a locality, mayor
ḥw – divine
ḥwt – royal administrative center, royal foundation
ḥwt-ꜥꜣt – royal agricultural center
ḥwt-wr(t) – royal executive/legal center
ḥwt-mḥꜥ – Lower Egyptian royal center
ḥwt-nbw – center for processing gold
ḥwt-šmꜥw – Upper Egyptian royal center
ḥwt-kꜣ – royal cult center
ḥwt-ṯḥnt – faience production center
ḥm-nzwt – serf of the king, servant of the king
ḥrj-tp – chief
ḥrj-tp ꜥꜣ n zpꜣt – great chief of the nome
ḥr-sbꜣ-ḫt – Horus-first-of-the-corporation-of-gods (epithet)
ḥr-tpi-ḫt – Horus-star-of-the-corporation-of-gods (epithet)
ḥsbw – work crew
ḥkꜣ – great (leader, governor)
ḥqꜣ ḥwt – governor of a royal center
ḥqꜣ ḥwt-ꜥꜣt – overseer of the great royal center
ḥtp dj nswt – "An offering that the king gives" (mortuary ritual formula)
ḥṯꜣ – bread
ḥḏ – mace; white
ḥḏt – white crown of Upper Egypt
ḫnrt – work center
ḫntj-š – palace attendants, bodyguards
ḫnw – the interior, inside
Ḫn-Nḫn – the interior of Hierakonpolis

z3 nzwt – son of the king
si3 – perception
swnw – towers (administrative unit)
sh3 – monument, memorial
sm3 šmʿ t3-mḥw – uniting Upper and Lower Egypt
sm3-t3wj – uniting the Two Lands, i.e., Upper and Lower Egypt
sr – giraffe, one who sees far, ruler
sr(w) – officials
sšm t3 – ruler of the land
stj – land of Nubia
špsy – august, noble
Šm3j – magnate
šmsw ḥr – the followers of Horus
šsp – perform (as in a miracle)
qnbtjw w – members of the council of the district
k3 – soul, ancestral spirit, essence
k3p – to cense, make offering to the divine
k3-nḫt – strong bull (royal epithet)
t3 mḥw – the Northland (in relation to Upper Egypt)
t3 nṯr – God's Land
t3ty – vizier
ṯnwt – census
ṯt – official
Dʿw – magnate, dignitary
ḏw – mountain
Ḏbʿwt – Buto (a locality)
ḏt – eternity, forever

Contributors

Mehmet-Ali Ataç
Department of Classical and Near Eastern Archaeology
Bryn Mawr College
101 North Merion Avenue
Bryn Mawr, PA 19010-2899
USA
matac@brynmawr.edu

Miroslav Bárta
Charles University
Czech Institute of Egyptology
Prague
Czech Republic
miroslav.barta@ff.cuni.cz

Dominique Charpin
Directeur d'études à l'EPHE (IVe s.) Orient Antique
Université Paris I
Centre Glotz 17 rue de la Sorbonne
75231 Paris Cedex 05
France
charpin@msh-paris.fr

D. Bruce Dickson
Department of Anthropology
Texas A&M University
College Station, TX 77843-4352
USA
dickson@tamu.edu

Eckart Frahm
Near Eastern Languages and Civilizations
Yale University
New Haven, CT 06520-8236
USA
eckart.frahm@yale.edu

Alan B. Lloyd
Classics, Ancient History, and Egyptology
Swansea University
Singleton Park
Swansea SA2 8PP
Wales
UK
A.B.Lloyd@swansea.ac.uk

Juan Carlos Moreno García
Centre de Recherches Egyptologiques de la Sorbonne – CRES
Université Paris–Sorbonne Paris IV
1 rue Victor Cousin
75230 Paris Cedex 05
France
jcmorenogarcia@hotmail.com

Ludwig Morenz
University of Bonn
Regina-Pacis-Weg 7
53113 Bonn
Germany
aegyptologisches.seminar@uni-bonn.de

Ellen Morris
Barnard College
Columbia University
3009 Broadway
New York, NY 10027
USA
emorris@barnard.edu

Beate Pongratz-Leisten
Institute for the Study of the Ancient World
New York University
15 East 84th Street
New York, NY 10028
USA
bpl2@nyu.edu

Michael Roaf
Ludwig-Maximilians-Universität München
Department für Kulturwissenschaften und Altertumskunde
Geschwister-Scholl-Platz 1
80539 München
Germany
Michael.Roaf@lrz.uni-muenchen.de

Walther Sallaberger
Ludwig-Maximilians-Universität
Department für Kulturwissenschaften und Altertumskunde
Institut für Assyriologie und Hethitologie
Schellingstr. 5
80799 München
Germany
WaSa@assyr.fak12.uni-muenchen.de

Joann Scurlock
History Department
Elmhurst College
190 Prospect Avenue
Elmhurst, Illinois 60126-3296
USA
r-beals@uchicago.edu

Acknowledgments

The work contained in this volume is the result of a four-day workshop entitled "Experiencing Power—Generating Authority: Cosmos and Politics in the Ideology of Kingship in Ancient Egypt and Mesopotamia" held in the University of Pennsylvania Museum of Archaeology and Anthropology November 2007. During the course of that week, fifteen scholars from the fields of Anthropology, Assyriology, and Egyptology shared their research, views, and expertise on questions relevant to the cross-cultural study of ancient kingship. After a fruitful week of papers and discussions, three participants—Manfred Bietak, D. Bruce Dickson, and Bradley Parker, along with Simon Martin of Penn Museum's American Section—presented their research in a series of open lectures at the Penn Museum.

The editors wish to thank the great many people whose help and encouragement aided in the successful arrangement of this working conference. As part of the University of Pennsylvania Museum's International Research Conference Program, then-Williams Director Richard Leventhal granted us the resources to organize a conference involving some of the world's most respected and innovative scholars to work on questions of interest to both specialized fields and to anthropology as a whole. Conference Series Director Holly Pittman generously gave of her time and energy in helping us plan and organize the conference and has since helped shepherd the publication of the conference volume to its completion. Many thanks are also due to our outside consultants Drs. David O'Connor and Richard Zettler for their many helpful suggestions during the planning and editing process. Unfortunately, due to time and academic constraints, some of our authors were not able to keep their contributions in this volume. For those who would like to refer to this work, Bradley Parker's paper, "The Construction and Performance of Kingship in the NeoAssyrian Empire," was published in *The Journal of Anthropological Research* in 2011.

We would also like to thank the Penn Museum personnel who made the conference sessions and associated events run smoothly and efficiently. Special thanks in this regard are due to Museum Events Staff Bethany Robblee Schell and Tena Thomason.

Finally, many thanks are due to the scholars themselves, some of whom traveled great distances to participate in this demanding conference workshop, for so generously giving of their insights, research, and time.

JANE A. HILL, PHILIP JONES, ANTONIO J. MORALES

Penn Museum International
Research Conferences

Foreword

For more than a century, a core mission of the University of Pennsylvania Museum of Archaeology and Anthropology has been to foster research that leads to new understandings about human culture. For much of the 20th century, this research took the form of worldwide expeditions that brought back both raw data and artifacts whose analysis continues to shed light on early complex societies of the New and Old Worlds. The civilizations of pharonic Egypt, Mesopotamia, Iran, Greece, Rome, Mexico, Peru, and Native Americans have been represented in galleries that display only the most remarkable of the Penn Museum's vast holding of artifacts. These collections have long provided primary evidence of many distinct research programs engaging scholars from around the world.

As we moved into a new century, indeed a new millennium, the Penn Museum sought to reinvigorate its commitment to research focused on questions of human societies. In 2005, working with then Williams Director Richard M. Leventhal, Michael J. Kowalski, Chairman of the Board of Overseers of the Penn Museum, gave a generous gift to the Museum to seed a new program of high-level conferences designed to engage themes central to the Museum's core research mission. According to Leventhal's vision, generating new knowledge and frameworks for understanding requires more than raw data and collections. More than ever, it depends on collaboration among communities of scholars investigating problems using distinct lines of evidence and different modes of analysis. Recognizing the importance of collaborative and multidisciplinary endeavors in the social sciences, the Penn Museum used the gift to launch a program of International Research Conferences that each brought together ten to fifteen scholars who had reached a critical point in the consideration of a shared problem.

During the three years until the spring of 2008, it was my privilege to identify, develop, run, and now oversee the publication of eight such conferences. The dozen or so papers for each conference were submitted to all participants one month in advance of the meeting. The fact that the papers were circulated beforehand meant that no time was lost introducing new material to the group. Rather, after each paper was briefly summarized by its author, an intense and extended critique followed that allowed for sustained consideration of the contribution that both the data and the argument made to the larger questions. The discussions of individual papers were followed by a day discussing crosscutting issues and concluded with an overarching synthesis of ideas.

Experiencing Power, Generating Authority is the edited proceedings of a conference of the same name held in the fall of 2007. It is the sixth of the conferences to see publication. As Series Editor, I look forward to one more volume that will appear in the near future. The publication of the results of these conferences allows the new knowledge and understanding that they achieved to be shared broadly and to contribute to the uniquely human enterprise of self understanding.

HOLLY PITTMAN
Series Editor
Deputy Director for Academic Programs, Penn Museum 2005–2008
Curator, Near East Section
Professor, History of Art
Bok Family Professor in the Humanities, University of Pennsylvania

Introduction

Comparing Kingship in Ancient Egypt and Mesopotamia

Cosmos, Politics and Landscape

JANE A. HILL, PHILIP JONES, ANTONIO J. MORALES

> If we refer to kingship as a political institution, we assume a point of view which would have been incomprehensible to the ancients . . . Whatever was significant was imbedded in the life of the cosmos, and it was precisely the king's function to maintain the harmony of that integration.
>
> — Frankfort 1948:3

INTRODUCTION

It is now more than sixty years since Henri Frankfort introduced his classic comparative study of rulership in ancient Egypt and Mesopotamia, *Kingship and the Gods*, with this basic distinction between the political and cosmic roles of kingship. This volume follows in Frankfort's footsteps in examining the relationship of kingship, cosmos, and politics in the context of ancient Egyptian and Mesopotamian civilization. Three millennia of recorded history and social traditions make ancient Egypt and Mesopotamia rich sources for a comparative study of the long-term political and social development of these two "pristine" cultures (for the most recent large-scale comparison, see Baines and Yoffee 1998). They were geographically near, while culturally quite distinct. For almost three thousand years, Egypt and Mesopotamia shared the concept of ultimate legitimate authority being invested in the single sacred office of kingship. This office was legitimized by the gods, demonstrated through ritual, and reinforced by tradition. Through this sacred office the ruler exercised the essential political authority of the state. Both ancient civilizations provide us a rich material record of royal monuments (civil and religious), iconography, and texts that eloquently define and frame the actions of the ruler: the context of his deeds, the purpose of his commissions, and the accomplishments achieved under his reign.

As Frankfort implies, however, the sacred aspects of kingship in both societies drive a wedge between the ancient evidence and modern attempts to understand it. Was it "the king's function to maintain the harmony of [the] integration" of human life with the cosmos, as Frankfort argued, or was it, as we would expect of our own rulers, to facilitate the integration of his human subjects with his own regime or with each other? In taking up this challenge, we join a debate that stretches back beyond him to, at least, the late 19th century (Feeley-Harnik 1985). In very broad outline, this debate has inspired three basic approaches to understanding the dichotomy: (*i*) privileging one of the cosmic and political orientations of kingship over the other; (*ii*) treating the two as separate but equal facets of kingship; and (*iii*) exploring the interaction between the two of them.

The first such approach attempts a definite answer to our question posed above. Beginning with the classic work of Sir James Frazer, *The Golden Bough* (1894; see also, Frazer 1900; 1905–1915; and 1922), there has been an on-going controversy in anthropology and history as to whether kingship in pre-modern societies should be considered fundamentally either cosmic or political. This debate has often spilled over, more or less overtly, into the study of ancient Egyptian and Mesopotamian kingship. Frazer postulated that kings had originally embodied the powers of nature and must therefore be sacrificed before their own physical decline affected the fertility of the world around. Much of this reconstruction seemed congruent with either extant Greco-Roman memories of Egypt and Mesopotamia or the material revealed with gathering pace throughout the 19th century by archaeology. Particularly with regard to the Egyptian evidence, prominent festivals such as the *Heb-Sed* seem to evoke Frazer's basic principle (Uphill 1965), while the figure of Osiris, known already to Frazer from Classical sources and utilized by him, seemed to be an archetypal "Dying and Rising" god (Otto 1968:24; Griffiths 1980). Mesopotamia fit Frazer's theories less obviously, but after the First World War, the so-called Myth and

Ritual school of scholars sought to apply a version of Frazer's ideas about cosmic kingship to both Egyptian and Mesopotamian rulers (Fairman 1955; Gadd 1933; Hooke 1933). Frankfort's *Kingship and the Gods* was a rejoinder to the Myth and Ritual school, although it is noteworthy that he judged Egyptian kingship to be significantly more cosmic in orientation than its Mesopotamian equivalent (Wengrow 1999). In general, Frankfort's views were congruent with those espoused by Assyriologists and his work elicited little controversy with respect to Mesopotamia. Traditionally, Assyriologists have tended to treat cosmic aspects of kingship as a mode of legitimation (Postgate 1995) or simple hyperbole (Kraus 1974). Where cosmic kingship was acknowledged, it was often contrasted with non-cosmic kingship in a different period or area (Labat 1939). For many Egyptologists, however, Frankfort's de facto endorsement of the cosmic view of Egyptian kingship provoked a fierce reaction in recent decades, beginning with Posener (1960).

Such a debate, however, risks either denying that a king and his subjects could think as rationally as ourselves or ignoring significant aspects of the source material for failing to replicate our own attitudes to such matters (Caldwell and Henley 2008). One obvious way to overcome this dilemma is simply to treat the cosmic and political aspects of a kingship as separate but equal facets of the institution without attempting to privilege one over the other (Lorton 1979, 1986; Charpin 2004:232–316; and note the remarks of O'Connor and Silverman 1995:xxv).

While avoiding the question of whether a kingship is ultimately political or cosmic does allow a more uninhibited exploration of both aspects, "it may be," as in the words of O'Connor and Silverman (1995:xxvi), "that there is yet a further mystery to be explored." Suggestive in this regard has been the work on medieval and early modern political and constitutional theory by Ernst Kantorowicz (1957) entitled *The King's Two Bodies*. Kantorowicz argued that the king was viewed as a mixture of individual holders of a kingship who were mortal and the office of kingship itself that was effectively immortal. Beyond this dichotomy, however, he was more focused on how the cosmic and political aspects of kingship were interwoven rather than how they could be distilled out. Moreover, he was concerned with exploring the ways in which the relationship between the divine world and the king changes over time. While such studies have been attempted in the ancient Near East (for example, Jones 2005; Machinist 2006), it is an open question whether the source material is abundant or well enough understood for our disciplines to be able to emulate Kantorowicz's work on the much more extensively studied history of Europe.

Each of these approaches has contributed much to our understanding of kingship both in traditional societies in general and Egypt and Mesopotamia in particular, but each has attendant problems. In organizing this book, we aimed to combine these approaches to the problem rather than utilize one to the exclusion of the others. While observing a division of labor between Egypt and Mesopotamia, we asked our contributors to focus on particular topics rather than to produce synthetic accounts of kingship in discrete periods or regions. We grouped those studies overtly into three clusters. The first two of these focused on the relationship of kingship to, respectively, cosmos and politics. In the final section, we focus on a topic where these two relationships seem automatically to merge: landscape. At the same time, we framed our investigations in terms of the experience of power and the generation of authority. In doing so, we were less interested in explicitly defining these terms and more interested in seeing how such general guidelines stimulated the crystallization of themes that cut across any reified dichotomy of cosmos and politics.

PART I: KINGSHIP AND COSMOS

At the end of the 4th millennium the emergence of civilization in Egypt and Mesopotamia brought about a series of transformations in the environment and society that culminated with the establishment of early polities and the consolidation of the institution of kingship. The complex forms of kingship attested at this time in both civilizations emerged from ideological motivations to control their territory and people, so that the king was able to respond to social, religious, and political concerns with both physical and transcendental powers (Beattie 1968; Feeley-Harnik 1985). Therefore, ideological constructions of kingship in Egypt and Mesopotamia defined the figure of the king as a multi-faceted sacred ruler with effective human authority, divine legitimacy, and supernatural attributes. The sacred nature of his office transcended the earthly political dominion and addressed religious issues of greater significance for the benefit of mankind (Mann 1986). In this manner, the sacred aspect of kingship acted as a cohesive factor in the development of the state (Coe 1982; Keatinge 1982), the comprehension of the divine, and the understanding of cosmic order.

The complexity of the royal institution reflects its socially accepted universal role and the king's ultimate responsibility—the preservation of order over chaos and constant rebirth over death. As the mission of the king was to guarantee political stability and cosmic balance (Young 1966), the principles of kingship were founded upon the relationship of the king to the gods. This association has stimulated an intense debate on royal divinity in general (Feeley-Harnik 1985; Quigley 2005), as well as in Egypt (O'Connor and Silverman 1995) and Mesopotamia (Brisch 2008). Although there is evidence linking the prominent position of the king in the cosmos as proof of his divinity (Frazer 1905, 1922), royal equivalence with the gods is not so patent, as several different examples indicate, e.g., son (*z3*) of Re, servant (*b3k*) of Amun, or flesh (*šīru*) of the god (see Charpin and Frahm, both this volume). Thus, the essential purpose of the king from a cosmic perspective is not so much to be an actual god, but rather to act as mediator between the gods in general and his people (Geertz 1980). The scholars whose work is presented in Part I of this volume have engaged in the analysis of the role of kingship as institutional guarantor of life and order for humanity, dealing with specific cases in Egypt and Mesopotamia that bring fresh perspectives—and pose new questions—to the long-standing debate about the divine nature of the king in these cultures.

In taking on the issue of the cosmic aspects of kingship, our contributors divided along disciplinary lines. Charpin, Frahm, and Scurlock focused on the nature of the divine connections enjoyed by the king. Morris and Morenz, in contrast, focus on how such images were created and promulgated.

Morris examines various early dynastic cultic objects from Early Dynastic Egypt, in particular the famous Narmer Palette. Although they differ in artistic conventions from later dynastic art, she sees the basic aspects of Egyptian kingship already encoded in these works. As such, she argues that the king fulfilled a number of both cosmic and political roles. The king is not an ordinary human being and various strategies emerged to support this view. Morris focuses on the use of scent, animal imagery, and association with ithyphallic divine figures to mark the king as extra-ordinary. Such motifs as the "four sacred animals" and the Followers of Horus emphasize the divine protection enjoyed by the king. However, the king himself also provides a charismatic center for the land: he defeats enemies abroad and crushes rebels within, he personifies the union of Upper and Lower Egypt within himself, and he is an administrator and bestower of largesse.

In delineating the means of separating the king from ordinary mortals, Morris notes the importance of the association of early Egyptian kings with the god Horus. Our next four chapters focus specifically on the issue of royal identification with a divine or at least superhuman figure. In doing so, they elucidate the wider significance such associations may have for the ideology of kingship in their respective cultures. Both Charpin and Frahm examine the relationship between Mesopotamian kings and the sun-god. As with the ancient Egyptians and many other societies, Mesopotamians felt a particular connection between the king and the sun. For them, the sun-god was associated with concepts of justice, and—as Charpin reminds us in his chapter—divination. Through a focus on the sun-god, Charpin explores the wider significance these two attributes have in Mesopotamian conceptions of the cosmos. He shows how for the king, this association has a number of implications. In terms of the extent to which the king is considered divine, Charpin argues that the dispensation of justice constitutes a situation in which the king is actually considered to embody a divine figure. Moreover, he sees this phenomena as reflected not only in literary texts but also in prosaic contexts such as letters and personal names. Through the association with justice, equations of the king with the sun-god imply responsibility as much as any augmentation of royal power through identification with the divine. The association with justice has a double aspect: a static one encapsulated in the concept of an unchanging cosmic order and a dynamic one of the ability to react to threats to this order and restore the cosmos to balance. Charpin also shows how the concepts of justice and divination themselves are not seen as the exclusive domain of the sun-god. They are also associated with other deities such as Adad, Ninsianna, and the moon-god.

Frahm deepens our understanding of the Mesopotamian identification of the king with the sun-god. Beyond explicit identification with the god, ritual actions of the king in important 1st millennium rituals mimic the movement of the solar body. Frahm points out that this identification of the king with a phenomenon of the daytime sky has a counterpoint in the king's identification with the planet Saturn in the nighttime sky. Whereas the sun provides an image of cosmic reliability, Saturn as a planet is subject to the vicissitudes of movement that characterize the night sky. As such, the two astral bodies represent two facets of kingship: on the one hand, the steady and reliable pivot of people's lives, on the other, a figure exposed to all the ups and downs of political life. Frahm further explores this celestial contrast between order and disorder in terms of two major 1st millennium mythic narratives, *Enuma Elish* and *Erra*, which utilize Jupiter and Mars respectively as embodiments of these forces.

Morenz focuses on cultic objects from Predynastic Egypt and the ways in which political messages can be conveyed through iconography in a preliterate culture. He identifies three major types of such objects: weapons, tools, and ornaments. These correspond respectively to rituals of victory, agriculture, and enthronement. From this he discerns both a military and a sacred aspect to earliest Egyptian kingship. Each aspect is encoded in contrasting types of animals depicted on ritual objects. Thus, for example, fierce animals such as bulls or lions exhibit an obvious reference to military prowess. Conversely, depictions of giraffes—conceptually associated with seeing or foretelling the future—and hybrid animals such as human-headed hyenas suggest a shamanistic ability to commune with the supernatural world.

Scurlock examines the mythological associations of Mesopotamian kings with the concept of death, chiefly in how they identity with the god Dumuzi. Although literary texts linking kings directly with Dumuzi are limited to the Old Babylonian period, Scurlock argues that the connection can be traced from at least the royal tombs of Ur in the Early Dynastic period (see also Dickson) down to the Neo-Assyrian period. For Scurlock, however, these matters are not just of mythological interest. She analyzes how the king's connections to the Netherworld shape the nature of kingship itself. In particular, she focuses on how the identification with Dumuzi—the archetypal shepherd—implied royal responsibility rather than an augmentation of royal power (see also Charpin).

PART II: KINGSHIP AND POLITICS

In our second section, the chapters focus on various political aspects of kingship in ancient Mesopotamia and Egypt. Traditional studies of Egyptian kingship frequently neglect the actual workings of the institution and the means by which it exercised power. In part, the reason for this is due to the types of information available through our preserved sources. For instance, scholars of 3rd millennium Mesopotamia focus on economy in large part because of the abundant nature of their preserved texts dealing with temple and palace economy, while the earliest information on kingship from Egypt is iconic, representational, and king-centered. It is perhaps because of these accidents of preservation that Frankfort's interpretation of Mesopotamian kingship as being a rational and political institution while the Egyptian version of the office was an irrational and religious institution has persisted so long in the literature (Wengrow 1999). Even so, in the earliest Egyptian representations and writings denoting kingship, it is the physical manifestation of the institution in the landscape—the Great House (*pr ꜥꜣ*)—which was no doubt of both economic and political importance that is used as a signifier of the office. It is also noteworthy that most of what we know about the reach of the power of the office of First Dynasty Egyptian kings comes from these same symbols (*serekhs*) scratched into pottery or engraved onto tags marking valuable trade goods shipped from within and beyond Egypt's borders and denoting official networks controlled by an administrative structure even during this early period.

In later periods official texts treating kingship in both Egypt and Mesopotamia deal in the symbolic and religious aspects of the office and much less in its mechanics, i.e., the means by which the king's authority is legitimated in the eyes of his subjects and how he wields power within the country. Detecting and interpreting the inner workings of government in any of the periods under discussion is extremely difficult and in many cases our surviving primary sources tend to be sparse, diffuse, or even mute on the social texts and subtexts behind issues such as the king's use of deadly force against his own subjects or the abandonment of one style of mortuary complex for another. The scholars whose work is presented in Part II of this volume have undertaken the difficult task of reconstructing the political and social structures through which the king's authority is generated and his power exercised. By looking beyond the bright light thrown by the figure of Shamash or "Son of Re" himself and into the lives of palace servants, priests, exorcists, bureaucrats, weavers, provincial headmen, and tax collectors, these authors draw back the curtain behind the throne to explain how and why the king creates, co-opts, and manipulates the social institutions of his world, and vice versa, in order to maintain order, inspire service, collect taxes and tribute, and exact obedience.

Moreno focuses on the integration of central and provincial elites prior to the New Kingdom. The Egyptian state seems large in size and stable over time, particularly when compared to contemporary Mesopotamian polities. Its foundation and periodic re-foundation seems to be effected by one particular region—Upper Egypt. Moreno argues that Egypt had a number of regional power centers and therefore that both the prominence of Upper Egypt in state formation and the ability of the center to integrate various provincial nuclei together cannot be taken for granted. He therefore begins by examining the initial creation of a pan-Egyptian state in the Predynastic period. He looks beneath the image of Upper Egypt as a monolithic bloc and instead seeks to elucidate the advantages that led one political component of that region—the city of Hierakonpolis—to unify initially its local region and ultimately the whole valley of Egypt (see also the chapters by Morris and Morenz). Looking mainly at the Old Kingdom, Moreno then traces the modes of regional integration that underpin the comparative stability of the ancient Egyptian state. Kings were able to mold local elites into orienting their economic and ideological interests to the central government. Moreno emphasizes the economic integration achieved by the creation of royal agricultural centers in the countryside and royal land grants to local temples (see also Bárta, this volume).

The economic relationship between palace and temple is taken up by Sallaberger in the contexts of early Mesopotamia. Traditionally, scholars have seen both institutions as examples of great households fulfilling similar economic roles and hence constituting potential rivals. Through an analysis of 3rd and 2nd millennia archives, Sallaberger argues that not only do palace and temple fulfill distinct economic roles, but that we also need to be aware of the different roles of "state" institutions at the provincial and central level. Temples produce food and utilitarian goods. In contrast, the palace was concerned with the distribution of prestige items such as metals, luxury textiles, exotic goods, and fine food. To do this, the palace—often utilizing provincial centers—requisitioned primary products from the temples at home and plundered or traded for raw materials and craft products abroad. These were then used to provide members of the elite—either directly or through the upkeep and supply of skilled craftsmen—with prestige goods. While Sallaberger specifically focuses on 3rd and 2nd millennium archives, he also sees his model as applicable to later states such as the Neo-Assyrian empire. As such, he suggests that the control and distribution of royal "treasure" constitutes not only a crucial means of mediating the relationship between king and elites, but also constitutes as fundamental an aspect of Mesopotamian kingship as, for example, supreme command of the army or ultimate control of territory.

Bárta analyses royal mortuary complexes of Egypt from the Fourth to Sixth Dynasties to illuminate the relationship between king and elite. He contrasts the laudatory picture of Old Kingdom monarchy propagated on behalf of the king to the evidence of changing patterns of elite tomb placement and the titulary of officials. The claims to overwhelming power found in royal propaganda are often belied by evidence on the ground. Early Fourth Dynasty royal pyramids are some of the most impressive structures ever created by an ancient civilization. By the end of the dynasty, however, these structures had become more modest in size and from the Fifth Dynasty onwards, the storerooms and administrative buildings attending the pyramids become much larger while the pyramids themselves become more modest structures. Utilizing the evidence of autobiographical mortuary stelae, Bárta traces the evolution of the administrative structure from one dominated by members of the royal family in the Fourth Dynasty to the emergence of a non-royal central bureaucracy in the Fifth Dynasty to the kings' attempts in the late Fifth and Sixth Dynasties to forge ties with the provincial elites as a means of loosening the control of the central elites. Lastly, he looks at how the Old Kingdom patterns of administration broke down during the First Intermediate Period and how the system was resurrected in the Middle Kingdom.

Pongratz-Leisten focuses on Neo-Assyrian kingship in the 7th century BCE. She analyzes the nature of the relationship between king and elites as the society attempts to create a royal figure that is independent of social and political frameworks (see also Morris, this volume). Nonetheless, such creation was undertaken by the elite members of these frameworks. Pongratz-Leisten sets out to identify these players and the king's relationship to them. She identifies the so-called scholars—experts in traditional science and lore—rather than the priesthood as the group delineating the king's intermediary role between gods and people. The master scholars of the Assyrian court create a mythological buffer for the king that leaves him dependent on their guidance in cosmic matters. In particular, the city of Assur, although no longer the capital, is turned into an ideological center of the polity effectively undercutting royal authority. Through a close analysis of the events implied by the well-known letter of Sargon II to the god Ashur, Pongratz-Leisten investigates the ways the king has to negotiate with the traditional capital in order to maintain his legitimacy.

Dickson examines the question of early state formation primarily through the prism of the royal tombs of Ur from Early Dynastic Mesopotamia. He positions his study in terms of the dichotomy between integration theory that sees state formation in terms of the managerial aspects of the emerging state apparatus and conflict theory that in contrast emphasizes the predatory aspects of this apparatus. The royal tombs include large numbers of retainers buried with the royal corpses. The original excavator, Sir Leonard Woolley, argued that these retainers went to their deaths willingly. Dickson, in contrast, argues that the imposition of a violent and unwilling death is much more congruent with what we know about other emergent state forms including the First Dynasty tombs at the royal cemetery at Abydos and the Early Dynastic elite cemetery at Saqqara (see Morris, this volume).

PART III: KINGSHIP AND LANDSCAPE

Frankfort saw the differences he perceived between Egyptian and Mesopotamian ideas of kingship as rooted in the contrasting physical environments of the two civilizations. The Mesopotamians thought in terms of cosmic instability, the Egyptians of cosmic stability. For Frankfort (1948:4–5) the difference he saw in a Mesopotamian view of an unstable cosmos with the Egyptian one of a stable cosmos was:

> curiously in keeping with the physiographical differences between the two countries. The rich Nile Valley lies isolated and protected between the almost empty deserts on either side, while Mesopotamia lacks clear boundaries and was periodically robbed and disrupted by the mountaineers on its east or the nomads on its west. Egypt derived its prosperity from the annual inundation of the Nile, which never fails to rise, even if the floods differ greatly in effectiveness. But Mesopotamia is, for much of its grazing, dependent on an uncertain rainfall and possesses in the Tigris an unaccountable, turbulent, and most dangerous river.

In the final section, our chapters explore the relationship between kingship and the physical environment, but from a rather different perspective. By focusing on the concept of landscape, we examine both the physical manifestation of the land and its casting by human hand and mind (Falconer and Redman 2009:1–2; Schama 1996; Smith 2003). The chapters draw together a number of the many dichotomies that underpin this volume: Egypt and Mesopotamia as distinct civilizations; cosmos and politics as alternative stimuli for royal actions; the experience of power and the generation of authority as subtly different processes contextualizing kingship. Frankfort structured *Kingship and the Gods* around the differences in physical landscape between Egypt and Mesopotamia. In focusing on the human reaction to and cultural appropriation of landscape, our contributors highlight similarities between the two civilizations. In keeping with many societies (Helms 1993), both Egypt and Mesopotamia conceptualized the lands beyond their own border as otherworldly regions that were the source both of power itself and the exotic products that so often signified it. Moreover, in cultures of restricted literacy and public oratory, manipulation of the landscape—both physically and figuratively—was often the most visible means of interaction between the subjects and rulers (Milano et al 2000; Thomason 2001, 2004).

The chapters by Roaf and Lloyd focus on the physicality of landscape, but as with Ataç in his study of landscape in art and literature, attention is paid to the ideological significance of landscape. Roaf in his account of royal building activity in Mesopotamia emphasizes the sheer diversity of kings and kingship throughout the course of the civilization. Despite this diversity, landscape and its manipulation by kings provided one common theme. Furthermore, there tended to be more emphasis on the king's spatial rather than, for example, genealogical status. Kings were generally rulers of particular places—whether a city, a country or even the whole world—rather than scions of a particular dynasty. Roaf focuses briefly on the territorial aspects of kingship and then more fully on the way royal building activities have an impact on the landscape. He emphasizes how fluid all relationships to the landscape were: concepts of territory evolved over time; the urge to surpass as well as simply emulate the building work of predecessors ensured that there was a constant evolution of such work. Moreover, there was a gradual change in emphasis as the interests of Mesopotamian kings switched over the millennia from temples to more "secular" works such as palaces, walls, canals, parks, and gardens. The modification of the landscape through building provides a way of connecting a king both to past and future. The structures themselves are a reminder of the power of past rulers and a means for current rulers to extend a visible reminder of their power into the future. The inscriptions contained within the structures enable current rulers to encounter the words of their predecessor and leave a means of communicating with their successors.

Lloyd analyzes five inscriptions from Wadi Hammamat, a quarrying area in the desert east of the Nile Valley: four Middle Kingdom inscriptions from Mentuhotep IV year 2 and one New Kingdom inscription from Ramses IV year 3 commemorating quarrying expeditions sent out to the wadi. He focuses on the conceptual world within which the Egyptians understood events taking place in the Eastern Desert rather than the events of the expeditions themselves. First, he examines the practicalities of the Wadi Hammamat. The wadi is a source of a number of raw materials including the greywacke stone that provides the focus for the expeditions he discusses. Beyond its own resources, the wadi also forms part of the transit route for precious goods from farther afield, particularly the fabled land of Punt. The area is of course desert and presents numerous and great obstacles to any expeditions that attempt to exploit the resources of the area. Lloyd argues that both sorts of text treat the Wadi Hammamat as a sacred area. Furthermore, the Egyptians viewed the world as full of imminent divine powers that could be either helpful or harmful. It was possible to enlist, placate, or repel these forces by ritual action. The desert to the east of the Nile was particularly associated with beneficent powers and with the sunrise. Some areas could be seen as especially numinous due to particular physical features. The Wadi Hammamat was one such area due to its associations with savior deities, its physical stillness, and the fact that successful expeditions "obviously" required local divine assistance. The stones quarried from the wadi are themselves imbued with sacred power. The religious conception of the expeditions makes possible their use as propaganda. Our texts emphasize the "miracles" (*bi3yt*) seen en route. The Egyptians considered such miracles as a signal that the king enjoyed divine approval.

Ataç examines both the vertical and horizontal dimensions of the cosmos. He focuses on the relationship between mythic or ritual elements as against real or historical ones in Neo-Assyrian royal art. Mythic or ritual elements such as the sacred tree or the antediluvian sages are juxtaposed with the depiction of more historical events. In the early Neo-Assyrian period, the two elements are kept spatially separate, but in the art of Sennacherib or Assurbanipal they tend to blend into one another. Rather than attempting to analyze the degree of realism implied in such juxtapositions, Ataç reads them through a prism of geography, cosmology, and their respective visual representations, in which he sees ritual or myth on the one hand and reality on the other as inseparable and blended. To do this, he looks first at concepts of the edge of the earth. He analyzes depictions of fabulous places beyond the edge of the known world in the Babylonian *Mappa Mundi* and the *Gilgamesh Epic*. He then examines the impact of these ideas on Mesopotamian conceptions of the oecumene. The lands beyond the oecumene are treated in Mesopotamian thought as exotic and chaotic, but also paradigmatic and paradisiacal. Mesopotamian royal titles such as King of Totality and King of the Four Quarters imply the integration of these fabulous areas in the body politic. Ataç sees this through the lens of the scholar of Medieval Islamic philosophy, Henri Corbin. Corbin theorized the existence in pre-modern thought of the "imaginal"—"real" places that could nevertheless only be apprehended through the imagination. It is the ideal role of an imperial administration to manifest the paradigmatic aspects of the imaginal at the center. Closely connected to the horizontally distant imaginal lands are the vertically inaccessible realms of the divine world. In particular, the Apsu, the mythical subterranean ocean of freshwater, blends into the horizontal imaginal. It is the home of the antediluvian sages who are the prime example of the paradigmatic sacred power necessary for the optimal well-being of the human center. Depictions of human landscape on Neo-Assyrian reliefs attempt to evoke a connection to the Apsu through depictions of the sages.

EXPERIENCING POWER, GENERATING AUTHORITY

As can be seen, our authors touch upon a wide variety of themes relating to the cosmic and political aspects of kingship. Here, we wish to draw out briefly five themes that cut across our initial categories and throw the relationship between the cosmic and political aspects of kingship into greater relief: violence, the circulation of goods, legitimation, royal death, and elite politics.

Violence

Frankfort's basic distinction between the relative peace and security of Egypt versus the environmental and geo-strategic vulnerability of Mesopotamia is symptomatic of a tendency to associate the cosmic pole of our comparison with passivity and the political one with violence. As our chapters highlight, however, the threat of violence underlies both the cosmic and political aspects of kingship. The gods are ever ready to deploy violence in the form of natural disasters or societal upheaval, while violence by the king or against him is a constant feature of human politics.

However, we need to distinguish between inaugural and standard phases of Egyptian and Mesopotamian states. For Morenz, violence constitutes one of the two main underlying metaphors expressing the power of the earliest royal figures known from Egypt. As Morris and—particularly—Dickson show, primeval states could deploy a shocking degree of actual violence in domestic contexts, especially in the form of human sacrifice. For example, year tags of the Egyptian First Dynasty rulers Aha and Djer have been interpreted as scenes of ritual sacrifice to the gods (Emery 1961:59, fig. 21) as they appear to depict submissive figures with blood pouring from their heads. Sacrificing fellow citizens to the king or the gods seems to be a rarer occurrence, though not necessarily in the early stages of state formation (Dickson, this volume). These incidents seem to fall into one of three categories: (1) the ritual killing of human beings as part of the offerings presented to the gods on a regular basis, or on special occasions, (2) the execution of criminals in punishment for a crime, and (3) retainer sacrifice, or the killing of domestic servants to bury them along with their master. While the origin of those sacrificed in the royal tombs of Ur remains uncertain, those sacrificed in Early Dynastic Egypt were certainly local residents. These blatant displays of violence were paralleled by gargantuan public works, most obviously in the great funerary enclosures of Egypt's first two dynasties.

As both Bárta and Morris demonstrate, the excesses of such early transitional stages needed to give way to more stable, less volatile and wasteful behaviors. After the First Dynasty in Egypt and after the period of the royal tombs of Ur in Mesopotamia, public displays of ritual, state sanctioned murder are relatively uncommon. Though textual evidence of some such cases do exist, they should perhaps be classified as hybrid examples of the state meting out capital punishment by performing acts of ritual sacrifice for the gods on special occasions (Willems 1990; Habachi 1963:39).

In terms of violence, there comes to be a clear distinction between "us" and "them." As Morris points out in the case of Old Kingdom Egypt, kings in standard state formations drew a distinct line between the domestic and foreign arenas. While violence against his own subjects was an ideologically sensitive matter, the king was generally expected to defeat foreign enemies in battle and exploit them in times of peace. Moreover, this aspect of his nature was heavily advertised to his subjects. At home, the threat of violence was always there, but in Egypt for example, the submission of the population to the king was conveyed artistically through the symbolism of small birds hung from the king's standards rather than any explicit depiction of royal violence against the king's subjects. Only with the breakdown of order in the First Intermediate Period and the need to re-establish the dynastic state, do we find overt depictions of Egyptians as victims of the king.

Booty claimed through victorious battle was often dedicated to the state's patron deity and texts describing the conquest of territory and the subjugation of foreign peoples were often couched in the terms associated with a divine charge of the king. Perhaps the most graphic case of which we have a record from ancient Egypt is the account of Amenhotep II who killed seven Syrian princes in the temple of Amun and had the bodies of six of them hung from the walls of Thebes, and another from the walls of a temple in Nubia (Breasted 1988: v.2 §797).

On the exterior walls of the temples themselves the king is shown maintaining the political world order by defeating the enemies of the state by the most violent of means. On the temple interiors he is shown maintaining cosmic order by propitiating the gods through prayers and offerings. By the larger-than-life display of the ruler murdering the outsider, the king is certainly fulfilling the role of "sacred monster" but the question of how realistic, if at all, these depictions are has long been a subject for debate (Girard 1972). Images of the king killing or humiliating foreigners are commonplace on many royal monuments. In ancient Egypt one of the earliest art works attributed to a ruler of the entire country—the Narmer Palette—shows the king crushing the skull of an Asiatic or Lower Egyptian rebel on one side and inspecting the battlefield—decapitated and emasculated enemies of the state arranged in neat rows before him—on the other side (Davis 1992; Morris, this volume). Similarly an early Mesopotamian monument, the Stele of the Vultures, visually equates violence committed by the king with the will of the divine by showing such acts being carried out by the earthly ruler on one side of the stele and the god grasping the enemies of the state in a great net on the other side of the monument (Winter 1985; Alster 2003–2004). Statues of prisoners and foreigners shown in painful and humiliating positions were a common decorative theme in Egypt's royal art, for example: Khasekhemwy's feet treading on the traditional enemies of the state (the "Nine Bows") on the first preserved royal statue or the carved heads of foreigners positioned below the balcony of the king's window of appearances at Medinet Habu so that when Ramses III appeared before the crowd he would be seen to be trampling his enemies (Murnane 1980:24). These and many other monuments from both cultures tell us that symbolic violence by the king was a widely accepted part of public life and was considered yet another aspect of the royal-divine discourse (de Heusch 1997).

However, in the case of Mesopotamia, there were limits to the royal exercise of violence even against outsiders. As Pongratz-Leisten (this volume) shows, in sacking the foreign sanctuary of Musasir, Sargon II of Assyria was subsequently unsure of whether he had automatic divine approval for his action or not.

Circulation of Goods

With regard to the more peaceful aspects of kingship, the chapters by Charpin, Frahm, and Scurlock illustrate one well-known cluster of roles that unite the cosmic and the political: the roles of judge and shepherd of the people reflected in the identifications of the king with the sun-god and Dumuzi. Here, however, we wish to highlight briefly another aspect of the peaceable side of kingship. For both civilizations, a core aspect of the relationship between humanity and the gods was the requirement that the former feed the latter and adorn their temples. This created a basic economic undercurrent whereby goods were transferred from the outside world into the temples. Fundamental to any exercise of kingship therefore was the need to interpose the king into this process and orient it, both materially and ideologically, around him so that the king stood at the center of an interconnected series of circulations that knit the cosmic and political realms together. Thus Morris describes how in Egyptian art, the king alone is depicted as sacrificing to the gods, ignoring the part played by the priests who largely filled this role in reality. Mesopotamian myths such as *Atrahasis* (Lambert and Millard 1969) emphasize the basic human obligation to feed the gods. In Mesopotamian religious rhetoric, organizing this activity remains an important legitimating act whether conceptualized as the work of the king or of one of the gods themselves (Jones 2005). Much of the administrative activity described in the chapters of Sallaberger, Moreno, and Bárta is ostensibly designed to provide temples with a means of fulfilling this human obligation.

Moreover, this system reaches beyond the borders of the homeland. As Sallaberger argues, it is the palace's responsibility to transform the staple products that characterize the economic output of cuneiform societies and exchange them abroad for prestige goods such as metals, precious stones, and exotic wood. As the products of distant lands, such materials possess their own charisma and are experienced as an infusion of the sacred into the ordinary world of the homeland. Lloyd and Ataç both elucidate the role of Egyptian monarchs in obtaining "sacred" materials from, for example, the Wadi Hammamat or Punt. Both these chapters bring out the close connection between obtaining material goods from the outer world along with less tangible benefits such as a general sense of the numinous or, more specifically, instantiating the primeval Absu in the royal palace. On a more prosaic level, as Sallaberger shows, controlling the flow of prestige goods constituted an important royal mechanism for manipulating elite opinion in both societies.

It is in this circulation of goods that we begin to discern some basic differences between the two civilizations. The model of the Egyptian economy presented by Moreno and Bárta involves the careful integration of central and local elites. In contrast, Sallaberger presents a model of Mesopotamian states in which the center extracts an annual tribute from the provinces with little if any integration of the two types of elite.

Legitimation

Legitimation is one of the most complex aspects of kingship. In particular, it provides the most comfortable arena to consider cosmic aspects of kingship for those who wish to follow a political perspective on the matter; irrespective of their content, correct relations with the divine world can be conceptualized as legitimating the king. Such relationships can involve the king being close to the gods or considered a god himself. It should be noted in any comparative study of Egyptian and Mesopotamian kingship that the issues facing the ruler from the earliest dynastic periods was essentially different in scope. Egypt, being a territorial state from its inception, required the ruler to knit together the interests of varying constituencies scattered along the 800 km length of the Nile Valley from the First Cataract to the Mediterranean. In comparison, early Mesopotamian political organization above the level of the city-state seems short-lived and shallow. As such, Mesopotamian kings were much more beholden to a single constituency.

Many of the features considered characteristic of Egyptian kingship—the identification of the king with the gods or a single god, for example—are adopted or at least become an issue in Mesopotamian kingship in periods when the king claims sovereignty over much wider territories and must therefore broaden his claim to legitimacy, either as a god himself or under the auspices of an ascendant deity such as Ashur.

Our chapters highlight three facets of legitimation: the king's need for divine approval; the king's self-legitimization; and finally, the king as a source of legitimacy for others. We see the need for outside legitimacy exemplified in terms of the king's relationship to both the gods, his own ancestors, and to his own subjects. In terms of the gods, there are appeals to both divine favor and divine status. The legitimacy of the king was established in the earliest periods of both cultures through association with the patron deity of a polity or city. As we see in Morris's account of the offerings of King Scorpion and Narmer, in Egypt the first and most obvious association of the king with a local cult was with the sky god Horus of Hierakonpolis (Kemp 2006:83–85).

The association with the patron deity is still evident in Mesopotamia in the way the god Ashur personified the Neo-Assyrian empire (Pongratz-Leisten, this volume). In such cases, while texts referring to the ruler associate him with a locality rather than the deity of the city, it is clear that some sort of endorsement by the local god or, more practically, by the local priesthood was necessary in order for a ruler to gain and retain power. Lorton (1979:463) has further suggested that in the case of Egypt's rulers this endorsement was purchased from the priesthoods of various local deities in the form of gifts and endowments to their temples. In essence, the king paid to have himself represented performing cultic activities for the deities of various temples. The prominent role played by the priesthood in the coronation of the king and the presentation of the symbols of his royal authority in both cultures required the endorsement of the priesthood. One example of this relationship is the symbolic role played by the shrines of Upper and Lower Egypt in the *Heb-Sed* ritual, indicating that all of these temples and their priests had essentially endorsed the reign of a particular ruler. An example of this endorsement being repaid is in the mortuary papyrus of Ramses III in which details of donations by the king to the major temples in the country are described (Grandet 1994). One of the first duties of a newly crowned pharaoh was to travel the length of the country visiting the major shrines and their gods along the way.

Examples of the importance of divine favor to kings can be found in Lloyd's account (this volume) of the interpretation of miracles seen by quarrying expeditions as examples of divine favor towards the king. Neo-Assyrian kings did not explicitly claim divinity, but as Ataç (this volume) shows, they surrounded themselves in their palaces with imagery of divine favor. Again, Pongratz-Leisten shows the mechanics of such divine favor were not always simple. Outside of our chapters, we may imagine Ramses II's Kadesh reliefs battling with a similar problem.

The extent to which kings could be considered divine has been a continual debate in the study of both ancient Egypt and Mesopotamia. To an extent, we avoided a direct engagement with this question, content to see what emerged from the contributions. Morris deals briefly with the Egyptian king's identification with Horus, and Morenz explicates preliterate representations of the king in which he is explicitly associated with animals identified with shamanistic or military might. Our Mesopotamian contributors deal more directly with the issues involved in royal identification with the divine. As such, they belie any belief that such identifications represent simple validations of the king. Charpin examines perhaps the most expected identification: that with the sun-god. He shows that this is no simple honorific, but instead embeds the king in a complex web of cosmic relations. The sun is the patron of divination as well as justice; the judicial aspect implies both tradition and innovation; and a series of other deities share in this aspect. As Frahm shows, this identification with the sun leads to a further identification with the planet Saturn. Scurlock (this volume) analyzes the other major equation with the divine experienced by Mesopotamian rulers, that with Dumuzi. As with the likeness to the sun-god, this serves to delineate the desirable characteristics expected of a ruler rather than to imbue the king with an extra aura of authority.

Kings however should not be seen as depending purely on appeals to the gods for their legitimacy. Their own actions can generate their own charisma. As Morris notes, the king's very presence, whether in the context of ritualized court life or of processions through the countryside generates its own form of charismatic legitimacy. Obviously, a king's ability to inspire loyalty through personal appearance alone would have limited effect in most of his kingdom. The large-scale building works described by Roaf or symbolic structures on the landscape such as the small early pyramidal buildings along the Nile mentioned by Moreno provide a means of representing royal presence in his physical absence.

Finally, in this volume, we see kings providing legitimacy for others. The right to burial close to royal tombs (Bárta), royal selection to run provincial temples (Moreno), and the distribution of prestige goods (Sallaberger, Bárta) all serve both to reward the recipients and augment their prestige in the eyes of their own subordinates.

Death of the King

As we see from our scholars' contributions, the point at which a specific king leaves the mortal world constitutes a significant moment. Conceptually, the end of one reign and the beginning of another involves the temporary cessation of normality (Charpin). Kings retained their individual identity after death to a much greater degree than ordinary mortals (Scurlock). The rituals and ritualized behavior that buried a dead king and inaugurated a new one were partly intended to ensure the old king's ghost did not threaten the living. This threat is amplified where the king's death was anomalous. Frahm and Scurlock show how the ghosts of Sargon II of Assyria—a rare instance of a Mesopotamian king dying on the battlefield—and his son, Sennacherib—assassinated by his own sons—haunted Neo-Assyrian politics after their untimely deaths. At its most extreme, as seen in the chapters of Dickson and Morris, the death of a royal figure was the occasion for mass-murder. While we may speculate as to the reason for the rapid emergence and disappearance of such customs, it is difficult to gauge whether this evolution involved an equally rapid change in the ideas on the relationship between kings and death.

While more stable state structures eschewed human sacrifice, royal death, especially in Egypt, provided an important aspect of kingship. The Egyptian pyramids, whether the elephantine creations of the Fourth Dynasty or the more compact examples of succeeding dynasties, form not only some of the more impressive human manipulations of the natural landscape, but as explored by Bárta, they provide a significant pivot for the circulation of goods through the Egyptian state system. Lloyd provides a snapshot of such activity in his account of the expeditions to Wadi Hammamat to obtain greywacke for royal sarcophagi. In a Mesopotamian context, Roaf reminds us of the way that the building and re-building of public structures provides a link across time between a king and his often long-dead predecessors.

Identification of dead Egyptian kings with the underworld deity Osiris reflects the cosmic dimension of integrating royal death into a functioning system of kingship. Similarly, in Mesopotamia royal identification with Dumuzi (Scurlock) and association with Gilgamesh, the legendary hero and judge in the Underworld, betray a similar need to integrate royal death into that system.

Elite Politics

Impinging on all our contributions is the issue of the king's relationship to various elite groups. Fundamentally, of course, this is usually seen in political terms and the chapters of Bárta, Moreno, and Sallaberger provide interesting pointers to significant differences in the dynamics of state forms in Egypt and Mesopotamia. Moreno and Bárta illustrate a long-term process of elite evolution in the case of the relatively stable and long-lasting polity of Old Kingdom Egypt. Originally, higher administrative functions are monopolized by members of the royal family. Gradually, royal family members are excluded from these offices by non-royal elite families based at the center. Eventually, members of the provincial elite gain access to the benefits of central authority, while members of the central elite attempt to build up provincial power bases less subject to royal control. While kings would obviously have an interest in promoting some turnover among their ostensible minions, it is unlikely that their sense of self-preservation was the only factor stimulating this process. Sallaberger describes a much more modular structure in early Mesopotamia than the Egyptian one divined by Moreno and Bárta. Relations between central and provincial elites were complicated by the fact that the latter were not integrated into the imperial structures such as the empires of Ur III or the Old Babylonian empire of Hammurabi, nor, despite some degree of colonization by central government organs (for example, Heimpel 2009), were they systematically replaced by central appointees. Provincial elites, therefore, aimed at secession from the system rather than competition with central elites within the system.

While kings would attempt to influence the centripetal and centrifugal forces structuring the relationship between central and peripheral elites to their own advantage, they could also take more drastic action. By physically moving their own seats of residence, they could automatically render previously central elites peripheral (Roaf, this volume). This could be to entirely new foundations such as Sargon II's new capital of Dur-Sharrukin or elevating an existing city to the status of capital, as did Sargon's son Sennacherib with Nineveh. During various stages of Egyptian history similar re-centering efforts were made by kings founding new capitals or royal residences including the founding of Memphis in the First Dynasty; the founding of Itjtawy in the early Twelfth Dynasty; and the founding of Akhetaten in the late Eighteenth Dynasty as a means of weakening the economic and bureaucratic power base of the Amun priesthood based at Thebes.

Other chapters introduce a cosmic dimension to the relationship of monarch and elite. Pongratz-Leisten highlights some of the tensions involved in such maneuvers in her examination of the relationship between Sargon II and the citizens of Assur, the old capital and the seat of the national deity. She contrasts the scholars who mediated the king's relationship with the divine world with other, more materially based elite groups such as army commanders, court eunuchs, or provincial administrators. The scholars' expertise in cosmic matters provided them with significant influence over royal policy. Moreover, as Ataç reminds us, the high politics of the Neo-Assyrian empire took place within buildings whose decoration mingled both political and cosmic concerns. For earlier periods, Morenz suggests that the consciousness of the intellectual elite of their role in the creation of the ideology of kingship may go deep into the past. Charpin introduces us to the issues involved for members of the royal family in dealing with the divinity or near-divinity of their royal relative.

CONCLUSION

The study of kingship in any ancient society is a complex one. There are few aspects of a civilization that do not have at least some bearing on the topic. By necessity, therefore, we had to be selective and chose to focus on comparing the monarchies of Egypt and Mesopotamia in terms of the relationship between their cosmic and political aspects. Any attempt at comparison naturally also involves a degree of contrast. In juxtaposing these two ancient civilizations, Frankfort emphasized contrasts: between the two civilizations and between cosmically oriented and politically oriented types of kingship. In introducing our authors' contributions, we have highlighted the commonalities between Egypt and Mesopotamia. In doing so, however, we acknowledge that there were also many differences. The politics/cosmos dichotomy is more complex. While we reject privileging one aspect over the other or using the antinomy to distinguish one example of kingship from another, we believe it retains a heuristic value. The blurring of the boundary between cosmos and politics requires, inter alia, a deeper understanding of each aspect individually; an examination of contexts that presuppose such blurring; and the identification and development of concepts that cut across the original division.

REFERENCES

Alster, B. 2003–2004. Images and Texts on the *Stele of the Vultures*. *AfO* 50: 1–10.

Baines, J., and N. Yoffee. 1998. Order, Legitimacy, and Wealth in Ancient Egypt and Mesopotamia. In *Archaic States,* ed. G. Feinman and J. Marcus, pp. 199–260. Santa Fe, NM: School of American Research.

Beattie, J.H.M. 1968. Kingship. In *International Encyclopedia of the Social Sciences*, ed. D.L. Sills, Vol. 8, pp. 386–89. New York: Macmillan.

Breasted, J.H. 1988. *Ancient Records of Egypt: Historical Documents*. Vol. 2, *The Eighteenth Dynasty*. London: Histories & Mysteries of Man Ltd.

Brisch, N., ed. 2008. *Religion and Power. Divine Kingship in the Ancient World and Beyond*. Oriental Institute Seminars 4. Chicago: The Oriental Institute of the University of Chicago.

Caldwell, I., and D. Henley. 2008. Introduction: The Stranger Who Would Be King. *Indonesia & the Malay World* 36:163–75.

Charpin, D. 2004. Histoire politique du Proche-Orient Amorrite (2002–1595). In Mesopotamien: *Die altbabylonische Zeit,* ed. P. Attinger, W. Sallaberger, and M. Wäffler, pp. 25–480. OBO 160/4. Fribourg: Academic Press.

Coe, M.D. 1982. Religion and the Rise of Mesoamerican States. In *The Transition to Statehood in the New World*, ed. G.D. Jones and R.R. Kautz, pp. 157–71. Cambridge: Cambridge University Press.

Davis, W. 1992. *Masking the Blow: The Scene of Representation in Late Prehistoric Egyptian Art*. Berkeley: University of California Press.

de Heusch, L. 1997. The Symbolic Mechanisms of Sacred Kingship: Rediscovering Frazer. *Journal of the Royal Anthropological Institute* 3:213–32.

Emery, W. B. 1961. Archaic Egypt. Harmondsworth, Middlesex: Penguin Books.

Fairman, H.W. 1955. The Kingship Rituals of Egypt. In *Myth, Ritual and Kingship. Essays on the Theory and Practice of Kingship in the Ancient Near East and in Israel*, ed. S.H. Hooke, pp. 74–104. Oxford: Clarendon Press.

Falconer, S.E., and C.L. Redman. 2009. The Archaeology of Early States and Their Landscapes. In *Polities and Power: Archaeological Perspectives on the Land-*

scapes of Early States, ed. S.E. Falconer and C.L. Redman, pp. 1–10. Tucson: University of Arizona Press.

Feeley-Harnik, G. 1985. Issues in Divine Kingship. *Annual Review of Anthropology* 14:273–313.

Frankfort, H. 1948. *Kingship and the Gods. A Study of Ancient Near Eastern Religion as the Integration of Society and Nature.* Chicago: University of Chicago Press.

Frazer, J.G. 1894. *The Golden Bough: A Study in Comparative Religion.* 2 vols. London: Macmillan.

———. 1900. *The Golden Bough: A Study in Magic and Religion.* 2nd ed. 3 vols. London: Macmillan.

———. 1905–1915. *The Golden Bough: A Study in Magic and Religion.* 3rd ed. 12 vols. London: Macmillan.

———. 1905. *Lectures on the Early History of the Kingship.* London: Macmillan.

———. 1922. *The Golden Bough: A Study in Magic and Religion.* London-New York: Oxford University Press.

Gadd, C.J. 1933. Babylonian Myth and Ritual. In *Myth and Ritual: Essays on the Myth and Ritual of the Hebrews in Relation to the Culture Pattern of the Ancient East*, ed. S.H. Hooke, pp. 40–67. Oxford University Press.

Geertz, C. 1980. *Negara: The Theatre State in Nineteenth-Century Bali.* Princeton: Princeton University Press.

Girard, R. 1972. *Le violence et le sacré.* Paris: Gallimard.

Grandet, P. 1994. *Le Papyrus Harris I (BM 9999).* Vol. I-II. Bibliothèque d'étude 109/1–2. Cairo: Institut Français d'Archéologie Orientale.

Griffiths, J. G. 1980. *The Origins of Osiris and His Cult.* Studies in the History of Religions 40. Leiden: Brill.

Habachi, L. 1963. King Nebhepetre Menthuhotp: His Monuments, Place in History, Deification and Unusual Representations in the Form of Gods. *MDAIK* 19:16–52.

Hallo, W.W. 1957. *Early Mesopotamian Royal Titles: A Philologic and Historical Analysis.* American Oriental Series 43. New Haven, CT: American Oriental Society.

Heimpel, W. 2009. *Workers and Construction Work at Garshana.* Cornell University Studies in Assyriology and Sumerology 5. Bethesda, MD: CDL Press.

Helms, M.W. 1993. *Craft and the Kingly Ideal: Art, Trade, Power.* Austin: University of Texas Press.

Hooke, S.H. 1933. The Myth and Ritual Pattern of the Ancient East. In *Myth and Ritual: Essays on the Myth and Ritual of the Hebrews in Relation to the Cul-*

ture Pattern of the Ancient East, ed. S.H. Hooke, pp. 1–14. Oxford: Oxford University Press.

Jones, P. 2005. Divine and Non-Divine Kingship. In *A Companion to the Ancient Near East*, ed. D. Snell, pp. 330–42. Malden, MA: Blackwell Publishing.

Kantorowicz, E.H. 1957. *The King's Two Bodies. A Study in Medieval Political Theology*. Princeton: Princeton University Press.

Keatinge, R.W. 1982. The Nature and Role of Religious Diffusion in the Early Stages of State Formation: An Example from Peruvian Prehistory. In *The Transition to Statehood in the New World*, ed. G.D. Jones and R.R. Kautz, pp. 172–87. Cambridge: Cambridge University Press.

Kemp, B. 2006. *Ancient Egypt: Anatomy of a Civilization*. 2nd ed. New York: Routledge.

Kraus, F.R. 1974. Altbabylonische Königtum. *Le Palais et la Royauté*, ed. P. Garelli, pp. 235–62. Rencontre Assyriologique Internationale 19. Paris: Librarie Orientaliste Paul Geuthner.

Labat, R. 1939. *Le caractère religieux de la royauté assyro-babylonienne*. Études d'Assyriologie 2. Paris: Librairie d'America et d'Orient.

Lambert, W.G., and A.R. Millard. 1969. *Atra-Ḥasīs: The Babylonian Story of the Flood*. Oxford: Oxford University Press.

Lorton, D. 1979. Towards a Constitutional Approach to Ancient Egyptian Kingship. *JAOS* 99:460–65.

———. 1986. The King and the Law. *Varia Aegyptiaca* 2:53–62.

Machinist, P. 2006. Kingship and Divinity in Imperial Assyria. In *Text, Artifact and Image: Revealing Ancient Israelite Religion*, ed. G.M. Beckman and T.J. Lewis, pp. 152–88. Brown Judaic Studies 346. Providence, RI: Brown Judaic Studies..

Mann, M. 1986. *The Sources of Social Power: A History of Power from the Beginning to A.D. 1760*. Cambridge: Cambridge University Press.

Milano, L., S. de Martino, F.M. Fales, and G.B. Lanfranchi, eds. 2000. *Landscapes: Territories, Frontiers and Horizons in the Ancient Near East*. Rencontre Assyriologique Internationale 44. 3 vols. Padova: Sargon srl.

Murnane, W.J. 1980. *United with Eternity: A Concise Guide to the Monuments of Medinet Habu*. The Temple of Khonsu 2. Chicago: Oriental Institute, University of Chicago.

Murnane, W. J. 1995. The Kingship of the Nineteenth Dynasty: A Study in the Resilience of an Institution. In *Ancient Egyptian Kingship*, ed. D. O'Connor and D.P. Silverman, pp. 185–217. PdÄ 9. Leiden: Brill.

O'Connor, D., and D.P. Silverman. 1995. Introduction. In *Ancient Egyptian Kingship*, ed. D. O'Connor and D.P. Silverman, pp. xvii–xxvii. PdÄ 9. Leiden: Brill.

Otto, E. 1968. *Egyptian Art and the Cults of Osiris and Amon*. London: Thames & Hudson.

Otto, E. 1969. Legitimation des Herrschens im pharaonischen Ägypten. *Saeculum* 20:385–411.

Posener, G. 1960. *De la divinité du Pharaon*. Cahiers de la Société Asiatique 15. Paris: CNRS–Imprimerie Nationale.

Postgate, J.N. 1995. Royal Ideology and State Administration in Sumer and Akkad. In *Civilizations of the Ancient Near East*, ed. J. Sasson, vol 1, pp. 395–411. New York: Simon and Schuster Macmillan.

Quigley, D., ed. 2005. *The Character of Kingship*. New York: Berg.

Schama, S. 1996. *Landscape and Memory*. New York: Vintage Books.

Smith, A.T. 2003. *The Political Landscape: Constellations of Authority in Early Complex Polities*. Berkeley: University of California Press.

Thomason, A.K. 2001. Representations of the North Syrian Landscape in Neo-Assyrian Art. *Bulletin of the American Schools of Oriental Research* 323:63–96.

———. 2004. From Sennacherib's Bronzes to Taharqa's Feet: Conceptions of the Material World at Nineveh. *Iraq* 66:151–62.

Uphill, E. 1965. The Egyptian Sed-Festival Rites. *JNES* 24:365–83.

Wengrow, D. 1999. The Intellectual Adventure of Henri Frankfort: A Missing Chapter in the History of Archaeological Thought. *AJA* 103(4): 597–613.

Willems, H. 1990. Crime, Cult and Capital Punishment (Mo'alla Inscription 8). *JEA* 76:27–54.

Winter, I.J. 1985. After the Battle Is Over: The Stele of the Vultures and the Beginning of the Historical Narrative in the Art of the Ancient Near East. In *Pictorial Narrative in Antiquity and the Middle Ages*, ed. H.L. Keesler and M. Shreve Simpson, pp. 11–32. Washington, DC: National Gallery of Art.

Young, M.W. 1966. The Divine Kingship of the Jukun: A Re-evaluation of Some Theories. *Africa* 36:135–53.

Cosmos

1

Propaganda and Performance at the Dawn of the State

ELLEN F. MORRIS

According to pharaonic ideology, the maintenance of cosmic, political, and natural order was unthinkable without the king, who served as the crucial lynchpin that held together not only Upper and Lower Egypt, but also the disparate worlds of gods and men. Because of his efforts, society functioned smoothly and the Nile floods brought forth abundance. This ideology, held as gospel for millennia, was concocted. The king had no supernatural power to influence the Nile's flood and the institution of divine kingship was made to be able to function with only a child or a senile old man at its helm. This chapter focuses on five foundational tenets of pharaonic ideology, observable in the earliest monuments of protodynastic kings, and examines how these tenets were transformed into accepted truths via the power of repeated theatrical performance. Careful choreography and stagecraft drew upon scent, pose, metaphor, abject foils, and numerous other ploys to naturalize a political order that had nothing natural about it. Some of these tactics were abandoned after they had served their purpose or began to inspire negative backlash, while others survived to be drawn upon by Augustus and his successors.

By the end of an extended Nile Valley cruise, it is common for tourists to express the sentiment that they don't care if they never see another Egyptian temple. From Aswan to Alexandria, the traveler encounters innumerable representations of Pharaoh in the largely homogenous (mostly) New Kingdom and Ptolemaic temples they are ushered through. They see statues that may vary a bit in posture (seated versus standing, primarily) or size (some were particularly large!), and reliefs that may differ slightly in subject matter (the king may be smiting a group of foreigners or he may be standing on a chariot and shooting into a tangled mass of them. Likewise, he may be offering before a deity, embracing a deity, or performing a ritual in divine company). In essence, however, in the temples that the tourist has toured, two primary messages have been driven home *ad nauseum*. The king is the aggressive defender of his people, and the king is the only mortal who is on the same plane with the divinities and who may enter into relations of reciprocity and affection with them.

Egyptologists see nuances that travelers might not. Notions of kingship clearly fluctuated according to periods and personalities. The pyramids at Giza and the colossal statues of Amenhotep III and Rameses II, for example, occupy one end of the pendulum of royal deification and aggrandizement, while kings who reigned in and around Egypt's Intermediate Periods and purportedly authored pensive ruminations expressing vulnerability and even loneliness sit at the other. Further, some kings are known to us as specific personalities given their excitement at the prospect of viewing a pygmy (Pepy II), their unusually big ears (Senusret III: "the better to hear you with"), their propensity to boast about feats of physical prowess in unusual ways (Amenhotep II), or their love of horses (Piankh). It is the humanness and individuality of various rulers that breathes life into Egyptian history and provides the pleasure in studying it. Even the most casual of those weary tourists that daily board their planes homeward, however, have passively grasped the foundational tenets of pharaonic kingship—so assiduously did the Egyptians curate them over millennia. It is the purpose of this chapter to address the foundation, dissemination, and eventual naturalization of these tenets.

The notion that pharaoh was absolutely essential to the proper functioning of Egypt's religious, military, and administrative endeavors existed from its "conception in the egg" in protodynastic times to its slow death under the absentee pharaohs of the Roman period. As it was not uncommon for pharaohs to ascend the throne as "nestlings" or to rule despite crippling disease or extreme old age, this illusion was vulnerable to an easy unmasking. Clearly, the state could function perfectly well with only the pretence of an authority figure at its apex. Further, even in those rare periods when Egypt was politically fragmented, the sun continued to rise and set, and the Nile flooded its banks and fertilized the soil. The question is: how did a small, newly powerful group at the dawn of the state convince the recently conquered population of the Nile Valley that the unapproachable stranger king they promoted was vital to the welfare of the world? Moreover, how did the single office of kingship usurp and maintain a hold over all of the most highly valued sources of social power?

To answer these questions, I will utilize three pioneering articulations of royal ideology as a springboard for a discussion of propaganda and performance (or, perhaps better, propaganda *in* performance). These three monuments—the Narmer Palette and two impractically large maceheads, dedicated by King Narmer and King Scorpion to the god Horus of Hierakonpolis—are deservedly well known. Perhaps ironically, considering that they predate the Early Dynastic Period, they surpass any extant monuments of that time in their ability to efficiently communicate the various roles of the king at this period and the belief systems that surrounded him. While these objects may have been meant for the eyes of the god, the scenes portrayed upon them, I argue, were dramatic rituals that conveyed in their performance five foundational ideological precepts. These messages, writ large on these three royal monuments, were simultaneously disseminated by other means, and evidently so inculcated the Egyptian worldview that they together constituted a set of truths that remained essentially unquestioned for millennia. Although there were plenty of revolts in ancient Egypt's history, we know of no revolutions. According to all available records, rebels within Egypt sought to *be* the king rather than to abolish kingship as an institution. Thus the fatigue of the modern tourist is a direct legacy of the success of Scorpion, Narmer, and the individuals who helped these kings and their successors in forging a new dominant paradigm.

THE MEDIUM: GIFTS TO BE GRASPED BY THE GODS

Before addressing the key visual messages carved into the three votive objects, it is important to provide background on the monuments and their makers. King Scorpion, who dedicated one of the large maceheads under discussion (see Fig. 1.1) to a temple that he may well have founded, is known primarily by virtue of this monument, though the scorpions that appear on many other items in the Main Deposit at Hierakonpolis and in other contemporary contexts may betray his sponsorship. Although it is not certain where, nor even when precisely, he ruled, the similarity in shape and style of his macehead to the other votive macehead under discussion (see Fig. 1.2) render it

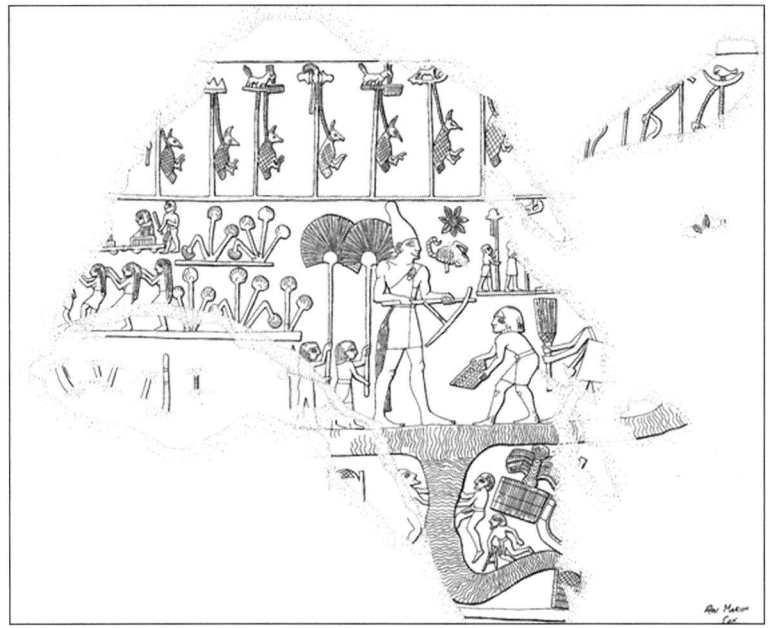

1.1. The Scorpion macehead Oxford, Ashmolean Museum E.3632 (after A.J. Spencer 1993:56, fig. 36. Drawing: Marion Cox).

extremely likely that he ruled just prior to Narmer, at the very cusp of the First Dynasty. Narmer's macehead is well known and his palette (see Fig. 1.3) is one of Egypt's most emblematic works of art. Narmer is also memorialized on a label discovered at Abydos (see Fig. 1.4), an ivory cylinder seal also from the Main Deposit (see Fig. 1.5), and a variety of other artifacts, including a

1.2. The Narmer macehead, Ashmolean E. 3631 (after Friedman 1992:31, fig. 12).

great many storage jar fragments discovered throughout Egypt and southern Canaan. His double grave in the royal cemetery at Abydos practically abuts his successor's sprawling mortuary monument, and there is much debate as to whether he or Hor-Aha should be equated with King Menes, who later Egyptians viewed as the first king to inherit the throne of Horus (Brunner 1982).

The two maceheads and the palette under discussion were discovered in a cache of occasionally precious and always enigmatic Naqada III and Early Dynastic artifacts deposited together under the floors of the temple of Horus, Egypt's archetypal legitimate god-king (Quibell 1900; Quibell and Green 1902; Adams 1995:54–75). Thus their findspot provides a rare window into the intended audience of these items. Like the foundation cylinders of later Mesopotamian kings, the messages written upon these votives were meant for an unearthly audience and for those Egyptians privileged enough to gain access to sacred ground. While such items may have been at times displayed to the kings' subjects (such as in religious processionals) or have been published on other media, there is no way of ascer-

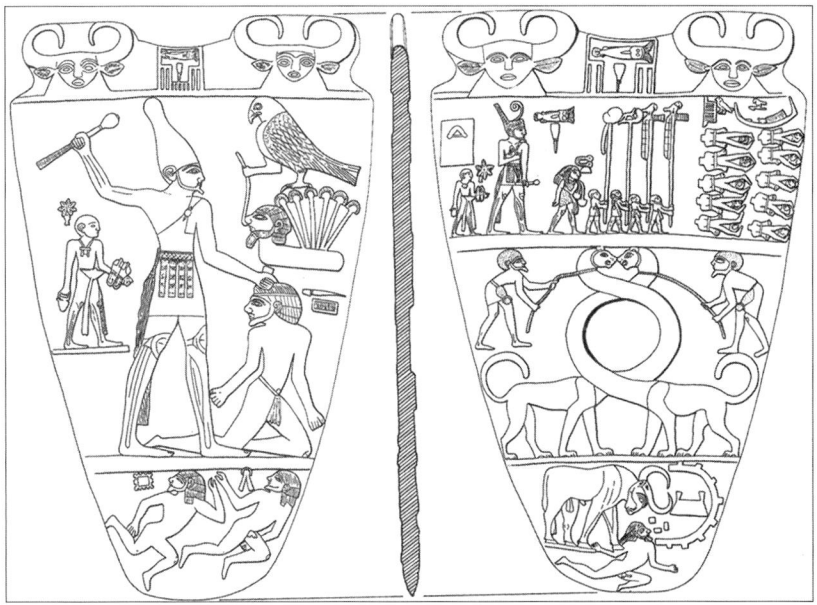

1.3. The Narmer Palette, Cairo J.E. 14716, C.G. 32169 (after Kemp 1991:42, fig. 12).

taining this, and John Baines (1994:78) is probably correct in questioning their traditional interpretation as state propaganda—at least in the sense that this term is usually employed.

That these items were explicitly fashioned as gifts for a god is also driven home by their extraordinary size, for their scale is not appropriate to humans. If the roughly contemporary colossi of Min discovered at Koptos may be taken as a rough guide for the envisioned size of at least some deities (i.e., in excess of 4 meters high), however, these presents were indeed perfectly scaled for a divine being (see Kemp 2000 and Fig. 1.6). The impractically large flint knives also discovered in the Main Deposit assuredly fell into this category (Quibell and Green 1902:6, pl. 3), and it is likely that the tradition of providing divinized entities with gifts appropriate to their stature can be traced at least as far back as the votive deposits of massive flint arrowheads discovered in association with an early Naqada II pillared structure in Hierakonpolis' earliest elite cemetery.[1] The god Seth, the

1.4. Narmer's label from Abydos. Drawing: author.

strongest of all gods, was known to have wielded a weapon weighing many thousands of pounds in his nightly combat against the forces of darkness (Te Velde 2001:269). For the mere mortals who glimpsed these votive maceheads that they had not the strength to wield—not to mention the gigantic palette presumably made to fit comfortably into the palm of a god's hand—the effect of their own miniaturization with respect to the cosmic world must have been vertiginous and humbling.

Votive gifts in Egypt as elsewhere were typically offered either as thanks for divine favors or in pious solicitation of them, and in many cases they were fashioned so as to appeal to aspects of a deity's character and/or to the type of favor requested (a phallus for fertility, etc.). The gift of the maceheads, then, may well have been a token of thanks for the victories whose aftermaths appear to be engraved upon them. On the Narmer Palette, which explicitly commemorates a victory, the king raises high his own mace to dispatch his prize prisoner. The word for mace (*ḥḏ*) was a homophone of the word "white" or "bright," which was used to designate the white Upper Egyptian crown (*ḥḏt*) that Narmer wore for this act of smiting and also the radiant whiteness that purportedly shone from the walls of the first capital at Memphis (Erman and Grapow 1929:206–11). This weapon, then, was entangled on multiple levels with concepts of kingship and served as a particularly fitting gift to be bestowed upon Egypt's celestial hawk-king by his earthly avatar. Certainly, the fact that pharaohs continued to grasp the mace in smiting scenes and statuary thousands of years after the weapon had become obsolete in contemporary warfare is a testament to the power of these early images, so imbued with symbolism, to endure.

THE MESSAGE: THE KING DOES NOT BELONG TO THE ORDINARY REALM OF HUMANKIND

Conventions of comparative size and physical placement on the two maceheads and on the palette drive home the point that the king's status was far divorced from that of even the highest officials of his kingdom (assuming that the ubiquitous *ṯt*-official and Narmer's sandal-bearer fall into this category). Thus, when standing, no other individuals reach as high as the king's waistband, due either to their artificial shrinkage or to their crouched and submissive stance. When he sits enthroned, as the king does in the Narmer macehead, it is atop a nine-stepped platform—perhaps symbolic of the nine gods of the ennead or decorated with the nine traditional enemies of Egypt that he would crush underfoot upon mounting the platform. Whatever his posture or placement, the message is unambiguous: the king towers above humanity. The same rules that bind flesh and blood do not apply to him.

Such artistic—and no doubt performative—chicanery in the service of visually communicating this ideology was adopted by virtually all subsequent kings. To this end, later pharaohs appeared before their subjects in elevated windows of appearance. They sailed in royal barques or rode chariots, while others walked, rowed, or ran beside them. Kings traveled also in raised palanquins, and when they held audience, even the greatest magnates of their kingdom laid flat and kissed the ground. The inscriptions of the Fifth Dynasty grandees Ptahshepses (the high priest of Ptah and the husband of a princess) and Washptah (a vizier and chief architect) go further in informing us that the very highest honor, bestowed separately upon both of these two great men and deemed worthy of memorializing for eternity in their mortuary inscriptions, was that the king had commanded them to kiss his foot rather than the earth in front of him (*Urk.* I:41,15; 53,2-3; Strudwick 2005:304–5, 318–20).

Indeed, the manner in which the literary character of Sinuhe narrates his audience with Senusret I suggests that such elaborate self-abasement in the royal presence was not an artifact solely of the Old Kingdom. "I found his Majesty on the great throne in the portal of electrum. Then I was stretched out prostrate, unconscious of myself in front of him, while this God was addressing me amicably. I was like a man seized in the dusk, my soul had perished, my limbs failed, my heart was not in my body. I did not know life from death" (Parkinson 1997:40). Lest it be thought that such paroxysms of dread awe in the royal presence were purely fictional, Senusret I's own vizier, a man named Mentuhotep, bore among his most vaunted epithets two that boasted of his privileged position with respect to the physical person of the king, namely "master of every wardrobe of Horus" and he "who approaches the limbs of the king" (Breasted 1988a:256, 257). Clearly the opportunity to touch the royal person or to touch royal things (such as the king's sandals!) was reserved for a very tightly guarded inner circle. And even within this circle, unauthorized touching (such as the accidental contact made between a priest and "keeper of accoutrements" and the king's scepter) was potentially of the direst consequence (*Urk.* I:232,5–16; Strudwick 2005:305–6).

In the Old Kingdom, the reigning king was termed not only a god but occasionally even a great god (*ntr ꜥꜣ*). Scholars disagree, however, on what the Egyptians actually meant by "god" (Was this term anticipatory of a transmutation that would only fully take place after death? Was it only the abstracted office of kingship that was divine? Or was the living king himself infused with a supernatural spirit?). For the earliest rulers especially, the extent of their divinity can only be guessed at, although the fact that in Khasekhemwy's fifteenth year a copper statue named High-is-Khasekhemwy was "born" (*mst*) suggests that it may have received cult attention prior to the death of the king, as certain statues of Old Kingdom rulers did (Baines 1995b:132). In the New Kingdom, of course, Amenhotep III, Tutankhamun, and Rameses II likewise bolstered their own reputations as living gods by commissioning named statues of themselves that were invested with the individual agency to hear prayers in their stead (Wilkinson 2000:PS r.V.4; Baer 1960:264–72; Habachi 1969:40–52; Wildung 1977:1–30).

Judging from the imagery engraved on the votives dedicated by Scorpion and Narmer, the literal and figural elevation of these kings above humanity leant itself to the cultivation of a divine aura. Interestingly, in the theatrics of sacred kingship, scent may have also been employed to serve the same purpose. If the king to some extent could not help resembling a human being, he could at least smell like a god. A recurrent trope in narratives of encounters with the divine in Egypt held that gods exuded from their pores the fragrance of the finest incense (Hornung 1982:133–34). It may be no coincidence, then, that one of the earliest items subject to taxation at the dawn of the state was a commodity called the "fragrance of Horus." Scent certainly played an important role in the coronation rites, for it was believed that the incense that suffused the heir apparent during the ceremonies was in turn emitted from his own skin following their completion. In a dramatized pre-enactment of a Middle Kingdom coronation, the actor depicting the god Thoth commanded the god-to-be, just prior to crowning him king, "Take you the fragrance of the gods [*censing*], that which cleanses, which has come out of yourself" (Frankfort 1978:130–32).

At the death of the pharaoh, when the king's sacred nature lost any ambiguity whatsoever, scent also played an enormous role, for the king wished to affirm that his sweat was the sweat of Horus and that his odor was the odor of Horus (Faulkner 1969:PT 508). To this end, it seems, no expense was spared. In excavating the First Dynasty King Semerkhet's royal tomb, Flinders Petrie speculated that "hundredweights" of perfumed unguents must have been poured at the entrance of the sepulcher and observed that "the scent was so strong in cutting away this sand that it could be smelt over the entire tomb" (1989 [1900]:14). This description calls to mind the congealed tar of scented substances that had been poured so generously over Tutankhamun's corpse that his body stuck fast to the floor of his coffin three millennia after burial (Carter 1972:140–41). This fragrance of Horus—no doubt dispensed with extra urgency to mask the stench of death—seems to have been employed as "proof" of the king's divinity even in the state's earliest days.

The king's intimate association with the god Horus, whose scent he shared, is emphatic in Narmer's monuments. On his macehead, for instance, the *serekh* implies that the king is Horus-in-the-palace (as opposed, perhaps, to Horus-in-the-temple or Horus-in-the-sky), while on the palette, the king's crown and the falcon-head of Horus both graze the sky as the two subdue their foes in parallel. Likewise, on a royal cylinder seal (see Fig. 1.5), Horus extends the sign of life to Narmer's personified catfish, which was engaged in the act of dominating prisoners with a long cudgel. The king's essential relationship with his divine counterpart—whose spirit no doubt entered the king's body upon coronation—was also emphasized by Early Dynastic rulers in their names, either directly (such as Hor-Aha—Horus-the-fighter) or obliquely (as one of the "two powers" that this god comprised together with his rival Seth) or simply by virtue of the name of the name itself (i.e., the Horus name, Anedjib's

1.5. Narmer's ivory cylinder seal from Hierakonpolis. Drawing: author.

Two Lords name, and perhaps the Golden Horus name as well). The designations of royal estates, also, regularly combined the name of the god Horus with an epithet (such as Horus-first-of-the-corporation-of-gods—*ḥr-tpi-ḥt*— or Horus-star-of-the-corporation-of-gods—*ḥr-sb3-ḥt*) (Wilkinson 1999:119, 121–22).

If Horus played a starring role as the divine avatar of the king, Scorpion and Narmer also appear to have promoted the idea that their beings were infused with the bone-crushing power of the wild bull. At least two of the first powerful kings of Hierakonpolis, buried in Locality 6 in the early Naqada II period, had taken sacrificed bulls with them to the grave, perhaps in order to materialize the metaphor of the king as the "strong bull" of his people (Friedman 2004:138; Warman 2004). Later at Hierakonpolis, on the Narmer Palette, a bull acts as the proxy of the king in ramming down the fortifications of an enemy city and trampling its inhabitant(s), and a similar motif is found on the nearly contemporary bull palette. While in these cases the bull is only an artistic motif, perhaps intended to be viewed by an extremely limited audience, Early Dynastic kings associated themselves more publicly with the figure of the bull in two very important festivals. The first, the running of the sacred Apis-bull of Memphis, was one of the more frequent festivals in Early Dynastic Memphis and coincided on occasion with the "dawn/appearance" of the Lower (or Upper) Egyptian King (e.g., Wilkinson 2000:PS r.III.12; PS r.IV.10; CF4 r.M.1). On these occasions, the feared and ferocious bull would have been unleashed in the same set of ceremonies as the Memphite king appeared in state, visually impressing the equation of the two entities upon the audience. The other festival of note, the *Heb-Sed*, occurred far less frequently, but it was the single most celebrated and fervently desired event of a king's rule. The festival was named after the ceremonial bull's tail that the king wore appended to his kilt, further attesting to the fundamental importance of the bull to the king's projected image.

Although the scenes depicted on Narmer's Palette and Scorpion's macehead cannot be definitively identified as components of the *Heb-Sed* festival, it is notable that both kings are depicted on these monuments wearing a bull's tail. This deliberate fusion of man and animal as presented on public occasions may have been part and parcel of the cross-culturally common practice of "creating a stranger" that occurs when obvious mortals have to be remade into divine kings (Feeley-Harnik 1985:280–81). Indeed, such a method of enhancing the elevated otherness of the king would have been particularly effective in an Egyptian context judging from the fact that by the Early Dynastic Period gods often appeared, like the king, as human-animal hybrids. Other powerful animals, such as the lion—which destroyed cities in tandem with the scorpion and the falcon on the cities palette, devoured foes on the battlefield palette, and appeared amongst the buried retinue of king Hor-Aha—also captured the Early Dynastic imagination and served as enduring metaphors for pharaonic power. It was with the bull, however, that the spiritual synergy between king and beast was most profound.

Before segueing from this discussion of the supernatural aspects of archaic kingship, as gleaned from these three monuments and Early Dynastic public performances, I want to return to the subject of the mace, this time as grasped by Narmer on his way to view the decapitated corpses of his foes on the palette. Sometimes, as Freud would have it, a mace is just a mace. The shape of this particular mace, the manner in which the king grasped its stem firmly in his left hand, and the angle at which it protruded from his body, however, together effectively evoke the world-creating act of the cosmic deity. According to the Heliopolitan tradition, this original begetting via the act of masturbation was accomplished by Atum and his hand. The pose of the Koptos Collosi and the fact that one of these statues may have borne Narmer's name etched into its body (Williams 1988:36–37), however, suggest that the king was here visually alluding to his own partial syncretism with the ever-virile ithyphallic Min. While it is certainly a stretch to envision the king performing any such act before an audience, the poses of the king and the poses adopted by (statues of the) gods quite likely mirrored one another and influenced the way the king may have carried his mace or posed in public.

THE MESSAGE: THE KING IS THE CHOSEN ONE OF THE GODS

If it remains somewhat unclear whether the first kings of Egypt were thought of as deities incarnate, the protective hovering vulture goddess on the Narmer macehead, the multiple supportive appearances of Horus, the dual depictions of the celestial cow-goddess that flank the king's name on the palette, and the shrines engraved in the background of scenes on the two maceheads make it quite clear that the king was under the protection of the deities and in an intimate relationship with them. Indeed, until the mid-2nd millennium the king was as a rule the only mortal portrayed directly interacting with the gods, much less enfolded in their embrace, as many of the kings prior to that point were commonly depicted. On the subject of decorum (or perhaps actual taboo), however, it is also vital to note that mere mortals did not depict the king on their own religious or commemorative monuments until the end of Egypt's Middle Kingdom (Baines 1995a:10; Silverman 1995:83), suggesting perhaps that while both king and god belonged to the same category, the sacred nature of the cosmic deities was perhaps less contested or easily tarnished.

The reliance of the king upon the gods and the (no doubt) public demonstration of their support for him in the earliest days of Egyptian kingship is also demonstrated by the ubiquitous presence on these three monuments of the four sacred standards, which seem to have accompanied the king in ceremonial contexts. So far as it is possible to ascertain, this assemblage of sacred fetishes served a number of purposes: symbolizing aspects of the king's own divine nature, signaling his alliances with the deities depicted, and perhaps simultaneously celebrating particularly important terrestrial alliances. The two falcons, for example, are found as early as the cities palette engaged with other royal avatars in the process of hacking up walled polities, and here as well as on our monuments they may signify the Two Lords, Horus and Seth. These deities, according to royal doctrine, abandoned their internal quarrel and threw their combined weight and spiritual personae behind the king such that the royal queen held the title "[She]-who-sees-Horus-and-Seth" (Te Velde 1967:68, 71). The dual falcons were also signifiers of the Coptite nome, however, and likely possessed a seat of worship there. If Koptos, in its key position as a powerful southern stronghold was instrumental in aiding the Abydene kings in their rise to supremacy, then the appearance of its city-symbol in royal processions should also be read as a special acknowledgment of the king's political supporters.

The other symbols that topped the remaining two standards also may be interpreted on multiple planes. The "cushion" was known as the king's *nḫn*, most convincingly argued to be his placenta and thus the materialized presence of his spiritual twin (i.e., *ka*—Blackman 1915). The word *nḫn*, however, is also a homonym of the Egyptian name for Hierakonpolis (Posener 1965:194–95) and may thus have constituted yet another avenue for the Abydene kings to emphasize their alliance with this highly influential former rival. Finally, Wepwawet, the Opener-of-the-Ways, appears like Horus to have acted as the divine personification of the legitimate king, and the bulbous sled this god stood upon was said to have been the vehicle that transported the deceased king to the next world. The god's close ties to the ruler in death likely stemmed from the fact that Wepwawet was one of the earliest gods worshipped at Abydos. The role of this city as the victor in the struggle for control of Egypt is well known, and it may be that the god's presence here acted as a visual reference to the origin of the new kings. There is yet another (perhaps less likely) possibility, however. Wepwawet also functioned as the god of Asyut, a polity whose location between Middle and Upper Egypt lent it a pivotal role in the battles for the reunification of the country in the First Intermediate Period. If the region of Asyut played an analogous role in Egypt's first unification, the prestigious positioning of its standard in the royal entourage might have visually acknowledged the martial support the king had received from the city and its god (Frankfort 1978:92–93; DuQuesne 2005:390–97).

As we know from the regular reappearance of these standards at *Sed* festivals throughout Egyptian history, the group was collectively known as the *šmsw ḥr*—the followers or attendants of Horus (or occasionally "The gods who follow Horus"). In later times the standards—perhaps because of their great antiquity—were closely identified with the divinized royal ancestors, who together endorsed the king's reign and granted him millions of years upon the throne. In the Turin Canon, for example, the *šmsw ḥr* designated the primordial kings that preceded Egypt's first mortal ruler and provided the direct link between his rule and that of the gods (Kaiser 1959; Baines 1995b:120, 125; Frankfort 1978:83–93). Together these standards served as a convenient cultic representation of the spirits of the seemingly innumerable individual kings who came before the reigning one and who bestowed upon him their blessing and divine aid. When first introduced in the protodynastic period, however, the standards almost certainly communicated to onlookers the message that the king's spiritual and political backers were the most powerful entities in the country.

Archaic year names and the official annals promote the idea that care for the gods, including perhaps divinized ancestors, was a supremely important royal responsibility. To this end the king proudly recorded—and indeed named whole years after—the birth of divine statues (e.g., those of Neith, Min, Anubis, Sed, and Mafdet). As we know from myriad later in-

1.6. Reconstruction of Min colossi (after Kemp 2000:225, fig. 13).

scriptions, new statues were created as the direct result of royal edicts, and it is thus fascinating to note that in sponsoring the statues of deities, a king was to some extent identifying himself with the sole creator. According to the tradition preserved in the Memphite Theology, gods came into being via the conceived thought and spoken word of the supreme god (Ptah in Memphis). "He gave birth to the gods; he made the towns; he established the nomes; he placed the gods in their shrines; he settled their offerings; he established their shrines; he made their bodies according to their wishes. Thus the gods entered into their bodies, of every wood, every stone, every clay, everything that grows upon him in which they came to be. Thus were gathered to him all the gods and their *ka*s, content, united with the Lord of the Two Lands" (Lichtheim 1975:55). Like the Early Dynastic king, Ptah resided in Memphis, bore royal titles, and created of his own initiative the bodies of the gods.

As part of his primordial cosmic duties, the typical Early Dynastic king also constructed new shrines and temples for the gods (e.g., the Thrones-of-the-Gods, the Mouth-of-Horus, The Goddess-Abides, and the Throne-of-Horus-the-Harpooner). Moreover, he periodically officiated at their most important festivals (e.g., the Sokar Festival, the Adoring-Horus-of-the-Sky Festival, and the *Sopdu* Festival). The creation of statues and the founding or embellishment of various cults, especially those cults most easily adapted to the new royal ideology, assuredly entailed also the establishment of generous endowments, as are elaborated in the more detailed redactions of the Fifth Dynasty annals (e.g., Wilkinson 2000:PS v.II.2; PS v.III.1; PS v.IV.3). By participating in festivals that were no doubt promoted as essential to the country's welfare, the king created a stage for himself on which to be actively viewed by a substantial segment of his subjects performing vital spiritual work on their behalf. Likewise, by liberally bestowing wealth upon local power centers, the king may have attempted to purchase the loyalty of these regions and, especially, that of their most influential citizens.

If founding divine statues and temples were the deeds of the creator deity and of the creators of the Egyptian state, it is hardly surprising that rulers emulated these same deeds throughout pharaonic history. This exultant enumeration of Horemheb's accomplishments immediately after ascending the throne illustrates how direct royal involvement in cultic affairs could be. It takes little imagination to envision how the bestowal of such largess upon the cults of deities, not to mention cultic office upon king's men, worked to shore up political and spiritual support for all manner of pharaonic activity.

> And lo, he set in order this land, organizing it after (the manner of) the time of Ra. He renewed the temples of the gods (from) the marshes of the Delta to Nubia. He fashioned all their images, distinguished above the original(s) and surpassing in beauty through what he did to them.... He sought out the precincts of the gods which were in ruins in this land and set them in order (even) as they were since the time of primal antiquity, and instituted for them regular offerings (on) every day, and every vessel of their fanes was fashioned in gold and silver. He equipped them with ordinary priests and lectors from the pick of the army, and opened up for them fields and herds equipped with all services, they rising up early to pay honor to Ra at the beginning of the morning every day: Do thou lengthen for us the kingship of thy son who does what pleaseth thy heart, Deserkheprure-setpenre, and mayst thou give him millions of jubilees [*Heb-Seds*] and set his victories over all lands like Horus son of Isis, even as he propitiates thy heart in On and thy Ennead join thee. (Gardiner 1953:15–16)

The royal gifts lavished upon the gods were evidently impressive enough to prompt their priests to wake up early in the morning to pray earnestly for the king's continued well-being!

Horemheb's inscription is interesting to us for a second reason—namely that all his good works for the gods unabashedly functioned as currency in the classic royal barter whereby benefactions for the gods were provided in expectation of divine assistance in military matters. Indeed, this cosmic trade may have been as old as the institution of kingship itself, for the inclusion of the shrine of Buto (*Dbꜥwt*) on the Narmer macehead in all likelihood indicated that a substantial portion of the prisoners and livestock arrayed before the king were to be donated to it. If so, we would have depicted on Narmer's two votive gifts the traditional royal cycle of reciprocity with the gods. On the palette, Horus aids (or animates) the king in battle, while on the macehead, the king returns to the gods a portion of the booty reaped from military victory as a token of appreciation for their support.

THE MESSAGE: THE KING IS THE CRUSHER OF REBELS AND THE EXPANDER OF THE ORDERED STATE

The Narmer Palette used to be read by scholars, and occasionally still is, as a symbolic narrative of Egypt's first unification. On the most visually striking side of the monument, Horus dominates a personified sign for the Northland (*tꜣ mḥw*), while the divine falcon's earthly counterpart—The King of Upper Egypt (*nswt*)—raises high his mace to deal a deathly blow to (as was often thought) the former leader of Lower Egypt. On the opposite side of the palette, act accomplished, Narmer assumes his well-won title—King of Lower Egypt (*bity*)—and processes out to the battlefield to observe the neatly decapitated remains of the vanquished army.

As our understanding of the complexities of Egyptian prehistory has grown, however, this simplistic reading has been challenged. Upper Egyptian (and Upper Egyptian-style) pottery in early levels at Buto, tags discovered in the royal tomb U-j at Abydos, *serekh*s on far-flung storage jars, and various other lines of evidence have convinced archaeologists that Egypt was more-or-less culturally unified and economically dominated by the southern kings some generations prior to the reign of Narmer. The palette, then, it is argued, could not have memorialized Narmer's victory over a united Lower Egyptian kingdom. Rather it must have represented either a symbolic (re) statement of a *fait accompli* (Wengrow 2006:204) or perhaps, if it were a recording of a real event, it depicted a victory against outsiders, such as Canaanites, Libyans, or perhaps even Nubians (e.g., Kaplony 2002:472).

Given the visual reference to a dominated Northland, the most likely reading of the palette is that it commemorates the king's victory over the polity depicted as being broken and entered by the horns of the bull-king on the bottom register of the front side. Certainly, Dreyer's recent discovery at Abydos of a label bearing a year name, in which Narmer is shown grasping the papyrus plants growing out of the head of a bearded prisoner, supports the idea that the scenes on the palette were in fact linked to a specific event (see Fig. 4; Dreyer et al. 1996:139). While it is not necessary to see in the palette the commemoration of the defeat of *the* King of Lower Egypt, it is not unlikely that Narmer is indeed shown defeating *a* Lower Egyptian kinglet, perhaps in a battle that was pivotal in establishing his uncontested control of the Delta. Certainly, the many "horizon A" *serekh*s discovered in the north during the Naqada III Period suggest that the idea of kingship was not restricted to the south, nor perhaps was it centralized in the north (Kaiser and Dreyer 1982: fig. 14; Köhler 2004:310). Seismic shifts in the power of the southern kings in and around Narmer's reign are clearly betrayed by the quantum leap in the geographic breadth and numerical saturation of his *serekh*s and also in the vast escalation in the size and opulence of those royal tombs erected following his reign. Thus it would appear likely that military ventures undertaken in his reign radically expanded his kingdom and that his successors were able to reap the substantial economic rewards of increased scale and security. Regardless, it is clear that the idea of the king as a fighter and a punisher (first witnessed perhaps in the Naqada II "Painted Tomb" at Hierakonpolis) was to emerge as a central tenet in the ideology of Early Dynastic kingship.

That Narmer and his successors were interested in projecting Egypt's influence not only over—but also beyond—the Nile Valley is demonstrated by the many *serekh*s bearing Narmer's name discovered in southern Canaan, often in conjunction with Egyptian enclaves (Braun 2002). Records from the reigns of Djer and Den, especially, demonstrate an interest not only in trading with but also in smiting easterners (Wilkinson 2000:PS r.III.2; CF1 r.II.5; CF5 r.L.2; Kaplony 2002:466). Nubia too seems to have incited avarice and aggression in Egypt's earliest pharaohs. The new kings prioritized the construction of the southern fortress at Elephantine, suggesting a clearly delineated vision of where Egypt's borders should officially be drawn. Further, victories such as those celebrated by Hor-Aha over Ta-Seti, and depicted in a graffito at Gebel Sheikh Suleiman by Scorpion and an unknown early ruler, resulted within a few generations in the total eradication of the rich and powerful kingdom at Qustul. With no rivals in the region, Early Dynastic and Early Old Kingdom rulers were left lords of a largely depopulated and eminently exploitable Lower Nubia (Wilkinson 1999:71–72, 178–81).

Egypt's third periphery was its western flank, and the word *Tjehenu*, which later signified this general area, appears already on the cities palette (albeit on the side depicting rows of animals, not the destruction of walled polities). This term presumably also designated the origin of the pinioned captives on Narmer's cylinder seal (see Fig. 1.5), and perhaps even (as witnessed by a sole *"nw"* element) that of the papyrus-headed prisoner on Narmer's label (see Fig. 1.4). If the latter identification is correct, as Dreyer et al. (1996:139) believe, it may be that the term originally designated the land into which the inhabitants of the western Delta who resisted Upper Egyptian authority fled to escape the tentacles of the state. In such a scenario, the inhabitants of *Tjehenu* would have simultaneously constituted both foreigners and rebels. Whatever the identity of the decapitated soldiers on the Narmer Palette, it is perhaps safe to assume that their nakedness, the severance of their heads from their bodies, the orderly arrangement of their corpses, and their official viewing by Narmer and his entourage were all designed to showcase the humiliation and eternal damnation that awaited enemies of the Egyptian state. Royal smiting, which was the fate reserved for the most socially important individuals of a conquered people, was likely also a publicly staged event, replete with its own abasement and horror.

Like the scribes that would later compile execration texts, the artisans that crafted the palette and the two maceheads under discussion made sure to assert the universal supremacy of the Egyptian king against *all* possible enemies, both internal and external. Under Narmer's feet on the palette, defeated representatives of cities and of villages or perhaps nomadic tribes are represented (i.e., the two categories of those-who-inhabit-walled-towns and those-who-do-not). The two sets of penned animals on the king's macehead—one wild and the other domesticated—may also symbolically represent the emic dichotomy between ordered Egyptians and disordered foreigners. Lest this last suggestion seem perhaps a reach, on the Scorpion macehead two sets of dominated entities dangle by the neck from the standards of the king's supporters (whether these are interpreted as divine, terrestrial, or—most likely—both). On one half of the macehead (according to the most plausible reconstruction) the standards suspend bows, presumably the canonical "nine bows" that together stood for the entire assemblage of Egypt's enemies. On the better-preserved section of the macehead, however, it is *rekhyt*-birds that swing by their necks. These lapwings, usually portrayed with wings pinioned behind their back and arms (!) raised in worship, designated the potentially rebellious classes within Egypt. Whether the papyrus plants that sprouted directly beneath the *rekhyt* on the Scorpion macehead were meant to signal their Lower Egyptian origin is unknown, but given the historical context, this is perhaps likely.

Explicit demonstrations of royal power directed toward an internal audience appear to have occurred periodically in the First Dynasty as the state worked to assert its authority. There is, for instance, the enigmatic record in the Palermo Stone of a ceremony in Djer's fourth year that was indicated by a lapwing with its throat severed—pictured in conjunction with the sign for "to cense" (*k3p*) and a seated figure (Wilkinson 2000:97–98, and fig. 1, PS r.II.6). Although the timing of this ceremony precludes an identification with the retainer sacrifices that took place at the time of the earliest dynastic burials, it is likely that the early state was here, as well, experimenting with how best to communicate the ideology that their new world order was worth dying for (Morris 2007). The scale of these funerary sacrifices reached an obscene pitch in the initial reigns of the First Dynasty, as hundreds of individuals were slain to bolster the otherworldly retinue of the dead king (compare Dickson, this volume, for discussion of a similar phenomenon in early Mesopotamia). Moreover, it is notable that within this impressive sample size of burials there is no osteological, archaeological, or inscriptional evidence to indicate that the victims were culled from the relatively expendable ranks of prisoners of war—quite the contrary. The bones, names, and depictions of those that escorted the deceased monarch to the afterlife are typically Egyptian.

With this in mind, it is of interest that three early First Dynasty labels from Saqqara and Abydos seem to depict the blood sacrifice of pinioned individuals in conjunction with mortuary imagery and that these bear the label "receiving (or taking—*šsp*) [from] the South and North" (Crubezy and Midant-Reynes 2000:30). It may be suggested, then, that sacrificial victims were consciously selected in state ceremony to serve as representatives from each of the Two Lands. Indeed, following from this observation, one wonders whether the statistically significant variance in the frequency and severity of porotic hyperstosis observed between the populations of retainers buried around the royal graves at Abydos and those that surrounded the valley temples may have been due to the fact that one group was traditionally harvested from the north and the other from the south (for the study on porotic hyperstosis, see Keita and Boyce 2006). The evident investment on the part of the King of Upper and Lower Egypt in emphasizing his own position as the lynchpin between the two lands will be addressed in the subsequent section.

The scale of the retainer sacrifices associated with royal funerals declined markedly as the First Dynasty wore on, presumably indicating that the state's point had been proven, or perhaps that the rulers began to realize that their message might be more receptively communicated if the killings abated. When instability again became an issue in Egypt during the waning years of Khasekhemwy's reign, however, massacres of Delta-dwellers were referenced in royal inscriptions yet again—interestingly, on statues recovered in the august company of the palette and maceheads in the Main Deposit at Hierakonpolis! While the smiting and wholesale slaughter of outsiders was to persist in Egyptian iconography right through and beyond the pharaonic period, the smiting of insiders—other Egyptians—largely disappeared from the artistic repertoire in favor of the more innocuous (and ubiquitous) image of *rekhyt*-birds, apparently content in their subdued state, worshipping the king. It is telling, however, that one of the rare exceptions to this rule—a scene of Nebhepetra Mentuhotep II smiting an Egyptian together with a Libyan, a Nubian, and an Easterner (Habachi 1963:39)—was fashioned by the very next individual to take a politically divided nation and forge it into the Kingdom of Upper and Lower Egypt.

THE MESSAGE: IN THE KING'S PERSON UPPER AND LOWER EGYPT ARE UNIFIED

On the two maceheads and the Narmer Palette the above message—assiduously perpetuated and elaborated upon by pharaohs over the ages—was already driven home. Narmer, of course, is seen in both an Upper and a Lower Egyptian crown on the palette, asserting his claimed sovereignty over both regions. Although he wears only a crown of Lower Egypt on the macehead, his dominance over the Two Lands was aptly signalled by the tutelary goddess of Upper Egypt, Nekhbet, who hovered in her aspect of vulture protectively just above his head. Finally, on the Scorpion macehead, the king is depicted in a crown of Upper Egypt, but Lower Egypt is visible in the multiple clumps of papyrus arrayed right behind him, and more than one scholar has suggested that this Upper Egyptian Scorpion would originally have faced a corresponding Lower Egyptian Scorpion on the portion of the macehead that is now all but entirely destroyed (see Baines 1995b:119).

By the reign of Djet, a short way into the First Dynasty, a new crown was developed that combined elements from the crowns of Upper and Lower Egypt to form together a single entity, known as the Two-Powers (*sekhemty*—Wilkinson 1999:73, 75, 196). The royal dominion over both the Delta and the narrow band of Nile Valley that stretched southward from it was similarly stressed in two of the four regnal names that kings utilized in the First Dynasty: the *nsw-bity* throne name and the Two Ladies name. The first of these combined the words for king associated with each of the two crowns, and the second referenced the protective goddesses Nekhbet of El-Kab and Wadjet of Buto, each of whom was also identified with the crown of her region and believed to infuse it with her spirit. Due to the divine nature of these crowns—goddesses in their own right—they typically dwelt in the two most sacred royal ancestral shrines in Egypt, namely the *Per-wer* of Hierakonpolis and the *Per-neser* of Buto (Frankfort 1978:95–97, 131). These shrines, although quite likely remodeled numerous times over the ages in brick and stone, continued to function as the twin hearts of the cult of kingship throughout Egyptian history and were represented in art and writing as reed shrines of the general type perhaps best typified by the predynastic temple HK29, excavated at Hierakonpolis (HK29—Adams 1999:373).

In royal ideology, then, if there were two crowns, it was important that they be melded into the single crown that sat upon the forehead of the king and infused him with the Two Powers. Likewise, from the First Dynasty onward the existence of the Two very different Lands was trumpeted, but primarily in order to enhance the luster of the royal act of unifying them. Indeed, the first duty of a newly crowned king was to ritually re-enact this foundational event. The First Dynasty annals tersely summarize the cardinal performative events of the coronation: "the appearance of the King of Upper Egypt and Lower Egypt; the union of the Two Lands (*smꜣ šmꜥ tꜣ-mḥw*); the procession around the wall (*pḥr hꜣ inb*)" (e.g., Wilkinson 2000:PS r.V.8; PS v.I.2; CF1 r.III.3). In the act of physically traversing the extent of the white walls of his capital city, the new king symbolically and publicly laid claim—as his ancestors had before him—to everything that existed within the country's borders.

The act of investiture that took place in the dual shrines of kingship served a similar purpose, for the regalia received was both sacred and infused with symbolism, much of it related to the king's unique position as the sole unifying symbol of his country. In the Pyramid Texts, for example, in an otherworldly enactment of his coronation, the king asks to receive the shepherd's crook, which functioned to materialize the word "ruler" (*ḥḳꜣ*) and to evoke the metaphor of the king as the caretaker of humanity (envisioned as the noble cattle of the god). The king explicitly asks to receive this crook—which was similar in shape assuredly to that carried by Narmer on his palette and also to the crooks of his predecessors buried in tombs U-547 and U-j at Abydos—so that "the head of Lower and Upper Egypt may be bowed" (Faulkner 1969:PT 222 + Dreyer 1998: pl. 36; Dreyer et al. 1996:21).

The king's role as the unifier of his country was not only stressed in his accession and in the regalia that he adopted as king, but it was ritually reaffirmed in the *Sed* Festival—the festival of the bull's tail—that served to revivify the king after (ideally) thirty years on the throne. This festival may well be depicted already on the Narmer macehead, judging from the king's enveloping garment, the presence of the boundary markers, the palinquin (of a type that in later *Heb-Sed* celebrations carried members of the royal family), and the Followers of Horus assembled on their standards. The incorporation of the latter two elements in conjunction with the king's tail and the female dancers may similarly suggest a *Sed* Festival setting for the imagery on the Scorpion macehead, although this is perhaps too bold a statement as royal ritual is not well understood for this early period. Finally, there is the third massive macehead discovered at Hierakonpolis in the Main Deposit, which depicts a king (probably Narmer or Scorpion) clad in *Sed* Festival robes, seated under a canopy, and wearing the crown of Lower Egypt (Quibell 1900: pl. 26A). For Early Dynastic kings, too, this ceremony appears from statuary, annals, and other inscriptions to have preoccupied much of their (often anticipatory) attention, as it would for pharaohs ever after (Jiménez Serrano 2002:42–78). It comes then as little surprise that Egypt's first elaborate stone masonry complex, commissioned by a Third Dynasty king named Netjerikhet (lit. The-Divine-One-of-the-Corporation-of-Gods), was largely devoted to enabling this king's spirit to celebrate millions upon millions of *Sed* Festivals.

As essentially a re-enactment of the king's own coronation—and by the same token a commemoration of the original unification of Egypt—*Sed*

Festivals essentially elaborated upon the script laid out for a coronation in the royal annals. On the Days of the White Crown and the Days of the Red Crown, the king made his appearance as a *nesu* and a *bity*. He ran a race encircling Egypt's symbolic boundary stones (which perhaps evoked in their shape the crenulations of the white walls of Memphis), and by the Third Dynasty at least he did this clutching the deeds to the country as a whole that had been bestowed upon him by the gods. In the course of the ceremony the king visited reed-built representations of the most important sanctuaries of the south and north, including the *Per-wer* and the *Per-neser*. He received again the most important symbols of office, and he processed in the company of the Followers of Horus. The intentional and ever increasing archaism of the rites and of their architectural setting was a key feature of the *Sed* Festival and one boasted about by the officials of Amenhotep III, who had intensively researched these rites in dusty archives (see generally Uphill 1965; Hornung and Staehelin 1974).

If the symbolism inherent in the coronation and the *Sed* Festival emphasized the king's role as the only personage capable of uniting the Two Lands, the very act of holding these ceremonies demonstrated this point. For these two central festivals of kingship, all the leading figures of the terrestrial and celestial realms came together to pay their respects to the king, to give him gifts, and to receive gifts in return. As the accumulator and the disburser of his country's wealth in these ceremonies and more mundanely in annual practice, the king thus served as the focal point of an extremely impressive administrative apparatus.

THE MESSAGE: THE KING IS THE HEAD OF THE ADMINISTRATION AND THE BESTOWER OF BOUNTY

A thriving bureaucracy that oversees the accumulation and distribution of surplus is a hallmark of state societies, and its presence appears to be indicated obliquely in the monuments of the earliest kings. The Scorpion macehead, for instance, depicts the king perhaps symbolically "cutting the ribbon" in the context of an agricultural project, presumably one intended to increase future food stores. Whether the king is depicted opening up a new irrigation canal or hacking up earth in preparation for planting is unclear, but the anticipated results of his efforts are not. Facing him, behind the man who proffers his basket to catch the king's earth, is a distinctively dressed official holding what looks to be a stylized sheaf of grain. This same official—variously labeled *t* and *tt* and often thought to be the forerunner of the *ṯȝty* vizier—likewise appears among the king's entourage on Narmer's macehead and palette. Significantly, when this official holds the grain on the Scorpion macehead and when he strides out to view the remains of the massacre on the Narmer Palette, he carries with him a scribal kit.

Writing at the dawn of the state was a very new and seemingly tightly monopolized technology. Excavations in Cemetery U at Abydos, and especially at the royal grave U-j, suggest that the first systematic employment of symbols to represent sounds and convey complex concepts occurred at the time that Upper Egypt was first unified and, thus, that unprecedented quantities of goods and information flowed toward the royal center. Like the use of cylinder seals to mark property, writing was almost certainly an administrative tool imported as a concept from Mesopotamia along with all manner of other precious commodities and exotic imagery (such as the snakey-necked felines on Narmer's Palette). Insofar as it is possible to tell from the many inscriptions recovered from U-j, scribes initially employed this technology predominantly to identify the provenience of goods destined to be property of the state (at least insofar as the state was embodied in the person of its dead king). Indeed, this situation seems to have persisted throughout the Early Dynastic Period, judging from the fact that such an overwhelming percentage of contemporary inscriptional evidence comes from the excavations of the royal tombs at Abydos and from the fabulously opulent tombs of the kings' intimates at Saqqara.

The position of the king as the focal point for accumulated surplus, whether agricultural or in the form of human and animal chattel, is brought out in the two maceheads, and it is thus perhaps to be expected that the officials appearing in the Early Dynastic inscriptional repertoire are predominantly those whose duties included the oversight of various royal estates and the collection and storage of resources more generally (Wilkinson 1999:111–33). Indeed, the internal colonization of the Delta with new revenue-producing domains, estates, and even whole towns began at this time full force, continued throughout pharaonic history, and ratcheted up in intensity yet again once Egypt fell under the rule of foreign powers.

The primary method employed by Egypt's first kings to assess and presumably partially requisition the wealth of their new subjects was a biennial tour of the country known in the annals as the Following of Horus, perhaps in reference to the four standards that accompanied the king or else simply to the spectacle created by the sight of a royal entourage on the move (perhaps best envisioned by the boat processions depicted in the Painted Tomb at Hierakonpolis, on the Turin Linen, on D-ware pots, on ivory knife handles, and in countless petroglyphs). This waterborne royal progress likely served many purposes, as it has for rulers throughout the world since states began. By touring his country, the monarch was able to make his (undoubtedly resplendent) presence known throughout his realm and to visually enforce the ideology that placed him above all other mortals and in the company of the gods (in the person of their standards). During his progress, the armed contingent of his entourage reminded his regional officials of who was in charge, and the king was simultaneously afforded the opportunity to inspect such men with an eye toward determining their loyalty and potential powerbase. On analogy to later royal travels, the tour undoubtedly also presented the king with an opportunity to pay his respects to the local deities in their temples and perhaps to arbitrate pressing legal matters (Baines 2006:271, 290; Breasted 1988b:91–92; Gardiner 1953:16; Kuhrt 1995:633).

More cynically, however, royal progresses traditionally offer an opportunity for the court to absorb for itself a substantial portion of local revenues in elaborate ceremonial contexts (by virtue of attending feasts and receiving "gifts") and to assess firsthand (in conjunction with knowledge gained from the Nile flood records) realistic expectations for future income. In the Early Dynastic Period, the Following of Horus often explicitly co-occurred with a census (*ṯnwt*), and the progress likely should be equated as well with the biennial cattle-count that eventually replaced it and with periodic inventories of specific sources of wealth such as people, fields, livestock, and minerals (e.g., Wilkinson 2000:PS r.III.4; PS r.V.3, 5; CF1 vII.1) that took place at a period when Horus no longer accompanied his tax collectors.

Presumably because showing the flag was no longer deemed necessary once kingship was an unquestioned norm and the country possessed a competent bureaucratic infrastructure, the Following of Horus ceased to be a regular practice by the advent of the Old Kingdom. The cessation may also have been, however, a bow to public opinion, as preparations to receive the king (above and beyond preparations to accumulate the expected taxes) could be burdensome. Under British rule the royal progresses of the Nyoro king in Uganda and Zaire were "frowned upon by the European district officials, who held that the Mukama used them as a means of economizing on his palace expenses. They were also growing increasingly unpopular with the people, who were required to contribute labor and foodstuffs to support them, and saw little or no return for their efforts, but they were important traditionally, both in enabling the Mukama to keep an eye on the activities of his chiefs of all ranks in their areas, and also in keeping him in touch with trends in public opinion throughout the country" (Beattie 1971:138). Given the fact that the Early Dynastic royal progress coincided with the original attempts of these kings to naturalize their rule and assert military, economic, and ideological control over their new subjects, it is of interest that the only other time when such royal progresses reappear in Egyptian history is in the reign of Thutmose III, precisely when this king was attempting to solidify and to systematize his control over a newly won and very unruly northern empire.

The amount of revenue garnered from nationwide taxation, from long-distance trade, and from battle (as hinted at by the undoubtedly exaggerated totals of cattle and livestock enumerated on the Narmer macehead) would have been staggering. Certainly, the vast quantities of wealth interred with the First Dynasty kings and with their closest companions buried in the mastabas at Saqqara provide one window onto its expenditure, and no doubt the maintenance of a sumptuous court in a newly created capital city likewise dented the coffers. Much that was accumulated, however, was likely redistributed to gods and priests, to nobles (in the form of boons that the king gave and in reward ceremonies), to workers on state projects and in state workshops, and to state functionaries of all sorts—including those in charge of recording such disbursements! (Compare Sallaberger, this volume, on Mesopotamian kings as the distributors of largesse.) Finally, lavish royal events such as coronations or *Sed* Festivals were well known for the distribution of the bounty that had been collected, as inscriptions and archaeological evidence at sites such as Malkata attest (Frankfort 1978:130, 132; Hayes 1951:31–40, 82–104, 156–83, 231–42; Hope 1977).

Whether the state's supply was intended also for crisis management, as in times of disastrous floods, is not known. Food relief, the construction of canals (such as might be represented on the Scorpion macehead), and other methods of agricultural intensification undoubtedly bolstered the legitimacy of regional leaders in the First Intermediate Period, and might be speculated to have done so as well at the dawn of the state, as evidence suggests that floods around this period were particularly unstable (Bell 1970). If the distribution of food to the hungry was indeed an important component of the king's mandate to rule, however, it is remarkable how little this message seems to have been promoted by the court, both in these early monuments and forever after. When royal largess is depicted in state-commissioned artwork, its subject is most often the king offering to the gods or showering golden baubles upon deserving nobles, rather than sharing royal larders with individuals in need. Clearly, then, the pharaoh did not promote himself primarily as man *of* and *for* the people, rather he more commonly boasted of his position as a man *of* and *for* the gods.

CONCLUSION

The messages that Scorpion and Narmer composed and communicated to the gods (and to those mortals privileged enough to enter Hierakonpolis' holiest temple) were largely the same ideological tenets that pharaohs promoted in religious and secular contexts for the following three millennia: the king was no ordinary mortal; he possessed access to the world of the gods and successfully solicited their blessings. The king used both force and an able administration to maintain order in his realm, and in his person he alone unified the dangerously disparate parts of his country. The sociologist Michael Mann (1986) has subdivided ultimate power into four potentially discrete spheres: ideological, military, economic, and political. Narmer and Scorpion, already prior to the First Dynasty, had usurped all of these and enfolded them into their own role as king.

Throughout the eons following the reigns of Scorpion and Narmer there were many variations upon these essential themes. The gods that gave the king their blessing (or even engendered him) differed such that at different periods or in different contexts the sun god or the god of one or another capital cities or anthropomorphized concepts might receive the most credit. Some kings stressed their own status as a divinity on earth, while others laid more emphasis upon their role as humanity's intercessor with the gods. All kings took credit for military victories, but some kings trumpeted them more and even accompanied their armies on the day of battle. The amount of resources funneled directly into the royal coffers and spending priorities also changed with administrations, as did the degree to which it was the king who made decisions as opposed to his councilors. For all of the rulers who adopted the red and white crowns and endeavored to rule Egypt, however, the legacy left to them had been articulated already on the outsized maces and palettes of two primordial rulers and in the ceremonies and performances they staged in order to publicize the foundational tenets of their new ideology.

NOTE

1.1 This cache, discovered in 2007, is as yet published only online. See http://www.archaeology.org/interactive/hierakonpolis/field07/6.html, accessed May 27, 2008.

REFERENCES

Adams, B. 1995. *Ancient Nekhen. Garstang in the City of Hierakonpolis*. Surrey: SIA Publishing.

———. 1999. Hierakonpolis. In *Encyclopedia of the Archaeology of Ancient Egypt*, ed. K. Bard, pp. 371–74. New York: Routledge.

Baer, K. 1960. *Rank and Title in the Old Kingdom: The Structure of the Egyptian Administration in the Fifth and Sixth Dynasties*. Chicago: University of Chicago Press.

Baines, J. 1994. On the Status and Purposes of Ancient Egyptian Art. *CAJ* 4 (1): 67–94.

———. 1995a. Kingship, Definition of Culture, and Legitimation. In *Ancient Egyptian Kingship*, ed. D. O'Connor and D.P. Silverman, pp. 30–47. PdÄ 9. New York: Brill.

———. 1995b. Origins of Egyptian Kingship. In *Ancient Egyptian Kingship*, ed. D. O'Connor and D.P. Silverman, pp. 95–156. PdÄ 9. New York: Brill.

———. 2006. Public Ceremonial Performance in Ancient Egypt: Exclusion and Integration. In *Archaeology of Performance. Theaters of Power, Community, and Politics*, ed. T. Inomata and L.S. Coben, pp. 261–302. New York: AltaMira Press.

Beattie, J. 1971. *The Nyoro State*. London: Oxford University Press.

Bell, B. 1970. The Oldest Records of the Nile Floods. *Geographical Journal* 136:569–73.

Blackman, A.M. 1915. The Pharaoh's Placenta and the Moon-God Khons. *JEA* 3:235–49.

Braun, E. 2002. Egypt's First Sojourn in Canaan. In *Egypt and the Levant. Interrelations from the 4th through the Early 3rd Millennium B.C.E.*, ed. E.C.M. van den Brink and T.E. Levy, pp. 173–89. New York: Leicester University Press.

Breasted, J.H. 1988a. *Ancient Records of Egypt I*. London: Histories & Mysteries of Man, Ltd. Reprint.

———. 1988b. *Ancient Records of Egypt II*. London: Histories & Mysteries of Man, Ltd. Reprint.

Brunner, H. 1982. Menes. *LÄ* IV, ed. W. Helck et al., pp. 46–48. Weisbaden: Harrassowitz.

Carter, H. 1972. *The Tomb of Tutakhamen*. New York: E.P. Dutton.

Crubezy, É., and B. Midant-Reynes. 2000. Les sacrifices humains à l'époque prédynastique: L'apport de la nécropole d'Adaïma. *Archéo-Nil* 10:21–40.

Dreyer, G. 1998. *Umm el-Qaab I. Das prädynastische Königsgrab U-j und seine frühen Schriftzeugnisse*. Mainz: Philipp von Zabern.

Dreyer, G., E.-M. Engel, U. Hartung, T. Hikade, E. C. Köhler, and F. Pumpenmeier. 1996. Umm el-Qaab. Nachuntersuchungen im frühzeitlichen Königsfriedhof 7/8 Vorbericht. *MDAIK* 52:11–81.

Dreyer, G, U. Hartung, T. Hikade, E.C. Köhler, V. Müller, and F. Pumpenmeier. 1998. Umm el-Qaab. Nachuntersuchungen im frühzeitlichen Königsfriedhof. 9/10 Vorbericht. *MDAIK* 54:77–167.

DuQuesne, T. 2005. *The Jackal Divinities of Egypt I: From the Archaic Period to Dynasty X*. Oxfordshire Communications in Egyptology VI. London: Darengo Publications.

Erman, A., and H. Grapow. 1929. *Wörterbuch der Ägyptischen Sprache III*. Leipzig: J.C. Hinrichs.

Faulkner, R.O. 1969. *The Ancient Egyptian Pyramid Texts*. Warminster: Aris & Phillips.

Feeley-Harnik, G. 1985. Issues in Divine Kingship. *Annual Review of Anthropology* 14:273–313.

Frankfort, H. 1978. *Kingship and the Gods. A Study of Ancient Near Eastern Religion as the Integration of Society and Nature*. Chicago: University of Chicago Press.

Friedman, R.F. 1996. The Ceremonial Center at Hierakonpoils HK29A. In *Aspects of Early Egypt*, ed. J. Spencer, pp. 16–35. London: British Museum Press.

———. 2004. Elephants at Hierakonpolis. In *Egypt at Its Origins. Studies in Memory of Barbara Adams*, ed. S. Hendrickx, R.F. Friedman, K.M. Cialowicz, and M. Chlodnicki, pp. 131–68. Leuven: Peeters.

Gardiner, A.H. 1953. The Coronation of King Haremhab. *JEA* 39:13–31.

Habachi, L. 1963. King Nebhepetre Mentuhotep: His Monuments, Place in History, Deification and Unusual Representation in the Form of Gods.

MDAIK 19:16–52.

———. 1969. *Features of the Deification of Ramesses II*. Glückstadt: J.J. Augustin.

Hayes, W.C. 1951. Inscriptions from the Palace of Amenhotep III. *JNES* 10:35–56, 82–104, 156–83, 231–42.

Hope, C. 1977. *Jar Sealings and Amphorae of the 18th Dynasty: A Technological Study*. Warminster: Aris & Phillips.

Hornung, E. 1982. *Conceptions of God in Ancient Egypt. The One and the Many*, trans. J. Baines. Ithaca: Cornell University Press.

Hornung, E., and E. Staehelin. 1974. *Studien zum Sedfest*. Basel: Edition de Belles-Lettres.

———. 1987. *Studies on the Middle Kingdom*. Budapest: Chaire de l'Égyptologie.

Jiménez Serrano, A. 2002. *Royal Festivals in the Late Predynastic Period and the First Dynasty*. Oxford: BAR International.

Kaiser, W. 1959. Einige Bemerkungen zur agyptischen Fruhzeit I: Zu den šmsw-ḥr. *ZÄS* 84:119–32.

Kaiser, W., and G. Dreyer. 1982. Umm el-Qaab. Nachuntersuchungen im frühzeitlishen Königsfriedhof. 2. Vorbericht. *MDAIK* 38:211–69.

Kaplony, P. 2002. The Bet Yerah Jar Inscription and the Annals of King Dewen—Dewen as "King Narmer Redivivus." In *Egypt and the Levant. Interrelations from the 4th through the Early 3rd Millennium B.C.E.*, ed. E.C.M. van den Brink and T.E. Levy, pp. 464–86. New York: Leicester University Press.

Keita, S.O.Y., and A.J. Boyce. 2006. Variation in Porotic Hyperostosis in the Royal Cemetery Complex at Abydos, Upper Egypt, a Social Interpretation. *Antiquity* 80, no. 307:64–73.

Kemp, B. 1991. *Ancient Egypt: Anatomy of a Civilization*. London: Routledge.

———. 2000. The Colossi from the Early Shrine at Coptos in Egypt. *CAJ* 10:211–42.

Köhler, E.C. 2004. On the Origins of Memphis—The New Excavations in the Early Dynastic Necropolis at Helwan. In *Egypt at Its Origins. Studies in Memory of Barbara Adams*, ed. S. Hendrickx, R.F. Friedman, K.M. Cialowicz, and M. Chlodnicki, pp. 295–315. Leuven: Peeters.

Kuhrt, A. 1995. *The Ancient Near East c. 3000–330 BC, Volume Two*. New York: Routledge.

Lichtheim, M. 1975. *Ancient Egyptian Literature I: The Old and Middle Kingdoms*. Berkeley: University of California Press.

Mann, M. 1986. *The Sources of Social Power: A History of Power from the Beginning to AD 1760*, Vol. I. Cambridge: Cambridge University Press.

Morris, E. 2007. Sacrifice for the State: Royal Funerals and the Rites at Macramallah's Rectangle. In *Performing Death. Social Analyses of Ancient Funerary Traditions in the Mediterranean*, ed. Nicola Laneri, pp. 15–37. Oriental Institute Seminars 3. Chicago: Oriental Institute.

Parkinson, R. 1997. *The Tale of Sinuhe and Other Ancient Egyptian Poems 1940–1640 BC*. New York: Oxford University Press.

Petrie, W.M.F. 1989[1900]. *The Royal Tombs of the First Dynasty, Part I*. London: Egypt Exploration Fund (reprint by Histories & Mysteries of Land).

Posener, G. 1965. Le nom de l'ensigne appelée "Khons." *RdE* 17:193–95.

Quibell, J.E. 1900. *Hierakonpolis I*. London: B. Quaritch.

Quibell, J.E., and F.W. Green. 1902. *Hierakonpolis II*. London: B. Quaritch.

Sethe, K. 1933. *Urkunden des Alten Reichs I*. Leipzig: J.C. Hinrichs'sche Buchhandlung.

Silverman, D.P. 1995. The Nature of Egyptian Kingship. In *Ancient Egyptian Kingship*, ed. D. O'Connor and D.P. Silverman, pp. 49–87. PdÄ 9. New York: E.J. Brill.

Spencer, A.J. 1993. *Early Egypt: The Rise of Civilisation in the Nile Valley*. Norman: University of Oklahoma Press.

Strudwick, N.C. 2005. *Texts from the Pyramid Age. Writings from the Ancient World* 16. Atlanta: Society of Biblical Literature.

Te Velde, H. 1967. *Seth, God of Confusion: A Study of His Role in Egyptian Myth and Religion*. PdÄ 6. Leiden: Brill.

———. 2001. Seth. In *Oxford Encyclopedia of Ancient Egypt III*, ed. D.B. Redford, pp. 269–71. New York: Oxford University Press.

Uphill, E. 1965. The Egyptian Sed-Festival Rites. *JNES* 24:365–83.

Warman, S. 2004. Predynastic Egyptian Bovid Burial in the Elite Cemetery at Hierakonpolis. In *Behavior Behind Bones. The Zooarchaeology of Ritual, Religion, Status and Identity*, ed. S.J. O'Day et al., pp. 34–40. Oxford: Oxbow Books.

Wengrow, D. 2006. *The Archaeology of Early Egypt: Social Transformations in North-East Africa, 10,000–2,650 B.C.* Cambridge: Cambridge University Press.

Wildung, D. 1977. *Egyptian Saints: Deification in Pharaonic Egypt*. New York: New York University Press.

Wilkinson, T. 1999. *Early Dynastic Egypt*. New York: Routledge.

———. 2000. *Royal Annals of Ancient Egypt. The Palermo Stone and Its Associated Fragments*. New York: Kegan Paul International.

Williams, B.B. 1988. Narmer and the Coptos Colossi. *JARCE* 25:35–59.

2

"I Am the Sun of Babylon": Solar Aspects of Royal Power in Old Babylonian Mesopotamia

DOMINIQUE CHARPIN[1]

In Mesopotamia, manifestations of light play a crucial role in the formulation of feelings. The face of one who is angry is "dark";[2] in contrast, one who is satisfied "radiates," sometimes occurring with the additional complement "as the sun." And so a woman who receives good news from the brother she thought dead states: "I rejoiced greatly so: 'Addiya is not dead, Addiya is living!' and I shined like the sun."[3] Another example can be found in a letter whose sender expects the king to visit the troops before he leads the expedition: "When my lord will stand in the assembly of his servants and his servants will see him, the heart of the soldiers will live. And when my lord will reach his goal with his troops, then the heart of his troops will shine like the sun."[4] In all those cases, we are dealing with metaphors.[5] On the other hand, the prologue of the famous *Code of Ḫammurapi* shows that the king identifies himself with the Sun-god. After enumerating the main cities of his kingdom, the king declares: "I am the Sun of the city of Babylon, who spreads light over the lands of Sumer and Akkad."[6] The sentence is unambiguous: Babylon is in the center of Ḫammurapi's kingdom, and from his capital he shines over all his territories. This feature is not an innovation of the Amorite period. Already at the end of the 3rd millennium, Shulgi proclaimed himself "Sun of his land," or "faithful god, sun of his land" (Seux 1967:46; s.v. ᵈutu). In the same way, Shu-ilishu of Isin described himself as the "Sun of Sumer." Such a conception of kingship, that is identifying the king with the Sun-god, influenced Babylonia as much as Assyria. Kurigalzu is described as "a judge who investigates matters" (Seux 1967:66; *s.v. dayyānu*). We also find the epithet "Sun of his land" in an inscription of Nebuchadnezzar I and the set phrase "Sun of all the human beings" in inscriptions of several Assyrian kings from Tukulti-Ninurta I onwards (references in Seux 1967:284). Nebuchadnezzar II is also described as "the one who like Shamash watches over every land" (Seux 1967:52; *s.v. barû*). When one considers the theme of the Sun-king, the period of El-Amarna immediately springs to mind, indeed for the Hittites the Sun also played a crucial role with sovereigns referring to themselves as "My sun." In this chapter, I shall not deal with the examples of Hittite kings nor Egyptian kings, which would, of course, require a lengthy comparison with Mesopotamian ideology.

The present contribution offers an interpretation of this solar image of the king, primarily during the Old Babylonian period. What I was not fully aware of at the beginning, but which is clear to me now through treating this theme in the context of this conference, "Experiencing Power—Generating Authority: Cosmos and Politics in the Ideology of Kingship in Ancient Egypt and Mesopotamia," is that the subject certainly has some connection with my own identity as, for the French, ever since the reign of Louis XIV kingship is immediately connected to the sun.

THE KING AND THE GOD SHAMASH

Shamash and Justice

In the Mesopotamian pantheon, each god was the patron of a special aspect of the universe: Gula was the mistress of health, Adad settled the rains, and so on. These aspects can be found in two different areas: in the prayers addressed to the gods, but also and perhaps even more in the curses that invoke them. The god Shamash is attested as a god of justice since the 3rd millennium.[7] The reason for such an association is explicitly given in the famous "Shamash Hymn."[8] Because the sun travels across the earth during the day, he sees all that is happening, even what is hidden from the eyes of men (Reiner 1985:72, line 58): "You are the one who brings light to the case of the evil and the criminal."

We also find that the rays of the sun are similar to a net that capture the evildoer: "Your brilliance overwhelms the earth like a net."[9] This explains why some oaths were sworn *ina saparrim*, literally "through/with a net."

Klaas Veenhof has explained that such oaths were sworn in the room of a Shamash temple where a net was hanging from the ceiling, symbolising the rays of the sun, which would capture any perjury committed.[10]

This close association of the Sun with justice explains why, high on the famous Stele of *Ḫammurapi's Code*, now in the Louvre, the god in front of whom the Babylonian king stands is the god Shamash. It is not Marduk, the main god of Babylon, as is sometimes stated.[11] It is true that in the prologue of the *Code*, the gods Anu, Enlil, and Enki entrust Marduk with omnipotence; after that, they fix the destiny of Babylon and finally that of Ḫammurapi. In the epilogue also, the king states that his stele is placed in his capital, Babylon, within Marduk's temple, the Esagil (Roth 1995:133–34, xlvii:59–78):

> In order that the mighty not wrong the weak, to provide just ways for the waif and the widow, I have inscribed my precious pronouncements upon my stela and set it up before the statue of me, the king of justice, in the city of Babylon, the city which the gods Anu and Enlil have elevated, within the Esagil, the temple whose foundations are fixed as are heaven and earth, in order to render the judgments of the land, to give the verdicts of the land, and to provide just ways for the wronged.

But just after this section—and before Marduk—Shamash is mentioned (Roth 1995:134, xlvii:79–xlviii:2):

> I am the king pre-eminent among kings. My pronouncements are choice, my ability is unrivalled. By the command of the god Šamaš, the great judge of heaven and earth, may my justice prevail in the land. By the order of the god Marduk, my lord, may my engraved image not be confronted by someone who would remove it. May my name always be remembered favorably in the Esagil temple which I love.

This passage has been very aptly commented on by Martha Roth (2002:40a): "The king has the separate backing of the gods Šamaš and Marduk—Šamaš to endorse Hammurabi's claim of justice and wisdom, and Marduk to endorse Hammurabi's right to erect the stela and its inviolability." In addition, we should clarify that the depiction of Shamash, high on the copy of the *Code* stele kept in the Louvre, has nothing to do with its provenance, almost undoubtedly Sippar, where Shamash was the main protecting divinity. Indeed we know that it is from Sippar that an Elamite conqueror of the 12th century took the stele as booty to bring to Susa, where the French excavation team found it in 1902 (André-Salvini 2003); and it is to my mind certain that the stele erected in the temple of Marduk in Babylon bore a similar representation. This stele of the Esagil, which we do not know, is certainly the original from which replicas were made and inscribed in order to be placed in the principal temples of the kingdom.[12] If the stele of the other temples had been modified, modifications would be occurring for both iconography and formulation: however the text of the Sippar copy (in the Louvre) mentions the introduction of the Stele in the Esagil of Babylon, not in the Ebabbar of Sippar.[13]

The connection between Shamash, god of justice, and Marduk, god of Babylon, can be found in three year names of successors of Ḫammurapi, which commemorate the proclamation of a redress (*mîšarum*) promulgated by the ruler:[14]

— year name 13? of Abi-eshuh:[15]
"Year: Abi-eshuh, the king, the humble prince, to whom Shamash listened, the ... of Marduk, remitted the debts from his country."

— year name 21 of Ammi-ditana:[16]
"Year: Ammi-ditana, the king, the fierce great ruler, beloved of Shamash and Marduk, remitted the debts that his country has incurred."

— year name 10 of Ammi-saduqa:[17]
"Year: Ammi-saduqa, the king, the loyal, obedient shepherd of Shamash and Marduk, remitted the debts of his land."

Shamash and Divination

Shamash was not only a god of justice. He played a crucial role for the sovereign in his exercise of power, a role which can appear to us to be a separate function, while for the Mesopotamians it was another facet of the same reality: he was the patron of divination.[18] The exercise of power was only possible with the constant use of divination, which enabled the king to make good decisions, whether in diplomacy or war.[19]

Divination and justice went hand in hand for Babylonians: in both cases, it was the fairness of the judgment that was important, whether it was a decision taken in the heavens or on earth,[20] as the ritual of the Old Babylonian diviners testifies. The prayer that they pronounced before sacrificing a lamb whose liver they will examine contains a hymn to Shamash (Starr 1983:30 and 37:9-2):

> O Šamaš, you have opened the locks of the gates of heaven; you went up a staircase of pure lapis lazuli.
> Lifting (it), you carry a staff of lapis lazuli in your arms for the cases that you judge.
> You judge the cases of the great gods; you judge the case of the beasts of the field; you judge the case of mankind.
> Judge today the case of so-and-so, son of so-and-so. On the right of this lamb (place) a true verdict, and on the left of this lamb place a true verdict.

We can also quote the curse against an evil king with which the *Code of Ḫammurapi* ends (Roth 1995:137–38, lines 14–40):

> "May the god Šamaš, the great judge of heaven and earth, who provides just ways for all living creatures, the lord, my trust, overturn his kingship; may he (= the bad king) not render his judgments, may he confuse his path and undermine the morale of his army; when divination is performed for him, may he (=Šamaš) provide an inauspicious omen portending the uprooting of the foundations of his kingship and the obliteration of his land; may the malevolent word of the god Šamaš swiftly overtake him, may he uproot him from among the living above and make his ghost thirst for water below in the Netherworld."

This passage shows particularly clearly the close association of justice and divination. Here an aspect of the relation of the king to divination that was not always correctly analysed unveils itself. It was recently stressed that "Hammurabi's belief in oracles was normal for the time" (Van De Mieroop 2005:115). However, we are not confronted here with a character trait:[21] scepticism toward the oracles' answer is never mentioned anywhere.[22] From this, it is not conceivable that Ḫammurapi is requesting a fabricated omen: by definition, an omen cannot be false (at worse it can be ambiguous, in which case the question will be repeated) (Charpin 1994). What Ḫammurapi asks of Shamash is an unfavorable omen: that is, a decision to afflict the future king by way of a curse should he not respect his work.

A letter from Mari shows us how, when Ḫammurapi launched his troops against Mashkan-shapir, he recalls the divine guarantee he had been given (ARM 26/2 385:13'-15'): "Now, I complained to Šamaš and Marduk and they constantly answered 'Yes!' I did not launch this attack without the consent of the gods." We find in the divinatory context the same divine duo—Shamash and Marduk—that we find in the *Code* in the context of justice.

It is for his dual title of keeper of justice and master of the future that Shamash was invoked in the context of alliance "treaties," which were in fact during the Old Babylonian period nothing more than sworn oath protocols (Charpin n.d.). The oath sworn by the king of Andarig, Atamrum, to Zimri-Lim of Mari starts thus (A.96; Joannès 1991 = LAPO 16 291): "By Šamaš of [the sky], Atamrum, son of Warad-Sîn, king of Andarig, so swore: 'I swear that from now on, as long as I live …'" When Ḫammurapi made an alliance with Zimri-Lim against the Elamite emperor who had invaded the Mesopotamian plain, the oath already sworn by the king of Mari was so described (A.4626; Charpin 1990b = LAPO 16 286):

> My lord (=Zimri-Lim) did not make an alliance with the Elamite lord. He raised for you his hand toward Šamaš through the *maṣhatum*-meal and the *saskûm*-meal and, as my lord already swore so: "I swear that I will not conclude a separate (peace) with the lord of Elam." That is what my lord swore.

The examples are numerous and one could quote a large number of them. We should remark on a very beautiful passage of the epic of Tukulti-Ninurta, where the Assyrian king invokes Shamash against his enemy, the Kassite king Kashtiliash, whom he believes has committed perjury through the non-respect of an oath which the kings of Assur and Babylon had previously sworn:[23]

> O Šamaš, lord […], I kept your oath, (and) feared your greatness. He who does not […] transgressed before your […], (but) I safeguarded your judgment. When our fathers made an agreement before your divinity, (and) established an oath between them, they invoked your greatness. You are the hero who since times past was the judge of our fathers, not changing (verdicts), and you are the god who now watches over our loy-

alty, setting (things) right. Why then, since past times has the king of the Kassites contravened your plan (and) your judgment? He has not feared your oath, has transgressed your command, has schemed falsehood. He has committed crimes against you, O Šamaš: be my judge! Bu[t as for him who] perpetrated no wrong against the king of the Kassites, a[ct favorably toward him]. By your great [command] grant victory to the one who keeps the oath. [For him who does not obey] your command, destroy his people in the defeat of the battle.

The ruling that the king requests, victory or defeat in battle, can be considered as a type of ordeal (Machinist 1978:218). In fact, the hymn to Shamash shows the role played by the Sun-god in the event of a river ordeal:[24] "You have raised from the river of the ordeal the [innocent] involved in a lawsuit."

THE KING, IMAGE OF SHAMASH ON EARTH

It is not by accident that Shamash as the patron of divination is called "master of decisions" (*bêl purussî*).[25] The relationship between the king and the god Shamash with regard to the exercise of justice does not rely on inspiration, but on imitation: as Shamash judges in the heavens and decrees the destiny of humankind,[26] so must the king on earth judge cases and issue verdicts for all his subjects.

Ḥammurapi's duty given to him by the supreme gods, Anu and Enlil, is clear: he must imitate the Sun-god. It is on that note that the first part of the prologue of the *Code* ends (Roth 1995:76–77, i 27–49): "At that time, the gods Anu and Enlil, for the enhancement of the well-being of the people, named me by my name: Hammurabi, the pious prince, who venerates the gods, to make justice (*mîšarum*) prevail in the land, to abolish the wicked and the evil, to prevent the strong from oppressing the weak, *to rise like the sun-god Šamaš over all humankind*, to illuminate the land."

Chance has it that the majority of sources dealing with this theme lead us to Ḥammurapi, however it is not a phenomenon that is exclusive to this king. With regard to his successor, we can note the existence of the name Samsuiluna-nūr-mātim (AbB 2 72:1), meaning "Samsu-iluna is the light of the land." We also note in an inscription of Samsu-iluna this epithet:[27] "who caused bright daylight to come forth for the numerous people." In fact, this theme is not exclusive to the kingdom of Babylon. In an oath of alliance sworn by the king Hazip-Teshup of Razamâ, we can read amongst the clauses (Eidem 2008:319, L.T.-2:v 6'-7'): "A verdict like divine [Šamaš (…)] I shall render."

Year name 1 of Ammi-saduqa (1646) is particularly important:[28] "Year: Ammi-saduqa, the king, faithfully went forth like the Sun-god Šamaš for the sake of his country and instituted the redress (*mîšarum*) for his countless people." This occurs at a time when the new king, in order to celebrate his accession to the throne, proclaims a *mîšarum*:[29] delinquent tributes to the palace are forgiven and private individuals who had not been able to repay their debts are relieved of their burden through an annulment, the possessions that they had to alienate are given back to them. It is important to emphasize that it is not ideology alone at play here; we have numerous texts that show the real enforcement of these decrees.[30] The proclamation of a *mîšarum* constituted a duty that the gods themselves expected of the new king; it took place at a ceremony during which the king lifted a gold torch. No texts (ritual or otherwise) describe this ceremony for which we only have three references. Witness to this is the plea of an individual who begins his petition with this call:[31] "When my lord raised high the golden torch for Sippar, instituting the redress (*mîšarum*) for Šamaš who loves him."

Another reference is contained in a loan contract dating from year 9 of Sin-muballit, wherein the scribe adds after the date:[32] "After the king raised high the golden torch." This means that the loan was agreed to after the promulgation of a *mîšarum* by Sin-muballit and is not affected by it (Kraus 1984:55).

The explanation proposed by S. Greengus, for whom "torches were used as a rapid signal, initially, to alert the population,"[33] does not seem convincing to me:[34] it is clearly specified that the king lifts up a torch *in gold*. We are in fact dealing here with a solar symbol.[35] A prayer to Shamash states:[36] "O Šamaš, your torch covers the lands (with light)!" A letter recently published links this ceremony of the "lifting of the torch" with the end of the mourning period following the death of the previous king; in that case Samsu-iluna (AbB 12 172:8'-10'): "The king promulgated a redress (*mîšarum*) for the land: he raised the golden torch for the land and ended the period of mourning of the land."[37] The new king rises over his land like the sun that, every morning, emerges from the realm of the dead and shines over the earth like a torch that dispels darkness. We further note that the king of Mari Zimri-Lim had sent as a present to Ḫammurapi of Aleppo for his accession to the throne, a solar disk (*šamšum*): the symbolic character of this gift seems very clear (Charpin 2008:90).

A letter sent to Zimri-Lim confirms the link between the proclamation of a *mîšarum* and the light that the king makes shine over the country (ARM 10 92 = LAPO 18 1211).

> Say to my lord: so (speaks) your servant Shewrum-parat. Without me learning it from your mouth, you made me a priestess when you sent me here. Well, where you are, I have been wronged (*hablâku*). Well then, sweep my tears! Sîn-mušallim wronged me: he took from me my nurse and now she lives with him. If at least it was my lord who took her from me and if she were living with him, I would be satisfied! But it is Sîn-mushallim who wronged me.
>
> Now, since you established the light for the country, establish it also for me! Give me my nurse, so that I pray for you in front of Addu and Hebat! May my lord not refuse me this woman.
>
> Here, I am you servant and your thing: place your name upon me!"

This letter was sent by a woman who had been part of the harem of Yasmah-Addu. A short time after his accession, Zimri-Lim had vowed her as a priestess, possibly to the god Addu of Aleppo.[38] But a certain Sîn-mushallim took possession of the servant of Shewrum-parat. We have a clear example here of what Addu mentions in his prophecy (see below): a wronged woman appealing to the king. What is very interesting from the perspective of this present colloquium is the phrase: "since you have established light (*nûrum*) for all the land." J.-M. Durand has interpreted this as a reference to the *mîšarum* proclaimed by Zimri-Lim shortly after his accession.[39] The argument contained in the letter seems to me to be the following: Shewrum-parat requests to benefit from that measure, even though she no longer lives in the kingdom of Mari.[40] The light of the Sun-king must extend even beyond the borders of his realm.

A last aspect allows for the underlining of a cosmic dimension of the duty given to the king. The sovereign is compared to a shepherd (sum. sipa; akk. *rê'ûm*). Indeed, in the Mesopotamian pantheon, the shepherd-god par excellence was Dumuzi (Fritz 2003). However, at the beginning of the 2nd millennium, it is Shamash before all who is the shepherd who helps shape the royal person. The hymn to Shamash titles the Sun-god thus (Reiner 1985:71, line 33). "Shepherd of the regions below, pastor of the regions above." Here again, the relationship between justice and divination is a close one: indeed, gods wrote their decisions on the liver of a lamb (Fincke 2006–2007:147, n. 109). The ritual of the diviner explicitly establishes a link between Shamash, shepherd-god, and the sacrifice of a lamb (YOS 11 23:18; Foster 2005:213): "Let the divine shepherd [=Šamaš] bring forward a sheep to the assembly of the great gods." In *Theodicy*, the sovereign, identified with the Sun-god, reassumes also his role as pastor:[41] "The shepherd, the sun of the people, pastured (his flock) like a god." What better place to quote S. Maul:[42] "Šamaš the Sun God, is accounted the 'Lord of the Above and Below,' he 'Who Sees All,' and, in consequence, 'Judge of Heaven and Earth' [*passim* in the prayers of the namburbi-rituals], since he travels by day over all the Earth and by night journeys through the regions beneath it." As the one who constantly and routinely circles the Earth, Shamash is the most striking element of dynamic order. For this reason he is reckoned to be the Guardian and Watchman of Creation; he sees to it that the universe—in the same manner as the sun—continues to move in its proper course. This role of the Sun-god as paragon and guardian is expressed by the epithet *muštēširu*, "He-who-guides-aright," an epithet that often appears in the namburbi-prayers. Shamash is supposed to guide people back into their proper course and to revoke the evil judgment against them. These remarks could be extended to apply to the king as it is exactly what he does when proclaiming a *mîšarum*:[43] *he makes his people go aright*. We can see in the name of year 2 of Abi-eshuh, who commemorates the *mîšarum* proclaimed by the king upon his accession:[44]

> Year: Abi-eshuh, the king, the beloved *shepherd* of Anum and Enlil, who looked toward Sumer and Akkad with a loyal eye, *led aright the feet of the people*, established [...], good will and reconciliation in his land, caused order (nì-gi-na) and redress (nì-si-sá) to exist and made the land to prosper.

Here we have a reference to the two dimensions of justice (Charpin 2004:308). *Kittum* (sum. nì-gi-na) is static: it is order, stability. On the contrary, *mîšarum* (sum. nì-si-sá) is dynamic: it is the correction of unfair situations.[45] As a good shepherd, the king goes in search of lost flock and sets them back on the right path: this royal image was so resilient in the Near-East that it was still alive at the time of Jesus Christ, who drew on it to be recognized as king.

THE "SUN KING," THE "FATHER KING," AND PROBLEMS OF DIVINE KINGSHIP

Does calling himself the "sun" make the king equal to the gods? We know how complex the question of divine kingship is.[46] Although even as one reads the texts without preconceptions, it really seems as if the sovereign, while exercising justice, could be considered as divine, as a plea illustrates:[47] "To you, O God, I have therefore come. (…) Just as my lord would not countenance the surrender of the weak (to the power of) the mighty, may all Sippar see that […] the mighty to injure the weak." Finkelstein believed this passage to be of no consequence (1965:238b, up to line 46): "Assuming that the addressee of this petition is the king (…), it need not cause any surprise that he should be addressed as a god: there need be no deeper implications in such an address than in the modern usage of 'Your Majesty,' 'Your Honor,' etc. (…). Note especially *šarru* UZU.DINGIR.MEŠ *šamši ša nišīšu* 'the king, flesh of the gods, sun of his people' (from *Ludlul* I), a characterization particularly appropriate here, where the king is petitioned to render judgment."[48] I am not so sure that we should minimize the impact of this passage. What appears most interesting is that we have here a case of divine kingship where the king does not appear in a literary text, but in a legal document.[49] The author of the petition is clearly well aware of phraseology, but he possesses it from within, so to speak: the end of the text, close in spirit to the prologue and epilogue of the *Code of Ḫammurapi*, does not constitute a quote, as Finkelstein had remarked. The passage of *Ludlul*, which he mentions in his commentary, seems to be particularly meaningful: the king who exercises justice is the "sun of his people" and as such he becomes identical to the gods.[50] The king is also the guardian of contracts: simply by taking an oath by the gods and the king whilst closing a contract joins the king to the divinities, even though his name is not generally preceded by the divine determinative.[51]

The personal names composed with kings' names can be examined in this light (Charpin 2004:261). Some are ambiguous. In the case of Abiešuh-kima-ilim (Klengel 1976:158; 3b) "Abi-eshuh is like a god," we are dealing with a comparison. But others are clearer, such as Ḫammurapi-ili "Ḫammurapi is my god" (ibid., 158; 1g),[52] or Ammiditana-iluni or Ammisaduqa-iluni "Ammi-ditana / Ammi-saduqa is our god" (ibid., 159; 4a, 5a). The question of divine kingship was often wrongly stated by scholars using absolute categories: was the king considered as a god or not? However, the vision that the Mesopotamians had of their society, and also of the whole universe, was *relative*: we are met with the same conceptual difficulties with categories such as *awīlum / muškēnum / wardum* (Kraus 1973). A minister can only speak on behalf of his king in certain contexts: while he remains his "servant" (*wardum*). We cannot consider him as a "slave" in the legal understanding of the term.[53] It is said in certain cases that the ambassador is the "body" (*pagrum*) of the king, when he is considered to be his personal representative; that is, he is to be treated as the sovereign who sent him would be. We can say that, for a formal mission, he is the embodiment of the king (ARM 26/1 21; Durand 1990b). In other cases, it is said that he is "the lips" of the king.[54] Everything is dependent on context: it is the same for the divine nature of the king. He can define himself as a "servant" (*wardum*) of a god as much as be considered to be "the flesh of the gods" (*šīr ilī*). The many types of names we find to designate the status of Zimri-Lim are significant: depending on circumstances, "kingship" (*šarrûtum*) alternates with "highness" (*elûtum*) or "divinity" (*ilûtum*) (Charpin 1988:223, text no. 391 note r). Working in reverse, it is the "permeability" between the realm of the gods and that of humans, which enables a divinity to embody a statue, even though it is fashioned by human hands (Dick 1999). If a statue, while incarnating an immortal god, can be destroyed, why could the king, even though mortal, not be of divine nature?

In another plea, the king from whom deliverance is petitioned is not called a god but a "sun." A woman named Kibsatum, held at Eshnunna against her will, asks Zimri-Lim that she be brought back to Mari. She begins her letter in a significant manner, calling out,[55] "For my liberation, you are my sun!" Bearing this perspective in mind, we should also collect the cases where the king is called "my sun" (*šamšī*) in the anthroponomy, as in the name Ḫammurapi-Shamshi.[56] Also, we have coherent onomastic groups, where we find the same predicate: with "my father" (*abī-*), "my lord" (*bēlī-*) or "my sun" (*šamšī*), we find "may he be everlasting!" (*-lû-dâri*), or again "may he live!" (*-lîbûr*).[57] We see that the daughters of the king Zimri-Lim speak to him using either "to my father" (*ana abiya*), or "to my lord" (*ana bêliya*), or "to my star" (*ana kakkabiya*),[58] or lastly "to my sun" (*ana šamšiya*).[59] These qualifying terms of the king as "sun" (*šamšum*) or "father" (*abum*) thus appear interchangeable.

THEME OF THE JUST KING AS FATHER TO HIS PEOPLE

We can see that the king in the exercise of justice considers himself explicitly as the father of his people. Indeed, we find in the epilogue of the *Code* (Roth 2002:39a, xlviii:3–19 and 20–38):

> May the wronged man who has a law case come before the statue of me, the king of justice, and may he read aloud my inscribed stela, and thus may he hear my precious pronouncements, and may my stela produce the law case for him; may he perceive his case; may he ease his heart, and (saying thus):
> "Hammurabi, the lord, *who is like a true father to the people*, submitted himself to the command of his lord Marduk and achieved victory for Marduk everywhere. He gladdened the heart of his lord Marduk, and he secured eternal well-being for the people and provided just ways for the land."

As always, this type of declaration must be questioned: are we not dealing with "propaganda"? Two texts seem to be revealing of the reality of this notion of the king as "father of his people." First we have a formula pronounced by the king Ammi-saduqa during the ceremony of the "cult of ancestors" (*kispum*).[60] Amongst the people he invites to eat and drink are the deceased with no family:[61] "All persons from East to West who have nobody to take care of them." We can here draw a parallel with a letter that shows that when someone died with no descendant, and if his father was still alive, it was he who must undertake the *kispum*:[62] "My son Sukkukum disappeared from me eight years ago and I did not know whether he was still alive and I kept making funerary offerings for him as if he were dead." In the *kispum* ritual, the king appears as the "father" of his people.

Also most revealing is the episode that we find in a letter to a king of Talhayum, to Zimri-Lim; it deals with female subjects of the king to whom he must give husbands (ARM 28 39; see Ziegler n.d.). We are clearly dealing with a matter where women, because of war, were separated from their families. The letter shows that Zimri-Lim will receive the *terhatum* (bride price) for these women, as was the case when a father married his daughter: he here plays the role of father to these women who are his subjects. The king is therefore, here as a last recourse, the father of his people: it is what the subject of Ḫammurapi must understand when he is brought to consult the stele of the *Code*. The king is both the sun and the father of his subjects.

THE OTHER GODS

I did not want to end this contribution without mentioning that justice was by no means the exclusive sphere of Shamash within the Mesopotamian pantheon. We will emphasize here the complementary aspects of Shamash and the Storm-god, Adad/Addu, as well as the astral deity of Venus (Ninsianna) and the Moon-god (Nanna/Sin).

Adad

Together with Shamash, Adad was the god of divination. The prayer of Old Babylonian diviners begins with the incantation: "Šamaš, lord of judgment; Adad, lord of extispicy-rituals and divination." In the same way, the oracle-queries (*tāwītum*) of the Old Babylonian kings begin with a call to "Šamaš lord of judgement, Adad, lord of divination."[63] Considering the close links that exist between divination and justice discussed above, it would be surprising if Adad did not have prerogatives in matters of justice. This thus far has not been extensively investigated,[64] but we can show it unfolding in many places. We have first of all to notice that Mîšarum, as a deity, was considered a son of Adad (Maul 1988:158).

The association of Shamash and Adad within the context of a *mîšarum* measure at the accession of the king is documented in the name of year 2 of Ammi-ditana:[65] "The year: Ammi-ditana, the king, the pious and obedient shepherd of Šamaš and Adad, the one who releases from corvée."

We will also note in the *Code of Ḫammurapi* the presence of a significant variant. Where the text of most manuscripts says[66] "by the command of Šamaš, the great judge of heaven and earth, may my justice prevail in the land," the variant reads[67] "by the command of Šamaš and Adad, judges of judgments and who render verdicts." The association of Shamash and Adad can be ascertained as early as the 3rd millennium in the context of alliance-agreements. D. Beyer noted that the treaty of Ebla with AbarSAL was placed under the double patronage of the Storm-god and the Sun-god, as was later the treaty of Tudhaliya IV and Kurunta of Tarhundasha or again the treaty between Hattusili III and Rameses II (Beyer 1995:32; Lambert 1997:86). We can add that this association is found at the time of the alliance between Ḫammurapi and Zimri-Lim against Elam. The oath that the king of Babylon was supposed to swear starts:[68] "Swear by Šamaš of heaven, swear by Adad of heaven! By these gods Hammurabi, son of Sin-muballiṭ, king of Babylon, (swore): 'From this day, as long as I live…'." The divinities invoked are Shamash and Adad, and not the political divinities of the parties, namely Marduk for Babylon and Itur-Mer and Dagan for Mari.[69]

Attestations of the Storm-god (Adad/Addu) as keeper of justice come especially from Aleppo. We know two prophecies in which the Storm-god of Aleppo requests of Zimri-Lim that he make sure he is accessible to his subjects. The first contains the promise of an extended and populated kingdom (FM 7 39:53–59):

> Whenever a wronged man or a wronged woman appeals to you, be present and judge their case! This is what I require of you. (If) you do what I have showed you and that you pay heed to my word, then I will give you the land from its east to its west and a country densely populated.

The second one starts in similar terms, but what follows is different (FM 7 38:(7'–17'):

> When anyone with a case appeals to you, saying: "I am despoiled," be present and judge his case! Satisfy him fairly! This is what I require of you. When you leave for a campaign, do not leave without having consulted the oracle. When I, in an oracle from me, have been present, you shall be able to go on a campaign; otherwise, do not walk through the door!

Once more, the indissoluble link between justice and divination appears clearly;[70] soon after having asked the king to be at the disposition of his subjects in order to render judgment, the god tells the king to consult him through diviners[71] before any military enterprise. We note the identical use of the verb "to stand, to be present" (*izuzzum*): the king must "be present" for his subjects (line 9'), and the god "will be present" (line 15') when the king consults him. This seems to be a kind of consequence: the god promises the king to give him favorable omen for his military campaign through "his being present" in the oracles, if the king "is present" to give justice. So that finally, the two phrasings of the prophecy are equal: the god promises the king the extension of his kingdom on the one hand, and successful military campaigns on the other.

Ninsianna

We know that Ninsianna, a goddess who corresponds to Venus, is—depending on the case—either male (cf. Heimpel 1998–2001:488a, and De Meyer 1989) or female (Reiner 1995:6, nn14 and 68). As an astral divinity, she is praised for her light. A hymn of the king of Isin Iddin-Dagan defines her as[72] "The respected one who fills heaven and earth with her huge brillance." An inscription of the king Rim-Sin refers to Ninsianna as[73] "god, whose station shines from clear heaven, whose light shines forth." We have an echo of this in a text found in the house of the gala-mah Ur-Utu at Sippar-Amnanum:[74] "Ninsianna, pure god, whose light fills heaven and earth."

Ninsianna is also closely linked to justice. The name of his temple at Ur is é-eš-bar-zi-da "House of True Decisions."[75] In the inscription of Rim-Sin that refers to it, Ninsianna is called[76] "Judge, supreme adviser, who distinguishes between truth and falsehood." The close relationship of Ninsianna with Shamash appears in the caption of this seal:[77] "Ninsianna, great lady of the sky, light that emerges over the land like Šamaš." In the hymn *Iddin-Dagan A*, we also note this passage (Jones 2003:295, lines 119–21): "She makes her order known and makes known evildoers, rendering an evil verdict for the evildoer and destroying the wicked. She looks favourably on the just and decrees a good fate for them." We can furthermore establish a special link between Ninsianna and divination. Based on an oracle-query (*tâwîtum*) also found in the house of Ur-Utu and which starts thus:[78] "O my lord Ninsianna, accept this offering, be present in my offering and place in it a portent of well-being and life for your servant Ur-Utu!" In principle, this type of text is addressed to Shamash and Adad, but we have here an exception, which must be held as significant.[79]

We therefore find in the case of Ninsianna the exact same characteristics as those of Shamash: we have a luminous deity, keeper of justice as well as of divination. It is not surprising that the two gods should be associated in a court case that takes place[80] "before Šamaš, Ninsianna and their *gamlum*-weapons."

Nanna/Sin

The god Nanna-Sin also has a special link to justice. This is based on the conception that the Mesopotamians had of the moon as a sort of nocturnal double of the Sun. In fact there was at Ur, city of the Moon-god, a specific building, the é-dub-lá-mah, sometimes called the "net," where oaths were taken.[81] We also have a "literary" text in Akkadian in which a man, a victim of injustice, appeals to Nanna putting special emphasis on the pronouncement this divinity gives in response to human injustice.[82] The text opens with a plea to Nanna (UET 6 402:1–2): "O Nanna, you are king of heaven and earth, I put my trust in you." At the end of the text, we find Nanna and Utu/Shamash together. In this instance, the presence of Utu/Shamash cannot be explained by his role as god of justice par excellence. Indeed the text says (UET 6 402:41–42): "Before Nanna, before Šamaš, he swore this: 'May I, Elali, be damned if I wrong Kussulu! May Elali have no heir before Nanna and Šamaš (if he wrongs)'." It is therefore as a divinity of Larsa that Shamash is here invoked as in this kingdom, oaths by Nanna (god of Ur) and Utu/Shamash (god of Larsa) were taken, as well as by the king.

The god Nanna is sometimes identified with a shepherd; however, the comparison to Shamash is not perfect as the flocks he is in charge of are not composed of ovines, but bovines (Veldhuis 1991:1). The nature of the Moon-god explains finally his very important place in matters of divination: eclipses played an essential role in this domain.[83]

CONCLUSION

There is a group of three astral deities—the sun (Shamash), the moon (Nanna/Sîn), and Venus (Inanna/Ištar as Ninsianna)—who shared common features: because of their position in the sky, they could oversee the earth and were patrons both of justice and divination. To these three gods was added the Storm-god Adad, as is evident in particular in the "prayer to the gods of the night" (Reiner 1995:68): "The gods and goddesses of the country—Šamaš, Sin, Adad and Ištar—have gone home to heaven to sleep, they will not give decisions or verdicts (tonight)." These four gods are also those who order the four chapters of the great divination series *Enūma Anu Enlil*.[84] It is not evident why Adad was paired with Shamash: his role as Storm-god does not explain his place in the Mesopotamian context. We generally consider the Storm-god as linked with rainfall, and it is true that a lot of his epithets allude to the fertility he brings (Schwemer 2001:699–716). Nevertheless, his most spectacular manifestation is of a luminous nature: the flash of lightning, glittering in a spectacular way. We can quote this epithet that describes Adad as[85] "lord of lightning, whose glow illuminates the universe."

The most typical representation of the Storm-god during the 2nd millennium is the famous stele of Ugarit, now in the Louvre, depicting Baal with a bolt in the left hand and a kind of club in the right hand; the waves at his feet depict the sea (Yam) against whom he is fighting.[86] And when the Storm-god of Aleppo reminded Zimri-Lim of the help he gave him, he stated:[87] "I put you back on the throne of your father and gave you the weapons with which I fought against the Sea (*têmtum*). I anointed you with the oil of my light[88] and nobody stood in front of you." Just after this historical-mythological reminder, the Storm-god asks Zimri-Lim to give a judgment for the people appealing to him, as we have already seen. As Jean-Marie Durand wrote (1993:54): "In the same way as Order triumphed over Chaos, the king has the first duty to give judgment."

I do not want the point of this chapter to be misunderstood: I do not propose that Mesopotamian kings of the beginning of the 2nd millennium were some sort of "pharaohs." I, nevertheless, have the feeling that the double dimension, both cosmological and divine, of their power has been underestimated until now, and I wanted to stress this aspect of their authority. In Babylon, the king was associated with the sun, and it is certainly not by chance if, during the 1st millennium, the ideogram used to designate the king was the number "twenty," the number associated with the Sun-god.[89] In Aleppo and in Mari, it was more the Storm-god Addu who was a model for the king.[90] But in both cases, the king received the same mission: give judgment, so that his country can "go aright." And we are in a way the heirs of this concept, since we still speak of "human *rights*."

NOTES

2.1 École Pratique des Hautes Etudes (UMR 7192). My warmest thanks to Nadia Ait Said Ghanem for her translation of my contribution.

2.2 *CAD* Ṣ records only one example in 1962 (Ṣ, p. 70b; mng 1.d.2':ARM 1 60:21), but there have been new ones since: see ARM 26/2 328:58 and 329:23' (and n. i p. 99).

2.3 A.3568: (10) … *li-ib-bi ma-di-iš ih-du* (11) *um-ma a-na-ku-ma* ᴵ*ad-di-ia ú-ul* ba-úš (12) ᴵ*ad-di-ia ib-ta-al-ṭám ki-ma* ᵈ*utu aw$_x$-wi-ir* (published in Ziegler n.d.).

2.4 Unpublished A.510: (9) *i-nu-ma be-lí i-na pu-hu-ur* ìr-meš-šu (10) *iz-za-az-zu-ma* ìr-meš-šu *i-ma-ru-šu* (11) *li-ib-bi ša* aga-ús *i-ba-al-lu-uṭ* (12) *ù ki-ma ša be-lí it-ti ṣa-bi-šu* (13) *a-na re-iš* a-šà-ma *il-li-ku* (14) *ù ki-ma* ᵈutu *lib-bi ṣa-bi-im i-na-wi-ir.*

2.5 I am citing these two examples as *CAD* N/1 (*s.v. namāru*) does not offer any example of this kind. To be noted in the article *šamšu* (Š/1, p. 336a) is: *amēlu šû kîma* ᵈ*šá-maš namir* "that man shines like sun-light," ABL 1396 = LAS 71 (= SAA 10 74), but the subject here is the heir to the throne after a purification rite.

2.6 Roth 1995:80 (v 4) ᵈutu-*šu* (5) ká-dingir-ra^ki (6) *mu-ṣe-ṣí nu-ri-im* (7) *a-na ma-at* (8) *šu-me-ri-im* (9) *ù ak-ka-di-im*. The context is as follows (iv 64–v 13): "The pious one, who prays ceaselessly for the great gods, scion of Sumu-la-El, mighty heir of Sin-muballiṭ, eternal seed of royalty, mighty king, Sun of the city of Babylon, who spreads light over the lands of Sumer and Akkad, king who makes the four regions obedient, favoured of the goddess Ištar, I am." "Babylon" here undoubtedly points to the city, and not the land (hence the translation "the city of Babylon").

M. Roth translates *šamšu* here as "solar disk," but I must admit that I fail to understand why. The term is written ᵈutu-*šu* on the Louvre stele, but the tablet of the prologue kept in the Louvre is written phonetically *ša-a[m-šu]* (Nougayrol 1951:75, iv 17). The term *šamšum* can mean a votive solar disk (*CAD* Š/A:338), but *CAD* has rightly listed this passage under the category "as epithet of Mesopotamian rulers" (337a).

2.7 We should not doubt this *pace* D. Katz (2006:120); see references collected in Sommerfeld 2006:4, nn. 8–9.

2.8 The standard edition is Lambert's 1960:121–38. See since then Reiner's translation 1985:68–84. The exact date of this composition is not known, but it is certain that it contains elements that go back to the Old Babylonian period.

2.9 Line 5 (cf. *CAD* Š/2:142b). Furthermore, see mentions of a "net" and a "trap" in lines 83–84 and 87, in a passage unfortunately badly preserved, and also in line 94.

2.10 See Veenhof's commentary 2003:326. For the location of the temple see Charpin 2005a. A new example of an *ina saparri* oath can be found in OECT 15 131:14 (cf. *RA* 101, 2007, p. 151).

2.11 Bottéro 1987:192 (= 1992:157). This hypothesis, which dates from C.J. Gadd (1948:90–91), should be abandoned: Gadd forgot the rays that emanate from the shoulders of the god and which permit him to be identified as Shamash without a doubt. Recently, U. Seidl asked whether this scene represents Ḫammurapi before the god Shamash, or whether one should instead consider the king as being represented before the cult statue of the god (Seidl 2001:120–21).

2.12 We know that fragments of other stelae were found in Susa: see the study of the possible joins by J. Laessoe, who concluded "that there were at least three stele editions of the text" (1950:181), including the complete stele. The stele of the Esagil could be "source X" (1950:184) on which would be based the other manuscripts; Laessoe himself had a different opinion (1950:186).

2.13 The iconography of the stele of the Code was recently discussed by G. Elsen-Novák and M. Novák 2006. The idea that Shamash hands to Ḫammurapi a calamus (p. 138) cannot work: the size and the form of the object do not fit at all; besides the text of the stele is carved in stone, not inscribed on clay. However, the idea that the diorite was carefully polished for light to glisten and thus allow for a glimmering effect (p. 142) is interesting. The matter was last discussed by K. Slanski 2007:51–54. For her, the "rod and ring" are the tools of the topographer: however it becomes difficult to follow that from this ensues that the king is the šar mîšarim.

2.14 For the concept of mîšarum, see below note 45.

2.15 Horsnell 1999:254: mu a-bi-e-šu-uh lugal-e nun sun₅-na lú ᵈutu-ke₄ giš in-na-an-tuk-tuk-a x x AŠ ᵈamar-utu-ke₄ ur₅-tuk kalam-ma-ni-ta ba²-an²-da²-ab²-du₈².

2.16 Horsnell 1999:298: mu am-mi-di-ta-na lugal-e en íb gu-la ᵈutu ᵈamar-utu-<bi-da->ke₄ ur₅-ra ma-da-ni ab-ak-ak-ke ba-an-da-ab-du₈-a.

2.17 Horsnell 1999:337: mu am-mi-ṣa-du-qá lugal-e sipa zi še-ga ᵈutu ᵈamar-utu-bi-da-ke₄ ur₅-ra kalam-ma-na (šu) bí-in-du₈-a.

2.18 See in general Jeyes 1991–1992. I did not have access to J. Polonsky, *The Rise of the Sun God and the Determination of Destiny in Ancient Mesopotamia*, unpublished Ph.D. diss., University of Pennsylvania, 2002 (cited by Jones 2005).

2.19 Charpin 2004:244–46. It is the kingdom of Mari that offers the more numerous and concrete examples of oracle-queries on behalf of the king (Durand 1988). But see also the oracle queries asked on behalf of the kings of Babylon, known through Neo-Assyrian copies (Lambert 1997 and 2007).

2.20 See Fincke 2006–2007. In her opinion, the similarity of divinatory treaties' composition and "codes of law," that is the casuistic presentation (protases/apodoses), is not only formal, but comes from a cohesive unitary conception of divination and justice. See again *infra* note 70.

2.21 The quote can be found in chapter 9, titled "Ḫammurapi's Character."

2.22 See Charpin 2004:245, n. 1252. The only example I know is the suspicion of an oracle's manipulation by a diviner from Mari expressed by the king of Qaṭna Ishi-Addu (unpublished M.6331, cited in Charpin and Ziegler 2003:101, n. 220).

2.23 Machinist 1978:76–79 (ii:13'-24'). From the Amarna period, treaties did not only bind the parties, but also their descendants, which was not the case in the Old Babylonian period (Charpin, In press b).

2.24 Reiner 1985:72, line 62. For river ordeals during the Old Babylonian period, see above all Durand 1988:509–39.

2.25 Tallqvist 1938:458 (who gives many other corresponding/analogous epithets).

2.26 A diviner who is about to commence his work says in his prayer to Shamash: "I am approaching the judgement," YOS 11 22:(9) … *e-ṭe-eh-hi* (10) *a-na di-nim* (Goetze 1968:25).

2.27 Frayne 1990:389 no. 8: (20) u₄ zalag-ga un-šár-ra-ba (21) íb-ta-an-è-a. Seux had translated following Poebel (*AfO* 9, p. 262): "Soleil qui fait jaillir la lumière sur son pays" (Seux 1967:460, transcribes utu u₄ etc.), but the divine determinative is missing.

2.28 Horsnell 1999:325: mu *am-mi-ṣa-du-qá* lugal-e ᵈutu-gin₇ kalam-ma-ni-šè zi-bé-eš im-ta-è-a un-šár-ra-ba si bí-íb-sá-sá-a. The translation of the verb si--sá by M. Horsnell ("he caused the people, in their totality, to prosper," justified in p. 325 note 2 should evidently be modified (especially since in p. 242 it is su—du₁₀ which is translated by "to make prosper" in the name of year 2 of Abi-eshuh). We should understand it word for word "he made his people go straight towards." It is surely a reference to the proclamation of a *mîšarum*, hence the translation "instituted the redress." The verb si-sá is here the equivalent of what we find elsewhere as nì-si-sá gar "to install/establish/institute/ a *mîšarum*." In the same way, in Akkadian, we find *šutêšurum* instead of *mîšaram šakânum*. That is how it occurs in the name of Zimri-Lim's year 2 at Mari: mu *Zimrî-Lîm Ah Purattim uštêšeru* "year when Zimri-Lim 'straightened' the banks of the Euphrates," i.e., when he instituted a *mîšarum* in the kingdom of Mari (see Charpin and Ziegler 2003:184n108).

2.29 The inescapable reference is Kraus 1984, where the texts of edicts are published with commentaries, the most complete being that of Ammi-saduqa. A new fragment of the edict of Samsu-iluna was published in Hallo 1995. See also Charpin 1987 and 2000a.

2.30 See Charpin 1990a (revised with additions in Charpin 2010: ch. 7) and Charpin 2000a.

2.31 The text, published in Finkelstein 1965, was revised as AbB 7 153; for a translation into French with commentary, see Charpin 2000b:91–92, no. 47. The king to whom the plea is addressed is Samsu-iluna: for the dating of this text as year 28 of Samsu-iluna (year of the proclamation of a *mîšarum*), see Charpin 2000a:202.

2.32 Finkelstein quoted the text in Finkelstein 1965:240 (later copied as CT 48 71). It is a loan of grain and silver. CT 48 71:(24) mu ús-sa i₇ ᵈa-a-/hé-gál (25) *wa-ar-ki šar-rum di-pa-ar* kù-GI (26) *iš-šu-ú*.

2.33 Greengus 1988:153b, following a hypothesis of Finkelstein (1965:236).

2.34 Besides, the use of torches is only attested for alerting populations of enemy invasions, which an omen calls *dipâr nikurtim* "a torch of hostility" (YOS 10 31 ix 50). See examples of Mari translated in Durand 1997 (249, 438), 1998 (nums. 491, 502–504, 507, 592, 622–623, 660, 683–684, 700) and 2000 (note 1273) and commentary in Durand 1998:303. For the astral symbolism of the torch, see note 120 (sum. izi-gar = *dipârum*).

2.35 This dimension was not touched upon by Kraus's commentary in Kraus 1984:70, but he did not yet have the most explicit example provided by AbB 12 172 (see below).

2.36 KAR 32 33, cited from *CAD* D:157a.

2.37 Lit. "he washed the sullied hair of the land." For the explanation of this translation, see Charpin 2000a:185, n. 1.

2.38 Based on the reconstruction of Durand 2000:412–13.

2.39 Durand 1985:415–16. For this *mîšarum*, see Charpin and Ziegler 2003:184, n. 108.

2.40 This geo-political dimension had not been taken into account in this otherwise very fine discussion of this letter by J.-M. Durand.

2.41 Lambert 1960:88, line 297: *re-e-um šamši niš ilišī ir['e]*.

2.42 Maul 1999:124, summarising Maul 1994:60–71 ("Der Rechtsstreit vor Šamaš").

2.43 This term is based on same root YŠR as the verb *ešêrum* from which derives the epithet *muštēširum*.

2.44 Horsnell 1999:242–44. The translation follows the text in Sumerian.

2.45 The traditional translation of *mîšarum* (nì-si-sá) as "equity" does not render this nuance. Also, Ph. Jones has opposed the retrospective aspect of Old Babylonian *mîšarum* to the prospective character of exemptions that appear to him to be more characteristic of later periods (Jones 2005). There are no chronological oppositions: the Old Babylonian period distinguishes between a remission (ama-ar-gi$_4$ / *andurârum*) and an exemption (šu-bar-ra / *šubarûtum*); cf. Charpin 1987:38, n. 10. Furthermore, the *andurârum* still existed in the first millennium (Villard 2007).

2.46 See notably Jones 2005 (with my observations in Charpin 2006:127). See henceforth the studies collected in Brisch 2008.

2.47 See *supra* note 30. AbB 7 153:(46) dingir *ka-ta ak-ta-aš-dam* (…) (50) *ki-ma en-šum a-na da-an-nim* (51) *ma-har be-lí-ia la iš-ša-ar-ra-ku* (52) UD.KIB.NUN^{ki} *ka-lu-šu li-mu-u[r]* x (53) *dan-nu a-na en-ši-im ha-ba-lim* x [x x x]. Kraus had described this text as "ein Gesuch an den König um Eröffnung eines Prozesses" (AbB 7, p. 128, n. 153 b). It also makes one think of a "letter-prayer" laid before the statue of Shamash in his temple at Sippar; for a similar example, see the plea to Nanna-Sin UET 6 402 (*infra*). There is however no reason why "my lord" (*bêlî*) in lines 49 and 51 should not be the king, as is clear in line 1 (cf. line 3 where we have "Šamaš who loves him" ^{d}utu *ra-i-mi-šu*).

2.48 Finkelstein added in a note: "Note especially *PBS* VI 2, No. 10 = *VAB* V, No. 292:4: ^{d}*Hammurapi* lugal-e, in the context of a legal suit actually brought before the king himself" (1965:238, n. 20).

2.49 We should therefore bring some nuance to the comments of Ph. Jones: "The literary nature of much of our evidence renders the concept of divine kingship even more suspicious. Surviving Old Babylonian administrative and commercial letters, contemporary with the bulk of our literary evidence for divine kingship, treated the king as a purely human figure" (Jones 2005:330–31).

2.50 Among other examples of *šīr ili*, we note a passage in the *Epic of Tukulti-Ninurta* (ref. in *CAD* Š/3:117 §c "referring to divine nature").

2.51 In the same perspective, N. Ziegler brought to my attention the atypical formula of blessings that is found in AbB 11 75:7: "May your well-being last before Šamaš, Marduk and my lord Ammi-ditana."

2.52 Note that CBS 8040 is the envelope of the letter now published as AbB 11 156.

2.53 The other counter examples quoted by Heimpel (1997:79n17) are not acceptable.

2.54 See ARM 26/1 35:14 with note d) and ARM 26/2 311:24 (with note c).

2.55 ARM 10 99 = LAPO 18 1192 (5) *aš-šum pa-ṭà-ri-ia at-ta-a* ^{d}utu-*ši* (6) *ta-ba-aš-ši*. For this woman and her story, see Ziegler 2007:289 note in FM 9 72:10".

2.56 Klengel 1976:157; 1b. We see already in Ur III Šulgi-šamši (*CAD* Š/1:337). Comparisons to the sun were not limited to the king. Note in particular the very beautiful letter of a *nadîtum* of Ninurta at Nippur, named Akatiya, addressed to her brother Sinni: "You truly are the sun, so let me warm myself in your heat; you truly are a cedar tree, so let the heat not burn me in your shadow!" (AbB 9 228: (16) *at-ta lu ša-am-šu-ma* (17) *ṣé-et-ka lu-uš-ta-ha-an* (18) *at-ta lu e-re-n[u]-u[m]-ma* (19) *i-na ṣi-li-ka ṣ[é-tum]* (20) *a-a ih-mu-ṭa-ni*). We observe however that the emphasis is put here on the warmth that the sun provides, and not on its light.

2.57 For Šamši-lu-dari or Šamši-libur, see ref. of *CAD* Š/1:337a.

2.58 Letters of Erishti-Aya (LAPO 18 1195–1198 and 1200–1201); of Inibshina (LAPO 18 1203–1206); of Kiru (LAPO 18 1223–1224, 1228); of Shimdatum (LAPO 18 1225); of Naramtum (LAPO 18 1235–1237). See also the letter LAPO 18 1233 (letter of Inbatum).

2.59 Letter of Erishti-Aya (ARM 10 39 = LAPO 18 1199).

2.60 BM 80328, published in Finkelstein 1966. See henceforth Radner's commentary in Radner 2005:89–90.

2.61 BM 80328: (36) *a-wi-lu-tum ka-la-ši-in* (37) *[i]š-tu* ^{d}utu-*è-a a-di*! ^{d}utu-*šú-a* (38) *ša pa-qí-dam ù sa-hi-ra-am la i-šu-ú*.

2.62 AbB 13 21:(5) ^{I}geštu$_2$-lá *ma-ri* (6) *iš-tu* mu 8-kam *ih-li-qà-an-ni-ma* (7) *ba-al-ṭú-us-sú ú-ul i-de-e-ma* (8) *ki-ma mi-tim ki-is-pa-am* (9) *ak-ta-as-sí-ip-šum*.

2.63 Starr 1983:30 (1) [^{d}utu *be*]-*el di-n[im]* ^{d}IM *be-el ik-ri-bi ù bi-ri-im* (text A, restored from text B, p. 122). The same formula is found in the prayer of the diviners published by Goetze 1968:25 (= YOS 11 22: 11). See the commentary in Starr 1983:44–46.

2.64 See however Schwemer 2001:221–22 (and the lengthy note 1534, which enumerates all the references where Shamash and Adad appear side by side) and Lambert 2007:15 ("Šamaš and Adad as a duo").

2.65 Horsnell 1999:274: mu *am-mi-di-ta-na* lugal-e sipa ní-tuk še-ga ᵈutu ᵈiškur-bi-da-ke₄ íl-la-du₈-a.

2.66 Roth 1995:134, xlvii:85–87.

2.67 CT 13 46 iii 11 *ina qibīt Šamaš u Adad dāianū dīnim pārisū purussē*. This is the manuscript e in Roth 1995:252 (Bu. 91-5,9, 221). This variant appears on a tablet of Ashurbanipal's library at Nineveh, but it may reproduce an Old Babylonian text. Indeed, during the Neo-Assyrian period, the oracle queries were questions asked to Shamash alone (Starr 1990), and no longer to Shamash and Adad as in the Old Babylonian period (cf. Lambert 1997:85); for the "modernization" of oracle questions, where Adad's presence was erased, see Lambert 1997:88, n. 7.

2.68 M.6435⁺ (Durand 1986:111–18 = LAPO 16 290): (1) ᵈutu *ša ša-me-e* [*t*]*a*-ma* (2) ᵈIM *ša ša-me-e* [*t*]*a*-m*[*a**]. Note that the restitutions of lines 1–2 of the *editio princeps* (taken as is in Lambert 1997:86, Heimpel 2003:512, and Lambert 2007:2) were corrected by Charpin 1990b:115, n. 29; the correction was (implicitly) supported by Durand 1997:452, n. 93.

2.69 Sometimes, the list of divinities invoked at the beginning of an oath is much lengthier: cf. LAPO 16 292 or 293.

2.70 This link is verified by the way the god, like the king, rendered a verdict and how diviners like judges were in charge of interpreting them: a comparison imposes itself between divinatory collections and the *Codes* (see in this regard Charpin 2005b, revised in Charpin 2010, ch. 6).

2.71 The expression *ina têrtiya* in FM 7 38:14' holds no ambiguity; see besides that FM 7 40:10-6'.

2.72 Jones 2003:294 (*Iddin-Dagan A* 8 nir-gál an-ki si gal si-a). To be noted also the term "holy torch who fills the heavens" (line 4: izi-gar kù an-e si-a-ra) and see lines 11–14: "When she radiantly ascends at evening, when she fills the heaven like a holy torch, when she stands in the heavens like Nanna and Utu, she is known by all the lands from South to North" (Jones 2003:295).

2.73 Frayne 1990:297–98, no. 18: (2) dingir an-sikil-ta gišgal-bi im-zalag (3) giš-nu₁₁-bi pa-è. We correct the translation by D. Frayne, who indicates everywhere "goddess" instead of "god" (cf. lugal line 16, which he gives as "my lord[sic!]").

2.74 De Meyer 1989:213–14, Di 761: (1) ᵈnin-si₄-an-na *i-lum el-lum* (2) *ša nu-úr-šu ša-me-e ù ki ma-lu-ú*.

2.75 George 1993:83, no. 261. This temple it would seem is located at Ur, as the two cones which bear Rim-Sin's inscription come from there.

2.76 Frayne 1990:297–98, no. 18: (10) di-ku₅ na-ri-mah (11) nì-zi nì-lul-la šid-šid.
2.77 Stol 1999:46–47, A 32065 sceau 1: ᵈNIN. ŠI₄.AN.NA / NIN GAL AN.NA ᵈUTU.GIN₇ / GIŠ.NUₓ KALAM.MA È.A.
2.78 De Meyer 1982. English translation in Reiner 1995:68 (see also Foster 2005:214).
2.79 Lambert 1997:85–86 simply qualifies this text as a "rarity."
2.80 Limet 1990:35, PUL 333: (5) igi ᵈutu ᵈnin-si₄-an-na (6) ù ga-am-la-ti-šu-nu. This text dates from 3/viii/Ḫammurapi 41, but cannot as yet be located. Note that the first witness is line 14 i-ṣí-qá-ta-ar, who bears in line 15 the title of ugula mu-ús-si-rù-meš; see about this matter Durand 1990a, who shows that the mussirum is a specialist of purifications and who particularly deals with the gamlum, a divine apotropaic weapon.
2.81 Veenhof 2003:324. For the "net" of Shamash, see *supra* note 9.
2.82 UET 6 402; re-edition Charpin 1986:326–29. English translation in Foster 2005:215–16.
2.83 See Rochberg-Halton 1987. For a Neo-Assyrian transcription of an Old Babylonian "oracle-query (*tâmîtum*) concerning the eclipse of Sin," see K.2884 (edited by Lambert 1997:94–95).
2.84 Following Virolleaud's arrangement. More precisely, the four sections are: omens linked to the Moon (Sin), those linked to the sun (Shamash), meteorological omens (Adad), and omens linked to the planets (with Venus-Ishtar to begin with); see Rochberg-Halton 1987:18.
2.85 *CAD* Š/2:143a: bē[l birqi ša šar]ūrūšu unamm[arū k]ibrāti. The beginning (bēl birqi) is missing in Schwemer 2001:714.
2.86 See Bordreuil and Pardee's commentary in Bordreuil and Pardee 1993:69–70. For the iconography of the "Smiting God," see Schwemer 2001:227.
2.87 FM 7 38: (1') … a-na giš-g[u-za é a-bi-ka] (2') ú-te-er-ka giš-tukul-[meš] (3') ša it-ti te-em-tim am-ta-ah-ṣú (4') ad-di-na-ak-kum ì ša nam-ri-ru-ti-ia (5') ap-šu-úš-ka-ma ma-am-ma-an a-na pa-ni-ka (6') ú-ul iz-z[i-iz].
2.88 J.-M. Durand considers *namrirûtum* to be derived from the root MRR, "to vanquish" (Durand 1993:53–54). I must say that I prefer connecting *namrirrû* to "awe-inspiring luminosity" (*CAD* N/1:237a–239b), which he envisaged without adopting it. Also note in this regard: "Die Kontexte sprechen eher für eine Lichterscheinung" (Schwemer 2001:226, n. 1566).
2.89 I thank S. Maul who underlined for me the importance of this fact in the context of this contribution.
2.90 It is indisputable that the Western Storm-god strongly influenced the figure of Marduk, as it is shown in *Enūma eliš*: see on this point the reflections of Durand

1993, followed by Schwemer 2001:226–37.

REFERENCES

André-Salvini, B. 2003. *Le Code de Hammurabi*. Paris: Réunion des Musées Nationaux.

Beyer, D. 1995. Les sceaux apposés sur les traités de l'ancien Orient: étude de cas. In *Les relations internationales. Actes du Colloque de Strasbourg 15-17 juin 1993*, ed. E. Frézouls and A. Jacquemin, pp. 27–40. Paris: de Boccard.

Bordreuil, P., and D. Pardee. 1993. "Le combat de Baʻlu avec Yammu d'après les textes ougaritiques." *MARI* 7:63–70.

Bottéro, J. 1987. *Mésopotamie. L'écriture, la raison et les dieux*. Paris: Gallimard. English trans. 1992: *Mesopotamia. Writing, Reasoning, and the Gods*. Chicago: Chicago University Press.

Brisch, N., ed. 2008. *Religion and Power: Divine Kingship in the Ancient World and Beyond*. Oriental Institute Seminars 4. Chicago: Oriental Institute Press.

Charpin, D. 1986. *Le Clergé d'Ur au siècle d'Hammurabi (XIXe–XVIIIe siècles av. J.-C.)*. Genèva-Paris: Droz.

———. 1987. Les décrets royaux à l'époque paléo-babylonienne, à propos d'un ouvrage récent. *AfO* 34:36–44 [available on www.digitorient.com].

———. 1988. Première partie. in *Archives Epistolaires de Mari I/2*, ed. D. Charpin, F. Joannès, S. Lackenbacher, and B. Lafont. *ARM 26/2*. Paris: Éditions Recherche sur les Civilisations.

———. 1990a. Les édits de "restauration"des rois babyloniens et leur application. In *Du pouvoir dans l'antiquité: mots et réalité*, ed. Cl. Nicolet, pp. 13–24. Paris-Genèva: Droz [available on www.digitorient.com].

———. 1990b. Une alliance contre l'Elam et le rituel du *lipit napištim*. In *Contribution à l'histoire de l'Iran. Mélanges offerts à Jean Perrot*, ed. F. Vallat, pp. 109–18. Paris: Éditions Recherche sur les Civilisations.

———. 1992. Les malheurs d'un scribe, ou de l'inutilité du sumérien loin de Nippur. In *Nippur at the Centennial. Papers read at the 35e Rencontre Assyriologique Internationale, Philadelphia 1988*, ed. M. deJ. Ellis, pp. 7–27. Occasional Publications of the Samuel Noah Kramer Fund 14. Philadelphia: S.N. Kramer Fund.

———. 1994. Deux agneaux pour la *piqittum* d'un devin paléo-babylonien de Sippar. *NABU* 1994/4.

———. 2000a. Les prêteurs et le palais: les édits de *mīšarum* des rois de Babylone et leurs traces dans les archives privées. In *Interdependency of Institutions and Private Entrepreneurs. Proceedings of the Second MOS Symposium (Leiden 1998)*, ed. A.C.V.M. Bongenaaar, pp. 185–211. MOS Studies 2. Leiden: Nederlands Instituut voor het Nabije Oosten.

———. 2000b. Lettres et procès paléo-babyloniens. In *Rendre la justice en Mésopotamie*, ed. F. Joannès, pp. 69–111. Paris: Presses Universitaires de Vincennes [available on www.digitorient.com].

———. 2004. "Histoire politique du Proche-Orient amorrite (2002–1595). In *Mesopotamien: Die altbabylonische Zeit*, ed. D. Charpin, D.O. Edzard, and M. Stol, pp. 25–240. OBO 160/4. Fribourg and Göttingen: Academic Press and Vandenhoeck & Ruprecht.

———. 2005a. Ṣurârum est-il le fils de son père? À propos d'un procès à Sippar-Amnânum." *NABU* 2005/3.

———. 2005b. Codes de lois et recueils divinatoires. *NABU* 2005/94.

———. 2006. Comment faire connaître la civilisation mésopotamienne. *RA* 100:107–30.

———. 2008 "Le roi est mort, vive le roi!" Les funérailles des souverains amorrites et l'avènement de leur successeur. In *Studies in Ancient Near Eastern World View and Society. Presented to Marten Stol on the occasion of His 65th birthday, 10 November 2005, and His retirement from the Vrije Universiteit Amsterdam*, ed. R.J. van der Spek, pp. 69–95. Bethesda, MD: CDL Press.

———. 2010. *Writing, Law and Kingship: Essays on Old Babylonian Mesopotamia*. Chicago: Chicago University Press.

———. n.d. Guerre et paix dans le monde amorrite. In *Krieg und Frieden im Alten Vorderasien. 52ᵉ Rencontre Assyriologique Internationale. Santag*, ed. H. Neumann et al. Wiesbaden: Harrassowitz. In press.

Charpin, D., and N. Ziegler. 2003. *Florilegium marianum V. Mari et le Proche-Orient à l'époque amorrite: essai d'histoire politique*. Paris: SEPOA.

De Meyer, L. 1982. Deux prières *ikribu* du temps d'Ammī-ṣaduqa. In *Zikir šumim. Assyriological Studies Presented to F. R. Kraus on the Occasion of His Seventieth Birthday*, ed. G. van Driel, Th. J. H. Krispijn, M. Stol, and K. R. Veenhof, pp. 271–78. Leiden: Brill.

———. 1989. Le dieu Ninsianna ou l'art de transposer les logogrammes. In *Archaeologia iranica et orientalis. Miscellanea in honorem Louis Vanden Berghe*, ed. L. De Meyer and E. Haerinck, pp. 213–21. Leuven: Peeters.

Dick, M.B., ed. 1999. *Born in the Heaven Made on Earth. The Making of the Cult Image in the Ancient Near East*. Winona Lake: Eisenbrauns.

Durand, J.-M. 1985. Les dames du palais de Mari à l'époque du royaume de Haute Mésopotamie. *MARI* 4:385–436.

———. 1986. Fragments rejoints pour une histoire élamite. In *Contribution à l'histoire de l'Iran. Mélanges offerts à Jean Perrot*, ed. F. Vallat, pp. 111–28. Paris: Éditions Recherche sur les Civilisations.

———. 1988. *Archives épistolaires de Mari I/1*. ARM 26/1. Paris: Éditions Recherche sur les Civilisations.

———. 1990a. *Mussirum*. *NABU* 1990/1.

———. 1990b. *šuke''unum* = "Prosternation." *NABU* 1990/24.

———. 1993. Le mythologème du combat entre le Dieu de l'orage et la Mer en Mésopotamie. *MARI* 7:41–61.

———. 1997. *Les Documents épistolaires du palais de Mari, tome I*. Littératures Anciennes du Proche Orient 16. Paris: Éditions du Cerf.

———. 1998. *Les Documents épistolaires du palais de Mari, tome II*. Littératures Anciennes du Proche Orient 17. Paris: Éditions du Cerf.

———. 2000. *Les Documents épistolaires du palais de Mari, tome III*. Littératures Anciennes du Proche Orient 18. Paris: Éditions du Cerf.

Ebeling, E. 1915–1923. *Keilschrifttexte aus Assur religiösen Inhalts I/II*. WVDOG 28 and 34. Leipzig: J.C. Hinrichs.

Eidem, J. 2008. Apum: A Kingdom on the Old Assyrian Route. In *Mesopotamia. The Old Assyrian Period*, ed. K.R. Veenhof and J. Eidem, pp. 265–352. OBO 160/5. Fribourg and Göttingen: Academic Press and Vandenhoeck & Ruprecht.

Elsen-Novák, G., and M. Novák. 2006. Der "König der Gerechtigkeit." Zur Ikonologie und Teleologie des "Codex Ḫammurapi. *BaM* 37:131–55.

Fincke, J. 2006–2007. Omina, die göttlichen "Gesetze" der Divination. *JEOL* 40:131–47.

Finkelstein, J.J. 1965. Some New *Misharum* Material and Its Implications. In *Studies in Honor of Benno Landsberger on His Seventy-Fifth Birthday, April 21, 1965*, ed. H.G. Güterbock and Th. Jacobsen, pp. 233–46. Chicago: University of Chicago Press.

———. 1966. The Genealogy of the Hammurapi Dynasty. *JCS* 20:95–118.

Foster, B.R. 2005. *Before the Muses. An Anthology of Akkadian Literature*. 3rd ed. Bethesda: CDL Press.

Frayne, D.R. 1990. *Old Babylonian Period (2003–1595 BC). Royal Inscriptions of Mesopotamia Early Periods* 4. Toronto: Toronto University Press.

Fritz, M. 2003. …und weiten um Tammuz. *Die Götter Dumuzi-Ama'ušumgal'anna und Damu*. AOAT 307. Münster: Ugarit-Verlag.

Gadd, C.J. 1948. *Ideas of Divine Rule in the Ancient Near East*. London: The Schweich Lectures of the British Academy.

George, A. 1993. *House Most High. The Temples of Ancient Mesopotamia*. Mesopotamian Civilization 5. Winona Lake: Eisenbrauns.

Goetze, A. 1968. An Old Babylonian Prayer of the Divination Priest. *JCS* 22:25–29.

Greengus, S. 1988. Review of F. R. Kraus, *Königliche Verfügungen in altbabylonischer Zeit*, Leiden, 1984. *JAOS* 108:153–57.

Hallo, W.W. 1995. Slave Release in the Biblical World in Light of a New Text. In *Solving Riddles and Untying Knots. Biblical, Epigraphic, and Semitic Studies in Honor of Jonas C. Greenfield*, ed. Z. Zevit, S. Gitin, and M. Sokoloff, pp. 79–93. Winona Lake: Eisenbrauns.

Harper, R.F. 1892–1914. *Assyrian and Babylonian Letters Belonging to the K[ouyunjik] Collections of the British Museum*. Chicago: University of Chicago Press.

Heimpel, W. 1997. Disposition of Households of Officials in Ur III and Mari. *Acta Sumerologica* 19:63–82.

———. 1998–2001. Ninsiana. *Reallexikon der Assyriologie* 9, pp. 487b–488a. Berlin and New York: de Gruyter.

———. 2003. *Letters to the King of Mari. A New Translation, with Historical Introduction, Notes, and Commentary*. Mesopotamian Civilization 12. Winona Lake: Eisenbrauns.

Horsnell, M.J.A. 1999. *The Year Names of the First Dynasty of Babylon*. Vol. 2, *The Year-Names Reconstructed and Critically Annotated in Light of Their Exemplars*. Hamilton: McMaster University Press.

Jeyes, U. 1991–1992. Divination as a Science in Ancient Mesopotamia. *JEOL* 32:23–41.

Joannès, F. 1991. Le traité de vassalité d'Atamrum d'Andarig envers Zimri-Lim de Mari. In *Marchands, diplomates et empereurs. Études sur la civilisation mésopotamienne offertes à Paul Garelli*, ed. D. Charpin and F. Joannès, pp. 167–78. Paris: Éditions Recherche sur les Civilisations.

Jones, P. 2003. Embracing Inanna: Legitimation and Mediation in the Ancient Mesopotamian Sacred Marriage Hymn Iddin-Dagan A. *JAOS* 123:291–302.

———. 2005. Divine and Non-Divine Kingship. In *A Companion to the Ancient Near East*, ed. D.C. Snell, pp. 330–42. Oxford: Blackwell.

Katz, Dina. 2006. Appeals to Utu in Sumerian Narratives. In *Approaches to Sumerian Literature. Studies in Honour of Stip (H.L.J. Vanstiphout)*, ed. P. Michalowski and N. Veldhuis, pp. 105–22. Cuneiform Monographs 35. Leiden: Brill.

Klengel, Horts. 1976. Hammurapi und seine Nachfolger im altbabylonischen Onomastikon. *JCS* 28:156–60.

Kraus, F.R. 1973. *Vom mesopotamischen Menschen der altbabylonischen Zeit und seiner Welt*. Amsterdam and London: North-Holland Publishing.

———. 1984. *Königliche Verfügungen in altbabylonischer Zeit*. Studia et Documenta 11. Leiden: Brill.

Laessoe, Jorgen. 1950. On the Fragments of the Hammurabi Code. *JCS* 4:173–87.

Lambert, W.G. 1960. *Babylonian Wisdom Literature*. Oxford: Oxford University Press.

———. 1997. Questions Addressed to the Babylonian Oracle. The *tamîtu* Texts. In *Oracles et prophéties dans l'Antiquité, actes du colloque de Strasbourg, 15–17 juin 1995*, ed. J.-G. Heintz, pp. 85–98. Paris: de Boccard.

———. 2007. *Babylonian Oracle Questions*. Mesopotamian Civilization 13. Winona Lake: Eisenbrauns.

Limet, H. 1990. Actes juridiques paléo-babyloniens. In *De la Babylonie à la Syrie, en passant par Mari. Mélanges offerts à Monsieur J.-R. Kupper à l'occasion de son 70ᵉ anniversaire*, ed. Ö. Tunca, pp. 35–58. Liège.

Machinist, P. 1978. The Epic of Tukulti-Ninurta I. A Study in Middle Assyrian Literature. Ph.D. diss., NELC, Yale University. New Haven, CT.

Maul, S.M. 1988. *"Herzberuhingungsklagen." Die sumerisch-akkadischen Eršaḫunga-Gebete*. Wiesbaden: Harrassowitz.

———. 1994. *Zukunftsbewältigung. Eine Untersuchung altorientalischen Denkens anhand der babylonisch-assyrischen Löserituale (Namburbi)*. Baghdader Forschungen 18. Mainz am Rhein: Philipp von Zabern.

———. 1999. How the Babylonians Protected Themselves against Calamities Announced by Omens. In *Mesopotamian Magic. Textual, Historical, and Interpretative Perspectives*, ed. T. Abusch and K. van der Toorn, pp. 123–30. Ancient Magic and Divination 1. Groningen: Styx Publications.

Neumann, H., et al., eds. n.d. *Krieg und Frieden im Alten Vorderasien. 52ᵉ Rencontre Assyriologique Internationale*. Santag. Wiesbaden: Harrassowitz. In press.

Nougayrol, J. 1951. Le prologue du Code Hammourabien d'après une tablette inédite du Louvre. *RA* 45:67–78.

Parpola, S. 1970–1983. *Letters from Assyrian Scholars to the Kings Esarhaddon and Assurbanipal*. AOAT 5. Kevelaer: Butzon & Becker.

Radner, K. 2005. *Die Macht des Namens. Altorientalische Strategien zur Selbsterhaltung. Santag 8. Wiesbaden: Harrassowitz.

Reiner, E. 1985. *Your Thwarts in Pieces Your Mooring Rope Cut: Poetry from Babylonia and Assyria*. Michigan Studies in the Humanities 5. Ann Arbor: Horace H. Rackham School of Graduate Studies.

———. 1995. *Astral Magic in Babylonia*. Transactions of the American Philosophical Society Vol. 85, Pt. 4. Philadelphia: American Philosophial Society.

Rochberg-Halton, F. 1987. *The Lunar Eclipse Tablets of Enūma Anu Enlil: Aspects of Babylonian Celestial Divination*. BAfO 22. Horn: Verlag Ferdinand Berger & Söhne.

Roth, M. 1995. *Law Collections from Mesopotamia and Asia Minor*. Writings from the Ancient World 6. Atlanta: Society of Biblical Literature.

———. 2002. Hammurabi's Wronged Man. *JAOS* 122:38–45.

Schwemer, D. 2001. *Die Wettergottgestalten Mesopotamiens und Nordsyriens im Zeitalter der Keilschriftkulturen. Materialien und Studien nach den schriftlichen Quellen*. Wiesbaden: Harrassowitz.

Seidl, U. 2001. Das Ringen um das richtige Bild des Šamaš von Sippar. *ZA* 91:120–32.

Seux, M.-J. 1967. *Épithètes royales akkadiennes et sumériennes*. Paris: Letouzay et Âné.

Slanski, K.E. 2007. The Mesopotamian "Rod and Ring." In *Regime Change in the Ancient Near East and Egypt from Sargon of Agade to Saddam Hussein*, ed. H. Crawford, pp. 37–59. Proceedings of the British Academy 136. Oxford: Oxford University Press.

Sommerfeld, W. 2006. Der Beginn des offiziellen Richteramts im Alten Orient. In *Recht gestern und heute. Festschrift zum 85. Geburtstag von Richard Haase*, ed. J. Hengstl and U. Sick, pp. 3–20. Philippika 13. Wiesbaden: Harrassowitz.

Starr, I. 1983. *The Rituals of the Diviner*. Bibliotheca Mesopotamica 12. Malibu: Undena.

———, ed. 1990. *Queries to the Sungod*. SAA 4. Helsinki: Helsinki University Press.

Stol, M. 1999. Tavolette paleo-babilones. In *Catalogo del Museo Egizio di Torino, Serie Seconda—Collezioni* IX, ed. A. Archi, F. Pomponio, and M. Stol, pp. 41–81. Turin: Cisalpino-istituto editoriale universitario.

Tallqvist, K.L. 1938. *Akkadische Götterepitheta*. Studia Orientalia 7. Helsingfors: Societas Orientalis Fennica.

Van De Mieroop, M. 2005. *King Hammurabi of Babylon. A Biography*. Malden, MA: Blackwell.

Veenhof, K.R. 2003. Fatherhood Is a Matter of Opinion. An Old Babylonian Trial on Filiation and Service Duties. In *Literatur, Politik und Recht in Mesopotamien. Festschrift C. Wilcke*, ed. W. Sallaberger, K. Volk, and A. Zgoll, pp. 313–32. Orientalia Biblica et Christiana 14. Wiesbaden: Harrassowitz.

Veldhuis, N. 1991. *A Cow of Sîn*. Library of Oriental Texts 2. Groningen: Styx.

Villard, P. 2007. L'(an)durāru à l'époque néo-assyrienne. *RA* 101:107–24.

Ziegler, N. 2007. *Les Musiciens et la musique d'après les archives de Mari*. Florilegium marianum 9. Paris: SEPOA.

———. n.d. "Kriege und ihre Folgen: Frauenschicksale anhand der Archive aus Mari." In *Krieg und Frieden im Alten Vorderasien. 52e Rencontre Assyriologique Internationale,* ed. H. Neumann et al. Santag. Wiesbaden: Harrassowitz. In press.

3

Rising Suns and Falling Stars: Assyrian Kings and the Cosmos

ECKART FRAHM[1]

In Book VI of his *City of God*, St. Augustine discusses, and eventually dismisses, an attempt by the famous Roman polymath Marcus Terentius Varro (116–27 BC) to classify various approaches to the divine (Dihle 1996). Drawing on concepts developed by the Stoic philosopher Panaetius, Varro distinguished between three dimensions of divinity: a cosmological dimension (*theologia naturalis*), a mythological dimension (*theologia fabularis*), and a political one (*theologia civilis*). As cosmic entities, gods represented elements of nature; in mythology, they appeared as protagonists of stories in which they interacted with other deities; and in their "political" capacity, they were associated with specific cities or countries and worshipped in local temples dedicated to them. Varro associated each of his three dimensions with specific professional groups. Philosophers, he argued, would focus on the cosmological, poets on the mythological, and priests and rulers on the political aspects of the divine world.

Even though derived from an analysis of the Greco-Roman pantheon, Varro's theory of a *"theologia tripertita"* can also serve as a useful investigative tool when one aims at a better comprehension of the theological concepts of other civilizations. Jan Assmann has applied it to the religion of ancient Egypt (Assmann 1991:16–18), and with similar justification, one can try to employ it when studying the deities of ancient Mesopotamia. The Babylonian god Marduk provides a good example. His divine statue, placed in the cella of the Esagil temple in Babylon, represents his political dimension, the planet Jupiter, closely associated with him, represents his cosmological qualities, and *Enūma Eliš*, the Babylonian *Epic of Creation* (Foster 2005:436–86) that describes how Marduk fought primeval monsters and created the world, provides the mythological context for his rise to prominence and power.

It is true that many Egyptian and ancient Near Eastern deities possessed only one or two of Varro's three dimensions. This applies especially to minor deities, but a few major gods were likewise deficient in this respect. Pharaoh Akhenaten, for instance, when implementing his new brand of solar religion during the Amarna period, propagated a deity, the Aten, that had an all-powerful cosmological presence but no political or mythological dimensions (Assmann 1991:243–53). In Assyria the god Ashur remained essentially limited, for many centuries, to the "political" quality of a god closely linked with his city, Assur, and the land of Assyria, both of which bore his name. Attempts to identify him with the god Enlil—and later with Marduk—in order to provide him with mythological and cosmological facets, never fully succeeded (Frahm 1997:282–88; Vera Chamaza 2002:71–167). Yet Ashur and the Aten were rather exceptional deities. The rule for the most powerful gods and goddesses of the ancient Near East was that they had some share in all the three dimensions outlined by Varro.

It has been frequently observed, most prominently by Henri Frankfort (1948), that in the ancient Near East, ideas about the gods were closely connected to the ideology of kingship. In accordance with the dialectics of "political theology" (Assmann 2002:15–27), Mesopotamian and Egyptian rulers would model their own image on that of the gods, while at the same time representations of the gods were to a significant extent projections onto the divine world of the political self-representation of those very rulers. Hence it is not surprising to rediscover traces of Varro's three dimensions in the sphere of earthly government.

This is most obvious with regard to the political dimension, which Varro, after all, had derived from the sphere of human power. The palaces from which Mesopotamian kings ruled their states were, despite a few conspicuous differences, in many ways the functional equivalents of the temples, and shared with them a number of architectural features. For instance, 1st millennium throne rooms, where subjects and foreign dignitaries would officially encounter the king, were designed very much like temple cellas, where worshippers would pray to the deity (Oppenheim 1977:327f.). Furthermore, as I will discuss further below, certain royal rituals are highly reminiscent of rituals carried out before the gods.

There is also evidence for what one might dub the "mythology" of political leaders. It finds its most obvious expression in the "autobiographical" inscriptions Mesopotamian kings left on lasting supports such as stone slabs, stelae, rock reliefs, or baked clay tablets and prisms. In Mesopotamia, unlike in Egypt, essentially only kings were entitled to this form of commemoration. The way many royal inscriptions (and a few royal "epics") describe the kings' heroic victories over dangerous enemies and their efforts to spread, mostly through building projects, civilization and progress is similar in style, form, and content to mythological tales such as the Sumerian *Lugal-e Epic* (van Dijk 1983) or the aforementioned *Epic of Creation*, where Marduk first vanquishes the forces of chaos and then creates heaven and earth, with the city of Babylon in its center (Maul 1991).

Last but not least, ancient Near Eastern royal ideology also possessed a cosmological dimension. It was a widespread belief that the rule of the king—and political affairs in general—had counterparts in certain celestial phenomena. These cosmological aspects of the ideology of kingship will be the topic of the following reflections, which will focus on evidence from the 1st millennium and especially the Neo-Assyrian period.[2] I will first explore the solar aspects of Assyrian (and Babylonian) kingship and then, in a second step, investigate some of its—far less obvious—astral features. Of course, I cannot claim to walk on altogether untrodden ground here. But despite earlier studies by Cassin 1968, Janowski 1989, Maul 1998, and quite a few others, the topic has not yet been fully exhausted.

Of all the heavenly bodies, it was, from early on, first and foremost the sun that provided the model for kingship in the pre-classical ancient world. As is well known, the close connection between the king and the sun received its most sophisticated politico-theological, ritual, and visual expressions in ancient Egypt, where it was the primary cornerstone of pharaonic self-representation at least from the Fifth Dynasty onwards (Assmann 1991:67–102). But solar theology played a significant role in Hittite and Mesopotamian politics as well. For Hittite kings, "my sun" served as an official title during the imperial period (Fauth 1979; Beckman 2002), while the most obvious evidence for the "solarization" of Mesopotamian rulers comes from personal names and royal epithets. Already during the Ur III period, people gave their children names like Šulgi-šamšī "(king) Shulgi is My Sun" (*CAD* Š/1:337). The Isin ruler Lipit-Ishtar claimed in a hymn extensively studied in Old Babylonian schools that "he walked along like (the sun-god) Utu," which made him "the brilliant light of the land" (^{d}utu-gin$_7$ du še-er-zid kalam-ma) (Vanstiphout 1978:36–37, line 3). Ḫammurapi of Babylon, who is invoked in personal names such as Ḫammurapī-^{d}Šamšī, referred to himself, in his famous law-code, as $^{(d)}$Šamšu Bābilim "sun(-god) of Babylon" (Borger 1979:6 and 9, v 4). This solar imagery was taken up by the Middle Assyrian king Tukulti-Ninurta I, who claimed to be "the one who shepherds the four quarters at the heels of (the sun-god) Šamaš" (ša kibrāt arba'i arki Šamaš irte''û) (Grayson 1987:233). Neo-Assyrian rulers used similar epithets. Ashurnaṣirpal II boasted that "his protection was spread like the sun's rays over his land" (ša kīma šarūr Šamši andillašu eli mātišu šuparruru) (Cifola 1995:190), and Adad-nirari II, Tukulti-Ninurta II, Ashurnaṣirpal II, Shalmaneser III, and Esarhaddon all claimed to be "the sun of all the people" (šamšu kiššat nīšī) (Cifola 1995:157; CAD Š/1:337a).[3]

Why were comparisons between the king and the sun so common, not only in Egypt and Mesopotamia, but also in the Hellenistic and Roman world, in Japan (where the Tenno was regarded as a descendant of the sun-goddess Amaterasu), and in Western political ideology? What is the *tertium comparationis* governing this association? It seems there are several qualities that make the sun particularly compatible with the ideology of kingship. First of all, the sun is by far the brightest heavenly body. Its radiance, called in Akkadian *birbirru*, *melammu*, *namrīru*, or *šalummatu*, is much more powerful than that of the moon, the planets, and the stars—just as the power of the king was supposed to surpass that of any other living being. The sun is, furthermore, visible everywhere. The great Babylonian hymn to Šamaš claims: "Your fierce light fills the lands to their limits" (*namrīrūka imlû siḫip mātāti*) (Lambert 1960:126–27, line 20). This solar omnipresence corresponds to an idea that became more and more predominant in Mesopotamian political thought over the centuries: that the rule of the king should be universally accepted. And finally, there is the great steadiness that characterizes the sun's course: "Regularly and without cease you traverse the heavens" (*tētenettiq ginâ šamāmī*), the Shamash hymn states (Lambert 1960:126–27, line 27). In this respect as well, the sun served as a model for the rule of the king.

The permanence of the presence of the sun, its static aspect, is expressed with the Akkadian term *kânu* "to be stable," while its regular movement, the dynamic element of the solar course, is referred to with the verb *ešēru* "to direct oneself steadily." Notions of stability and regularity were closely connected, in the Assyro-Babylonian worldview, to the idea of righteousness, a concept for which the Akkadian language uses the word pair *kittu u mīšaru* "truth and justice" (lit. "steadiness and directedness"), terms derived from *kânu* and *ešēru* (Maul 1998:65–67). An Esarhaddon inscription, referring, somewhat unusually, not only to the sun but also to the moon, declares: [*Sîn u*] *Šamaš ilāni maššūte aššu dēn kitte u mīšari ana* [*māti*] *u nīšī šarāku arḫišamma ḫarrān kitte u mīšari ṣabtūma* "[(The moon-god) Sîn and] (the sun-god) Šamaš, the twin gods, kept from month to month the path of steadiness and directedness, so that the people would be granted lawsuits steeped in truth and justice (lit. "steadiness and directedness") (Borger 1956:2, i 31–36). The earthly agent responsible for this administration of justice was of course no one else but the king, which explains why Ḫammurapi is portrayed together with the sun-god on his law stele and why various Assyrian kings, to designate their legal functions, bear the epithet "securer of justice (*muštēširu*) for the people," likewise derived from *ešēru* (for examples, see Cifola 1995:189). The great significance the people of the ancient Near East ascribed to the judicial role of the sun-god explains why Mesopotamian kings normally invoke Šamaš in the context of domestic politics, when trying to extol their role as benefactors of their people, but only rarely refer to the sun when they describe the annihilation of enemies in times of warfare.

It is important to note that all the references to the sun-like qualities of Mesopotamian kings I have mentioned so far can be classified as tropes. They are either comparisons—"his protection is like the sun's rays"—or metaphors (Streck 1999:30–53) accompanied by conditional statements: the king is "the sun(-god) of Babylon," of "all the people," or of the individual who addresses him. These qualifications seem to indicate the non-literal character of the solar imagery and to limit its area of application. The king, it appears, is neither the real sun nor is he the sun-god; but if compared to other human beings, he holds a position that is analogous to the position the sun (and the deity representing it) holds among the heavenly bodies.

Yet to define the nature of the relationship between Babylonian and especially Assyrian kings on one hand, and the sphere of the gods on the other, as merely metaphorical and free of "ontological" implications is not as accurate as it may first seem. As recently shown in considerable detail by Peter Machinist (2006), there can be little doubt that the kings in question were believed to share certain divine attributes in a far more immediate way. Of the various god-like aspects of Assyrian kingship that Machinist discusses, I would like to briefly reinvestigate here one in particular: the designation of the ruler as the ṣalmu, or "image," of a deity.

A letter sent in 669 by the well-known scholar Adad-šumu-uṣur to the Assyrian king Esarhaddon (680–669) claims: *šarru bēl mātāti ṣalmu ša ᵈŠamaš šū* "The king, the lord of the lands, is the very image (ṣalmu) of Šamaš" (Parpola 1993:no. 196, rev. 4–5). A similar statement, again by Adad-šumu-uṣur, occurs in another letter, which refers to the Assyrian king Ashurbanipal (669–630), Esarhaddon's successor, as "the very image of (the god) Bēl" (*šarru bēlī ṣalam Bēl-ma šū*) (Parpola 1993:no. 228, line 19).[4] These invocations of divine archetypes manifesting themselves as "images" in the person of the king[5] recall the Platonic concept of abstract forms or ideas having their specific counterparts in the lower orders, and bring to mind the Christian maxim *rex imago dei*, which defined the "political theology" of the Middle Ages (Kantorowicz 1997 [1957]: 504). Yet as pointed out in recent discussions, mostly by art historians (Winter 1997; Bahrani 2003:123–48), a ṣalmu is more than a mere "image" in the modern sense of the word. It is, in a culture where "the world of appearance and the world of essence are the same" (Bahrani 2003:134), quite literally a "re-presentation," that is, to take up a distinction established by Hans Belting (1994), something that serves as a medium not so much of likeness but rather of presence. For those accustomed to such a way of semiotic reasoning, a ṣalmu contained, in an (almost) physical sense, at least some of the qualities that characterized its model.

We therefore have to be more nuanced. Calling the Assyrian king a ṣalmu of Šamaš implies that his solar aspects possessed a degree of reality that went significantly beyond the realm of the merely metaphorical. Some textual references seem, in fact, to indicate that the king was regarded as little less than an "incarnation" of the sun-god. An explicit statement to this effect, *šarru šīr ilāni Šamaš ša nīšīšu* "The king is the flesh of the gods and the sun-god of his people," can be found in *Ludlul* I 55 (Lambert 1960:32). The letter Cole and Machinist 1998, no. 46, rev. 12-14, after calling the king "an image of Marduk," seems to make a similar point, but the context is not completely clear; the passage reads: [*šarru*] *be-lí a-bat-su ki-i šá* dingir-meš / [*gamrat*(?) x x] x uzu-meš dingir-meš ᵈutu / [x x x x] "The word of [the king], my lord, [*is*] just as [*final*] as that of the gods [...] the flesh of the gods, Šamaš

[...]." Finally, the Middle Assyrian Tukulti-Ninurta epic, before praising the king as "an eternal image of Enlil" (ṣalmu Enlil dārû), claims that he is to be "reckoned as flesh godly in his limbs" (mani itti šīr ilāni mi-na-a-šú) (Lambert 1957–1958:50, lines 16, 18; Machinist 2006:163–64). The last two references point towards conceptual links between Assyro-Babylonian ideas about incarnation on one hand and ṣalmu on the other, a connection also implied by various texts characterizing the materials from which divine images (ṣalmu) were made as šīr ilāni, "flesh of the gods" (CAD Š/3:117).[6]

It was in part through ritual that the king acquired his reputation of sharing certain qualities of Šamaš—and god-like qualities in general. Rituals are cultural acts based not only on words, or *legomena*, but also on deeds, or *dromena,* as well as on "things shown," *deiknymena*, and the transformations they bring about transcend what a simple speech act, such as a comparison in a royal inscription, can achieve. The Catholic ritual of the Eucharist, infused by the doctrine of "transubstantiation," is a good example.[7] Even though the Mesopotamian kings of the 1st millennium, unlike some of their predecessors between the late Akkad and the Isin-Larsa period, no longer wrote their names with a divine determinative, they still participated in rituals that imbued them with a divine aura.

One of the most significant royal rituals of 1st millennium Mesopotamia was the so-called Bīt-rimki or "house-of-bathing" ritual (Laessoe 1955; Farber 1987:245–55; Janowski 1989:81–84). It began before dawn with a purification of the king that took place in his palace, and continued with several ablutions in seven "houses of bathing"—reed huts that had been erected in the countryside outside the city. The first of these ablutions took place in the moment when the sun rose, and was accompanied by prayers to the sun-god. The other six ablutions, which followed later during the day, were likewise performed in conjunction with such prayers, those in Sumerian spoken by the exorcist and those in Akkadian uttered by the king. The main purpose of the ablutions and the prayers to Šamaš was to free the king of every feasible physical or psychological ailment. But the Bīt-rimki ritual seems to have had an additional goal: to present the king, as he proceeded through the seven "houses of bathing," as an avatar of the sun traversing the various stations of its celestial course. So Bīt-rimki, apparently, not only aimed at providing the king with the protection of the sun-god, but also at establishing in a tangible way the close functional similarities between the sun and the ruler.

Another Mesopotamian royal ritual seems to have been administered to turn the king, quite literally, into an "image," or ṣalmu, of a god—just as Adad-šumu-uṣur had described him in the aforementioned letters. The ritual in question, known as mīs pî, i.e., "washing of the mouth," was normally performed when a newly fashioned statue of a deity, before being placed in a temple, had to be imbued with life to make it viable (Walker and Dick 2001). On such occasions, usually at night, the mouth of the divine image was ritually opened and cleaned, a practice also attested in ancient Egypt. Something very similar happened in the course of the so-called Bīt-salā'-mê ritual with certain accoutrements of the Mesopotamian king (Berlejung 1996; Ambos, n.d.). Bīt-salā'-mê, which originated in Babylonia but was also carried out for the last rulers of Assyria, can be described as a sort of re-investiture ritual, performed annually in the month of Tashritu (VI) to prepare the king for his participation in the Akītu festival later in the month. After having spent the night, stripped of his insignia, in a reed-hut symbolically representing a prison (a nice example of the separation stage of a *rite de passage*), the king emerged in the morning renewed and reborn with the rising sun. He then donned his garments, was returned his insignia, including his scepter and his crown, and took his seat on the royal throne. Even though the aforementioned mouth-washing ritual was applied, not to the king himself, but (in a nocturnal ceremony preceding his re-investiture) to his garments and his throne, the analogies with the rites performed on the occasion of the induction of a divine image seem very strong. The royal garments and the royal throne were, after all, objects of greatest importance when it came to the visual representation of royal power

That the divine features projected onto the king on the occasion of his (re)-investiture had a particularly pronounced solar component—at least during the Neo-Assyrian period—can be inferred from Ashurbanipal's so-called coronation hymn, which begins with an invocation of Šamaš and refers to a blessing for the king that was pronounced while a censer was placed before the sun-god (Livingstone 1989:no. 11, line 1, rev. 3; see also Arneth 1999).[8] Likewise of interest is that a bronze helmet with Assyrian motifs from the Guttmann Collection—whose authenticity, however, is subject to some doubt—shows a coronation scene with the Assyrian king depicted directly under a winged sun-disk (Berlejung 1996:35).

Returning to the concept of divine "dimensions" discussed at the beginning of this chapter, one could argue that the "political dimension" of the sun-god was represented not only by images (*ṣalmu*) of Šamaš worshipped in temples (Woods 2004), but also by the very person of the king, who functioned as a kind of "living image" of the sun-god (and perhaps a few other important deities as well).[9] It increased the complexity of this elaborate system of symbolic associations that one of the most powerful ancient Near Eastern iconographic symbols of the sun, the winged sun-disk, often associated with depictions of kings, was apparently called ^{d}*ṣalmu* in Akkadian, perhaps because it was regarded as the sun's "divine image" *par excellence* (Dalley 1986).

It should be noted that there were also actual statues of Neo-Assyrian kings, which were displayed in temples. Some of them functioned as votive statues, that is, as representations of the ruler put up before images of gods in order to pay, unceasingly, homage to them and, in return, receive their blessings. Yet cultic and other texts mentioning a ^{d}*ṣalam-šarri*, lit. "a deified image of the king," seem to indicate that other statues of Neo-Assyrian rulers, just as the royal images of earlier phases of Mesopotamian history, received offerings and prayers themselves (Winter 1992; Cole and Machinist 1998:xiii–xv; Machinist 2006:170–82).

Strong monarchical structures tend to generate tensions between royal ideology on the one hand, and the realities of the political scene on the other. To describe these tensions, Ernst Kantorowicz, in his study of "the king's two bodies" (1997 [1957]), established his famous distinction between the royal "body politic" and the royal "body natural." Mesopotamian kings of the 1st millennium, however powerful, were not exempt from having a body natural. Esarhaddon, for instance, the addressee of one of the aforementioned letters sent by Adad-šumu-uṣur, was a very sick man during the last years of his life, suffering from both physical and psychological disorders. In fact, Adad-shumu-usur's praise of him as "the very image of the sun-god" is accompanied by, and related to, complaints about the king actually behaving quite unlike that god. For days, Adad-šumu-uṣur grumbles in his letter, Esarhaddon had stayed in the dark, indulging in a depressed state of mind and eating and drinking nothing. Now it was high time for him, the writer insists, to get back on track (Parpola 1993:no. 196, rev. 5-19). We encounter here a rather pronounced contrast: the ideal *roi soleil* invoked by Adad-šumu-uṣur in rev. 4-5 of his letter had little to do with the real Esarhaddon, whose personal condition was wretched.

The Mesopotamian *literati* used various strategies in order to reconcile the contingencies brought about by the fragile nature of the royal "body natural" with the prestige-oriented ideology of kingship. One was the development of cosmological concepts that went beyond solar theology and focused instead on a close observation of the moon, the stars, and, most importantly, the planets, heavenly bodies that were less luminous than the sun and followed erratic paths. This night-side of the cosmos mirrored, far more accurately than the solar course, the complexities of the king's life and actual royal politics. Unlike the sun, which combined strength, steadiness, and directedness and therefore served as a symbol of absolute power and justice, the stars, with their mysterious appearances and disappearances, became the reference points of a symbolic system that was capable of also representing the uncertainties and risks that threatened the fate of the land and its ruler.

From the second half of the 2nd millennium BC onwards, the observation of the night sky became more and more a major concern, one might even say an obsession, of the Mesopotamian *literati*. Extispicy, until then the dominant method of divination (by use of animal entrails), lost much of its prestige to astrology. Thousands of putative celestial observations, many of them completely unrealistic from an astronomical point of view, were collected in the large astrological omen series *Enūma Anu Enlil*, which provides ample evidence for the potentially dangerous implications of certain astral phenomena. To illustrate this point, I quote here, more or less at random, a short passage of Jupiter omens from the series:

> [If Jupiter] comes close [to] a planet, wolves will bar the roads of the land. [If Jupiter] leans [against] a planet ... the cattle will be reduced. [If Jupiter] becomes steady [*in*] *front of* a planet ... a great army will fall (Reiner and Pingree 2005:42-43, rev. 4'-6').[10]

The crisis on earth predicted by the apodoses of these omens is announced, and to some extent created, by the cosmic "crisis" described in the protases. Jupiter, the planet of Marduk and as such normally a beneficial cosmic force, means bad luck when seen with another planet, and so the outcome of the three foregoing omens is inauspicious.

To be sure, Assyrian kings and their scribes and counselors frequently invoked what they believed were the positive and auspicious characteristics of stars and constellations. Esarhaddon, for instance, writes in an inscription from Ashur that on the occasion of his accession, "Venus, the brightest of the stars, appeared in the West [in the path] of the (stars) of Ea, reached its hypsoma, and disappeared, in order to stabilize the land and reconcile its gods"[11] (Borger 1956:2, i. 39–ii. 5).

The "celestial writing" (*šiṭir burūmê/šamê*) represented by the stars could, furthermore, serve as a model and archetype for the topographical setting of temples and royal cities (see *CAD* Š/3:146a; Janowski 2003). Thus, one of Esarhaddon's Babylon inscriptions describes the newly built Esagil temple in Babylon as "a palace of the gods, mirror (*maṭlat*) of the Apsu (the subterranean sweet water horizon), equivalent (*tamšīlu*) of the Esharra temple, counterpart of the dwelling of Ea (*meḫret šubat Ea*), and equivalent of the Ikû constellation (Borger 1956:21, lines 47–51). Here, partly in accordance with ideas articulated in Enūma eliš and the Babylonian Akītu liturgy (Linssen 2004:219, 228, lines 273–75), several cosmological entities are claimed to have been the model of Babylon's greatest temple, among them the constellation of the Field Star (Ikû), which corresponds to Pegasus. When Esarhaddon's father Sennacherib, between 690 and 681, restructured the Ashur temple in Ashur in order to create a cultic infrastructure that fit his religious reform plans, the Esagil served in several respects as a model for the new building. Probably inspired by its astral features, Sennacherib erected a number of gates around a new eastern courtyard of the temple of Ashur and gave them names that refer to stars and constellations, such as "Gate-of-the-wagon-star" or "Gate-of-the-path-of-the-(stars)-of-Enlil" (Pongratz-Leisten 1994:60–63).

Astral references can also be found in Sennacherib's accounts of his massive efforts to rebuild and enlarge the city of Nineveh, which became the greatest metropolis of its time during his reign. Sennacherib describes the city with the following words:

> Nineveh, the exalted cult center, the city beloved of Ishtar, wherein are all the rites of gods and goddesses, the everlasting foundation, the eternal base, whose plan had been designed from of old and whose structure had been made beautiful along with [or: in accordance with] the celestial writing [*šiṭir burūmê*], a fine-looking place, a dwelling of mystery, where all kinds of artistic craftsmanship and all the rituals, the secret of Lalgar [a synonym of Apsu, the subterranean abode of Ea], had been brought together [or: were studied][12] (Frahm 1997:72, lines 1–10).

It is not completely clear in what respect Sennacherib thought the outline of Nineveh corresponded to "celestial writing," but it is possible that *šiṭir burūmê* is another oblique reference to the constellation Ikû, a square of somewhat uneven proportions, which might have been regarded as a prefiguration of the rectangular shape of Mesopotamian cities. In any case, Assyrian capitals were apparently in some way conceptualized as "heavenly cities" (Maul 1997).

In another display of their belief in astral power, the Assyrian kings Sargon II and Esarhaddon, in order to record their names and titles, occasionally used a newly devised pictographic script that was, in ways not yet fully understood, connected to the "heavenly writing" of stars and constellations (Finkel and Reade 1996; Scurlock 1997; Roaf and Zgoll 2001; Frahm 2005:50[28]). Esarhaddon describes the characters of this writing system as "*lumāšē* (that is, "astral constellations"), the counterparts of (the writing of) my name" (Borger 1956:28, lines 11–12).

All these references, direct or indirect, to the beneficial qualities of stars and constellations should not distract us, however, from the ambivalent nature Assyrian and Babylonian kings and scholars ascribed to the heavenly bodies that populate the night sky. A comparison between two of the most influential Babylonian mythological epics of the first millennium BC, the *Enūma eliš* and the *Erra* epic (Foster 2005:436–86, 880–911), both eminently political and, at the same time, cosmological texts, makes it quite clear that astral configurations could represent not only harmony but also chaos. *Enūma eliš* was modeled upon the older *Lugal-e* epic but turned the terrestrial outlook of that text into a far more astral-oriented vision. It reports how Marduk created the stars, which were dominated by Jupiter-Nēbiru, his own celestial avatar, as a clockwork of perfect and harmonious order. The *Erra* epic, in contrast, in many respects a "counter-text" to *Enūma eliš*, shows how that harmony is dissolved and how the stars, first and foremost the "Fox star" (Mars), mirror the destruction and confusion that rules on earth once Marduk has gone to the Netherworld and Erra has grabbed the reins of power.

Babylonian and Assyrian scholars regarded Mars as the most dangerous of the planets. Not only the *Erra epic*, but also many planetary omens from the series *Enūma Anu Enlil* demonstrate that Mars was deemed a notoriously ill-boding celestial body, associated with pestilence and war (Reynolds 1998). Whenever Mars came into contact with a normally auspicious celestial body or constellation, danger seemed in store. Lunar eclipses were likewise events of grave consequence and required, under certain circumstances, the enthronement of a substitute king who would absorb the evil forces that were otherwise bound to attack the regular ruler (Parpola 1983:xxii-xxxii).

Phenomena related to the sun are, of course, mentioned in *Enūma Anu Enlil* as well, especially in tablets 23(24)–35(36), and they played a role in the practice of astrology during the Neo-Assyrian period. An occultation of the sun that took place in the course of a solar eclipse was, unsurprisingly, a reason for grave concern. Quite a few sun-related omens mentioned in letters and reports addressed to Late Assyrian kings were, however, treated rather strangely by their senders. The astrologers, scholars, and priests who discussed them re-interpreted them as pertaining, not to the sun, but to a completely different celestial body: the planet Saturn. In the report Hunger 1992, no. 48, for example, Nabû-aḫḫē-erība, commenting on his observation that Mars had passed below Saturn,[13] quotes an omen whose protasis reads: "If the Wolf star reaches the sun,"[14] and then provides a foundation for this rather surprising reference by explaining: "The Wolf star is Mars; [the star of the sun] is Saturn."[15] The same equation is found in astrological commentaries and other reports (see Brown 2000:68–70, 73; and Al-Rawi and George 2006:46–47), some of which specify that Saturn, because of its association with the sun, is also closely connected to the king. Thus, the report Hunger 1992, no. 95, rev. 1-7 claims:[16] "Tonight, Saturn approached the moon. Saturn is the star of the sun, and the relevant interpretation is as follows: It is good for the king. The sun is the star of the king."[17] Saturn was normally called *kayyamānu* "the steady one," a name that reflects, according to David Brown, "the planet's slow, indeed saturnine (though not necessarily gloomy) movement" (2000:69). *Kayyamānu* derives from *kânu*, which is the basis of *kittu*, one of the aforementioned key concepts of Mesopotamian royal ideology, and it therefore comes as no surprise that the planet features as *kakkab kitti u mīšari*, "star of truth (or: steadiness) and justice (or: directedness)," in a prayer from the ritual text for the Akītu festival from Babylon (Linssen 2004:220, 229, line 307). The prayer in question addresses Saturn, together with many other celestial bodies, among them the sun and the moon, as a manifestation of Bēl-Marduk. Saturn is also identified with the constellation Zibānītu, Libra or The Scales (see Hunger 1992:no. 39, line 3: ^{mul}*zi-ba-ni-tu*$_4$ [^{mul}*udu-idim-sag-uš*]), which represents yet another symbol of justice linked to royal ideology, and with the heroic warrior god Ninurta (Brown 2000:61, 69f.).

The association of the king with the planet Saturn is thus well established. But unlike the relationship between the king and the sun, its cosmological implications seem somewhat precarious. After all, Saturn is the dimmest of the planets known in antiquity; difficult to recognize, the Assyrians and Babylonians also called it the "black star," a rather unfavorable epithet in a civilization where darkness was usually regarded as inauspicious (Brown 2000:69, 73).[18] Esarhaddon's overextended sojourn in the dark, which seemed so inappropriate to Adad-shumu-usur, is far more reminiscent of Saturn than of the sun.

Given the ambivalent character of Saturn and other heavenly bodies populating the night sky, it is not surprising that, besides the aforementioned references, Babylonian and Assyrian texts allude only rarely to connections between stars and the ruling king. This is in marked contrast to Egypt, where Pharaoh is repeatedly associated with various stars and constellations, especially Orion (Albani 2004:67–73). One noteworthy astral reference to the king in the cuneiform textual record is the address of the ruler as *kakkabī* "my star" in the Old Babylonian Mari correspondence. Mostly attested in letters sent to the ruler by female family members, *kakkabī* seems to be a more intimate address than the epithet *šamšī* "my sun," likewise attested in the Mari corpus (Moran 1969:33; see also Charpin, this volume). Another reference to a king associated with a star can be found in an unpublished Neo-Assyrian letter from the Yale Babylonian Collection, probably dating to the reign of Esarhaddon, which mentions a dream in which the city-overseer of Ashur sees a star (*kakkubu*) "in the midst of the father of the king."[19] The symbolic implications of this surprising image remain, unfortunately, unclear. The late Middle Assyrian text *KAR* 158 might provide, in vii 2, yet another link between the Assyrian king and a star. The relevant line reads: "rise like the *morning* star," and represents the *incipit* of a song that may or may not address the king.[20]

The most influential astral reference to a 1st millennium Mesopotamian king, likewise referring to a celestial body rising at dawn, can be found not in a cuneiform text but in the Bible. In Isaiah 14, the famous mocking dirge about the end of "the king of Babel," we read in verse 12: "How you are fallen from heaven, Bright one, Son of Dawn (Hebr.: *hêlēl ben šāḥar*); how you are cut down to the earth, you who laid the nations low." Few verses in the Bible have given rise to so many fanciful interpretations. Modern scholars have explained the enigmatic *hêlēl ben šāḥar*, which English translations usually render as "Day Star, Son of Dawn," as, alternatively, a reference to: the Canaanite god ʿAttar; the Canaanite-Arabian moon-god *hll*/Hilâlu; the head of the Mesopotamian pantheon Enlil/Illil; the Greek god Phaeton; the morning star; the moon; the sun; and even Halley's Comet (see Etz 1986; Gallagher 1994; Jensen 1997; Spronk 1998; Poirier 1999; Albani 2004; and Watson in van der Toorn, Becking, and van Der Horst 1999:392–94). None of these theories can be proven, and the passage remains essentially enigmatic. Yet it seems quite clear that the image used here is that of a celestial body, luminous and impressive at first, but then, not unlike the stars mentioned in Is. 13:10, doomed to fall from its heavenly station.

The interpretation of the political context of the Isaiah passage is debated as well, yet despite some problems (see Olyan 2006), evidence indicates that the allegedly "Babylonian" king whose downfall Isaiah 14 describes was, originally, no king of Babylon at all, but rather the Assyrian ruler Sargon II (Ginsberg 1968; Frahm 1999). Isaiah 14:19 reports that the king in question had been "cast out, away from [his] grave, like loathsome carrion, clothed with the dead, those pierced by the sword." Whereas this description is quite compatible with what we know about the sad end of Sargon, who had died on the battlefield and whose body had not been recovered, no such tradition is attached to a king of Babylon. First Isaiah was a contemporary of Sargon II, which makes the connection even more likely.

It is quite feasible that the reference to *hêlēl ben šāḥar*, despite its possible links to Canaanite mythology, can be read as a deliberate critique of the cosmological foundations of Mesopotamian royal ideology. The Hebrew Bible is, in fact, for the most part rather suspicious of the astral sciences of the East and their political implications; passages such as Isaiah 47:13-14, a polemical invective against Babylonian celestial divination, and Jer. 10:2 make this quite clear. Astrology is explicitly prohibited in Deut. 18:10, and the difficult verse Amos 5:26 blames the Israelites for worshipping "Sikkût, your king, and Kiyyûn, your *image(s)*, the star (of) your gods" (*'t skwt mlkkm w't kjwn ṣlmjkm kwkb 'lhjkm*). Sikkût can probably be identified with Sakkut, a god of Elamite origin popular in the eastern Mesopotamian city of Dēr, while Kiyyûn is Kayyamānu, the Akkadian version of Saturn that we have encountered earlier.[21]

The short passage in Isaiah 14:12 about *hêlēl ben šāḥar* had a remarkable reception history (Jensen 1997; Kelly 2006). Translated as Heosphoros in the Septuagint and as Lucifer in the Latin Vulgata (which renders the verse as *"quomodo cecidisti de caelo lucifer qui mane oriebaris corruisti in terram qui vulnerabas gentes"*), Hêlēl Son of Dawn was linked by Origen to the "lightning from heaven" to which Satan's fall is compared in Luke 10:8. Hêlēl thus became one of the archetypes of a new, and highly influential, Christian re-conceptualization of the forces of evil, in which the devil was regarded as a fallen angel of enormous power. We have here yet another example of history taking the form of a comedy (or tragedy) of errors: The image of the devil that lay people and clerics of the Western world internalized for centuries is based in part on a non-literal, and clearly mistaken, interpretation of a cosmological metaphor used in the Bible to characterize a Babylonian (and in an earlier version most probably Assyrian) king.

In the official discourse of their own sphere, Assyrian kings were of course never portrayed as falling stars. Instead, they claimed, as we have seen, that they resembled the rising sun, and they implemented their status as "living images" of the sun-god, the patron of justice, through elaborate rituals. But in the astrological omen texts consulted by the kings and their scholars, the complex nocturnal movements of the moon, the planets, and the stars served as an image of a different, and more realistic political world, a world in which kings could be defeated, deposed, and even killed if things went wrong.

NOTES

3.1 I would like to thank the organizers and participants of the conference for their comments on a preliminary draft of this paper. For information on the Bīt-salā'-mê ritual, discussed further below, I am much indebted to Claus Ambos.

3.2 Earlier phases of the Mesopotamian discourse on politico-cosmological matters are covered in this book by Dominique Charpin's contribution.

3.3 It should be noted that the onomastic type that identifies someone as "my sun" is not only attested with royal names, but also with theonyms. Examples include the names Aššur-šamšī "(the god) Ashur is my sun," and Ištar-šamšī "(the goddess) Ištar is my sun" (Dalley 1986:98).

3.4 See also the proclamation [*šarru bēlī ṣala*]*m Marduk šū* in the letter Cole and Machinist 1998: no. 46, rev. 11; the name of the sender is lost. In yet another letter, Parpola 1993: no. 207, rev. 9–13, Adad-shumu-usur describes man as a shadow of god, while the king equals him more fully: [*š*]*a qa-bu-u-ni am-me-ú* / [*m*]*a-a gissu dingir a-me-lu*

Rising Suns and Falling Stars: Assyrian Kings and the Cosmos 113

/ [u?] gissu ˡᵘ*a-me-le-e* / [*a*]-*me-lu* : lugal : *šu-ú* / [*k*]*al*! *mu-uš-šu-li šá* dingir "Now as to that saying, 'Man is a shadow of god, [*and*] man *is* a shadow of *man*'—(that man, i.e. the one of whom man is a shadow) is the king, (for) he is the perfect likeness of god" (the translation of this difficult passage follows for the most part Machinist 2006:173–74). The word *muššulu*, used to define the relationship between king and god at the end of the passage, is, interestingly, also known as a term for "mirror." Note, furthermore, that Izi G, 56-57 equates *mu-ša-lum* and *ṣalmu* (see *CAD* Ṣ: 79a). For other references to the Neo-Assyrian king's status as an "image" of god, see Parpola 1983:112; Cole and Machinist 1998:xxii n12; and Machinist 2006:170–82.

3.5 The concept of manifestation is also known from Mesopotamian ideas about individual gods representing the whole pantheon, expressed in personal names such as Aššur-ṣalam-ilāni "Ashur is the image of the gods" (Neo-Assyrian, VAT 10050: 7 (unpubl., courtesy K. Deller) and Ea-ṣalam-ilī "Ea is the image of the gods" (Neo-Babylonian, see Tallqvist 1905:56); cf. also the name Gabbi-ilāni-Aššur "All the gods are (manifest in) Ashur" (PNA 1/II:414).

3.6 The well-known writing of the word *šarru* "king" with the cuneiform sign "20," the sacred number of the sun-god, is likewise of interest in this context. For Mesopotamian scribes, both the graphemic rendering of a word and its phonemic realization transcended the merely conventional; they denoted their object by nature, in an act of immediate signification (Bottéro 1974). Hence the writings of *šarru* as "20" indicate a belief, on the part of the scribes, that the links between the solar and the royal spheres were indeed very close.

3.7 For more elaborate thoughts on the function of ancient Near Eastern rituals, and references to various definitions of the term "ritual," see Winter 1992:16–17.

3.8 In rev. 5-8, the hymn invokes various royal accoutrements, among them the crown and the throne, and claims they were given to the king by the most powerful deities of the Mesopotamian pantheon. The passage has parallels in a short myth (Mayer 1987) that describes the creation of the king as separate from that of man, indicating that the Babylonians and Assyrians regarded the former as an *ens sui generis* (Deller 1987).

3.9 Note, for example, that the Late Assyrian kings renewed their semi-divine position also by wearing the crown of the god Ashur, called Bēl-agê, when showing themselves to the crowd in the southwestern courtyard of the Ashur temple during the annual Akītu festival in the month of Nisannu (Menzel 1981: T 49-50, lines 23–25). The god Ashur, on the other hand, was invoked as "king" in the coronation ritual performed on the occasion of the ascension of a new Assyrian ruler (Machinist 2006:157–59), indicating that the borders between the royal and the divine spheres were permeable in both directions.

3.10 [DIŠ *Nēbiru ana*] ᵐᵘˡudu-idim te ur-bar-ra a-rá kur tar-meš / [DIŠ *Nēbiru ana* (...)] ᵐᵘˡudu-idim *i-mid* ... *bu-lu₄* tur-*ir* / [DIŠ *Nēbiru ana* i]gi? ᵐᵘˡudu-idim *i-ku-un* ... erim gal šub-*ut*.

3.11 *Dilbat nabât kakkabāni ina Amurri* [*ina ḫarrān*] *šūt Ea innamirma ša kunnu māte ša*? *sullum ilāniša niṣirtu ikšudamma itbal*.

3.12 *Ninua māḫāzu ṣīru ālu narām Ištar ša napḫar kidudê ilāni u ištarāti bašû qerebšu temmennu darû duruš ṣâte ša ultu ulla itti šiṭir burūmê eṣrassu eṣretma šūpû šindūšu ašru naklu šubat pirište ša mimma šumšu šipir nikilti gimir pelludê niṣirti Lalgar šutābulū qerebšu*.

3.13 [ᵐᵘˡ]*ṣal-bat-a-nu ina šap-*[*la*] / [ᵐ]ᵘˡudu-idim-sag-uš *e-*[*te*]*-et-iq*.

3.14 [DIŠ ᵐᵘˡur-bar-ra ᵈutu] kur-*u*ᵈⁱᵏ⁻šᵘ⁻ᵘᵈ.

3.15 [ᵐᵘˡ]ur-bar-ra ᵐᵘˡ*ṣal-bat-a-nu* / [mul ᵈutu] ᵐᵘˡudu-idim-[sag-uš].

3.16 *mu-šu* gi₆ *an-ni-i-ú* / ᵐᵘˡudu-idim-sag-uš *a-na* ᵈ30 / *iq-ṭi-ri-ib* ᵐᵘˡudu-idim-sag-uš / mul: ᵈutu *šu-ú* / *ki-i an-ni-i-e* / *pi-še-er-šú* sig₅ *šá* lugal *šu-u* / ᵈutu mul *šar-ri šu-u*.

3.17 In Hunger 1992: no. 39, rev. 5-6, Nabû-aḫḫē-erība states that "the sighting of Saturn [is a good sign] for the king my lord" (*ta-mar-tú ša* ᵐᵘˡudu-idim-[sag-uš sig₅] / *ša* lugal en-*ia šu-u*). In the letter Parpola 1993: no. 51, rev. 8–9, it seems that Saturn (the name is lost in a break) is identified as "the star of the king." ᵐᵘˡlugal or Regulus, the "king-star," (which is different from "the star of the king") seems to have played a fairly minor role in Mesopotamian astrology; together with Saturn, it occurs in *SAA* 8, 40.

3.18 Brown holds that "evil = black" is an "eurocentric equation," but it should be noted that, in Mesopotamian extispicy, and not only there, dark color was consistently regarded as a bad sign (see Koch-Westenholz 2000:42, on *tarāku*).

3.19 *ina libbi abišu ša šarri* (YBC 11382, line 32, to be published by the present author).

3.20 *upḫa kī kakkab še-*[*e-ri*] For the reading, not completely certain, see *CAD* K:48a; and *CAD* N/1:266a .

3.21 Amos 5:26 and the two gods mentioned there have been discussed in recent years by, among others, M. Stol, in van der Toorn, Becking, and van Der Horst 1999:478 (s.v. "Kaiwan") and 722-23 (s.v. "Sakkuth"), R. Borger (1988), and Sh. Paul (1991:194–98). Paul suggests an emendation to 't skwt mlkkm w't kjwn kwkbkm ṣlmj 'lhjkm, which would yield the translation: "Sikkût, your king, and Kiyyûn, your star, the graven images of your gods"). The Masoretic vocalization of the two divine names is clearly artificial and apparently based on the vowel pattern typical of Hebrew words for idols and abominations, such as *gillul*. This chapter is not the place for a full reinvestigation of the matter, but I would like to briefly discuss here yet another so far, to my knowledge, unexplored possible approach to this much-debated passage. *ṣlm* has been regarded, by most exegetes (see, however, Paul 1991:196, n81), as the well-established term for "image," even though the apparent plural ending -*j* remains difficult. There is, however, a different possibility. As pointed out above, Stephanie Dalley (1986) has shown that according to Mesopotamian, Syrian, and northwest Arabic sources, the sun-god was occasionally called (ᵈ)*ṣalmu* in the ancient Near East. In a passage from the lexical list ḪAR-gud, this very name is associated with Saturn, the planetary avatar of the sun: mul gi₆ = an-*sa-lam*dùl = ᵈsag-uš ᵈutu "The black star (*kakkabu ṣalmu*) is *ṣalmu*, (which is) Saturn (Kayyamānu) (which in turn is) the sun(-god)" (see MSL 11, 40, lines 39–41, Brown 2000:69). Is it feasible that the sequence *kjwn ṣlmjkm kwkb* in Amos 5:26 was somehow inspired by the same chain of associations that underlies the ḪAR-gud entry?

In contrast to the Biblical passages critical of the astral sciences practiced in the East, the creation account of Gen. 1 refers to the heavenly lights as "signs" (1:14), displaying a somewhat more generous attitude towards astrology. The same seems to hold true for Job 38:31–33, with its mention of the Pleiades, Orion, the Bear, and "Mazzaroth" (< Akk. *mazzaltu* "position [of celestial constellations]").

REFERENCES

Albani, M. 2004. The Downfall of Helel, the Son of Dawn: Aspects of Royal Ideology in Isa. 14:12.13. In *The Fall of the Angels*, ed. C. Auffarth and L.T. Stuckenbruck, pp. 62–86. Themes in Biblical Narrative 6. Leiden: Brill.

Al-Rawi, F.N.H., and A.R. George. 2006. Tablets from the Sippar Library 13: *Enūma Anu Ellil XX. Iraq* 68:23–57.

Ambos, C. n.d. *Der König im Gefängnis und das Neujahrsfest im Herbst: Mechanismen der babylonischen Herrscherlegitimation im 1. Jahrtausend v. Chr. und ihre Geschichte.* In preparation.

Arneth, M. 1999. "Möge Šamaš dich in das Hirtenamt über die vier Weltgegenden einsetzen. Der "Krönungshymnus Aššurbanipals" (SAA 3,11) und die Solarisierung des neuassyrischen Königtums. *Zeitschrift für altorientalische und biblische Rechtsgeschichte* 5:28–53.

Assmann, J. 1991. *Ägypten: Theologie und Frömmigkeit einer frühen Hochkultur.* Stuttgart: Kohlhammer Verlag.

———. 2002. *Herrschaft und Heil: Politische Theologie in Altägypten, Israel und Europa.* Frankfurt am Main: S. Fischer.

Bahrani, Z. 2003. *The Graven Image: Representation in Babylonia and Assyria.* Philadelphia: University of Pennsylvania Press.

Beckman, G. 2002. "My Sun-God" Reflections of Mesopotamian Conceptions of Kingship among the Hittites. In *Ideologies as Intercultural Phenomena*, ed. A. Panaino and G. Pettinato, pp. 37–44. Melammu Symposia 3. Milan: Associazione Culturale Mimesis.

Belting, H. 1994. *Likeness and Presence: A History of the Image before the Era of Art*. Chicago: University of Chicago Press.

Berlejung, A. 1996. Die Macht der Insignien: Überlegungen zu einem Ritual der Investitur des Königs und dessen königsideologischen Implikationen. *UF* 28:1–35.

Borger, R. 1956. *Die Inschriften Asarhaddons, Königs von Assyrien*. BAfO 9. Graz: Selbstverlag des Herausgebers.

———. 1979. *Babylonisch-assyrische Lesestücke*. 2nd ed. AnOr 54. Rome: Pontificium Institutum Biblicum.

———. 1988. Amos 5,26, Apostelgeschichte 7,43 und Šurpu II, 180. *ZAW* 100:70–81.

Bottéro, J. 1974. Symptômes, signes, écritures en Mésopotamie ancienne. In *Divination et rationalité*, ed. P. Vernant, pp. 70–197. Paris: Éditions de Seuil.

Brown, D. 2000. *Mesopotamian Planetary Astronomy-Astrology*. CM 18. Groningen: Styx.

Cassin, E. 1968. *La splendeur divine: Introduction à l'étude de la mentalité mésopotamienne*. Paris: Mouton & Co.

Cifola, B. 1995. *Analysis of Variants in the Assyrian Royal Titulary from the Origins to Tiglath-pileser III*. Dipartimento di Studi Asiatici Series Minor 47. Naples: Istituto Universitario Orientale.

Cole, S.W., and P. Machinist. 1998. *Letters from Priests to the Kings Esarhaddon and Aššurbanipal*. SAA 13. Helsinki: Helsinki University Press.

Dalley, S. 1986. The God Ṣalmu and the Winged Disk. *Iraq* 48:85–101.

Deller, K. 1987. Assyrische Königsinschriften auf "Perlen." *NABU* 1987/101.

Dihle, A. 1996. Die Theologia tripertita bei Augustin. In *Geschichte—Tradition—Reflexion (Fs. M. Hengel)*, ed. H. Cancik, M. Hengel, and H. Lichtenberger, pp. 183–202. Tübingen: J.C.B. Mohr.

Etz, D.V. 1986. Is Isaiah XIV 12-15 a Reference to Comet Halley? *VT* 36:289–301.

Farber, W. 1987. Rituale und Beschwörungen in akkadischer Sprache. In *Texte aus der Umwelt des Alten Testaments* II/2^1, ed. O. Kaiser, pp. 212–81. Gütersloh: G. Mohn.

Fauth, W. 1979. Sonnengottheit (^{D}UTU) und "Königliche Sonne" (^{D}UTU$^{\check{S}I}$) bei den Hethitern. *UF* 11:227–73.

Finkel, I.L., and J.E. Reade. 1996. Assyrian Hieroglyphs. *ZA* 86:244–68.

Foster, B. 2005. *Before the Muses: An Anthology of Akkadian Literature.* 3rd ed. Bethesda: CDL Press.

Frahm, E. 1997. *Einleitung in die Sanherib-Inschriften.* BAfO 26. Wien: Selbstverlag für Orientalistik der Universität Wien.

———. 1999. Nabû-zuqup-kēnu, das Gilgameš-Epos und der Tod Sargons II. *JCS* 51:73–90.

———. 2005. Observations on the Name and Age of Sargon II and on Some Patterns of Assyrian Royal Onomastics. *NABU* 2005/44.

Frankfort, H. 1948. *Kingship and the Gods: A Study of Ancient Near Eastern Religion as the Integration of Society and Nature.* Chicago: University of Chicago Press.

Gallagher, W.R. 1994. On the Identity of Hêlēl Ben Šāḥar of Is. 14:12-15. *UF* 26:131–46.

Ginsberg, H.L. 1968. Reflexes of Sargon in Isaiah after 715 B.C.E. *JAOS* 88:49–53.

Grayson, A.K. 1987. *Assyrian Rulers of the Third and Second Millennia BC (to 1115 BC).* Royal Inscriptions of Mesopotamia, Assyrian Periods 1. Toronto: University of Toronto Press.

Hunger, H. 1992. *Astrological Reports to Assyrian Kings.* SAA 8. Helsinki: Helsinki University Press.

Janowski, B. 1989. *Rettungsgewißheit und Epiphanie des Heils.* Neukirchen-Vluyn: Neukirchener Verlag.

———. 2003. Der Tempel als Kosmos: Zur kosmologischen Bedeutung des Tempels in der Umwelt Israels. In *Egypt: Temple of the Whole World / Ägypten—Tempel der gesamten Welt (FS J. Assmann),* ed. S. Meyer, pp. 163–86. Studies in the History of Religions 97. Leiden: Brill.

Jensen, J. 1997. Helel ben Shaḥar (Isaiah 14:12-15) in Bible and Tradition. In *Writing and Reading the Scroll of Isaiah: Studies in an Interpretive Tradition,* ed. C.C. Broyles and C.A. Evans, pp. 330–56. Supplements to Vetus Testamentum 70. Leiden: Brill.

Kantorowicz, E. 1997 [1957]. *The King's Two Bodies: A Study in Mediaeval Political Theology.* Princeton: Princeton University Press.

Kelly, H.A. 2006. *Satan: A Biography.* Cambridge: Cambridge University Press.

Koch-Westenholz, U. 2000. *Babylonian Liver Omens: The Chapters Manzāzu, Padānu and Pān tākalti of the Babylonian Extispicy Series mainly from Aššurbanipal's Library.* CNI Publications 25. Copenhagen: Museum Tusculanum Press.

Laessoe, L. 1955. *Studies on the Assyrian Ritual and Series bît rimki.* Copenhagen:

E. Munksgaard.

Lambert, W.G. 1957–1958. Three Unpublished Fragments of the Tukulti-Ninurta Epic. *AfO* 18:38–51.

———. 1960. *Babylonian Wisdom Literature*. Oxford: Clarendon Press.

Linssen, M.J.H. 2004. *The Cults of Uruk and Babylon: The Temple Ritual Texts as Evidence for Hellenistic Cult Practices*. CM 25. Leiden: Brill/Styx.

Livingstone, A. 1989. *Court Poetry and Literary Miscellanea*. SAA 3. Helsinki: Helsinki University Press.

Machinist, P. 2006. Kingship and Divinity in Imperial Assyria. In *Text, Artifact, and Image: Revealing Ancient Israelite Religion*, ed. G. Beckman and Th.J. Lewis, pp. 152–88. Brown Judaic Studies 346. Providence: Brown University Press.

Maul, S.M. 1991. "Wenn der Held (zum Kampfe) auszieht ...": Ein Ninurta-Eršemma. *OrNS* 60:312–34.

———. 1997. Die altorientalische Hauptstadt: Abbild und Nabel der Welt. In *Die orientalische Stadt: Kontinuität, Wandel, Bruch*, ed. G. Wilhelm, pp. 109–24. CDOG 1. Saarbrücken: Harrassowitz.

———. 1998. Der assyrische König–Hüter der Weltordnung. In *Gerechtigkeit: Richten und Retten in der abendländischen Tradition und ihren altorientalischen Ursprüngen*, ed. J. Assmann, B. Janowski, and M. Welker, pp. 65–77. München: Fink.

Mayer, W. 1987. Ein Mythos von der Erschaffung des Menschen und des Königs. *OrNS* 56:55–68.

Menzel, B. 1981. *Assyrische Tempel*. StP SM 10. Rome: Biblical Institute Press.

Moran, W.W. 1969. New Evidence from Mari on the History of Prophecy. *Biblica* 50:15–56.

Olyan, S.M. 2006. Was the "King of Babylon" Buried before His Corpse Was Exposed? Some Thoughts on Isa 14,19. *ZAW* 118:423–26.

Oppenheim, A.L. 1977. *Ancient Mesopotamia: Portrait of a Dead Civilization*. Rev. ed. by Erica Reiner. Chicago: University of Chicago Press.

Parpola, S. 1983. *Letters from Assyrian Scholars to the Kings Esarhaddon and Aššurbanipal*. Vol. 2. AOAT 5/2. Kevelaer/Neukirchen-Vluyn: Butzon & Bercker.

———. 1993. *Letters from Assyrian and Babylonian Scholars*. SAA 10. Helsinki: Helsinki University Press.

Parpola, S., et al. 1998. *The Prosopography of the Neo-Assyrian Empire*. Neo-Assyrian Texts Corpus Project. Helsinki: Helsinki University Press.

Paul, S.M. 1991. *Amos: A Commentary on the Book of Amos*. Minneapolis: Augsburg Fortress Publishers.

Poirier, J.C. 1999. An Illuminating Parallel to Isaiah XIV 12. *VT* 49:371–89.

Pongratz-Leisten, B. 1994. *Ina šulmi īrub: Die kulttopographische und ideologische Programmatik der akītu-Prozession in Babylonien und Assyrien im 1. Jahrtausend v. Chr.* BAfO 16. Mainz: Philipp von Zabern.

Reiner, E., and D. Pingree. 2005. *Babylonian Planetary Omens Part Four*. CM 30. Leiden: Brill/Styx.

Reynolds, F. 1998. Unpropitious Titles of Mars in Mesopotamian Scholarly Tradition. In *Intellectual Life in the Ancient Near East*, ed. J. Prosecký, pp. 347–58. CRRAI 43. Prague: Academy of Science of the Czech Republic–Oriental Institute.

Roaf, M., and A. Zgoll. 2001. Assyrian Astroglyphs. *ZA* 91:264–95.

Schwemer, D. 2007. *Abwehrzauber und Behexung: Studien zum Schadenzauberglauben im alten Mesopotamien*. Wiesbaden: Harrassowitz Verlag.

Scurlock, J.A. 1997. Assyrian Hieroglyphs Enhanced. *NABU* 1997/92.

Spronk, K. 1998. Down with Hêlēl! The Assumed Mythological Background of Isa. 14:12. In *"Und Mose schrieb dieses Lied auf": Studien zum Alten Testament und zum Alten Orient (Fs. O. Loretz)*, ed. M. Dietrich and I. Kottspieper, pp. 717–26. AOAT 250. Münster: Ugarit-Verlag.

Streck, M.P. 1999. *Die Bildersprache der akkadischen Epik*. AOAT 264. Münster: Ugarit-Verlag.

Tallqvist, K.L. 1905. *Neubabylonisches Namenbuch zu den Geschäftsurkunden aus der Zeit des Šamaššumukīn bis Xerxes*. Actas Societatis Scientiarum Fennicae 32/2. Helsingfors/Leipzig: August Pries.

van der Toorn, K., B. Becking, and P.W. van Der Horst. 1999. *Dictionary of Deities and Demons in the Bible*. 2nd ed. Leiden: Brill.

van Dijk, J. 1983. *LUGAL UD ME-LÁM-bi NIR-GÁL: Le récit épique et didactique des Traveaux de Ninurta, du Déluge et de la Nouvelle Création*. Leiden: Brill.

Vanstiphout, H.L.J. 1978. Lipit-Eštar's Praise in the Edubba. *JCS* 30:33–61.

Vera Chamaza, G.W. 2002. *Die Omnipotenz Aššurs: Entwicklungen in der Aššur-Theologie unter den Sargoniden Sargon II., Sanherib und Asarhaddon*. AOAT 295. Münster: Ugarit-Verlag.

Walker, C.B.H., and M.B. Dick. 2001. *The Induction of the Cult Image in Ancient Mesopotamia*. SAALT 1: Neo-Assyrian Text Corpus Project. Helsinki: University of Helsinki Press.

Winter, I. 1992. "Idols of the King": Royal Images as Recipients of Ritual Action in Ancient Mesopotamia. *Journal of Ritual Studies* 6:13–42.

———. 1997. Art in Empire: The Royal Image and the Visual Dimensions of Assyrian Ideology. In *Assyria 1995: Proceedings of the 10th Anniversary Symposium of the Neo-Assyrian Text Corpus Project*, ed. S. Parpola and R.M. Whiting, pp. 359–81. Helsinki: Helsinki University Press.

Woods, C. 2004. The Sun-God Tablet of Nabû-apla-iddina Revisited. *JCS* 56:23–103.

4

Texts before Writing

Reading (Proto-)Egyptian Poetics of Power

LUDWIG D. MORENZ

INTRODUCTION: ON READABILITY

The idea of reading is much older than writing. Mesolithic hunters read footprints of animals and Neolithic farmers interpreted the sky as well as various other phenomena such as the flight of birds to predict the future. A more specific sense of reading is preserved in various divinatory practices. For example, sacral specialists in various cultures predict the future by reading the stars and their movements. While we can date this concept to the middle of the 3rd millennium BC in Mesopotamia, this practice is probably much older than its recording in writing.

Another conceptualization analogous to writing is the oracular reading of cracks in animal bones we know particularly from China (Keightley 1978). Early in human history people developed hermeneutic strategies with a view to helping them protect themselves from danger, supplying sufficient foodstuffs, or predicting the future. Furthermore, it may be more than pure chance that in China a substantial amount of early writing is closely associated with the oracular bones just mentioned. In the modern era this concept of reading lost something of its magic but at the same time dramatically changed when Galileo wrote: "Nature's great book is written in mathematical symbols."

According to an inscription of Gudea (the ruler of the ancient Mesopotamian city-state Lagash ca. 2100 BC) not only are the gods stars in heaven, but heaven is specifically conceptionalized as a tablet of blue stone on which *the world* is written. This Borghesian transposition of culture into nature is an expressive metaphor on the power of writing and celestial prototypes for life on earth. Furthermore, we know the Greek etiology of Palamedes inventing writing by graphically imitating the flight of the birds or the Chinese myth of the cultural hero Cang Jie, who invented letters after observing the footprints of wild animals. These are just mythological motifs and not simple historical memories, but they point out remarkable associations of letters important for a philosophy of writing.

Every development of writing—be it in Egypt, Mesopotamia, China, or Mesoamerica—has its own specific cultural setting. Thus, various culturally specific components played a distinctive role in this very complex process. Nevertheless, the very ancient and even pre-human idea of a certain *readability of the world* (Blumenberg 1979) was an essential mental precondition for the development of writing. In all cases of evolving significatory systems, we can see a long path from natural signs—such as the footprints of wild animals—via partially altered signs—such as the cracks in oracular bones thrown into the fire—to consciously created iconic and symbolic signs. In the late 4th millennium BC a certain de-iconization of the sign generated a new technology of communication. This transition from pictures to script is marked by stressing the phonetic aspect of various signs via the rebus principle. Some signs were transformed into semiographically empty designators of the sound—i.e., phonograms. This development was probably a small step for a man but a giant leap for mankind, which seems to have taken place first around 3200 BC in the Nile Valley (Morenz 2004). Writing was of great importance for ancient Egypt from the late 4th millennium BC onwards, generating a substantial part of the Egyptian cultural identity.

PICTURES AND NARRATIVES.
READING PROTO-DYNASTIC SEMIOPHORES

Reading, in terms of understanding the message of a cluster of images in a fairly precise way, predated writing. Thus, the ceremonial palette from ancient Hierakonpolis (Fig. 4.1; Oxford, Ash. E.3924) is understandable not just as a pictorial composition, but also as a distinct "royal" narrative exploring the metaphorical power of the images.[1] In this chapter, I will pres-

Texts before Writing: Reading (Proto-) Egyptian Poetics of Power 123

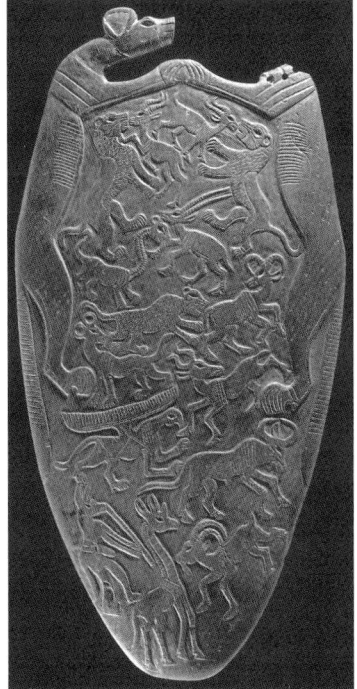

4.1. Ceremonial palette, Oxford, Ashmolean E.3924 (after Quibell and Green, 1900–01, 2:41, pl. 28).

ent an archaeo-semiotic case study of this remarkable object to understand the relationship between semiotic systems and power in late pre-dynastic Egypt. This way of encoding messages can be seen as "familienähnlich" (L. Wittgenstein) to writing.

The palette under discussion belongs to a group of objects classified as semiophores—objects of meaning (Pomian 1987)—which includes ceremonial palettes, maces, combs, knives, or sickles (Asselberghs 1961). These objects gradually developed during the 4th millennium BC from being purely functional to primarily representative of meaning (Figs. 4.2 and 4.3; Morenz 2005a). They are typically prestigious products of the (proto-) Egyptian elite culture of the later 4th millennium BC; it is likely that they also played a sacral role.

The palette, for example, may have served in the preparation of ritual eye paint. The circular depression in the center of one side of the palette indicates a usage for grinding the cosmetic paste. In the social practice of

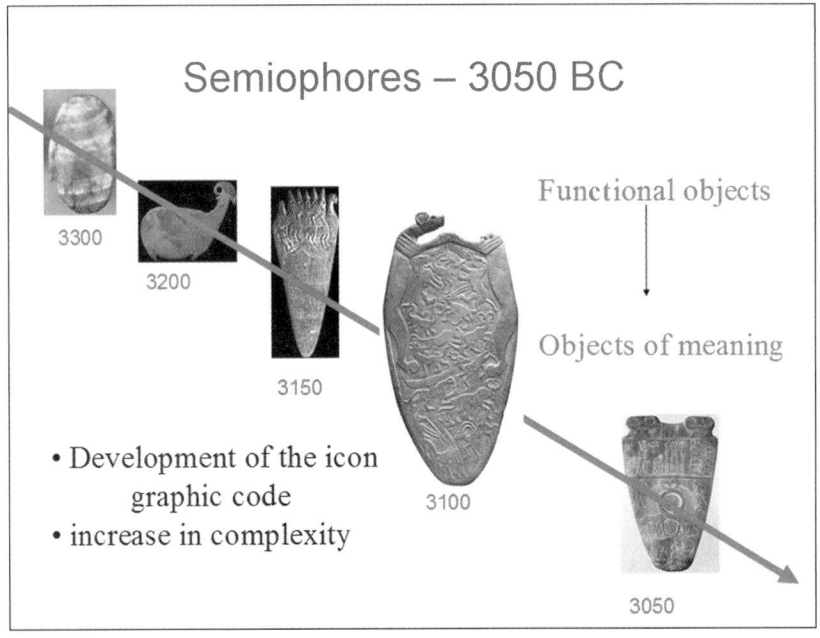

4.2. Development of Semiophores. Illustration: author.

ruler-fashioning, this eye paint served to generate the awe-inspiring gaze of the ruler. We can therefore assume a close interrelation between specific ritual performances and the visual and cognitive acts of viewing and reading, between social practice and symbolic meaning. The act of viewing these semiophores was heavily determined by social codes and specific sacral conditions generated by the ritual. Concerning the interaction between the beholder and the sacral object, we may compare the ceremonial palette with other sacral objects. As with a Christian altarpiece, the problems of gaze and awe are present in the interpretation between the beholder and the sacral object.[2] Like most ceremonial palettes, this palette was decorated on both sides. In order to be visible in its entirety such a large palette with decoration on both sides had to be handled in a particular way. We can only guess how these palettes were exhibited and where they were stored in practice. Were they on temporary display during festivals or were they permanently visible in a sacral space? These are questions essential for a proper understanding, but impossible to answer at our current state of knowledge.

Texts before Writing: Reading (Proto-) Egyptian Poetics of Power   125

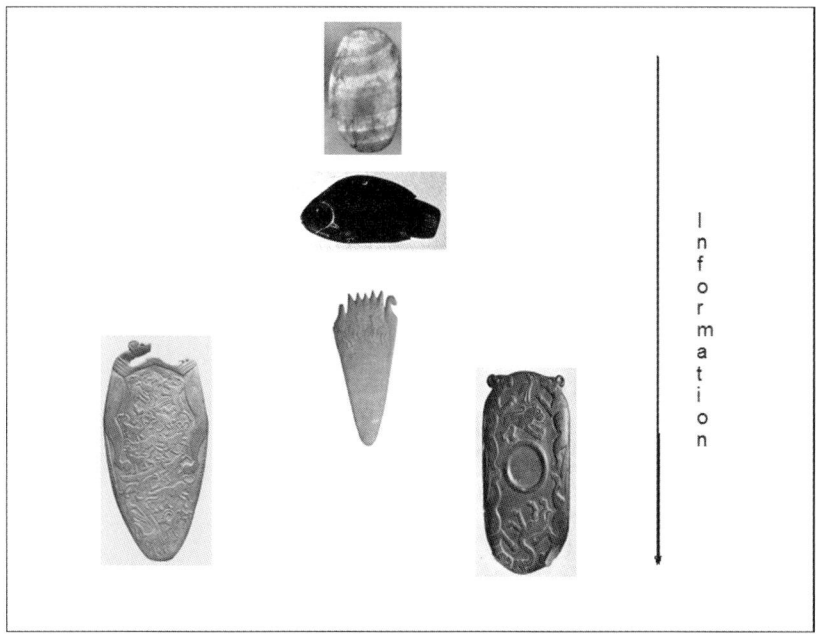

4.3. Development of semiophores in the 4th millennium. Illustration: author.

Deciphering the messages of these semiophores requires a close reading of each individual object in its cultural context. They are themselves products of significant changes in the society of the times that witnessed the emergence of a distinctly "Egyptian" high culture involving the growing stratification of the proto-Egyptian society. They were created by a new group of *professional* artists who were attached to the ruling elite of the proto-Egyptian city-states. These specialized meaning-makers developed skills that required a specific training in the various levels of codified imagery, which can be deduced to be the product of an active discourse between popular culture and the emerging high culture (see Pongratz-Leisten, this volume).

One especially important textual format in early Egypt as well as early Mesopotamia was the presentation of information in lists. Traditional research has often specifically related them to the sphere of writing, but they may have an older oral setting. As early as the 4th millennium both societies were complex enough to require inventories for administrative and ideological purposes (early examples for lists of conquered territories are discussed in Morenz 2004:172–74). From cross-cultural comparison, we know that various oral cultures used orally transmitted lists (Vansina 1985). So the conceptual organization of words—or images—in lists may well predate the origin of writing in Egypt as well as in Mesopotamia. Pictorial lists, or more precisely a list-like organization of a composition, can be seen in various rows of animals on some proto-Egyptian objects. One example is provided by the Davis comb (Fig. 4.4). Here the list is already modified by distinct individual signs, such as the star, providing additional information (Morenz 2004:114–15). A complex example is provided by the knife-handle from Abu Zeidan (Fig. 4.5). The handle is made of ivory. It is decorated with ten rows of animals on each side. Here we can distinguish three different categories of animals (Huyge 2004):

Natural animals:	most animals on the comb
Constellation of animals:	elephant above entwined serpents (side A 1)
Imaginary animals:	ibex-tilapia (A 7) and elephant-vulture (B 1).

Furthermore, this knife-handle decoration contains additional signs such as the *sr*-giraffe, a stick (or a snake, identification not entirely certain), a star, and a catfish. These iconic signs are not just pictorial elements but are

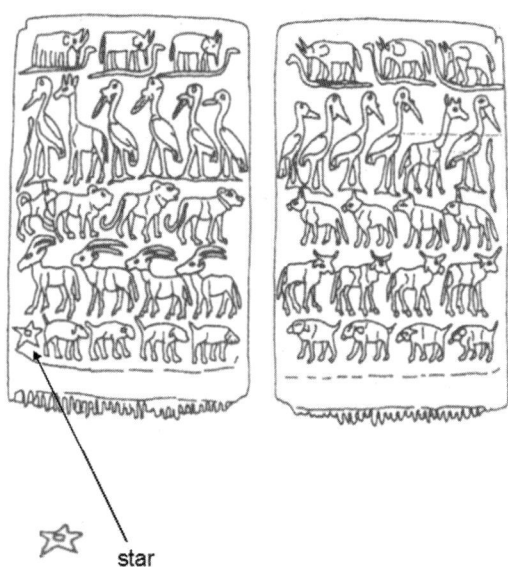

4.4. Davis comb (MMA 30.8.224); rows of animals = iconographic list (after Hayes 1953:28, fig. 20).

Texts before Writing: Reading (Proto-) Egyptian Poetics of Power   127

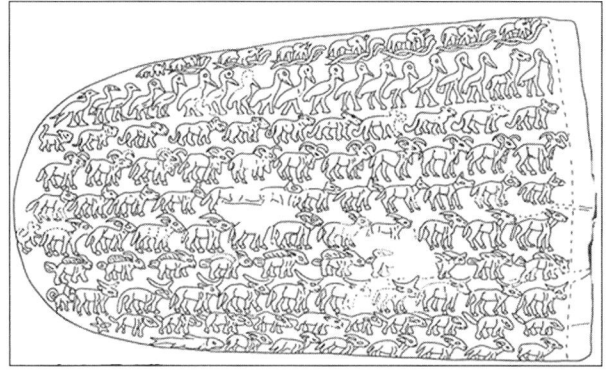

4.5. Knife-handle from Abu-Zeidan, Brooklyn Museum 09.889.118 (after Needler 1984:154).

readable in a more specific way. The star and some of the other signs point to the sphere of sacral rulership, while the catfish seems to represent the name of the individual ruler. His name can probably be identified as Nar (I).

The same sign CATFISH represents the name of the famous Nar(-meher) who lived some generations later and is known from a ceremonial mace-head, palette, and various other objects (Wilkinson 2000). This king CATFISH = Nar (I) is probably the first person we know by name from proto-Egyptian history.[3] A similar reading seems possible for the Pitt-Rivers knife-handle (see Fig. 4.6) where again a catfish follows a row of emblematic elephants above snakes (Morenz 2004:187–88). Both knifes may therefore belong to an otherwise unknown ruler Nar (I).

The whole composition of the Abu Zeidan knife-handle can be understood as a sort of encyclopedic listing generating a mental landscape to contextualize the rulership of Nar (I). We can observe an attempt to grasp the world iconically. These images do not just mirror reality but we might better understand them as a sort of world-making in the sense of N. Goodman (1978). At this point we should briefly discuss the semiotic status of the fabulous animals, such as the snake-headed panther, the griffin, or the ibex-tilapia. These animals belong to a code aiming at a specifically metaphoric readabilty. This new combination of elements from the natural world implies a fictionalization and autonomy which exceeds mimesis. Thus, the combination of a mammal with a fish in the strange ibex-tilapia seems to refer to a transgression of boundaries. Even if the specific reading remains problematic, we can certainly infer a strong readability.

All these semiophors have a role in a complex relationship between society, author, customer, and recipients (Eco 1990, 1996, and 1999) even if we lack various data for specific interpretations. Therefore, the various ways of reception (Jauß 1992) must remain predominantly conjectural since we know nothing about their empirical readers. The relationship between meaning and various social realities—e.g., the relation between individuals and institutions (Bourdieu 1994)—may be very complex but it must be discussed in a broader context of all the available data from protodynastic Egypt. Nevertheless we can assume various levels of graphic codes in the proto-Egyptian society in-between high culture and popular culture, with various degrees of mutual exchange and diffusion.

A CEREMONIAL PALETTE FROM HIERAKONPOLIS CELEBRATING ROYAL STRENGTH

The palette we are now going to discuss in detail (see Fig. 4.7) is made of dark gray schist. It is 42 cm high and 22 cm wide. It is unusual both in terms of its decoration and outstanding size. It was found in the main deposit of the temple from ancient Hierakonpolis, one of the major political, economic, and sacral centres in the second half of the 4th millennium BC (Friedman 1996; see also Morris and Moreno, this volume). The deposit dates from the Fifth Dynasty. Here various objects from the Pre- and Early Dynastic period were stored away. A typology based on style and semiotics dates it to somewhere between 3200–3050 BC, most probably around 3100 BC.

Texts before Writing: Reading (Proto-) Egyptian Poetics of Power   129

4.6. Pitt-Rivers knife-handle, British Museum EA 68512 (after Asselberghs 1961).

The Jackal-Human Hybrid

A jackal-human hybrid creature playing the flute is depicted on the lower left side (Fig. 4.7). He wears a conspicuous penis-sheath (Baines 1975). The jackal-human hybrid is the sole figure with a (semi-)human appearance on the palette and is therefore of particular importance in understanding the composition on this semiophore.

The iconography of this hybrid has no known direct parallel in Egyptian art, but we may note that playing the long flute[4] was an important element in performance in the context of an Egyptian court. This becomes quite clear from the Fourth Dynasty statue of the court musician Ipi playing the flute (Sourouzian 1999). From the Middle Kingdom onwards playing the flute became less prestigious and other instruments were more regularly used in cultic contexts (Hickmann 1977:266). The *aulos* signified *ecstasis* for the Greeks (Zaminer 2000:547–49).[5] We may assume a similar connotation for this proto-Egyptian flute, especially because the jackal-human hybrid is dancing with his left foot raised up. This iconographic element therefore signifies ecstasy. In addition to this, for the Egyptians the jackal implied the idea of transition (Neumann 1997) and this notion is specifically expressed by the figure of the jackal-human hybrid. Furthermore the *jackal* was conceptualized as companion of the king. The standard with a jackal on top was the most important royal standard. It may be an emblem of the archaic royal residence from Abydos (Morenz 2002), but it also implies the idea of "opening the ways" (*wp w3.wt*). Thus the jackal was closely associated with the royal sphere.

Furthermore, in many cultures the flute and similar instruments are considered not merely to be musical instruments, but are sometimes quite clearly gendered as well.[6] Concerning the jackal-human hybrid, we might now consider the relation between the action of playing the flute and his conspicuous

penis-sheath. Various cultures create similar imageries independently from each other. Thus in rock art, phallic flute players are quite well known figures. A popular example from the American Southwest Pueblo rock art and pottery is the Kokopelli, a hunchbacked flute player with an exceptionally large phallus (Fig. 4.8; Hays-Gilpin 2004:19–20, 141–45). The motif of the flute-playing animal exercising power and charming others can be traced back to Upper Paleolithic cave art.

As a common denominator of these examples of dancing animal-human hybrids making music, we may think of an old shamanistic substratum. Shamanism might have played a greater role in the Neolithic and Chalcolithic period in the Nile Valley, while, on this proto-Egyptian ceremonial palette, the action of playing the flute together with the wearing of the

4.7. Jackal-human hybrid playing the flute, detail of ceremonial palette; Ashmolean E.3924.

4.8. Kokopelli (hunchbacked flute-player); Southwestern Puebloan rock art (after Hays-Gilpin 2004:19–20, 141–45).

penis-sheath may specifically refer to the idea of masculinity, domination, and festival.⁷

The anthropomorphic jackal has some relatives in other hybrids shown on this palette: the griffin and the snake-headed panthers (Fig. 4.9). Both these imaginary animals fall under the heading *"marvels of the East"* (Wittkower 1983). Considering their historical and iconographic origin they may be Iranian or possibly Mesopotamian creatures, which entered the proto-Egyptian iconographic repertoire in the second half of the 4th millennium BC. The snake-

4.9. "Marvels of the East," details of ceremonial palette; Ashmolean E.3924.

headed panther disappeared from the iconographic repertoire of the Egyptian high culture in the Early Dynastic Period, while the griffin represented the Pharaoh on some monuments from the Old Kingdom. The group of imaginary animals placed in the desert were reintroduced into elite tomb decoration of the Middle Kingdom probably as a conscious renaissance (Morenz 2002).

The Status of the Sign "Giraffe"

Let us now turn to the giraffe (Fig. 4.10). The giraffe was prominent in Pre- and Protodynastic Egyptian art but marginalized in the later tradition. This development was probably due to gradual climatic changes that forced the animal southwards. The giraffe, as an animal of memory, was possibly transformed into the semi-mythical *sedja*-beast we know from the Middle Kingdom (Vernus and Yoyotte 2005:631 sub *animaux fantastiques*). Such changes in meaning are typical phenomena of long-term cultural processes and we may note a similar development with regard to the elephant. Both these animals were related to Protodynastic rulership and this connection to the early rulers may have contributed to their mythical status in later Egyptian history.

4.10. Giraffe, detail of ceremonial palette; Ashmolean E.3924. *sr(w)* – "giraffe," *sr* – "ruler" = "the farsighted one, the one who forsees."

On this palette the image of the giraffe represents more than just the animal. The Egyptian name for the giraffe is *sr(w)*—actually an epithet meaning "the one who sees far," involving a pun with the Egyptian verb *sr* "to see far, predict" (Vernus and Yoyotte 2005:144 sub *giraffe*). In Egyptian *sr* is also the

Texts before Writing: Reading (Proto-) Egyptian Poetics of Power 133

word for ruler and may go back to the verb *sr*, thus designating the ruler as the far-sighted man (discussion in Morenz 2004:114–15, 199–200):

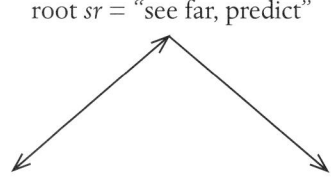

"The one who sees far" = ruler   "The one who sees far" = giraffe.

The image of the giraffe is thus tied to a complex of meaning involving the qualities of the ruler. The reading of the *sr*-giraffe as a rebus for *sr*-ruler indicates a distinctly metaphorical dimension of the whole composition.

The Pictorial Litany Celebrating the Ruler's Dominance

But how does this interpretation contribute to our understanding of the composition of this side of the palette in its entirety? The upper part shows various pairs of animals (see Fig. 4.13; for identification, cf. Osborn and Osbornová 1998:2):

- lion + gazelle
- lion + gazelle
- snake-headed panther (serpopard) + oryx-antelope
- leopard + goat

The pairs combine a dominant animal with a subordinate one, indicating a theme of dominance of the strong over the weak. This provides an easily comprehensible pictorial language. Again these elaborated versions of just one motif are readable as conveying a variation on one major theme.

Below this we see a single hyena-dog and a griffin attacking a gnu-antelope, another variation of the same pattern. The sequence of dominant animals—lion, serpopard, leopard, griffin—seems to indicate that natural and imaginary animals are conceptionalized as interchangeable.

The hyena-dog and griffin attacking a gnu-antelope are followed by a bull. Already in early Egyptian art, as on the ceremonial palette of Narmeher (for this reading of the royal name instead of the common Nar-mer, cf. Morenz 2004:3), the bull was conceptualized as an icon of power and

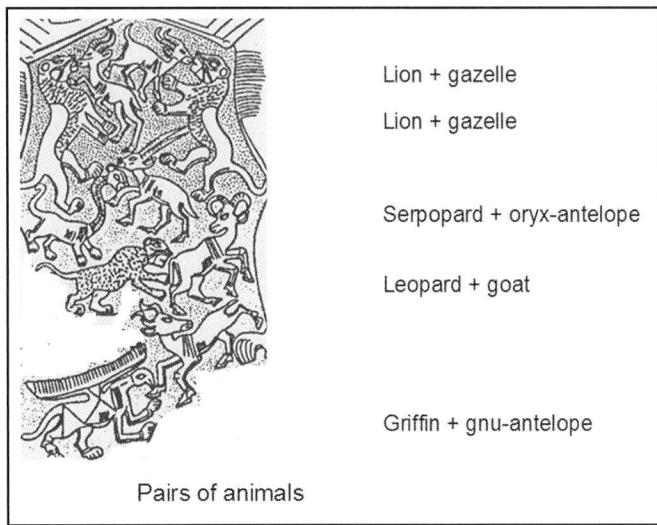

4.11. Distribution of animals on ceremonial palette, Ashmolean E.3924. Illustration: author.

the king was called "strong bull" (*k3-nḫt*) in the royal protocol.[8] Furthermore, this interpretation finds support in the observation that the strong, victorious animals move from left to right, while the weak, subjugated ones move from right to left.[9] In Egyptian art there is a clear preference for the movement from left to right, somehow the direction of the victorious (cf., e.g., the ceremonial palette of Nar-meher; discussion in a broader context in Ennenbach 1996; Weigl 2001; and Luschey 2002). The hyena-dog also belongs to the sphere of domination and corresponds intra-pictorially to the hyena-dogs surmounting the palette and the hyena-dogs on the other side of the palette. Looking at the whole composition, its appearance without a counterpart is surprising, but essentially it seems to function as a space-filler creating an intra-pictorial link to the other side of the palette and the animals framing the composition. In a reading of the whole composition the bull belongs quite clearly to the semantic triangle, making it a quadrangle with the basic topic of rulership. The spatial layout is elaborated to a high degree here and is thus readable. On the other hand, the artist has managed to relate the individual figures to each other and to the limited space. The specific position and pose of each individual figure depends on the surrounding figures, creating a strong intrapictorial net.

We can understand the composition on this side of the palette as an iconic litany of triumph with the structure *X does Y*. The images in this composition convey a subject (strong animals), a verb (subduing/killing), and an object (weak animals as prey). The verb is represented by the interaction between subject and object. But is this combination of images just a linear translation of a verbal narrative into a pictorial form? It suggests a sort of semantic triangle:

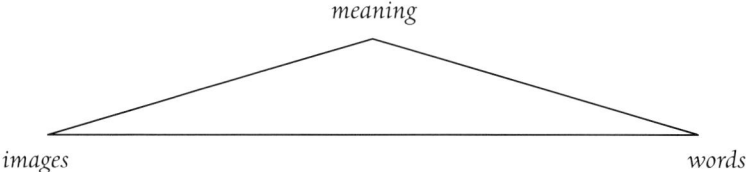

This pictorial composition does not have to go back literally to an individual verbal prototype but nevertheless it is very easy to verbalize. Furthermore, we may assume litanies of this kind to have been performed orally from a pre-Egyptian date on. The praise of the ruler's strength was probably an important motivation in the development of this genre.

Other examples can be cited which reinforce the interpretation of this palette as a readable litany. The Protodynastic knife handle from Gebel el-Tarif (Fig. 4.12; on Protodynastic ceremonial knife-handles: Dreyer 1999) shows four pairs of animals with the stronger always attacking the weaker one, such as the lion attacking the oryx.[10] Among these animals we find a griffin attacking an ibex (for identification of the animals: Osborn and Osbornová 1998:7 sub 1-12).[11] These four pairs of animals are again readable as a little litany of "written" boustrophedon. This layout in boustrophedon—running in alternate directions—creates a distinct textuality in its expression of one chain of events. Yet another example for a sequentially organized boustrophedon is the Protodynastic Davis comb (MMA 30.8.224; see Fig. 4.13). Here the end of the sequence is marked by the sign of a star, probably some sort of proto-writing reference to the sacral world.[12] This compositional device was popular in a number of other cultures, but was only popular in Egypt in the Proto- and Early Dynastic period. It became marginalized during the development of writing in the Nile Valley. Later on this principle was more rarely applied in Old Kingdom tomb decoration.

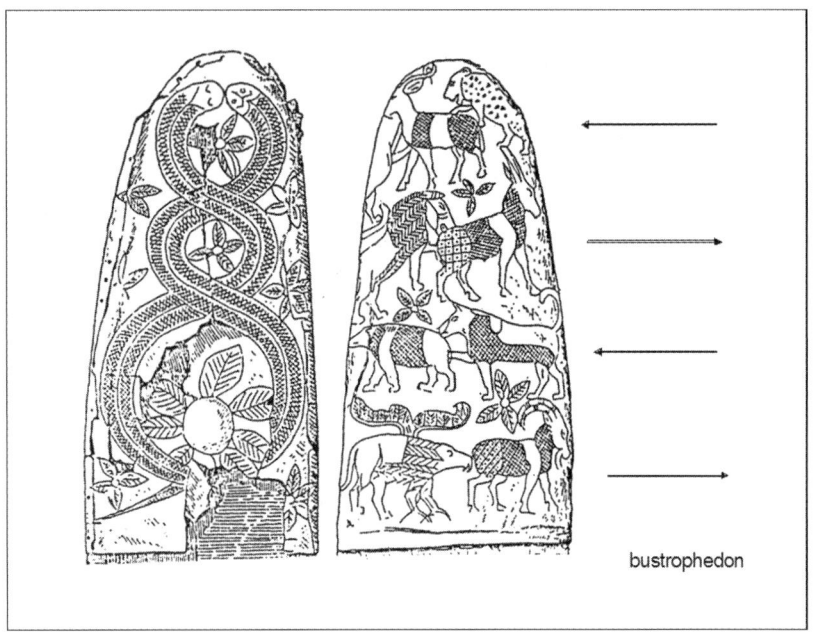

4.12. Knife-handle from Gebel el-Tarif (after Vandier 1952, fig. 366).

4.13. Reading the Davis comb, MMA 30.8.224. Illustration: author.

What can be said about the readability of these animals and their semiotic status? They are not just natural animals, but as symbols of *royal* dominance they can be interpreted as icons of power. The distinct desert setting does not seem to imply a specific geographical reference but can be interpreted more easily as a rhetorical strategy expressing strength over the untamed. The awe-inspiring wild or even fabulous nature of these creatures served as a source for the urban and elite imagery of power.

Considering the aesthetic and semiotic quality we can assume a careful planning of the whole composition. This ceremonial palette bears witness to the high standard of Protodynastic courtly art, and it represents a meaningful organization of readable images that predates writing.

Enacting the Litany, Bridging the Gap between the Object and Its Viewer

We may consider this litany to be enacted by the jackal-human hybrid playing the flute. He represents the intellectual elite engaged in the production of meaning, as he shapes the status of the potentate in rituals, words, or images. These specialists in knowledge were of particular importance in molding the high culture. The semiophores such as the palette under discussion bear witness to their work and interests.

By entering onto the scene, the beholder—probably a member of the elite familiar with its code—may have partly merged with the flute-playing hybrid. This particular creature with a semi-human appearance may have been a focal point of identification for the elite bridging the gap between the object and the individual beholder.

The ceremonial palettes address more than just one sense, especially the eye (decoration) and the skin (tool for preparing eye-paint). During the 4th millennium the secondary function of these palettes—that of visual address—became more and more important. These semiophores belong to the sphere of pre-aesthetics (art before art) in which beauty and semantics are used to convey a sacro-political message. Theoretically we can distinguish two major functions of these palettes: (a) use in ritual and (b) display. As objects for display they may have addressed the humans as well as the gods. The uses of the palettes in rituals and for display are by no means exclusive. On the contrary, cross-cultural comparison indicates that this double function of ceremonial objects is a widespread phenomenon.[13] Thus we can assume a close interrelation between the use in ritual and the act of reading. Reading these scenes may have implied a certain ritual or performative dimension.

The palettes were just one part of a set of sacro-political insignia. We can distinguish three different groups of semiophores—weapons, tools, ornaments. They correspond to central festivals celebrating the ruler—enthronement, victory, agricultural rituals.

Picturing Protodynastic Conceptions of Power

In Protodynastic as well as Pharaonic Egyptian ideology the ruler combined aspects of sacral as well as military leadership. This ceremonial palette expresses the incarnation of both aspects of power within a single person. The dominant animals such as lion, leopard, and griffin refer to the aspect of military leadership. This theme is complemented by the sacral dimension embodied in the giraffe and the jackal-human hybrid playing the flute. Combining these two potentially conflicting aspects in a single person can be understood as a claim to absolute power (Baudrillard 1976). It embodies a very specific form of the universal poetics of power in which the real is as imagined as the imaginary (Geertz 1973).

These ceremonial objects embed the potentate within the sacral sphere, and so contribute to his superhuman status as a bridge between gods and humankind. The composition of this palette does not seem to refer to a single event such as a specific war but more generally to an ideological constellation. It shows a *Weltbild* expressed in a non-verbal litany. We may understand this monumental composition not to be commemorative but performative. To interpret this pictorial litany the conception of performativity (Searl 1969) seems to be more fruitful than the common Egyptological designation as *magical*, although it nevertheless includes the supposed "magical" wish that the message might become and remain *real*.

To quote Clifford Geertz (1973), the palette presents a story we tell ourselves about ourselves and thus it is a distinct exponent of culture. This semiophore was made in the age of gradual transition from a proto-writing period to an early writing period in the Nile Valley, but still contains an iconic *language game* ("Sprachspiel"). The borders between proto-writing and early writing were clearly not well defined, which suggests an extended process of transition. The viewer needs a high visual literacy to read the palette in all its details. On the other hand, we can assume that the basic message of royal dominance was quite easily intelligible.

Power seems to have a tendency to dramatize itself while the specific form depends very much on the development of media. Thus the process of preparing ritual eye-paint on these semiophores combines the aspects of ritual and reading. The symbolic significance of the ritual act of putting on make-up is reflected by the iconic celebration of rulership. Thus the iconic text interprets the ritual while the ritual provides the cultic context for the story. The messages on these semiophores are far more complex than the earlier ones, although they are constrained by specific graphic conventions. Their highly formalized code, which included proto-writing, created a distinct clarity greater than that of the older pictorial messages, which we find in tomb decoration, on rocks, or on pottery.

Royal Ideology and Individual Rulers. Identifying Two Kings from Protodynastic Hierakonpolis

Here I have discussed the distinct visibility of words before writing. Furthermore, I have argued that coherent texts were not only composed before writing and performed orally, but in a specific context of high culture they were graphically fixed and monumentalized as well. One could also discuss cultural specifics of the neuro-cognitive triangle of eye–brain–vision. On the other hand a close reading of the individual objects may reveal very basic facts of Egyptian history such as names of the rulers from the kingdom of Hierakonpolis.

The palette with the flute-playing hybrid creature was created for a specific ruler from Hierakonpolis, one of the proto-Egyptian predecessors of SCORPION (II) and Nar-meher. On the other side of the palette his personal name is indicated by the sign of an ostrich above the heads of the snake-headed panthers (Fig. 4.14); its position (Davis 1992:82) indicates a specific meaning. Like the giraffe, the ostrich is not just a pictorial element, but a sign in proto-writing. Most of the known names of Proto- and Early Dynastic rulers are names of animals, which inspire awe in some way (SCORPION, CROCODILE, SNAKE, etc.: Morenz 2005a). Furthermore, the place of this supposed name finds a close parallel in the name IBIS on the Louvre palette (Fig. 4.15; Louvre E 11052; cf. O'Connor 2002:11–12; and Morenz 2005b) which was also found in Hierakonpolis. The personal name creates a specifically individual dimension (the status of names is discussed in Kripke 1981). Thus we can refer to these palettes as the ceremonial palettes of OSTRICH and SCORPION.

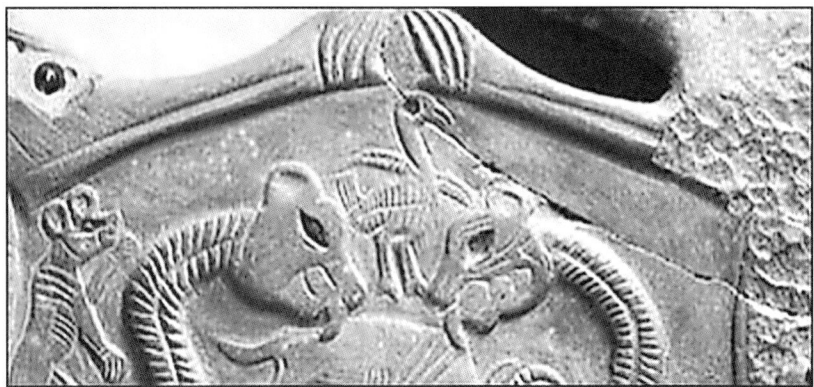

4.14. Detail of ostrich on the ceremonial palette, Oxford, Ashmolean E.3924. Photo: author.

4.15. Detail of ibis on the ceremonial palette, Louvre E 11052. Photo: author.

The kingdom of Hierakonpolis (Egyptian *Nḫn*) constituted a Protodynastic polity. From a slightly later period we have a brief king-list of Hierakonpolis (Morenz 2004:105–10), but so far it remains impossible to define the specific position of King OSTRICH of Hierakonpolis within this list. In reading and contextualizing the palette we find out his name and begin to understand his status and royal ideology. Furthermore we can probably understand him as a (or probably the) predecessor of King IBIS known from the slightly later Louvre palette.

Texts before Writing: Reading (Proto-) Egyptian Poetics of Power 141

These two roughly contemporary ceremonial palettes celebrated the kings OSTRICH and IBIS, who so far are unknown to Egyptology. Other ceremonial palettes were also produced for specific rulers such as the well-known SCORPION (II) and Nar-meher.[14] The most elaborate ceremonial palettes served as royal insignia of the Proto- and Early Dynastic rulers and were probably used in several festivals. This setting opens new perspectives for our understanding of the formation of Egyptian royal ideology as well as politics and art.

THE REPRESENTATION OF POWER AND THE DEVELOPMENT OF MEDIA

In a cross-cultural perspective we may note that texts before writing were also created in Mesopotamia and Elam at more or less the same time and in a comparable socio-economic environment. Our main source is seals and seal impressions, particularly from Susa and Uruk. By analogy with the speech-act as defined by J.L. Austin (1978), the act of sealing can be interpreted as a prewriting act or as a writing act indicating a responsible presence and thus personalizing and authorizing things and messages (Macho 2005).

The origin of the ancient Near Eastern cylinder seal can be traced back to the production of cylindrical stone cores (for early seals, see Pittman

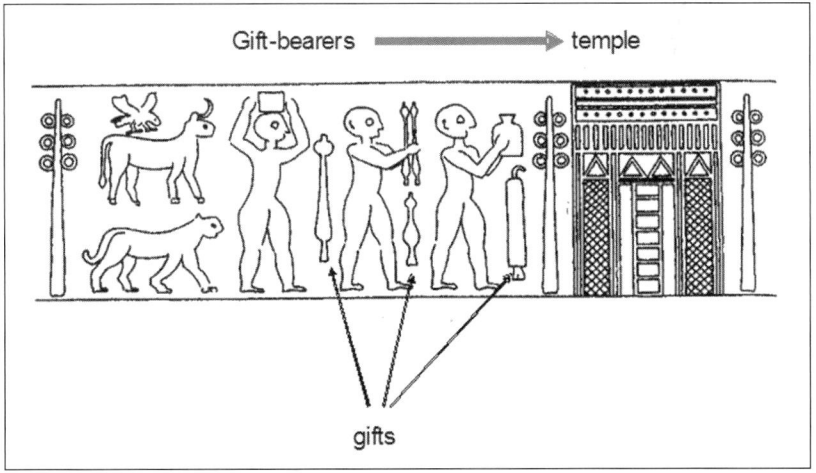

4.16. Pictorial "text" on a cylinder seal impression from Uruk; iconic narrative of offering (after Pittman 1994, fig. 5a).

2001). If decorated with an element, these cylinder seals could be rolled over a clay surface to produce a sequence in a kind of register. In a next step this was extended to rolling seals where not only one figure but several varying figures could be depicted. The variants of a procession of gift-bearers could then be shown. This textual scheme can be explained primarily as a list—listing the gift-bearers—but possibly as a litany too. This exotic variety stresses the aspect of pomp and circumstance in a festival. As a third step, this schema was developed further by the introduction of an objective to the procession—namely the ruler or a sacral building (see Fig. 4.16). Thus, both interaction and—through the differentiation of figures by size—hierarchy were introduced into the scenes.

Indeed, among the seal-pictures from the late Uruk period, quite complex ones can be found which can be interpreted as iconic litanies, such as the animal-seal shown in Fig. 4.17. Here pairs of animals are shown symmetrically around an imaginary central axis. All four pairs symbolize the dominance of the strong over the weak in the same way as the Egyptian semiophores discussed above. Moreover this picture can also be understood as a boustrophedon.

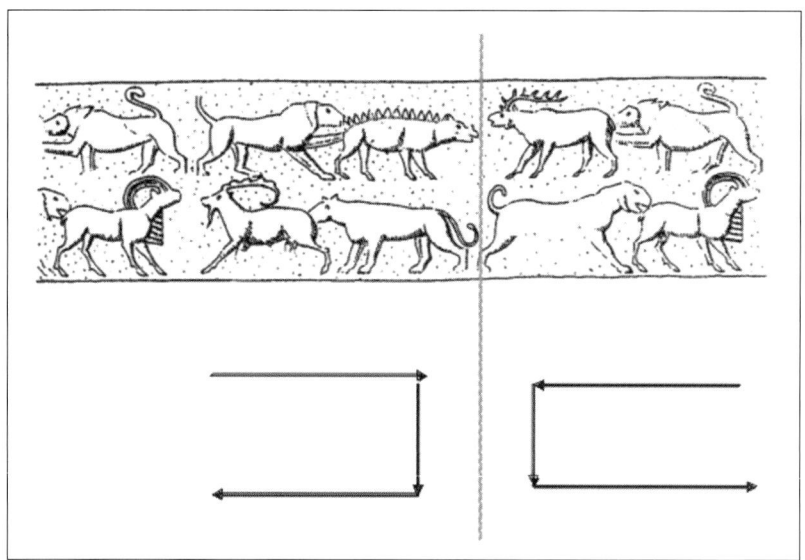

4.17. Cylinder seal from Uruk; symmetrical composition in boustrophedon (after Frankfort 1955, fig. 7E).

Texts before Writing: Reading (Proto-) Egyptian Poetics of Power 143

4.18. Cultic vessel from Uruk, Baghdad Museum 19606 (after Roaf 1999:61).

This culminated in the monumental stone vase from Uruk (see Fig. 4.18) in which pictorial and scriptural elements in a narrower sense were fused into a distinctively readable entity (cf. recently Bahrani 2001). The layout of the elements, organization in registers, and regular sequences offered medial prerequisites that could be conceptionally used and contributed enormously to the development of a reading gaze. In this case mediotechnological development follows technical preconditions, but the very realization of their opportunities and its productive utilization constitutes a fundamental and exceptionally fruitful cultural achievement.

The specific iconic textuality was indeed developed under socio-economically analogous conditions in Mesopotamia and the Nile Valley during the second half of the 4th millennium BC, but, it seems, more or less independent of each other. This textuality stood on the threshold of a comprehensive development of media that, among other things, led to the formation of a normative metrological system and culminated in the emergence of writing. The structural similarities between Mesopotamia and Egypt during that time were such that prescriptorial texts served to represent power. So this is a convincing example of the close interconnectedness of socio-economic structures, discourses, and medio-technological prerequisites.

On the other hand, we find similar textual constellations of iconic elements on a Caucasian silver vessel of the Maikop culture (Fig. 4.19) dating to the Early Bronze Age. However this culture never developed or adopted a script. In human history the transition from readable iconic texts to writing proper never occurred automatically.

4.19. Cultic vessel from Maikop culture, Hermitage Museum. Drawing: author.

NOTES

4.1   The use of pictorial metaphors can be traced back to the early Neolithic period: Morenz and Schmidt 2009.

4.2   Following the outstanding research of Ernst Gombrich (1960), the analysis of visual cultures made new advancements in the last decades: Baxandall 1985 and 1995; Belting 2008. In an art-historical as well as neuro-psychological perspective, special emphasis is given to the beholders share and active engagement in the act of viewing.

4.3   Most of the names of the Protodynastic and Early Dynastic rulers contain references to awe-inspiring animals: Morenz 2005a.

4.4   The ancient Egyptian long flutes were 100–120 cm long, had 4–6 finger holes but

> *Texts before Writing: Reading (Proto-) Egyptian Poetics of Power*   145

       no mouthpiece, and were made of bamboo; cf. in contemporary Egyptian popular music, the *Nay* and the *Uffata*.

4.5   Looking at the shape of a flute, some sort of Freudian symbolism may appear obvious, but one should be aware that different cultures develop quite different conceptualizations of objects and actions, and relate them differently to gender or other categories (Lakoff 1987).

4.6   According to the Greek myth of the unfortunate Marsyas (Visser 1999), Athena angrily threw away the double-*aulos* when seeing her distorted face mirrored in the water.

4.7   We note a similar case for the sign of a man shooting an arrow (labels Abydos Uj 45–48). This iconic sign is an early hieroglyph that is phonetically readable as *stj* designating the territory of ancient Nubia. This man is depicted with a conspicuous penis-sheath. Aspects of gender in the early hieroglyphic script are discussed in Morenz 2008.

4.8   The epithet "strong bull" (*k3-nḫt*) was used regularly in the royal names of the Eighteenth Dynasty, but the bull was related to Egyptian kingship in iconography as well as in phraseology much earlier. Thus, it is a pictorial metaphor of pharaonic dominance that the king tramples upon an enemy, as we already know from the lower register of the palette of Nar-meher.

4.9   There are two exceptions, the lion on the upper right (clearly due to the demands of symmetry) and the hyena-dog functioning as a sort of space filler. Its position is dictated by the available space.

4.10   Another element within this sequence of animals is the rosette. It is more than just a space-filler, but it seems to refer to the sacral sphere. Furthermore, it creates an intrapictorial link to the other side of the knife-handle where nine rosettes and two entwined serpents are depicted. We may understand the rosette as a pictorial element or even as a sign of proto-writing. Probably it designates the king as the rosette on the monuments of the kings SCORPION and Nar-meher (discussion in Morenz 2004).

4.11   One might however doubt their identification of the attacked animal in row 3 as a bear.

4.12   Another element of proto-writing on this object is the stick at the beginning of the second row of animals. Furthermore, we may understand the giraffe as a rebus-writing for *sr*-ruler. The giraffe is somewhat singled out among the other animals because it is depicted just once on each side of the comb. This may point to its function as a rebus.

4.13   Cf. the use of the bronze vessels in early China: Wu Hung, *Monumentality in Early Chinese Art* (Stanford, 1995: Stanford University Press); and L. von Falkenhausen, *Chi-*

nese Society in the Age of Confucius (1000–250 BC): The Archaeological Evidence, Ideas, Debates, and Perspectives 2 (Los Angeles, 2006: Cotsen Institute of Archaeology, University of California).

4.14 I suggest the following correlation of ceremonial palettes to kings:

Kingdom of Abydos:

– anonymous ruler of Abydos	Lion Hunt Palette
– name lost	battlefield palette
– name lost	Bull Palette

Kingdom of Hierakonpolis:

– OSTRICH	Oxford, Ash. E.3924
– IBIS	Louvre E 11052
– SCORPION (II)	Buto Palette
– Nar-meher	Nar-meher; united kingdom of Abydos and Hierakonpolis

REFERENCES

Asselberghs, H. 1961. *Chaos en Beheersing: documenten uit het aeneolithisch Egypte*. Documenta et monumenta Orientis antiqui 8. Leiden: E.J. Brill.

Austin, J.L. 1978. *How To Do Things with Words*. Cambridge, MA: Harvard University Press.

Bahrani, Z. 2001. *The Women of Babylon. Gender and Representation in Mesopotamia*. London: Routledge.

Baines, J. 1975. ꜥAnkh-Sign, Belt and Penis Sheath. *SAK* 3:1–24.

Baudrillard, J. 1976. *L'echange symbolique et la mort*. Paris: Editions Gallimard.

Baxandall, M. 1985. *Patterns of Intention: On the Historical Explanation of Pictures*. New Haven: Yale University Press.

———. 1995. *Shadows and Enlightenment*. New Haven: Yale University Press.

Belting, H. 2008. *Florenz und Bagdad. Eine westöstliche Geschichte des Blicks*. Munich: C.H. Beck.

Blumenberg, H. 1979. *Die Lesbarkeit der Welt*. Frankfurt am Main: Suhrkamp.

Bourdieu, P. 1994. *Soziologische Fragen*. Frankfurt am Main: Suhrkamp.

Davis, W. 1992. *Masking the Blow. The Scene of Representation in Late Prehistoric Egyptian Art*. California Studies in the History of Art 30. Berkeley: University of California Press.

Dreyer, G. 1999. Motive und Datierung der prädynastischen Messergriffe. In *L'art de l'Ancien Empire égyptien*, ed. C. Ziegler, pp. 195–226. Paris: Documentation Française.

Eco, U. 1990. *Lector in fabula. Die Mitarbeit der Interpretation in erzählenden Texten.* Munich: Deutscher Taschenbuch Verlag.

———. 1996. *Zwischen Autor und Text. Interpretation und Überinterpretation.* Munich: Deutscher Taschenbuch Verlag.

———. 1999. *Die Grenzen der Interpretation.* Munich: Deutscher Taschenbuch Verlag.

Ennenbach, W. 1996. Über das Rechts und Links im Bilde. *Zeitschrift für Ästhetik und allgemeine Kunstwissenschaft* 41:5–57.

Frankfort, H. 1955. *The Art and Architecture of the Ancient Orient.* New Haven: Yale University Press.

Friedman, R. 1996. The Ceremonial Centre at Hierakonpolis, Locality HK 29A. In *Aspects of Early Egypt*, ed. A.J. Spencer, pp. 16–35. London: British Museum Press.

Geertz, C. 1973. *The Interpretation of Cultures. Selected Essays.* New York: Basic Books.

Gombrich, E.H. 1960. *Art and Illusion.* New York: Pantheon Books.

Goodman, N. 1978. *Ways of Worldmaking.* Hassocks: Harvester Press.

Hayes, W.C. 1953. *The Scepter of Egypt: A Background for the Study of the Egyptian Antiquities in The Metropolitan Museum of Art. Part I: From the Earliest Times to the End of the Middle Kingdom.* New York: Harper & Brothers.

Hays-Gilpin, K.A. 2004. *Ambiguous Images. Gender and Rock Art.* Gender and Archaeology Series 7. Walnut Creek, CA: Altamira Press.

Hickmann, E. 1977. Flöte. in *LÄ* II:265–67.

Huyge, D. 2004. A Double-Powerful Device for Regeneration: The Abu Zaidan Knife Handle Reconsidered. In *Egypt at Its Origins. Studies in Memory of Barbara Adams*, ed. S. Hendrickx, R.F. Friedman, K.M. Cialowicz, and M. Chlodnicki, pp. 823–36. OLA 138. Leuven: Peeters en Departement Oosterse Studies.

Jauß, H.R. 1992. Rezeption, Rezeptionsästhetik. *HWP* 8:996–1004.

Keightley, D.N. 1978. *Sources of Shang History: The Oracle-Bone Inscriptions of Bronze Age China.* Berkeley: University of California Press.

Kripke, S.A. 1981. *Name und Notwendigkeit.* Frankfurt am Main: Suhrkamp.

Lakoff, G. 1987. *Women, Fire and Dangerous Things: What Categories Reveal about the Mind.* Chicago: University of Chicago Press.

Luschey, H. 2002. *Rechts und links. Untersuchungen über Bewegungsrichtung, Seitenordnung und Höhenordnung als Elemente der antiken Bildsprache.* Tübingen:

Ernst Wasmuth.

Macho, T. 2005. Handschrift—Schriftbild. Anmerkungen zu einer Geschichte der Unterschrift. In *Hand, Schrift, Bild. Paragrana: Internationale Zeitschrift Historische Anthropologie, Beihefte* 1, ed. T. Bernhart and G. Gröning, pp. 111–20. Berlin: R. Oldenbourg Verlag.

Morenz, L.D. 2002. Mytho-Geographie der vier Himmelsrichtungen—Drei bzw. vier Fabelwesen in zwei Gräbern des ägyptischen Mittleren Reiches und ägyptisch-altorientalische Kulturkontakte. *WdO* 32:20–32.

———. 2004. *Bild-Buchstaben und symbolische Zeichen. Die Herausbildung der Schrift in der hohen Kultur Altägyptens*. OBO 205. Freiburg: Vandenhoeck & Ruprecht.

———. 2005a. Genese und Verwendungskontext archaischer Prunk-Objekte in Ägypten. *GM* 206:49–59.

———. 2005b. Zoophore Herrschernamen. Auf Spurensuche nach neuen protodynastischen Potentaten. *WZKM* 95:119–37.

———. 2008. Fest-Schreibungen von Gender im Herausbildungsprozeß der Hieroglyphenschrift. In *Egypt at Its Origins 2. Proceedings of the International Conference "Origins of the State. Predynastic and Early Dinastic Egypt," Tolouse (France), 5th–8th September 2005*, ed. B. Midant-Reynes and Y. Tristant, pp. 937–73. OLA 2. Leuven: Uitgeverij Peeters.

Morenz, L.D., and K. Schmidt. 2009. Große Reliefpfeiler und kleine Zeichentäfelchen. Ein frühneolithisches Zeichensystem in Obermesopotamien. *LingAeg* 8:13–31.

Needler, W. 1984. *Predynastic and Archaic Egypt in the Brooklyn Museum*. Brooklyn: Brooklyn Museum.

Neumann, E.W. 1997. Überlegungen zur Rolle von Gott Upuaut bis zum Ende des Mittleren Reiches. MA thesis, Institut für Ägyptologie, Universität Leipzig.

O'Connor, D. 2002. Context, Function and Program: Understanding Ceremonial Slate Palettes. *JARCE* 39:5–25.

Osborn, D.J., and J. Osbornová. 1998. *The Mammals of Ancient Egypt*. The Natural History of Egypt, Vol. 4. Warminster: Aris & Phillips.

Patch, D.C. 2011. *Dawn of Egyptian Art*. New York: Metropolitan Museum of Art.

Pittman, H. 1994. Toward an Understanding of the Role of Glyptic Imagery in the Administrative Systems of Proto-Literate Greater Mesopotamia. In *Archives Before Writing*, ed. P. Ferioli, E. Fiandra, G.G. Fissore, and M. Frangipane, pp. 177–203. Rome: Centro Internazionale di Ricerche Archeologiche Antropologiche e Storiche.

———. 2001. Mesopotamian Intraregional Relations Reflected through Glyptic Evidence in the Late Chalcolithic 1–5 Periods. In *Uruk Mesopotamia and Its Neighbors: Cross-Cultural Interactions in the Era of State Formation,* ed. M.S. Rothman, pp. 403–43. *School of American Research Advanced Seminar Series.* Santa Fe: School of American Research Press.

Pomian, K. 1987. *Collectionneurs, amateurs, curieux: Paris-Venise, XVIe–XVIIIe siècles.* Paris: Editions Gallimard.

Quibell, J.E., and F.W. Green. 1900–1901. *Hierakonpolis.* 2 vols. London: Egypt Exploration Fund.

Roaf, M. 1999. *Cultural Atlas of Mesopotamia and the Ancient Near East.* New York: Facts on File, Inc.

Schmidt, K. 2006. *Sie bauten die ersten Tempel. Das rätselhafte Heiligtum der Steinzeitjäger.* München: C.H. Beck.

Searl, J.R. 1969. *Speech Acts.* Cambridge: Cambridge University Press.

Sourouzian, H. 1999. La statue du musicien Ipi jouant de la flûte et autres monuments du règne de Snofrou à Dahchour. In *L'art de l'Ancien Empire égyptienne,* ed. C. Ziegler. Paris: Documentation Française.

Vandier, J. 1952. *Manuel d'archéologie égyptienne. Tome premier: Les époques de formation.* Paris: Éditions A. et J. Picard.

Vansina, J. 1985. *Oral Tradition as History.* Madison: University of Wisconsin Press.

Vernus, P., and J. Yoyotte. 2005. *Bestiaire des pharaons.* Paris: Librairie Académique Perrin.

Visser, E. 1999. Marsyas. *Der Neue Pauly* 7:955.

Weigl, S. 2001. Die Richtung des Bildes. *Zeitschrift für Kunstgeschichte* 64:449–74.

Wilkinson, T.A.H. 2000. What a King Is This: Narmer and the Concept of the Ruler. *JEA* 86:23–32.

Wittkower, R. 1983. "Roch": Ein orientalisches Ungeheuer auf einem niederländischen Stich. In *Allegorie und der Wandel der Symbole in Antike und Renaissance,* ed. R. Wittkower, pp. 180–85. Cologne: DuMont Reiseverlag.

Zaminer, F. 2000. Musikinstrumente V, Griechenland. *Der Neue Pauly* 8:543–51.

5

Images of Tammuz

The Intersection of Death, Divinity, and Royal Authority in Ancient Mesopotamia[1]

JOANN SCURLOCK

"The king is dead, long live the king." In ancient Mesopotamia as elsewhere, kings had a special relationship with death and with immortality. What follows will attempt to answer the following questions. How were royal dead different from ordinary dead? What powers did the gods confer on the king during his lifetime? What happened to royal power when kings died? What exactly did it mean to be a divine king? Did it matter whether you were a god yourself or a king appointed by the gods? What difference did it make which god or gods you were or were associated with? How can we, who believe in neither kings nor gods, understand any of this?

KINGLY EVEN IN DEATH: MESOPOTAMIAN KINGS AND THE AFTERLIFE

King or not, all humans are mortal. When mortals died in ancient Mesopotamia, two souls, the "ghost" (*eṭemmu*) and the "spirit" (*zaqiqu*) separated from the body. The latter was pitiable, but essentially nothing but wind. The former lingered about the bones and was gotten to the Netherworld (imagined as a sort of prison with seven gates) by the simple expedient of burying the body in a tomb (usually placed beneath the floor of the house) where it could continue to receive funerary offerings for as long as any trace of the bones persisted (Katz 2007). Only those dead who were personally known to their descendents—fathers and mothers, brothers and sisters, and grandfathers and grandmothers—retained their individuality after death. The dead of no-longer-remembered relatives seem to have melted together into a sort of corporate ancestor referred to as the *eṭem kimti* or as the *eṭemmu* (ghost) of one's *kimtu*, *nišūtu*, and *salātu* (agnatic kin and cognatic kin) (Scurlock 1995). Ghosts, provided that they were properly cared for, were weak and powerless. If, however, (s)he had died some unhappy death and/or managed to escape burial and/or did not receive funerary offerings, (s)he was a real problem to surviving relatives and whoever else happened to come his or her way (Scurlock 1997).

A king who died by violence was an angry ghost correspondingly more dangerous than an ordinary person's ghost and entitled to especially elaborate burial rites and funerary offerings (Kramer 1991). This done, however, unless his grave was disturbed, a king's ghost was, again in principle, ineffectual in the land of the living. A dead king was, however, still a king. What distinguished Mesopotamian monarchs from their subjects in the Land of No Return was that they had the privilege of attending on Ereshkigal, queen of the Netherworld, as a sort of court (Barrett 2007:9). Some of them, like Gilgamesh and Dumuzi, became judges of the dead. What is more remarkable is that the shades of kings and queens remained individuals even in death (Katz 2003:121–22).

This deluxe afterlife was achieved by two strategies: providing the deceased monarch with particularly splendid grave goods and arranging for funerary offerings to be made to individual monarchs, invoked by name, in perpetuity. A fragment of a Neo-Assyrian inscription records a royal burial (which would have been in Ashur beneath the floors of the royal palace), giving a list of the grave goods, including gold and silver dishes, unridden horses (a gift for Gilgamesh), and all sorts of tiaras and garments (McGinnis 1987). Actual grave goods from the tombs of Assyrian queens (beneath the floors of the royal palace at Kalḫu) included gold diadems, gold earrings, armlets, and anklets, cups and bowls, rock crystal vessels, and the remains of richly embroidered linen sewn with gold rosettes (Damerji 1991). A touching and little known detail: before the grave was closed up, the other women of the harem apparently threw their earrings onto the body in a last farewell (McG. Gibson, pers. comm.). As for individual remembrance, this was achieved by reading out the names of all the royal ancestors as part of the funerary offering ceremony. One of the kinglists from the Old Babylonian period indicates that it was used for this precise purpose (Millard 1997).

Mesopotamians believed that kings were possessed of *melammu* or divine radiance, which literally overwhelmed their enemies like the ravages of a storm (*CAD* M/2:9–12; Machinist 2006:159, n. 28,160–64, 169–70; Ataç 2007; Winter 2008:84–85). Fortunately, this *melammu* was generally lost at death, but there were exceptions.

Sennacherib, according to the Netherworld vision of Kumaya, was not only still individual and still a king; he was in some sense still alive. He seems not to be part of the throng about Ereshkigal, but living with the head of the Assyrian pantheon, Ashur, presumably in the eternal garden imitating Mount Lebanon mentioned prominently in the text. His body, normally not an issue with ghosts, is protected by no less than three gods and his *melammu* is still fully active in the upper world to the terror of his successors who dare to reverse his policies: "Whoever of you closes his ears to his words, tastes what is forbidden, and tramples on what is holy—the *melammu* of his terrifying kingship will speedily overwhelm you until you are (but) wind!" (Livingstone 1989: no. 32, r. 22–27).

Was this taken seriously? Yes, indeed; the only example of the inclusion of human beings in a funerary offering known from ancient Mesopotamia is Ashurbanipal's slaughter of the conspirators captured at Babylon on the spot where his grandfather Sennacherib had been murdered (Tsukimoto 1985:112–14, and note 405). Those so sacrificed had nothing to do with the death of Sennacherib, but they were regicides. According to Ashurbanipal, a number of prominent Babylonians had led Ashurbanipal's brother Shamash-shum-ukin, who was king of Babylonia, to revolt. Later, when the revolt failed, in the ultimate act of treachery and cowardice, they[2] threw him into the flames of his palace, declining to do the honorable thing and die with him (Asb A iv 50–58, 70–73).

The idea of killing regicides to placate an angry royal ghost is surprisingly widespread. Alexander the Great executed his father's alleged assassins at his father's tomb (Justin, *Epitome* 11.2.1). The Roman emperor Augustus is usually thought of as a charming and pacific fellow, but not when it came to avenging his adopted father. "The leader (of the revolt) and some others obtained pardon, but most of the senators and knights were put to death. And the story goes that they did not merely suffer death in an ordinary form, but were led to the altar consecrated to the former Caesar (Julius Caesar) and were there sacrificed—three hundred knights and many senators, among them Tiberius Cannutius, who previously during his tribuneship had assembled the populace for Caesar Octavianus" (Dio XLVIII 14.3–4; cf. Suetonius, *Augustus* 15).

One might have thought early modern Europe would be more "civilized," but one would have been wrong. In 1649, Claude Saumaise, then Europe's greatest historian, advocated killing Puritans on the grave of Charles I in the following words: "Surely the blood of a great King … calls to its revenge all monarchs and princes of the Christian World. Nor can they appease his spirit more worthily than by … slaying as victims at the tomb of the saintly dead, those most outrageous beasts who conspired for the murder of so great a king." (Durant and Durant 1963:227–28).

Sennacherib died by violence at the hands of his own sons, and thus was a prime candidate for an angry royal ghost that needed something above the ordinary to keep him quiet. This is not, however, the whole story. Ashurbanipal was, after all, not Sennacherib's son but his grandson, and surely the Babylonians, however guilty in the horrible death of Shamash-shum-ukin, had nothing to do with Sennacherib, nor are they accused of complicity in his murder. Why are they not being sacrificed to the ghost of Shamash-shum-ukin, the king whom they killed? And why are they being sacrificed to the ghost of Sennacherib, the king whom they did not kill?

In Kumaya's vision, the only policy that comes readily to mind which was violated by *his son* Esarhaddon and which Sennacherib could be counted on to act beyond the grave to protect was Ashur's judgment that Babylon must fall to rise no more. The disaster of the Shamash-shum-ukin revolt might have seemed a confirmation that Esarhaddon's rebuilding policy was a dismal failure even on a purely mundane level. Ashurbanipal, nonetheless, fully intended to rebuild Babylon after the suppression of the revolt. He thus found himself in the position of once again violating Sennacherib's mandate in the worst possible way, and in need of something rather dramatic to buy off an unusually armed and dangerous royal ghost. What better offering under the circumstances than Babylonian regicides, the spiritual if not lineal descendents of those prominent Babylonians whose treacherous turning over of another Assyrian prince, Ashur-nadin-shumi, their king, to the invading Elamites had brought down upon Babylon the wrath of Ashurbanipal's grieving grandfather, Sennacherib (Grayson 1991:118).

What is interesting is that Ashurbanipal chose to take his option to override what might seem the ultimate exercise of absolute power—relegating the ancient city of Babylon to permanent nonexistence, despite the fairly obvious fact that there was literally nobody, particularly not at Babylon, in any position to force him to do anything other than whatever he pleased with those who, from his point of view, had done him every conceivable wrong. Ashurbanipal made sure to consult with the god Ashur and to receive his imprimatur on the rebuilding of the shrines of Akkad (Livingstone 1989: no. 44, r. 19–25). Perhaps Ashurbanipal also took inspiration from the *Marduk Prophecy*. This apparently first person narration by Marduk, head of Babylon's pantheon, portrays this god as particularly fond of the city of Ashur, where he was a guest of Tukulti-Ninurta I. It also describes the rescue of the Marduk statue by Nebuchadnezzar I from Elam in such a way as to promise that, if any future king, say Ashurbanipal, were to rebuild Babylon and the temple Esagil after terrible troubles, say the Shamash-shum-ukin revolt, Marduk would reward him with total victory over Elam and, most importantly, extraordinary peace and prosperity in the land: "The grass of winter (will last) till summer. The grass of summer will last to winter. The harvest of the land will thrive. The marketplace will prosper … Brother will love his brother. A son will fear his father as his god … A man will regularly pay his taxes" (Longman 1997). This sounds like fantastic royal propaganda, but we know that esoteric texts of this sort were typically for internal consumption only.

HOW DIVINE A KING?

The Assyrian king was never divine; the god Ashur was the true king of Assyria,[3] and the human king, whatever his title, was merely the faithful servant of his god (Frankfort 1948:228–30; Machinist 2006:153–59, 183–88). This relationship is depicted on the throne room reliefs of Ashurbanipal II, where the god Ashur floats above Ishtar's tree and the dual image of the human king (Winter 2003:253). Ashur's representation (*ṣalmu*) shows him riding on the winged disk of the god of justice, Shamash. At the center of this winged disk is the carnelian ring of power (*šibirru*; see below) through which the rod-like body of Ashur himself passes (Livingstone 1989:5). Translated into a sentence, the throne-room relief proclaims: Ashur is king, and Ashurbanipal his earthly (and mortal) counterpart.

 The Assyrian king was bound by a covenant (*adê*) with Ashur (Parpola 1997: no. 3 ii. 10–32) which guaranteed his continued exercise of power on condition that he not only dispense justice but keep prices as low as possible so that everybody could afford grain, oil, and wool, the basic necessities of life (Livingstone 1997a). He was literally the creation of the gods (Machinist 2006:160–62, 166–69) and, as pointed out by Charpin and Frahm in this volume, in the Old Babylonian and later periods, the god of justice, Shamash, was the divine patron of kingship with whom the king was in some sense identified (Machinist 2006:164, 171–73).

When a Mesopotamian king was imagined as Shamash, this was as the "image" or "flesh," i.e., the body of the god (Machinist 2006:160–63, 170–75), a sort of mobile and speaking cult statue (Walker and Dick 2001:6–8), as if literally cast from bronze (Tigay 2003). To explain: for ancient peoples generally, a statue or other object associated with a god, such as his bed or throne, were spirited entities capable of influencing the god with whom they were associated and the recipients in their own right of offerings (Porter 2006). Similarly, the statues of kings were objects of veneration and recipients of offerings intended for the royal funerary cult (Holloway 2002:188–90; cf. Frankfort 1948:302–6; Winter 1997:359–81; Machinist 2006:175–82).

Statues were not, however, gods, properly speaking. In addition to the god's spirit for which they constituted a corporeal casing, statues contained a lower order of spirit, a body-spirit which, like the human ghost (*eṭemmu*), lasted only as long as the body to which it was attached. When a statue was destroyed, this body-spirit simply ceased to exist. In both the Hebrew Bible and its Greek translation, body-spirits are carefully differentiated from the Spirit of God. What the original anti-iconic dialectic was arguing was not that statues were lifeless (such an assertion dates the text in which it appears to the Persian period or later). Instead, the point was that a statue was inhabited only by its own body spirit (Hebr. *nephesh*; Greek *eidolon*) and did not, nor could it, contain a divine spirit (Hebr. *ruah*; Greek *psuche*), which is why it was no use applying to it for help (cf. Lapinkivi 2004:133–37, 139–45).

Egyptian kings were actually gods; Mesopotamian kings would qualify, literally, only as idols (>*eidolon*). A Mesopotamian king consorted with gods, but was in no position to call the shots; even if he was a god's body, your body has a limited ability to ignore you. Shamash was a god of justice, which essentially meant that the king had to be a font of justice as well. If he failed to perform his duties as monarch, the choice and creature of the gods though he was, his divine soul would abandon him and choose to inhabit another. In practical terms, the gods would occasion a successful revolt, which would topple him and replace him with the new divine favorite (Frankfort 1948:237–40).

Assyrian kings accepted this situation as just the way things were. Indeed, the right of the people to enforce good government is directly underwritten by Sargon II of Assyria, himself the beneficiary of what is portrayed in his own inscriptions as a divinely sanctioned popular revolution against an unjust king:

> Because they listened to my words and followed my advice … and came to lend me support, Assur the city (which had been granted) exemption of dues by old dynasties, the exalted cult city which Ashur its lord chose for the four quarters, band of heaven and earth, which has no equal, whose inhabitants from times past did not know *ilku* and *tupšikku* service—Shalmaneser (V), who did not fear the king of the universe, did evil things to this city and imposed upon its people *ilku* and *tupšikku* service in a painful way and he treated the people as *ḫupšu*-soldiers, but [Ashur], the Enlil of all the gods, terminated his reign in his grave anger; me, Sargon, the king, he elevated; he let me take over scepter, throne (and) royal headgear—for the purpose of setting up the throne firmly and making my dynasty stable, I established their exemption from dues. (*Assur Charter*:28–36 [Saggs 1975])

Interestingly, the curse formula at the end eschews the usual list of curses for the wish that the violator be himself overthrown in a rebellion (*Assur Charter*:42–43, see Saggs 1975.

In the inscriptions of the same king, reference is also made to the fact that "protecting the poor and the weak" included a duty to protect ordinary citizens from oppression by the king's own government officials:

> In accordance with the meaning of my name (i.e. Šarru-kên "the king is upright"), which the great gods bestowed on me—namely to protect righteousness and justice, to guide well the disabled and not to oppress the weak, I reimbursed the owners of the fields of this town with silver or bronze according to the purchase documents, and in order not to create bad feelings in those who would not want to take the silver, I gave them field(s) corresponding to their former field(s) wherever they preferred to have them. (Fuchs 1994:39–40, lines 50–52)

Similarly, regarding the prayers addressed by Assyrian kings to their gods, one would think that, when all alone in the palace and able to ask for any favor, the Assyrian monarch would let you know what he was really thinking. It is, then, striking in how many of the private prayers addressed by Ashurbanipal to the gods, he asks to be given truth and justice with which to shepherd his people (Livingstone 1997a, 1997b).

A millennium earlier, Lipit-Ishtar, ruler of Isin, was a king who claimed to be a god in his own right, yet on clay cones meant to be buried into the foundations of a temple storehouse where nobody but the gods and future monarchs repairing the building could read them, he calls himself "humble shepherd" and claims as his sole accomplishment to have "established justice" in the land of Sumer and Akkad (Frayne 2000b). The reference is to his laws which were promulgated, as he says because: "the gods An and Enlil called Lipit-Ishtar to the princeship of the land … in order to establish justice in the land, to eliminate cries for justice, to eradicate enmity and armed violence, to bring well-being to the lands of Sumer and Akkad" (Roth 2000b:411).

Shulgi, the greatest of the preceding dynasty of divinized rulers, apparently became a god-king by spending the night on a specially prepared bed with the goddess Inanna('s statue) (Klein 2006:127–28, n. 53; Lapinkivi 2004:69–77) in the Sacred Marriage.[4] Yet what is striking about Shulgi is the extent to which his endless boasting emphasizes the practice of what even we would recognize as good government. Indeed it would be accurate to say that his royal propaganda mill defined for the rest of Mesopotamian history what exactly were the basic duties and responsibilities of kingship. In his court, where he heard cases in five languages, "the orphan was not delivered up to the wealthy or the widow to the mighty" (Klein 1995:846–56; cf. Klein 2006:126–27).

He was not, of course, inventing anything. The ethics and ideals of government, which he claimed to epitomize were first developed in Sumerian city-states, and have all the hallmarks of a tight-knit community where everybody takes care of everybody else.[5] In warfare, the city turns into an army; if walls or public buildings need putting up, the city turns into a work detail. If expenses need to be met, everybody makes a contribution. And the rich and the powerful use their wealth and power to protect, and if necessary feed, poorer members of the community. The job of *ensis* (city-state rulers) and kings was simply to coordinate and enforce these basic rules of community solidarity (Roth 2000b:411) and a good *ensi* like Uruinimgina even made it his job to keep taxes at the lowest possible level: "From the border of the divine Ningirsu to the sea, there was no tax collector! ... Uruinimgina made a compact with the divine Ningirsu that the powerful man would not oppress the orphan (or) widow" (Hallo 2002).

Greek democracy this was not; not even a "primitive" one, but it was a form of popular government, which is sometimes referred to as "functional democracy." What this means is that the people, and not the ruler, decide what their government is supposed to do. Add to this the fact that citizens of a Sumerian city, like those of the cities of ancient Greece, valued a "freedom" in their relations to their fellow citizens which meant that individuals were free to do whatever they pleased only so long as they did no harm to themselves or others: "I established freedom for the Akkadians and resident aliens in the lands of Sumer and Akkad ... I did not deliver the man with but one shekel to the man with one mina (60 shekels) ... I did not impose orders. I eliminated enmity, violence and cries for justice. I established justice in the land. If a man murders another man, they shall kill that man, etc.[a series of laws follows]" (Roth 2000a:409). That a civilized person could be anything other than a "slave" to the law was so inconceivable that even Enlil, the autocratic ruler of the Sumerian divine assembly, whose very "word" was law, as we know from the myth of *Enlil and Ninlil* (Black et al 1998–2006:1.2.1), fell afoul of the laws which he himself had made and was dispatched in disgrace to the Netherworld, being allowed to return only by leaving behind a substitute, per the regulations of the Land of No Return (Scurlock 2006:62–65).

If the *ensi* failed to do his job, even religion gave its imprimatur to a carefully managed revolt. In *Atrahasis*, the Igigi gods, angered by being given too much work to do by their king Enlil, not only go on strike, but they besiege his house as an angry mob, threatening to kill him. Although the ringleader is later executed, Enlil acknowledges the justice of their cause, gives in to the demands of the Igigi gods, and creates mankind to do their work (Dalley 1991:9–18).

DUMUZI, DEATH, AND SACRIFICE

But surely Shulgi did not become a divine king just so that he could give himself an endless round of jobs to perform and in order to open himself and his successors to the legitimate exercise of the ultimate check on royal power? The answer to this quandary lies with Tammuz or, as they called him in Sumerian, Dumuzi. According to Mesopotamian tradition, Dumuzi was a mortal shepherd who became a god and/or king by virtue of his relationship with the goddess Inanna/Ishtar who, as goddess of liminality (Harris 1991), had both transformations in her gift (van Buren 1944:52; Frankfort 1948:296–97; Kramer 1959:199; Renger 1972–75; Alster 1972:14–15; Fritz 2003:88–91, 162–63; Lapinkivi 2004:39–40, 43; Klein 2006:128).

But why Dumuzi? If a god who died or a divinized human was all that was required, there was actually a fairly wide choice. To be the sky-god Anu had little to recommend it unless you favored being flayed and having your blood die the sky red (Livingstone 1989: no. 38, 17–22). Nergal was master of the Netherworld and a truly grand god, perhaps a bit too grand to risk offending, assuming of course, that he was actually around at the time. Inanna/Ishtar, like the West Semitic Baal, went to the Netherworld and was able to return, but the bald fact was that they both lost the battle with death. Ereshkigal stripped and killed Inanna/Ishtar and hung the corpse up on a peg, and she would have stayed dead if the other gods had not intervened (Kramer 1963:491). Besides, Inanna/Ishtar was more female than male. Atrahasis (Ut-Napishtim), the Babylonian Noah, had been made immortal, but he lived far away at the source of the rivers (Foster 1997b:460), so he might as well have been dead.

Of course, Dumuzi was one of Shulgi's ancestors of whom he might plausibly be what we would call a reincarnation (Kramer 1969:62–63). Connection with him thus provided a legitimizing link with former kings, and the extensive mourning rites performed annually for him could be seen as an extension of the royal ancestor cult (Fritz 2003:89, n. 333; 231, n. 885; 240–42; 265–72; 365–68). However, in this case, the passing over by Shulgi of Gilgamesh as this legitimizing link with the past is truly puzzling.

As is pointedly mentioned in the Gilgamesh Epic, Dumuzi was rewarded for his attentions to the goddess Ishtar by being packed off to the Netherworld alone and before his time. Gilgamesh, by contrast, was a partly divine human being and a king who managed to die peacefully in bed (as Shulgi aspired to do) and who, after his timely death, became a judge in the Netherworld. He was also, like Dumuzi, one of Shulgi's ancestors, not to mention a great hero renowned throughout the ancient Near East due largely to the efforts of Shulgi's propaganda machine. Why claim to be Gilgamesh's brother (Klein 2006:123–24; Michalowski 2008:36–38) when you can be the man himself?

So why Dumuzi? Popular belief in the modern West, inspired directly or indirectly by Frazer (1914), sees Tammuz as a dying god of fertility (Frankfort 1948:281–99; Fritz 2003:17–45, 361–68; Klein 2006:127–28). On the surface, this is patently absurd. Dumuzi was a god of shepherds (Fritz 2003:97–102, 112–13, 121–23, 127–29, 131–32, 150, 281; Kramer 1969:68–72) to whom one prayed to have lots of cattle and sheep in the pen (Frayne 2000c). His only connection with agricultural fertility (Farber 1997:512) came in the form of the dung dropped by grazing sheep onto the fields. Yet the laments for Tammuz were, insofar as we can tell, performed exclusively by agriculturalists. What, then, are we to make of this? Settled folk hysterical over the loss of the pastoralist's flocks? A fertility cult, which celebrates the death of nature? A royal ancestor-fertility cult that makes no mention of the provision by the ancestors of royal offspring?

To be fair to Frazer, he actually meant to characterize his "dying god" as a Christ analogy (J.Z. Smith 2005 [1987]:2536; M.S. Smith 1998:312; Mettinger 2001:16). Like Christ, the dying god is a god-king, and like him he dies and is mourned but ultimately triumphs over death (Jacobsen 1949:215; Parpola 1997: nn. 123–25, 127; Lapinkivi 2004:149–51). Returning to the notion of Shulgi becoming divine king as specifically Dumuzi (Alster 1972:15, n. 31; Gurney 1962:156; Klein 2006:123, 128–29, 131; cf. Jacobsen 1997b; Fritz 2003:163–64; Lapinkivi 2004:35, 39–41, 44–45, 52), what, apart from providing an intensified link between mankind and the gods (Frymer-Kensky 1992:50–58, 62; Klein 2006:129), will have been the object of the exercise?

It made a great deal of sense for Ur III and First Dynasty of Isin kings to claim divinity in order to justify the submission of the rest of southern Mesopotamia to their rule. If they were not gods, why should *they* be rulers and not the *ensis* of other, formerly independent cities, which rivaled their own? This grasping for unquestioned authority in the face of internal division (Klein 2006:129, 131; Michalowski 2008) would also be in consonance with the king's close relationship with hero-gods such as Ninurta whose monster-slaying activities culminating in leadership of the gods have been seen as justification for royal absolutism in the face of foreign enemies (Foster 2007:182; cf. Frankfort 1948:220). Making the divine king specifically Dumuzi would have had the added bonus of allowing the human king to triumph over death, the ultimate definition of absolute power.

Verisimilitude is not, however, to be mistaken for truth. We are now in a position to understand to what extent the dying and resurrected god is appropriate. In fact, Dumuzi does *not* triumph over death (Gurney 1962:151–53; Yamauchi 1966; J.Z. Smith 2005 [1987]:2538–39), as might indeed have been gathered from the texts of the laments themselves (Jacobsen 1961:209–10) as well as the accompanying myth of *Inanna's Descent* (Sladek 1974). Being looked at with the look of death apropos of taking Inanna's much deserved place in the Land of No Return is hardly a promising start to immortality.

The Mari letter, which is often quoted as evidence of Dumuzi's resurrection (Mettinger 2001:201–2; Parpola 1997: n. 127; Lapinkivi 2004:151), should be removed from the argument. When the full context is examined (Marello 1992), it becomes clear that the author is praising himself for his refusal to give up no matter what, in contrast to the lazy good-for-nothing whom he is addressing. This man who has, by his own account, escaped death ten times over in Ahuna and yet persists in remaining there and doing his job is indeed like Dumuzi who is killed every year yet persists in coming back to the temple of Anunītum (a by-form of Inanna) from whence he will once again be shipped off to the Land of No Return to take her place. Note that the spring timing for Dumuzi's return, which is allegedly mentioned in the letter, is based solely on a restoration.

Dumuzi's half of the year alternation with his sister Geshtinanna, like statements in cultic commentaries about a descent of Nergal on the 18th of Du'uzu and his return on the 28th of Kislimmu (Mettinger 2001:189–90, 204), cannot be taken at face value. Geshtinanna was scribe of the Netherworld, and Nergal its king; neither of them can really have been allowed to spend more than a few days away from home and above ground, without, so to speak, all hell breaking loose. As with the strange myth of *Inanna and Shukaletuda* (Volk 1995) in which the goddess seems to be helplessly absent in the Abzu when she ought to be avenging herself on her rapist, mysterious presences and absences of essential divinities are best explained in terms of astral mythology (Cooley 2008). In other words, what is probably being referred to in the Nergal and Inanna passages are the heliacal rising and setting of Nergal's planet and Venus phenomena associated with the goddess Ishtar.

Dumuzi, too, had an astral dimension. He was not Orion, as is often stated in the older literature, but was instead associated with the constellation known in Mesopotamia as The Hireling. This had its heliacal rising in the first month of the year, and eventually became the first sign of the Zodiac (Foxvog 1993; Fritz 2003:247–48). The Hireling was hence the "doorkeeper" of the other stars, which is why Dumuzi is called "gatekeeper of the highest heaven" in *Adapa and the South Wind* (Lapinkivi 2004:149). When Shulgi is described as going up to heaven as "doorkeeper" (Hallo 2002; cf. Lapinkivi 2004:46–47, 151), this presumably means that he was imagined as becoming Dumuzi's constellation. The alternation beween Dumuzi and Geshtinanna, then, refers to the period of visibility of Dumuzi's constellation of The Hireling (when Geshtinanna was imagined as taking his place in the Netherworld). None of these astral references is what would normally be meant by death and resurrection (M.S. Smith 1998:274).

Neither is the wailing for Dumuzi a death and resurrection festival. The assertion that it was, which is often found in the older literature, is based on the assumption that many if not all major Mesopotamian divinities were somehow Tammuz (Langdon 1914; Witzel 1935:vi–xxi; Frankfort 1948:281–94; Moortgat 1949) and/or that Marduk died and was resurrected in the Babylonian New Year's Festival (Langdon 1923:32–56; Jensen 1924; Zimmern 1926; Frankfort 1948:313–33). Although Marduk paid an annual visit to the Netherworld and to the Heavens during this festival, he neither died nor was resurrected; instead, he wrested control of the Netherworld from Nergal and Ereshkigal and of the Heavens from Anu.

Not only was he *not* Dumuzi but, according to a late lamentation, it was Marduk who was responsible for Dumuzi's premature death (Hallo 1997). Since Marduk is frequently referred to by his title of Bēl or "lord," this is presumably the origin of the notion among the Sabeans of Harran that Tammuz was murdered by his master (Lapinkivi 2004:150, n. 713). Similarly, in the Ugaritic Baal Epic, it was Mot and not Baal who was cut and winnowed like so much ripe grain (M.S. Smith 1998:276–77).

The 1st millennium wailing for Dumuzi might be more accurately described as a resurrection and death festival in which Dumuzi "comes up" for three days accompanied by the ghosts of the dead who have taken this opportunity to visit living relatives (Scurlock 1992; cf. Yamauchi 1966:13–15; Fritz 2003:236–38; Lapinkivi 2004:42). "On the day when Dumuzi comes back up, (and) the lapis lazuli pipe and the carnelian ring come up with him, (when) male and female mourners come up with him, the dead shall come up and smell the incense offering" (Dalley 1997a:383–84). Alas, at the end, all must return home. Put in Christian terms, the 1st millennium cult of the "dying god" would be the equivalent of having Easter Sunday *precede* Good

Friday so, Easter Friday, Holy Saturday, and Good Sunday rather than Good Friday, Holy Saturday, and Easter Sunday.

Nor is this apparent inversion likely to be a 1st millennium innovation. Ur III Umma had what is probably the best candidate for a resurrection festival (Mettinger 2001:200). However, Dumuzi had to be fetched by boat from the Netherworld (Cohen 1993:186–87), and, contrary to the generally accepted notion that this fetching was to usher in Dumuzi's alleged half-year above the earth (Cohen 1993:186–88, 478–79; Lapinkivi 2004:149–50), the celebration of his Sacred Marriage with Inanna was followed with dizzying suddenness by official mourning for his demise (Sallaberger 1993:257–64). The interval between the fetching and the mourning is not known, but it was not a long one, and possibly even three days as in the 1st millennium mourning rites, the only difference being that the Sacred Marriage had to be accommodated in the earlier version. It is also noteworthy that a number of Sumerian Sacred Marriage texts distinctly cross Dumuzi's death with his marriage (Lapinviki 2004:42, 46–47), suggesting that Dumuzi, in all periods, came up only to return once more to his Netherworld prison.

Opening the gates of the Netherworld to permanently release the dead like Christ Triumphant is actually invoked as a possibility in ancient Mesopotamia—but as the worst thing that could possibly happen (Yamauchi 1966:12). "If you do not send that god to me," threatens Ereshkigal, "according to the rites of Erkalla and the great Earth, I shall raise up the dead, and they will eat the living. I shall make the dead outnumber the living!" (Dalley 1997b:388). Similarly Ishtar on her descent to the Netherworld: "If you do not open the gate for me to come in, I shall smash the door and shatter the bolt, I shall smash the doorpost and overturn the doors, I shall raise up the dead and they shall eat the living. The dead shall outnumber the living!" (Dalley 1997a:381). And was not overpopulation due to human fertility (Kilmer 1972) so displeasing to the gods that it motivated them to attempt to destroy mankind in the great flood? (Foster 1997a).

Ereshkigal, of course, had the power to open the gates of the Netherworld whenever she pleased; so too, as we know from the *Erra Epic*, did Marduk. The latter even exercised his right periodically, unleashing Erra, the god of plague, whenever the "peoples' noise" and the trampling of cattle indicated that there were too many people in the land (Dalley 1997c:405–8). The result was not eternal life for the blessed but its opposite: horrible and undiscriminating death. The fevers attributed to Marduk and his byforms in the medical corpus produce massive bleeding and are inevitably fatal (Scurlock and Andersen 2005:486–87). What endeared Marduk to his constituents was not his justice but his mercy (Machinist 2006:170–71), and in his Akītu festival he was annually subjected to what I have termed a covenant sacrifice (Scurlock 2002:400–401), which, like the Abrahamic covenant, bound him to provide benefits to his people and to exercise his powers with restraint, sparing always a remnant. In short, absolute power exercised absolutely did not make a good king of the gods any more than it made a good king of men (Jacobsen 1949:150–57).

THE SIGNIFICANCE OF THE GRAIN

What made Adonis (equated with Tammuz by Frazer 1914:6–7) the dying and resurrected god of fertility was the grain that played such an important part in his cult (Frazer 1914:229–32). For Frazer, the point of Adonis' mourning rites, typically carried out by women, was *not* sorrow at the natural decay of vegetation under the heat of summer (*contra* Frankfort 1948:282, 288, 291, 293–94; Kramer 1969:107) but the guilt felt by agriculturalists at the bald fact that they had violently destroyed and eaten the divine corn spirit whose annual sacrifice preserved them from starvation (Frazer 1914:231–32; cf. Jacobsen 1961:194–95, 197, 201–3, 205–7, 211–12).

At first glance, Frazer's analysis is quite compelling, at least when applied to a post-Ur III/First Dynasty of Isin context. Umma had what is probably the best candidate for a resurrection festival connected with the Sacred Marriage (Mettinger 2001:200) and, true to paradigm, Dumuzi the shepherd's gifts to his new bride included grain and flour in addition to the expected sheep and goats, wood and reeds (Sallaberger 1993:258–59; Lapinkivi 2004:63–64).

In the Old Babylonian period, when the Sacred Marriage was no longer celebrated, the annual mourning rites continued, and continued to be associated with grain offerings. By Samsuiluna 23, groats were being issued for the "day of the binding of Dumuzi" (Lapinkivi 2004:29, n. 121). Large quantities of grain were also issued to mourning women for the rites of Du'uzu at 2nd millennium BCE Mari (Alster 1999:831; Mettinger 2001:200–201). What is more, the 1st millennium BCE rites of Dumuzi that survived in Harran until the 10th century CE also provide a striking parallel to the classical cult of Adonis (Gurney 1962:159–60; Mettinger 2001:202; Lapinkivi

2004:150–51, and n. 713). This prominence of grain is conventionally interpreted to mean that Dumuzi was, at least in 1st millennium Assyria, a grain god (Fritz 2003:361, and n. 1561) and/or that "the spirit of the corn" was one of his (late) manifestations (Jacobsen 1961:201–2).

Grain has a specific symbolism for early Christian apologists, and has long been used to provide a salvation analogy readily comprehensible to the popular imagination. Grain is a dead thing, yet when it is buried in the earth, it comes to life and grows again. Similarly, humans believing in Christ may appear to be dead and to be buried in the earth, yet they too will rise again to eternal life. Or, to quote Frazer, "(Attis is the) ripe grain wounded by the reaper, buried in the granary, and coming to life again when it is sown in the ground" (Frazer 1914:279).

A simplistic reading of such an analogy is, obviously, fertility of crops equals, by extension, fertility of animals and people. This inevitably led to the re-interpretation of the rites of Dumuzi, Adonis, etc., as fertility cults, complete with human sacrifice and cultic prostitution, which formed a milestone on the road leading from savagery to civilization (Pisi 2001:32–36). Or, to put it more kindly: "Christianity accepted Tammuz symbols—commonly presumed to be the symbols of a dying Savior who rose again—as it has always accepted any pre-Christian conception which represents a striving in the dark after the revelation finally given in Christ" (Saggs 1962:468). Unfortunately for Frazer, as we have seen, neither resurrection nor fertility was envisaged by the rites of Dumuzi.

What is most interesting about all of this is that, in spite of it all, Frazer was not wrong in seeing the dying god as a Christ analogy (similarly, Mettinger 2001:217–22), as is specifically revealed by the way in which grain is used in the 1st millennium rites of Dumuzi. The grain that represents the dying god is neither eaten nor planted in the earth, as it should be by the women-centered lamentation-cum-fertility scenario, but parched and strewn about, or a dolly is soaked in beer until it sends up sprouts in order to make Dumuzi come up (Scurlock 1992). This motif is already present in the Sumerian Sacred Marriage texts; one of the love poems compares Dumuzi to sprouted lettuce (Kramer 1969:95–96; Lapinviki 2004:34–35) and another mentions Inanna sprinkling the water (of life) on the ground in order to make Dumuzi, her *mes*-tree over whom she will weep with the lyre, sprout (Lapinviki 2004:35, cf. 36). This image of the dead coming to life is a vivid evocation of the effects of even light rainfall in a semi-desert environment.

Frazer notes numerous classical references to the "Gardens of Adonis" in which wheat, barley and lettuce were made to sprout (1914:236). The sprouted grain appears as a Christ symbol among Eastern Rite Christians; it is prepared on St. Barbara's day in time for the grain to have sprouted by Christmas (Rogers 1989 [1865]:363). A similar custom is attested in Persia in connection with Naurouz (Massé 1954 [1938]:139, 156–57). In all cases, the sprouts soon withered (as indeed they were intended to) and were subsequently discarded (cf. J.Z. Smith 2005 [1987]:2536).

This parallelism among the various rituals of the sprouts is particularly striking since Eastern Rite Christians also celebrate the three days of Easter with mourning rites involving, as with the wailings for Dumuzi, the setting up of a funeral bed. "At the top of the nave, just below the chancel-step, stood a bier and upon it lay the figure of the Christ, all too death-like in the dim light" (Lawsen 1910:574–76).

The referent here is not, obviously, Christ Triumphant, who died in order to live, but the Suffering Servant and Lamb of God, who lived in order to die; a young man taken before his time as a sacrifice for others. To put it in other words, the desired benefit is a reconciliation with God rather than the acquisition of eternal life as such. It is for this reason that the grain which is offered to Dumuzi or Adonis or Christ is deliberately sprouted so that it will never grow in the earth or produce seed. Similarly, the eggs which one hunts at Easter have been boiled or have had the contents removed and are delivered by an animal, the rabbit, which is proverbial for its fecundity but which does not produce eggs.

Striking in these cases is the deliberate canceling or inversion of fertility symbols. Contrast the rituals associated with Demeter and Persephone, which were, variously, rites ensuring agricultural fertility (Demeter was the goddess of grain) and a death and resurrection cult leading to a deluxe afterlife for the participants (the Eleusinian mysteries). The festival of Chthonia as performed by the Hermionians (Pausanius 2.35) involved a mock marriage rite in which children dressed in white and garlanded with flowers of mourning escorted four frisky heifers (representing the teen-aged girls who accompanied Persephone to the Netherworld for her forced marriage with Hades). The heifers disappeared into the Temple one by one as if into a bridal chamber and the doors were closed behind them. Four old women awaited, who sacrificed the heifers in the manner of the harvest, using sickles and taking care that the animals all fell on the same side like a row of grain. What we have here in a true women-centered lamentation-cum-fertility rite connected with grain is an analogy between the bride who dies to her natal family (and is mourned by her womenfolk) in order to provide men with progeny and the grain which dies but nonetheless provides the seed for the next year's harvest. Here, the death of the corn spirit (Persephone) is represented symbolically by animal sacrifice, the exact inverse of the rites of Adonis and Dumuzi.

As with the bread and wine of Christian communion, the grain that forms the focus of the rites of Dumuzi and Adonis is a symbolic form of animal sacrifice of which the god is the (unwilling) victim. As Walter Farber has shown, the goat which was Ishtar's favorite offering and whose heart was torn out and burned before her was understood to represent Dumuzi (Farber 1977:64–67:20, 30). Unlike communion, however, Dumuzi's was a sacrifice, which was never meant to be consumed by his worshippers. Far from bringing benefits, it was charged with transferred evils and thus prepared only to be discarded. Nonetheless, the fact that reconciliation with God is still a *sine qua non* for salvation makes these rites appropriate for Christians.

As with Christian communion, Dumuzi's sacrifice was one from which the human community expected to benefit and it was indeed to receive this benefit that the rites were performed. Dumuzi's 1st millennium festival was timed to coincide with the departure of pastoralists from the Mesopotamian flood plain for summer pastures in the mountains to the east. Every year, when he departed for the Netherworld (also located conceptually in the Eastern mountains to which the pastoralists were headed), he took with him all the evils that plagued mankind. He was literally imagined as herding them off with him like so many sheep (Farber 1977:152–53:171–188).

Although evils plaguing mankind were not necessarily the products of sin (meaning moral offences punished by the gods with illness), many were, and so in at least a limited sense Dumuzi could be seen as taking away the sins of the world. To benefit, however, it was necessary to engage in the mourning rites for Dumuzi; otherwise, you were the one who would be carried off to take Ishtar's place in the Netherworld (Alster 1999:832–33). This is as close to the notion of a universal salvation contingent on accepting moral responsibility for the fact that Christ died for your sins as one could hope to find. Since, in fact, Christianity grew up in the Greek east, at a time when wailings for Tammuz were still practiced, the resemblance is probably not entirely accidental. The focus on women as participants in the cult of Dumuzi/Tammuz is neither a sign of the insignificance of the rites nor of their exclusively popular character (*contra* Kutscher 1990), but a natural outgrowth of the virtual monopolization by women of rites de passage including particularly mourning for the dead. Curiously similar is the tendency, remarked on in all periods of European history, for participants in the Mass to consist primarily of women.

THE PERILS OF IDENTIFICATION WITH DUMUZI

For the human king to be a Christ Triumphant is one thing, to be a Suffering Servant, quite another. Mesopotamian kings did not aspire to die for others or at least not on the spot with one salient exception. When an eclipse occurred which portended disaster for king and country, a substitute king was appointed (Frankfort 1948:262–65). As we know from the preserved parts of the ritual, and from references in Neo-Assyrian letters, the substitute king died and went to the Netherworld along with his queen and court on a mission to take with him the evil portended by the eclipse, allowing the real king (who had been pretending to be a gardener in the interim) to safely reassume his throne (Parpola 1993: nos. 351–52).

The custom was very old in Mesopotamian culture and is still the best explanation for the famous "royal cemetery" at Ur (see Dickson, this volume), which was not, contrary to normal practice, under the floors of the palace but located in a city dump, and is full of objects invoking Ishtar and Dumuzi (Barrett 2007:30–35). Particularly striking are statuettes of a goat in lapis, the color of Dumuzi as well as of his staff of kingship (Dalley 1997d:453). This goat stands on its hind legs to feed on a tree whose branches end in Ishtar's rosettes. Here once again, we have Dumuzi's goat (Barrett 2007:32) and Ishtar's tree in a representation strikingly parallel to the Biblical image of the ram in the thicket.

Blue, Dumuzi's color (Barrett 2007:25–27), is the color of the Netherworld. Ishtar's color is red (Barrett 2007:25–27), the color of life and divinity, silently symbolizing the fact that Dumuzi died so that Ishtar might live. When offerings were made to astral divinities, a red cloth was spread; for ghosts, the color was blue-green (*LKA* 136:15). The throne of Nergal, king of the Netherworld, was made of lapis lazuli fitted in silver and gold or, to be more precise, it was a piece of wood colored with white, yellow, and blue paste which became lapis set in silver and gold when he took it below (Dalley 1997b:385–86). Note also that the standard of the moon god Nanna of Ur was also of lapis lazuli, fitted in silver and gold (Frayne 2000a:247).

The jury is still out on whether or not participation in the substitute king ritual was voluntary. Damage to the bones combined with evidence of boiling (Pitman, pers. comm.; see now Baadsgaard et al. 2011) would suggest a practice of excarnation, which, however unpleasant, will have taken place after death. In any case, inclusion provided real benefits for the sacrificed, whether they appreciated them or not. As with Easter pageants in the Spanish diaspora, where the person playing the role of Christ submits to being whipped and crucified, it was presumably thought that such sacrifice would translate to a better life in the otherworld, where ordinary people might have the chance to continue to play the role of the royal court round Ereshkigal like real kings and queens. As may be seen from the grave goods, those who died there were expected to spend their afterlives dressed in splendid garments riding about in chariots and participating in an endless round of feasting accompanied by the finest music. What was perhaps more important, there were no agricultural tools or weaving paraphernalia, which means that never again would they have to do any useful work (Barrett 2007:102–4).

But what about Shulgi? Eventually, he hoped to become a star like Dumuzi (Foxvog 1993; cf. Klein 1995:855; Michalowski 2008:38; Lapinkivi 2004:41, 46–47), but that was after living a long and happy life, marrying various mortal wives and concubines, and having lots of children, things which the real Dumuzi never got to do and no husband of Ishtar could imagine getting away with. Indeed, in one of the Sumerian "love poems," Dumuzi is actually made to swear an oath not to touch another woman (Sefati 1997:541).

How to achieve the impossible? Inanna would have to be sent off in disgrace in order for Shulgi to thrive. In other words, kings who celebrated the Sacred Marriage with Inanna were hoping for all the rewards of connection with the divine without having to suffer Dumuzi's speedy and untimely death in the process. To paraphrase Severn Darden's professor Walther von der Vogelweide, they were trying to find out what would have happened if the hero had read the book *before* going on the journey (Darden 1961). To judge from what evidence we currently have from later celebrations of the festivals of Nisannu and Tashritu, as well as from Ur III and First Dynasty of Isin hymns and the Sumerian lamentation series, Shulgi was imagined as having left his marriage bed to go off and defeat the enemies of Sumer under the aegis of Enlil's son Ninurta. The ever fickle Inanna seems to have used this opportunity to start a clandestine affair of her own, but was caught red-handed and ultimately sent packing. With her out of the way, Shulgi was free to marry whom he pleased, and was introduced into the divine assembly by his patron, Ninurta, to have his destiny decreed as king (Scurlock, forthcoming).

Ninurta was, of course, the son of Enlil, the king of heaven and earth and head of the Sumerian pantheon. Although a very important god in his own right, and himself decreed king in the assembly of the gods, he is mostly seen as a faithful and obedient servant of his father, and it is in his father's name and not his own that his victories are won (Annus 2002). The similarity of this father/son relationship to the proper role of the pious king and his god made Ninurta a patron of kingship already with Shulgi. Later, after the rise of Marduk to the head of the pantheon, Marduk's son Nabû took over the role of dutiful son and patron of kingship for Babylonian kings (Annus 2002:15–16; cf. Machinist 2006:160–61).

Divine election on merit was a much more glorious, and manly, way of acquiring kingship (divine or otherwise) than marriage with Ishtar, which explains why so little fuss is made about Dumuzi even in the Ur III period (Kutscher 1990). For Old Babylonian and later monarchs, Ninurta was the appropriate patron for the sovereign as commander in chief and mighty hunter. The sun-god, Shamash, clearly outshone his rivals as patron of kingship as a font of justice. Nonetheless, when it comes to royal legitimation, the more the merrier. However de-emphasized, Dumuzi remained a god and a shepherd who had ruled as king (Fritz 2003:165–66) and thus a paradigm for kingship (Fritz 2003:160), and to be a good king was always to be a "good shepherd."

THE GOOD SHEPHERD: MESOPOTAMIAN KINGSHIP AND ETHICAL RESPONSIBILITY

So what was the point? It is now appropriate to understand what Mesopotamians meant when they characterized a king as a "good shepherd" like, if not identical with, Dumuzi and why Gilgamesh was not chosen to play this role. Gilgamesh was a handsome young hero, but he was a reprobate ruler—running off at all times to fight monsters with whom he had no quarrel and whom he treated dishonorably, putting onerous burdens on people because he wanted to amuse himself and worse, deflowering every virgin in town with a "I'll do whatever I please" attitude. Not only that, but he had the ill grace to insult the goddess Ishtar, divine patroness of his city Uruk, when she offered him her favors (George 1999; Katz 1997). In other words, Gilgamesh was the ultimate autocrat (Davenport 2007) whose churlish behavior was excused only by his age and inexperience.

Dumuzi, by contrast, was the "sun god of the people" (Lapinviki 2004:43) and a good shepherd (Lapinviki 2004:44), who was distinctly subordinate to the realm of the gods, not to mention "dependent on the love and blessing" of his wife (Klein 2006:131), and he could safely be left behind to tend to Sumer while Inanna/Ishtar was off trying to conquer the Netherworld. Nothing is said about any complaint from his subjects; Dumuzi was terribly punished not for deflowering their virginal daughters but for not mourning Ishtar's deeply deserved demise and enjoying himself with the palace slave girls (Fritz 2003:109–10, 282), a sport to which any human king who was not married to Inanna/Ishtar would have felt himself perfectly entitled. To be Dumuzi or like Dumuzi, then, was not to evade the onerous duties of kingship but to embrace them, and to suffer the ultimate penalty for failure.

As Giovanni Lanfranchi notes, "When making important decisions, the king is always subject to the gods' judgment; if he commits a mistake or a 'sin,' he will have to pay personally. The king is thus treated as a person who assumes the risk of decision or acts on behalf of others than himself (his subjects); as such, he is courageous, generous, voluntarily acting as a possible scapegoat, and ready to sacrifice. He is, after all, the best shepherd of his herd" (Lanfranchi 2003:107; cf. Frankfort 1948:258–61). As Lanfranchi further points out, the fact that the king had been given bad advice by his councilors by no means exonerated him (2003:101–3). In other words, kingship in Mesopotamia was not ideologically about power but about responsibility. According to the *Eridu Genesis*, as restored from a Neo-Assyrian fragment, kings were created by the mother goddess Belet-ili (Livingstone 1997c). This was not before but after the creation of mankind. Why was mankind created? To do the work of the gods (Klein 1997). And why were kings created? To supervise their labor (Jacobsen 1997a:514).

The Old Babylonian and later periods see the emergence of Shamash as the divine patron of kingship par excellence. As pointed out by Charpin in this volume, Shamash was not only the god of justice, but he was also a "good shepherd" who wielded Dumuzi's lapis lazuli staff to judge cases human and divine. Moreover, whether his successors chose to follow Shulgi into divinity or not, Dumuzi remained symbolically identified with human kingship even as late as the Neo-Assyrian period (Lapinkivi 2004:30). As we mentioned earlier, on Ashurbanipal II's palace reliefs, in the throne room just behind the emplacement for the royal throne (Paley and Sobelewski 1997: pl. 46), the king is shown on both sides of the sacred tree (Winter 2003:253), a direct reference to the common motif of Ishtar as a tree flanked on both sides by Dumuzi's goat.

Similarly, a Neo-Assyrian tile panel from Nimrud's Fort Shalmaneser shows at the bottom two facing kings on either side of Ashur and, above this scene, two bulls flanking Ishtar's sacred tree. The predominant color of the panel is blue, Dumuzi's color (Winter 2003:257). This iconography is echoed in early Christian mosaics from Syria, which depict a cross or Tree of Life flanked by two lambs or bulls or lions, representing Christ as Lamb of God and Heavenly King.[6]

The symbols of Assyrian kingship frequently shown in the process of being handed over by Ashur or other gods were a rod (*haṭṭu*) and a ring (*kippatu* in Babylonia but *šibirru* in Assyria).[7] These may be seen as originating in surveying tools used by the monarch to build temples and symbolically dispense justice (i.e., make things go aright; Slansky 2007), and, as pointed out by McGuire Gibson (pers. comm.), they are also tools used by herdsmen to control their animals. Symbolically, the lapis rod evoked Dumuzi and represented good government; the carnelian ring, which is always mentioned *after* the rod, evoked Ishtar and represented the divine power (*melammu*) which was given to the king by the gods and which enabled him to do his job. Or, as Adad-nirari II put it: "(the great gods) put into my hands the scepter for shepherding the people, ... wound round my head the *melammu* of kingship" (Machinist 2006:169–70).

However godlike, then, Assyrian kings were always kings of responsibility and not kings of power. Sennacherib died the worst possible death only to live eternally in a paradise garden (Polinger Foster 2004–2005) with his heavenly father. Even in death, he remained possessed of divine power to intervene in human affairs (Livingstone 1989: no. 32, r. 22–27).

However, even Sennacherib was not rewarded for his spectacular exercise of power in the destruction of Babylon and the smashing of Marduk. This is not actually mentioned in Kumaya's vision. Instead, what is given as the reason for Ashur's favor, and what was the living Sennacherib's proudest achievement, was his gardens: his Akītu-house garden for Ashur (Livingstone 1989: no. 32, 24), his hanging garden Palace Without a Rival and his massive aqueduct projects which created a line of public parks and turned the city of Nineveh into one giant garden, as he says, so that those ignorant people with nothing between their ears (*OIP* 2, 108:85) would no longer have to look to the sky and pray for rain:

> That they might plant orchards I subdivided some land in the plain above the city into plots of 2 acres each for the citizens of Nineveh, and gave it to them. To increase the vegetation from the border of Kisri to the plain about Nineveh, through mountain and lowland, with iron pickaxes I cut and directed a canal. For a distance of 1.5 double hours of land, the waters of the Khosr, which from of old sought too low a level, I made to flow through those orchards in irrigation ditches. (*OIP* 2, 97–98:88–90)

> The wealth of the mountain and all lands, all the aromatics of the land of Hatti, bitter herbs among which fruitfulness was greater than in their (natural) habitat, all kinds of mountain vines, all the fruits of all the lands, aromatics and fruit trees, I set out in great numbers… To arrest the flow of these waters, I made a swamp and set out a canebrake within it. Igiru-birds, wild swine, beasts of the forest I let loose therein… At the dedication of the palace, I drenched the foreheads of the people of my land with wine, with sweetened beer I sprinkled their hearts. (*OIP* 2, 113–116:viii, 17–76)

In short, it was his creation of an earthly paradise for his people and not his free exercise of power, however justified, which entitled him to an eternal paradise in the other world.

CONCLUSION

In sum, Mesopotamian kings retained their status and individualism in death. Living kings, whether divine or not, received divine powers from the gods who appointed (or married) them. Even when the king became a god, however, that god was imagined as like Dumuzi, a divinized human being who came to life and died annually to benefit others. The correct Christian analogy for Dumuzi as dying god and Heavenly King is not Christ Triumphant, an image of absolute power rejected by ancient Mesopotamians, but the Suffering Servant or Good Shepherd who is willing to give his life to protect his flock. Our own political system is predicated on the notion that government is about power, which makes it essential for the ruled to ensure that that power is, insofar as is possible, used to everybody's benefit. Ancient Mesopotamian kingship was predicated on the notion that government is about responsibility, which made it essential to define what those responsibilities were and to see to it that kings fulfilled them.

NOTES

5.1 I wish to thank Steven Holloway and Richard Beal for reading preliminary drafts of this paper and for making many helpful additions and corrections. I would also like to thank members of the workshop from whom I received many helpful suggestions. Any errors which remain are, of course, my own.

5.2 Ashurbanipal has the gods doing this; presumably he means that the gods caused the Babylonians to do this, a fact that shows that Shamash-shum-ukin deserved what happened to him, but did nothing to exonerate the perpetrators of the dreadful deed.

5.3 Livingstone 1997a:473, 15 should read: "Ashur is king, Ashur alone is king!"

5.4 For a very nice argument that the Sacred Marriage whereby the king married Inanna was not—*contra* Frankfort 1948:295–99; Kramer 1959:199; Kramer 1969:49–66; and Foster 2007:201—about fertility and kingship, see Cooper 1993, especially p. 91 (cf. Renger 1972–75). Cooper's arguments are supported by the fact that what are identified as the ritual texts for the Sacred Marriage by Kramer imagine Inanna as giving her spouse life and kingship as his reward for pleasing her in the bedroom (Kramer 1963:502, 504, 507; cf. Lapinkivi 2004:44, 45, 47–48, 50–54). Fritz 2003:325–28, 361–68 argues for both fertility and legitimation of kingship via the ancestor cult (cf. Pisi 1995).

5.5 With Elizabeth Stone (2005), we must not be too hasty in assuming that this necessarily translated to oppression of the countryside. Weber's parasite city model is based on ancient Rome, which began, by its own account, as a den of robbers.

5.6 See http://198.62.75.1/www1/ofm/fai/FAIrasas.html, accessed October 14, 2008.

5.7 *CAD* Š/II 377–78 translates it as a "staff," but it appears paired with the actual word for staff and is an Assyrian form of Babylonian *šewerru*: "ring."

REFERENCES

Alster, B. 1972. *Dumuzi's Dream: Aspects of Oral Poetry in a Sumerian Myth, Mesopotamia*. Copenhagen Studies in Assyriology 1. Copenhagen: Akademisk Forlag.

———. 1999. Tammuz. In *Dictionary of Deities and Demons in the Bible*, ed/ L/ Vam Der Toorn, B. Becking, and P.W. Van Der Horst. 2nd ed. Leiden: Brill.

Annus, A. 2002. *The God Ninurta*. SAA 14. Helsinki: Helsinki University Press.

Ataç, M.A. 2007. The *Melammu* as Divine Epiphany and Usurped Entity. In *Ancient Near Eastern Art in Context (Fs. Winter)*, ed. J. Cheng and M.H. Feldman, pp. 295–313. Culture and History of the Ancient Near East 26. Leiden: Brill.

Baadsgaard, A., J. Monge, S. Cox, and R.L. Zettler. 2011. Human Sacrifice and Intentional Corpse Preservation in the Royal Cemetery of Ur. *Antiquity* 85:27–42.

Barrett, C.E. 2007. Was Dust Their Food and Clay Their Bread? *JANER* 7(1): 7–65.

Black, J.A., G. Cunningham, J. Ebeling, E. Flückiger-Hawker, E. Robson, J. Taylor, and G. Zólyomi. 1998–2006. *The Electronic Text Corpus of Sumerian Literature*. http://etcsl.orinst.ox.ac.uk/. Oxford.

Cohen, M.E. 1993. *The Cultic Calendars of the Ancient Near East*. Bethesda: CDL Press.

Cooley, J.L. 2008. Inana and Šhukaletuda: A Sumerian Astral Myth. *Kaskal. Rivista di storia, ambienti e culture del Vicino Oriente Antico* 5:161–72.

Cooper, J. 1993. Sacred Marriage and Popular Cult in Early Mesopotamia. In *Official Cult and Popular Religion in the Ancient Near East*, ed. E. Matsushima, pp. 81–96. Heidelburg: C. Winter.

Dalley, S. 1991. *Myths from Mesopotamia*. Oxford: Oxford University Press.

———. 1997a. The Descent of Ishtar to the Underworld (1.108). In *Context of Scripture*, ed. W.W. Hallo and K.L. Younger, Vol. 1, pp. 381–84. Leiden: Brill.

———. 1997b. Nergal and Ereshkigal, Standard Babylonian Version (1.109). In *Context of Scripture*, ed. W.W. Hallo and K.L. Younger, Vol. 1, pp. 384–89. Leiden: Brill.

———. 1997c. Erra and Ishum (1.113). In *Context of Scripture*, ed. W.W. Hallo and K.L. Younger, Vol. 1, pp. 404–16. Leiden: Brill.

———. 1997d. Etana (1.131). In *Context of Scripture*, ed. W.W. Hallo and K.L. Younger, Vol. 1, pp. 453–57. Leiden: Brill.

Damerji, M.S. 1991. The Second Treasure of Nimrud. *Bulletin of the Middle East-*

ern Culture Center in Japan 5:9–16.

Darden, S. 1961. Free Will and Necessity in the Light of Oedipus Rex or What Would Have Happened to Oedipus if He Had Read the Book before Going on the Journey. In *The Sound of My Own Voice and Other Noises*, LP recording. Chicago: Mercury.

Davenport, T. 2007. An Anti-Imperialist Twist to the Gilgamesh Epic. In *Gilgamesh and the World of Assyria*, ed. J. Azize and N. Weeks, pp. 1–23. Ancient Near Eastern Studies Supplement 21. Leuven: Peeters.

Durant, W., and A. Durant. 1963. *The Age of Louis XIV*. The Story of Civilization 8. New York: Simon & Schuster.

Ebeling, L. 1953. *Literarische Keilschrifttexte aus Assur*. Berlin: Akademie-Verlag.

Farber, G. 1997. The Song of the Hoe (1.157). In *Context of Scripture*, ed. W.W. Hallo and K.L. Younger, Vol. 1, pp. 511–13. Leiden: Brill.

Farber, W. 1977. *Beschwörungsrituale an Ishtar und Dumuzi*. Wiesbaden: Franz Steiner.

Foster, B.J. 1997a. Atra-hasis (1.130). In *Context of Scripture*, ed. W.W. Hallo and K.L. Younger, Vol. 1, pp. 450–53. Leiden: Brill.

———. 1997b. Gilgamesh (1.132). In *Context of Scripture*, ed. W.W. Hallo and K.L. Younger, Vol. 1, pp. 458–60. Leiden: Brill.

———. 2007. Mesopotamia. In *A Handbook of Ancient Religions*, ed. J.R. Hinnells, pp. 161–213. Cambridge: Cambridge University Press.

Foxvog, D.A. 1993. Astral Dumuzi. In *The Tablet and the Scroll (Fs. Hallo)*, ed. M.E. Cohen, D.C. Snell, and D.W. Weisberg, pp. 103–8. Bethesda: CDL Press.

Frankfort, H. 1948. *Kingship and the Gods: A Study of Ancient Near Eastern Religion as the Integration of Society and Nature*. Chicago: University of Chicago Press.

Frayne, D. 2000a. Shu-ilishu (2.93). In *Context of Scripture*, ed. W.W. Hallo and K.L. Younger, Vol. 2, pp. 246–47. Leiden: Brill.

———. 2000b. Lipit-Eshtar (2.95). In *Context of Scripture*, ed. W.W. Hallo and K.L. Younger, Vol. 2, p. 247. Leiden: Brill.

———. 2000c. Rim-Sin (2.102A). In *Context of Scripture*, ed. W.W. Hallo and K.L. Younger, Vol. 2, p. 252. Leiden: Brill.

Frazer, J.G. 1914. *The Golden Bough: A Study in Magic and Religion*. Part IV: vols. 5–6, *Adonis, Attis, Osiris: Studies in the History of Oriental Religion*. London: Macmillan.

Fritz, M.M. 2003. "… und weinten um Tammuz": Die Götter Dumuzi-Ama'ušumgal'anna und Damu. AOAT 307. Münster: Ugarit-Verlag.

Frymer-Kensky, T. 1992. *In the Wake of the Goddesses: Women, Culture and Biblical Transformation of Pagan Myth*. New York: The Free Press.

Fuchs, A. 1994. *Die Inschriften Sargons II. aus Khorsabad*. Göttingen: Cuvillier Verlag.

George, A. 1999. *The Epic of Gilgamesh*. London: Penguin Press.

Grayson, A.K. 1991. Assyria: Sennacherib and Esarhaddon. In *The Cambridge Ancient History*, 2nd ed., ed. J. Boardman et al., Vol. 3(2): 108–41. Cambridge: Cambridge University Press.

Gurney, O.R. 1962. Tammuz Reconsidered: Some Recent Developments. *JSS* 7:147–60.

Hallo, W.W. 1997. A Neo-Babylonian Lament for Tammuz (1.118). In *Context of Scripture*, ed. W.W. Hallo and K.L. Younger, Vol. 1, pp. 419–20. Leiden: Brill.

———. 2000. Reforms of Uru-Inimgina (2.152). In *Context of Scripture*, ed. W.W. Hallo and K.L. Younger, Vol. 2, pp. 407–8. Leiden: Brill.

———. 2002. The Death of Shulgi (3.143). In *Context of Scripture*, ed. W.W. Hallo and K.L. Younger, Vol. 3, p. 315. Leiden: Brill.

Harris, R. 1991. Inanna-Ishtar as Paradox and Coincidence of Opposites. *History of Religions* 30:261–68.

Holloway, S. 2002. *Aššur Is King! Aššur Is King!* Culture and History of the Ancient Near East 10. Leiden: Brill.

Jacobsen, T. 1949. Mesopotamia: The Cosmos as a State. In *Before Philosophy: The Intellectual Adventure of Ancient Man*, ed. H. and H.A. Frankfort et al. Baltimore: Penguin.

———. 1961. Toward the Image of Tammuz. *History of Religions* 1:189–213.

———. 1997a. The Eridu Genesis (1.158). In *Context of Scripture*, ed. W.W. Hallo and K.L. Younger, Vol. 1, pp. 513–15. Leiden: Brill.

———. 1997b. The Sacred Marriage of Iddin-Dagan and Inanna (1.173). In *Context of Scripture*, ed. W.W. Hallo and K.L. Younger, Vol. 1, pp. 554–59. Leiden: Brill.

Jensen, P. 1924. Bēl im Kerker und Jesus im Grabe. *OLZ* 1924:574–80.

Katz, D. 1997. Gilgamesh and Akka (1.171). In *Context of Scripture*, ed. W.W. Hallo and K.L. Younger, Vol. 1, pp. 550–52. Leiden: Brill.

———. 2003. *The Image of the Netherworld in the Sumerian Sources*. Bethesda: CDL Press.

———. 2007. Sumerian Funerary Rituals in Context. In *Performing Death: Social Analyses of Funerary Traditions in the Ancient Near East and Mediterranean*, ed. N. Laneri, pp. 167–88. Oriental Institute Seminars 3. Chicago:

Oriental Institute.

Kilmer, A.D. 1972. The Mesopotamian Concept of Overpopulation and Its Solution as Reflected in the Mythology. *OrNS* 41:160–77.

Klein, J. 1995. Shulgi of Ur: King of a Neo-Sumerian Empire. In *Civilizations of the Ancient Near East*, ed. J.M. Sasson, Vol. 2, pp. 843–57. New York: Simon & Schuster.

———. 1997. Enki and Ninmah (1.159). In *Context of Scripture*, ed. W.W. Hallo and K.L. Younger, Vol. 1, pp. 516–18. Leiden: Brill.

———. 2006. Sumerian Kingship and the Gods. In *Text, Artifact and Image: Revealing Ancient Israelite Religion*, ed. G. Beckman and T.J. Lewis, pp. 115–31. Brown Judaic Studies 346. Providence: Brown University Press.

Kramer, S.N. 1959. Sumerian Literature and the Bible. *Analecta Biblica* 12:185–204.

———. 1963. The Sumerian Sacred Marriage Texts. *Proceedings of the American Philosophical Society* 107:485–527.

———. 1969. *The Sacred Marriage Rite*. Bloomington: Indiana University.

———. 1991. Death of Ur-Nammu. *Bulletin of the Middle Eastern Culture Center in Japan* 5:193–214.

Kutscher, R. 1990. The Cult of Dumuzi. In *Bar-ilan Studies in Assyriology Dedicated to Pinhas Artzi*, ed. J. Klein and A. Skaist, pp. 29–44. Ramat Gan: Bar-ilan University.

Lanfranchi, G.B. 2003. Royal Responsibility in the Neo-Assyrian Period. *Eretz Israel* 27:100–110.

Langdon, S. 1914. *Tammuz and Ishtar*. Oxford: Oxford University Press.

———. 1923. *The Epic of Creation*. Oxford: Oxford University Press.

Lapinkivi, P. 2004. *The Sumerian Sacred Marriage in the Light of Comparative Evidence*. SAA 15. Helsinki: Helsinki University Press.

Lawsen, J.C. 1910. *Modern Greek Folklore and Ancient Greek Religion*. Cambridge: Cambridge University Press.

Livingstone, A. 1989. *Court Poetry and Literary Miscellanea*. SAA 3. Helsinki: Helsinki University Press.

———. 1997a. Assurbanipal's Coronation Hymn (1.142). In *Context of Scripture*, ed. W.W. Hallo and K.L. Younger, Vol. 1, pp. 473–74. Leiden: Brill.

———. 1997b. An Assurbanipal Hymn for Shamash (1.143). In *Context of Scripture*, ed. W.W. Hallo and K.L. Younger, Vol. 1, p. 474. Leiden: Brill.

———. 1997c. A Late Piece of Constructed Mythology Relevant to the Neo-Assyrian and Middle Assyrian Coronation Hymn and Prayer (1.146). In

Context of Scripture, ed. W.W. Hallo and K.L. Younger, Vol. 1, pp. 476–77. Leiden: Brill.

Longman III, T. 1997. The Marduk Prophecy (1.149). In *Context of Scripture*, ed. W.W. Hallo and K.L. Younger, Vol. 1, pp. 480–81. Leiden: Brill.

Machinist, P. 2006. Kingship and Divinity in Imperial Assyria. In *Text, Artifact and Image: Revealing Ancient Israelite Religion*, ed. G. Beckman and Th.J. Lewis, pp. 152–88. Brown Judaic Studies 346. Providence: Brown University Press.

Marello, P. 1992. Vie Nomade. In *Florilegium marianum (Fs. Fleury)*, ed. J.M. Durand, pp. 115–25. Memoires de NABU 1. Paris: Société pour l'Étude du Proche-Orient Ancien.

Massé, H. 1954 [1938]. *Persian Beliefs and Customs*. New Haven: Human Relations Area Files.

McGinnis, J. 1987. A Neo-Assyrian Text Describing a Royal Funeral. *SAAB* 1(1): 1–12.

Mettinger, T.N.D. 2001. *The Riddle of Resurrection: "Dying and Rising Gods" in the Ancient Near East*. Coniectanea Biblica: Old Testament Series 50. Stockholm: Almqvist & Wiksell.

Michalowski, P. 2008. The Mortal Kings of Ur: A Short Century of Divine Rule. In *Religion and Power: Divine Kingship in the Ancient World and Beyond*, ed. N. Brisch, pp. 33–45. Chicago: The Oriental Institute.

Millard, A. 1997. Babylonian King Lists (1.134) In *Context of Scripture*, ed. W.W. Hallo and K.L. Younger, Vol. 1, p. 462. Leiden: Brill.

Moortgat, A. 1949. *Tammuz: der Unterblichkeitsglaube in der altorientalischen Bildkunst*. Berlin: Walter de Gruyter.

Paley, S.M., and R.P. Sobelewski. 1997. The Outer Façade of the Throne Room of the Northwest Palace of Ashurnasirpal II at Nimrud (Kalhu). In *Assyrien im Wandel der Zeiten (XXXIX RAI)*, ed. H. Waetzoldt and H. Hauptman, pp. 331–35. Heidelberg: Heidelberger Orientverlag.

Parpola, S. 1993. *Letters from Assyrian and Babylonian Scholars*. SAA 10. Helsinki: Helsinki University Press.

———. 1997. *Assyrian Prophecies*. SAA 9. Helsinki: Helsinki University Press.

Pisi, P. 1995. Il dio Lugal-URUxKÁR^{KI} e il culto degli antenati regali nella Lagaš pre-Sargonica. *Orientis Antiqui Miscellanea* 2:1–40.

———. 2001. Dumuzi-Tammuz:Alla ricerce di un dio. In *Quando un dio muore: morti e assenze divine nelle antiche tradizioni mediterranee*, ed. P. Xella, pp. 31–62. Verona: Grafiche Fiorini.

Polinger Foster, K. 2004–2005. The Hanging Gardens of Nineveh. *Iraq* 66-67(1): 207–20.

Porter, B.N. 2006. Feeding Dinner to a Bed: Reflection on the Nature of Gods in Ancient Mesopotamia. *SAAB* 15:307–31.

Renger, J. 1972–1975. Heilige Hochzeit. In *Reallexikon der Assyriologie* 4, pp. 251–59. Berlin: Walter de Gruyter.

Rogers, M.E. 1989 [1865]. *Domestic Life in Palestine*. London: Kegan Paul International.

Roth, M. 2000a. The Laws of Ur-Namma (Ur-Nammu) (2.153). In *Context of Scripture*, ed. W.W. Hallo and K.L. Younger, Vol. 2, pp. 408–10. Leiden: Brill.

———. 2000b. The Laws of Lipit-Ishtar (2.154). In *Context of Scripture*, ed. W.W. Hallo and K.L. Younger, Vol. 2, pp. 410–14. Leiden: Brill.

Saggs, H.W.F. 1962. *The Greatness that Was Babylon*. New York: New American Library.

———. 1975. Historical Texts and Fragments of Sargon II of Assyria. 1. The "Aššur Charter." *Iraq* 37:11–20.

Sallaberger, W. 1993. *Der kultische Kalender der Ur III-Zeit*. Berlin: Walther de Gruyter.

Scurlock, J.A. 1992. K 164 (*BA* 2:635): New Light on the Mourning Rites for Dumuzi. *RA* 86:53–67.

———. 1995. Death and the Afterlife in Ancient Mesopotamian Thought. In *Civilizations of the Ancient Near East*, ed. J.M. Sasson, Vol. 3, pp. 1883–93. New York: Simon & Schuster.

———. 1997. Ghosts in the Ancient Near East, Weak or Powerful. *Hebrew Union College Annual* 68:77–96.

———. 2002. Animal Sacrifice in Ancient Mesopotamian Religion. In *A History of the Animal World in the Ancient Near East*, ed. B.J. Collins, pp. 389–403. HdOr 64. Leiden: Brill.

———. 2006. But Was She Raped?: A Verdict Through Comparison. *NIN* 4:61–103.

Scurlock, J.A., and B.R. Andersen. 2005. *Diagnoses in Assyrian and Babylonian Medicine*. Urbana: University of Illinois Press.

Sefati, Y. 1997. The Womens' Oath (1.169A). In *Context of Scripture*, ed. W.W. Hallo and K.L. Younger, Vol. 1, pp. 540–41. Leiden: Brill.

Sladek, W.R. 1974. Inanna's Descent to the Netherworld. Ph.D. diss., Johns Hopkins. Ann Arbor, MI: UMI.

Slanski, K.E. 2007. The Mesopotamian "Rod and Ring." In *Regime Change in* the Ancient Near East and Egypt from Sargon of Agade to Saddam Hussein, ed. H. Crawford, pp. 37–59. Proceedings of the British Academy 136. Oxford: Oxford University Press.

Smith, J.Z. 2005 [1987]. Dying and Rising Gods. In *The Encyclopedia of Religion*. 2nd ed. Vol. 4, pp. 2535–40. Detroit: Thomson Gale.

Smith, M.S. 1998. The Death of "Dying and Rising Gods" in the Biblical World: An Update, with Special Reference to Baal in the Baal Cycle. *JSOT* 12:257–313.

Stone, E. 2005. Mesopotamian Cities and Countryside. In *The Companion to the Ancient Near East*, ed. D.C. Snell, pp. 141–54. London: Blackwell.

Tigay, J.H. 2003. Divine Creation of the King in Psalms 2.6. *Eretz Israel* 27:246–51.

Tsukimoto, A. 1985. *Untersuchungen zur Totenpflege (kispum) im alten Mesopotamien*. AOAT 216. Kevelaer: Butzon & Bercker.

van Buren, E.D. 1944. The Sacred Marriage in Early Times in Mesopotamia. *OrNS* 13:1–72.

Volk, K. 1995. *Inanna und Šukaletuda: Zur historisch-politischen Deutung eines sumerischen Literaturwerkes*. Wiesbaden: Harrassowitz Verlag.

Walker, C.B.F., and M.B. Dick. 2001. *The Induction of the Cult Image in Ancient Mesopotamia: The Mesopotamian Mis pî Ritual*. SAALT 1. Helsinki: University of Helsinki Press.

Winter, I. 1997. Art in Empire: The Royal Image and the Visual Dimensions of Assyrian Ideology. In *Assyria 1995. Proceedings of the 10th Anniversary Symposium of the Neo-Assyrian Text Corpus Project*, ed. S. Parpola and R.M. Whiting, pp. 359–81. Helsinki: Neo-Assyrian Text Corpus Project, University of Helsinki Press.

———. 2003. Ornament and the Rhetoric of Abundance in Assyria. *Eretz Israel* 27:252–64.

———. 2008. Touched by the Gods: Visual Evidence for the Divine Status of Rulers in the Ancient Near East. In *Religion and Power: Divine Kingship in the Ancient World and Beyond*, ed. N. Brisch, pp. 75–101. Chicago: The Oriental Institute.

Witzel, P.M. 1935. *Tammuz-Liturgien und Verwandtes*. AnOr 10. Rome: Pontifical Biblical Institute.

Yamauchi, E.M. 1966. Additional Notes on Tammuz. *JSS* 11:10–15.

Zimmern, D.H. 1926. *Das babylonische Neujahrsfest*. Der Alte Orient 25. Leipzig: J.C. Hinrichs'sche Buchhandlung.

Politics

6

Building the Pharaonic State

Territory, Elite, and Power in Ancient Egypt in the 3rd Millennium BCE

JUAN CARLOS MORENO GARCÍA

The aim of this chapter is to study some general trends dealing with the historical construction and transformation of the state administration and its relationship to royal office in ancient Egypt during the 3rd millennium BCE. Pharaonic Egypt has usually been considered an anomaly: nearly from the very beginning it emerges as an unified state encompassing a considerable territory by the standards of ancient polities, especially when compared with the relatively reduced palatial systems and city-states of the ancient Near East in the 3rd millennium or with the Greek *poleis* prior to the 5th century BCE. Moreover the Egyptian state seems to have been a remarkably solid one, when centuries of unity and apparent stability were broken only by occasional and rather limited episodes of crisis (the "intermediate periods"), immediately followed by a reunification which lasted for some centuries again. This stability is particularly noteworthy within the historical context of the Near East in the 3rd millennium BCE, especially when one thinks about contemporaneous and similar but rather ephemeral episodes of state building such as the Akkad empire or the Ur III kingdom.

Another fact which has drawn the attention of historians is the political primacy of Upper Egypt as a reserve of "statehood" for most of Pharaonic history, especially as this region was the focus of the political unification of the country after the Predynastic, the First Intermediate, and the Second Intermediate periods. Even after the end of the New Kingdom this region

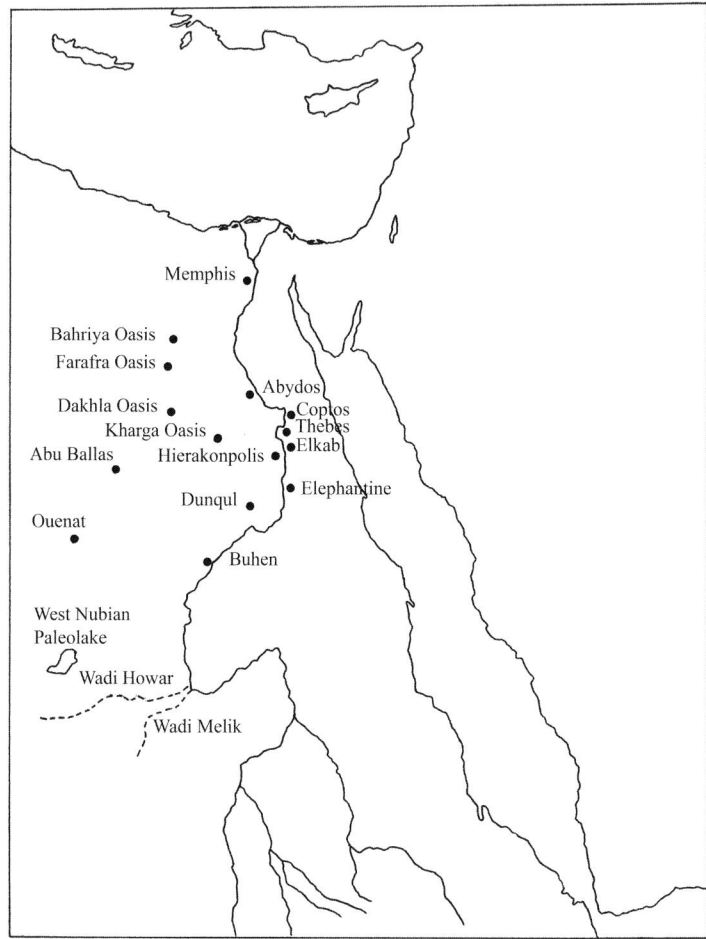

6.1. Map of Egypt and the Western Desert.

continued its autonomous existence for some centuries, while the forces of unification were usually led by external actors (Nubians, Assyrians, Achaemenids, Macedonians) or by the new but contested power of the Saite kings, themselves relying on foreign elements such as Greek mercenaries or international trade. But this kind of "regional determinism" may just be a mirage which, in addition to the apparent stability of the kingdom, diverts the focus of research from the very core of the problem: how the state was built and preserved and what were the means employed by the pharaoh to tie together in the long term so large a territory with its many regional foci of power, especially as the provinces regularly rose as alternative centers of authority. The answer to these questions calls for a rethinking of the early Pharaonic state and introducing authority, politics, and territorial organization as key elements of analysis.

THE ORIGINS OF THE PHARAONIC STATE: THE RISE OF HIERAKONPOLIS IN CONTEXT

The origins of the Pharaonic state are difficult to trace because of the scarcity of archaeological and written records and their uneven geographical distribution, being concentrated mostly in a limited number of cemeteries whose urban contexts are largely unknown. Meagre as this evidence might be, Egyptologists accept that some centers of political power arose about the last third of the 4th millennium in several Upper Egyptian localities like Hierakonpolis, Naqada, and Abydos, and that the kings of Abydos accomplished the political integration of the country and the control of neighboring areas through military expeditions against Nubia and the establishment of some kind of commercial "colonies" in southern Palestine which are attested just before and immediately after the unification of the country. However, recent discoveries at Hierakonpolis show that some kind of political authority was already in place at this locality in the first half of the 4th millennium as it displayed its emerging power in an elaborated form, including a life-size statue (Harrington 2004; Jaeschke 2004; for another Predynastic larger than life-size statue from Hierakonpolis, cf. Quibell and Green 1902:15, pl. 57), remarkable "royal" tombs, and complex ritual centers. These tombs precede the first royal burials at Abydos by several centuries and they raise many questions about the relationship between Hierakonpolis (the first "royal" local center?) and Abydos (from whence the first pharaohs came). The importance of Hierakonpolis, at least as a venerable ritual center, was recognized by later pharaohs who built quite impressive monuments there, such as Khasekhemwy, or enriched the local sanctuary with their statues, such as Pepi II. As for Naqada, many clay-sealings dating from Naqada IIb-c have been recovered from a very specific location at South Town, perhaps a kind of institutional or "communal" sector, since most of the clay administrative devices were primarily used for internal control of storage facilities. Even if the funerary evidence from this period indicates an increase in social stratification, Naqada remained a small town

(Di Maria 2007; Fattovich 2007). One can speculate that after the initial development of Hierakonpolis, Abydos became a kind of Predynastic "Memphis of the south," a new political center which arose in a fluvial basin far larger than that existing at Hierakonpolis and better positioned for controlling the exchange network with the Levant, as well as the northern areas of the Nile Valley being progressively integrated into the kingdom. After the consolidation of the united monarchy the capital was moved farther north, to the area of Memphis, where the control of the newly incorporated rich region of the Delta could be more easily accomplished. In any case, the recent discoveries at Hierakonpolis show that some kind of "royal" authority or primitive chiefdom existed about 3700 BCE, well before the Predynastic kings of Abydos, and one can infer that the model for the conquest and territorial organization of the kingdom could have first arisen in southernmost Egypt, in the region later known, precisely, as *Ḥn-Nḥn* "the interior of Hierakonpolis."

The regional role played by Hierakonpolis may be better understood in the light of new archaeological discoveries. First of all, the *serekhs* of some Predynastic rulers have been found in the deserts surrounding the city, at Wadi Mineh, Wadi Qash, and Wadi Um Balad (Eastern Desert), at Gebel Tjauti and west of Armant (Western Desert). They have also been found at distant places like Gebel Sheikh Suleiman in Nubia or the Kharga Oasis (Ikram and Rossi 2004), which confirms that some Predynastic polities were powerful enough to extend their influence far beyond the immediate area of the Nile Valley where they were based, towards the Red Sea, the western oases or Nubia, not to mention Palestine. The vessels from Dakhla found in the tomb of a chief of Abydos dating from Naqada II or the ceramics from the Naqada culture excavated in the Dakhla Oasis support this interpretation (Hartung and Hartmann 2005; Hope 2006). In this context Hierakonpolis appears as a crossroads of land and fluvial ways, connecting the east-west desert routes to the south-north axis of the Nile which led to Nubia and Palestine. The discovery of the bones of a young elephant recalls, in a rather unusual way, the importance of the contacts with the Sudan (Friedman 2004).

Second, the wide distribution of artifacts like the Clayton rings reveals that pastoral populations traveled extensively through the Eastern Sahara and the Nile Valley during the 4th and early 3rd millennium BCE thanks to the more humid conditions then prevalent in this region (Kuper 2007). The Megalake Chad covered a surface of about 350,000 km^2 during this period, whereas the West Nubian Palaeolake measured about 5,500 km², the Wadi Howar carried perennial water at least in its high and middle sections, and permanent settlers are attested in remote regions like Gilf el-Kebir. One should also mention the fact that the water emblems carved inside a rectilinear sign discovered at The-Water-Mountain-of-Redjedef, about 100 km southwest of Dakhla Oasis, were also discovered at Gala el-Sheikh in the Wadi el-Howar, about 700 km south of Dakhla. These emblems probably do not represent an Egyptian hieroglyph but rather some kind of symbol used by native populations (Kröpelin and Kuper 2006–2007). This vast area offered better conditions for cattle breeders and for the circulation of people and goods (Jesse et al. 2007). Nubians played an active role in this area; they are attested not only in the Nile Valley but also in the Western Desert (Lange 2004a, 2004b) and in southernmost Egypt, including Hierakonpolis. In fact, as Gatto has stressed, Upper Egypt and Lower Nubia and their cultural entities were not in opposition to one another, but in the Predynastic period were still expressions of the same cultural tradition, with strong regional variations, particularly in the last part of the 4th millennium BCE (Gatto 1996, 2000). In later periods Hierakonpolis remained a focus of ritual and burial activities for Nubian populations (Friedman 1992, 2000, 2001; Giuliani 2006). The discovery of more rock art with exciting ritual scenes in the area of Gebel Ouenat suggests that some kind of proto-Egyptian religious belief system could have left traces there around 4000 BCE (Le Quellec 2005). The importance of Nubian activities and Nubian contacts with Egypt are also conspicuous at the Qustul necropolis, a burial center for powerful Nubian chiefs whose tombs display astonishing wealth, including high-quality Egyptian artifacts. These rulers likely controlled Lower Nubia, which would have formed a political unit prior to the beginning of the Egyptian First Dynasty.

Third, the gradual worsening of climatic conditions of the Eastern Sahara, in a context of increasing aridity, could have led to the gradual disappearance of the pastoral activities and human settlement in this region and, as a consequence, the progressive abandonment of many of the land routes. The Nile then became the most important, but by no means the only, route through which to make contacts and exchanges. The eventual decline of Hierakonpolis and the rise of Abydos as the new emergent political power might be understood as the consequence of the movement of the center of political activity north to a location better situated for controlling this increasingly crucial axis of communication, as well as exploiting the rich agricultural potential of Middle Egypt and the trade routes to Palestine where many Egyptian factories or commercial centers were founded before the beginning of the First Dynasty (Van den Brink and Levy 2002). Keeping in mind the importance of Hierakonpolis as a ceremonial center during the Archaic period, one can suggest that its rulers simply moved to Abydos. In fact, the political initiatives of the last Predynastic Upper Egyptian rulers seem to have pursued the aim of eliminating any rival in the Nile. The conquest of the Delta and the campaigns against Nubia resulted in the destruction of the proto-state centered in Qustul and the emergence of Egypt as a single polity encompassing the lower section of the Nile Valley. Egypt's capital was moved farther to the north, to Memphis, in order to better assert its control over an extensive area that covered more than 50 percent of the agricultural land of the country. The construction of a fortress at Elephantine represents the culmination of the aggressive Egyptian attitude toward her southern neighbors. Nevertheless, Nubians are attested at Elephantine and other localities south of Armant during the Thinite period, and this circumstance prevents us from considering the area of Aswan as a sealed border between two different cultural areas.

TERRITORIAL ORGANIZATION AND ELITE CO-OPTING AT THE BEGINNING OF THE OLD KINGDOM

The discovery of thousands of seal stamps in the tomb of Khasekhemwy, the last king of the Second Dynasty, reveals the early existence of some kind of territorial organization, since some historical provinces are mentioned together with administrative titles and the names of the king (Engel 2006). Nevertheless the ink inscriptions on the vessels from the funerary complex of Pharaoh Djoser (about 2686–2667 BCE) as well as the seal stamps from Elephantine dating from the Third Dynasty are the most important sources for the study of the basic features of the territorial organization of the kingdom at this early date (Pätznick 2005).

First, these brief texts reveal the existence of a network of royal agricultural centers (the *ḥwt-ꜥꜣt* being the most frequently attested whereas the *ḥwt* are also mentioned) which coexisted with the *pr* "domains" of some individuals. Some of these royal domains bear the name of the god Horus (Engel 2004), and some of the institutions whose name is composed with

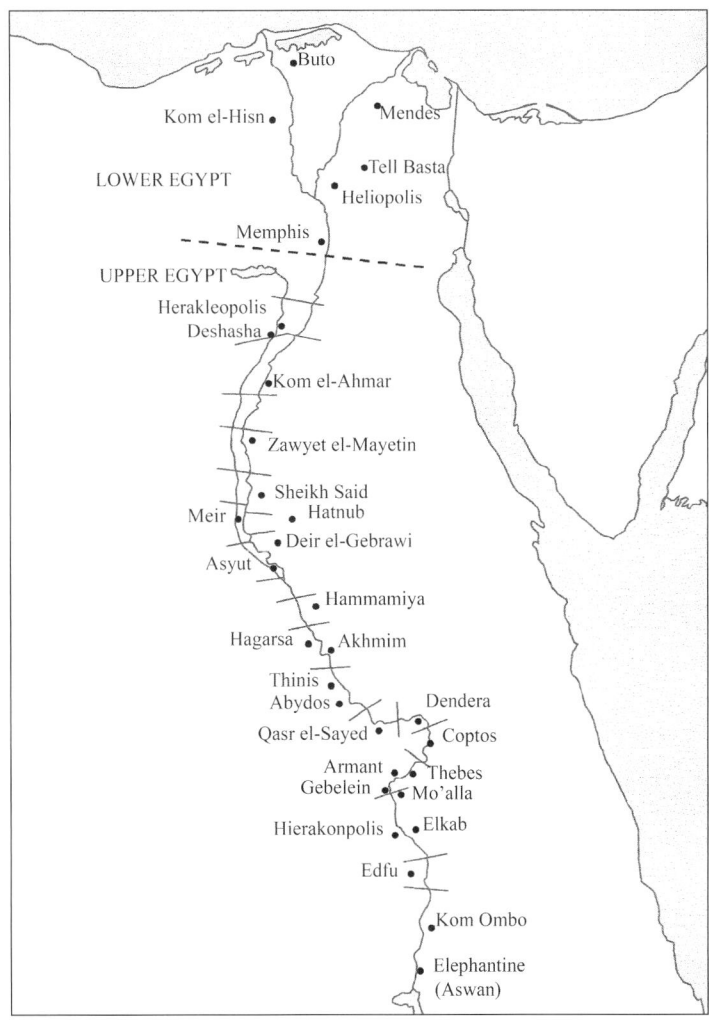

6.2. Map of Egypt in the 3rd millennium BC.

the element *ḥwt* were perhaps some kind of specialized royal workshop like the *ḥwt-mḥꜥ*, *ḥwt-ṯḥnt*, or *ḥwt-šmꜥw* known from later inscriptions. The ink texts from another enormous set of vessels, recovered at Abydos and dating from the Second Dynasty, confirm this model as they mention institutions named after the element *ḥwt*, like the *ḥwt-nbw* or the *ḥwt-wr(t)* (Regulski 2004). It seems that the territorial organization of the kingdom consisted of a duality of agricultural centers belonging to the crown. The first of these were the *ḥwt-ꜥꜣt* and *ḥwt*, which were administered by royal officials called *ḥqꜣ ḥwt-ꜥꜣt* and *ḥqꜣ ḥwt*. The second were the *pr* domains administered by individuals whose links to the royal administration are poorly understood, since it is impossible to determine if they were local magnates who exercised a personal control over the territorial units called *pr* or if they were royal agents in charge of the administration of these circumscriptions. Another problem is our ignorance of the exact geographical distribution of these centers and circumscriptions: were they evenly scattered over the country or were they only prevalent in specific regions because of their strategic and/or economic importance? As regards this important question, our understanding of the role of provincial governors or of specific nome leaders is rather limited. Only the *sšm tꜣ* played an active role as can be inferred from their frequent mention in the ink inscriptions, but it is impossible to ascertain the geographical extent of their authority or the scope of their activities (Moreno García 1999:233–38).

Second, the seal stamps from Elephantine show that this locality played the role of royal fortress and trade center in the southernmost frontier of the kingdom, and that its officials were supplied by institutions from the area of Abydos (Pätznick 2005). Third, the archaeological remains of several small step pyramids have been recovered at some localities in Upper and Middle Egypt—perhaps significantly not in the Delta—thus asserting the local symbolic presence of the crown (Seidlmayer 1996:122–25). This early evidence confirms the importance of a territorial organization based more on a network of royal centers scattered all over the country than on a structure of provinces clearly marked out and controlled by local governors. The titles of the Delta governor Metjen, from the very beginning of the Fourth Dynasty (about 2620 BCE), show that the administrative organization of Lower Egypt, where royal centers like *ḥwt-ꜥꜣt* or *ḥwt* were gradually replacing the *pr* circumscriptions, was far from complete even some centuries after the political unification of the country (Sethe 1933:1–7).

Nevertheless, increasing archaeological evidence reveals that the local elite of the Third Dynasty (2686–2613 BCE) were powerful enough to build great tombs (mastabas, rock-cut tombs) in styles recalling the royal centers at Memphis and Abydos, as the old evidence from Beit Khallaf or Reqaqnah, or the more recent finds from Thebes, Elkab, and the El-Bersheh area show (Arnold 1976:11–18; Vörös 2002:207; Huyge 2003). These tombs at this early date raise the question about the integration of the local elite in the governmental apparatus or about the nature of their ties with the central administration. It seems clear that their collaboration with the monarchy was essential to rule and preserve the kingdom, even if the visibility of the local magnates is much less evident than in later periods, when their decorated tombs became a prominent and symbolic landmark of the provincial landscape. The inscriptions of Khor el-Aqiba in northern Nubia are a good illustration of this problem: these texts, dated from the Fourth Dynasty (2613–2498 BCE), record the expeditions led by two *rḫ nzwt* "acquaintances of the king" from the seventeenth nome of Upper Egypt and from the fourteenth nome of Lower Egypt (López 1967). We know virtually nothing about the history or the social hierarchies of the seventeenth nome of Upper Egypt during the Old Kingdom. Similarly, the sources concerning the provincial elite of the Delta are very scarce and usually limited to a handful of documents from the Memphite necropolis such as funerary inscriptions and administrative papyri. Once again sealing stamps are an invaluable source of information about these elusive provincial elite, as some Early Dynastic examples found at Mendes show (Redford 2008). Scarce as this evidence is, these inscriptions prove nevertheless that local magnates collaborated with the monarchy and took over important functions, even if they did not leave behind or use the kind of monuments one would usually associate with the ruling elite. Perhaps they constituted an informal autonomous authority, not fully integrated in the official administration, and only mobilized for some specific tasks, like the recruitment of workers or military contingents. Later inscriptions, like the autobiography of Weni of Abydos, enumerate the local authorities who contributed to a military expedition abroad, whereas Imeny, the Middle Kingdom governor of Beni Hassan, proclaims that he led a contingent from his own nome three times, both for military and architectural purposes in the service of the king. Later sources also confirm that the "mayors" (*ḥȝtj-ʿ*) participated alongside the local contingents of workers (*ḥsbw*) in activities organized by the state.

We can infer that the territorial authority of the pharaoh during the early phases of the Old Kingdom existed as a combination of a network of local centers founded at strategic points and of local authorities tied to the monarchy in a more or less informal way, not necessarily designated by the rank and function titles so typical of the central royal administration, and with titles referring only rarely to activities carried out in a given, precise area. Their access to the kind of prestigious items normally displayed by the ruling elite (decorated tombs, inscribed objects, high quality workmanship, etc.) seems to have been rather limited. Signs of royal patronage are rare, even if a few local officials could afford a statue, precious vessels (Brunton 1927:11–12, pl. 18), or even a mastaba. Examples of this type of patronage can be found in Thebes where two mastabas dating from the beginning of the Fourth Dynasty and from the Fifth Dynasty are known (Ginter et al. 1998), and in Mendes where the mastabas of Nefershutba and his son Ahapuba are dated around the reign of Neferirkara (Cody 2008:54). Nevertheless, contacts with the palatial sphere may sometimes be inferred from the archaeological record. Bowls of precious stone and vessels inscribed with the name of Pharaoh Sneferu, from the beginning of the Fourth Dynasty (2613–2589 BCE), have been recovered in Upper Egypt localities like Elkab, Naga ed-Der, El-Mahâsna, Reqaqnah, and Gebel el-Teir among others. They were probably prestigious gifts delivered by the king to some prominent provincial potentates well established in areas like Elkab, Abydos, and the 16th nome of Upper Egypt, the same provinces where the small step pyramids and remarkable non-royal tombs were also built during the Third Dynasty (Willems 2008:82).

Later sources state that co-opting select members of the most powerful provincial families, marrying provincial women, giving princesses in marriage to high officials, creating royal cult centers in the nomes (like the *ḥwt-k3*), donating fields to local sanctuaries, or enhancing the circulation of the palatial culture in the nomes seem to have been the most common means employed by pharaohs to reinforce their political and symbolic power. Through these methods the king continuously (re)created a "national" ruling elite tied to the monarchy who benefited both economically and symbolically from their collaboration with the monarch. In spite of the scarcity of sources, it is possible to find some traces of the validity of this policy in the earlier periods of the Old Kingdom: the Fourth Dynasty king Menkaura (2532–2503 BCE) was remembered as the donor of a field of about one acre to the temple of Hathor at Tehna (again in the 16th nome of Upper Egypt) (Sethe 1933:24–31), whereas the exceptionally decorated tomb—according to the provincial standards of the Fourth Dynasty—of Kai-Khent of El-Hammamiya belonged to a couple bearing the titles of "son of the king" and "daughter of the king," (El-Khouli and Kanawati 1990). In this respect the oldest papyrological archive, the Gebelein papyri of the later Fourth Dynasty, is of the greatest importance. The documents concern a domain (*pr-ḏt*) embracing several villages presumably granted, as usually was the case with domains of this kind, to an official. The inhabitants of the domain were administratively classified, frequently designated by occupation or "fiscal" categories like *ḥm-nzwt* or "serf of the king," and constrained to work and deliver items to the state (Posener-Kriéger and Demichelis 2004). What makes this fascinating set of documents so exceptional is that they illuminate, at this early date, the nature of the links between the local potentates and the crown: granting villages and a work force to a local official implied in no way a loss of revenues or power for the central administration. Quite the contrary, it asserted its control over the provincial resources, helped by local magnates who became thus integrated into the administrative and economic structure of the kingdom, and whose economic power and political authority were thus enhanced and legitimized thanks to their collaboration with the monarchy. This mutually fruitful relationship also allowed the king to define the local elite, to nourish the ranks of the bureaucracy, and to tie the local magnates closely to a network of personal relations encompassing all the country and dominated by the central figure of the pharaoh. Later inscriptions mention that, apart from these measures, the creation of local institutions like temples or *ḥwt* were key to the stability of the kingdom, as they were foci of royal authority and allowed the provincial elite, tied to the monarchy, to grow around them. The royal donations of fields to the provincial temples recorded in the Old Kingdom annals, for example Tehna, suggest that the pharaohs of the Fourth Dynasty maintained close links with at least some local sanctuaries and with the priestly elite who ruled them. Actually, prestige items belonging to priests are among the rare sources evoking the provincial elite during the Third and Fourth Dynasties, like the high-quality vessels of Nemti-hetep of Qau or the statues of Nefershemem of Elkab (Brunton 1927: pl. 18; Wildung 1999).

PROVINCIAL TEMPLES, *ḤWT*, AND THE FORMATION OF THE LOCAL ELITE IN THE OLD KINGDOM (2685–2125 BCE)

Until the end of the Fifth Dynasty, about 2375 BCE, sources relating to the local authorities and the nature of their links with the central administration are very scarce. Only rarely the brief development of an elite provincial cemetery, the titles of some dignitaries, or the discovery of rather sparse but precious administrative evidence—like the fragments of lists of officials exerting territorial responsibilities in the Neferirkara papyri (Posener-

Kriéger 1976: 397–400)—cast light on some aspects of the administration of the provinces before the Sixth Dynasty. To the extent that this evidence is representative, it is possible to infer that royal centers like the *ḥwt-ꜥȝt*, the towers *swnw*, and the agricultural domains of the crown *nwt mȝwt* (literally "the new localities") continued to dot the Egyptian landscape and helped to assert the presence of the king's authority, in a formal way (Moreno García 1999:233–41; 2006b).

The temples continued to receive considerable amounts of land from the pharaoh, sometimes accompanied by workers (*mrt*) and production centers (*pr-šnꜥ*) (Sethe 1933:235–49). The discovery of royal monuments at localities with great political or symbolic importance allows us to glimpse the continuity of the contacts between the court and the local magnates, even if the administrative titles of the officials or the surviving inscriptions have left no trace of these links. However, the royal decrees found at Abydos and El-Bersheh, the pillar of Userkaf at Tod, and the statues of Neferirkara and Isesi at Karnak and Abydos, respectively, suggest that the invisibility of the local elite is more perceived than real, and that their role in the stability and the politics of the kingdom justified the pharaohs displaying locally the kind of prestige investment (land donations, "artistic" creations) which legitimized both the role of the king and the local authority exerted by the provincial potentates. This evidence is invaluable as it shows the continuity of the links tying the Memphite court to the provincial elite, even if the details, regional variants, and precise nature of these contacts remain largely unknown before the Sixth Dynasty. It also helps explain why the nomes or the provincial officials became so conspicuous in the Sixth Dynasty sources. For the first time they simply became more visible, even if they were nothing more than the heirs of their largely invisible predecessors of the Third to Fifth Dynasties. Lastly, it also helps balance the picture of the organization of pharaonic power in a period where the sources issuing from the Memphite area are so prevalent in the epigraphic and monumental record. Inscriptions from the tomb of Nikaankh of Tehne are a good example of the role played by the royal land allocations to provincial temples, as well as by the agricultural centers of the crown, in framing local elites tied to the pharaoh. At the beginning of the Fifth Dynasty, this provincial official and his family succeeded in controlling both the local temple of the goddess Hathor and the royal agricultural centers of the crown in the province as *jmj-r nwwt mȝwt* "overseer of the new localities" and *jmj-r pr n ḥwt-ꜥȝt* "administrator of a great *ḥwt.*" The texts in Nikaankh's tomb also describe the confirmation of the former donation of a field, granted during the Fourth Dynasty, by the kings of the Fifth Dynasty, thus showing the continuity of the royal policy in this region over time (Sethe 1933:24–31).

But it is only from the end of the Fifth Dynasty forward (about 2350 BCE) that the growing number of inscriptions and decorated tombs allow the local

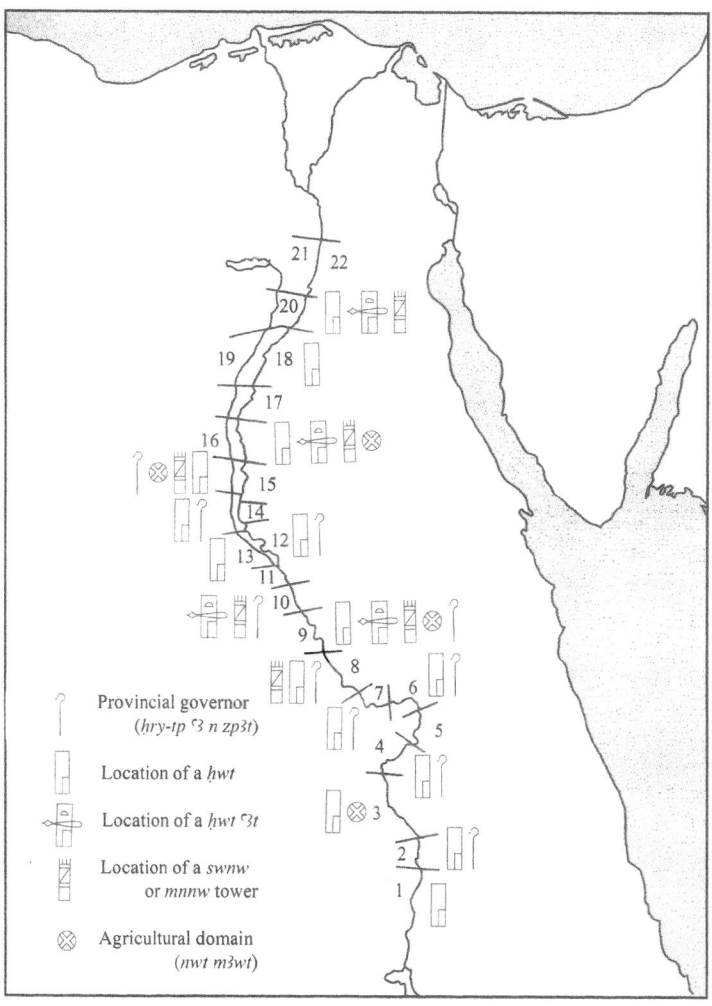

6.3. Provincial administration in 19 Upper Egyptian nomes (Dynasties IV–VI, ca. 2600–2180 BC).

elite, for the first time, to surface in many areas of Upper Egypt in quantities great enough to permit us to draw some sociological and political conclusions. Temples and agricultural royal centers (*ḥwt*) were now the main foci of the local and royal governing authority in the provinces, and the access to these institutions became a fundamental source of economic power and legitimacy for local leaders. At the same time, the aim of these centers—particularly the *ḥwt*-foundations—was to make the royal domination of a region effective through "islands of authority," especially over the richer agrarian zones or the more strategic areas of the Nile Valley (Viso 2006:176–77). The shaping of these "islands of authority" was subordinated to the raising of tribute and the establishment of political power structures into which the local leaders could be incorporated (Moreno García 2004, 2005a).

Private inscriptions state that the *ḥqꜣ ḥwt* or "governor of a *ḥwt*" was a state official appointed by the administration. The inscriptions in Metjen's tomb, from the early Fourth Dynasty, reveal that a *ḥwt* could control several villages, whereas the autobiography of Ibi of Der el-Gebrawi states that extensive fields of about 50 ha provided with workers and cattle were administered by a *ḥwt*, a fact confirmed by the ritual texts where the *ḥwt* appear as administrative centers asserting their control over several fields and domains (Moreno García 1999, 2001a). The role played by the *ḥwt* in providing the agents of the king with supplies is illustrated by the inscriptions of Hatnub, which mention the resources delivered by the local *ḥwt* to the teams of workers sent to the quarries, the organization of the expeditions by an overseer of *ḥwt*, or the close relationship between the *ḥwt* and the agricultural domains *nwt mꜣwt* (graffiti 1 & 6: Anthes 1928; cf. also Sethe 1933:87, 2). In short, temples and *ḥwt* were part of a network of economic and production centers spread all over the country and controlled by the crown. Their production was usually at the disposal of the king's officials as is stated in the letter sent by Pharaoh Pepy II to Harkhuf of Aswan: "Orders have been brought to the governor(s) of the new localities, the companion(s) and the overseer(s) of priests to command that supplies be furnished from what is under the charge of each from every *ḥwt* belonging to a processing center and from every temple without making any exemption" (Sethe 1933:131, 4–6).

As for the highest position in a temple, the *jmj-r ḥm(w)-nṯr* or "overseer of prophets," it was usually held by local magnates and controlled by powerful provincial families who sometimes exercised a *de facto* monopoly over this title. In fact, the control of the local temples appears to be an important foundation for the relationship between the provincial elite and the central state, as well as in the local balance of power. The donations of land by the pharaoh increased the patrimony held by the sanctuaries, and the building of royal chapels (ḥwt-k3) or the delivery of royal statues transformed the temples into foci of royal ideology. But, at the same time, these measures allowed for integrating the local magnates into the governmental apparatus of the kingdom and for establishing a local elite devoted to the service of the king, interested in collaborating with the monarchy and educated in the values of the palatial culture as the autobiography of Qar of Edfu proclaims (Moreno García 2004). This means that the temples were also an instrument for selecting the representatives of the crown at a local level, for enriching them through their access to the fields and revenues of the sanctuaries, and for breaking the solidarity of the local dominant families. Under this system some local elites now had new opportunities to enhance their social position by developing an individual career in the administration, especially after a period of training and education in a palatial environment at the capital, becoming thus more autonomous from the constraints and strategies imposed by their kin. The case of El-Hawawish is a good example of this procedure. The dominant family of this area was composed of several branches; firstborns of the main branch controlled the local temple as well as the dignity of the position of "great overlord of the nome," while their brothers were employed in secondary positions. As for the descendants of the minor branches, they were usually employed in the central administration of the kingdom, where on two occasions they reached the position of vizier.

Occasionally, a combination of epigraphic sources from both the Memphite area and El-Hawawish allows us to glimpse how this system operated (Moreno García 2005b). This is true in the case of Tjeti-Kaihep, an official who lived during the Sixth Dynasty and whose autobiography indicates that he entered in the service of the king when he was a young man. Some inscriptions from El-Hawawish state that he was the son and brother of two great overlords of the nome. The titles borne by Tjeti-Kaihep are rather exceptional for a provincial official, as he was responsible for the Double Treasury, chief of the royal harem, and Great Seer, among other dignities, which point to a career one would expect to be continued at the highest level in the central administration. It is also probable that a tomb built at the royal necropolis of Saqqara for a high official from El-Hawawish was, in fact, intended for him. Nevertheless, Tjeti-Kaihep returned to his province, where he became great chief of the nome and chief of priests, thus combining the highest responsibilities over both the nome and the local temple dedicated to the god Min, as his family had been doing for several generations. Tjeti's unexpected return to El-Hawawish may be interpreted as the consequence of the premature death of his older brother without an heir, and it also suggests that he preferred to ensure the control of the traditional local base of power of his family instead of developing a high-ranking career in the capital. Finally, another official of lesser rank from the same nome went to Memphis, perhaps in order to replace Tjeti or just to support the interests of the leaders of the province at the royal court, among other possibilities. In fact, several officials from El-Hawawish are attested in the Memphite cemeteries. What makes Tjeti-Kaihep's case so exceptional is that it provides us a rare insight into the strategies of power pursued by a provincial elite family at both the local and palatial level.

If Tjeti's inscriptions present the promotion and the alternative strategies of power available to a high-ranking provincial magnate, the decrees of Coptos, on the other hand, constitute an example of "elite building" and the co-opting of lower-ranking local leaders. This important set of inscriptions, dating for the most part from the Sixth Dynasty, show how the usual procedure of donating fields to a local sanctuary was immediately followed by the appointment of some members of the local elite (including the chiefs of villages), together with some officials, to the council in charge of administering the agricultural domain just founded. Thus village chiefs appear as essential intermediaries between the central administration and the local potentates, on the one hand, and the peasant population, on the other (Moreno García 1998). The terminology concerning their categories or social rank is nearly absent in the official sources, and the texts evoking them usually employ rather general terms like "chief" (*ḥrj-tp*) or "great one" (*wr*). Yet the absence of sources and their stereotypical representation in the iconography of the elite tombs should not make us forget that they were essential links in the chain of command tying the palace to the villages. Sometimes, local elites were rich enough or had the right contacts to provide prestige items for themselves, like the statues of the governors Ankhudjes and Yankh (Moreno García 2001b). But in other cases the sources state only that a plurality of chiefs was present in a given nome at the same time, thus indicating that a "great chief of a nome" was probably the most eminent leader among his local peers. Only once are the texts a little more explicit about the social rank of one of these chiefs. A graffito discovered in Nubia at Sayala states that the overseer of craftsmen, Irunetjeru, was the father of the governor of Hierakonpolis Reniqer (Satzinger 2006:140–41). Finally, there is another group of provincial magnates for whom the sources remain nearly silent—the *jmj-r pr* "overseer of a domain," the administrators of the domains of the elite. Only two examples demonstrate their importance as members of a local sub-elite indispensable for ruling the affairs of the high rank leaders (Moreno García 2001b): a collective appeal to the living preserved in an inscription from Qasr el-Sayed which is addressed to them and to the chiefs of the villages, and a Theban inscription from the First Intermediate Period, in which a scribe boasts of having worked for some overseers of a domain.

These texts contribute to a more balanced understanding of the ways in which power and authority were asserted at a local level. Even when the official sources insist on the apparent all-encompassing role played by the agents and bureaus of the pharaoh, it must be remembered that the effectiveness of the royal administration was only possible thanks to the collaboration of local leaders more or less integrated into the political, economic, and ritual apparatus controlled by the king. Many other aspects, like the extent of the patronage networks, the formation of local and palatial factions, or the informal ways in which authority and power were spread from top to bottom and vice-versa remain largely unknown. But the monarchy tried to tie the local leaders closely to the ritual and prestige circuits focusing on the king. In fact, an appointment as (temporary) priests or *ḫntj-š* in the royal temples of the capital appears conspicuously in the private and official inscriptions as a source of honor and income, as the inscription of Sabni of Aswan or the lists of administrators of Lower Egypt in the Abusir archive show.

In contrast to the temples, the *ḥwt* was seldom a path to social promotion to the highest offices of the state during the Sixth Dynasty. However, in the more limited sphere of the provincial world the *ḥwt* played an economic role important enough to enhance the position of the officials in charge of these centers, as the monuments of the local *ḥqꜣ ḥwt* show with greater frequency from the beginning of the Sixth Dynasty on. One of the rare exceptions to this rule was Mehu of Mendes, a *ḥqꜣ ḥwt* who managed to become vizier and to bequeath this position to his descendants, probably thanks to his contacts with the royal family and with some high officials in the palatial circles, like the noble Shepsipuptah mentioned on the lintel of his tomb (Moreno García 2006a). However, the overwhelming majority of sources at our disposal indicate that temples played an important role in defining the local elite whose prestige, revenues, and contacts with the central, palatial elite were largely dependent on their integration into the provincial sanctuaries. As a counterpart, there also existed the possibility that control of the temples by the same families for several generations involved an increasing degree of autonomy in the long term resulting in the gradual erosion of the authority exercised by the royal administration. Nevertheless, as the royal decrees of Coptos show, the temples were considered institutions dependent on the royal administration, since the pharaohs built royal chapels (ḥwt-kȝ) in the provincial sanctuaries and financed them with their own resources; they could also abolish the privileges (i.e., fiscal exemptions) temporarily granted to the cult centers. Additionally, numerous royal agents and bureau chiefs frequently demanded workers, including the priests themselves, and a variety of goods from the temples.

Temples and *ḥwt* certainly contributed to building up and defining the provincial elite, but this was only one aspect of the complex relationships between local leaders, provincial institutions, and the state, because the local elite also participated in building and defining the state. In fact the growth of the governmental apparatus in the nomes opened new opportunities for provincial magnates, which could eventually lead to the development of spheres of power increasingly independent of the central authority, especially when the channels for delegating power became less fluid and these institutions could be used primarily for the promotion of specifically local interests. The growth of the local resources could not only increase the tribute due to the state but also enrich some local potentates whose positions became thus enhanced. Yet temples or *ḥwt* never became private possessions, and the revenues of the local dominant families seem to have been dependent, in a significant way, on their ties with the state and its institutions. The "traffic" in official positions, such as priest or mayor, and revenues granted by the state or its institutions, such as shares of allotments, priestly services, etc., figure prominently in the funerary arrangements of the elite, as attested in later sources. Additionally, access to official positions or promotions in the administration or the court opened new possibilities for enrichment and contacts much larger than those available at a local level.

In fact, it is very difficult to discern the existence of big private landowners from the available records. Inscriptions also express the desire of successful officials to transfer their wealth uniquely to their heirs, without the interference of the broader family (i.e., the brothers of the official), thus breaking the solidarity of kin affiliation and weakening its collective interests. Both circumstances probably explain why periods of political crisis were not followed by the emergence of some kind of feudal system, as the sources of official revenues could become scarcer or less centrally controlled but never private property. It probably also explains why the state succeeded in reorganizing itself after periods of crisis, when the local officials could usurp royal prerogatives or divert "public" resources to their own benefit when no central authority was in place, but they never became private property owners. Hence a crisis of the state was usually followed by the development of a multiplicity of micro-states, not by the collapse of the state concept and the subsequent rise of feudal lords.

REGIONAL VARIANTS AND THE REALITIES OF LOCAL POWER AT THE END OF THE 3RD MILLENNIUM

The general model just discussed exhibits considerable local nuances and regional variants which highlight the importance of the informal ties between the local elite and the royal court, usually hidden behind the rigidity of rank and titles or the standardized art of the period.

First of all, no "great overlords of the nome" are attested in the Delta or in the northernmost provinces of Middle Egypt. However, the concentration of *ḥq3 ḥwt* "governor of a *ḥwt*" in the Memphite necropolis, as opposed to the regular distribution of their colleagues in the Upper Egyptian elite cemeteries, suggests different models of territorial administration were adopted for Lower and Upper Egypt. It appears that in Lower Egypt more direct control was exercised within a 200 km radius of the capital at Memphis. Nevertheless, epigraphic evidence shows that the co-optation of members of the local elite was a common practice in the north as well as in the south. Both Weni of Abydos and Mehu of Mendes had the dignity of vizier bestowed on them. Yet the Delta seems to have been administered in a more centralized way. The titles of Metjen, from the beginning of the Fourth Dynasty, reveal a landscape where the *pr* domains, each one encompassing several localities, were being replaced by royal centers—usually *ḥwt-*

ꜥ3t, but also ḥwt—which controlled the same areas. The full administrative organization of the Delta seems to have been longstanding, not immune from occasional uprisings, as recorded in the monuments of Narmer and Khasekhemwy, and probably stimulated by the enormous architectural projects of the monarchy in the Memphite area and the production centers that were needed to support them. Specialized economic centers in the Delta like Kom el-Hisn provided livestock for the capital, whereas localities like Mendes, Tell Basta, or the Eastern Delta contain architectural evidence for the existence of local elites with ties to the court. Later ink inscriptions on the blocks of the Middle Kingdom pyramids in the Fayum area show a similar pattern of territorial administration, owing to the fact that corvée labor came from the localities and domains of Middle and Lower Egypt, the regions more directly governed by the monarchy.

Conversely, the relationship between the local authorities, the provincial institutions (temples, ḥwt), and the pharaoh displays greater variability in Upper Egypt, probably as a result of the local distribution of power. Royal centers, like the ḥwt, were for the first time frequently attested south of Akhmim from the beginning of the Sixth Dynasty, and the local elite played an important role in the affairs of the kingdom. Magnates like Qar of Edfu were educated in the royal court whereas many provincial viziers came from localities just south of Akhmim. The creation of the position of jmj-r Šmꜥw "overseer of Upper Egypt" probably was a consequence of the growing importance of the South, its resources and its leaders. It is also true that in some provinces where the local temples played a prominent role, the most archetypal royal center, the ḥwt, was absent (Coptos) or nearly absent (Akhmim, Elkab), whilst in others it was common that both institutions were controlled by a single official. A division of functions among local magnates is also evident in certain provinces, like El-Hawawish, since some officials bore titles representing central administration offices while others monopolized local dignities like those of chief of the provincial sanctuary or great overlord of the nome. The study of some cases may cast some light on the regional differences between nomes and also on the nuances of the balance of power between the royal administration and the families of local leaders.

Akhmim offers again a unique wealth of sources. At the end of the Fifth Dynasty the inscriptions from the main provincial necropolis at El-Hawawish reveal that the prevalent local conditions were not different from those of other Upper Egyptian localities (Moreno García 2005b). Royal agricultural centers like the *ḥwt-ꜥꜣt* "the great *ḥwt*" or the *nwt mꜣwt* "new localities" were well attested in the nome as well as titles concerning the organization of the work force of the province (*jmj-r zꜣw Šmꜥw* "overseer of the phyles of Upper Egypt," *jmj-r wpt jdw* "overseer of missions of the young men," *wr 10 Šmꜥw* "greatest of the ten of Upper Egypt"). The only "overseer of works of the king" (*jmj-r kꜣt nt nzwt*) of the nome lived during the Fifth Dynasty, like four out of the five *rḫ nzwt* "acquaintance of the king" known at El-Hawawish, a title usually held by the local agents of the crown working for the central administration (*ḥwt wrt, pr nzwt*) during this period. But important changes intervened from the beginning of the Sixth Dynasty, when a new family whose local onomastic shows no contact with the former administrators of the nome exerted a true monopoly over the functions concerning the temple or the newly created position of *ḥrj-tp ꜥꜣ n zpꜣt* "great overseer of the nome." Another contemporaneous feature is the increasing prominence of the temple of Min as the main economic institution of the area, to the point that it was not necessary to found royal centers (like the *ḥwt*). Some rather exceptional titles evoke the fields, workers, offerings, or processing centers of the sanctuary of Min (Moreno García 1998). In contrast, no traces either of *ḥwt* or of agricultural centers of the crown are attested at the necropolis during the Sixth Dynasty. It seems as if the elevation of the new dominant family was accompanied by a transfer of goods from the royal sphere to the temple, a movement well attested at Coptos, for instance, but not on so large a scale. This circumstance is particularly noteworthy as *ḥwt* are nevertheless documented in two other minor necropolises of the nome, thus suggesting the existence of several foci of power in this area where El-Hawawish enjoyed a unique position. In any case, this situation cannot be claimed as evidence of the weakness of the royal authority in the nome, as many members from the minor branches of the dominant family worked for the central administration and often became viziers, whereas high officials from the main branch lived and worked at Memphis before returning to Akhmim, like Tjeti-Kaihep mentioned above. Even a royal chapel was founded in the temple and its construction was financed with the resources of the central administration. The underlying reasons for the special circumstances at El-Hawawish are rather difficult to ascertain, but it has been suggested that a queen called Iput, from the beginning of the Sixth Dynasty, could have come from this nome.

No *ḥwt* are attested at Coptos and only one at Elkab. El-Hawawish,

Coptos, and Elkab display a rather limited number of the royal agricultural centers that are so characteristic of the other nomes of Upper Egypt, perhaps because of the overwhelming importance of the temples in these regions (Moreno García 2004). The dominant sanctuaries at Coptos and Elkab were governed by true dynasties of chief of priests and, in the case of Elkab, the complex genealogy of the dominant local family can be reconstructed in detail: the main branch controlled the more important ritual functions whereas the minor ones had a limited access to the temple or were employed in the service of the central administration. In these three cases the local temple seems to have reached a position important enough to block in some way the foundation of the *ḥwt* royal centers, even if these sanctuaries and the dominant families at their head were also well integrated in the royal administration (Moreno García 2005b).

In other cases, the fortune of a local family of magnates was inextricably linked to their relationship with the royal family. The wealth displayed by the tombs of Meir, in Middle Egypt, is a good example. They belonged to a family of viziers and high-ranking courtiers who shared a common feature with El-Hawawish in that no vizier bore the title of "great chief of the nome." The same trait is also evident at Abydos. In this locality some leaders reached exceptionally high positions in the kingdom when a family of local magnates successfully became viziers over three generations, the famous Weni being the most prominent of them (Richards 2002; Herbich and Richards 2006). But the balance of power in the nome seems to have been regulated by the same considerations prevailing in Akhmim or Meir, since the functions of "great chief of the nome" and vizier were separated, the first one being unusually held by magnates (*Jbj*, *Ḏꜥw*/*Šmȝj* and *Ḏꜥw*) from a distant locality, Der el-Gebrawi, where they were buried. Lastly, two ladies from Abydos, the sisters both called Ankhnespepi, became queens and mothers of Merenra and Pepy II whereas their mother and brother (Nebet and Djau) became viziers. These magnates were connected with Weni's son, and the presence of so many viziers, probably belonging to the same broad family, in a single nome could be explained by their kin ties with the royal family. This was, not surprisingly, a favored means of increasing social status and accumulating power, as in the case of Shemai of Coptos, a vizier and overseer of Upper Egypt who married a princess late in the Old Kingdom.

Contacts with the royal family, the co-optation of provincial leaders into the administration, and clientele networks between the court, magnates, and minor officials were ways in which social mobility among the elite was encouraged. Conversely, these relationships avoided the consolidation of a hereditary feudal class of landowners because the wealth and social position of the magnates depended largely upon the continuity of the state. These characteristics probably underlay such concepts as *rḫ nzwt* "acquaintance of the king" or, in some cases, *zȝ nzwt* "son of the king," wherein ranks and functions were expressed in terms of kinship and where the agents of the king were ideally considered members of a peculiar household, the *pr-ʿȝ* "great house" (i.e., the state). The creation of such an elite class is particularly well documented at the beginning of the Sixth Dynasty, a troubled period when the accession of a new line of Egyptian kings was marked with numerous difficulties and created the need for framing a new palatial circle. The first reigns of this dynasty saw the murder of Pharaoh Teti and the accession of an usurper to the throne (both events are known through later traditions). In addition to these irregularities, texts tell us of the destitution of some courtiers, the prosecution of a queen, the destruction of the monuments of many officials in Teti's pyramid necropolis, the marriage of several high officials with princesses, an astonishingly high mobility in some of the most important functions of the state (like that of vizier), the very high positions reached by young officials, an absence of information about the families of several high dignitaries in their tombs, multiple marriages of the Pharaoh Pepy I (often with women of provincial origin), the creation of the position of *jmj-r Šmʿw* "overseer of Upper Egypt," the expansion of the title of *ḥqȝ ḥwt* "governor of a *ḥwt*" in the provinces, and the nomination of "great chiefs of the nome" in many provinces of Upper and Middle Egypt where they were buried (Moreno García 2006a). Many provincial officials (like Weni of Abydos, Tjeti-Kaihep of Akhmim, Qar of Edfu, Khentikaupepi of Dakhla) describe in their autobiographies their education or promotion at the court, while others left in their Memphite monuments some traces of their provincial origin (like Mehu of Mendes or some officials from Akhmim and Abydos).

In short, the pharaohs of the Sixth Dynasty seem to have expanded their base of power by means of incorporating themselves into the state apparatus of provincial leaders and new groups of dignitaries that were not linked to the traditional powerful Memphite families, like those of Ptahhotep/Akhethotep, Senedjemib, or Akhethotep. The new role played by the nomes and their apparent vitality, especially in Upper Egypt, betray a gradual change in the territorial balance of power. The South experienced an increase of resources, administrative organization, and urban life which was not accompanied, at least on such a scale, by a similar movement in the Delta. On the other hand, the sharp contrast between, say, the Third and the Sixth Dynasty, in terms of the presence of private monumental architecture in Upper Egyptian localities, reflects the growing importance of this region. Simultaneously the diffusion of the official culture and its products (decorated tombs, statues, inscribed objects, stelae, coffins) touched a broader spectrum of social groups, probably because most of the provincial tribute was now administered locally and this provided new possibilities for accumulating both wealth and power at a local level.

The expansion of the network of *ḥwt* is perhaps the best expression of these changes, especially as they were also founded in some areas of Upper Egypt where no other royal centers are attested before the Sixth Dynasty. They also provided a useful instrument for gathering tribute and mobilizing the local work force. When the "*ḥwt* and temple model" is placed in the *longue durée*, it can be observed that the earlier inscriptions record the pre-eminence of the *ḥwt-ꜥꜣt*, whereas the *ḥwt* played a rather more modest role, a situation which still prevailed during the Fourth and Fifth Dynasties. But from the Sixth Dynasty on, the *ḥwt* were ubiquitous in nearly all provinces of Upper Egypt, with few exceptions, and the Delta, judging by the high number of *ḥqꜣ ḥwt* buried at Memphis. Conversely, the royal centers formerly prevalent in the countryside, like the *ḥwt-ꜥꜣt* or the towers called *swnw*, disappear from the epigraphic record. The title *ḥqꜣ ḥwt* became a very common one, with nearly two hundred holders of this function attested in the monuments, and formal descriptions of the rural landscape in private tombs began to include the *ḥwt* as one of its main constituents (Moreno García 1999, 2007). While all these changes point to a higher degree of involvement of the monarchy in the agrarian economy of the nomes, they also suggest that the reinforcement of the royal presence in Upper Egypt required the collaboration of the local elite through the enhancement of their official status.

The predynastic cultural and political unification of the country was a relatively quick one, and it allowed for a sudden increase in the available agricultural and tributary resources placed at the disposal of the crown, especially in Middle and Lower Egypt. However, the economic and administrative organization of the new spaces incorporated into the kingdom took several centuries, and it was not until the Sixth Dynasty that a network of royal centers (the *ḥwt*) effectively encompassed all of Egypt and allowed for the development of local royal agents who became more and more rooted in the nomes they administered and emotionally attached to their local family cemeteries instead of the traditional royal necropolis at Memphis (Moreno García 2006b).

THE CRISIS OF THE FIRST INTERMEDIATE PERIOD AND ITS AFTERMATH

Recent research shows that the First Intermediate Period is nothing like the "dark age" suggested by the traditional historiography (Moeller 2005; Seidlmayer 1990; Moreno García 1997). In fact, the urban development, the rise of new polities around localities like Dara, Thebes, Herakleopolis, or Ezbet Rushdi, the wealth displayed in many provincial cemeteries, the innovations in the artistic and epigraphic domains, and the broad social access to prestige goods formerly restricted to the administrative elite, may be interpreted as the culmination of the long-term provincial growth of Upper Egypt, as well as the consequence of the increasing imbalance of power between this region and the Memphite and Delta areas. Both regions became the foci of the Theban and Herakleopolitan kingdoms, respectively, which fought for supremacy in the Nile Valley after the end of the unitary monarchy of the Old Kingdom, and it is noteworthy in this respect that the nucleus of the Herakleopolitan policy did not lay in the Delta nor in the venerable Memphite area, which remained under their control, but in provincial areas like Siut, Bersheh, and, of course, Herakleopolis itself. In fact, the northern kingdom appears to be the heir of the former pharaonic monarchy and its traditions, as it encompassed the area formerly administered directly from Memphis (i.e., Lower Egypt and the northernmost area of Middle Egypt), while its power outside this zone continued to depend on the cooperation of nomarchs. In any case, the "regionalization" of power gave the local lower elite an opportunity to enhance both their status and social values, especially in the South, as inferred from the epigraphic record (Moreno García 1997). The social position of the nomarchs seems to have been relatively downplayed outside the Herakleopolitan kingdom, which reinforces the impression that their authority and prestige were closely linked to the existence of a central government. In contrast, the governors of localities (ḥqꜣ), the "greats" (wr), the chiefs (ḥrj-tp), or the military leaders (jmj-r mšꜥ) emerged as respected local authorities. Finally, the crisis of the pharaonic authority led to the dissolution of its institutions in the rebel areas around Thebes. For instance, Redikhnum of Dendera proclaimed that officials (srw) and governors of ḥwt were appointed by the Theban kings in the zones under their control, whilst Henenu and other Theban high officials re-established the fiscal organization in the South. Even the chief priests of Coptos assumed the functions traditionally carried out by the agents of the king until the re-establishment of a strong authority in the South. But the role of the ḥwt in the Theban kingdom seems to have been relatively ephemeral, as few governors of ḥwt are known at the beginning of the Middle Kingdom. The institution never recovered the prominence it had previously enjoyed.

Nevertheless the ḥwt was remarkably durable in the administrative imagination of the ancient Egyptians. For about a millennium it had been a typical element of the rural landscape, only to disappear at the beginning of the Middle Kingdom. But later proverbs and inscriptions (cf. *The Eloquent Peasant*, *The Duties of the Vizier*, or the so-called triumphal inscription of Pyankhi, from the 1st millennium BCE) and even the funerary phraseology of the tombs, continued evoking the ḥwt and its governors, the ḥqꜣ ḥwt, as an archetypal element of the countryside. Temples and royal centers continued to be the main poles of the state authority in the nomes during the Middle Kingdom, the only difference being that the work-centers ḫnrt replaced the ḥwt and the provincial sanctuaries began to be built on a larger and richer scale. Yet it seems that the ḫnrt were neither as conspicuous nor as broadly distributed as the ḥwt (Quirke 1988). Another difference is the gradual disappearance of the "great overlords of the nome," since provincial families seem not to have retained such a prestigious local official position as they became more and more integrated into the central government's apparatus (Franke 1991; Willems 2007:83–113). This circumstance is probably linked to the fact that minor local territorial entities began to play a significant administrative role, like the domains (rmnjjt) of some officials and private persons, or the localities and their districts, as one can infer from the frequent mentions of qnbtjw w "members of the council of the district" or hꜣtj-ꜥ "chief of a locality" in administrative contexts. Even the loss of the former importance of the nomes in favor of the wꜥrt "regional circumscription" also recalls the supra-provincial role played by officials like the *jmj-r Šmʿw* "overseer of Upper Egypt" during the Old Kingdom. In short the territorial administration appears fragmented into small spatial units during the Middle Kingdom, where the local royal centers or the powerful provincial families tied to the court were gradually fading and were no longer playing their traditional role of intermediaries between the palace and the nomes. In this context the central power became more and more blurred in a multitude of small but numerous local spheres of decision which led to the final disintegration of the kingdom, as it occurred at the end of the Old Kingdom.

As for the provincial sanctuaries, they continued to be significant institutions in Upper Egypt, perhaps because the relative scarcity of agricultural land in southernmost Egypt precluded the appearance of landowners or powerful royal centers, and contributed to preserving the goods and privileged position of the temples as economic institutions and repositories of legitimacy, especially when the central power collapsed. The pharaohs of the Middle Kingdom built extensively in the sanctuaries of this region, usually with expensive materials and a rich ornamental program. This situation contrasts sharply with their scarcity at Memphis and the Delta or with the humbler provincial constructions of the 3rd millennium (Habachi 1963). It is possible that the kings found sounder support in Upper Egypt than in Lower Egypt or Memphis, which did not regain its earlier status of capital city. Perhaps this relationship was fostered by the military protection provided during the critical periods which followed the Old and Middle Kingdoms, when, for example, armed incursions of Nubians and foreigners were recorded in Abisko, El-Kab, and Thebes. The ties of the pharaohs with powerful local families linked to the temples are also well attested, as they made royal grants to the sanctuary of Heqaib at Aswan or allowed the governors of Elkab to record their private transactions in stelae (i. e., the *Stèle juridique*) which were placed in Karnak temple. The provincial Upper Egyptian sanctuaries remained important sources of power in the Second Intermediate Period, and the kings intervened in their internal affairs (Coptos), reorganized their agricultural domains (Medamud or Elkab), put members of the royal family at the head of important ritual offices (Karnak), and erected stelae in them (Karnak). Temples became a solid source of support for the kings since royal centers like the *ḥwt* or *ḫnrt* never recovered their former role as counterweights of the sanctuaries, especially after the end of the Middle Kingdom. The consequences of this trend for the future of the monarchy would prove serious, when the temple of Amon at Karnak became an exceptionally rich and powerful institution during the New Kingdom (Ullmann 2007) and provided the foundation of a state controlled by high priests who escaped the authority of the pharaohs during the Third Intermediate Period.

REFERENCES

Anthes, R. 1928. *Die Felseninschriften von Hatnub*. Leipzig: Georg Olms Verlagsbuchhandlung.

Arnold, D. 1976. *Gräber des Alten und Mittleren Reiches in El-Tarif*. Mainz am Rhein: Philipp von Zabern.

Brunton, G. 1927. *Qau and Badari I*. London: B. Quaritch.

Cody, M.E. 2008. An Old Kingdom Bowl from Mendes in the Brooklyn Museum: A Preliminary Investigation of Its Archaeological Context. In *Servant of Mut. Studies in Honor of Richard A. Fazzini*, pp. 53–62. PdÄ 28. Leiden: Brill.

Di Maria, R. 2007. Naqada (Petrie's South Town): The Sealing Evidence. In *The International Conference on Heritage of Naqada and Qus Region*, ed. H. Hanna, pp. 65–78. Naqada: ICOM-CC-Wood.

El-Khouli, A., and N. Kanawati. 1990. *The Old Kingdom Tombs of El-Hammamiya*. Sydney: The Australian Center for Egyptology.

Engel, E.-M. 2004. The Domain of Semerkhet. In *Egypt at Its Origins. Studies in Memory of Barbara Adams*, ed. S. Hendrickx, R.F. Friedman, K. M. Ciałowicz, and M. Chłodnicki, pp. 705–10. OLA 138. Leuven: Peeters.

———. 2006. Die Entwicklung des Systems der ägyptischen Nomoi in der Frühzeit. *MDAIK* 62:151–60.

Fattovich, R. 2007. Exploration at South Town by the Naples Oriental Institute (1977–1986). In *The International Conference on Heritage of Naqada and Qus Region*, ed. H. Hanna, pp. 46–56. Naqada: ICOM-CC-Wood.

Franke, D. 1991. The Career of Khnumhotep III of Beni Hasan and the So-called 'Decline of the Nomarchs.' In *Middle Kingdom Studies*, ed. S. Quirke, pp. 51–67. New Malden: SIA Publications.

Friedman, R. 1992. Pebbles, Pots and Petroglyphs: Excavations at HK64. In *The Followers of Horus. Studies Dedicated to Michael Allen Hoffman*, ed. R. Friedman and B. Adams, pp. 99–106. Oxford: Oxbow Books.

———. 2000. Pots, Pebbles and Petroglyphs, Part II: 1996 Excavations at Hierakonpolis Locality HK64. In *Studies in Ancient Egypt in Honour of H. S. Smith*, ed. A. Leahy and J. Tait, pp. 101–8. London: Egypt Exploration Society.

———. 2001. Nubians at Hierakonpolis: Excavations in the Nubian Cemeteries. *Sudan & Nubia* 6: 20–24.

———. 2004. Elephants at Hierakonpolis. In *Egypt at Its Origins. Studies in Memory of Barbara Adams*, ed. S. Hendrickx, R.F. Friedman, K.M. Ciałowicz, and M. Chłodnicki, pp. 131–68. OLA 138. Leuven: Peeters.

Gatto, M.C. 1996. Contacts between the Nubian 'A-Groups' and Predynastic Egypt. In *Interregional Contacts in the Later Prehistory of Northeastern Africa*, ed. L. Krzyzaniak, K. Kroeper, and M. Kobusiewicz, pp. 331–34. Poznan: Poznan Archaeological Museum.

———. 2000. The Most Ancient Evidence of the 'A-Groups' Culture in Lower Nubia. In *Recent Research into the Stone Age of Northeastern Africa*, ed. L. Krzyzaniak, K. Kroeper, and M. Kobusiewicz, pp. 105–17. Poznan: Poznan Archaeological Museum.

Ginter, B., J.K. Kozlowski, M. Pawlikowski, and J. Sliwa. 1998. *Frühe Keramik und Kleinfunde aus El-Târif.* AVDAIK 40. Mainz am Rhein: Philipp von Zabern.

Giuliani, S. 2006. Nubian Evidence in Hierakonpolis. In *Acta Nubica. Proceedings of the Tenth International Conference of Nubian Studies*, ed. I. Caneva and A. Roccati, pp. 223–27. Rome: Ist. Poligrafico e Zecca dello Stato.

Habachi, L. 1963. King Nebhepetre Menthuhotp: His Monuments, Place in History, Deification and Unusual Representations in the Form of Gods. *MDAIK* 19:16–52.

Harrington, N. 2004. Human Representations in the Predynastic Period: The Locality HK6 Statue in Context. In *Egypt at Its Origins. Studies in Memory of Barbara Adams*, ed. S. Hendrickx, R.F. Friedman, K.M. Ciałowicz, and M. Chłodnicki, pp. 25–44. OLA 138. Leuven: Peeters.

Hartung, U., and R. Hartmann. 2005. Zwei vermutlich aus der Westwüste stammende Gefässe im prädynastischen Friedhof U in Abydos. *MDAIK* 61:211–18, pl. 36.

Herbich, T., and J. Richards. 2006. The Loss and Rediscovery of the Vizier Iuu at Abydos: Magnetic Survey in the Middle Cemetery. In *Timelines. Studies in Honour of Manfred Bietak,* vol. I, ed. E. Czerny, I. Hein, H. Hunger, D. Melman, and A. Schwab, pp. 141–149. OLA 149. Leuven: Peeters.

Hope, C.A., G.E. Bowen, W. Dolling, C. Hubschmann, P. Kucera, R. Long, and A. Stevens. 2006. Report on the Excavations at Ismant el-Kharab and Mut el-Kharab in 2006. *BACE* 17:23–67, pls. 1–12, figs. 1–16.

Huyge, D. 2003. An Enigmatic Third Dynasty Mastaba at Elkab. *EA* 22:29–30.

Ikram, S., and C. Rossi. 2004. An Early Dynastic *Serekh* from the Kharga Oasis. *JEA* 90:211–14.

Jaeschke, H.F. 2004. The HK6 Statue Fragments. In *Egypt at Its Origins. Studies in Memory of Barbara Adams*, ed. S. Hendrickx, R.F. Friedman, K.M. Ciałowicz, and M. Chłodnicki, pp. 45–66. OLA 138. Leuven: Peeters.

Jesse, F., B. Keding, N. Pöllatii, M. Bechhaus-Gerst, and T. Lenssen-Erz. 2007. Cattle Herding in the Southern Libyan Desert. In *Atlas of Cultural and Environmental Change in Arid Africa*, ed. O. Bubenzer, A. Bolten, and F. Darius, pp. 46–49. Africa Praehistorica 21. Cologne: Heinrich Barth Institut.

Kröpelin, S., and R. Kuper. 2006–2007. More Corridors to Africa. In *Mélanges offerts à Francis Geus*, ed. B. Gratien, pp. 219–29. CRIPEL 26. Villeneuve d'Ascq: Université Charles de Gaulle–Lille 3.

Kuper, R. 2007. "Looking Behind the Scenes"—Archaeological Distribution Patterns and Their Meaning. In *Atlas of Cultural and Environmental Change in Arid Africa*, ed. O. Bubenzer, A. Bolten, and F. Darius, pp. 24–25. Africa Praehistorica 21. Cologne: Heinrich Barth Institut.

Lange, M. 2004a. Nubier in der Wüste—Fundplätze des 5. Und 4. Jahrtausends vor Chr. in der Laqiya-Region (NW-Sudan). *Archäologische Informationen* 27(1):169–77.

———. 2004b. Wadi Shaw 82/52: A Peridynastic Settlement Site in the Western Desert and Its Relations to the Nile Valley. In *Nubian Studies 1998. Proceedings of the Ninth International Conference of Nubian Studies*, ed. Timothy Kendall, pp. 315–24. Boston: Northeastern University.

Le Quellec, J.-L. 2005. Une nouvelle approche des rapports Nil-Sahara d'après l'art rupestre. *Archéo-Nil* 15:67–74.

López, J. 1967. Inscriptions de l'Ancien Empire à Khor El-Aquiba. *RdE* 19:51–66.

Moeller, N. 2005. The First Intermediate Period: A Time of Famine and Climate Change? *Ägypten und Levant* 15:153–67.

Moreno García, J.C. 1997. *Études sur l'administration, le pouvoir et l'idéologie en Égypte, de l'Ancien au Moyen Empire*. Ægyptiaca Leodiensia, 4. Liège: Université de Liège.

———. 1998. La population *mrt*: une approche du problème de la servitude en Egypte au IIIe millénaire, *JEA* 84:71–83.

———. 1999. *Ḥwt et le milieu rural égyptien du IIIe millénaire. Economie, administration et organisation territoriale*. Bibliothèque de l'École des Hautes Etudes—Sciences Historiques et Philologiques, 337. Paris: Honoré Champion.

———. 2001a. L'organisation sociale de l'agriculture dans l'Egypte pharaonique pendant l'Ancien Empire (2650–2150 avant J.-C.). *JESHO* 44:411–50.

———. 2001b. *Ḥqȝw* "jefes, gobernadores" y élites rurales en el III milenio antes de Cristo. Reflexiones acerca de algunas estatuas del Imperio Antiguo. In *. . . Ir a buscar leña. Estudios dedicados al Profesor Jesús López*, ed. J. Cervelló Autuori and A.J. Quevedo Alvarez, pp. 141–54. Aula Ægyptiaca Studia, 3. Barcelona: Aula Ægyptiaca.

———. 2004. Temples, administration provinciale et les élites locales en Haute-Égypte: la contribution des inscriptions rupestres pharaoniques de l'Ancien Empire. In *Séhel entre Égypte et Nubie. Inscriptions rupestres et graffiti de l'époque pharaonique*, ed. A. Gasse and V. Rondot, pp. 7–22. Montpellier: Université Paul Valéry–Montpellier III.

———. 2005a. Élites provinciales, transformations sociales et idéologie à la fin de l'Ancien Empire et à la Première Période Intermédiaire. In *Des Néfererkarê aux Montouhotep. Travaux archéologiques en cours sur la fin de la VIe dynastie et la Première Période Intermédiaire*, ed. L. Pantalacci and C. Berger-el-Naggar, pp. 215–28. Lyon: Maison de l'Orient et de la Méditerranée.

———. 2005b. Deux familles de potentats provinciaux et les assises de leur pouvoir: Elkab et El-Hawawish sous la VIe dynastie. *RdE* 56:95–128.

———. 2006a. La tombe de *Mḥw* à Saqqara. *Chronique d'Egypte* 161-162:128–35.

———. 2006b. La gestion sociale de la mémoire dans l'Egypte du IIIe millénaire: les tombes des particuliers, entre utilisation privée et idéologie publique. In *Dekorierte Grabanlagen im Alten Reich—Methodik und Interpretation*, ed. M. Fitzenreiter and M. Herb, pp. 215–42. London: Golden House Publications.

———. 2007. The State and the Organization of the Rural Landscape in 3rd Millennium BC Pharaonic Egypt. In *Aridity, Change and Conflict in Africa*, ed. M. Bollig, O. Bubenzer, R. Vogelsang, and H.-P. Wotzka, pp. 313–30. Colloquium Africanum, 2. Cologne: Heinrich-Barth-Institut.

Pätznick, J.-P. 2005. *Die Siegelabrollungen und Rollsiegel der Stadt Elephantine im 3. Jahrtausend v. Chr.* BAR S1339. Oxford: Archaeopress.

Posener-Kriéger, P. 1976. *Les archives du temple funéraire de Néferirkarê-Kakaï (les papyrus d'Abousir).* Cairo: IFAO.

Posener-Kriéger, P., and S. Demichelis. 2004. *I Papiri di Gebelein: Scavi G. Farina 1935*. Turin: Ministero per i Beni e le Attività Culturali.

Quibell, J.E., and F.W. Green. 1902. *Hierakonpolis. Part II*. London: B. Quaritch.

Quirke, S. 1988. State and Labour in the Middle Kingdom. A Reconsideration of the Term *ḫnrt*. *RdE* 39:83–106.

Redford, D.B. 2008. Some Old Kingdom Sealings from Mendes: I. In *Servant of Mut. Studies in Honor of Richard A. Fazzini*, ed. S.H. D'Auria, pp. 198–203. Leiden: Brill.

Regulski, I. 2004. Second Dynasty Ink Inscriptions from Saqqara Paralleled in the Abydos Material from the Royal Museums of Art and History (RMAH) in Brussels. In *Egypt at Its Origins. Studies in Memory of Barbara Adams*, ed. S. Hendrickx, R.F. Friedman, K. M. Ciałowicz, and M. Chłodnicki, pp. 949–70. OLA 138. Leuven: Peeters.

Richards, J. 2002. Text and Context in Late Old Kingdom Egypt: The Archaeology and Historiography of Weni the Elder. *JARCE* 39:75–102.

Satzinger, H. 2006. Felsinschriften aus dem Gebiet von Sayâla (Ägyptisch-Nubien). In *Timelines. Studies in Honour of Manfred Bietak*, vol. III, ed. E. Czerny, I. Hein, H. Hunger, D. Melman, and A. Schwab, pp. 139–47. OLA 149. Leuven: Peeters.

Seidlmayer, S.J. 1990. *Gräberfelder aus dem Übergang vom Alten zum Mittleren Reich. Studien zur Archäologie der Ersten Zwischenzeit*. SAGA 1. Heidelberg: Heidelberger Orientalverlag.

———. 1996. Town and State in the Early Old Kingdom: A View from Elephantine. In *Aspects of Early Egypt*, ed. Jeffrey Spencer, pp. 108–27. London: British Museum Press.

Sethe, K. 1933. *Urkunden des ägyptischen Altertums, I. Urkunden des Alten Reiches*. Leipzig: J. C. Hinrichs'sche Buchhandlung.

Ullmann, M. 2007. Thebes: Origins of a Ritual Landscape. In *Sacred Space and Sacred Function in Ancient Thebes*, ed. P.F. Dorman and B.M. Bryan, pp. 3–25. SAOC 61. Chicago: The Oriental Institute of the University of Chicago.

Van den Brink, E.C., and T.E. Levy, eds. 2002. *Egypt and the Levant. Interrelations from the 4th through the Early 3rd Millennium BCE*. Leicester: Leicester University Press.

Viso, I.M. 2006. Central Places and the Territorial Organization of Communities: The Occupation of Hilltop Sites in Early Medieval Northern Castile. In *People and Space in the Middles Ages, 300–1300*, ed. W. Davies, G. Halsall, and A. Reynolds, pp. 167–86. Studies in the Early Middle Ages, 15. Turnhout: Brepols.

Vörös, G. 2002. Hungarian Excavations on Thot Hill at the Temple of Pharaoh Montuhotep Sankhkara in Thebes (1995–1998). In *5. Ägyptologische Tempeltagung, Würzburg: 23.–26. September 1999*, ed. H. Beinlich, J. Hallof, H. Hussy, and C. von Pfeil, pp. 201–11. Ägypten und Altes Testament Bd. 33. Akten der ägyptischen Tempeltagungen, Bd. 3. Wiesbaden: Harrassowitz.

Wildung, D. 1999. La Haute-Égypte, un style particulier de la statuaire de l'Ancien Empire? In *L'art de l'Ancien Empire égyptien*, ed. C. Ziegler, pp. 335–53. Paris: La Documentation Française.

Willems, H. 2007. *Dayr al-Barshā*. Vol. I, *The Rock Tombs of Djehutinakht (No. 17K74/1), Khnumnakht (No. 17K74/2), and Iha (17K74/3). With an Essay on the History and Nature of Nomarchal Rule in the Early Middle Kingdom*. OLA 155. Leuven: Peeters.

———. 2008. *Les Textes des Sarcophages et la démocratie. Éléments d'une histoire culturelle du Moyen Empire égyptien*. Paris: Éditions Cybèle.

7

The Management of Royal Treasure

Palace Archives and Palatial Economy in the Ancient Near East

WALTHER SALLABERGER[1]

The argument of this contribution starts with a methodological consideration of "palace archives," administrative archives found in palaces, which by their specific composition reflect the political, social, economic, and religious role of the ruler. Palace archives of the ancient Near East, such as those from Early Dynastic Ebla, Ur III Puzrish-Dagan, Old Babylonian Mari, Hittite Hattusa, and Neo-Assyrian Nimrud as well as many others, deal with specific goods, namely silver and other metals, textiles, and delicacies; furthermore, these goods are not handled in the same way by any other organization, including the temples. Therefore the complex of production, exchange, and distribution of these prestigious goods may be labeled a "palatial economy." The kinds of goods, the ways of acquisition, and the procedures for distribution remained basically constant during the two millennia documented in cuneiform archives. The following discussions always begin by using the evidence from Ebla and include examples from the Ur III empire or the Old Babylonian period, but the basic principles detected can easily be applied to other palace archives, as surveys of similar texts reveal.

PALACE ARCHIVES

Archaeological undertakings have unearthed not only architectural vestiges of ancient Near Eastern palaces and fragments of their original inventories, but also the remains of the originally rich holdings of inscribed clay tablets stored in these palaces. As it is to be expected in the cuneiform world, most of these are administrative texts documenting the economic resources handled by the palace. The first question to be asked is which kinds of administrative documents are to be expected in an ancient Near Eastern palace. Though most documents can be described as registrations of transactions (incomes and deliveries) and as inventories, the objects treated deserve closer attention.

The Archive from Palace G at Ebla

The point of departure is the oldest, and probably the most complete, palace archive ever discovered, the main archive of the Early Dynastic Palace G at Ebla, dating to the 24th century BC. Palace G was destroyed in the great wars that eventually paved the way for the rise of Sargon of Akkade (Archi and Biga 2003). In the court of reception, close to the staircase leading to the inner parts of the palace, the Italian archaeologists led by Paola Matthiae discovered several archives in 1975–76. The location near the entrance characterizes administrative archives, since this is the place where the palace interacted with the outside world and it was here the transactions took place that were documented in administrative texts.[2]

Obviously the administrative archives of a palace directly reflect its economy. In this regard a palace can first be viewed as a large household, an *oikos*. Its personnel had to be maintained, and here especially the production, distribution, and consumption of grain was of crucial importance. A series of texts was found in a separate small room at Ebla (L. 2712; see Milano 1990) documenting the expenditure of cereals and beer to the inhabitants and guests of the palace. This text group can be compared to the Sargonic so-called beer and bread texts or the Ur III "messenger texts" and many other similar administrative texts, all dealing with an exact report of the food and beer given out to permanent and temporary members of the household. The "beer and bread texts" of the palace of Ebla thus provide a detailed account of the persons present at the palace at a given time, including the women of the court, messengers, artists, and craftsmen.[3]

The main archive room (L. 2769) with its thousands of tablets was likewise situated in the so-called court of reception. According to the overview of the archive by Ebla's epigrapher Alfonso Archi (Archi 2003a) it housed the following groups of tablets.

Table 7.1 Overview of the Main Archive (L.2769) from Palace G at Ebla (24th c. BC)

1. Correspondence (including correspondence with other city states, see Fronzaroli 2003; partly in vestibule L. 2875)
2. International and internal legal regulations (selection; see Fronzaroli 2003)
3. Management of the holdings of the palace and of the state (mostly early texts, incomplete)
    3.1. Management of agricultural land, products and personnel (see Milano 1996)
    3.2. Management of animal herds (see Archi 1984)
4. Administration of palace goods
    4.1. Annual collective accounts* concerning the delivery of metals (especially silver) and textiles (mu-du texts)
    4.2. Annual collective accounts concerning the expenditure of metals (especially silver) (= AAM)
    4.3. Monthly collective accounts concerning the expenditure of textiles and metals (especially silver) (= MAT)
    4.4. Accounts concerning single transactions of metals or textiles
    4.5. Monthly collective accounts concerning the expenditure of meat for consumption (see Pettinato 1979)
5. Religious practice:
    5.1. Incantations (e.g. ARET 5, 8–19)
    5.2. Rituals of the ruler (ARET 11)
6. Education and literature:
    6.1. Literary texts including texts in Sumerian (ARET 5, 20f. etc.)
    6.2. Lexical lists of the Mesopotamian tradition, Eblaite lists, school texts (MEE 3 and 4 etc.; see Archi 1992)

---

*Since the annual and monthly administrative texts of Ebla repeat the full contents of various single transactions, they are labeled "collective" instead of "summary" accounts. Monthly or annual "summary" accounts, on the other hand, present totals of the various categories (as e.g. in the Ur III animal texts from Puzrish-Dagan).

The presence of the chancery documents (nos. 1 and 2 in Table 7.1) proves that this archive is *directly* linked with the center of political power. Comparable palace archives (e.g., Old Babylonian Mari) also included documents concerning the administration of labor, conscriptions, and levies. But since administrative tablets were also found in other sectors of the Ebla palace, the main archive did not contain the complete documentation.

Within the main archive L.2769 of Ebla the documentation of the "luxury goods" metals and textiles takes by far the most space. Almost 600 large tablets list the monthly expenditure of textiles with or without objects in silver or other metals (MAT). The expenditure of objects of silver and gold, as well as those of tin and copper, was recorded in some 35 large annual documents (AAM), among these the largest administrative texts with thirty columns on each side, each containing several hundred text boxes. The annual income in gold, silver, and textiles was documented in another group of more than 30 large tablets. Several hundred smaller tablets concern individual expenditures or deliveries or special accounts of metals and textiles (Archi 2003a:35–36). To these groups, one has to add some 20 texts about animals for slaughter (ibid., 28–29).

The documentation of "luxury" goods constitutes not only the largest group of administrative documents by far within the central archive of the palace of Ebla, but it can also be singled out by the size of its documentary coverage. The term "documentary coverage refers to the extent to which the network of administrative transactions is matched by the creation of written records" (Postgate 2001:184). This pertains to the amount of information about the objects and the participants of a transaction that was considered relevant for the ancient tablet scribes; sometimes it sufficed to note a total of objects (e.g., animals) and the entrepreneurs involved, in other cases the scribe described each object and identified each person delivering or receiving the commodities. This documentary coverage is closely related to the "administrative reach," namely "the extent to which the central administration controlled the economic transactions in which it was involved," as defined by Postgate (2001:183–84). With regard to silver and textiles in the Ebla documentation each single transaction was carefully noted. The texts indicate the exact weight of metal objects or the number and quality of textiles, they identify recipients by name and/or profession, and they describe the exact place and the circumstances of the delivery.

The fact that the administration noted each single detail in these texts becomes more relevant as in other sectors the Ebla administration adopted a different perspective. In the management of animals (Archi 1984), to cite just one example, no texts deal with the actual control of single herds and their herdsmen,[4] but instead the documents list high numbers of animals with various persons. Thus sometimes officials were listed as the persons responsible for the animal herds; in other cases herding controllers,[5] who organized the distribution and composition of the herds and the collection of wool, were employed. This internal distribution of tasks, however, was not recorded in the documents of the palace.

The "luxury goods" of the palace archives include all that is rare and expensive: gold and silver, and the rings, cups, or bowls made from such metals; precious clothes; or fine delicacies such as fresh fruit, meat, wine, or flour made from wheat instead of barley. Obviously, it is not always possible to draw a clear-cut distinction between these palace luxury goods and goods in everyday use. Textiles, for example, were used by everyone and silver served as currency in economic transactions and so it was not exclusively a luxury good.

Archives of the Crown or Excavated in Palaces

Ebla's is the earliest of a series of palace archives in the cuneiform cultures. In the 3rd millennium, relevant documents in larger quantities stem mainly from the Third Dynasty of Ur (2110–2003 BC). In this relatively federalist state important parts of the administration of the crown sector were not situated in the capital Ur, but in the center of Puzrish-Dagan, situated close to Nippur; most of the documents from this site deal with the administration of animals kept for meat (Sallaberger 2003–04), but there is also a small royal archive dealing with gold and silver and objects made of precious metal (Sallaberger 1999:240–52; Paoletti 2010).

Among the palace archives from the Old Babylonian period or Middle Bronze Age, those from Mari are without doubt the most important ones. There the royal correspondence was found in rooms between the two main courts; the administrative documents stem from rooms around the Court of the Date Palm, near the entrance to the inner quarters, and near secondary entrances (Durand 1985). Again, a large part of the administrative documentation deals with textiles, with precious metals, or a variety of foodstuffs and delicacies destined for the royal table.[6]

The same luxury goods appear also in texts from other Old Babylonian palaces: the administrative documents from the palace of Sin-kashid in Uruk include a significant group of metal texts;[7] some texts about textiles were discovered in the palace of Shusharra (modern Shemshara) in Northern Mesopotamia (Lower Zab);[8] an archive dealing with oil was found at Shubat-Enlil (Tell Lailan), the capital of the empire of Upper Mesopota-

Table 7.2 Luxury goods in the archives of Ebla, Puzrish-Dagan (Ur III), and Mari

Early Dynastic Ebla (24th century BC)	Ur III Puzrish-Dagan (21st century BC)	Old Babylonian Mari (18th century BC)
silver and other metals (full documentation)	silver and other metals (treasure archive)	silver, metals (single documents, inventories)
textiles (full documentation)		textiles
animals for slaughter	central bookkeeping of animals	animals for slaughter
(wine)		delicacies for the royal table (*naptan šarrim*), wine, oil

mia;[9] and among the documents from the palace at the site of Tell ar-Rimah one notes an archive dealing with wine.[10] The same holds true for palace archives of the Late Bronze Age (second half of the 2nd millennium), such as those from Alalakh, Nuzi,[11] and Hattusa,[12] and of the 1st millennium, like the Neo-Assyrian archives of Nineveh and Nimrud[13] and the lists of oil expenditure from Nebuchadnezzar's Southern Palace in Babylon (Pedersén 2005a, 2005b).

The documentation itself may differ. For example, texts about the production of luxury goods like those for which Mukannishum was responsible at Mari or the craft archives from Ur (time of Ibbi-Suen of Ur) or Isin (time of Ishbi-Erra and Shu-ilishu of Isin) have not been stored in the main archive of Ebla, whereas the detailed summary tablets are unique to Ebla.

A basic type of account which appears in most palace archives records the expenditure of palace goods, always including the relevant details about the goods, identifying the persons involved, and often naming the circumstances of the transaction. The full administrative reach underlines the direct participation of the palace in these transactions and shows that no other organization was involved.

The Exclusive Documentation of Precious Goods in Palace Archives

Archival texts of every kind—administrative, juridical, or epistolary—obviously reflect the economic transactions and other activities of the organization in whose realm they were written, so an archive as a whole can be regarded as a written documentation of the respective organization.[14] The composition, the thematic orientation, and the administrative reach of archives found in palaces lead to the following conclusion: the administration of the above-mentioned "luxury goods," above all non-perishable and storable textiles and precious metals, but also oil and delicacies, formed a central task of the royal palace. The prototypical palace texts are the detailed documents of expenditure of palace goods. This continuously and constantly holds true for the ancient Near East, independent of possible political differences and independent of the natural resources occurring either in the southern alluvial plain dependent on irrigation agriculture or in the northern rainfall zone. This evidence of the palace archives alone demands an investigation of the phenomenon.

Although the analysis presented here will be based on administrative documents, these luxury goods are dealt with in other texts as well, namely in the correspondence of the rulers[15] and in royal inscriptions. As examples one may cite on the one hand the international political correspondence found at Amarna, which deals with the exchange of valuables such as lapis lazuli, horses, or gold between rulers of different countries, and on the other hand the textual and pictorial representation of the tribute delivered to Assyrian kings.

The documentation concerning the distribution of silver, textiles, and other precious goods is not only found in royal palaces through the ages, but, more importantly, such documentation can only be found there. Of course silver or textiles may appear in any archive. But only the palace and no other organization was able to handle such expensive items on such a scale that they regularly had to be documented in administrative texts. Throughout history, this distinguished the palace from the temples, which did not distribute these goods; the temples as economic organizations managed the agriculture and they received valuable donations from the ruler including gold and silver objects and thus served as a kind of treasure house.

Temples

Unfortunately, no major temple archive of the Early Dynastic period has been found that might provide a direct comparison. The so-called Bawu temple archive of Girsu is the documentation of the e_2-mi_2, the "female quarter," the household of the lady of Girsu, the ruler's wife (Bauer 1998).

Its more than 1600 Old Sumerian administrative texts deal mainly with subsistence economy, the management of persons and agriculture. Jewelry does appear in the context of care for the temples: the lady of Girsu dedicated bronze vessels, necklaces, and other metal objects to the goddesses of the state of Lagash during their festivals, as she did for the statues of her predecessors.[16] This is the prototypical situation: the ruler, his family, and to a lesser extent other members of the society dedicated votive gifts, among these jewelry and other valuables, to the temples. In those transactions the ruler played the active part, whereas the temples only served as repositories.

Evidence especially from later periods demonstrates how the temples handled their treasures; instructive examples include Assur, the Ebabbar of Sippar, and Uruk's Eanna. In these temples craftsmen were employed to produce or to repair the valuable clothes, jewellery, and other utensils for the cult. But despite the internal handling of the valuable materials, expenditure lists like those from the palace archives seem to be missing in temples. The importance of temples in the control of people and of agricultural labor cannot be disputed; however, they did not actively control the politically important treasures.

Tell Beydar, a Second Rank Town of the Ebla Period

Other organizations also did not handle the "palace goods," as we defined them above, in the same way the palace did, even if the respective administration encompassed a whole town or province. It may suffice to point to a few contrasting examples from the 3rd millennium.

The texts from Nabada/Tell Beydar stem from the central administration of the town and its surroundings and thus illustrate the case of a second-rank town at the time of the Ebla archives. The administration deals with agricultural production and the management of persons, but does not deal with palace goods. Wool is collected from the community's sheep flocks, but the texts do not treat textile production. A good case in point is the distribution of animals: equids were stationed near Tell Beydar but actually belonged to the economic realm of the ruler. This is even reflected in the popular imagery of animal terracottas, since sheep dominate the finds from Tell Beydar, whereas in the capital Nagar/Tell Brak equids, the animals of the ruler, were much more common (see Pruß and Sallaberger 2003–2004).

The Early Dynastic Household of the Lady of Girsu (e_2-mi_2)

The already mentioned Early Dynastic e_2-mi_2 archive of the lady of Girsu includes only a handful of documents that deal with silver and bronze. Silver was invested in foreign trade and entrusted to merchants,[17] but even here the silver was sometimes provided by the ruler himself (e.g., DP 513, 516). Gift exchange of palace goods between the ladies of various city-states is documented in a few cases (e.g., RTC 19: Adab; VS 27 98: Dilmun; DP 511: aromatic resins for the lady's mother), but for these single transactions no standardized text format was developed as it was for more common procedures of the household like the distribution of rations or of offerings. Perhaps the most impressive list of prestige goods among the e_2-mi_2 texts—personal gifts for a prince at his marriage—states that the source of the wealth was the sovereign Lugalanda himself (DP 75).

There is no doubt where the texts pertaining to silver and other metals were kept: in the archive of the "palace" (e_2-gal) of the ruler, the $ensi_2$, or lugal of Girsu. So, for example, copper and oil were delivered to the palace (DP 343), here the weighing of the copper from Dilmun[18] took place, and the lady of Girsu Sasa gave metals to the merchant from the palace (VS 14 43).

In addition to silver and gold, textiles feature prominently in the palace archives. A large number of female personnel of the lady's household at Girsu were employed in textile production. Rations of wool and occasionally textiles were distributed to the employees (e.g., DP 171, 192–194; VS 14 181; VS 27 9), whereas the expenditure of more elaborate clothes was basically restricted to dedications to (the statues of) ancestors at festivals (e.g., DP 73, 77, 78; VS 14 163, 164). The production of textiles thus did not entail the right to control their distribution.

Whereas the Ur III royal archives from Puzrish-Dagan deal with the luxury goods of meat and silver, the provincial archives of Girsu and Umma concentrate on the subsistence economy. It is therefore no coincidence that the Shara-isa archive from Girsu of the time of Gudea treats palace goods, since this was a period when the ruler of Girsu was politically independent.

Umma, Provincial Capital under the Third Dynasty of Ur

The substantial differences between the royal palace and the provincial center can most clearly be demonstrated for Umma, capital of a core province of the state of the Third Dynasty of Ur. The thousands of archival texts from Umma stem clearly from the center of the province, the seat of its governor (ensi$_2$). An Ur III governor enjoyed relatively large independence in the internal organization of his province, whether it concerned agriculture and economy, the cult in the local sanctuaries, or judicial matters. A province was, however, obliged to deliver goods to the crown and to fulfill compulsory service in state organizations (cf. Sharlach 2004), and the provincial governor was not integrated into the army, which was completely under royal control.

The sector of animal husbandry and the expenditure of animals for slaughter clearly show the difference between the provincial and the state economy. At Umma, animals were offered in the local cults and they were delivered to the state as contributions, but no gifts to persons such as those recorded in Puzrish-Dagan are known from Umma (see Sallaberger 2003–2004:60 with reference to the evidence collected by Stępień 1996).

The rare example of expenditures of textiles or silver to messengers at Umma (e.g., MVN 16 960; Santag 6 127) in the same way as it was practiced at a royal court is indicative for our purpose. The habit of gift-giving was not restricted to the palace and therefore such a document at Umma does not come as a surprise; but only the royal court deals with these presents on a large scale, so that the relevant documents from Umma can easily be recognized as exceptions among the standard documentation on basic goods.

Concerning silver, the most prominent commodity handled by the palace, two recently published large documents from Umma are especially instructive. They deal with the annual income and expenditure of silver for two consecutive years (D'Agostino and Pomponio 2005). The first part of each text lists the sources of silver in the provincial treasury. The central office of the province of Umma received silver from the sale of local products, from numerous persons as taxes for the usufruct of agricultural products, and as payment of outstanding obligations. The sources for silver of Umma's "fiscal office" (cf. Steinkeller 2003:42 and passim) are also enumerated in the balanced accounts on the merchants' activities (Snell 1982). Another example is the balanced account of silver by Ur-E'e, the administrator of the district of Apishal (TCL 5 6045): silver came from the irrigation tax on fields (maš a-šà$_3$-ga), from repaid debts of the shepherds, and from (the sale of) bird wings, wool, dates, apples, and bran.

Similarly at Puzrish-Dagan the shepherds had to deliver silver to the royal treasury as balance of payment for their outstanding debts in cattle (cf. Paoletti, 2008). Such a payment in silver for obligations in commodities is already well attested in the Early Dynastic e_2-mi_2 archive of the lady of Girsu. Silver came from the shepherds (e.g., RTC 27, VS 14 65) and was delivered instead of a lost cow (DP 103) or instead of outstanding fish deliveries (VS 14 20). Land rents were also paid in silver (e.g., VS 14 175) as was, as a rule, the irrigation tax on fields (maš a-ša$_3$-ga) (RTC 75, VS 14 170; see Steinkeller 1981:130–33).

The two Umma texts for Šu-Suen year 9 (BdI E-1) and the following year Ibbi-Suen 1 (BM 106050) list not only the income, but also the expenditure of the total of silver that was collected during these years (see Table 7.3).

Only a minor part of the silver collected in many tiny sums from within the province was actually used there. Much of this silver (12.2% and 31.4%,

Table 7.3 Silver at Ur III Umma: the situation in the province (amounts given in minas, shekels, and grains; e.g., 23, 43, 105 = 23 minas [ma-na] and 43 shekels [giĝ$_4$] and 105 grains [še]). Texts published by D'Agostino and Pomponio 2005

	BdI E-1 (Šu-Suen 9)*	BM 106050 (Ibbi-Suen 1)
Total income	22, 28, 110.5	21, 16, 146
Total expenditure (calculated)	23, 43, 105 = 100%	20, 54, 122 = 100%
mašdaria-tax for royal festivals	18, 45, 000	14, 15, 000
statue of Šu-Suen, royal messenger	2, 00, 000	
sub-total royal sector	20, 45, 000 = 87.4%	14, 15, 000 = 68.1%
cultic standards in Umma province	0, 05, 090 = 0.4%	0, 05, 090 = 0.4%
at disposal of merchants	2, 53, 015 = 12.2%	6, 34, 032 = 31.4%

* Apparently, the account is correct as far as the minas and shekels are concerned, however there is slight difference of grains. Expenditure total = 23, 43, 105, whereas income (saĝ-niĝ$_2$-gur$_{11}$-ra) 22, 28, 110.5 + overdraft (diri) 1, 15, 42.5 = 23, 43, 153. The account for Šu-Suen 9 includes some special expenditures at the death of Šu-Suen and the coronation of Ibbi-Suen.

respectively) was then handed over to merchants. This sector is amply documented by the balanced accounts concerning the merchants' activities, which brought gold and other metals, resins, and various other exotic materials to Umma (see Snell 1982). A fixed sum, effectively less than half of a percent of the annual silver income, was stored in the form of "standards" in the main temples of the city-state.

The major part, namely 87.4% and 68.1% of the province's silver income, was delivered to the royal state cult and thus ultimately destined for the crown. At the time of the coronation of Ibbi-Suen in the tenth month of the year Shu-Suen 9, the province had to pay an extraordinary donation for a royal statue and a gift to the royal messenger, who brought the news of the new king's coronation. But most silver was converted into gold for nose rings which decorated the oxen at the state festivals at Ur (Sallaberger 1993, 1:167–69); perhaps the gold rings entered the temple of Nanna at Ur during the ceremony called "the opening of the house of silver and lapis lazuli" (Sallaberger 1993, 1:185–86). In the case of Ur under its Third Dynasty it is actually known that the treasures stored in the temples could ultimately serve the state, since Ibbi-Suen a few years later spent the treasures from the temples of Ur to buy grain from Isin for his starving population. UET 3 702 (xii. month, year Ibbi-Suen 13) lists more than 36 minas of gold of various qualities, ca. 74 minas of silver, 620 minas of bronze, and 587 minas of copper for "the purchase from Isin."

This perspective from Umma, the capital of an important province of the state of Ur, clearly underlines the central role of the treasure archive of Puzrish-Dagan as the written documentation of a royal organization.[19]

This survey could also be extended to later periods. In the Old Babylonian period, for example, one could point to the silver delivered by the entrepreneurs, who managed the enterprise of the palace in various economic branches (cf. Renger 2000; Stol 2004:919–44). Here again the palace dealt with the silver, gold, and other luxury items.

1.4. "Great Household Archive" vs. "Palace Archive"

The simple question about the goods treated in cuneiform texts from palaces thus leads to a categorization of archives and organizations. A label like "Great Household archive," which Benjamin R. Foster used for Sargonic Girsu (1982) and which may apply to the Pre-Sargonic e_2-mi_2 as well, is not precise enough to describe the archive of a royal palace. According to

Foster, the "great household" differs from the "household" in "degree and scope"; its archive would include "the 'agricultural circle' . . . and industrial, husbandry, commercial, and military records as well. Such archives can have a wider horizon, including not only a city and its hinterland . . ."; furthermore "a political ruler can appear as principal in the records" (1982:10–11).

Ebla has taught us a different lesson: the treasures of the state, the palace goods, could *only* be managed actively by the political ruler. Their collection as taxes, gifts, and booty and their distribution as gifts and donations may be regarded as a true "materialization" of the political duties of a ruler, including both domestic and foreign politics. This is definitely a difference in quality, not quantity, and it should warn us against stressing the household metaphor beyond its limits. Although the palace of the ruler is *also* a household (see above 1.1., the example of Ebla), its archives reflect its unique function within the state.

The differentiation of archives proves to be essential for an evaluation of the institutions active in Mesopotamia. Without the documentation of a palace archive it is almost impossible to detect the central economic and political activities of a ruler. Another example from the secondary literature may be cited in this regard: "Mesopotamian kingship contrasts strongly with that of Egypt . . . It seems that kings were at first elite landowners, perhaps important figures in community assemblies, who progressively assumed more power as war leaders and who bought land from corporate landholding groups . . . In pre-Sargonic land-sale documents . . . the buyer of the land is often a ruler or high official . . . These documents show the strong difference from Egypt in how early Mesopotamian kings were able to gain power, labor, and resources. The Mesopotamian king was a local lord whose acquisition of power was internal and unrelated to conquest outside his own state" (Baines and Yoffee 1998:207). Yoffee bases his interpretation of kingship on royal inscriptions and on the evidence of land-sale documents, without elucidating the proper place of these documents in the economy and politics of the period. The presence of archives like the one from the e_2-mi_2 of Girsu and the role of temples in the management of agricultural land then leads to the following statement: "In the earlier Mesopotamian states . . . the major economic units were palace estates and temple estates . . . The economic history of Mesopotamia must be written in terms of the dynamic forces of struggle among these economic sectors, and of degrees of intersection and cooperation among them" (Baines and

Yoffee 1998:225). The management of the agricultural resources and the interaction between temple, palace, and other institutions in this realm is a central topic of Mesopotamian economic history; but after the detection of the specific palatial economy this interaction is set into a different perspective: since the ruler alone disposed of the valuable treasures of the state, the struggle for primary resources must have seemed less threatening for him.

To sum up, the management of silver and gold and of other precious or "luxury" goods is largely dominated by the royal palace; this is reflected in the palace archives. The royal treasure can thus be seen as a defining feature of kingship in the same way as the army or control of the land was. This clear-cut distribution of resources also negates the assertion that early Mesopotamian temples should be regarded as politically leading institutions.

VALUE OF THE PALACE GOODS

The precious palace goods did not serve the basic needs of food and clothing and were not used as everyday tools, but they stand out both for their value and their "uselessness." The cuneiform documents provide a complete overview of the composition and extent of royal treasures, in a way that archaeological remains will never be able to convey. Textiles are completely lost and precious metals to a large part, from the archaeological record, although pictorial representations can compensate for this loss to a modest degree. But even the most detailed representations of clothes and the most beautiful gold vases do not reveal how such objects were valued in their original setting. Precisely this information is given by the documents as the next section will show.

Indications of Value

The value of a commodity is attributed to it in its social setting. There is extensive literature on the topic of value (e.g., Appadurai 1986, Graeber 2001, Myers 2001). For the ancient Near East, Pollock (1983) has presented a strictly archaeological point of view. Unfortunately, the unrivalled wealth of cuneiform sources for a discussion of "value" in an ancient culture has been hitherto neglected and this section intends to identify and to present a few relevant aspects.

The documentation of the palace goods serves as a copious and informative source both for the enumeration of the valued goods and for the commodity value of the goods. Concerning the first point, the detailed treatment of, for example, meat for consumption in royal archives is already a first and important indicator for its high value in the contemporary world. Concerning the commodity value, the best indicators are the price equivalents in silver, which are available for most commodities in the extensive administrative archives of the 3rd millennium. (In the treatment below these silver prices are sometimes transformed into other equivalents like work days of hired men in order to allow a better evaluation.)

According to the textual evidence various factors determined the value of these palace goods:

— the "material" itself, a value based on convention, restricted access, and rarity (examples: meat, silver, wine)

— the foreign provenience indicating a special quality (examples: clothes from Mari at Ebla, equids from Nagar)

— the expense of labor (examples: gold and silver jewels, daggers, or vessels; textiles).

The character of meat as a luxury good becomes clear from the fact that meat is missing from rations lists or the composition of meals in the messenger stations of Mesopotamia. Nevertheless, documents from royal and state archives list up to thousands of cattle and tens of thousands of sheep (Sallaberger 2003–2004:48). We know the prices of some delicacies. At Ebla, a liter of wine cost 0.6 shekel (ca. 4.8 gr) of silver (Archi 1993:32); one and a half liters could have been exchanged for a sheep. This role of wine as a luxury good—against the more common beer—has been well known in modern research and is treated in depth in several contributions (e.g., Milano 1994).

Not only food but also the draught animals at the royal court had to be of exquisite quality. At Ebla, much favored were special equids (KUNGA$_2$), probably a cross-breeding of domesticated donkeys and wild onagers, which were acquired at Nagar in Upper Mesopotamia (modern Tell Brak) at a distance of almost 400 km as the crow flies. These hybrids were infertile, and thus such an expensive animal could only be used during its lifetime and not for breeding. Still, for one head, 5 minas of silver were paid, five times the usual price of an equid of the same breed (KUNGA$_2$) at Ebla, and enough to obtain about one hundred sheep (assuming an average price of 3 shekels; 1 sheep is 1 to 7 shekels each). A gift for the travel itself (NIG$_2$.KASKAL) was not included in the price, since it was listed separately in the documents. More than once, the palace of Ebla sent out for these most expensive equids; the remote place of origin increased their value and prestige (see e.g., Sallaberger 2000:394 and note 7).

Concerning objects of silver and gold, the value of the material itself is more relevant. The treasury texts of the Third Dynasty of Ur from Puzrish-Dagan deal largely with gifts of silver rings to dignitaries or envoys. The number and weight of the rings varies, but a typical gift may consist of two silver rings of 8 shekels each, i.e., 16 shekels.[20] If this amount is converted according to the exchange rates of everyday business, well known from the sale documents of the period, it corresponds to the average purchase price of two slaves (cf. Steinkeller 1989:135–38) or the hire of a worker for more than two years,[21] or the grain and wool rations for five adult male workers for a whole year.[22]

Table 7.4 Royal gift of silver rings converted to everyday values

Royal gift of	Corresponds to
2 silver rings weighing 8 shekels each = 16 shekels	price of 1 male slave (ca. 10 shekels) plus 1 ox (ca. 6 shekels)
	or: 1 hired worker for more than 2 years (annual rate 7.6 shekels)
	or: grain and wool rations for 5 grown-up male workers for a year (annual rate 2.8 shekels)

In the context of the treasure archive, the rings appear to be a modest good, but a closer look reveals that they were indeed royal gifts of enormous value.

Textiles are, for us, the goods which are most difficult to evaluate. The documents, from Ebla, Mari, or other places, feature rich and subtly differentiated descriptions of textiles; at least the kind of cloth, its color, and quality were noted (cf. Sallaberger 2009). Using a diversified vocabulary, these subtle variations reveal immediately the actual importance of this differentiation and of the hierarchic ranking of textiles. Textiles were especially esteemed when they came from foreign places—for example, clothing from Mari at Ebla or from Yamkhad in Old Babylonian Mari.

2.2. Labor as a Factor of Value

The value of the textiles was partly determined by the quality of the wool, but to a greater extent by the expense of labor. Administrative texts record the time spent by female weavers. A few examples may suffice to illustrate this (from Waetzoldt 1972:138–40):

90 to 360 work days for flouncy cloth (^{tug}guz-za)

150 to 355 work days for niĝ$_2$-lim$_4$-cloth

780, 960, 1080, or 1200 work days for special cloths

In the production of textiles two women worked at the same loom. So for the most elaborate textiles two women worked for about two years and they could produce only two niĝ$_2$-lim$_4$-cloths per year. Regarding the long time required for their production, the most elaborate textiles must have been richly decorated and covered with ornaments.

Precious vessels of broze, silver, and gold were described in the administrative records in even greater detail than the textiles, thus providing relevant information besides the simple weight of the objects. Here, we find references to figurative decoration, inlays in other materials, or granulation. The descriptions of the bronze vessels in administrative texts from Mari are remarkable for their detail; they have been treated in an exemplary study by Guichard (2005). So the value of a good was determined not only by the material and its place of origin, but, in the case of textiles and metal vessels, also by its design and by the time and workmanship invested in its manufacture.

With these observations the economic dimension pertaining to the palace goods becomes obvious. It is the enormous expense of labor invested in their production that adds to their value. Without doubt labor was probably the most important (and most underestimated) factor of the economy of the ancient world. Concerning the role of labor in what he called prestige economy ("*Prestigewirtschaft*") in ancient Egypt, Morenz 1969 wrote: "Since labor together with the corresponding factor 'time,' which was wastefully exploited according to modern conceptions, was the most important economic power in the pharaonic empire,"[23] and in connection with the use of personnel in the cult, "Therefore personnel has to be extricated from the total workforce (we repeat: the most important economic factor in ancient Egypt), which wholly or partially takes charge of the society's duties vis-à-vis the deities."[24]

The economic documents of the ancient Near East also allow quantification in this regard. A striking example is provided by the personnel

Table 7.5 Number of personnel in the palace at Ebla after Archi 1988:135–36; here listed in decreasing order of the average number of persons. (The right-hand column gives the actual figures with the number of attestations other than one in brackets.)

Profession	Average	Attestated Numbers
"metal workers," SIMUG	491.4	460, 480, 500 (5×)
"carpenters," NAGAR	155.4	140 (6×), 142, 152, 160, 260
"slaves", DUMU.NITA-DUMU.NITA URDU$_2$-URDU$_2$	135	120 (2×), 140, 160
"(of) possessions," ZA$_x$, "of Ibbizikir"	80	80 (4×)
"personal attendants of the lord," PA$_4$.ŠEŠ EN	66.7	42 (3×), 56 (2×), 78, 80 (4×), 98
"producer of arrows," (LU$_2$ ^{ĝeš}TI)-^{ĝeš}TI	63.1	60 (3×), 65 (5×)
"agents of Ibdulu"	56.8	40 (2×), 60 (7×), 68
"(of) possessions of the king," ZA$_x$ EN	55.1	16, 40 (2×), 60 (3×), 66 (5×)
"overseers of teams of equids," UGULA SUR$_x$ KUNGA$_2$	55	43, 47, 60 (4×)
"agents," MAŠKIM	44.5	29, 60
"agents of (vizier) Ibbizikir"	42.2	40 (7×), 50 (2×)
"agents of Dubuhu-Hadda (the son of vizier Ibbi-zikir)"	40	40
"doctors," ^{a}AZU	38.7	30, 40 (4×), 42
"dancers," NE.DI	28	28 (2×)
"musicians," NAR	27	26 (5×), 27, 29, 30
"couriers," (LU$_2$) KAŠ$_4$-KAŠ$_4$	24.6	16, 20 (4×), 26, 29 (3×), 37
"agents of HaguLum (overseer of the palace)"	18.8	10, 20 (7×)
"barbers," KINDA	14	14
"dirge singers," BALAĜ-DI	9	9 (4×)

working in the palace of Ebla. These people appear as recipients of their annual cloth or wool ration in the monthly expenditure documents of textiles (MAT, cf. above).

According to the lists of workers, on average almost five hundred metal workers were employed by the palace of Ebla. This was by far the largest group of its male working personnel; the groups following in size were much smaller, the carpenters comprising 140–160 men, the "slaves" about 140 men. Even if some of the smiths were employed in the production of work tools and weapons, the majority of them were probably devoted to diligent and artistic work on objects made from precious metals. It also has to be kept in mind that this army of specialized craftsmen, producing "useless" luxury goods, had to be supported by the national economy.

At Ebla an exact quantification of the personnel employed directly by the palace is possible. The evidence from other palace archives does not contradict this concentration of artisans at the royal court. A well-known example is the workshops of the royal palace of Mari under the command of Mukannishum (Rouault 1977; cf. Durand 1997:221–82).

ACQUISITION OF PALACE GOODS

Production, Tax, Tribute, Gift, and Booty

Palace goods could be produced at the palace itself, as is indicated at Ebla by the metal workers in the palace (see above and Table 7.5) and by the weavers engaged in textile production (e.g., Milano 1990:338). A large part of the goods arrived at the palace as taxes, tribute, and gifts from dependent organizations, cities, or provinces: examples are the annual accounts of the delivery of metals and textiles from Ebla (see Table 7.1, no. 4.1) and the delivery of silver from the province of Umma in the form of donations for the cult (see above, Table 7.3). Acquisition by trade will be treated below, whereas the reciprocal exchange of gifts with other rulers will not be considered here but will form the subject of a separate article to be published elsewhere (see note 1). Finally, royal treasures were always a target of military expeditions, as is impressively testified not only by the enumerations in Neo-Assyrian royal inscriptions but as is already documented for the time of Zimri-Lim of Mari with the hunt for the treasure of Shamshi-Adad (Eidem 1994). But any successful military campaign could increase the crown's possessions through the spoils of war, including movable property, cattle and other livestock, and prisoners of war for whom sizable ransoms might be paid: the high sums recorded may indicate that this was a major goal of ancient Near Eastern warfare (cf. Waetzoldt 2003 for Old Babylonian Mari and Shehna, Archi 2003b for Ebla).

For the various ways that prestigious objects were acquired, it may suffice to refer to a passage from the Broken Obelisk of Ashur-bel-kala (1073–1056) dealing with rare and exotic animals (Grayson 1991:A.0.89.7): the king himself hunted wild bulls, elephants, and other animals, catching some animals alive for breeding in Assyria; he had merchants acquire exotic animals (iv 26–27); and finally the king of Egypt sent a crocodile, a monkey, and other beasts as diplomatic gifts (iv 29–30).

The flow of goods to the palace has not yet been studied adequately. For the early periods, which are the focus of this contribution, one would think of the delivery lists of Ebla (MU.DU texts), the transfer of animals to Puzrish-Dagan (for which a quantitative evaluation of the sources has not been carried out; cf. e.g., Sallaberger 1999:267), or the deliveries (šūrubtum) of textiles and metals to the Mari palace. The study of the relative importance of the various ways of acquisition such as production, confiscation, tax, tribute, gift, or booty would contribute to a better understanding of the palatial economy.

Paola Paoletti (2008) has studied the deliveries of silver to the crown as documented in the treasure archive of Puzrish-Dagan:

The high amount of silver from the herdsmen as compensation for outstanding debts of animals certainly resulted from the function of Puzrish-Dagan as the administrative center for the royal cattle. More silver was transferred from the workshops or from the palace, but the documents of

Table 7.6 Specified income of silver in the Drehem treasure archive after Paoletti 2008; amounts given in talents, minas, and shekels; e.g., 2, 18, 15 = 2 talents (gun$_2$), 18 minas (ma-na), and 15 shekels (giĝ$_4$)

payment for arrears on animals	11 texts	1, 26, 37 (ca. 43.6 kg)
income for the sale of gold	4 texts	2, 18, 15 (ca. 69.1 kg)
booty, tribute, retrieved goods	8 texts	14, 58, 15 (ca. 8 kg)

this archive hardly ever mention the supplier's name without identifying the kind of income, a text type not treated by Paoletti (2008).

Purchase and Trade

Trade as a means to acquire precious goods was based on the investment of silver and so has left its traces in the administrative documents. The annual expenditure documents for metals from Ebla (AAM, see Archi 1996) provide a unique source to investigate the use of royal treasures in great detail. These Ebla documents list every expenditure of silver and the silver equivalents of expenditures of gold, tin, and copper of the palace of Ebla during one year. Of the few texts published so far, two are fairly well preserved so that they can be analyzed in this context: the annual accounts of the years Ibbi-zikir 5, MEE 10, 29 (75.1918), and Ibbi-zikir 10, MEE 12, 36 (75.2429), according to the relative chronology established by Archi and Biga (2003:9). Each of these has more than 170 individual entries. In this context we are only interested in the relative amount of silver spent for "purchase" (NIG$_2$.SAM$_2$) during a year:

According to the accounting system used by the administrative texts, all silver and gold objects whatever their form and decoration were weighed and the only thing that counted for the administration was the pure weight of metal. Silver might be disbursed as a gift, as a votive donation to the deities, or as payment in a purchase, and all these transactions are noted in substantially the same format and in the same context in the administrative texts. Although silver was perceived as a weighed material by the administration, the objects themselves differed according to their

Table 7.7 Amounts of silver expended for trade by the palace of Ebla during the years Ibbi-zikir 5 and 10. The silver is rounded to minas (1 mina corresponds to ca. 0.47 kg)

	Total of silver distributed (as far as text is preserved)	Total of silver according to the total given in the text	Silver for purchase
MEE 10 29, year Ibbi-zikir 5	434 minas	(449 minas)	108 minas = 25%
MEE 12 36, year Ibbi-zikir 10	351 minas	(362 minas)	66 minas = 19%

actual use. For purchase, simply the weight is indicated and thus silver coils or other forms of silver were used (cf. Paoletti 2008 for the Ur III evidence).

A considerable part of the silver of Ebla, a fifth or even a fourth of the total silver expenditures of the palace, was used for purchases (see Table 7.6). Perhaps one would expect that the treasures of the country collected in the palace would be used to acquire *necessary* materials and for investments in economic production. The following goods were purchased according to the two selected annual accounts:

a) MEE 10, 29, Ibbi-zikir 5: 108 minas spent for purchase, i.e., 24% of total expenditures

Table 7.8a Expenditure of silver for purchases for one year according to the selected annual accounts of Ebla, measured in minas and shekels (e.g., 3, 10 = 3 minas 10 shekels)

Agricultural products	0, 35	"straw" (ŠE IN.BUL$_5$)
	1, 18	"straw" (ŠE IN, etc.)
	0, 05	goats
Delicacies	0, 40	a vegetable (^{ga}GARAŠ$_3$^{sar} KUR^{ki})
Equids	3, 04	donkeys (IGI NITA)
	30, 00	KUNGA$_2$ equids
Stones	4, 00	lapis lazuli
Textiles	0, 06	clothes for apprentice scribes
	0, 34.5	128 white belts for the "slaves"
	65, 12	textiles from the markets
Unclear	2, 00	A-A

b) MEE 12, 36, Ibbi-zikir 10: 66,16.8 minas spent for purchase, i.e., 19% of total expenditures

Small sums were disbursed for agricultural products such as straw and for livestock such as goats and donkeys which might have been used for transport. But large amounts were spent on delicacies, lapis lazuli (4 minas in Ibbi-zikir 5), the expensive KUNGA$_2$ equids of the royal wagons (30 and 15

Table 7.8b Expenditure of silver for purchases for one year according to the selected annual accounts of Ebla, measured in minas and shekels (e.g., 3, 10 = 3 minas 10 shekels)

Delicacies	1, 00	a vegetable (gaGARAŠ$_3$sar KUR)
	0, 05.5	wine (ĜEŠTIN)
	0, 01	fish (KU$_6$.KU$_6$)
Equids	15, 00	KUNGA$_2$ equids (hybrids)
Textiles	0, 25	100 white belts for the 'new slaves'
	45, 02	textiles from the markets
Wool	1, 33.3	280 "stones" of wool from Mari
	3, 10	440 "stones" of wool from the markets

minas), and above all, textiles (65 and 45 minas), thus corresponding exactly to the usual well-known luxury goods. Especially considering the large-scale production of textiles at the palace of Ebla itself (see above) and its control of enormous flocks of sheep, the extensive purchase of clothing and even wool on the market may come as a surprise.[25]

Other archives largely confirm this picture from Ebla. Within the Ur III treasure archive the purchased goods were gold and cedar resin, but also copper and tin.[26] Mari matches our expectations closely: silver was exchanged for gold and for the metals used to produce bronze, namely copper and tin, as well as for lead, but in addition resins, wool, and lapis lazuli were purchased.[27]

The merchants acquired the materials that were not found in Mesopotamia, namely wood and resins, precious stones and metals, in the surrounding mountain ranges. A large part of overland trade was thus linked with the prestige economy of the palace. It may be added that the sub-centers also participated in a similar way in this trade of prestige goods. According to the annual silver accounts of Umma (discussed above with Table 7.3), 12% to 30% of the silver delivered to the provincial capital was handed over to the merchants in order for them to acquire materials in the eastern mountain regions, in particular resins, which were used mainly for scented oil (Snell 1982).

The administrative texts from the ancient Near Eastern palaces thus indicate the context and the extent of the acquisition of "exotic" materials and also the exchange of such materials as diplomatic gifts. At Ebla as well as in the other archives, the same commodities appear in the same contexts—both as gifts and as objects of trade. Therefore a substantial distinction between a trade in commodities and a transfer of goods through gift-giving is not appropriate for the understanding of ancient (and other) socio-economic systems, as has already been argued by scholars like Wagner-Hasel (2000, especially chapter 1) and by Reden (2003:2–4).

The cuneiform texts do, however, make a sharp terminological distinction between "purchases" (at Ebla NIĜ$_2$.SAM$_2$) and the "giving" of gifts (NIĜ$_2$.BA)—including votive offerings to deities, which were sometimes explicitly called "gifts." The legal act of *purchase* is carried out by merchants, working on behalf of the palace; it is always focused on the goods, there is a fixed relation between the values of the exchanged goods, and this exchange takes place without delay. These features stand in clear contrast to *gifts* which are focused on the person, have no fixed relation of values, and where the delay in the exchange is an essential part of the procedure.

Certainly the imported goods were valued in various regards: "The colour of a semi-precious stone, its religious aura and associations with specific deities; the distance travelled by the material; the hardships involved in its procurement; the status of the bearer—these and other overtones were undoubtedly heard and understood by those who witnessed the conspicuous display of materials which came to Mesopotamia from, in many cases, great distances" (Potts 2007:124). Such a perspective on the palace goods, despite its undeniable merits, tends to obliterate the distinction between the economic value and the estimation of a good. The high esteem of certain materials in a specific cultural context was ultimately the driving force behind why merchants were sent to obtain these goods. But for the ancient Near Eastern administration prices in silver were determined for the palace goods, whether exotic, luxurious, or prestigious, and so they could and can be compared with basic commodities such as barley or with work days. The same object could be considered both as a valuable royal gift (with all the associated cultural overtones) and as a commodity (that could be included in the accounts of the administration or could be bought or sold).[28]

Storage and Distribution

The silver and textiles brought to the palace were stored in its treasure chambers and thence distributed according to actual needs. At Ebla, the

Table 7.9 Table 7.9 Silver "expended" (E_3) and "stored/present" ($AL_6.\hat{G}AL_2$) in the palace of Ebla (amounts per year in minas) after Archi 1996:73; dates according to Archi and Biga 2003:8–9; MEE 10 29 and MEE 12 36 added

Year (counted after "vizier")	Text	Silver expended (E_3)	Silver present/ stored ($AL_6.\hat{G}AL_2$)
Ibrium 15	75.2502	273.46	437
Ibbi-zikir 1	75.1860 = MEE 10, 20	573	430
Ibbi-zikir 5	75.1918 = MEE 10, 29	449.20	630
Ibbi-zikir 10	75.2429 = MEE 12, 36	369	1109
Ibbi-zikir 11	75.2507	442	1200

annual accounts of expenditure of metals (AAM) indicate the relation between stored and distributed goods.

At Ebla, the treasure was constantly growing. According to the tabulation of Archi (1991:217) 5561 kg of silver and 179 kg of gold were delivered to the palace during ten years when Ibbi-zikir was vizier. This is an average of 556.1 kg (ca. 1183 minas) of silver, whereas 17.9 kg of gold equal ca. 89.5 kg silver (standard ratio 1:5; ca. 190 minas), thus a total of ca. 1373 minas silver (value) per year. Accordingly, the "silver present" ($AL_6.\hat{G}AL_2$) should correspond to the silver delivered (MU.DU) the same year but not expended (E_3). However, an exact calculation of the treasure of Ebla must be postponed until all the relevant texts are published.

A considerable portion of the expensive luxury goods, acquired with much effort from various sources, was distributed for various purposes. This agrees with the character of prestige goods, which have to be ostentatiously disbursed in order for them to produce the desired effect of excessive splendor and thereby to confer power and status. This principle of conspicuous consumption, the multiple presentations of the acquired goods, has become widely known since Th. Veblen's brilliant analysis of the "Theory of the leisure class" (Veblen 1899; cf. the second part of this essay).

The amount of silver distributed as gifts from the treasure as documented by the administrative texts underlines the general tenor of this chapter: the royal treasure, the "king's chest" (*pisan šarrim*) as it was called at Old Babylonian Mari, was not "dead" silver hidden in the palace, but was itself an instrument of government, carefully managed and exploited according to the political and economic circumstances.

THE POLITICAL AND ECONOMIC RELEVANCE OF PALACE GOODS

Luxury goods—textiles, silver and gold, meat, and special edible delicacies—are primarily found in one specific context, namely the palace. The management of royal treasure, which can hardly be seen as a static hoard, may be called the palatial economy.[29] This sector of the economy emerges most clearly from the perspective of consumption, which was dictated by the needs of the king and his court. As will be discussed elsewhere (see note 1), specific segments of the society participated in the consumption of the palace goods, which were distributed by the king according to actual political requirements.

The Reach of the Palace Economy

The expenditure of palace goods, which was based on political considerations, ultimately determined the economy of the crown and thus the state. Documentation of deliveries to the palace show how revenues were collected from different economic organizations. As exemplified in the annual silver balances of Umma (Table 7.3) numerous branches converted their primary goods of every kind into tiny sums of silver, which were collected by the province and then delivered to the state in the form of donations to a religious festival. Furthermore, hundreds of workers were directly employed in the production of the palace goods. Palace goods were bought on the markets from other producers, and merchants were essential for the distribution of these goods over wide distances.

So when we focus on their production, it is clear that the palace goods did not remain restricted to an elite or to the court, but pertained to the economy and politics of the whole country: a considerable part of the labor force and of the surplus of goods of the country were used to obtain and produce the palace goods, commodities which were extremely valuable but not intended for daily use. One has to underline the fact that textiles were bought by the ruler in the markets, which directly attests to the production of prestige goods also by other organizations or even by private handicraft (see above, Sallaberger 2008). Furthermore, the purchase of products by the palace represents one of the ways in which silver was distributed within the population.[30] Keeping this in mind, the high percentage of silver spent by the palace to acquire textiles at the markets (see Table 7.7) has to be evaluated not only as an expression of the ruler's insatiable desire for luxury, but also at the same time and perhaps no less significantly as a program to support de-centralized production.

Investigating Consumption as a Heuristic Principle

Although the palatial economy is well documented in the cuneiform archives, this prominent sector of the economy has never been treated nor has its importance been recognized. The reason for this neglect can easily be identified in the traditional perspectives of the investigation of social and economic history, namely as a form of history "from below"—thus concentrating on subsistence economy, and on production (in Marx' tradition), and on exchange (mostly in the Polanyi school)—and the almost total neglect of consumption as a heuristic principle.

A contribution by Renger (2007), who generally bases his analysis on economic exchange, may serve as an example of a very recent summary of the economy of ancient Mesopotamia. In this view, all economic organizations in the empire of the Third Dynasty of Ur are seen as parts of the "household of the ruler" (Renger 2007:190) without attaching any importance to the patent differentiation between the palace and the province as is clearly indicated in the archives (see above). According to Renger the ruler's household encompassed "individual households of the ruler, members of the royal family, high priests and the highest officials of the realm for their personal support." Sectors of the economy produced a surplus which "served exclusively ostentatious and prestige purposes" (Renger 2007:195); this refers to the palatial economy, with the substantial difference that the collection and distribution served essential socio-political purposes of the state (support of the army, diplomatic gifts, purchases, etc.; see the second part of this study).

The Application of the Model of Palace Economy

As noted above, the management of silver and gold, of textiles, and of other precious or "luxury" goods is largely dominated by the royal palace; this is reflected in the palace archives. Royal treasure thus can be seen as a defining feature of kingship in the same way as the army or the control of the land are. In the section above (Acquisition of Palace Goods), evidence has been presented showing how the acquisition of goods destined for the palace treasure affected the economy of the whole state, if one considers first of all the collection of silver in various economic branches, the workforce employed in production, purchases in the local markets besides the merchants active in long-distance trade.

The model of the palatial economy presented here has been developed out of an analysis of palace archives of the late 3rd and early 2nd millennium. Other palace archives from later periods do not contradict the basic conclusions, but of course differences existed in the respective environments. Silver was definitely more widespread from the Old Babylonian period onwards, the relationship between palace and temple or between the royal palace and seats of governors may have varied, and also the political and economic roles of palaces did not remain the same. An Early Dynastic palace of a city-state certainly did not function at the same level as for example Sennacherib's palace at Nineveh.

The spread of silver, textiles, and other prestigious goods in the society is essential for the recognition of their value. The widespread circulation of silver in the society, as exemplified by its use in sales and loans already in the Early Dynastic period, is a precondition for collecting silver for the crown. Therefore it is hard to draw a sharp borderline between the specific handling of silver within the palatial economy, i.e., the management of royal treasure, and any other use of silver or textiles. A single document may be ambiguous in this regard, and only a larger group of texts may reveal their institutional origin. As repeatedly indicated above, the prototypical palace texts are the detailed documents of expenditure of palace goods with their total administrative coverage of the objects concerned, the recipients, occasion, and circumstances.

Elements of the royal management of treasure are not restricted to the palace, since the principles of prestige and of gift-giving are shared by the society. Thus some documents of the Old Babylonian period have been identified that register the expenditures for banquets by notables and donations to their clients.[31] The extent to which other institutions act similarly or differently from the crown may contribute to an analysis of their socio-political relationship with the ruler. A few examples in this direction have been given concerning the handling of palace goods by the lady of Girsu in Early Dynastic times or by the provincial government of Umma under the kings of Ur. Only the recognition of the idealizing model of the concentration of palace goods at the crown leads to further questions, for example, about the goldsmiths of the god Ashur (cf. Radner 1999): were they simply employed for work at the Ashur temple commissioned by the king or should they be regarded as a "realization" of the ideological role of the god Ashur as the ruler of the Assyrian empire and his temple as his "palace"?

This chapter has concentrated on the management of palace goods and has underlined their relevance for the state's economy and for society as a whole. This does in no way negate the social and political importance of the subsistence economy. On the other hand, despite the dominant role of the temples in the management of agriculture in the 3rd millennium, it has become evident that the temples definitely do not exert a political power similar to that of a royal palace. This perspective allows us to differentiate more exactly between the various institutions and organizations in the ancient Near East instead of accepting them simply as various realizations of "households." Some notes have been made above on the differences between palace and temple, capital and second-rank towns, royal and governor's archives, and between prestige goods handled by the king and those handled by the governor.

Finally, one may ask if the palatial economy as described here characterizes a special type of state or kingship. The three examples chosen stem from different contexts: Early Dynastic Ebla may be described as a city-state, Puzrish-Dagan represents the royal administration of the empire of the Third Dynasty of Ur, which comprises a number of former city-states, and in the ideology of the kingship of Mari, tribal affiliation plays a central role. The management of royal treasure thus can be seen as a defining feature of kingship independent of the composition or scope of the state. The acquisition of the goods in the state and their strategic distribution according to the actual political situation are undisputed prerogatives of the king in the ancient Near East.

NOTES

7.1 The text prepared for the meeting in Philadelphia under the title "Prestige and Loyalty: The Political Dimension of Palatial Economy in the Ancient Near East" turned out to be too long to be included in this volume. Therefore, it was decided to present here its first part on palace archives and palace goods in revised form and to publish the second part on the distribution of royal gifts elsewhere. The arguments of this contribution were first presented in a lecture on "Gifts of the Ruler" developed between 2000 and 2003. The article has benefitted from discussions after lectures at Berlin, Munich, Venice, Oxford, the Johns Hopkins University, Yale University, later at Munich within the Graduate College "Formen von Prestige in Kulturen des Altertums," especially with Sitta von Reden, and during the symposium at Philadelphia.

7.2 This topographic situation is not restricted to palace archives; note for example the scribal rooms near the entrance to the Ur III Inana temple at Nippur (Zettler 1992:67–86).

7.3 Milano 1990 published the texts as "ration lists," but both the present writer (in April 2004 at a symposium celebrating the fortieth anniversary of the excavations of Ebla by Paolo Matthiae) and Lucio Milano himself (in May 2005 at a symposium on labor organized by Piotr Steinkeller and Michael Hudson) came to the conclusion that the Ebla texts cannot be labeled "ration lists," which deal with grain distributed to the clients of an organization according to their respective rank and labor. In ancient Near Eastern studies the term "rations" is used instead of a more appropriate "salaries." The correct identification of the Ebla beer and bread documentation invalidates the assumption of a difference in the system of labor between Ebla and Southern Mesopotamia (as it had been proposed by Milano 1989:90; for differences between Mesopotamian ration lists and Ebla see also Milano 1996:145: "le fait signifiant est que l'on est en présence d'un système *sui generis*, tant du point de vue de l'enregistrement comptable, que dans sa substance").

7.4 Such a documentation of the management of single herds and their herdsmen is found among the roughly contemporary texts from Tell Beydar (Sallaberger 2004), typically enough a second-rank city under the capital Nagar (which thus corresponds to Ebla).

7.5 *PA.MUNSUB*, corresponding to Ur III šuš$_3$ and later *NA.GADA*.

7.6 The comparisons for Mari are based on cursory readings of the administrative texts published in *ARM* 7, 9, 11, 12, 18, 21 to 25, 31, and articles published in *MARI* 3 and 7.

7.7 See the full list of the publications in Charpin 2004:410; for the metal texts see especially Sanati-Müller 1990: no. 87ff., and *ead*. 1993: nos. 202, 203; for textiles *ead*. 1994: no. 206 (textiles), see ibid. p. 325 on wool as rations, for production, but also as present (niĝ$_2$.ba) especially for special services (*inūma* ...).

7.8 Eidem 1992, e.g., texts like nos. 109 (jewels, textiles, and oil for the royal court), 110 (textiles for the lady), 123–124 (textiles), 132 (textiles, shoes, and silver).

7.9 Van De Mieroop 1994.

7.10 Dalley, Walker, and Hawkins 1976: nos. 250–266.

7.11 See e.g., Mayer 1978.

Palace Archives and Palatial Economy in the Ancient Near East 249

7.12 Siegelová 1986:328ff., including the summary pp. 360–62: the administrative texts of Hattusha concern mostly textiles, but also jewels.

7.13 *SAA* 7 and 11, *CTN* 1–3.

7.14 This functional definition of an archive overcomes the problems of defining an archive either by find spot or by text types.

7.15 Starting with the correspondence of Ebla, for example the famous Hamazi letter *ARET* 13, 3 about the exchange of wood for equids.

7.16 Sumerian verb a ru; *DP* 69–72; *VS* 14 13; *BIN* 8 390; and *DP* 74; cf. Selz 1995:199–200.

7.17 E.g., *RTC* 25; *MVN* 3 10; Nik 1 292, 293, 300, 310, 313; *DP* 517.

7.18 *VS* 14 30, control of goods of Dimtur in the palace ("234 minas of copper, property of Dimtur, which the merchant Ur-Enki has brought from Dilmun. Prince Lugalanda weighed it in the palace."); cf. *VS* 14 194.

7.19 The (imprecise) view that the Umma and Girsu archives belonged to the "state administration" of the Ur III economy is so deeply rooted in Assyriology that e.g., Postgate 2001 used the Umma documentation for a comparison of palace-centered systems.

7.20 A few examples: *AUCT* 1 176 (Ūta-mīšaram), 942 (one female singer and a dirge singer), *JCS* 10, 30 no. 10 and 31 no. 11 (an attendant, sugal$_7$), *TrDr* 83 (a foreign messenger).

7.21 A hired worker received 6 liters (sila$_3$) grain per day and he had to live on this income. One worker (ĝuruš) received 2160 liters grain per year, worth 7.2 shekels (300 liters or 1 kor grain equals 1 shekel silver), plus wool of 4 minas, worth 0.4 shekels, thus an annual total value of 7.6 shekels (cf. Waetzoldt 1987:134).

7.22 Rations could be complemented by additional sources of income. Twelve monthly rations of a standard of 60 liters (sila$_3$), thus 720 liters worth 2.4 shekels, plus the wool ration worth 0.4 shekels (cf. preceding note).

7.23 "Da diese [sc. die menschliche – W.S.] Arbeitskraft, zusammen mit dem ihr korrespondierenden und für moderne Begriffe im Raubbau verwirtschafteten Faktor 'Zeit,' die wichtigste ökonomische Potenz im Pharaonenreich gewesen ist" (Morenz 1969:21–22).

7.24 "Darum muß aus der Summe der Arbeitskräfte (wir wiederholen: des wichtigsten ökonomischen Faktors im alten Ägypten) ein Dienstpersonal freigesetzt werden, das ganz oder teilweise die Pflichten der Gesellschaft gegenüber den Göttern übernimmt" (Morenz 1969:31–32).

7.25 On the markets of Ebla see Biga 2002; see also Sallaberger 2008.

7.26 For (the purchase of) gold see Paoletti in print; copper: *AUCT* 1 661; tin: *AUCT* 2 289; stones: *CT* 32 25; cedar resin: *TCNY* 45.

7.27 Cf. the literature cited by Charpin 2004:471–72 and the overview by Michel 1996, which lists the objects of trade, but without an evaluation of the quantitative aspect.

7.28 Reden 2003:60 discusses the re-evaluation of objects according to their context, so that "singular" objects may become commodities for trade.

7.29 This is to be separated from the "enterprise of the palace" (German: *Palastgeschäft*), a specific form of entrepreneurship described for the Old Babylonian period.

7.30 See above on Ebla and note Wilcke 2007 on the governor of Umma buying goods in his province.

7.31 See the examples from Mari (especially the house of the diviner Asqudum), Sippar, and Larsa listed by Charpin 1996:222–23.

REFERENCES

Appadurai, A. 1986. Introduction: Commodities and the Politics of Value. In *The Social Life of Things. Commodities in Social Perspective*, ed. A. Appadurai, pp. 3–63. Cambridge: University Press.

Archi, A. 1984. Allevamento e distribuzione di bestiame ad Ebla. *Studi Eblaiti* 7:45–81, figs. 3–20.

———. 1988. Zur Organisation der Arbeit in Ebla. In *Wirtschaft und Gesellschaft von Ebla,* ed. H. Hauptmann and H. Waetzoldt, pp. 131–38. HSAO 2. Heidelberg: Heidelberger Orientverlag.

———. 1991. Ebla. La formazione di uno stato del III millennio a. C. In *La Parola del Passato* 46:195–219.

———. 1992. Transmission of the Mesopotamian Lexical and Literary Texts. In *Literature and Literary Language at Ebla*, ed. P. Fronzaroli, pp. 1–29, pls. 1–10. Quaderni di Semitistica 18. Firenze: Università di Firenze, Dipartimento di Linguistica.

———. 1993. *Five Tablets from the Southern Wing of Palace G–Ebla*. Syro-Mesopotamian Studies 5(2). Malibu: Undena Publications.

———. 1996. Les comptes rendus annuels de métaux (CAM). In *Mari, Ébla et les Hourrites. Dix ans de travaux*, ed. J.-M. Durand, pp. 73–99. Amurru 1. Paris: ERC.

———. 2003a. Archival Record-Keeping at Ebla 2400-2340 BC. In *Ancient Archives and Archival Traditions. Concepts of Record-Keeping in the Ancient World*, ed. M. Brosius, pp. 17–36. Oxford: University Press.

———. 2003b. Minima eblaitica 17: níg-du$_8$ "price for release; ransom." *Nouvelles assyriologiques brèves et utilitaires* 2003(70).

Archi, A., and M.G. Biga. 2003. A Victory over Mari and the Fall of Ebla. *JCS* 55:1–44.

Baines, J., and N. Yoffee. 1998. Order, Legitimacy, and Wealth in Ancient Egypt and Mesopotamia. In *Archaic States,* ed. G.M. Feinman and J. Marcus, pp. 199–259. Santa Fe, NM: School of American Research Press.

Bauer, J. 1998. Der vorsargonische Abschnitt der mesopotamischen Geschichte. In *Mesopotamien: Späturuk-Zeit und Frühdynastische Zeit,* ed. P. Attinger and M. Wäfler, pp. 429–585. OBO 160/1. Freiburg, Schweiz: Universitätsverlag; Göttingen: Vandenhoeck & Ruprecht.

Biga, M.G. 2002. Les foires d'après les archives d'Ébla. In *Recueil d'études à la mémoire d'André Parrot,* ed. D. Charpin and J.-M. Durand, pp. 277–88. Florilegium Marianum 6. Paris: SEPOA.

Charpin, D. 1996. Maisons et maisonnées en Babylonie ancienne de Sippar à Ur. Remarques sur les grandes demeures des notables paléo-babyloniens. In *Houses and Households in Mesopotamia. Papers Read at the 40th Rencontre Assyriologique Internationale Leiden, July 5-8, 1993,* ed. K.R. Veenhof, pp. 221–28. Leiden: Nederlands Instituut voor het Nabije Oosten.

———. 2004. Histoire politique du Proche-Orient amorrite (2002–1595). In *Mesopotamien: Die altbabylonische Zeit,* ed. P. Attinger, W. Sallaberger, and M. Wäfler, pp. 25–480. OBO 160/4. Fribourg: Academic Press; Göttingen: Vandenhoeck & Ruprecht.

D'Agostino, F., and F. Pomponio. 2005. Due bilanci di entrate e uscite di argento a Umma. *ZA* 95:172–207.

Dalley, S., C.B.F. Walker, and D. Hawkins. 1976. *The Old Babylonian Tablets from Tell al-Rimah.* London: British School of Archaeology in Iraq.

Durand, J.-M. 1985. L'organization de l'espace dans le Palais de Mari: Le témoignage des textes. In *Le Système palatial en Orient, en Grèce et à Rome,* ed. E. Lévy, pp. 39–110. Strasbourg: AECR.

———. 1997. *Documents épistolaires du palais de Mari. I.* Littératures anciennes du Proche-Orient 16. Paris: Éditions du Cerf.

Eidem, J. 1992. *The Shemshara Archives 2. The Administrative Texts.* Historisk-filosofiske Skrifter 15. Copenhagen: Munksgaard.

———. 1994. Raiders of the Lost Treasure of Samsī-Addu. In *Recueil d'études à la mémoire de Maurice Birot,* ed. D. Charpin and J.-M. Durand, pp. 201–8. Florilegium Marianum 2. Paris: SEPOA.

Foster, B.R. 1982. Archives and Record-Keeping in Sargonic Mesopotamia. *ZA* 72:1–27.

Fronzaroli, P. 2003. *Testi di Cancelleria. I rapporti con le città*. ARET 13. Roma: Missione Archaeologica Italiana in Siria.

Graeber, D. 2001. *Toward an Anthropological Understanding of Value. The False Coin of Our Own Dreams*. New York: Palgrave publishers.

Grayson, A.K. 1991. *Assyrian Rulers of the Early First Millennium BC I (1114–859 BC)*. Royal Inscriptions of Mesopotamia, Assyrian Periods 2. Toronto: University of Toronto Press.

Guichard, M. 2005. *La vaisselle de luxe des rois de Mari. Matériaux pour le Dictionnaire de Babylonien de Paris 2. ARM 31*. Paris: ERC.

Mayer, W. 1978. *Nuzi-Studien I. Die Archive des Palastes und die Prosopographie der Berufe*. AOAT 205(I). Kevelaer: Butzon & Bercker, and Neukirchen-Vluyn: Neukirchner Verlag.

Michel, C. 1996. Le commerce dans les textes de Mari. In *Mari, Ébla et les Hourrites. Dix ans de travaux*, ed. J.-M. Durand, pp. 385–426. Amurru 1. Paris: ERC.

Milano, L. 1989. Le razioni alimentari nel Vicino Oriente antico: per un'articolazione storica del sistema. In *Il pane del re. Accumulo e distribuzione dei cereali nell'oriente antico*, ed. R. Dolce and C. Zaccagnini, pp. 65–100. Bologna: Cooperativa Libraria Universitaria Editrice.

———. 1990. *Testi amministrativi: Assegnazioni di prodotti alimentari*. ARET 9. Roma: Missione Archaeologica Italiana in Siria.

———. 1994. Vino e birra in Oriente. Confini geografici e confini culturali. In *Drinking in Ancient Societies. History and Culture of Drinks in the Ancient Near East*, ed. L. Milano, pp. 421–40. History of the Ancient Near East Studies 6. Padova: Sargon.

———. 1996. Ébla: Gestion des terres et gestion des ressources alimentaires. In *Mari, Ébla et les Hourrites. Dix ans de travaux*, ed. J.-M. Durand, pp. 135–71. Amurru 1. Paris: ERC.

Morenz, S. 1969. *Prestige-Wirtschaft im alten Ägypten. Sitzungsberichte der Bayerischen Akademie der Wissenschaften, Philosophisch-historische Klasse*. Jahrgang 1969, Heft 4. München: Beck.

Myers, F.R. 2001. Introduction: The Empire of Things. In *The Empire of Things. Regimes of Value and Material Culture*, ed. F.R. Myers, pp. 3–64. Santa Fe: School for Advanced Research Press.

Paoletti, P. 2008. Elusive Silver? Evidence for the Circulation of Silver in the Ur III State. *Kaskal* 5:127–58.

———. 2010. Der König und sein Kreis. Das *staatliche Schatzarchiv der III. Dynas-*

tie von Ur. Unpublished doctoral diss., Ludwig-Maximilians-Universität München.

Pedersén, Olof. 2005a. *Archive und Bibliotheken in Babylon*. Abhandlungen der Deutschen Orient-Gesellschaft 25. Saarbrücken: Saarbrücker Druckerei und Verlag.

———. 2005b. Foreign Professionals in Babylon: Evidence from the Archive in the Palace of Nebuchadnezzar II. In *Ethnicity in Ancient Mesopotamia. Papers Read at the 48th Rencontre Assyriologique Internationale Leiden, 1–4 July 2002*, ed. W.H. van Soldt, 267–71. Leiden: Nederlands Instituut voor het Nabije Oosten.

Pettinato, G. 1979. *Culto ufficiale ad Ebla durante il regno di Ibbi-sipiš*. Orientis antiqui collectio 16. Roma: Istituto per l'Oriente.

Pollock, S. 1983. *The Symbolism of Prestige. An Archaeological Example from the Royal Cemetery of Ur*. Ph.D. diss., Univ. of Michigan, Ann Arbor.

Postgate, J.N. 1979. The Economic Structure of the Assyrian Empire. In *Power and Propaganda. A Symposium on Ancient Empires*, ed. M.T. Larsen, pp. 193–221. Mesopotamia 7. Copenhagen: Akademisk Forlag.

———. 2001. System and Style in Three Near Eastern Bureaucracies. *Economy and Politics in the Mycenaean Palace States*, ed. S. Voutsaki and J. Killern, pp. 181–94. Cambridge Philological Society Suppl. 27. Cambridge.

Potts, D.T. 2007. Babylonian Sources of Exotic Raw Materials. In *The Babylonian World*, ed. G. Leick, pp. 124–40. New York: Routledge.

Pruß, A., and W. Sallaberger. 2003–2004. Tierhaltung in Nabada/Tell Beydar und die Bilderwelt der Terrakotten als Spiegel von Wirtschaft und Umwelt. *AfO* 50:293–307.

Radner, K. 1999. *Ein neuassyrisches Privatarchiv der Tempelgoldschmiede von Assur*. Studien zu den Assur-Texten 1. Saarbrücken: Saarbrücker Druckerei und Verlag.

Reden, S. von. 2003. *Exchange in Ancient Greece*. 2nd ed. London: Duckworth.

Renger, J. 2000. Das Palastgeschäft in der altbabylonischen Zeit. In *Interdependency of Institutions and Private Entrepreneurs. Proceedings of the Second MOS Symposium (Leiden 1998)*, ed. A.C.V.M. Bongenaar, pp. 153–83. Leiden: Nederlands Historisch-Archaeologisch Instituut te Istanbul.

———. 2007. Economy of Ancient Mesopotamia. A General Outline. In *The Babylonian World*. ed. G. Leick, 187–97. New York: Routledge.

Rouault, O. 1977. *Mukannišum. L'administration et l'économie palatiales à Mari. Transcription, traduction et étude historique*. ARM 18. Paris: Geuthner.

Sallaberger, W. 1993. *Der kultische Kalender der Ur III-Zeit*. Untersuchungen zur

Assyriologie und Vorderasiatischen Archäologie 7. Berlin: W. de Gruyter.

———. 1999. Ur III-Zeit. In *Mesopotamien: Akkade-Zeit und Ur III-Zeit*, ed. P. Attinger and M. Wäfler, pp. 119–390. OBO 160/3. Freiburg, Schweiz: Universitätsverlag; Göttingen: Vandenhoeck & Ruprecht.

———. 2000. Nagar in den frühdynastischen Texten aus Beydar. In *Languages and Cultures in Contact*. ed. K. Van Lerberghe and G. Voet, pp. 393–407. OLA 96. Leuven: Peeters.

———. 2003–2004. Schlachtvieh aus Puzrish-Dagān. Zur Bedeutung dieses königlichen Archivs. *JEOL* 38:45–62.

———. 2004. A Note on the Sheep and Goat Flocks. Introduction to Texts 151–167. In *Third Millennium Cuneiform Texts from Tell Beydar (Seasons 1996–2002)*, ed. L. Milano, pp. 13–21. Subartu 12. Turnhout: Brepols.

———. 2008. Rechtsbrüche in Handel, Diplomatie und Kult. Ein Memorandum aus Ebla über Verfehlungen Maris (ARET 13, 15). *Kaskal* 5:93–110.

———. 2009. Von der Wollration zum Ehrenkleid. Textilien als Prestigegüter am Hof von Ebla. In *Der Wert der Dinge. Güter im Prestigediskurs,* ed. B. Hildebrandt and C. Veit, pp. 241–78. Münchner Studien zur Alten Welt 6. München. Herbert Utz Verlag.

Sanati-Müller, S. 1990. Texte aus dem Sînkāšid-Palast. Dritter Teil: Metalltexte. *BaM* 21:131–213.

———. 1993. Texte aus dem Sînkāšid-Palast. Sechster Teil: Texte verschiedenen Inhalts III. *BaM* 24:137–84.

———. 1994. Texte aus dem Sînkāšid-Palast. Siebenter Teil: Texte verschiedenen Inhalts IV. *BaM* 25:309–40.

Selz, G. 1995. *Untersuchungen zur Götterwelt des altsumerischen Stadtstaates von Lagaš*. Occasional Pub. of the Samuel Noah Kramer Fund 13. Philadelphia: University of Pennsylvania Museum.

Sharlach, T. 2004: *Provincial Taxation and the Ur III State*. Cuneiform Monographs 26. Leiden: Brill & Styx.

Siegelová, J. 1986. *Hethitische Verwaltungspraxis im Lichte der Wirtschafts- und Inventardokumente*. Praha: Národní Muzeum.

Snell, D.C. 1982. *Ledgers and Prices. Early Mesopotamian Merchant Accounts*. Yale Near Eastern Researches 8. New Haven: Yale University Press.

Steinkeller, P. 1981. The Renting of Fields in Early Mesopotamia and the Development of the Concept of "Interest" in Sumerian. *Journal of the Economic and Social History of the Orient* 24:113–45.

———. 1989. *Sale Documents of the Ur-III-Period*. Freiburger Altorientalische Studien 17. Stuttgart: Franz Steiner Verlag.

———. 2003. Archival Practices at Babylonia in the Third Millennium. In *Ancient Archives and Archival Traditions. Concepts of Record-Keeping in the Ancient World*, ed. M. Brosius, pp. 37–58. Oxford: University Press.

Stępień, M. 1996. *Animal Husbandry in the Ancient Near East. A Prosopographic Study of Third-Millennium Umma.* Bethesda, MD: CDL Press.

Stol, M. 2004. Wirtschaft und Gesellschaft in altbabylonischer Zeit. In *Mesopotamien: Die altbabylonische Zeit,* ed. P. Attinger, W. Sallaberger, and M. Wäfler, pp. 641–975. OBO 160/4. Fribourg: Academic Press; Göttingen: Vandenhoeck & Ruprecht.

Van De Mieroop, M. 1994. The Tell Leilan Tablets 1991. A Preliminary Report. *Orientalia* 63:304–44.

Veblen, T. 1899. *Theory of the Leisure Class*. [Numerous reprints.]

Waetzoldt, H. 1972. *Untersuchungen zur neusumerischen Textilindustrie*. Rome: Istituto per l'Oriente.

———. 1987. Compensation of Craft Workers and Officials in the Ur III Period. In *Labor in the Ancient Near East,* ed. M.A. Powell, pp. 117–41. American Oriental Series 68. New Haven, CT: American Oriental Society.

———. 2003. Zahlung von Lösegeld in Šehnā. In *Festschrift für Burkhart Kienast zu seinem 70. Geburtstage dargebracht von Freunden, Schülern und Kollegen,* ed. Gebhard Selz, pp. 707–16. AOAT 274. Münster: Ugarit-Verlag.

Wagner-Hasel, B. 2000. *Der Stoff der Gaben. Kultur und Politik des Schenkens und Tauschens im archaischen Griechenland*. Frankfurt am Main: Campus-Verlag.

Wilcke, C. 2007. Markt und Arbeit im Alten Orient am Ende des 3. Jahrtausends v. Chr. In *Menschen und Märkte. Studien zur historischen Wirtschaftsanthropologie*, ed. W. Reinhard and J. Stagl, pp. 71–132. Vienna: Böhlau Verlag.

Zettler, R.L. 1992. *The Ur III Temple of Inanna at Nippur. The Operation and Organization of Urban Religious Institutions in Mesopotamia in the Late Third Millennium B.C.* Berliner Beiträge zum Vorderen Orient 11. Berlin: Dietrich Reimer Verlag.

8

Egyptian Kingship during the Old Kingdom

MIROSLAV BÁRTA

If you doubt our might, look at our buildings.

—Ryszard Kapuściński, *Imperium*

INTRODUCTION

In my view, this brief statement relating to the inscription left behind by Timur over one of the gates of Samarkand is one of the most suitable metaphors that can be successfully applied to the Old Kingdom state, society, and royal landscape. It refers both to the city's monuments themselves and to the way the city managed to manifest its superiority over the surrounding political landscape (Smith 2003:271ff.).

Looking at Old Kingdom history through the prism of the 21st century and from a distance of more than 4,000 years, one is very much tempted to look at the ancient Egyptian society of the day as a quite stable system with a preset hierarchical structure and predefined mode of rule and government, lacking any substantial development in terms of status, structure, and competence. After all, pyramids were built during the whole period and the ideology of the pharaoh preserved its formal features almost intact. But is this really so? Do we have the means to identify some significant and potentially meaningful development within the spheres of royal ideology, kingship display, the administration of the state, and the society itself? After all, each of these aspects is essential for a proper assessment of Old Kingdom kingship. In this chapter I shall show that these aspects were very closely related and never ceased to interact. Simultaneously, it will be shown that the notion of kingship developed in a rather dynamic way and amply reflected changes within society.

Contrary to some recent attempts to define kingship through the king himself (Silverman 1995), the present study focuses on kingship as reflected through royal tombs—icons of ancient Egyptian kingship—the wealth of preserved title strings of high officials of the state, wealthy non-royal tombs of high officials who were essential in the perpetuation and upkeep of kingship, and the mechanism of interaction between the king and his officials and specifically how this relationship can be observed in terms of social status display. It will be shown that both the residential and provincial elites were essential for maintaining the idea of the kingship (for a similar approach, see Garcia Moreno in this volume and compare also the study by Pongratz-Leisten on the same issue in Assyria).

As indicated by Baines and Yoffee (1998:212–14), order, legitimacy, and wealth are best suited to characterize the major trends in the development of ancient Egyptian society dominated by the notion of kingship. In their formulation, "order exploits wealth for legitimacy" (1998:235). Ancient Egyptian kingship stands, for understandable reasons, at the center of Egyptological research since the early 1920s when the famous tomb of the king "Tut" was brought to light (Engnell 1943, Frankfort 1948, and most recently Brisch 2008).

Henri Frankfort's fundamental study was aimed at tracing the political and economic functions of kingship in the ancient Near East and Egypt and it became a milestone in the study of the subject. Today, however, we know more about various aspects of archaic states and different institutionalized forms of kingship in cultures across the ancient world. Therefore a more systematized approach may be used in dealing with different aspects of kingship in the context of similar cultures. In addition, today's Egyptology does not need to dwell only on official sources and state propaganda and thus a more "profane" approach may be worth pursuing.

To begin with, the most prominent roles of ancient Egyptian kingship and the king, similar to, for instance the Maya and Zapotec civilizations, may be schematically characterized as follows (Marcus 1992, Baines 1995:13–19):

1. to reinforce the preordained world and cosmic order,
2. to link the ruling king to royal ancestors and divine beings,
3. to legitimize the right to rule with deeds appropriate to royalty.

Simultaneously, based on the official written and iconographic sources pertaining to the definition of Old Kingdom kingship, it can be claimed that the ancient Egyptian king was considered to be:

1. a godly creature begotten by the god (Ra),
2. guarantor and keeper of order and the country's unity and prosperity, i.e., of the natural cycle in nature and the world order which came into being as a consequence of the act of creation,
3. mediator between the ordinary mortal people and the gods,
4. messenger and executor of the gods' will and instructions.

Therefore kingship itself can be, in a simplified way, understood as "rulership by a single individual holding a supreme office in a lifelong tenure, most often succeeding on a hereditary principle and wielding—or not, as the case may be—great personal power" (Baines and Yoffee 1998:205) or, also, as "a prerequisite for civilized existence" which "was conceived to represent a god-given and divinely established order and the king acted as its guardian against chaos" (Kurth 1992:30).

To these features one may add the characteristics of divine kingship (spiritual domination and hierocratic organization), the king having an exclusive relationship with the god, controlling religious benefits and owning the whole of Egypt: her resources, water, land, people, and products (for the terms and details see Weber 1978:54–56). The king himself can be labeled as a spiritual dimension of his community and a self-contained "sacred space." State rituals or rites can be viewed not only as a "measure of the king's divinity… [but also as] the measure of the realm's well being" (Geertz 1980:129). These two aspects actually have been demonstrated to be the same thing (for a discourse on these last aspects see Geertz 1980:121ff.; for the specifically Egyptian concept along these lines see Assmann 2006).

Yet, we have always examined kingship as if our predefined characteristics distilled from the available evidence conform to the latest development of the discipline. As far as Old Kingdom kingship is concerned, we may consider ourselves to be quite fortunate as we now have published evidence that basically validates our points of departure in the definition of kingship. As the case may be, paradoxically one of the best definitions of Old Kingdom kingship and its specific demonstrations comes from a royal mortuary temple that has never been decorated because of the premature death of the king. The mortuary temple, discovered by the Czech mission in Abusir (Verner et al. 2006), belongs to the Fifth Dynasty king Raneferef.

Raneferef passed away after only one to two years on the throne with grave consequences. Construction of his pyramid and mortuary temple had barely begun and thus a decision was made to convert his pyramid into a "primaeval hill." His mortuary temple was roughly finished in mud brick and the architect had to refrain from building the causeway and the valley temple, which are otherwise indispensable elements of the royal mortuary complex. In order to ascertain the proper manifestation of the most important aspects of the king and kingship throughout the temple, a very unusual solution was found: the decoration was executed in faience inlays fastened to wooden furniture.

The program was reconstructed by R. Landgráfová who was able to identify the following themes preserved in the decoration (2006:16–52):

1. Identification of the king, his representations, names, titles, and epithets.

2. Acceptance of the king by the deities, the king being embraced by them, given life by the gods or goddesses suckling him.

3. Legitimization of the king such as coronation, purification, and *sed* festival.

4. The king guaranteeing order/*maat*: offering to deities, visiting gods' chapels, and uniting the country (*smꜣ-tꜣwj*).

5. Funerary sustenance of the king including processions of offering bearers, displays of offerings, and slaughtering scenes.

6. Apotropaic scenes consisting of the killing and trampling of enemies, hunting scenes, slaughtering scenes.

Even a quick comparison of the identified scenes with what was emphasized at the beginning of this study shows clearly that here we have a distilled official presentation of kingship in its most significant forms.

Following the enumerated characteristics above, it comes as no surprise that the developing idea of kingship and most of all its maintenance and constant refinement and readjustment according to the current trends operating the society of the day, positively influenced the process of state formation and was essential in stimulating the development of social stratification, representational arts, and technology. Last but not least, it fostered the invention of a new means of demonstrating power, control, and expansion, the art of writing and the art of representation (Davis 1992, Dreyer, Hartung, and Pumpenmeier 1998).

The Fourth Dynasty represents a milestone in the development of royal mortuary complexes. Simultaneously it may be claimed that it opened, and relatively quickly exhausted, one avenue of kingship development: power display and mythological ruler identification. It was V.G. Childe who emphasized that extraordinary "royal tombs ... will be found to belong to a single transitional stage in the development of the societies concerned— to the period when the kinship organization appropriate to barbarism was breaking down to make room for a territorial State" (Childe 1945).

This is what we can observe well throughout the history of the 3rd millennium BCE. In a certain sense it is only during the Fifth and Sixth Dynasties that we can discern real proliferation of the central administration and its bureaucratic elite. The following discussion will demonstrate that the Old Kingdom state was fully configured only at the end of the Fourth Dynasty when all essential institutions of the state were formed and fully operational. Whereas the Fourth Dynasty may be considered, given the building of giant and unparalleled mortuary complexes, to be abnormal, the Fifth and Sixth Dynasties are more likely to be characterized as "standard state phase." In a sociological sense, only now the concept of "Herrschaft" was fully developed as it meant *"zunehmende* Entpersonalisierung, zunehmende Formalisierung, zunehmende Integrierung" (Popitz 1986:42). We will see that the decline of the state at the end of the Sixth Dynasty resulted in the opposite tendencies: personalization, multiplication, and disintegration.

In order to make the case of the Fifth and Sixth Dynasty clear, I use evidence from several independent sources that, combined, provide rather a coherent picture of the epoch under examination. These comprise royal mortuary architecture, non-royal tomb development and decoration, administration, and religious concepts that best illustrate the subject of this study. Last but not least, as was emphasized above, one should bear in mind that these spheres constantly and mutually interacted and developed in the never-ending process of internal conflicts and/or contradictions, readjustments, and refinements. Paradoxically, I shall defend the view that it is not the inherent characteristics of kingship itself (which are so difficult to define precisely from our modern perspective, as we are still lacking some substantial information), but rather the way it was manifested through other components of society that are of vital importance for the current discourse on kingship in the Old Kingdom and especially of the Fifth and Sixth Dynasties. In most cases, I am relating the subsequent Fifth and Sixth Dynasty developments to the preceding Fourth Dynasty because only through this comparison do important differences emerge which are significant to our understanding of Old Kingdom kingship and its development.

Independent evidence provided by the royal monumental architecture, non-royal tomb development, and administrative titles will be assessed and compared. Through it I will demonstrate that despite the clear differences in the nature of the evidence, the conclusions indicated create a rather homogenous picture, especially when compared against the political development of the period.

MEDIATING KINGSHIP THROUGH MONUMENTAL ARCHITECTURE

From the Old Kingdom period there are preserved twenty-two royal tombs in the shape of a pyramid. They were built at the following principal sites: Abu Rawash, Giza, Zawyiet el-Aryan, Abusir, Saqqara, Dahshur, and Meidum (Edwards 1993, Hawass 2003, Lehner 1997, Stadelmann 1985 and 1990, Vallogia 2001, Verner 2002). These monuments immediately became exclusive symbols of unlimited royal dominance and superiority. They were characterized by their location on the western bank of the Nile, usually sitting on the highest places on the western horizon and thus embodied the idea of transition and connection between the profane and divine world personified by the king and his royal deeds (Arnold 1999). A brief comparison of the Fourth, Fifth, and Sixth Dynasty monuments illustrates clearly the complicated process of transformation that was expressed through their architectural and decorative concepts.

For most of the Fourth Dynasty there is a clear observable tendency to build larger and larger royal tombs as size seems to be the decisive factor marking their exclusive and superior existence (in contrast to the following periods) (Fig. 8.1). This concept repeats itself later in Egyptian history also, specifically during the New Kingdom in the case of the royal tombs in the Valley of the Kings, and was called by E. Hornung "Erweiterung des bestehenden" (1982:37–38). Sneferu, the first king of the Fourth Dynasty, is known to have built three pyramids during his reign. The first pyramid is located in Meidum, close to an old residential center and a caravan route connecting the Nile valley with the Fayum Oasis (for details see Bárta 2005a). The Meidum pyramid is also the first ancient Egyptian funerary complex of the king having the canonical number of components: the valley temple, the causeway (not yet roofed), mortuary temple, and the pyramid protecting the burial of the king.

In the sixteenth year of his reign Sneferu moved his principal necropolis to Dahshur, to the north of Meidum. Reasons for his decision are not certain: yet the site is much closer to the capital of Memphis and maybe the king wished to build a new and larger (one side of the square base of the Bent pyramid measures 188 m compared to 144 m of the Meidum pyramid) and, by shape, the first true pyramid. During the pyramid's construction, at a height of about 46 m, there appeared cracks within the masonry and the architect was forced to reduce the steep slope of the side walls from 54 degrees to 43 degrees. Consequently, it was decided to build yet another, third pyramid. This pyramid was conceived as an even larger construction (one side of the base being 220 m), but the slope of the walls was from the very beginning lessened to 43 degrees. This last pyramid probably became the final resting place of the king.

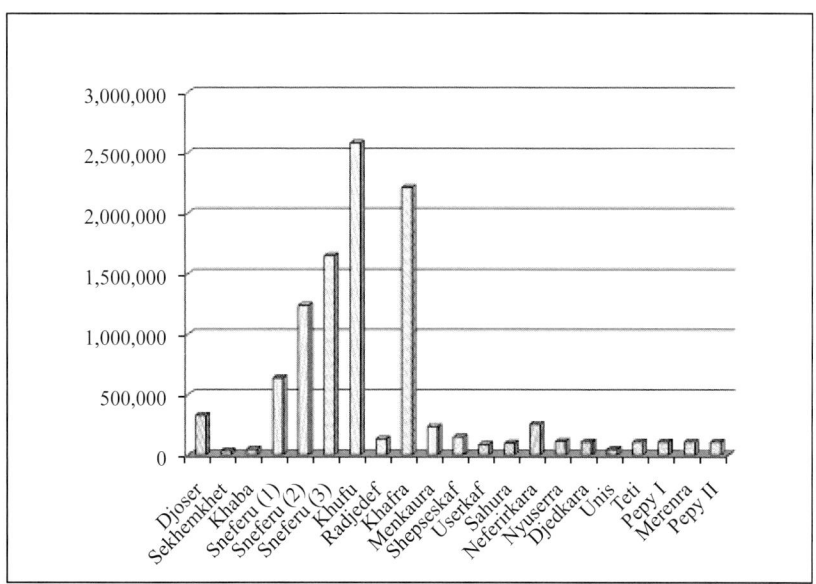

8.1. Volume of the Old Kingdom pyramids (in cu. meters).

Bearing in mind the experiences with the constructions of Sneferu's pyramids, his son Khufu, feeling compelled to build a mortuary monument surpassing those of his father, decided to relocate and establish his own necropolis at Giza. This is the only site that had solid bedrock capable of carrying the weight of his intended monument. Khufu launched an unparalleled single building project, designing a tomb with a base of 230.33 m which stood originally 146.6 m high with a volume of some 2,500,000 m^3 of stone. His achievement is by far the largest complete funerary monument attested from ancient Egypt.

It is clear that such an ambitious project as Khufu's pyramid complex represented a challenge not only for the king himself, but above all for the administrative system and the economic capacity of the country. There are indications (see below) that Khufu followed the parsimonious policy introduced by his father of standardizing the size of mastabas that his family members built around his pyramid and limiting their decoration to simple slab stelae (Manuelian 2003).

Khufu's successors seem to follow what in the meantime became a well-approved practice: to keep close to the solid limestone bedrock. Radjedef built a pyramid north of Giza at Abu Roash (one side of the pyramid base being 106 m) north of Giza. Rakhef/Khafra returns to Giza and builds the second largest pyramid in Egyptian history, this time with a base of 215 m, a height of 143.5 m, and a volume of 2,211,096 m^3. His successor Baka leaves for Zawyiet el-Aryan and it is estimated that his unfinished pyramid had a base of about 210 m. The last pharaoh situating his monument in Giza was Menkaura (with a pyramid measuring 102 x 104 m in ground plan, 65 m high, with a volume of 235,183 m^3).

Following Menkaura's reign a new, innovative trend led to the construction of significantly smaller pyramids. The principal factors that led to this decision may be of a practical nature (such as location of the pyramid with regard to the economic base and the availability of suitable bedrock). It is also important to realize that all the existing pyramids of the period following the Fourth Dynasty are situated in the vicinity of Memphis on the sites of Abusir and Central and South Saqqara—these sites contain almost 75 percent of all existing pyramids of the period. The expression of modes of power and status through the sheer size of the monument was, however, replaced by an increased symbolism in the complexes themselves. Also, some significant changes took place in the substructure of the tombs as they were newly expanded with storerooms (Roth 1993:45).

The clear trend towards the relatively small-scale pyramids of the Fifth and Sixth Dynasties practically becomes a paradigm during the Sixth Dynasty, starting with the reign of Teti, when the ground plans of the pyramids are strictly standardized (square base side measuring 78 m). This is the time when the smallest Old Kingdom pyramids were built and when the storerooms in these mortuary temples take up by far the largest portion of the built areas.

During the reign of the second king of the Fifth Dynasty, Sahura, another major change in the concept of the royal mortuary complex takes place. Hand in hand with the sudden decrease in the pyramid's size goes a tendency to emphasize the decorative program of the complex, thus favoring an increase in the symbolism of the royal tomb. The clear example is the mortuary complex of Sahura in Abusir. His temple comprised some 370 running meters of decoration whereas some of the most important kings of the Fourth Dynasty decorated only a small part of this area. Sneferu, for instance, reserved only 64 running meters for his complex's decoration, his son Khufu some 100 m, and the direct predecessor of Sahura, king Userkaf, had only about 120 m of relief decoration (Arnold 1999:98).

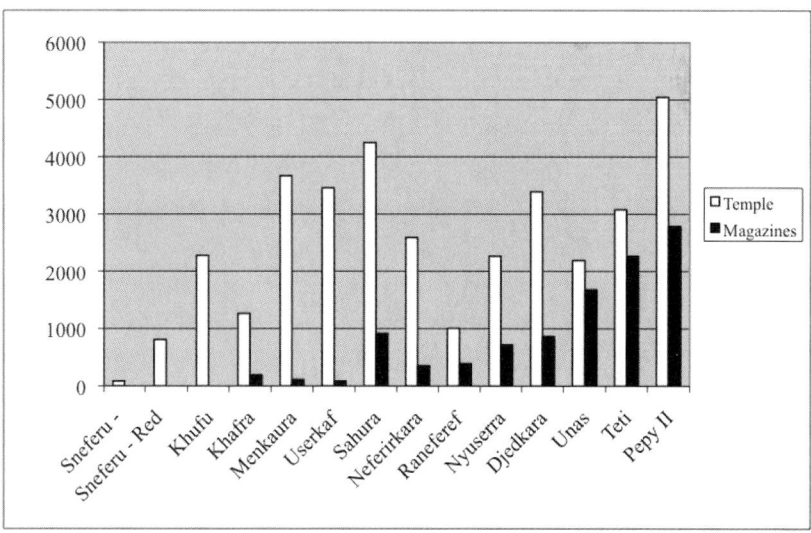

8.2. Comparison of the built area of individual funerary temples of the Old Kingdom kings and the areas of the storerooms within them (in sq. meters).

In addition to the relief decoration, the shift in priorities found its material expression in temple storerooms. From the reign of Sahura onwards there is a strong tendency to expand areas reserved for storerooms within the mortuary complexes, an indication that the daily cult carried out in them had gained in importance (Fig. 8.2). Sahura's storerooms cover 916 m^2 of the whole 4,246 m^2 of the temple's area. From the reign of Neferirkara onwards there is a clear tendency to an almost linear growth of the built area of the storerooms. Once again, this policy stands in marked contrast with earlier Fourth Dynasty development. Sneferu's pyramid temple in Dahshur covered an area of about 800 m^2 with virtually no space reserved for storerooms, as was the case with Khufu's temple covering an area of more than 2,000 m^2. Storerooms start to appear during the reign of Khafra (less than 200 m^2 of the 1,265 m^2 of the temple's built area). This tendency is illustrated not only by the area covered by these structures in individual mortuary temples but also by the papyrus archives recovered in the mortuary temples of Neferirkara (Posener-Kriéger 1979) and Raneferef (Posener-Kriéger, Verner, and Vymazalová 2006). The records contain reports of regular shipments of provisions for the offering cult of the king.

NON-ROYAL TOMBS

At the same time that Sneferu was dealing with his huge construction works in Meidum and Dahshur, vital changes took place on many different levels of the culture and society of the day. This development must be observed against the backdrop of a heavily exploited economy—most of the resources of which were channeled into state building projects like the pyramids. The consequences of this practice may be observed in several domains of human activity of the time, especially in the sphere of non-royal mortuary cults and architecture economization where some major innovations took place.

In Meidum three new socially significant classes of pottery that expand the Old Kingdom vessel inventory were identified, including miniature bowls and plates and the so-called Meidum ware. Whereas Medium ware was probably invented to imitate and replace expensive stone vessels for the cult and funerary equipment of wealthy officials of the day (Bárta 2006a), miniature vessels were developed solely for the upkeep of the daily cult for both royal and non-royal persons: miniature plates for symbolic amounts of food and miniature bowls for beverages (Bárta 1995a). From the technological point of view the miniatures are the first pottery vessels produced on the faster potter's wheel and thus a clear example of how development in social and religious requirements may instigate technological change like the invention of the pottery wheel.

In accordance with these changes and shifts in priorities the architecture of non-royal tombs developed. Scrutiny of the early Fourth Dynasty evidence shows that prior to Sneferu's building activities in Dahshur, tombs built for members of the royal family in Meidum covered incredible areas of several thousand square meters. For example, the tomb of the vizier Nefermaat and his wife Atet (M 16) covered an area of 6,048 m², the mastaba M 17 was 5,512 m², and Tomb M6 of Rahotep and Nofret was 3,203 m². Contemporary Saqqara tombs are smaller but still cover impressive areas—their size ranges from 470 to 1,431 m² (Bárta 2006b).

However, the cemetery built for Sneferu's family members at Dahshur shows strict standardization in terms of size, approximating 600 m² of the built area (Stadelmann and Alexanian 1998:304). Moreover, it is during the reign of Sneferu that the first offering formulae (the so-called *htp dj nsw* formulae) appear in non-royal tombs. Last but not least, the substructure of the tombs undergoes profound reduction in size and complexity leading to a single underground burial chamber which contrasts with the earlier plan of multiple large-scale subterranean rooms imitating the ground plan of a house. Finally, beginning in the reign of Sneferu, the location of the tombs of the highest officials of the state depended heavily on the siting of the king's mortuary complex—a rule that remained in operation for most of the Fourth Dynasty (Roth 1993:42ff.). Sneferu's son Khufu followed the same trend, applying the same policy of tomb standardization and strictly limiting the decoration of individuals' tombs in the cemetery. Only the so-called slab stelae were used for several years during the first part of his reign as a kind of substitute for tomb decoration, containing all the essential elements for ensuring an official's afterlife (Manuelian 2003).

To some extent, and in parallel to the Fourth Dynasty development, we may claim that during the Fifth and Sixth Dynasties the development in the royal sphere was also reflected in the non-royal level. In contrast to the preceding period, non-royal cemeteries of the middle to late Old Kingdom develop more loosely with significantly less dependence on royal tomb location. From the reign of Nyuserra on, one can observe a marked increase in the number of wealthy tombs of the highest officials of the state, some even incorporating elements from royal architecture (Bárta 2004). It is precisely during this period that the Osiris concept becomes accessible to non-royal persons when previously it was reserved solely for the king. Thus every mortal could after his death become Osiris (Bárta 1995b). This process is sometimes called, for the lack of more appropriate terminology, the "democratization of the afterlife." It comes as no surprise that shortly after losing its formerly exclusively royal prerogative over the Osiris myth, royal burial chambers inside the pyramids are decorated with Pyramid Texts through which the institution of kingship again attempted to set itself apart from the rest of the population.

Already tombs at the end of the Fourth and the beginning of the Fifth Dynasty are more fully decorated, being limited by the ground plan of the chapel. The onset of changes within non-royal architecture may be best illustrated by the tomb of the Vizier Ptahshepses at Abusir which dates to the reign of Nyuserra. Ptahshepses was the first official of non-royal origin to adopt a wide variety of architectural elements from royal mortuary complexes and apply them to his private monument. His mastaba incorporated the following royal elements: a monumental columned portico almost 10 m high, a statue room with three niches, a large-scale open offering court, an east-west offering chapel, a boat room, and an angular vaulted ceiling over the burial chamber (Bárta 2005b). Even the sarcophagi of Ptahshepses and his wife Khamerernebty were of the same style as the ones prepared for the Abusir kings (Verner 1994:173–92). Some of the innovations introduced by Ptahshepses were, in their turn, adopted by other viziers and high-ranking officials. For example, Ty did so in his Saqqara tomb even before the end of Nyuserra's reign. An innovative trait of non-royal tomb architecture during this period includes courtyards which took up a considerable part of the tomb compound. It was there that important ceremonies for the afterlife of the tomb-owner are likely to have taken place. This interpretation is supported by the presence of offering altars in the courtyards. Structurally, they are comparable in their function and significance with courts in the pyramid temples of the Fifth and the Sixth Dynasty kings (Bárta 2005a).

These features clearly indicate the increasing importance and independence of elite tomb-owners during the Fifth Dynasty. This importance is reflected in the decoration of their tombs, not in their monumentality in terms of their size, but through their symbolism as manifested in architectural design, decoration, and equipment.

During the same time (e.g., the reign of Nyuserra) another type of tomb developed, called "the family tomb," that was designed for the poorer echelons of Egyptian society. The term "family tomb" refers to a tomb with a row (or several rows) of burial shafts embedded in the masonry of the superstructure and designed for burials of the whole family. In most cases these tombs do contain a higher number of burials. Shafts in these tombs were usually sited west of a single offering chapel devised for the cult of the entire family. A family tomb may have been used for several generations of the same family, including both male and female members. The superstructure was filled with shaft openings, some of them unused. Though there was formal uniformity of individual burials in the tomb, marked differences existed, which are possibly indicative of individual social status. These differences include the depth of the burial shafts and the type and size of the burial niche/chamber.

Aside from these two principal types of tombs associated with two distinctive echelons of society, there was yet another family tomb design incorporating individual tombs or chapels arranged around a single gathering place, in most instances an open court, provided that the family members were wealthy enough to afford their own tombs/chapels. Once again, the purpose of such a facility was to secure the family cult and stress family bonds.

The emphasis placed on kinship realized through three different tomb forms might perhaps best be explained by the fact that many offices at the various levels of state administration became hereditary at this time. This made it necessary to highlight the relationship between individual family members. In many cases these relatives at one time held the same offices.

Pepy I was one of the last kings during whose reign large non-royal tombs were still being built, for example those of Mereruka, Ankhmahor, Ptahhotep, and Mehu. This explains why family tombs were so popular—more and more wealth, influence, and offices were becoming concentrated in the hands of families of high-ranking officials. There is also a clear relationship between administrative reforms and this development. It is during this same period that many powerful officials move their tombs to the provinces because it was apparently more important to demonstrate their ties with the local elite than to be present at the royal residential cemeteries.

ADMINISTRATION

Today, one of the major sources for examination of ancient Egyptian state administration are the chains of titles used by ancient Egyptian officials. Basically, two different theories on how these chains are to be interpreted exist. Following K. Baer, they represent strings of titles/offices that were acquired by their owners during their careers (Baer 1960:35). According to N. Strudwick, they can be viewed as sets that were held by the official during the time he was building his tomb (Strudwick 1985:172) and this is the view applied in this study. The bulk of the evidence used here is based on a database developed by the Czech Institute of Egyptology for the purpose of study of ancient Egyptian administration during the Old Kingdom.

The beginning of the Fifth Dynasty marked the start of a new era in terms of both political and administrative development in the country, which has also been called a "significant administrative calibration" (Papazian 2005:111). We may observe that new settlements were built and the title of "overseer of new settlements" came into being (see Moreno Garcia, this volume). The beginning of the Fifth Dynasty provides evidence that some significant changes were taking place on the administrative level as well. The inscriptions preserved in the non-royal tombs indicate clearly that officials of non-royal origin took over high administrative offices. They were responsible for both the administration of the state and of the royal residence, but also maintained cults in the royal mortuary complexes. This development probably had its roots in a sudden "opening-up" of state administration. While during the Fourth Dynasty the highest offices of state and court were reserved for privileged members of the royal family, from the Fifth Dynasty onward members of the royal family seem to have been excluded from state affairs and therefore an ever-increasing number of officials of non-royal origin were entrusted with offices in state administration (Helck 1986:18–23). This is reflected most notably in the rank of vizier. Whereas, down to the end of the Fourth Dynasty, it was exclusively a member of the royal family who held the office of vizier, from the early Fifth Dynasty onward the office was associated with officials of non-royal origin. Out of seventeen viziers attested down to the end of the Fourth Dynasty, only three (we do not always have complete titularies of these men preserved) did not claim the title "king's son" or its expanded and even more important variant "the oldest son of the king (of his body)." During the following Fifth and Sixth Dynasties these titles occur in the vizier's titulary only once.

Several titles gained in importance during the administrative reforms at the very beginning of the Fifth Dynasty. In line with the increase in the number of officials in charge of state offices, there was a clearly diversified spectrum of individual office holders during this period. Down to the end of the Fourth Dynasty there was a limited and quite homogeneous group of high-ranking officials active at court, but from the outset of the Fifth Dynasty one can observe a quick increase in offices in the royal residence held by officials of lower social status (Bárta 1999a).

To illustrate these new conditions, I would like to point to the example of the title *"keeper of the secrets* + an office," a title emphasizing the duty of its holder to be discrete where his specific state office was concerned. It is one of the titles that occurred infrequently during the Fourth Dynasty and proliferated during the Fifth Dynasty. The title was, down to the end of the Fourth Dynasty, used rarely as members of the royal family and high-ranking officials took for granted their duty to keep the secrets of the king and his court to themselves. After all, they were the only few representatives of the "profane world" that were in frequent contact with the sacred king. This is also why there are only eleven holders of this title attested from this period (Rydström 1994). The duty to keep secrets of the royal court came into prominence at the beginning of the Fifth Dynasty, when persons of non-royal origin and lower rank became associated with service to the king. From the Fifth Dynasty, we know of 96 holders of the title, and this number shrank during the Sixth Dynasty when the king tried to regain his authority and curb the influence and power of his officials (Bárta 1999b).

In order to pay all these officials, it was necessary to increase the size of store-rooms in the pyramid complexes because most officials at the court of Memphis worked simultaneously for some of the royal mortuary cults (Bárta 1999a). It is probably not by chance that from the onset of the Fifth Dynasty, the royal annals emphasize endowments made by the kings for individual temples of gods throughout the country (Wilkinson 2002:152ff.).

During the reign of Nyuserra the wealth of individual officials increased enormously. Nyuserra's successor created the office of overseer of Upper Egypt, probably out of the need to gain more effective control over remote regions of the country and officials living there (Martin-Pardey

1976:152). Thus, it is in this transitional time of Nyuserra and Djedkara that we can trace two opposing trends: one towards the usurpation of ever more power and influence by officials and their families, and the other towards curbing the power of these officials by the king. The situation reflected in the architecture of tombs belonging to different social categories of officials is further borne out by their titles. Nyuserra (and his successors) tried to put limits on the ever-increasing independence of wealthy officials, as shown by the growing number of private landholdings. Nyuserra and his successors also seem to have reduced the number of high officials—a trend that is discernible in the long series of titles held simultaneously by high-ranking officials of the time. Of equal significance is that, from the reign of Menkauhor or Unas onward, viziers started acting as inspectors of the priests who performed funerary rites in royal pyramid complexes (Strudwick 1985:308–9, Table 29). All this gives the impression that an increasing number of duties were concentrated in the hands of several powerful officials, a situation as potentially dangerous as a large number of middle-ranking officials with fewer offices. It is not by chance that we see from Djedkara onwards each king on the throne introducing his own set of administrative policy reforms designed to preserve the idea of centralized kingship despite the fact that in reality its power had already started to be curtailed.

The same line of evidence may be found in the governmental reforms which are known to have occurred during the Old Kingdom. Most of them date to the later Fifth and Sixth Dynasties. Also of vital significance is the fact that most of these reforms were directed toward the provinces of Upper Egypt so as to neutralize centrifugal tendencies. Following is a short overview of the various programs taken (Kanawati 1980).

1. Reforms of Djedkara:

Creation of the office of overseer of Upper Egypt. Introduction of the second office of vizier for Upper Egypt (nome 9—Akhmim). Establishing three administrative centers for the control of one of the most economically important nomes of Upper Egypt (10, 15, and 20). For the first time officials are buried in the provinces.

2. Reforms of Unas (end of the Fifth Dynasty):

Reverts to the central administration, no nobles are known to be buried in the provinces. Continues the policy of two viziers, but this time both reside in Memphis.

3. Reforms during the Reign of Teti (beginning of the Sixth Dynasty):

Installation of two viziers in Memphis, each one with separate and specific responsibilities in the provinces: revenues and works. Establishment of the seat of the vizier in Upper Egypt located in Edfu. Beginning of the practice of high officials being buried at Elephantine on the southern frontier of Upper Egypt.

4. Reign of Pepy I:

Pepy I marries two daughters of the Abydos official Khui and his wife Nebet, probably for political reasons in an attempt to regain control over Upper Egypt. In time, his wives become the mothers of the future kings Merenra and Pepy II.

5. Reign of Merenra:

Dating to his reign are many burials of nomarchs throughout Upper Egypt attesting to the increasing political and economic importance of individual nomes (nomes 1–Elephantine, 2–Edfu, 4–Thebes, 5–Coptos, 6–Dendereh, 7–Qasr el-Sayed, 8–Abydos, 9–Akhmim, 12–Deir el-Gebrawi, 14–Meir, 15–Sheikh Said, 16–Zawiyet el-Mayetin, 18–Kom el-Ahmar/Sawaris, 20–Deshasha).

6. Reforms of Pepy II:

During the first half of his reign: the office of the overseer and vizier of Upper Egypt are held by the family of Khui in Abydos.

Years 25–35 of his reign: the office of overseer of Upper Egypt is removed and the title is granted to most Upper Egyptian nomarchs who become responsible for tax collection under the supervision of the southern vizier. At Thebes and Meir he created central granaries, and possibly a third one at Abydos. Nomarchs of these nomes held the title "overseer of the granaries."

Second half of his reign: many nomarchs combine their titles with that of "overseer of priests." The nomarchs lose the title "overseer of Upper Egypt." The governor of Meir becomes the only overseer of Upper Egypt and the vizier of the south.

7. *Eighth Dynasty:*
Nomarchs continue to combine administrative and priestly titles and rise to the rank of "hereditary prince." Nomarchs of Thebes gain control over nomes 1–4. End of the united country.

How to evaluate these reforms? They certainly must be related to other spheres of society of the day. As such, they validate our assumption that there was a gradual erosion of the central government and the roots of kingship which can be identified as early as in the reign of Nyuserra. Also there had to be an external reason making these reforms necessary, and the increasing internal problems within the administration of the distant parts of the country in Upper Egypt are accountable for it. This may be further corroborated by the fact that, unlike the Fourth Dynasty when most of the funerary domains were located in Upper Egyptian provinces, during the Fifth and Sixth Dynasties they continually declined in number (Kanawati 1980:9, fig. 3). This may also be a consequence of the fact that during the Fifth and especially during the Sixth Dynasty the kings were not able to gain full control of the provinces. This contradicts the previously accepted hypothesis that the Sixth Dynasty pharaohs were in complete control of the provinces.

CONCLUSIONS (*"Circumstances are the social context"*)

We have reached the point when some conclusions are unavoidable. First of all, it should be repeated that it is only during the Fourth Dynasty when we witness a fully constituted archaic Egyptian state and the institution of kingship. The Third Dynasty was surely essential for completing the last major steps leading to a full-fledged state with its own bureaucratic apparatus, hierarchically structured society, and means of keeping order, increasing wealth, and streamlining legitimacy.

The Fourth Dynasty may be characterized as an apogee of the preceding formative development. Its main characteristic was family-run autocratic rule with exclusive concentration of power and wealth in the person of the king. This situation is rapidly modified at the beginning of the Fifth Dynasty when the highest offices in the state are handed over to persons of non-royal origin, when the pyramids decrease drastically in size and when many elaborate non-royal tombs appear, expanding their decorative programs and, later, changing their design completely in accordance with political and religious innovations.

In general, one may say that, from the beginning of the Fifth Dynasty, kingship becomes more "socially obliged," i.e., high- and middle-ranking officials and priests are entitled through their offices, which are indicated by their titles, to share and partake of a much greater portion of the state's revenues than ever before.

It is an interesting development, especially considering that the late Fifth and the Sixth Dynasty tombs of the highest officials feature on their walls many named subordinates, a way of depicting real historical persons and embedding them in a specific social system and hierarchy. One cannot escape the impression that this is yet another way of sharing economic revenues with those one step down on the social ladder, i.e., instead of the king sharing largesse with his high officials, revenues of high officials are being shared with *their* lower subordinates. Before us runs a complicated web of social networks based on patron-client relationships.

Simultaneously it may be claimed that the disappearance of gigantic state projects of the Giza pyramids style brought with it neither a significant relief to the economy nor any sort of retreat from the sacred kingship concept. The sophistication of the royal mortuary complexes now designed to represent the basic concepts of kingship in a more delicate and refined manner posed no fewer economic demands. Moreover, a substantial portion of the state's income went into the pockets of high officials in the form of natural payments (bread, beer, meat, and cloth, to mention just the most prolific commodities) as a consequence of the *Opferumlauf*. This is how the class of high officials was gaining greater control of state affairs and the flow of economic potential (for parallels cf. Flannery 1999).

The burden of the state-sponsored economy can be best illustrated by just one fragmentary document which survived from the Abusir Archive of the king Raneferef (Document 48 A$^{1-3}$) (Posener-Kriéger, Verner, and Vymazalová 2006: pls. 47–48, 264–66, and 382). The incompletely preserved text records deliveries from the temple of Ptah in Memphis within the course of a seventeen-day period, probably on the occasion of a religious feast. The totals of individual commodities can be summarized as follows: 952 $ht3$-bread pieces, *pzn*-bread, 408 jars filled with beer, 68 pieces of fowl, 136 pigeons, and 221 oxen (13 pieces a day).

This situation in ancient Egypt of the Fifth and Sixth Dynasties can be considered parallel with some Mesoamerican civilizations (Chase and

Chase 1992). As in ancient Egypt, Chase and Chase have been able to show that a significant growth of the classic Maya elite led to the collapse of this civilization. Moreover, this elite class was able to usurp some features formerly connected exclusively with the ruler, such as taking captives. At the same time, the elites were originally formed only in the central places of individual states and later spread to provincial areas, becoming more and more independent (Chase 1992).

At the same time, the Fifth and Sixth Dynasties may be characterized as a period when the former boundaries between the royal family and elite families were becoming less and less discernible because of a new policy of marrying royal daughters to non-royal high officials in the reigns of kings Userkaf, Nyuserra, Teti, and Pepy I. These kings apparently expected these officials to pay for this royal association through dedicated service.

It was R. Müller-Wollermann in 1986 who identified five endogenous factors that may be used to characterize the end of the Old Kingdom (Müller-Wollermann 1986; for a similar line of argument see Kaufman 1988). These are as follows:

— Crisis of identity: the way that the ruling group is accepted.

— Crisis of participation: who takes part in state administration and how.

— Crisis of penetration: inability of the executive to control the state's administration and economy.

— Crisis of legitimacy: the authority and ability to enforce decisions made.

— Crisis of distribution: the effectiveness of the redistribution of economic sources.

According to Müller-Wollermann, it is the crises of identity and distribution which are linked directly to the increasingly independent high officials of the state. Generally, we could also call this trend a *personalization of power and rule* and the general failure of the state machine to establish and to maintain the *norms and standards of the ancient Egyptians in every possible walk of life*.

To these we may now add two more critical factors: the land-ownership crisis and the significant worsening of the climate. It was R. Gundlach, among others, who drew attention to the fact that throughout the Old Kingdom more and more land was transferred from the state to the funerary, non-taxable domains whose only *raison d'etre* was to provide economic means for the upkeep of both royal and non-royal cults (Gundlach 1998:227ff.). Analyses of the palaeoecological data—Nile flood deposits on the island of Elephantine and the entomological finds in Abusir South indicate that during the Sixth Dynasty there was a major climate change that resulted in desertification in the immediate vicinity of the Nile Valley (Seidlmayer 2001; Bárta and Bezděk 2008). Thus it seems likely that a long-term growing crisis of the society and state in Egypt was, in its terminal stage, accelerated by environmental factors.

Two years after the study by Müller-Wollermann, J.A. Tainter (1988:42) sorted out in similar fashion eleven general criteria that may be generally cited as major collapse factors, and some of which are applicable to ancient Egypt, including insufficient response to circumstances, class conflict, societal contradictions, elite mismanagement or misbehavior, social dysfunction, and economic factors.

It has been almost a rule that when discussing some of the basic features connected with the decline of the Old Kingdom state, there are critics claiming that there are no indications of such a process. Looking at the Fifth Dynasty from the First Intermediate Period perspective, we can observe, however, that bureaucracy underwent a major development precisely during this time, both in terms of its purpose and structure. By its purpose I mean that the bureaucracy is understood as a tool to maximize efficiency. Its structure is socially based and encompasses functional specialization of the system composed of departments. Its basic tools of organization are written records, centralization, hierarchy, and professional specialists (Morony 1987:7). Along these lines, one may agree that as the Old Kingdom was approaching its final stage during the Sixth Dynasty, we clearly observe the decline of its efficiency and the fact that the interests of the bureaucrats started to be radically different from those of the rest of society. Similarly, the bureaucrats failed to exercise the same degree of control over the state and its internal development (comp. Morony 1987:9–10). As a consequence, the centrality of the 3rd millennium—be it a Residence, a deified king, or central institutions—disappears. Centrality is defined as "The center, or the central zone, is a phenomenon of the realm of values and beliefs. It is the center of the order of symbols, of values, and beliefs which govern the society" (Shils 1972:93). The principal characteristic of Shil's centrality concept is the fact that it influences all those who create the given society (1972:93).

The preceding lines of argument developed out of an analysis of archaeological evidence and written, non-literary inscriptions that were in most cases in no direct relationship to the official modes of kingship presentation. This approach has advantages, in my opinion. Simultaneously, its inherent weakness is that the conclusions drawn from it differ from the picture portrayed through the official propaganda. As such, it must be tested carefully against the still prevalent picture of the Old Kingdom as a solid, well consolidated hierocratic empire, strong and efficient down to the reign of Pepy II at the end of the Sixth Dynasty. Similarly, the external factors contributing to the weakening of the central administration and the king's authority, most prominently climate change, must be brought into the discussion as there is no doubt today that the decline of the Old Kingdom state phase of ancient Egyptian civilization coincided with major climatic change and an almost two-centuries-long dry spell in the northern hemisphere (cf. Dalfes, Kukla, and Weiss 1997, Issar and Zohar 2004, Bárta and Bezděk 2008).

What we have at the moment is a vivid picture of how kingship developed and manifested itself during the Old Kingdom, the manifold forms of its presentation and a rather clear process of its gradual erosion, but also the modes through which kingship reacted to actual historical situations. The way kingship manifested itself through monumental tomb complexes; the way it preserved the order by administering the country; and the way it legitimized itself by legitimizing the status, and later on the afterlife, of numerous high officials, should be illustrative enough.

Acknowledgments

This study was supported by the Charles University Scientific development programme No. 14: Archaeology of non-European areas, Sub-project: Ancient Egyptian civilization research: cultural and political adaptations of the North African civilizations in Antiquity (5,000 BCE–AD 1,000).

REFERENCES

Arnold, Do. 1999. Royal Reliefs. In *Egyptian Art in the Age of the Pyramids*, pp. 83–102. New York: The Metropolitan Museum of Art.

Assmann, J. 2006. *Ma'at: Gerechtigkeit und Unsterblichkeit im alten Ägypten*. Munich: Beck.

Baer, K. 1960. *Rank and Title in the Old Kingdom*. Chicago: University of Chicago

Press.

Bailey, F.G. 1965. Decisions by Consensus and Committees: With Special Reference for Village and Local Government in India. In *Political Systems and the Distribution of Power*, pp. 1–20. London: ASA Monographs.

Baines, J. 1995. Kingship, Definition of Culture, and Legitimation. In *Ancient Egyptian Kingship*, ed. D. O'Connor and D.P. Silverman, pp. 3–47. PdÄ 9. Leiden: Brill.

Baines, J., and N. Yoffee. 1998. Order, Legitimacy, and Wealth in Ancient Egypt and Mesopotamia. In *Archaic States*, ed. G.M. Feinman and J. Marcus, pp. 199–260. Santa Fe, NM: School of American Research Press.

Bárta, M. 1995a. Pottery Inventory and the Beginning of the IVth Dynasty. *GM* 149:15–24.

———. 1995b. Archaeology and Iconography: *Bedja* and *Aperet* Bread Moulds and "Speisetischszene" Development in the Old Kingdom. *Studien zur Altägyptischen Kultur* 22:21–35.

———. 1999a. The Title Property Custodian of the King during the Old Kingdom Egypt. *ZÄS* 126:79–85.

———. 1999b. The Title Inspector of the Palace during the Egyptian Old Kingdom. *Archiv Orientální* 1999(1): 1–20.

———. 2004. The Sixth Dynasty Tombs in Abusir. Tomb Complex of the Vizier Qar and His Family. In *The Old Kingdom Art and Archaeology*. Proceedings of the Conference held in Prague, May 31-June 4, 2004, ed. M. Bárta, pp. 45–62. Prague: Academia.

———. 2005a. Location of the Old Kingdom Pyramids in Egypt. *CAJ* 15(2): 177–91.

———. 2005b. Architectural Innovations in the Development of the Non-royal Tomb during the Reign of Nyuserra. In *Structure and Significance: Thoughts on Ancient Egyptian Architecture*, ed. P. Jánosi, pp. 105–30. Vienna: Verlag der Österreichischen Akademie der Wissenschaften.

———. 2006a. The Pottery. In *Abusir IX. The Pyramid Complex of Raneferef. I: The Archaeology*, ed. M. Verner, pp. 289–324. Prague: Academia.

———. 2006b. The Transitional Type of Tomb in Saqqara North and Abusir South. In *Texte und Denkmäler des ägyptischen Alten Reiches*, ed. W. Schenkel and S. Seidlmayer, pp. 1–22. Berlin: Achet Verlag.

Bárta, M., and A. Bezděk. 2008. Beetles and the Decline of the Old Kingdom. In *Chronology and Archaeology in Ancient Egypt (the Third Millennium B.C.) Proceedings of the Conference Held in Prague, June 11–14, 2007*, ed. M. Bárta and H.

Vymazalová. Prague: Czech Institute of Egyptology.

Brisch, N.M., ed. 2008. *Religion and Power: Divine Kingship in the Ancient World and Beyond.* University of Chicago Oriental Institute Seminars No. 4. Chicago: Oriental Institute, University of Chicago.

Chase, D.Z., and A.E. Chase, eds. 1992. *Mesoamerican Elites. An Archaeological Assessment.* Norman: University of Oklahoma Press.

Chase, A.E. 1992. Elites and the Changing Organization of Classic Maya Society. In *Mesoamerican Elites. An Archaeological Assessment*, ed. D.Z. Chase and A.E. Chase, pp. 30–49. Norman: University of Oklahoma Press.

Childe, V.G. 1945. Directional Changes in Funerary Practices during 50,000 Years. *Man* 3–4:13–19.

Dalfes, H.N., G. Kukla, and H. Weiss, eds. 1997. *Third Millennium BC Climate Change and Old World Collapse.* Berlin: Springer.

Davis, W. 1992. *Masking the Blow: The Scene of Representation in Late Prehistoric Egyptian Art.* Berkeley: University of California Press.

Dreyer, G., U. Hartung, and F. Pumpenmeier. 1998. *Umm el-Qaab I: das prädynastische Königsgrab U-j und seine frühen Schriftzeugnisse.* AVDAIK 86. Mainz am Rhein: Verlag Philipp von Zabern.

Edwards, I.E.S. 1993. *The Pyramids of Egypt.* Harmondsworth: Penguin Books.

Engnell, I. 1943. *Studies in Divine Kingship in the Ancient Near East.* Uppsala: Almqvist & Wiksell.

Feinman, G.M., and J. Marcus. 1998. *Archaic States.* Santa Fe, NM: School of American Research Press.

Flannery, K.V. 1999. Process and Agency in Early State Formation. *CAJ* 9:1, 3–21.

Frankfort, H. 1948. *Kingship and the Gods: A Study of Ancient Near Eastern Religion as the Integration of Society and Nature.* Chicago: University of Chicago Press.

Geertz, C. 1980. *Negara: The Theatre State in Nineteenth-Century Bali.* Princeton: Princeton University Press.

Gundlach, R. 1998. *Der Pharao und sein Staat. Die Grundlegung der ägyptischen Königsideologie im 4. und 3. Jahrtausend.* Darmstadt: Wissenschaftliche Buchgesellschaft.

Hawass, Z., ed. 2003. *The Treasures of the Pyramids.* Cairo: American University in Cairo Press.

Helck, W. 1986. *Politische Gegensätze im alten Ägypten.* Hildesheimer ägyptologische Beiträge 23. Gerstenberg: Hildesheim.

Hornung, E. 1982. *Tal der Könige.* Frankfurt: Artemis Verlag.

Issar, A.S., and M. Zohar. 2004. *Climate Change: Environment and Civilization in the Middle East*. Berlin: Springer.

Kanawati, N. 1980. *Governmental Reforms in Old Kingdom Egypt.* Warminster, England: Aris & Phillips.

Kapuściński, R. 1994. *Imperium.* New York: Knopf.

Kaufman, H. 1988. The Collapse of Ancient States and Civilisations as an Organisational Problem. In *The Collapse of Ancient States and Civilizations*, ed. N. Yoffee and G.L. Cowgill, pp. 219–35. Tucson: University of Arizona Press.

Kurth, A. 1992. Usurpation, Conquest and Ceremonial: From Babylon to Persia. In *Rituals of Royalty: Power and Ceremonial in Traditional Societies*, ed. D. Cannadine and S.R.F. Price, pp. 20–55. Cambridge: Cambridge University Press.

Landgráfová, R. 2006. *Abusir XIV. Faience Inlays from the Funerary Temple of King Raneferef. Raneferef's Substitute Decoration Programme.* Prague: Czech Institute of Egyptology.

Lehner, M. 1997. *The Complete Pyramids.* London: Thames and Hudson.

Manuelian, P. Der. 2003. *Slab Stelae of the Giza Necropolis.* New Haven, CT: Peabody Museum of Natural History of Yale University; Philadelphia: University of Pennsylvania Museum of Archaeology and Anthropology.

Marcus, J. 1992. Royal Families, Royal Texts: Examples from the Zapotec and Maya. In *Mesoamerican Elites. An Archaeological Assessment*, ed. D.Z. Chase and A.E. Chase, pp. 221–41. Norman: University of Oklahoma Press.

Martin-Pardey, E. 1976. *Untersuchungen zur altägyptischen Provinzialverwaltung bis zum Ende des Alten Reiches.* Hildesheimer ägyptologische Beiträge 1. Gerstenberg: Hildesheim.

Michalowski, P. 1987. Charisma and Control: On Continuity and Change in Early Mesopotamian Bureaucratic Systems. In *The Organization of Power. Aspects of Bureaucracy in the Ancient Near East,* ed. M. Gibson and R.D. Biggs, pp. 55–68. SAOC 46. Chicago: The Oriental Institute of the University of Chicago.

Morony, M.G. 1987. "In a City Without Watchdogs the Fox Is the Overseer": Issues and Problems in the Study of Bureaucracy. In *The Organization of Power. Aspects of Bureaucracy in the Ancient Near East*, ed. M. Gibson and R.D. Biggs, pp. 7–18. SAOC 46. Chicago: The Oriental Institute of the University of Chicago.

Müller-Wollermann, R. 1986. Krisenfaktoren im ägyptischen Staat des ausgehenden Alten Reichs. Diss., University of Tübingen. Tübingen.

Papazian, H. 2005. *Domain of Pharaoh: The Structure and Components of the Economy of the Old Kingdom.* Ph.D. diss., University of Chicago. Ann Arbor, MI: UMI.

Popitz, H. 1986. *Phänomene der Macht: Autorität—Herrschaft—Gewalt—Technik.* Tübingen: Mohr.

Posener-Kriéger, P. 1979. Les Papyrus d'Abousir et l'economie des temples funéraires de l'Ancien Empire. In *State and Temple Economy in the Ancient Near East I. Proceedings of the International Conference Organized by the Katholieke Universiteit Leiven from the 10th to the 14th of April 1978*, ed. E. Lipiński, pp. 133–51. OLA 5. Leuven: Departement Oriëntalistiek.

Posener-Kriéger, P., M. Verner, and H. Vymazalová. 2006 *Abusir XIII. The Pyramid Complex of Raneferef. The Papyrus Archive.* Prague: Czech Institute of Egyptology.

Richards, A.I., and A. Kuper, eds. 1971. *Councils in Action.* Cambridge Papers in Social Anthropology no. 6. Cambridge: University Press.

Roth, A.M. 1987. The Organization and Functioning of the Royal Mortuary Cults of the Old Kingdom in Egypt. In *The Organization of Power. Aspects of Bureaucracy in the Ancient Near East*, ed. M. Gibson and R.D. Biggs, pp. 133–40. SAOC 46. Chicago: The Oriental Institute of the University of Chicago.

———. 1993. Social Change in the Fourth Dynasty: The Spatial Organization of Pyramids, Tombs, and Cemeteries. *JARCE* 30:33–55.

Rydström, K.T. 1994. *Ḥrj sštȝ*: "In Charge of Secrets:" The 3000-Year Evolution of a Title. *Discussions in Egyptology* 28:53–94.

Schmitz, B. 1976. *Untersuchungen zum Titel s3-njswt: Königssohn.* Bonn: Habelt Verlag.

Seidlmayer, S.J. 2001. *Historische und moderne Nilstände: Untersuchungen zu den Pegelablesungen des Nils from der Frühzeit bis in die Gegenwart*, Berlin: Achet Verlag.

Shils, E. 1972. Center and Periphery. In *The Constitution of Society*, ed. E. Shils. Chicago: University of Chicago Press.

Silverman, D.P. 1995. The Nature of Egyptian Kingship. In *Ancient Egyptian Kingship*, ed. D. O'Connor and D.P. Silverman, pp. 49–92. PdÄ 9. Leiden: Brill.

Smith, A.T. 2003. *The Political Landscape: Constellations of Authority in Early Complex Polities.* Berkeley: University of California Press.

Stadelmann, R. 1985. *Die ägyptischen Pyramiden. Vom Ziegelbau zum Weltwunder.* Mainz am Rhein: Philipp von Zabern.

———. 1990. *Die grossen Pyramiden von Giza.* Graz: Akademische Druck- u. Verlagsanstalt.

Stadelmann, R., and N. Alexanian. 1998. Die Friedhöfe des Alten und Mittleren

Reiches in Dahschur. *MDAIK* 54:293–317.

Strudwick, N. 1985. *The Administration of Egypt in the Old Kingdom: The Highest Titles and Their Holders*. Studies in Egyptology. KPI.

Strudwick, N. 2005. *Texts from the Pyramid Age*. Atlanta, GA: Society of Biblical Literature.

Tainter, J.A. 1988. *The Collapse of Complex Societies*. Cambridge: Cambridge University Press.

Vallogia, M. 2001. *Au coeur d'une pyramide. Une mission archéologique en Égypte*. Lausanne-Vidy, Switzerland: Musée de Lausanne-Vidy.

Verner, M. 1994. *Forgotten Pharaohs, Lost Pyramids: Abusir*. Prague: Academia.

———. 2002. *The Pyramids. The Mystery, Culture, and Science of Egypt's Great Monuments*. Cairo: American University in Cairo Press.

Verner, M., P. Posener-Krieger, and H. Vymazalová. 2006. *Abusir IX: The Pyramid Complex of Raneferef. The Archaeology*. Prague: Czech Institute of Egyptology, Charles University in Prague, and Academia.

Weber, M. 1978. *Economy and Society: An Outline of Interpretive Sociology,* ed. G. Roth, C. Wittich, and E. Fischoff. Berkeley: University of California Press.

Wilkinson, T.A.H. 2002. *Royal Annals of Ancient Egypt: The Palermo Stone and Its Associated Fragments*. London: Kegan Paul International.

9

All the King's Men: Authority, Kingship, and the Rise of the Elites in Assyria

BEATE PONGRATZ-LEISTEN

In an article published in 1986, Hayim Tadmor with great sagaciousness discussed the question of the accountability of the king to the elites in the heyday of the Assyrian Empire (8th and 7th centuries BCE). In his investigation of the roles played by the nobility and the scholars, he moved beyond the figure of the king and addressed the crucial aspect of the organization of power in the monarchical system of Assyria in the 1st millennium BCE (Tadmor 1986:203–24). The structure of the elites and their interaction with one another and the king are very difficult to discern, as royal commemorative inscriptions barely mention any representatives of these groups. Nonetheless, as Tadmor points out, allusions in the *Babylonian Chronicle* (Grayson 2000:iv, 29; Glassner 2004:202, no. 16) referring to Esarhaddon's killing of numerous magnates who had conspired against him, and in texts such as the *Sin of Sargon* in which the scholars impose their will onto the king (Tadmor, Landsberger, and Parpola 1989:3-51) provide an inkling of the role which the nobility and the scholars must have played in state affairs (Tadmor 1986:207). In his article dedicated to Tadmor in an anniversary volume, Giovanni Lanfranchi (2003:100–110) approached the question of monarchical power while exploring the notion of royal responsibility. His point of departure is the hierarchical order of power structures as conveyed in the order of responsibilities prescribed in the Assyrian international treaties and loyalty oaths: these put the king on top, followed by his family and his entourage which included the scholars, and only at the end, his people. Lanfranchi argues that in the Sargonid Period various cultural strategies served to strengthen "the independence of the king from his contemporary political and social framework" and, consequently, "institutionally, the king would be provided" with what he calls a "protected non-responsibility" as he was not subject to any political judgment. Thus politically, the king "would assume a totally independent and practically tyrannical position" (2003:106).

With their respective approaches Tadmor and Lanfranchi have broadened the study of the nature of Mesopotamian kingship which used to focus primarily on the question of whether the king was divine or not (Labat 1938, Engnell 1943, Frankfort 1978, Jones 2005:330-342; Brisch 2008). The role of the elites in a monarchical system is a fascinating question and, as illuminated by the foregoing discussion, very much depends on the philosophical underpinnings of the respective scholar. While Tadmor begins with the notion of the king's accountability to the elites, Lanfranchi brings the concept of the king's responsibility for his actions to the fore which, according to his view, eventually results in the total independence of royal power. Nevertheless the question remains, who were the agents creating the cultural strategies destined to protect the king from any open disapproval, and what was the nature of the king's relationship with these people? In tackling this question I would like to take still another view and introduce the notion of power and authority.

As demonstrated by Max Weber, it is important to keep in mind that power and authority are not necessarily combined in one agency. Instead they are relational concepts which even in a monarchical system are built on constellations and interdependencies (1976:28). Although in Mesopotamia kingship is considered to be of divine origin, and although in the ideological discourse, power and authority are combined in one agency and the king is presented as the sole agent, in reality he had to rely on professional experts for mundane and religious matters. In other words, the king had to defer authority and rely on expert advice. This also pertains to the central building blocks of royal self-representation composed of text, image, and ritual. A glance at the history of Assyria reveals that the king cannot be held solely responsible for the discourse surrounding his supreme status or even deification within society. Here, the scholars partake in the authoritative voice by shaping the image of the king and defining his alliances with the divine world generated by means of kinship relations and intense communication (Machinist 2003:117–37). While circumscribing his distinct status and presenting his actions as divinely inspired, religious and scholarly authority, consequently, reinforces the image of a pyramidal power structure which in reality was dominated by a network of interdependencies.

However, the scholars not only continue a longstanding tradition linked with the shaping of the royal image but cultivate a specialized discourse that also confers authority on them. Numerous examples in literature and epistolary literature prove that the political and scholarly elites constantly strove to position themselves in the direct entourage of the king in order to profit from the privileges of the top few. Beyond their expertise in particular fields, their authority rested on their skill in manipulating the system to their own advantage. In literature, the *Enmeduranki Legend* (Lambert 1967) offers a beautiful example of the diviners constructing this kind of close interdependency by defining the king as the conduit of the divine knowledge to be passed directly on to them. In the ritual domain, numerous scholarly experts, diviners and exorcists alike, competed with each other to prove their competence to support the king in his role of maintaining the harmonious equilibrium between heaven and earth, and they did so by means of preventative methods such as purification rituals of all kinds to avert portentous signs.[1] While constantly investing an immense effort in preserving the king's immunity against all kinds of threatening forces, these omen experts and ritual professionals concomitantly built their monopolies of expertise.

In my considerations, I intend to narrow Tadmor's focus on the top end of this political hierarchy and investigate the interaction of the king and the elites in creating the city of Assur as the crystallization of Assyrian cultural identity. After some preliminary comments on the nature of the scholarly and religious elites and their impact on this process, the written communication between the king and the god Ashur, with a focus on *Sargon II's Report to Ashur on His Eighth Campaign,* will serve as an illustrative example for my discussion.

As the territorial state and later empire of Assyria grew out of the city state of Assur, the assumption of a conscious effort to uphold the central status of Ashur might seem beside the point. However, with the expansion of Assyria during the second half of the 2nd millennium the political and religious centers did not necessarily overlap anymore, and thus the investigation into the nature of the city of Assur as a cultural and religious metropolis throughout Assyrian history represents a question worth pursuing. While the name of Assyria constructed with the name of the city (*māt*

Aššur^{KI}) "reflects the ideological centrality of the city of Assur, and the city-god, henceforth also the national god, who bears the same name," efforts were still needed on the operational level to maintain the central status of the city and of her elites in a time when the king resided either in Nimrud, Khorsabad, or Niniveh (Postgate 2002:1–12,).

Many strategies contributed to producing this social and cultural nexus, among them the monthly deliveries to the Ashur temple from all the provinces of the empire, state ritual, the self-definition of the king as belonging to the seed of Assur, and the written communication between the king and the god Ashur. The first libraries of the Middle Assyrian period found in the Anu-Adad temple and in the Ashur temple (Weidner 1952–1953:197–215)[2] can be considered part of this effort.

The prime producers of the ideological discourse were the scholars in the direct entourage of the king who, although experts in a particular discipline, were also in command of the entire body of cultural knowledge as expressed in the media of image, text, and ritual and shaped the world view of the time. As stressed by Simo Parpola, the chief scholars of the various disciplines formed part of the direct entourage of the king and advised him in state matters,[3] unlike the priests whose duties remained confined to the cult. Text, image, and ritual illustrate that the fundamental political principle as formulated in the Assyrian coronation ritual dominated royal self-representation and action: the Assyrian ruler in his role of the chief šangû of the god Ashur had to secure Ashur's kingship by means of his cultic and political performance. The political-religious concept of the asymmetrical relationship between Ashur and the Assyrian ruler who primarily acted as the steward of the god and was king (šarru) only in relationship to the rest of the people also shaped the political-religious landscape. Once Assyria had expanded from a former city state into a territorial state, the religious center and the political center were not congruent anymore. While the cult of the god Ashur remained centered on the city of Assur, Tukulti-Ninurta I (1233–1197 BCE) was the first to move the political capital away from Assur, a step that then became the rule in the 1st millennium BCE. However, as acutely observed by Marc Van De Mieroop, it seemed to have made a difference whether the king explicitly boasted of the newly founded city as his own creation as did Sargon II, or whether he represented his work "as an extension of something that already existed" (Van De Mieroop 1999:327–39, 337) and which thus could be considered the original work of the gods as promulgated in Mesopotamian tradition. We can only guess what tensions among the elites must have resulted from the separation between the religious and the political center, and so Assyria offers a fascinating example of the dynamics of power and authority, i.e., of the interaction between the political elites, the scholars, and the clergy of the temples in securing their positions within the interdependencies of the monarchical system. The princes, magnates, and dignitaries, the royal advisers, military commanders, provincial governors, and court eunuchs are exactly the social groups listed in omen series and loyalty oaths that could pose a danger to the king. While the scholars would not directly engage in regicide, they nonetheless could jeopardize his position by not reporting to him the result of their observations either in extispicy or in observational astronomy; even worse, they could share their knowledge with the enemy of the king as attested for an haruspex and two astrologers working in Babylon who were accused by the king's son of conniving with the Elamites (Parpola 1972:21–34). Constant reporting to the king from all parts of his empire therefore was of prime importance and as such was stipulated in the loyalty oaths.

The content of the private libraries of the respective scholars as well as their contributions to building the royal libraries in Nineveh reflected in the epistolary literature and inventory tablets shows that the capacities of these scholars reached far beyond their operational skills in divination and cultic performance. This is not the place to discuss at length the content of the library of the chief exorcist at Assur (Maul 2003a), which mainly dates to the late Sargonid period (Pedersen 1985:4257; Hunger 1968:19f; Baker 2000:623f, no. 26). Numerous tablets bear the name of the chief exorcist, Kisir-Ashur, son of Nabu-bessunu, exorcist of the Ashur temple, and give witness to his career starting as a young student (LÚ.ŠAMAN.LÁ TUR) and continuing as a young exorcist (MAŠ.MAŠ TUR), until he reached the position of the chief exorcist of the Aššur temple (MAŠ.MAŠ É ^{d}Aššur) himself (Baker 2000:623). A cursory glance at the richness of his collection of texts already suffices to provide a notion of his erudition and of his potential in positioning himself within the top strata of the citizenry in Assur. The exorcist's library included most of the series listed in the *Exorcist's Manual*, incantations and commentaries to incantations, numerous medical prescriptions, lexical lists, god lists, hemerological texts, the astronomical series MUL.APIN, state rituals, as well as cultic commentaries commenting on passages of these state rituals and literary texts such as tablets of the *Erra Epic* and *Lugal-e*, as well as fables. It is noteworthy that beyond texts that in one way or the other either pertained to the cult or to the education of students, his library also contained the *Weidner Chronicle,* the *Marduk Prophecy,* and the *Shulgi Prophecy,* i.e., texts which all in one way or the other deal with the consequences of neglecting the cult of the chief deity, in these cases Marduk and Enlil, *Sargon's Report on His 8th Campaign* as well as *Sargon's Geography,* and the *Synchronistic King List* which lists Assyrian and Babylonian kings together with their chief scholars. Further text categories were represented by an exemplar of the *adê*-treaty for Sin-shar-ishkun, texts concerned with the topography of Assur, and decrees, some of them copied by his own hand.

Beyond his broad knowledge in theological, cultic, as well as political matters, the variety of these texts attests to a particular interest in the role of the Aššur temple as the major institution besides the palace. This scholar was responsible for managing the cult of the Aššur temple in the religious center of Assyria and, as illustrated by the colophons of the tablets referring to the rank of the scribes who had copied the tablets, was also committed to the education of students. The yearly performance of the state rituals formed an essential part of the official cult and required the presence of the Assyrian ruler as well,[4] meaning that for some weeks during the year the king had to stay in Assur and, consequently, directly deal with the chief exorcist in one way or the other. The library thus provides a notion of the exorcist's intellectuality and erudition as well as his potential power in interfering with the king's daily affairs.

A similar case could be made for some diviners in northwestern Syria in the second half of the 2nd millennium BCE. The content of their libraries exposes a variety of text categories comparable to that of the exorcist at Assur. This pertains to the house of the haruspex (*barû*) in Emar,[5] which although close to the temples, seemed to have represented an independent institution for the compilation and collection of texts as well as for educational purposes. The content of his library, which included a large number of Akkadian, Sumerian, Hurrian, and Hittite texts, goes far beyond the reference library of a diviner and suggests that this person, similar to the exorcist in Assur, was responsible for organizing the cult of Emar (see also Fleming 1992:126ff.). It is tempting to include the house of the diviner in Ugarit (Pedersén 1998:74–76) in this discussion because it likewise contained a broad array of text categories transcending the skills of extispicy.

The case I would like to make is that we do not necessarily need administrative documents and letters to prove the broad range of activities of diviners, astrologers, and exorcists, their responsibilities in managing the cult, and their share in shaping the world view of the time. Already the archaeological evidence from their private libraries suffices for us to postulate the existence of a social group which beyond organizing the local cult might have been involved in the affairs of daily politics. My point is that the archaeological and textual evidence of the second half of the 2nd millennium and 1st millennium Assyria greatly differs from the evidence attested for later Babylonia, when such a broad range of competences was reduced to the administration of cultural memory that seems to have moved to the temple. The libraries of the families of exorcists in Uruk (Pedersén 1998:212–13) represent the only exception so far, as they included, beyond medical and magic texts, also astrological and astronomical knowledge as well as literary texts. Yet, they are still different from the available evidence in Assur, as no ritual texts have been found in their libraries, and, consequently, no involvement in the management of the local cult or advising the king in state affairs can be assumed.

Beyond magic and ritual, divination and observational astronomy formed the two other major fields of expertise which served the ideological consolidation and actual stabilization of royal power. A cursory glance at the correspondence between the king and his astrologers must suffice to provide an idea of how strongly the activities of these scholars were linked with the decision-making and daily activities of the king.[6] In addition to writing purely astrological and astronomical reports and providing hemerological information, the astrologers were heavily involved in the organization of the cult in general and in the performance of the ritual of the substitute king (*SAA* X:1–4, 11, 12, 89, 90) in particular; furthermore, they had a say in the fashioning of divine statues (*SAA* X:27) and the divine tiara (*SAA* X:41), as well as in the organization of cultic festivals (*SAA* X:19, 20) and rituals (*SAA* X:93, 95, 98, 106) including the ritual of the *taklimtu* (*SAA* X:9, 18) which was part of the funerary ritual for members of the royal family, and prayers for the king and his sons (*SAA* VIII:102). Other duties included taking care of outstanding deliveries for offerings (*SAA* X:96), offerings (*SAA* VIII:112), as well as the condition of the Ashur temple (*SAA* X: 21). Political events such as the performance of the oath-taking (*SAA* X:5–7), a journey of the king (*SAA* X:44), the visit of a prince (*SAA* X:49, 52, 53, 73,

74, 85), and the appointment of officials (*SAA* X:110, 116, 118) were likewise part of their responsibilities. Again, the array of the duties of the diviners and astrologers indicate their authority within the organizational system of power.

Cult and divination as conduits of the divine voice in the form of astrology, prophecy, dream oracles, and extispicy are the primary domains through which an entire class of experts defines its position within the hierarchical structure, segregating themselves from the rest of the population by claiming the exclusivity and even secrecy of their knowledge.[7] Their involvement in the daily political affairs bespeaks their potential power in not only shaping the world view but also in the actual operations of power. Most of the diviners and astrologers resided in the respective residences of the kings (Pongratz-Leisten 1999:163ff., 193–94), if they were not sent into other cities of the empire to perform their observations. Nonetheless, their education and intellectuality explains the capacity of elite figures such as the chief exorcist to crystallize the spheres of social and cultural identity (Eisenstadt 1973:4) in the city of Assur throughout Assyrian history. As interpreters of the divine will and guardians of the body of cultural knowledge, their authority was primarily based on a particular expertise which, in its indispensability to political power, allowed them to position themselves within the power network. Their shrewd intertwinement of religious expertise and skills in the exercise of operational power enabled them to define the seat of the national god Ashur as the nexus of authority, even when political power was settled elsewhere.

Beyond the authoritative voice of the intellectuals, two other powerful groups strove to join the political game: the court officials, as represented by the magnates and the royal eunuchs, and the clergy of the temples, two groups whose power rested on large economic resources partially derived from the palace. The importance of these groups can be inferred from their attendance at the coronation ritual which took place in the Ashur temple. During the coronation ritual, prior to the investiture of the king, the *šangû*-priest strikes the cheek of the king reminding him explicitly of the kingship of Ashur—"Ashur is king, Ashur is king"—a gesture that recalls the rites performed prior to the "negative confession" of the king during the New Year festival in Babylon. The king then prostrates himself in front of Ashur and rolls on the ground before he is handed the regalia of kingship. Once in office the king reappoints his magnates. With the performance of these particular ritual gestures, the coronation ritual reaffirms the structure of monarchical power in Assyria, and the various social groups actively commit to their particular role in relation to the monarch. While Lanfranchi is certainly right in his assertion that such gestures cannot be interpreted as a periodical assessment or institutional limitations of kingship (2003:106), they nonetheless are symbolic performances meant to remind the individual king of his responsibility towards the gods in acting in harmony with the cosmic order and in maintaining the social order.[8]

All these groups, the scholars included, tacitly acknowledged the hierarchical relations of power and actively contributed to its symbolic system. Scholars, temple personnel, magnates, and high officials of the bureaucratic apparatus were both the agents and the audience of public manifestations of authority and power. They all actively engaged in the production and reproduction of the ceremonial etiquette, the code of gestures, officially prescribed rites, and language of power (Bourdieu 1991:112). Therefore to focus either on systems of domination or propensities for submission only (Lincoln 1994:122) distorts the social reality to be explored. Rather than viewing authority as an *entity* one should explore it under the aspect of producing an *effect* "that is operative within strongly asymmetric relations of speaker and audience" (Lincoln 1994:116).

However, notwithstanding the fact that the political and scholarly elites complied with the monarchical system, they grew more and more self-confident. While the king strove to maintain absolute control and authority, he simultaneously had to cope with the growth and proliferation of monopolies in the political, scholarly, and cultic arenas. The increasing self-confidence of the elites shows in their appropriation of certain fields of discourse,[9] symbols of power and prestige, constituting themselves as agents in the machinery of the empire. The epistolary literature between the Assyrian king, scholars, and political professionals exhibits this boost to those with special expertise and demonstrates that the monarchical system only kept functioning because of the close cooperation and interdependencies between the top strata of the societal hierarchy. While the king could exercise physical force and replace the individual, he still was dependent on the machinery as a whole which served to define and maintain his supremacy and immunity. Nonetheless, these elites had no interest in contesting or abolishing the monarchical system, because "the legitimacy of kingship was unquestionable" (Lanfranchi 2003:106). This view is supported by the fact that it is exactly in that historical moment of the Sargonid period that we observe the most sophisticated symbolic system to uphold supreme royal status.

With its expansion during the 8th and 7th centuries BCE the Assyrian empire develops an effective network of communication based on the king's road that was built for the rapid and safe transfer of messages and trade. Both Mario Liverani and Simo Parpola have stressed the significance of the communication system for administering and controlling the empire (Liverani 1984:107–15; Parpola 1987:xiii). Letters between the political elites in the provinces and the king and reports of any kind sent by anybody who had dealings with the king were the usual modes of communication and represented an effective means of control. Absolute control was imperative because digression from the law of primogeniture, the violation of international agreements, and internal strife threatened to shake the confidence in the legitimacy of the individual king during the Sargonid period. Lanfranchi rightly argues that "internal opposition might easily connect sacrilegious and shocking enterprises with political and military failures and with the tragic royal deaths" (2003:106), as in the case of Sargon's death in the battlefield and Sennacherib's murder at the hand of his son. Therefore strategies such as "stressing the image of the 'wise king,'" legitimizing the monarch by the notion of the extreme antiquity of his dynasty and presenting the king's action as divinely inspired, served to protect the king from any political criticism (Lanfranchi 2003:106). As I have argued elsewhere, the communication between the king and the gods by means of the divinatory techniques performed by the scholars who so strongly dominated royal self-representation at the time must be considered a product of this Realpolitik of control based on the network of communication (Pongratz-Leisten 1999:319).

Moreover, it is exactly in this period that the textual production revolving around the figure of the king grew more and more diverse and sophisticated. Tadmor even speaks of a regicentric literature (1986:205). What is striking is that dialogue, rather than the narrative form, turns into the preferred literary framework to illustrate the close relationship between the king and the gods. The move into new discursive modes shows in the secondary textualization of prophecy in the collective oracle tablets (Parpola 1997), as well as in the *Fictive Dialogue between Ashurbanipal and Nabû* in which the author compels the audience to engage in a dynamic and new reception of the already known form of the oracle (Livingstone 1989: no. 3). Typical of these new compositional frameworks is their retrospective viewpoint in contrast to the prospective viewpoint of the oracles. The retrospective perspective of these compositions links them to historiographic textual production, a literary framework that pertains to the written communication between the king and the god Ashur as well (Pongratz-Leisten, In press).

In its mode and asymmetrical relationship, the "written communication" between the king and the god mirrors the communication between the king and the elites. It draws on the fictive dialogue but forms text categories of its own: the *royal report to the god Ashur* and *Ashur's letter to the king*. Both text categories are of eminent importance for our understanding of the interaction and interdependency between the king and the religious elites of the city of Assur. These two text categories must be distinguished from the *letter prayers* of the Old Babylonian period dedicated by individuals to a variety of gods (Michalowski 1993, Michalowski 2011, Pongratz-Leisten 1999:213ff.) and letters sent to the god or by the god during a military campaign, evidence for which exists in a ritual text (Menzel 1981:38 rev.vi 1–14; Deller 1987:229–38; Pongratz-Leisten 1999:222–26), and in royal inscriptions (Pongratz-Leisten 1999:224–25). The practice of such interim reports is also attested in the *Anzû Myth* (Foster 2005:571, tablet II 86).

By contrast the *royal report to the god* and the *letter of the god* represent two text categories which were written after the campaign and thus concluded the communicative process between the king and the gods. The previous channels of communication included astrological omens, dream oracle and prophecy, as well as extispicy which all happened prior to and during wartime (Pongratz-Leisten 1999:277–85). Royal reports and divine letters do not seem to have been the rule in a military campaign. Rather they were written in the case of severe violations of tacit and explicit international agreements and fratricide, i.e., in cases when the action of the king was in need of an overruling divine command that sanctioned the royal deed. As already observed by A. Leo Oppenheim, Sargon II, with his letter to the god Ashur, "offers here an argument in his defense, an argument that anticipates a human reaction which the reference to a divine pronouncement is meant to counter" (1960:133–47, 137). Although one might say that the pillage of temples was a regular part of the devastating measures of destruction inflicted upon the defeated enemy by the Assyrian kings, Sargon II's pillaging of the temple of the Urartean national god Haldi, which was located in Musasir and served as the cultic center for the coronation ceremonies of the Urartean kings, was considered a sacrilegious act requiring divine sanction in the eyes of his contemporaries.

Some short remarks on the form of these text categories will contribute to a better understanding of their function. The king's report to the god, although concerned with the account of a military campaign, differs from the ordinary royal inscriptions insofar as it might either have an introductory section addressing the god and perhaps other parties, as well as a postscript reporting on the casualties.[10] Furthermore, it might use poetic language as does Sargon II in his report on his eighth campaign to Urartu or introduce some kind of an unusual discussion on the theme of royal responsibility as does Esarhaddon's report on his campaign to Shubria (Bauer 1931:234–59; Leichty 1991:52–57; Lanfranchi 2003).

By contrast, the *letter of the god* quotes literally from the reports of the kings sent to them before and might even refer to them with the formula *ša tašpuranni* "according to what you wrote to me" (Livingstone 1989: text nos. 41–43; Pongratz-Leisten 1999:220). Because of this formula I suggest restricting the term "letter of the god" to the texts of the 1st millennium which clearly identify the god as the sender of the letter. The letters of gods and royal reports have five typical features:

1. Both text categories reflect a written communication according to the sender–recipient model.

2. In the letter of the god, the god is supposed to be the sender, in the royal report it is the king who is the sender.

3. Formally, both text categories resemble the letter style, while the king may address the god Ashur in a longer eulogy.[11] The letters of gods omit the address to the king but the discursive mode of the dialogue is maintained in the direct speech addressed to the king. Several letters of gods use the formula *ša tašpuranni* "according to what you wrote to me."

4. Both text categories resemble the royal inscriptions in terms of content. The royal report is written in the first person and uses the past tense, as do royal inscriptions.

5. The letter of the god refers to the deeds of the king in the second person, while divine interference is described in the first person. It likewise uses the past tense.

Unlike the oracles of Ishtar which (even in their written transmission) aim at maintaining the illusion of a direct communication of speech between goddess and king, with the goddess performing a commissive speech act that expresses her commitment and obligation towards the king, the discursive form of the letter of Ashur is that of a commemorative narrative. The commemorative style of the letter and its similarity in content links the letter of the god to the commemorative inscriptions and the royal reports and does qualify it as a historiographic document relating the deeds of the king in a retrospective perspective. The letter of the god literally quotes from the royal report and modifies phraseologies only insofar as it adds prepositional elements that refer to the king in the second person thus creating the impression of a fictive dialogue. Beyond these modifying elements the god appropriates actions originally performed by the king. An excerpt out of Ashur's letter to king Ashurbanipal may serve as an example: "Because of the evil deeds [which Shamash-shum-ukin] committed against you, I pulled out the foundations of his royal throne, over[threw] his reign and [comma]nded the dispersal[12] of the entire land of Akkad." The royal inscription thus remains the basic phraseological structure which was subject to two forms of editorial revision to create the framework of the letter of the god: (1) the author intersperses the former royal report with legitimizing formulae which make the deeds of the king appear as being performed by the command of the god; and (2) by framing the whole text as a divine response to the king's report, the author evokes a situation of dialogue between god and king.

However, since there is no deficit in knowledge, the fictive dialogue between king and god does not aim at the exchange of information; rather, the goal of this interaction is to consolidate the relationship between king and god and, consequently, to re-establish the harmonious balance between the divine and earthly worlds with, however, a contemporary and posterior audience in mind (Pongratz-Leisten 1999:284). In the following, I posit that Ashur's positive answer sanctioning the king's deed was a prerequisite for the king to be allowed access to the Ashur temple and perform his triumphal procession. Sargon II's letter to the god Ashur in which he reports on his eighth campaign to Urartu will serve to make my case. Its introductory section as well as its postscript, in particular, will allow us to speculate about the aspect of the king's accountability to the elites and their involvement in the king's communication with the gods. Both sections are in form and content already familiar from Shalmaneser IV's report to Ashur, with one important exception: Shalmaneser IV (782–772 BCE) lists only the god Ashur and the gods dwelling in the Ashur temple as recipients of his letter; it is only Sargon II (722–705 BCE) who also includes the city of Assur and its citizens in his greeting formula:

1. To Ashur, father of the gods, great lord who dwells in Ehursag-galkurkurra, his great abode, hail, all hail!
2. To the gods of destinies and the goddesses who dwell in Ehursag-galkurkurra, their great abode, hail, all hail!
3. To the gods of destinies and the goddesses who dwell in the city of Aššur, their great abode, hail, all hail!
4. To the city and its people, hail, all hail, to the palace located in it, hail, all hail!
5. For Sargon, the pure priest, the servant who reveres your great divinity and his army, all is well.[13]

The fact that Sargon II includes in his address the elites of Assur—this is probably what is meant by "its people" (*nišēšu*)—reflects exactly the change that must have occurred after Tiglath-pileser III (744–727 BCE) had succeeded in turning former vassal states into provinces of the Neo-Assyrian empire, thus significantly extending the borders of the Assyrian empire. Not only had the bureaucratic apparatus been enlarged in its highest ranks, the political change informed the cultural discourse as well, as illustrated by the newly introduced text categories. The scholars, in shaping the world view and managing the communication between the gods and the king, had to create a cultural discourse that reflected the political achievements and harmonized them with the cosmic order. However, it was exactly the demand for the intense communication between the gods and the king and its public display that made the scholars indispensable to the king. It promoted their monopolies in divinatory techniques, in shaping the state ritual, and in elaborating text and iconographic programs in order to immunize the monarch against any human judgment.

The introductory formula, which is modeled after the phraseology of Neo-Assyrian letters, led Oppenheim to assume that the letters to the god "were written, not to be deposited in silence in the sanctuary, but to be actually read to a public that was to react directly to their contents" (1960:143). The public Oppenheim imagined was the priesthood, the city as a corporate unit represented by the elders, as well as all its inhabitants. However, the "priesthood" itself consisted of cultic functionaries who were rather confined in their cultic and administrative duties, and it is questionable whether beyond the šangû of Ashur and the šangûs of other gods[14] one can define them as a strong component among the social groups of Assur. The role of the scholars was certainly more incisive. Whether the elders who presumably consisted of the heads of the wealthy merchant families in the Old Assyrian period still played a role in Middle Assyrian times has been already questioned by Tadmor (1986:205). While Oppenheim's interpretation is very suggestive, there is no proof and, in fact, no need for such a public setting. What is more, nobody in the Aramaic environment of the time probably would have been able to follow this text in its unusual lexicography. Instead, Sargon's claim of publicity can be compared to Hammurabi's claim of addressing his people in the stele bearing his laws which was set up in the courtyard of the temple and, consequently, only accessible to the functionaries and cultic specialists linked with it. As I will show in the following, it is rather the colophon which helps in illuminating the prospective audience and the agents behind the scene.

The body of Sargon II's report following the opening epistolary formula has the narrative form typical of a royal inscription, albeit unusual in its "poetic language, plays on words, and elaborate figures of speech" (Foster 2005:790). Subsequent to the detailed report on his campaign against Urartu, at the very end, Sargon describes his decision to send the army home. Only accompanied by his elite troops he takes an unusual route via Musasir to destroy the temple of the god Haldi, chief god of the Urartian pantheon, where the Urartian kings were crowned, to kidnap its gods, and take all its belongings. The account ends with a five-line colophon which is unusual for the epistolary text category but typical of texts that belong to the stream of tradition. However, instead of declaring the tablet the king's property, the tablet is said to belong to the chief scribe of the king who is explicitly introduced as scholar of Sargon II.

Subsequently, in some way this text must have found its way into the library of the chief exorcist of the Ashur temple who must have had a particular interest in the figure of Sargon II. Note that *Sargon's Geography*, too, was part of this library, a text that portrays Sargon II as the follower of the great king of the past, Sargon of Agade, and his creation of an imaginary empire of nearly cosmological dimensions, a notion that transpires in Sargon's report on his eighth campaign as well (Pedersén 1986, II:44). The colophon of the text reads as follows:

426 One charioteer, two horsemen, and three scouts (of those who) were killed.
427 I made Tab-shar-Ashur, the chief-steward, send the men (who bring) first rate messages (^{lú}EME.SAG^{meš}) to Ashur, my lord.
428 Tablet of Nabu-shallim-shunu, chief scribe of the king, chief tablet scribe,[15] scholar of Sargon, king of Assyria,
429 First born son of Harmakki, royal scribe, a native of Assur
430 (The report) was delivered in the eponym year of Issar-duri, governor of Arrapha.

I will refrain here from the various renderings of line 427[16] which is complicated because of the fact that in other royal reports to the god Ashur the term *lisānu rēštu* (^{luz}EME.SAG^{meš}) might be used without the determinative lú and could be translated with "first rate message." Furthermore, scholarly opinion hinges upon the question as to whether to translate the verb *ultēbila* in the first or third person singular: "I made send" or "he (Tab-shar-Ashur) made send)." The 1st person possessive pronoun "my lord" induced me to assume Sargon II as the subject of this sentence.

What is of interest for our discussion on the relationship between the Assyrian king and the elites is that this colophon mentions several parties that are involved in Sargon II's report to the god. One is Nabû-shallim-shunu, the king's scholar who obviously composed the tablet, and the other is the chief steward and treasurer Tab-shar-Ashur who, according to the information gleaned form epistolary literature, was responsible for inspections of all kinds, work assignments to palaces and temples in various cities, and was involved in political affairs (Parpola 1987:41–74). Unfortunately Sargon II's scholar Nabû-shallim-shunu is scarcely known. He is, however, mentioned in a text which reports on his partaking in offerings and purification ceremonies performed in the Ashur temple prior to Sargon II's triumphal procession (Wiseman 1952:61–71; Driel 1969:200–204). These activities in the Ashur temple took place on the 21st of the month Kislimu or Sebetu. If we assume that the date for the king's triumphal procession to the Ashur temple was set in the eleventh month Shabatu, as mentioned in the later ritual text A 125 for Ashurbanipal,[17] then the textual evidence suggests that the chief scribe had to perform some preparatory rites to allow for the king to enter the city after his military campaign. Whether it was

Nabû-shallim-shunu who brought the report of the king before Ashur on this particular occasion must remain, of course, pure speculation. However, the royal report must have reached the Ashur temple at some point before Sargon II's triumphal entry into the city, as in other cases we do have a letter of the god which must have been written in response to the royal report. All the evidence available in conjunction with the postscripts of the letters of gods to the king suggests the following reconstruction of various steps needed for the king to be allowed to enter the city of Assur after his military campaign:[18]

1. The king's scribe wrote a report on the king's campaign
2. the king sent somebody with the report to Assur;
3. At some point purification rites had to be performed at the Ashur temple to allow for the triumphal entry of the king, in Sargon II's case by his chief scribe.
4. Ashur sanctified the report in the form of an oracle as may be deduced from the subscript *mihrat dibbī* [*Aššur*] "copy of the words of [Ashur]" in Ashur's letter to Ashurbanipal SAA 3 44;
5. this oracle was rewritten into a letter of a god in response to the king on the basis of the royal report; and
6. finally the letter of the god was sent to the king
7. who then was allowed to perform his triumphal procession and enter the Ashur temple.

This reconstruction puts the king and the god, i.e., the institutions of the palace and the temple, center stage and reduces the participation of the political elites to an auxiliary function. The restricted number of royal reports to the gods or letters of gods to the king suggests that this particular kind of communication was only performed when royal action was in absolute need of divine sanction, i.e., in the case of the abduction of the gods of the enemy and the destruction of their sanctuaries as described in the letter of Sargon II to Ashur, and in the case of fratricide as described in Esarhaddon's report to Ashur about his campaign to Shubria (Bauer 1931:234–59; Borger 1967:§68; Leichty 1991:52–57). Divine sanction is spoken in Ashur's letter to Ashurbanipal regarding the rebellion of Ashurbanipal's brother Shamash-shum-ukin who was governor of Babylonia and was killed by Ashurbanipal during the civil war.

The fact that Sargon II's treasurer and scholar are only mentioned briefly in the colophon should not delude us as to the extent of involvement of the religious and political elites in this exchange between the king and the god. Nor should the fact that the text was found in the library of the chief exorcist carrying a colophon of a scholar instead of the king lead us to assume that we are dealing with a text of a private nature written by a scribe to celebrate the king's success as has been suggested by Louis D. Levine. Although the library contains tablets of the Middle Assyrian period and the late 8th century BCE, it probably originates only in the time of Ashurbanipal which points to the secondary or even tertiary storage of the text (Pedersén 1986:44–45; Maul 1994:159). The texts assembled in this library and the fact that it served as an educational training center for young scribes demonstrates that the interests of the chief exorcist reached far beyond the performance of the purification rites at the Ashur temple, qualifying him as the central figure in organizing the cult of the Ashur temple and collecting, compiling, and producing the body of cultural knowledge of the time. Long ago, Parpola (1971:3ff.) as well as Tadmor (1981:31) cautioned us against mistaking the title "chief scribe" as denoting a functionary who is only a scribe in the technical sense of the word. On the contrary, the colophon testifies to the high degree of involvement of the scholar responsible for the cultic affairs performed at the temple of Ashur, who, together with the treasurer, carried out the steps necessary to allow Sargon II to enter the city.

The relationship between Sargon II and his scholars as well as with the religious elites in Assur is difficult to grasp. It seems that in addition to Sargon II's treasurer, his governor Tab-sil-Esharra (Parpola 1987: nos. 75–109), performed most of the tasks which should have required the presence of Sargon II in Assur. Note that with regard to the king's cooperation with the religious elites, in his commemorative inscriptions Sargon II tends to emphasize two major deeds which one could read as mutually exclusive or, in fact, related to each other. One is his explicit mention of his ceremonial performance of the New Year festival according to the model of a Babylonian king after his conquest of Babylonia as narrated in his annals (Fuchs 1994:156 lines 320–321). The other is his establishment of the tax-exempt status not only for the traditional Babylonian cultic centers but also for the cities of Assur and Harran proclaimed in a text which in Assyriological literature is known as the *Assur Charter* (Chamaza 1992:21–33). While one could interpret this text as an expression of Sargon II's personal interest in the city of Assur, it seems more likely to assume that at the end of the 8th century BCE the political and religious elites of Assur had achieved a status of monopoly and independence that enabled them to claim such privileges. Whatever Sargon II has done or not done to arouse the indignation of the citizenry of Assur, he seems to have avoided visiting the city even for state rituals. Some figures must have possessed the power to even regulate his entry on the occasion of his triumphal procession which after all normally included the offering of at least part of the booty to the Ashur temple. Esarhaddon's effort to ingratiate himself with the elites of Assur in his inscriptions by emphasizing that he also composed or perhaps just confirmed the charter of Assur ([ka]ṣir kidinnūt BAL.TIL^{ki}) is a further example in support of the king's accountability to the elites of the cultic center of Assyria (Borger 1967:81, §53).

The question therefore is whether the process as reconstructed for Sargon II's report to the god Ashur with the emphasis on the authority of Assur's political and religious elites represents a normal case which could be assumed already for the time of Shamshi-Adad V and Shalmaneser IV, or whether the fact that it was stored in the exorcist's library signified that it was meant to serve as a model for future kings to remind them of the fact that the victory in the end is Ashur's. In both cases, religious authority, if not capable of limiting royal arbitrary behavior and hubris, nonetheless proves to be a major factor in furthering the positive image and prestige of rulership and thus in contributing to the stability of political power. By means of ritual as performed in the king's triumphal procession to the Ashur temple, the religious elite reinforced the message of Ashur's kingship and the king's stewardship as proclaimed in the Assyrian coronation ritual. Denying the king the right to perform his duty as the chief *šangû* of the god Ashur at some point must have been detrimental to individual rulership and a reason why the king would make an effort to engage the various parties in a network of power rather than acting in a tyrannical way. The effect ritual can bear upon political power then is more than protecting the king from any culpability resulting from political mistakes in performing his office (Lanfranchi 2003:104). Ritual takes on a corrective force, as it reminds the king of his personal responsibility. However, in the process of textualizing the king's deeds, the scholars eventually shaped the cultural memory of the individual king. Unfortunately we do not have a letter of the god Ashur sanctioning Sargon II's pillage of the sacred center of the Urartian kings. Thus we cannot tell whether the religious elite of Assur made an effort from their side to manipulate the system of communication to support the harmonious balance between earthly and heavenly powers which would then translate into the relationship between the city of Assur and the king. The final scholarly assessment is expressed in the text of the *Sin of Sargon* which, as has been stressed by Tadmor and Lanfranchi, is a product of the scholarly milieu and implies that Sargon II as well as his son Sennacherib had to answer for their deeds with an untimely death on the individual level.[19]

To conclude, the Assyrian scholars of the Sargonid period in assuming their role as transmitters and producers of symbolic systems and cultural practices played a key role in shaping power relations by creating the authority of kingship. While political elites can choose to ignore their scholarly advisors, in the end they cannot escape their cultural definition of the universal order and their judgment. Modern underestimation of the impact of the ancient scholars might have to do with the fact that intellectuals are considered a part of the humanistic intelligentsia (artists, writers, academics) rather than including the fields of law and medicine as well as the ones of the technical intelligentsia (craftsmanship, engineering, divination, observational astronomy).[20] The Assyrian experts are neither intellectuals in the French sense, nor scholars in ivory towers, nor simple scribes, which makes it so difficult to translate the terms *tupšarru*, generally rendered as "scribe," and *ummânu*.[21] Their combination of technical and pragmatic skills with cultural knowledge turned the intellectual into a significant agent within the network of power.

NOTES

9.1 G.E.R. Lloyd (1996:40) describes a similar practice performed in the Chinese empire.

9.2 W. G. Lambert (1976:85-94, 85 n. 1) argued against the building of a library under Tiglath-pileser I because the find spot also contained tablets from the 1st millennium BCE. O. Pedersén (1985:29-41; 1998:83f) did not commit himself to either position. See now Maul 2003b. The categories of 'private' or 'institutional' when applied to temple libraries prove to be of limited value, as the colophons of tablets found in 'temple libraries' generally do not refer to a them as 'property of'. Rather they identify the various scholars as their scribes and owners, see Clancier 2009 and Frahm 2011:262ff.

9.3 See the comments of Simo Parpola in the introduction to *Letters from Assyrian and Babylonian Scholars* (Parpola 1993).

9.4 This is reflected in the title of the elder members of the family of the exorcist which is MAŠ.MAŠ *ša bīt Aššur*.

9.5   Known under the misnomer "Temple of the Diviner," see O. Pedersén, *Archives and Libraries in the Ancient Near East 1500–300 B.C.* (Bethesda, MD: CDL Press, 1998), 61–64, with further bibliography; Fleming 2000:13–45; and Cohen 2009.

9.6   The following passage is taken from Pongratz-Leisten 1999:34.

9.7   For the most recent commentary on the notion of secrecy regarding scholarly knowledge, see Lenzi 2008.

9.8   Here I slightly deviate from Giovanni Lanfranchi who discusses the notion of responsibility as being linked with the personal conscience of the king "who should feel involved in the consequences of his decisions or acts through the risk of penalty of death brought on by the gods" (2003:107).

9.9   See, for example, the appropriation by the chief eunuch Mutaris-Ashur of certain epithets usually reserved for the king, such as "wise," "expert in battle," "man of authority"; Grayson 1996 184:16–21, and Tadmor 2002:603–11.

9.10   See the royal reports sent by Shalmaneser IV (RIMA 3 A.0.105.3) and Sargon II's report (TCL 3).

9.11   This is the case in Ashurbanipal's letter to Assur reporting on his campaigns against the Arabs, see Pongratz-Leisten 1999:241–45.

9.12   Contrary to A. Livingstone (1989, SAA 3 44:3-4), I prefer to render *sapāḫu* with "dispersal" instead of "destruction."

9.13   F. Thureau-Dangin 1912: lines 1–5; for a new edition see Mayer 1983; a new translation has been supplied by B. Foster 2005:790–813; for a discussion of the letter, see Oppenheim 1960, Zaccagnini 1981, and Levine 2003.

9.14   For this professional group, see Menzel 1981, I:130–208 with a list of *šangûs* known by name.

9.15   For *giburu* Foster 2005:813 refers to Reiner and Civil 1967:200.

9.16   Line 427 reads: ^{lú}EME.SAG^{meš} ^{m}DÙG.GA.IM-^{d}A-šur ^{lú}AGRIG GAL-ú ina UGU ^{d}A-šur be-lí-ia ul-te-bi-la.; for the various translations see Levine 2003:118n18.

9.17   The text is dated to the time of Ashurbanipal and matters could have been completely different under his reign. See Menzel 1981, 2: no. 24 i 5. For the interrelationship of these events, see G.B. Lanfranchi 1990:230–31 and n99.

9.18   The idea of a fictive dialogue between king and god performed first in the royal report after a military campaign and second in the letter of the god to the king contradicts the idea of Oppenheim (1960) who claimed that the royal report was read on the occasion of the king's entry into the city of Assur.

9.19   See Lanfranchi 2003:107 for the distinction between the *institutional* and *personal* figure of the king, and his emphasis that it is the private person of the king who eventually pays.

9.20 For these distinctions see David Swartz's discussion of Bourdieu's approach to the intellectual (1997:222).

9.21 P. Zanker (1995) has the same problem with defining the intellectual in Classical antiquity.

REFERENCES

Baker, H.D. 2000. *The Prosopography of the Neo-Assyrian Empire*, Vol. 2(1) H-K. Helsinki: The Neo-Assyrian Text Corpus Project, University of Helsinki.

Bauer, Th. 1931. Ein Erstbericht Asarhaddons. ZA 40:234–59.

Borger, R. 1967. *Die Inschriften Asarhaddons, Königs von Assyrien*. Osnabrück: Biblio-Verlag.

Bourdieu, P. 1991. *Language and Symbolic Power*. Cambridge: Harvard University Press.

Brisch, N., ed. 2008. *Religion and Power. Divine Kingship in the Ancient World and Beyond*. Chicago: The Oriental Institute of the University of Chicago.

Vera Chamaza, G.M. 1992. Sargon II's Ascent to the Throne: the Political Situation. *State Archives of Assyria Bulletin* VI:21–33.

Clancier, Ph. 2009. *Les bibliothèques en Babylonie dans la deuxième moitié du 1er millénaire avant J.-C.* Münster: Ugarit Verlag.

Cohen, Y. 2009. *The Scribes and Scholars of the City of Emar in the Late Bronze Age*. HSS 59. Winona Lake, IN: Eisenbrauns.

Deller, K. 1987. Assurbanipal in der Gartenlaube. *BaM* 18:229–38.

Driel, G. van. 1969. *The Cult of Aššur*. Assen: van Gorcum.

Eisenstadt, S.N., ed. 1973. *Intellectuals and Tradition*. New York: Humanities Press.

Engnell, I. 1943. *Studies in Divine Kingship in the Ancient Near East*. Uppsala: Almqvist & Wiksells.

Fleming, D. 1992. *The Installation of Baal's High Priestess at Emar*. Atlanta: Scholars Press.

———. 2000. *Time at Emar. The Cultic Calendar and the Rituals from the Diviner's House*. Winona Lake, IN: Eisenbrauns.

Foster, B.R. 2005. *Before the Muses*. 3rd ed. Bethesda, MD: CDL Press.

Frahm, E. 2011. *Babylonian and Assyrian Text Commentaries*. Münster: Ugarit-Verlag.

Frankfort, H. 1978. *Kingship and the Gods*. 2nd ed. Chicago: University of Chicago Press.

Fuchs, A. 1994. *Die Inschriften Sargons II. aus Khorsabad*. Göttingen: Cuvillier Verlag.
Glassner, J.-J. 2004. *Mesopotamian Chronicles*. Atlanta, GA: Society of Biblical Literature.
Grayson, A.K. 1996. *Assyrian Rulers of the Early First Millennium BC, 2 (858–745 BC)*. Royal Inscriptions of Mesopotamia, Assyrian Periods 3. Toronto: University of Toronto Press.
———. 2000. *Assyrian and Babylonian Chronicles*. Repr. Winona Lake, IN: Eisenbrauns.
Hunger, H. 1968. *Babylonische und assyrische Kolophone*. Neukirchen-Vluyn & Kevelaer: Verlag Butzon & Bercker and Neukirchner Verlag.
Jones, P. 2005. Divine and Non-Divine Kingship. In *A Companion to the Ancient Near East*, ed. D.C. Snell, pp. 330–42. Malden/Oxford: Blackwell Publishing.
Labat, R. 1938. *Le caractère religieux de la royauté assyro-babylonienne*. Leiden: A. Maisonneuve.
Lambert, W.G. 1967. Enmeduranki and Related Matters. *JCS* 21:126–38.
———. 1976. Tukulti-Ninurta I and the Assyrian King List. *Iraq* 38:85–94.
Lanfranchi, G.B. 1990. *I Cimmeri. Emergenza delle elites militari iraniche nelle Vicino Oriente (VIII-VII sec. a. C.)*. Padua: Sargon srl.
———. 2003. Ideological Implications of the Problem of Royal Responsibility in the Neo-Assyrian Period. *Eretz-Israel* 27:100–110.
Leichty, E. 1991. Esarhaddon's "Letter to the Gods." In *Ah, Assyria...Studies in Assyrian History and Ancient Near Eastern Historiography Presented to Hayim Tadmor*, ed. Mordechai Cogan and Israel Eph'al, pp. 52–57. Jerusalem: The Magnes Press.
Lenzi, A. 2008. *Secrecy and the Gods. Secret Knowledge in Ancient Mesopotamia and Biblical Israel*. SAAS XIV. Helsinki: The Neo-Assyrian Text Corpus Project.
Levine, L.D. 2003. Observations on "Sargon's Letter to the Gods." *Eretz-Israel* 27:112–19.
Lincoln, B. 1994. *Authority: Construction and Corrosion*. Chicago: The University of Chicago Press.
Liverani, M. 1984. The Growth of the Assyrian Empire in the Habur/Middle Euphrates Area. *AAAS*: 107–15.
Livingstone, A., ed. 1989. *Court Poetry and Literary Miscellania*. SAA 3. Helsinki: Helsinki University Press.
Lloyd, G.E.R. 1996. *Adversaries and Authorities. Investigations into Greek and Chinese Science*. Cambridge: Cambridge University Press.

Machinist, P. 2003. The Voice of the Historian in the Ancient Near Eastern and Mediterranean World. *Interpretation* 57:117–37.

Maul, S.M. 1994. *Zukunftsbewältigung. Eine Untersuchung altorientalischen Denkens anhand der babylonisch-assyrischen Löserituale* (Namburbi). Mainz: Philipp von Zabern.

———. 2003a. Wie die Bibliothek eines Assyrischen Gelehrten wiederersteht. In *Wiedererstehendes assur. 100 Jahre deutsche Ausgrabungen in Assyrien*, ed. J. Marzahn and B. Salje, pp. 175–82. Mainz: Philipp von Zabern.

———. 2003b. Die Reste einer mittelassyrischen Beschwörerbibliothek. In *Literatur, Politik und Recht in Mesopotamien: Festschrift für Claus Wilcke*, ed. W. Sallaberger, K. Volk und A. Zgoll, pp. 181–94. Wiesbaden: Harrassowitz.

Mayer, W. 1983. Sargons Feldzug gegen Urartu - 714 v.Chr. *MDOG* 115:65-132.

Menzel, B. 1981. *Assyrische Tempel*. 2 vols. Rome: Istituto Biblico.

Michalowski, P. 1993. *Letters from Early Mesopotamia*. Society of Biblical Literature Translations Series. Atlanta: Scholars Press.

———. 2011. *The correspondence of the Kings of Ur: an Epistolary History of an Ancient Mesopotamian Kingdom*. Mesopotamian Civilizations 15. Winona Lake, IN: Eisenbrauns.

Oppenheim, A.L. 1960. The City of Assur in 714 B.C. *JNES* 19:133–47.

Parpola, S. 1971. *Letters from Assyrian Scholars, Part II A Introduction and Appendices*. Kevelaer: Butzon and Bercker.

———. 1972. A Letter from Šamaš-šum-ukīn to Esarhaddon. *Iraq* 34:21–34.

———. 1987. *The Correspondence of Sargon II, Part I. Letters from Assyria and the West*. SAA I. Helsinki: Helsinki University Press.

———, ed. 1993. *Letters from Assyrian and Babylonian Scholars*. SAA X. Helsinki: Helsinki University Press.

———. 1997. *Assyrian Prophecies*. SAA IX. Helsinki: Helsinki University Press.

Pedersén, O. 1985. *Archives and Libraries in the City of Assur Part I*. Uppsala: Almqvist & Wiksell.

———. 1986. *Archives and Libraries in the City of Assur, Part II*. Uppsala: Almqvist & Wiksell.

———. 1998. *Archives and Libraries in the Ancient Near East 1500–300 B.C.* Bethesda, MD: CDL Press.

Pongratz-Leisten, B. 1999. *Herrschaftswissen in Mesopotamien. Formen der Kommunikation zwischen Gott und König im 2. und 1. Jahrtausend v. Chr.* SAAS 10. Helsinki: The Neo-Assyrian Text Corpus Project.

———. n.d. "The Writing of the God" and the Textualization of Neo-Assyrian

Prophecy. In *I Am No Prophet*, ed. A. Lange et al. In press.

Postgate, J.N. 2002. The Land of Assur and the Yoke of Assur. In *Expanding Empires. Cultural Interaction and Exchange in World Societies from Ancient to Early Modern Times*, ed. W.F. Kasinec and M.A. Polushin, pp. 1–12. Wilmington, DE: Scholarly Resources.

Reiner, E., and M. Civil. 1967. Another Volume of Sultantepe Tablets. *JNES* 26(3): 177–211.

Swartz, D. 1997. *Power & Culture. The Sociology of Pierre Bourdieu*. Chicago and London: The University of Chicago Press.

Tadmor, H. 1981. History and Ideology in the Assyrian Royal Inscriptions. In *Assyrian Royal Inscriptions: New Horizons in Literary, Ideological and Historical Analysis.*, ed. F.M. Fales, pp. 13–33. Rome: Instituto per L'Oriente.

———. 1986. Monarchy and the Elite in Assyria and Babylonia: The Question of Royal Accountability. In *The Origins and Diversity of Axial Age Civilizations*, ed. S.N. Eisenstadt, pp. 203–24. Albany: State University of New York Press.

———. 2002. The Role of the Chief Eunuch and the Place of Eunuchs in the Assyrian Empire. In *Sex and Gender in the Ancient Near East: Proceedings of the 47th Rencontre Assyriologique Internationale, Helsinki, July 2–6, 2001*, ed. S. Parpola and R.M. Whiting, pp. 603–11. Helsinki: Neo-Assyrian Text Corpus Project.

Tadmor, H., B. Landsberger, and S. Parpola. 1989. The Sin of Sargon and Sennacherib's Last Will. *State Archives of Assyria. Bulletin* 3:3–51.

Thureau-Dangin, F. 1912. *Une relation de la huitième campagne de Sargon (714 av. J.-C.)*, TCL III. Paris: Paul Geuthner.

Van De Mieroop, M. 1999. Literature and Political Discourse in Ancient Mesopotamia. Sargon II of Assyria and Sargon of Akkade. In *Munuscula Mesopotamica. Festschrift für Johannes Renger*, ed. B. Böck, E. Cancik-Kirschbaum, and T. Richter, pp. 327–39. AOAT 267. Münster: Ugarit-Verlag.

Weber, M. 1976. *Wirtschaft und Gesellschaft*. 5th ed. Tübingen.

Weidner, E. 1952–1953. Die Bibliothek Tiglatpilesers I. *AfO* 16:197–215.

Wiseman, D.J. 1952. The Nimrud Tablets 1951. *Iraq* 14:61–71.

Zaccagnini, C. 1981. An Urartean Royal Inscription in the Report of Sargon's Eighth Campaign. In *Assyrian Royal Inscriptions: New Horizons*, ed. F.M. Fales, pp. 259–94. Rome: Instituto per l'Orient.

Zanker, P. 1995. *The Mask of Socrates. The Image of the Intellectual in Antiquity*. Berkeley: University of California Press.

10

Kingship as Racketeering

The Royal Tombs and Death Pits at Ur, Mesopotamia, Reinterpreted from the Standpoint of Conflict Theory

D. BRUCE DICKSON

> Here the question arises; whether it is better to be loved than feared or feared than loved. The answer is that it would be desirable to be both but, since that is difficult, it is much safer to be feared than to be loved, if one must choose ... Men have less hesitation in offending a man who is loved than one who is feared, for love is held by a bond of obligation which, as men are wicked, is broken whenever personal advantage suggests it, but fear is accompanied by the dread of punishment which never relaxes.
>
> — Niccolo Machiavelli, *The Prince*

This chapter focuses on the connection between sovereignty, violence, and inequality—and fear—evident in the ancient Mesopotamian institutions of kingship. The Royal Tombs and Death Pits of the Early Dynastic IIIb period (ca. 2450–2350 BCE, see Marchesi and Marchetti 2011:8, 64–65) at the site of Ur are used as an exemplar. Until the recent discovery of proof to the contrary (Baadsgaard et al. 2011), the interpretation of the Royal Tombs and Death Pits at this site by their excavator, Sir Leonard Woolley (1934), was long influential. Woolley implies that the people sacrificed when the Ur dynasts were buried went willingly to their deaths out of loyalty, devotion, and faith in the dead monarchs. In this chapter, Conflict theory is used to re-interpret the early Mesopotamian kingship and state and to suggest that these twin institutions constitute a kind of racketeering. Conflict theory presumes that profound inequalities in power exist, both between social systems and within them. Such inequality fosters competition over scarce resources of all kinds between individuals and between groups of individuals. Conflict theorists consider that the primary role of the state is to maintain the dominance of one segment of society over the others. Ur's kings may indeed have been strong and their subjects loyal, but it is equally likely that these rulers were weak and vulnerable and practiced ritual sacrifice in order to terrorize a restive citizenry and thereby preserve elite dominance of society.

L'UNITÉ SE FAIT TOUJOURS BRUTALEMENT

For the 19th century French savant Ernest Renan, historical (and, by extension, archaeological) research has a serious public relations problem: inevitably such investigation digs up the acts of violence that occur at the beginning of any political unit, even those which have had the most beneficial consequences. Unity is always achieved brutally (Renan 1947[1882]: 891, author's translation).

The public relations problem faced by those who would excavate (figuratively or actually) this foundational violence stems from what Farmer calls the "erasure of social memory" (2004:307). Simply put, the perpetrators—or at least the winners—have chosen to forget and their descendants prefer to keep it that way. But toujours? Always? Perhaps. Or perhaps not. That, surely, is a critical theoretical and empirical question. Let us approach it first theoretically and then empirically.

TWO THEORIES ACCOUNTING FOR THE RISE AND PERSISTENCE OF STATES

Understanding and explaining the emergence and survival of complex states and civilizations in the ancient Near East has long been a scholarly preoccupation. In his review of the contribution of anthropology to the question,

Elman Service (1977) recognizes two major theoretical approaches: Integration theory and Conflict theory.

Integration theory is derived from functionalism or structural functionalism as well as general systems theory and cultural ecology. In this perspective, state institutions emerge as a more complex level of social and economic integration in response to new problems and challenges presented by, for example, the requirements of irrigation (Wittfogel 1957), population growth (Carneiro 1967), competition with other social systems (Carneiro 1970, see Dickson 1987), the need to organize long-distance trade (Rathje 1971), the interaction over time in Egypt between the quality of leadership, external warfare, level of upper class extraction, and fluctuations in the Nile river's seasonal inundation of its floodplain (Butzer 1980), and so forth. Thus, in Integration theory, the state emerges as a mechanism through which its citizens adapt to their social and physical environment. The effectiveness (or lack of same) of its institutions and its leaders in performing those adaptive tasks determines whether any particular state will survive.

Conflict theory begins with the presumption that profound inequalities in power exist, both between social systems and within them. Such inequality fosters competition over scarce resources of all kinds. Conflict theorists consider this competition—which often leads to violence and warfare—to be the prime mover in the emergence of states. Competitive struggles may be between would-be external conquerors and those they would dominate (ibn Kaldun 1957 [1377]) or between classes or other segments within a society (Engels 1972 [1884]). The state emerges out of these struggles; it persists if its leader can maintain a stable or dynamic equilibrium between the various conflicting parties. Groups and individuals who benefit from the particular structural equilibrium solution that results strive to see that arrangement maintained (cf. Collins 1974, 1975; Dahrendorf 1959, 1968; Simmel 1964; Gluckman 1968).

Of course, Integration theory and Conflict theory are not mutually exclusive perspectives; both provide important insights into the question of state origin and persistence. However, speaking of ideology in social science generally, Paul Diesing asserts that "the strength of a perspective consists of its ability to bring certain aspects of society into clear focus, thereby making their empirical study possible; the weakness of a perspective results from the way it distorts or hides other aspects of society" (1982:l2).

In my view, contemporary explanations of the rise and persistence of the ancient Near Eastern state have fully and effectively utilized Integration theory in generating conclusions (for example, Flannery 1972, Cohen and Service 1977, Claessen 1978, Skalnik 1978). However, by focusing on the integrative or functional role played by state organizations, scholars—particularly those of a New Archaeology or "processual" persuasion—have tended to neglect to test the alternative hypotheses drawn from Conflict theory about the nature of these early states. Integration theorists, hypothesizing that Near Eastern states were interconnected, adaptive systems, have tended to be indifferent to the notion that such polities were likely riven with deep internal social conflict and competition over scarce resources.

PROTECTING THE POLITY INSIDE AND OUT

Whatever else they can or cannot do, states must perform two essential "functions" if they are to persist and survive. First, they must control or at least ameliorate violence within their territories—sometimes to the point of making internal war against their own subjects—or at least some of them. Second, they must be capable of waging external war against their neighbors and competitors. According to Charles Tilly, it matters little whether we take violence in a narrow sense, such as damage to persons and objects, or in a broad sense, such as violation of people's desires and interests; by either criterion, governments stand out from other organizations by their tendency to monopolize the concentrated means of violence (Tilly 1984). "Accept our power," warns the government "and we will protect you from worse violence—of which we can give you a sample, if you don't believe us" (Mann 1986:l00).

Integration theorists consider the concentration and monopolization of power as part of the state's role in protecting society from its surrounding external threats and insulating it from internal disorder. Yet, things are rarely that simple. What if the threat of external violence is due to the state's own actions abroad? Or worse, utterly of the state's own creation? What if external warfare or the control of internal violence directly serves the interests of the ruling elite or some other segment of society? Circumstances of this sort are difficult to address by means of Integration theory.

For example, over the last 15 years or so, the government of the African nation of Zimbabwe has turned what was once the business and agricultural dynamo of Central Africa into an inflation-ridden basket case. This chaotic self-wounding has in large part been due to government confiscation of the large-scale, white-owned farms that once fed the country and made Zimbabwe a net food exporter. At the same time, the government has violently cleared huge squatters' camps populated by peoples it perceives as hostile to it. Government security forces have driven these squatters into the countryside to face penury and death. How can we account for this state-sponsored economic failure, internal chaos, and selective violence save through Conflict theory? As Michael Wines reports in the *New York Times* (August 3, 2007): "While 11 million or more people descend into destitution; a tiny slice of the population is becoming ever more powerful and wealthy at their expense . . . Zimbabwe is fast becoming a kleptocracy, and the government's seemingly inexplicable policies are in fact preserving and expanding it."

Correspondingly, the sole strategy of the Zimbabwean elite and those dependent upon them is to hold onto power by any means in the midst of this expanding poverty and chaos and, in doing so, maintain control of the mineral and agricultural assets and other resources which they have appropriated. Admittedly, Zimbabwe is a state in extremis but this is precisely what makes its circumstances interesting here. As the Zimbabwean state teeters on the brink of collapse, the actions and interests of its controlling elite—obscured in ordinary times—are laid bare.

THE STATE AS PROTECTION RACKET

The prominent Conflict theorist Charles Tilly makes the mordant observation that, the more closely we study social history, "the more coercion by officials resembles coercion by criminals, state violence resembles private violence, authorized expropriation resembles theft" (1984:12). That is, for Tilly, the "protection" offered by states is a kind of racketeering.

One doesn't have to go very far to find an illustration of Tilly's view. Sudhir Venkatesh (2008) provides a great deal of it in his memoir of the dissertation field work he did in Chicago during the crack epidemic of the 1990s. Venkatesh worked with the Black Kings, a street gang which at that time controlled drugs, prostitution, and extortion in The Robert Taylor Homes, a sprawling public housing project on Chicago's South Side. In addition to their criminal marketing activities, the Black Kings effectively "governed" the Taylor complex and the surrounding area by protecting it from other gangs and operating as a police force, a taxing agency, and, more occasionally, as a charitable and civic foundation. In Venkatesh's account, local residents either passively tolerated the gang or were actively complicit in its activities. Of course, they had little choice. The gang maintained a tight monopoly on coercive force in the projects, and the police were nowhere to be found. The striking thing about the situation that Venkatesh describes is that it turns Tilly on his head: in the Taylor projects, coercion by criminals resembles coercion by the state, private violence resembles state violence, and theft dresses up like authorized expropriation. Moreover, we are left with the impression that the Black Kings' "governance" of the Robert Taylor public housing complex provides us with an unsettling model of the dawn of governance in the early state: very likely, it too was a kind of extortion racket.

In the remainder of this chapter, I use Conflict theory in the reinterpretation of the archaeological evidence from the celebrated Royal Tombs and Death Pits at the site of Ur in southern Mesopotamia. Of course, these mortuary remains are among the most dramatic evidence of state-sponsored ritualized violence in the entire Mesopotamian archaeological record. Interpretation of the Royal Tombs and Death Pits has generally been done from an integrative perspective. In my opinion, viewing the graves from this perspective has obscured our recognition of the social conflict and state violence that very probably produced them.

THE GREAT CEMETERY AT UR

The ancient site of Ur is located along a former course of the Euphrates River near An Nasiriya, a modern city in southern Iraq. Archaeological evidence recovered at the site indicates that occupation there began in the 'Ubaid period (ca. 5500–4200 BCE) and continued until sometime in the 4th century BCE. Although Ur's political fortunes waxed and waned during this long occupation, the site itself remained throughout one of the most significant and most venerated places on the southern Mesopotamian alluvium (Woolley and Moorey 1982, Cohen 2005).

Ur was excavated between 1922 and 1934 in an expedition sponsored jointly by the British Museum and the University of Pennsylvania Museum of Archaeology and Anthropology. The celebrated British archaeologist

Sir C. Leonard Woolley was overall director of the project. Excavation work in the Great Cemetery at Ur took place during five field seasons between 1926 and 1932 (Woolley 1934:6–8). This fieldwork resulted in the opening of a total of 1,850 graves most of which were single interments with few grave goods. However, 16 large graves found in the earliest portion of the cemetery proved very different from the rest. It was Sir Leonard's view that these 16 interments constituted the resting place of Ur's royalty (1934:33). These graves were larger and more lavishly provisioned than all the others, but Woolley's interpretation of them was not based simply on the richness of their contents. As he points out, 14 of the 16 showed evidence of having been robbed in antiquity so "their wealth must be taken on credit." The attribute that sets these 16 graves apart is that all of them contain multiple skeletons. In 10 of the 16, large, substantially built stone and/or brick burial tombs with one or more chambers are also present. Sir Leonard labeled these 10 "Royal Tombs." Six of the 16 graves containing multiple interments lack tombs. Woolley refers to these simply as "Royal Death Pits." It is his opinion that these 6 Royal Death Pits originally contained tombs but that grave robbers had destroyed them long ago.

The 10 Royal Tombs each contain—or presumably had once contained—the remains of a central or primary individual lain within a tomb chamber. The remains of one or more additional skeletons within most of these tombs indicate that the principal individual had not been interred alone but that sacrificial victims had been placed in the tomb at the some time (Baadsgaard et al. 2011). Additional individual skeletons are found buried in unroofed sunken courtyards that either surround the tombs or are built adjacent to them. Skeletal remains are also found in the shafts leading down to some of the tombs suggesting that sacrifices continued to be made as the tomb and death pit complex was refilled. Thus, both the peculiarities of the structure of these graves together with the evidence that grim rituals accompanied the interment of their primary burials makes these 16 graves unique in the cemetery at Ur. As noted, from the outset of their discovery Sir Leonard regarded these 16 features to be the graves of royalty and much of what he later wrote of Ur was predicated on this premise. Nonetheless, to this day the actual identities of the primary interments in the so-called Royal Graves and Death Pits remain an open question (cf. Dickson 2006:129–31; Marchesi 2004).

THE PUTATIVE ROYAL INTERMENTS IN GRAVES PG 789 AND PG 800

Of all the 16 Royal Graves and Death Pits, Woolley seems to have been particularly impressed by PG 789 and PG 800. The stone and brick tomb in PG 800 is located at one end of a deep, rectangular death pit that measures 4 by 11.75 m. Beneath this pit is a second death pit and a second tomb, PG 789. The tomb in PG 789 measures 4 by 1.8 m and is also built of stone and mud brick (Woolley 1934:62). In spite of the apparent superimposition of the death pits, the tombs in PG 789 and PG 800 are built next to one another on about the same level. These two burial complexes produced rich grave goods and the skeletal remains of at least 86 human beings. Only fragments of the bones of the principal occupant of the tomb in grave PG 789 were recovered. The bulk of the skeleton was missing. This absence, coupled with the disorder evident inside the tomb, suggests that the body had been removed and the associated grave goods plundered at some time in antiquity. Woolley believed that the robbery of this first tomb most likely took place during construction of the second one adjacent to it in grave PG 800.

PG 789

Looted or not, the tomb in grave PG 789 yielded valuable objets d'art. Recovered within the structure was the celebrated "Silver Boat," a model of a watercraft not unlike the modern Iraqi faradas (Bahrani 1995:1637); a wooden statue covered with gold leaf, shell, and lapis lazuli which Woolley named "The Ram in the Thicket" and connected to the Biblical story of Abraham and Isaac; and a number of other, equally extraordinary artifacts. The huge 5-by-10 m death pit adjacent to the tomb yielded skeletal remains of some 63 adults as well as two wheeled vehicles, complete with the bones of the draft animals that had drawn them (Woolley 1934:62–65). Woolley concluded that all of these individuals had been sacrificed and interred—along with the rich grave goods, vessels, food, clothing, wagons, and musical instruments—at the time that the primary interment was placed in the tomb.

PG 800

Unlike the tomb in PG 789, the burial structure in PG 800 still held its primary occupant and showed no signs of having been looted. This rectangular structure measures 4.35 by 2.8 m and is built of limestone slabs and mud bricks. Upon opening it, Woolley found it contained a raised platform, or bier, on which lay a skeleton still wearing an elaborate headdress made of a long band of gold, gold leaves, carnelian rings, lapis lazuli beads, and a five-pointed golden barrette decorated with gold and lapis lazuli flowers. A huge pair of crescent-shaped gold earrings once hung from the person's ears and the entire upper part of the body had been covered with jewelry made of gold and semi-precious stones (Woolley 1934:84–87).

By the right shoulder of this skeleton, excavators found three lapis lazuli cylinder seals. Inscribed on one seal is the name Pu-abi and the title NIN (Woolley 1934:88). When applied to mortal women, the Sumerian word NIN is generally translated as "queen" (Moorey 1977:27; Marchesi 2004)). From this, Woolley inferred that Pu-abi was the name of the primary interment, that she was queen of Ur at the time of her death, and that she was most likely the wife of the primary interment or "king" buried in the adjacent tomb in PG 789. The second cylinder seal bore the name A-bara-gi and Woolley inferred that this was the name of that royal husband. Two additional skeletons crouched or lay on the tomb floor at the head and foot of the raised platform. From their elaborate headdresses, Woolley concludes that these were maids or ladies-in-waiting to Pu-abi (1934:84). A third skeleton lay alongside the bier. The small knives and a whetstone associated with this individual led Woolley to the conclusion that this was the skeleton of a male. Skull fragments of a fourth individual were also recovered in the tomb (1934:88).

Although excavated to a depth of 7 m below the modern ground surface, the bottom of the PG 800 courtyard just reached the roof top of the tomb of Pu-abi that is set within it. The floor of this courtyard had been lined with reed mats, and it is connected to the ground surface above by a steep earthen ramp (Woolley 1934:73). A sledge, with the bones of the two onagers who presumably had once pulled it, was found in this courtyard together with the skeletons of 26 people, all of whom appear to be adults. Ten of these skeletons are thought to be females because they were found wearing lavish headdresses and jewelry nearly as complex and beautiful as that of Pu-abi herself (Bahrani 1995:1636). Five others, associated with weapons and wearing helmets, are thought to be male soldiers. The bones of 5 individuals, mixed with or near those of the onagers, are presumed to be those of male grooms or sledge drivers. Three skeletons, at least one of whom is presumed to be male, were found near a large wardrobe chest. Thus Woolley concluded that 12 women, 11 men, and 3 persons of unknown sex were interred along with Queen Pu-abi in PG 800. Unfortunately, these gender attributions can never be confirmed as all but a tiny fraction of the skeletal material excavated from the vast cemetery at Ur was discarded (Molleson and Hodgson 2003:91–93).

ACCEPTABLE DEATH: WHO DID AND WHO DID NOT DESCEND INTO THE DEATH PITS?

In his various professional and popular writings about the Great Cemetery at Ur, Woolley offers an extraordinary interpretation of the Royal Death Pits and Royal Tombs: the people buried with the primary interments descended into the grave pits and died there, if not willingly, at least passively. According to Sir Leonard, one could not but remark the peacefulness of the bodies; all were in order, not only set out in neat rows but individually peaceful; there was no sign of violence, not even such disturbance of the delicate headdresses of the women as was almost bound to result did the wearer merely fall; they died lying or sitting (Woolley 1934:35–36). But what was the source of that passivity? The social or occupational roles of the individuals sacrificed and interred in the Royal Graves hold some clues.

These people "seem to be only the immediate household staff of the buried dignitary. There is no evidence of children and no clear evidence of the self immolation of wives at their husband's funeral. Where men may be securely identified among the human victims they are usually armed guards, grooms or charioteers…" (Moorey 1977:35). The class asymmetry of this status distribution is obvious. Only members of the "lower orders," presumably the least powerful members of society, descended into the death pits. Pollock (1991:177) suggests that many of these people may have been menial laborers who "belonged" to the public institutions like the temple or the palace and, in return for their labor, received subsistence rations. Molleson and Hodgson's recent analysis of the entire surviving skeletal sample collected by Woolley at Ur reaches conclusions consistent with Pollock's hypothesis (2003:91). According to them, 16 skulls or whole skeletons in this sample collection apparently came from the Royal Cemetery. Of these 16 specimens, 2 appear to have been soldiers and 8 were presumably attendants to various central figures buried in the Royal Graves and Death Pits. The skeletons of 4 of the 8 attendants, specimens PG211, PG1573, PG1648a, and

PG1648d, were found to exhibit extraordinary degrees of shape alteration, robusticity, and muscle development rarely observed in skeletal populations anywhere else. Bones are most readily modeled by forces imposed upon them while the individual is still growing. Molleson and Hodgson (2003) consider it likely therefore that the exceptional skeletal alterations observed in these four Ur attendants had resulted from the relentless performance—beginning in childhood—of activities like charioteering (specimen PG 1573) and the carrying of heavy loads on the head or back (specimens PG211, PG1648a, and PG1648d). In Molleson and Hodgson's view, evidence of such heavy and intensive labor at such an early age "implies a role specialization that amounts to child labor, even slavery" (although note the scepticism of Pollock 2007a:214n14). Yet, whoever these attendants were, it seems clear who they were not. At Ur, neither royal spouse nor royal offspring seems to have accompanied the king or queen in the grave; noble courtiers, high temple officials, viziers, and generals do not appear to have been required to attend the royal personage in the afterlife. Such injustice need come as no surprise. After all, the formation and maintenance of elites, and then of elites within elites, lie at the heart of civilizations: inequality is fundamental. In the most ancient civilization, elites controlled material and symbolic resources but were scarcely subject to cultural requirements to disburse them in fulfillment of social obligations (Baines and Yoffee 1998:234). Neither, it would seem, were Ur's elite obliged to make ultimate sacrifices or fatal *beaux gestes*.

Interestingly, a similar arrangement between elite and commoner may have pertained in Egypt in the late Predynastic and Early Dynastic periods. During those early periods, the political and cultural center of the emerging Egyptian state was evidently located at Abydos (*3bḏw*) in Upper Egypt (see Morris, this volume). Pharaohs of the earliest dynasties of this nascent state were buried in the Royal Necropolis at Umm el Qa'ab in the western desert a few kilometers beyond Abydos proper. At the turn of the last century, seven large tomb-pits, each with associated small tomb-pits, were excavated in the Royal Necropolis by the redoubtable English archaeologist Sir W.M. Flinders Petrie (1900, 1901). Petrie recognized these tomb complexes as belonging to royalty and dated them to the First Dynasty. In more recent times, extensive work has been done in Umm el Qa'ab by the Deutsches Archäologisches Institut under the direction of Günter Dreyer. Each of the seven main tombs consists of a rectangular pit, the sides of which are lined with mud brick. Storage chambers were built against these mud-brick walls and a large wooden coffin or tomb shrine was formerly located in the center of each pit. Roofs of timber and matting were built over the tombs and the complexes were then covered by earth mounds.

What is significant from our perspective is that each of the central or royal tombs is surrounded by rows or clusters of smaller pits roughly large enough to accommodate a single individual. Like the central tomb-pits, these subsidiary tombs had been largely robbed in antiquity. Nonetheless human skeletal remains, stone and pottery grave goods, and animal bones were recovered from some of them. Presumably these small subsidiary tombs were built to contain the burials of individuals sacrificed at the time of the interment of the royal figure in the central tomb-pit. The number of these putative sacrifices is highest at the beginning of the First Dynasty. The earliest of the seven tomb-pits, identified as belonging to the Pharaoh Djer, has some 338 subsidiary burials associated with it. This number is never surpassed at Umm el Qa'ab. By the Second Dynasty, the practice of human sacrifice on the occasion of a royal interment seems to have disappeared altogether (Kemp 1966:18–19). While the sacrificial nature of the subsidiary burials in the graves and death pits at Ur seems well established, we can never be entirely certain that individuals buried in the various groupings of small subsidiary tombs at Umm el Qa'ab were laid to rest simultaneously with the central interment in each of the central tomb-pits. However, recent excavations of subsidiary graves surrounding First Dynasty royal enclosures at Abydos indicate that those burials were all sealed at the same time (O'Connor 2009:172–73) strengthening the possibility that the Umm el-Qa'ab subsidiary burials were also sacrificial. A fair conclusion seems to be that early state rulers both in Mesopotamia and in Egypt felt compelled to demonstrate their power through the murder of their subjects. Ernest Renan's notion that "l'unité se fait toujours brutalement" again seems prescient.

CONTINUA OF VIOLENCE

What are we to make of the grisly remains Woolley recovered at Ur? Are they an aberration unique to Ur and to a narrow slice of the site's history as some specialists claim? Or, as the tombs at Umm el Qa'ab suggest, are they rather specific examples of a much larger and more general pattern in human behavior and social development? Here again, some contemporary explorations of conflict and violence offer insight.

Scheper-Hughes and Bourgois (2004) provide a schema for understanding the horrendous warfare, genocide, and violence of our own times. In their view, violence is more than simply "the expression of illegitimate physical force against a person or group of persons." Rather, they see it "as encompassing all forms of the 'controlling process' (Nader 1997) that assault basic human freedoms and individual or collective survival." For Scheper-Hughes and Bourgois, violence in society is not to be understood as a discrete category of phenomenon (2004:22); rather it should be seen as forming a continuum of social control that progresses incrementally from depersonalization, institutional confinement, and acceptable death to outright physical violence. For these authors, continua of violence are built into the very fiber or structure of states. Violence within them is, in this sense, "structural violence."

Structural violence is particularly evident in societies "characterized by poverty and steep grades of social inequality" (Farmer 2004:307). This is so because in such settings it is easy for the individuals and groups that benefit from the existing asymmetry of the social arrangements to strive to maintain them by "reducing the socially vulnerable into expendable non-persons and assuming the license—even the duty—to kill, main, or soul murder" (Scheper-Hughes and Bourgois 2004:19). Under such circumstances, Farmer asserts, "structural violence is violence exerted systematically—that is, indirectly—by everyone who belongs to a certain social order" (2004:307).

BLOOD AS SOLVENT

A solvent is a liquid that creates a solution by dissolving solid, liquid, or gaseous material. Blood is a kind of social solvent in that executions or other forms of murderous violence can produce "solutions" to dilemmas faced by kings and states. As Stalin is reputed to have said, "No man, no problem." The rulers of the earliest states of the Near East would no doubt have agreed. However, in the foundation stages of those ancient polities, blood was not only commonly spilt, it was commonly spilt in public. In most early states, execution or sacrifice before the crowd was part of what Randall Collins (1974:436) calls the "dominant ceremonial order."

I have called such bloody public ceremonies "theaters of cruelty and terror" (Dickson 2006). Surely the ritual sacrifices that took place at Ur fit the category perfectly. In my view, such public spectacles were the material and public expression of powerful systems of ideas that emanated from the institutions of power. As noted earlier, Laura Nader (1997) calls these systems of ideas, "controlling processes." An example of such a controlling process from the ancient Near East would be the idea that the king is the "archenemy of chaos" charged with eliminating anarchy and disorder. What better solution to the problem of chaos and anarchy than the solvent of blood? Apply the solvent and disorder becomes order, confusion becomes predictability. Through the practice of public violence and the simultaneous propagation of systems of ideas that underwrite it, individuals and groups are persuaded not just to accede to their own domination, but to participate in it.

REVISITING THE DEATH PITS

The bodies in the Death Pits were arranged like dolls in a sinister doll house or actors in a mortal tableau. What are we to make of them? Beginning with Sir Leonard Woolley, these arrangements have been interpreted as reflecting the nature of social relations within the Ur city state. In his view—and in the views of many of the scholars who have followed him—the people sacrificed at Ur along with the dynasts went willingly to their deaths out of loyalty, devotion, and faith in the dead monarchs (cf. Pollock's [2007a, 2007b] recent interpretation of the role in this process played by loyalty to, and personal dependence upon, the great households at Ur).

Such an interpretation is consistent with the view of the state fostered by Integration theory. In order for the state to remain effective as a mechanism of adaptation to the social and physical environment of the southern alluvium, it must confirm that its government persists despite the death of its mortal ruler. Given the gravity of the situation, this confirmation must be carried on in the most convincing and dramatic manner. For at least some of its citizens, loyalty to king and state—and perhaps the promise of a reward in the afterlife—trumps loyalty to life.

In my view, Conflict theory, combined with contemporary ideas like structural violence, violence as continua, and the state as a protection racket gives us a greater understanding of the Royal Tombs and Death Pits. Such a perspective also expands our understanding of the nature of social life at Ur in particular and in the early states of Mesopotamia and the Near

East in general. The reflection of structural violence in the Royal Tombs and Death Pits seems clear: the people who were placed in them were likely menial laborers, grooms, charioteers, common soldiers, and the attendants of the primary burials. In sum, only "the socially vulnerable," only "expendable nonpersons" found their way into these graves and death pits. Royal spouses, noble courtiers, high priests, generals, or other members of Ur's elite are nowhere to be found. The injustice of this arrangement is palpable and reflective of a society with a steep grade of inequality.

Modern experience teaches that built into the very structure of unequal societies are continua of violence through which people at the lower strata incrementally move from depersonalization, institutional confinement, and acceptable death to outright physical violence. That is, social inequality creates structures that lead to murder and grant elites license to perform it. What clearer evidence than the Royal Tombs and Death Pits do we need in order to conclude that such was the order and nature of social life at Ur?

REFERENCES

Baadsgaard, A., J. Monge, S. Cox, and R.L. Zettler. 2011. Human Sacrifice and Intentional Corpse Preservation in the Royal Cemetery of Ur. *Antiquity* 85:27–42.

Bahrani, Z. 1995. Jewelry and Personal Arts in Ancient Western Asia. In *Civilizations of the Ancient Near East*, Vol. 111, ed. J.M.Sasson, J. Baines, G. Beckman, and K.S. Robinson, pp. 1635–45. New York: Macmillan.

Baines, J., and N. Yoffee. 1998. Order, Legitimacy, and Wealth in Ancient Egypt and Mesopotamia. In *Archaic States*, ed. G.M. Feinman and J. Marcus, pp. 199–260. Santa Fe, NM: School of American Research.

Butzer, K.W. 1980. Pleistocene History of the Nile Valley in Egypt and Lower Nubia. In *The Sahara and the Nile*, ed. M.A.J. Williams and H. Faure, pp. 253–80. Rotterdam: A.A. Balkema.

Carneiro, R.L. 1967. On the Relationship between Size of Population and Complexity of Social Organization. *Southwestern Journal of Anthropology* 23:234–43.

———. 1970. Theory of the Origin of the State. *Science* 169:733–38.

Claessen, H.J.M. 1978. The Early State: A Structural Approach. In *The Early State*, ed. H.J.M. Claessen and P. Skalnik, pp. 533–96. The Hague: Mouton Publishers.

Cohen, A. 2005. *Death Rituals and the Development of Early Mesopotamian King-*

ship: Toward a New Understanding of Iraq's Royal Cemetery of Ur. Leiden: Brill.

Cohen, R., and E. Service. 1977. *Origins of the State*. Philadelphia: ISHI.

Collins, R. 1974. Three Faces of Cruelty: Toward a Comparative Sociology of Violence. *Theory and Society* 1:415–40.

———. 1975. *Conflict Sociology: Toward an Explanatory Science*. New York: Academic Press.

Dahrendorf, R. 1959. *Class and Class Conflict in Industrial Society*. Stanford, CA: Stanford University Press.

———. 1968. *Essays in the Theory of Society*. Stanford, CA: Stanford University Press.

Dickson, D.B. 1987. Circumscription by Anthropogenic Environmental Destruction: An Expansion of Carneiro's (1970) Theory of the Origin of the State. *American Antiquity* 52(4): 709–16.

———. 2006. Public Transcripts Expressed in Theatres of Cruelty: The Royal Graves at Ur in Mesopotamia. *CAJ* 16(2): 123–44.

Diesing, P. 1982. *Science and Ideology in the Policy Sciences*. New York: Aldine.

Engels, F. 1972 [1884]. *The Origin of the Family, Private Property and the State*. New York: International Publishers.

Farmer, P. 2004. An Anthropology of Structural Violence. *Current Anthropology* 45(2): 307–10.

Flannery, K. 1972. The Cultural Evolution of Civilizations. *Annual Review of Ecology and Systematics* 3:399–426.

Gluckman, M. 1968. The Utility of the Equilibrium Model in the Study of Social Change. *American Anthropologist* 70:219–37.

Ibn Khaldun. 1956 [1377]. *The Muqaddimah: An Introduction to History*. New York: Pantheon Books.

Kemp, B.J. 1966. Abydos and the Royal Tombs of the First Dynasty. *JEA* 52:13–22.

Mann, M. 1986. *The Sources of Social Power.*, Vol. 1, *A History of Power from the Beginning to A.D. 1760*. Cambridge: Cambridge University Press.

Marchesi, G. 2004. Who Was Buried in the Royal Tombs of Ur? The Epigraphic and Textual Data. *Orientalia* n.s. 73:153–97.

Marchesi, G., and N. Marchetti. 2011. *Royal Statuary of Early Dynastic Mesopotamia*. Mesopotamian Civilizations 14. Winona Lake, IN: Eisenbrauns.

Marcus, M.I. 1994. Dressed to Kill: Women and Pins in Early Iran. *The Oxford Art Journal* 17(2): 3–15.

Molleson, T., and D. Hodgson. 2003. The Human Remains from Woolley's Excavations at Ur. *Iraq* 65:91–129.

Moorey, P.R.S. 1977. What Do We Know about the People Buried in the Royal Cemetery? *Expedition* 20:24–40.

———. 1994. *Ancient Mesopotamian Materials and Industries: The Archaeological Evidence*. Oxford: Oxford University Press.

Nader, L. 1997. Controlling Processes: Tracing the Dynamic Components of Power. *Current Anthropology* 38(5): 711–37.

O'Connor, D.B. 2009. *Abydos: Egypt's First Pharaohs and the Cult of Osiris*. London: Thames & Hudson.

Petrie, W.M.F. 1900. *Royal Tombs of the First Dynasty, 1900. Part I*. Egypt Exploration Fund Memoir 18. London: Egypt Exploration Fund.

———. 1901. *Royal Tombs of the Earliest Dynasties, 1901. Part II*. Egypt Exploration Fund Memoir 21. London: Egypt Exploration Fund.

Pollock, S. 1991. Of Priestesses, Princes and Poor Relations: The Dead in the Royal Cemetery of Ur. *CAJ* 1(2): 171–89.

———. 2007a. Death of a Household. In *Performing Death: Social Analyses of Funerary Traditions in the Ancient Near East and Mediterranean*, ed. N. Laneri, pp. 209–22. Oriental Institute Seminars 3. Chicago: The Oriental Institute of the University of Chicago.

———. 2007b. The Royal Cemetery of Ur: Ritual, Tradition, and the Creation of Subjects. In *Representations of Political Power: Case Histories from Times of Change and Dissolving Order in the Ancient Near East*, ed. M. Heinz and M.H. Feldman, pp. 89–110. Winona Lake, IN: Eisenbrauns.

Rathje, W. 1971. The Origins and Development of Lowland Classic Maya Civilization. *American Antiquity* 36:705–15.

Renan, E. 1947– [1882]. Qu'est-ce qu'est une nation? In *Oeuvres complètes,* Vol. 1, ed. H. Psichari, pp. 891–900. Paris: Calmann-Lévy.

Scheper-Hughes, N., and P. Bourgois. 2004. Introduction: Making Sense of Violence. In *Violence in War and Peace*, ed. N. Scheper-Hughes and P. Bourgois, pp. 1–31. Malden, MA: Blackwell.

Service, E. 1977. Classical and Modern Theories of the Origins of Government. In *Origins of the State*, ed. R. Cohen and E. Service, pp. 21–34. Philadelphia: ISHI.

Simmel, G. 1964. *The Sociology of Georg Simmel. Translated, edited, and with an introduction by Kurt H. Wolff*. New York; Collier-Macmillan.

Skalnik, P. 1978. The Early State as a Process. In *The Early State*, ed. H.J.M. Claessen and P. Skalnik, pp. 597–618. The Hague: Mouton.

Tilly, C. 1984. *Big Structures, Large Processes, Huge Comparisons*. New York: Russell Sage Foundation.

Venkatesh, S. 2008. *Gang Leader for a Day: A Rogue Sociologist Takes to the Streets*. New York: Penguin.

Wittfogel, Karl. 1957. *Oriental Despotism*. New Haven, CT: Yale University Press.

Woolley, C.L. 1934. *Ur Excavations Volume II: The Royal Cemetery: A Report on the Predynastic and Sargonid Graves Excavated Between 1926 and 1931*. London and Philadelphia: Publication of the Joint Expedition of the British Museum and of the Museum of the University of Pennsylvania to Mesopotamia.

Woolley, C.L., and P.R.S. Moorey. 1982. *Ur of the Chaldees: The Final Account of the Excavations at Ur*. Rev. ed. London: Herbert.

Landscape

11

Mesopotamian Kings and the Built Environment

MICHAEL ROAF

INTRODUCTION

In this chapter I explore certain aspects of the relationship between the rulers of Mesopotamia and the built environment. In particular I consider the intentions and effects of their building activities, by which the kings sought to alter their environment and the perception of this environment. In this rather discursive paper I first consider some territorial aspects of Mesopotamian kingship and then consider the role that Mesopotamian rulers played in changing the appearance of this territory by their architectural creations.[1]

MESOPOTAMIAN KINGSHIP

Mesopotamian rulers were (re)presented in text and image both as energetic builders and as pious servants of the gods and these two aspects of kingship came together in the frequent building and rebuilding of the temples in the territories under their control. The expenditure could be considerable, and while in some senses it might be looked on as an investment whereby the favor of the gods was secured, in other cases it is presented as a royal duty, incumbent on the ruler without any immediate payback.

Mesopotamian royal ideology as it appears in the texts belonged to a strong, long-lasting tradition: age-old rulers such as Gilgamesh, Sargon,

Shulgi, Shamshi-Adad, and Hammurabi served as models for later rulers. Their memory was preserved in the scribal schools of Mesopotamia and belonged to the so-called stream of tradition.[2] Despite sharing models of ideal—or at least successful—kingship, in reality the nature of kingship throughout the two millennia from 2500 to 300 BC was very diverse.

The meanings subsumed in the term "Mesopotamian kingship" are disparate,[3] and, while there might have been "ideal" Mesopotamian rulers, there was neither a typical nor a normative one. Every ruler had his own character and this individual personality affected the way he governed.[4] Politics is the art of the possible and each ruler even within a single family operated within a system of changing political relationships and thus was forced to adapt his policies to the prevailing circumstances. The characterization of the rulers of states in Mesopotamia between 2500 and 300 BC as "Mesopotamian rulers" is in my opinion no more enlightening than describing Augustus, Nero, Frederick Barbarossa, Lorenzo di Medici, Joseph Bonaparte, Victor Emmanuel II, and Pope Benedict XVI as "Italian rulers."

Similarly I would question the utility of the phrase "the ideology of Mesopotamian kingship." There were different ideologies in different reigns and regions: scholars have particularly distinguished Middle and Late Assyrian kingship from earlier Assyrian kingship and from Babylonian kingship.[5] In some instances we can document changes in the ideology within a single reign: this is most obvious in the deification of Naram-Sin of Agade and of Shulgi of Ur some years after they had first claimed the title of king. No doubt there were also different ideologies current in a single reign adhered to by different groups within Mesopotamian society. These ideologies in so far as we can recognize them have no features that can be characterized as exclusively Mesopotamian and few non-trivial features[6] in common that can be described as Mesopotamian.

Kingship in ancient Mesopotamia had many different facets and different aspects are reflected in the multifarious titles that the rulers took and in the statements included in their royal inscriptions (Seux 1967). Various words in various languages and dialects were used to label the king: *lugal, en, ensi, šarru, iššakku, malku,* etc. The precise meanings of these terms are debated and indeed differed at different periods and in different regions. The titles may be qualified in various ways such as great king, mighty king, and king of kings. Frequently these titles are associated with geographical criteria which may be general, for example, King of the Four Quarters, King of

All, King of the Lands, etc., or specific referring to territories, such as King of Sumer and Akkad and King of the Land of Ashur, or individual cities, such as King of Ur and King of Babylon, or particular peoples, such as King of the Amorites.

An early Mesopotamian concept of kingship was intimately connected with the idea of place. According to the *Sumerian King List* originally composed at the end of the 3rd millennium BC, kingship descended from heaven and was given by the gods not to an individual, nor to a family, a tribe, or a territory, but to a city (Jacobsen 1939, Glassner 2004:117–27).[7] Kingship was according to this view transferred from one city to another in succession.[8] After the flood, the reason given for the change of dynasty was either that the city was "smitten with weapons" or that its "term of office was abolished" and both cases had the same consequence, namely "its kingship was carried to" a new city.

From the late 3rd to early 2nd millennium BC the city of Nippur had a special, preeminent role, which was not acknowledged in the *Sumerian King List*. Control of Nippur, the seat of the temple of the god Enlil, the head of the early Sumerian and Babylonian pantheon, was seen as a sign of the legitimacy of a ruler's claim to be the rightful ruler of the whole of Babylonia.

A further geographic dimension to Mesopotamian kingship was played by the city of Kish in the later Early Dynastic period. Kingship of Kish, or at least the use of the title King of Kish, apparently implied divinely sanctified rule over other southern Babylonian city rulers. The Old Akkadian rulers transformed the title King of Kish into the title *šar kiššati* "king of all," "king of the universe." This title and the title *šar kibrāt arba'i* or *šar kibrāt erbetti* often conveniently but incorrectly translated as King of the Four Quarters were used by Mesopotamian kings from the Agade period (ca. 2300 BC) to the Achaemenid period. The exact implications of these two titles have been discussed and it has been suggested that the title *šar kiššati* referred to the cosmological realm and the title *šar kibrāt arba'i* to the terrestrial (Glassner 1984:26–29). In both contexts the implication is that the Mesopotamian ruler had authority over all the countries in the world. This is of course only a theoretical claim; Realpolitik acknowledged the legitimacy and authority of other regimes, whose rulers were also entitled as kings of particular territories.

Babylonian king lists and chronicles classified Mesopotamian rulers into dynasties based on the cities or countries which they governed. The names of most of the early dynasties are the names of cities with the determinative for city, not for land. The ruler of the city was the divinely ordained king and changes in ruling family did not affect the city as the seat of kingship. Thus the *Chronicle of Early Kings* (Grayson 1975:155; Glassner 2004:270–73) recorded that "Erra-imitti, king [of Isin] installed Enlil-bani, a gardener, as substitute king on his throne. He placed the royal tiara on his head. Erra-imitti [died] in his palace when he sipped a hot broth. Enlil-bani, who occupied the throne, did not give it up [and] so became king." This story may well be apocryphal but, at least when the *Chronicle* was composed, the scribe did not see Enlil-bani's non-royal origins as grounds for doubting the legitimacy of his assumption of the kingship.

In the king lists and chronicles later dynasties were often identified by the countries the rulers came from: thus the Sealand (KUR A.AB.BA), Babylonia (KUR *Kar-Duniaš*), Assyria (KUR *Aššur*), Chaldaea (KUR *Kaldi*), and Persia (KUR *Parsu*).[9] Rulers of Babylonia in their own inscriptions were, however, more frequently referred to as king of Babylon or of Agade (written without the determinative KUR) rather than king of the land of Babylonia. This development is clearly related to the development from city states to territorial kingdoms, but it should be remembered that unlike the city which remained fixed as the focus of a city state, the territorial kingdoms had no constant topographical extent and their borders changed according to the political realities. Nevertheless the rulers did not willingly acknowledge the existence of rebellions or independence movements within their territories until they had been put down. The royal ideology did not always reflect the true state of affairs: for example, Persia's rule over Egypt was implicitly claimed by the presence of an Egyptian supporting the royal dais on the tomb reliefs of not only the Persian kings who actually ruled Egypt, but also the 4th century BC Persian rulers during whose reigns Egypt was enjoying independence (Schmidt 1970: fig. 50).

TERRITORIES AND KINGDOMS

The territories controlled by ancient rulers are today often depicted on a two-dimensional map as areas with definite edges (e.g., Roaf 1990).[10] In the modern world, in which frontiers are often marked by walls or fences[11] and in which international law gives this view legitimacy, this is not unreasonable. Ancient polities could have natural geographical borders such as coastlines and river banks or, to a lesser extent, mountainous regions, but other boundaries between different states were often less clear-cut. The status of many frontier settlements was ambivalent and this uncertainty does not only result from the inadequacy of our sources. The attempt to construct maps showing the territorial extent of particular Mesopotamian kingdoms is an unreliable project. Not only are there large areas about which we have insufficient information, but the ancient sources record contradictory opinions about the allegiances of settlements. Such international disputes survive in the modern world: for example, maps produced in Iran include Bahrain and maps in Syria include the Hatay as part of their national territories. Ancient borders were certainly less definitely defined than those in the modern world. Control of the holy city of Ardini, for example, was claimed by the rulers both of Urartu and of Assyria, who called it Musasir, and its rulers vacillated between acknowledging the authority of the neighboring major powers.

Even regions within a larger kingdom could claim a degree of autonomy. In the Assyrian version of the inscription on the statue of Adda-it'i from Fakhariyeh he is described as *šaknu,* governor (i.e., vassal) of the Assyrian king, but in the Aramaic version he has the title *mlk* and is apparently an independent ruler of Sikanu (Abou Assaf, Bordreuil, and Millard 1982). Such nuances can often be proposed but seldom confirmed. A map labeled in Assyrian cuneiform would presumably have shown the city of Sikanu within the Assyrian Empire while one labeled in Aramaic produced in Sikanu could well have shown the same territory as independent from Assyria.

The territories controlled by Mesopotamian rulers can be classified as consisting of a homeland, the region which traditionally belonged to the polity, and conquered territories, which were recognized as having previously belonged to other kingdoms, and are commonly called by modern scholars core and periphery and sometimes thought to be characteristic of the empires rather than territorial nation states. These regions did not remain static over time: territories which had previously been independent could be incorporated into the homeland. There were no doubt differences in opinion about the status of a particular region. The majority of the provinces that formed the empire of the Third Dynasty of Ur had been previously independent city states and some of them achieved independence once again with the fall of the Ur dynasty. The power base of the Ur III kings may have been concentrated in the cities of Ur and Uruk, but the core of the Ur III Empire is normally taken to be the lowland provinces that paid the so-called *bala* tax in agrarian produce as opposed to the periphery that paid the *gun mada* tax in animals (Steinkeller 1986).

Rulers of Eshnunna in the 18th century BC claimed in their titles that they had enlarged the kingdom of Eshnunna. Assyrian kings added their conquests to the territory of Assyria. In the 13th century BC the Middle Assyrian king Tukulti-Ninurta I's epithets included "capturer of enemy lands, extender of borders" (Grayson 1987:240 A.0.78.2 lines 9–10), and he cursed a future ruler who abandoned his newly founded royal residence Kar-Tukulti-Ninurta: "May the god Ashur, my lord, . . . diminish his borders." Tiglath-pileser I stated in his prisms which commemorated his rebuilding of the Anu-Adad Temple in Ashur (Grayson 1991:13–14 A.0.87.1 lines 59–61) that "I added territory to Assyria (and) people to its population. I extended the border of my land and ruled over all their lands" (i.e., the lands of the rulers defeated by Tiglath-pileser). Sargon II at the end of the 8th century BC "set his eunuchs over them (i.e., the lands conquered by Sargon) as governors," "imposed on them the yoke of my sovereignty," and "imposed on them tribute and tax like Assyria's" (Luckenbill 1926–1927, 2:54 §102, 55§104; Fuchs 1994:56, 357, 56, 301). Thus in the royal inscriptions the Assyrian Empire did not consist of a well-defined core and periphery. The reality was, however, rather different. The statuses of the various provinces were not equal and from the 9th century to the early 7th century there was a regular order for the governors reflected in the sequence of eponyms. Although the Assyrian king maintained palaces complete with royal households in the provinces, which he visited when he traveled through his empire, he lavished more attention on the royal residences in the heartland of Assyria. Indeed as we will see the provincial governors were responsible for contributions of materials and labor for royal building projects in the homeland.

THE EDIFICE COMPLEX OF MESOPOTAMIAN RULERS

In the above discussion of Mesopotamian kingship I suggested that there are few non-trivial features of kingship in ancient Mesopotamia that can be characterized as typically Mesopotamian. There is, however, one common feature of the ideologies promulgated by Mesopotamian rulers (or by the scribes in their service) that could be considered quintessentially Mesopotamian, namely that the most important sources of information about these ideologies are those associated with the construction of buildings and other monuments. The vast majority of royal inscriptions from Mesopotamia are building inscriptions. These include inscriptions written or stamped on the bricks used in the buildings, display inscriptions, and foundation documents and door sockets buried under the floors or within the thickness of the walls. These texts, in addition to listing the king's titles and qualities, normally record details of the king's building activities and often the specific project for which the text was composed. In some kingdoms, such as that of Mittani in the 15th and 14th centuries BC, it appears that it was not the custom to deposit foundation inscriptions: the absence of such texts has had the result that our knowledge of the activities of the rulers of Mittani is extremely small.[12]

In addition, the majority of visual images of the king were created for specific locations within buildings.[13] These include the stone reliefs, glazed bricks, mural paintings, and plaques that adorned the palace and temple walls, the decorated bronze bands on the gates, and the statuettes intended for foundation deposits, as well as most stelae, *kudurrus*, and statues, which were erected in particular architectural contexts. For example, of the nineteen inscriptions of Hammurabi, king of Babylon, that were edited in the *Royal Inscriptions of Mesopotamia* project (Frayne 1990:332–57) all except two are either building inscriptions or are fragmentary and might have been building inscriptions; the exceptions are a fragmentary inscription probably belonging to a victory stele and an inscription reading E_2.GAL *ha-am-mu-ra-pi*, literally "palace of Hammurabi" but meaning "the property of Hammurabi" on two bronze mace heads from Tell Muhammad.

Further information about the building activities of the rulers is given in the official year names, which were normally used in Babylonia between the mid-3rd and mid-2nd millennia BC. The year names as well as having a purely practical role in the dating of documents also had a propagandistic purpose. The events commemorated in them were chosen to increase the prestige of the ruler (Horsnell 2003, 2004). While constrained by the actual events that had taken place in the previous year, the topics chosen included military successes, dynastic marriages, installations of priests or priestesses, dedication of cultic equipment, and various building projects. These projects embraced the rebuilding of temples or palaces, city walls and gates, digging of canals, etc. These are essentially the same types of building projects that were recorded in the royal inscriptions. For example, a third of the events commemorated in the year names of Gudea ca. 2100 BC (Edzard 1997:27–28) concerned the building of temples and a canal.

The following discussion will consider certain aspects of Mesopotamian rulers and the built environment: I do not consider all these features to be particularly Mesopotamian, although the preoccupation of Mesopotamian royalty with building projects might be thought of as typical of Mesopotamian kingship. Instead I see this essentially as the product of our sources and more characteristic of the Mesopotamian cuneiform scribal tradition, which produced texts written for the same purpose over hundreds or even thousands of years, than of the ideology of the kings, whom these scribes served. Since these genres included building inscriptions of various types we are better informed about the building activities of Mesopotamian rulers than those of rulers in regions where royal constructions were not furnished with descriptive inscriptions written on materials and deposited in places where they survived.

Our knowledge of the hundreds of rulers in Mesopotamia is uneven. The exact number of rulers cannot be calculated. In his study of the Amorite kingdoms of Mesopotamia, Dominique Charpin (2004) listed the names of more than four hundred rulers in the period from ca. 2000 to 1600 BC. No doubt there were many more rulers whose names have not been handed down to us. In many cases we know little else about these rulers than their names, the name of their kingdom, and the approximate period in which they lived. In the better documented cases we can trace the history of their reigns and have considerable knowledge of their deeds and of the constructions that they commissioned. In some cases the building activities of the king were immense. Inscribed bricks of Naram-Sin, king of Agade, have been found in Tell Brak and throughout southern Mesopotamia, and texts describe the temples he built in Agade, as well as his elaborate restoration of the temple area of Nippur, which according to a later tradition led to his downfall. Gudea, ruler of Lagash, is one of the most familiar of Mesopotamian rulers and he appears to have devoted all the resources of his kingdom to the beautification of the city of Girsu, building some 15 temples including the vast Eninnu, the temple of the god Ningirsu (Suter 2000). His personal interest in architecture is shown in the detailed description of the building process in his cylinder inscriptions and in the seated statue that shows him as an architect with a plan of one of his commissions on his knee. Ur-Namma, founder of the Third Dynasty of Ur, constructed massive ziggurats in Eridu, Ur, Uruk, and Nippur, and temples in Girtab, Abiak, Marad, and Akshak, and palaces for himself and the *entu* priestess in Ur, as well as rebuilding the city walls and digging canals for the same city. The Kassite king Kurigalzu I at the beginning of the 14th century BC carried out extensive building works at Ur, Uruk, and Isin as well as creating a completely new settlement called Dur-Kurigalzu with the best-preserved ziggurat and temple complex in Mesopotamia and the largest of all ancient Mesopotamian palaces, that eventually came to cover some 400,000 square meters.

Assyrian kings were renowned as builders, particularly Ashurnasirpal II whose rebuilding of the city of Kalhu is attested in numerous inscriptions and in the excavated remains, and the father, son, and grandson Sargon II, Sennacherib, and Esarhaddon who constructed the royal residences of Dur-Sharrukin and Nineveh and rebuilt the city of Babylon. Nebuchadnezzar, king of Babylon, also devoted much of the wealth of Babylonia in the restoration of Babylon and other Babylonian cities, as well as constructing two cross-country walls linking the Tigris and Euphrates in order to protect Babylon from the danger of flooding. Darius, king of Persia, not only added to the buildings constructed by Cyrus at Pasargadae and built the palatial complex in Susa but undertook similar work at Persepolis, Hamadan, and perhaps also in Babylon. Such obsessive urges demonstrated by these rulers as well as others to create a new built environment are sometimes attributed to them having an edifice complex.

Naming the compulsive mania of leaders to commemorate themselves in the construction of buildings as examples of an edifice complex does not mean that it was not an effective political and social tool. The Mesopotamian royal edifice complex attempted to ensure the ruler would be remembered and praised by associating his name with architectural constructions which it was planned would last for years, possibly centuries, and when in the course of time the structure was rebuilt the inscriptions left in the walls and foundations would be incorporated into the new structure and the ruler's contribution would still be remembered. Name, fame, repute, and prestige are closely related concepts in many cultures including that of Mesopotamia (see recently, Radner 2005a).

The main types of structure recorded in the royal inscriptions are temples, palaces, city walls and gates and streets, cross-country walls, and agrarian projects such as canals, gardens, and parks. In most cases these activities were the refurbishment or the rebuilding of pre-existing buildings or structures, but sometimes, particularly with cross-country walls and canals, the endeavours were new. In rare cases new settlements were founded or the building was so extensive that its function was radically changed.

Temples

The earliest and the most frequent of royal commissions were for the building or reconstruction of the temples of the gods. Normally the ruler rebuilt an existing shrine. In Assyria, according to the building inscriptions, the site was normally excavated to the bottom of its foundation pit and the temple was rebuilt in its entirety from its bottom to its top and it was decorated in a fashion more splendid than before. Archaeological excavations, however, reveal remains of earlier temples and it seems that the preparatory excavation was not as thorough as the texts suggest.

In southern Mesopotamia it was a common custom to preserve the foundations of previous temples when the temple was rebuilt. The walls of the new temple were built above the lower courses of the walls of the old temple which were often preserved by filling the spaces between them with brick. Archaeological excavations have revealed the remains of numerous re-buildings of temples often cut down to the same height. This seems to have been carried out because of the danger that, even if the appropriate rituals were undertaken, the god living in the temple might be angered by the complete destruction of his or her house (for discussion, see Winter 2000). In most cases the new temple did not follow exactly the same plan as the earlier one, though Neo-Babylonian rulers claimed to have rebuilt temples not deviating by an inch from the earlier plans.

New foundations no doubt required special precautions. The Oval Temple in Khafajeh showed the extreme lengths resorted to in order to purify a site, by digging out a huge pit and filling it with thousands of tons of pure earth. An idea of the elaborateness and extent of the ceremonies that were required can be found in the detailed descriptions contained on Gudea's enormous inscribed cylinders that tell of the rituals required for the purification of the site of the Eninnu Temple in Girsu (Edzard 1997:68–106).[14] Similar rituals, perhaps more extensive or perhaps less so, would have been carried out in the course of any building project.

The builders of temples requested later rulers, who might rebuild the temple, to preserve and rebury their foundation inscriptions (Grayson 1987:255 A.0.78.11 lines 53–81):

> I (Tukulti-Ninurta I) completed (the temple of Ishtar) from top to bottom and deposited my inscriptions. May a later prince when that temple becomes old and dilapidated, restore (it and) make (it) resplendent. May he anoint with oil my inscriptions, make sacrifices (and) return (them) to their places. (Then) the goddess Ishtar will listen to his prayers. As for the one who removes my inscriptions and my name: May the goddess Ishtar, my mistress, break his weapon (and) hand him over to his enemies.

There are several cases when a king searched for and found earlier foundation inscriptions and recorded the fact. In some building inscriptions the previous history of the building is outlined. For example, Adad-nirari I recorded that the Ishtar Temple in Ashur had been built by Ilu-shuma and restored by Sargon I and Puzur-Ashur III (Grayson 1987:150 A.0.76.15 lines 5–15). It is possible that this information was derived from the discovery of foundation inscriptions or inscribed bricks. When his son Shalmaneser I restored the building, he repeated the information in Adad-nirari's inscription almost word for word in his own foundation document (Grayson 1987:195 A.0.77.61 lines 5–14). The inscription was re-deposited by Shalmaneser's son Tukulti-Ninurta I together with his own foundation inscriptions (Ellis 1968:99 and 190).

The last native king of Babylon, Nabonidus, who rebuilt the temples of the moon god in Ur and Harran as well as the temple of the sun god in Sippar, was particularly obsessive in his search for evidence about the earlier temples and their builders (Beaulieu 1989, Schaudig 2001). He recorded that in his investigation of the Sin Temple at Harran (Schaudig 2001: 421-2, 438): "The inscription written in the name of Ashurbanipal, king of Assyria, I found and did not alter. I anointed it with oil, performed a sacrifice, placed it with my own inscription, and returned it to its place."

Palaces

Not surprisingly Mesopotamian rulers invested considerable resources in creating palaces which would provide a suitable setting for their kingship (for previous studies, see Garelli 1974, Lackenbacher 1982, 1990).[15] As Van De Mieroop (1997:78) wrote, "The buildings were often enormous in size, and considerable energy was expended on their construction and decoration. They were a powerful symbol of royal might."

In Mesopotamia the words used for palace were also sometimes used to describe temples, which were thought of as the residences of the gods. In the earliest texts, the sign AB was used, and in the later Sumerian texts, the word e_2-gal (etymologically "big house") which was borrowed as *ekallu* in Akkadian texts. Like temples, palaces were not merely buildings where ceremonies took place but were also institutions. They were above all the residences of the king, his family, and his staff, the place where the king held audience and dispensed decrees. But in addition they could contain administrative offices, workshops, prisons, treasuries, shrines, and graves.

As the residence of the king they required security: entry was restricted not only to the palace as a whole but also to the inner apartments where the residential part of the palace was situated. In Akkadian a distinction was made between the outer part of the palace the *bābānu* (gate area) and the *bītānu* (house area). They were often placed on the strongly fortified citadel and often had thick buttressed walls that might have been for defense but could also have been for show, as other official buildings exhibited such features.

Unlike temples in the Ubaid period which were built to a similar tripartite plan as houses, palaces were built with different plans even though on occasion a palace might contain a temple or chapel of the conventional plan or a temple might contain a throne room suite typical of palace architecture. It is indeed difficult to recognize palaces in the early periods. It was once thought that the palace as a building type emerged only in the later Early Dynastic period, but several scholars would now see residences of rulers in some of the remarkable buildings in the Eanna precinct in Uruk and have attributed a palatial function to the so-called Administrative Building at Jemdet Nasr.

Archaeologists have investigated a number of buildings from the second half of the Early Dynastic period and from the Agade period that they have identified as palaces in Eridu, Kish, Mari, Beydar, Tell Bi'a, Tell Chuera, Tell al-Wilaya, Tell Asmar, Khafajeh, and Tell Brak (Miglus 2004:241–44). They share few features in common and their plans do not conform to a common model. Strangely, both in Eridu and in Tell Mozan the palaces consisted of two parts with almost identical ground plans placed side by side. From administrative and economic texts of the Early Dynastic period we know that there were palaces (e_2-gal) in Ur, Shuruppak, Girsu, Mari, and perhaps Zabalam, and in the Agade period palaces are attested in Adab, Umma, Girsu, Isin, Susa, and Nippur. In early Early Dynastic Ur, the palace seems to have had a less important economic role than the temple though it is difficult to assess the relative importance of palace versus temple from the surviving documentation (Sallaberger 2004:200–202). It is also difficult to be certain in the Early Dynastic period whom the é.gal served and whether the ruler of a city, particularly one who had a priestly title, resided in the main city temple; but "from the Akkad dynasty on," as Postgate (2004a:195) has stated, "we know of no case where a Mesopotamian ruler did not rule from a palace."

We are less well informed about the building of palaces by early Mesopotamian rulers than we are about the building of temples because it was not standard practice before the Middle Assyrian period to leave building inscriptions in the foundations and walls of palaces. This means that the dating of excavated palaces must be based on archaeological evidence such as the construction techniques or the finds in them. In some cases this has led to widely varying dates being given to the structures. For example, the suggested dates of the construction of the Old Palace at Ashur vary some 500 years between the Agade period and the reign of Shamshi-Adad (most recently Miglus 2004:247). Similarly, which rulers were responsible for which parts of the so-called Palace of Zimri-Lim in Mari remains conjectural. Some palaces were constructed using inscribed bricks.

This, however, can be misleading. Many bricks bore short inscriptions such as E_2.GAL KN (KN = king's name) or KUR KN which might be interpreted literally as the palace of the named king since the signs E_2.GAL and KUR were used to write the word *ekallu* "palace," but in this case these signs are better interpreted as meaning "belonging to" or "property of" (Postgate 2004b:216). In other cases such as the so-called Palace of Bel-shalti-Nannar at Ur (now read as En-nigaldi-Sin or En-nigaldi-Nanna), it has been suggested that the bricks were intended for the building of the *giparu*, the residence of the *entu*-priestess, but were surplus to requirements and used by a local governor in the construction of his residence.

The king was not restricted to a single palace. The kings of the Third Dynasty of Ur had palaces in their three most important cities, Ur, Uruk, and Nippur. The construction of the Ehursag palace in Ur was sufficiently important to have provided the name of the 10th year of the reign of Shulgi. Bricks inscribed "Shulgi . . . built the Ehursag, his beloved house" were used in the construction close to the main temples in Ur and a hymn was composed praising the king and his palace. Assyrian kings had palaces in all the important provincial capitals which had a full staff and a well-equipped harem ready in case the king should visit (Radner 2006). In Assyria, only the king and his heir had palaces (E_2.GAL; *ekallu*): the residences of the other members of his court were described as houses (E_2; *bītu*) (Postgate 2004b:218).

The credit for building temples or palaces was normally given to the ruler, who was aided by the gods. Even Shamash-shum-ukin, king of Babylon, wrote his inscriptions in the name of his brother Ashurbanipal, king of Assyria and nominally his senior. In some instances too, local governors are mentioned, as, for example, Sin-balassu-iqbi in Ur or Shamash-bel-usur, the governor of Kalhu who claimed credit for the throne dais that was built in Fort Shalmaneser in Kalhu (Nimrud). The reality behind the monarch's claim can be perceived in the correspondence relating to the construction of the new royal residence of the Assyrian king Sargon II at Dur-Sharrukin, where the construction of different parts of the fortification walls was assigned to different high officials and provincial governors, who had to provide both the raw materials and the necessary manpower to complete their allotted tasks (Parpola 1995).

There seems in the surviving building inscriptions to be an increasing interest on the part of the monarch in the construction of his palaces and civic works, such as cross-country walls, canals, parks, and gardens,[16] during the 1st millennium BC, with a corresponding diminution of interest in temples.[17]

Renaming and Founding Cities

The seat of royal power was the palace, which in common usage might refer not only to the building but also to the king himself and to his government (like the White House). As stated earlier cities too received the attention of the kings and were used by them as part of the royal propaganda and ideology. The easiest way to associate a ruler with a settlement was to name it after him and this was frequently done: the most economical method was to take a pre-existing settlement and to rename it: for example, Kar-Sulmanu-Ashared (Kar-Shalmaneser, Masuwari, Til Barsip), Kar-Sharrukin (Harhar), Kar-Ashur-ahu-iddina (Sidon), Dur-Sin-ahhe-eriba eshu (New Fort Sennacherib = Alihu [location uncertain]).

Naming of settlements after spouses or ancestors or other famous figures, e.g., Laodikea, Apamea, Leningrad, Alexandria, does not seem to have been the normal practice in ancient Mesopotamia though the chief gods are often named: Kishessim and Dur-Abi-hara in the province of Gambulu were renamed as Kar-Nergal and Dur-Nabu in the reign of Sargon II. Shalmaneser III, probably after its reconquest in 856 BC, renamed "Ana-Ashur-uter-asbat, the town that the people of Hatti call Pitru" (Radner 2005b).

Infrequently Mesopotamian rulers created new cities or centers. For most of the history of Mesopotamia, the founding of cities as well as the building or rebuilding of palaces and temples, the carving of rock reliefs or the erection of stelae, the commission of divine cult statues and of human statues was a royal prerogative restricted to the rulers and occasionally their immediate relatives.[18] This restriction on the commissioning of major works of art to the king was a feature of Mesopotamian civilization from the 4th millennium to the Islamic period, with only short intervals in the Early Dynastic period and in the Parthian period when a more extended group of highly placed individuals were allowed to commission statues which were placed in the temples of the time.

The adoption of such practices by non-royal persons is normally interpreted as a sign of royal weakness and the usurpation of the king's powers.[19] In reality as stated above it may well have been local officials such as city or provincial governors using the resources under their control, who actually commissioned and carried out the work.

Some of these new foundations were named after the founding monarch as, for example, Dur-Kurigalzu, Kar-Tukulti-Ninurta, Kar-Ashurnasir-

Table 11.1 Selected major new foundations or centers so extensively rebuilt by rulers of Mesopotamia that they would hardly have been recognizable as the same site.

Name of ruler	Name of foundation
Sargon of Agade	Agade
Kurigalzu I	Dur-Kurigalzu
Tukulti-Ninurta I	Kar-Tukulti-Ninurta
Ashurnasirpal II	Kalhu
Sargon II	Dur-Sharrukin
Sennacherib	Nineveh
Cyrus	Pasargadae
Darius	Persepolis, Susa

pal, Dur-Sharrukin (Table 11.1).[20] These new foundations or refoundations often were intended as the principal residence of the monarch and for that reason are often referred to as the capital city of the kingdom or empire. This is perhaps in two ways incorrect, an anachronistic misnomer. The capital in the sense of the seat of government was where the king was and traveled with the king as was the case in many kingdoms, for example in medieval England. Thus no city or palace was the exclusive capital but many settlements in which the king had a palace were described as *āl šarruti* the city of kingship. Since Assyria was a theocracy, the ruler was the god Ashur and the city of Assur was where his residence was. The religious capital of all Mesopotamian states was the seat of the state god, i.e., his temple. Thus, Babylon was the religious capital of Babylonia as long as Marduk was acknowledged as the leader of the gods, although when Marduk was "godnapped" by the Hittites or by the Assyrians, Babylon must have lost its status as religious capital.

The second misconception is that the capital must have been a city. Van De Mieroop (1997:12) cites a book on European urbanization (de Vries 1984:11) in order to establish what a city is:

> [There are] commonly accepted quantifiable dimensions that distinguish cities from other forms of settlement: population size, density of settlement, share of non-agricultural occupations and diversity of non-agricultural occupations. All four of these criteria are continuums, so that one must draw a line at some point dividing cities from non-cities. This cannot help but be arbitrary. But a settlement must score sufficiently high in all four of these criteria to be a city, a requirement that does not make the task easier but does reflect the existence of a broadly shared intuitive understanding of what constitutes an urban place.

While most of the traditional so-called capitals of the ancient Near East fulfill these criteria, some of the new foundations would be better described as extensive palatial complexes because archaeological investigation has not revealed evidence of a large population or of dense settlement. This applies not only to the centers in Mesopotamia but also, for example, to the Hittite and Urartian "cities," as well as the "capitals" of the Persians at Pasargadae, Persepolis, and Susa (Roaf 2007).

DESIGN

Two contradictory principles governed the choice of royal building projects. The first and more common is that the ruler should follow the traditions of his ancestors and that the rebuilt structure should follow as closely as possible the original building (Roaf 2000, Winter 2000). Nabonidus in his attempt to rebuild the Ebabbar, the temple of the sun god Shamash at Sippar, was determined to find the authentic original temple since a previous attempt at rebuilding had failed because the king had not followed the correct plan (Schaudig 2001:422–23, 438 Sippar Cylinder ii.46–59):

> For Shamash, the judge of heaven and the netherworld, concerning Ebabbar ["shining house"], his temple which is in Sippar, which Nebuchadnezzar, a former king had rebuilt and whose old foundation deposit he had looked for but not found—yet he rebuilt that temple and after forty-five years the walls of that temple had sagged—I became troubled, I became fearful, I was worried and my face showed signs of anxiety.
>
> While I led Shamash out of its midst and caused him to dwell in another sanctuary, I removed the debris of that temple, looked for its old foundation deposit, dug to a depth of eighteen cubits into the ground and then Shamash, the great lord, revealed to me the original foundations of Ebabbar, the temple which is his favorite dwelling, by disclosing the foundation deposit of Naram-Sin, son of Sargon, which no king among my predecessors had found in three thousand and two hundred years.

The second principle is that the ruler should exceed his predecessors and do something that his predecessors had not succeeded in achieving. Thus the Assyrian king Esarhaddon in describing the construction of his palace (Luckenbill 1926–1927, 2:268 §698; Borger 1956:61 A.VI.2-6): "I built mighty palaces for my royal abode. A castle, 95 great cubits in length, 31 great cubits in width, such as none of the kings who went before, my fathers, had built, I constructed." In the first case, if we were to take the inscriptions literally the design was predetermined, but of course this was not the case. There were numerous decisions that had to be taken in the rebuilding and the eventual structure would not have been an exact copy of the previous building.

With "new builds" the choices were undoubtedly less prescribed. Tradition was no doubt still important in determining design, but the king and his architects and designers had the opportunity to incorporate into the design features which were specific to the wishes of the king. Such features are probably inexplicable to the modern scholar. Irene Winter (1981, 1983) attempted to unravel the motivation behind the decorative program used in the Palace of Ashurnasirpal II in Kalhu; although her specific explanations are unconvincing (Roaf 2008), it is probable that similar reasons lay behind the design decisions. A better documented modern example shows the difficulty in recognizing such features. In the construction of the Mosque of the Mother of All Battles in Baghdad there were four 43 m high outer minarets designed to look like Scud missiles: the number 43 was chosen because of the 43 days of bombing that preceded the ground attack on Iraqi forces in 1991. The four inner minarets, which imitated the barrels of AK-47 assault rifles, were 37 m high and there were 28 water jets in the pool with the outline of the Arab world that surrounds the dome of the mosque. Taken together these give the date of birth of Saddam Hussein, April 28, 1937, April being the fourth month of the year. That such numerical considerations could be taken into account in the design of the king's monuments is shown by a passage in several inscriptions of Sargon II describing the construction of Dur-Sharrukin: "I made the naming of my name the measurement of its wall 16,280 cubits." The interpretation of this statement is still disputed but, since the first four signs used to write the measurement 16,280 cubits consisted of the sign ŠAR$_2$ (3600) repeated four times, it is possible that this part should be read as the king's name and one of his most important titles "Sargon, king of all."[21]

FINANCING THE BUILD

Although the rebuilding or beautification of buildings was both a royal prerogative and a royal duty, not all Mesopotamian rulers exercised these rights. Presumably this was at least partly dependent on the personality and priorities of the ruler. But it was also highly correlated with the availability of resources. Building is expensive in materials and labor and most of the rulers whose building activities are well attested were also successful military commanders who had replenished their treasuries through booty and the supply of manpower through the capture of prisoners of war. This pattern is clearly seen in the inscriptions of the Assyrian kings between the 11th and the 9th centuries BC (Table 11.2).

Table 11.2 Assyrian kings and their building inscriptions from the 11th to the 9th centuries BC (after Roaf 2001: fig. 4).

Assyrian king	Ashur	Nineveh	Other cities
Tiglath-pileser I (1114–1076)	ITPW	ITPWCG	[Tabetu* IP]
Asharid-apil-Ekur (1075–1074)	-	-	-
Ashur-bel-kala (1073–1056)	SIPWCG	I	Apqu P; Saqa P; Sikkatu P
Eriba-Adad II (1055–1054)	SI	I	-
Shamshi-Adad IV (1053–1050)	SIT	IT	-
Ashurnasirpal I (1049–1031)	I	-	-
Shalmaneser II (1030–1019)	S	-	-
Ashur-nirari IV (1018–1013)	-	-	-
Ashur-rabi II (1012–972)	-	-	[Shadikanni† C]
Ashur-resh-ishi II (971–967)	S	-	[Shadikanni †T]
Tiglath-pileser II (966–935)	S	-	-
Ashur-dan II (934–912)	IPW	-	Kalzi IP; districts of his land P
Adad-nirari II (911–890)	ITW	IP	Apqu P; Shibaniba IP
Tukulti-Ninurta II (890–884)	ITPW	IP	Nemed-Tukulti-Ninurta P; Kahat IP
Ashurnasirpal II (883–859)	SITP	ITP	Apqu IP; Imgur-Enlil ITP; Kalhu ITPWCG; Shibaniba IP; Tushhan PW

S inscribed stele found in the Stelenreihe in Ashur
W wall or gate erection mentioned in a text
I building inscription or inscribed brick found at the site
C canal digging mentioned in a text
T temple building mentioned in a text
G garden planting mentioned in a text
P palace construction mentioned in a text
* built by Ashur-ketti-lesher, the ruler of Tabetu in the reign of Tiglath-pileser I
† built by Bel-eresh, the ruler of Shadikanni in the reign of Ashur-rabi II or Ashur-resh-ishi II

This is of course a circular argument: the majority of inscriptions were building inscriptions and our knowledge of the military activities of the kings is dependent on the survival of inscriptions, in which they could be recorded. Theoretically it is possible that those rulers whose building activities were not recorded in inscriptions were also militarily successful. But in the extant inscriptions the extensive builders were also extensive conquerors.

There were two Mesopotamian rulers, Gudea and Nabonidus, who boasted greatly about their building activities, but who showed little military prowess. And, although the coffers of the Neo-Babylonian treasury were no doubt bursting after the successful campaigns of Nabopolassar and Nebuchadnezzar, the extensive building activities of this latter ruler might well have emptied them. Gudea and his predecessors would have profited from the agricultural wealth of their kingdom and from its fortunate position at the head of the Persian Gulf which would have allowed the rulers to gain profit from the trade in that region. But it is noticeable that like that of mad king Ludwig II of Bavaria their kingdoms barely survived their deaths: in all three cases the edifice complexes of their rulers may have led to the extinction of their kingdoms.[22]

CONCLUSION

The reasons for the undertaking of building projects by Mesopotamian rulers were often not stated. Often an old building was said to have become dilapidated. While one might think that that was in itself a good reason for the rebuilding, since buildings are sometimes said to have been dilapidated for decades,[23] there must have been reasons which delayed the rebuilding and these may have been economic. Equally it may well be that often the building was recognized as dilapidated only after the decision had been taken to rebuild it.

Sometimes the ruler reported that the building or rebuilding was undertaken in fulfilment of a divine command. Tukulti-Ninurta's new complex (Kar-Tukulti-Ninurta) to the north of Assur was built because (Grayson 1987:273 A.0.78.23 lines 88–98):

> the god Ashur, my lord, requested of me a cult centre on the bank opposite my city, the *desired object* of the gods, and he commanded me to build his sanctuary. At the command of the god Ashur, who loves me, I built before my city, Assur, a city for the god Ashur, on the opposite bank, beside the Tigris, in uncultivated plains (and) meadows where there was neither house nor dwelling, where no ruin hills or rubble had

accumulated and no bricks had been laid.

Divine approval was sought through divination before the decision to build was taken (Luckenbill 1926-1927 vol. 1: § 200, Pedersén 1990: 706)[24]: "Because the god Ashur, my lord, loved Mount Epih, his mountain, and because he commanded me to build in it a lofty dwelling, I (Tukulti-Ninurta) asked for his (Ashur's) firm yes." The rulers are seldom explicit about their reasons for constructing palaces or new ceremonial centers beyond a general statement that it was to be a royal residence (Postgate 2004b:212–16 for the Assyrian palaces). Darius described the motivation for the construction of the citadel at Persepolis: "By the grace of Ahuramazda I built this citadel. And Ahuramazda was of such a mind, together with all the gods, that this citadel (should) be built. And (so) I built it secure and beautiful and adequate, just as I was intending to" (DPf: 7–18). Here Darius credits Ahuramazda and the gods with the decision to build but reveals in the last phrase that his intentions fortunately coincided with those of the gods.

A more direct statement of the will of the ruler is included on the inscription on a baked brick found in the debris of the throne room of Sargon II's new royal residence built in the last decades of the 8th century BC (Jacobsen 1936:129): "Sargon, king of the world, king of Assyria (says): 'Because I wanted to, I built a city. Dur-Sharruken I c[alled] its name. An ideal palace, which in the four [quarters of the world] does not have one rivaling it, [I built] in its midst.'" Clearly one intention of the ruler was to construct an impressive building and thereby to increase the prestige of his reign. The fame of Zimri-Lim's palace in Mari reached as far as Ugarit 500 km away (Gates 1984:70). Tukulti-Ninurta described his new palace and temple complex as follows: "I built the wall of Kar-Tukulti-Ninurta, the great cult centre, *(to inspire)* awe for my lordship" (Grayson 1987:270 A.0.78.22, lines 52–53).

Five hundred years later, Sargon II described the decoration of his palace and the intended effect (Luckenbill 1926–1927, 2: §84; Fuchs 1994:240–41, 354): "On great slabs of limestone I carved the towns which my hands had captured and I had them set up around the walls; I made them objects of astonishment from one end of the world to the other." Not only Sargon, but also his son Sennacherib, called his palace "Palace without a rival." And even today, divorced from their original setting and deprived of the color and atmosphere of the Assyrian court, the gigantic carvings are still able to impress us.

Architecture is perhaps the most obvious way to indicate the enduring power of a ruler: it shows at the same time that the ruler had the necessary resources at his command to create the monument and it serves as a visible demonstration of the activities of the ruler that lasted long after his death. The ziggurats, which still dominate the skylines of many ancient Mesopotamian cities after thousands of years of erosion, would when newly constructed have glistened under the glare of the bright Mesopotamian sun and have been a constant reminder for miles around that the ruler of that city had the power and resources not only to control the lives of his subjects but also to change the shape of the land itself.

NOTES

11.1 The organizers of the conference made the following suggestions for Session VI: Kingship and Territory: "This session would involve the arrangement of territory within the kingdom through the founding and movement of capitals and cities, the construction of new administrative or religious centers in regions or provinces. Discussion should touch on the differences in the ways that Mesopotamians and Egyptians socially defined their internal space and how it affected their national identity as well as how they defined and categorized the "other." Analysis of the symbolic geography imposed by the royal authority through religious and ideological factors might also be discussed.

"The examination of the connections between the central administration and regional powers might help to define the reactions of territory dwellers whose lives are transformed by royal activity. Additionally, the notion of a city as a 'home' or seat of kingship itself could be addressed as well as what were the political, social and cosmological justifications for its movement." In my contribution I have not felt able to consider all these aspects. I have concentrated on the building activities of the king, and placed less emphasis on investigating "the ways that Mesopotamians . . . socially defined their internal space and how it affected their national identity as well as how they defined and categorized the 'other'." As the reader will observe I am skeptical that the available sources can assist us in making meaningful speculations about matters such as identity, alterity, and symbolic geography in ancient Mesopotamia. The investigation of these subjects, in my opinion, will only lead to interesting conclusions when specific, well documented cases are studied in detail.

11.2 The extent to which the recorded scribal tradition reflected the political realities is difficult to assess. The exercise of power consists of a complex set of relationships and the ability of a ruler to govern is dependent on the acquiesence of his subjects or at least on the support of certain factions. (It is customary at this point to insert a reference to the four dimensions of social power—ideological, economic, military, and political—developed by Michael Mann [1986]. Alternatively, according to choice one can mention: Marx, Weber, Bourdieu, or some other social theorist.) It is easy to be sceptical and assume that much of the discourse in the cuneiform texts is nothing more than the self-serving propaganda of the priestly elite. The rulers did not write their royal inscriptions, though they may sometimes have insisted on changes and the scribes would have, of course, only supplied texts which they thought would not incur the disapproval and censure of the ruler. Thus attributing the military successes of Babylonian, Assyrian, or Persian rulers to the benevolence of Marduk, Ashur, or Ahuramazda might seem merely formulaic. No doubt there were realists/ atheists who did not follow the priests (there is a letter to Esarhaddon saying that the scholars at the court of the Assyrian king told his father Sennacherib what he wanted to hear rather than reporting accurately the events predicted by the stars (Parpola 1993:87 No. 109 lines 4-r.8)), but at the same time religion was certainly a driving force in society. When gods spoke to Gudea or Nabonidus in dreams (their irregular accession to the kingship may have encouraged the gods to communicate directly with them, as well as to the populace, whose choice elevated them to the throne) or in other ways communicated their desires to their earthly representatives, we should not dismiss these events merely as psychological delusions or as Machiavellian manipulations of the superstitions of their subjects, but we should consider the possibility that they were the result of deeply held beliefs. Human beings have an apparently infinite capacity for self-deception. Three hundred years after the Enlightenment, George Bush and Tony Blair both received personal messages from god. In an interview some years ago, a Chinese surgeon, who had just performed the first successful re-attachment of a severed hand, attributed his achievement to the fact that he was fortified by the thoughts of Chairman Mao. This was no doubt politically expedient but it was perhaps also true.

11.3 A similar problem is the identification of "the Mesopotamian city." For an opinion about the usefulness of the term see Van de Mieroop 1997:xiii–xiv; for the problems in its application, see the rest of the book.

11.4 Despite attempts by scholars to identify such character traits from the official royal inscriptions, the only convincing sources are either less formulaic contemporary documentation or external sources. Once such traits have been identified it is possible to see reflections of this in royal inscriptions but this may again be self-deception.

11.5 Eva Cancik-Kirschbaum (Berlin) "Des Königs Körper" lecture given in the Assyriologisches Kolloquium of the Institut für Assyriologie, Munich University, on 5 February 2002. In theory, at least, there is a clear distinction between theocratic and non-theocratic governments: in practice, however, it does not seem to have made much difference. It could be argued that the Assyrian king as *iššakku* was the representative of the god Ashur and a substitute for the god and was therefore in a more powerful position than that of a ruler appointed by the gods.

11.6 Characteristics such as being chosen by the gods, pious, militarily successful, physically unblemished, male, etc., are almost universal features of kingship.

11.7 An exception was the transfer of the kingship to Gutium, which was qualified either as the "army of Gutium" or as the "land of Gutium." The Sumerian word which we conveniently translate as dynasty is *bala* meaning "reign, term of office." The Akkadian word which we conveniently translate as dynasty is *bītu,* a word which covers a much wider semantic field, including "house, building, family."

11.8 This fiction created various inconsistencies such as the same ruler appearing in more than one dynasty and contemporary rulers ruling different cities separated by rulers who were their predecessors or successors. These anomalies were not thought to have been obstacles to the theory.

11.9 *The Dynastic Chronicle* (Glassner 2004:126–35) records the Dynasty of Bazi (originally a place name) as a personal name, therefore as a family or tribal dynasty.

11.10 Gordon Childe (1994:99) in a letter to Soviet archaeologists published after his death stated that "maps showing distributions by shading or outlines are suitable instruments for vulgarization, not for knowledge." He was referring to maps showing cultural attributes, but his dictum may be applied equally to maps showing ancient territories.

11.11 This is not necessarily to be associated with the worldwide presence of Windows and Gates.

11.12 Royal decrees of the Mittanian rulers of the 15th and 14th centuries BC have been discovered in archaeological excavations, but no building inscriptions. This might be attributed to the accident of discovery but since no such inscriptions have come to light through the activities of site robbers, it is plausible to suggest that they did not exist.

11.13 The exceptions include rock reliefs, cylinder and stamp seals, and, less commonly, terracottas and perhaps statuettes.

11.14 If Edzard (1997:88) was right in suggesting that originally there were at least three cylinders, then we should realize that what is preserved must be augmented by additional performances which were described in the missing parts of the cylinders.

11.15 A useful up-to-date summary of the textual and archaeological evidence about Mesopotamian palaces can be found in the *Reallexikon der Assyriologie und Vorderasiatische Archäologie* sub Palast (especially Postgate 2004a, 2004b, Sallaberger 2004, Edzard 2004, Jursa 2004, and Miglus 2004).

11.16 These important royal building works deserve detailed treatment.

11.17 Nabonidus, religious fanatic and last ruler of the Neo-Babylonian dynasty, stands out as a possible exception (Beaulieu 1989).

11.18 A similar but less strict restriction was in effect in Egypt (Baines 1994).

11.19 This has been suggested for Nergal-eresh, Shamshi-ilu, Bel-harran-bel-usur, and Shamash-resh-usur, though we now know that the last named was the independent ruler of Suhu and not an Assyrian governor.

11.20 This is an incomplete list and the practice continued long after the last scribe stopped writing cuneiform: e.g., Seleucia, Bishapur, Saddam City renamed Sadr City when the ruler was deposed.

11.21 A similar suggestion was made by Fuchs (1994:295). The interpretation of the $ŠAR_2$ sign as standing for *šarru* "king" found in the first part of Sargon's name and in the title *šar kiššati* "king of all" presents no problems, since it is often written with the homophone sign LUGAL = $ŠAR_3$. The sign $ŠAR_2$ is a logogram for *kiššatu* (see Zgoll and Roaf 2002 for this title in the glazed brick panels of Sargon). A possible explanation of the complete measurement is in preparation.

11.22 Paul Zimansky (1995, 2005) has proposed a similar scenario for the end of the Urartian kingdom through the excessive building activities of Rusa son of Argishti.

11.23 Tukulti-Ninurta I in his inscription commemorating his restoration of the temple of the goddess Dinitu (ARI 1 §742) stated that the "temple had been dilapidated, crumbled and in ruin since the reign of Adad-nirari," his grandfather who died 30 years before Tukulti-Ninurta became king.

11.24 I am grateful to Grant Frame for providing me with this reference and explaining why this text was not included in Grayson 1987.

REFERENCES

Abou Assaf, A., P. Bordreuil, and A.R. Millard. 1982. *La statue de Tell Fekherye et son inscription bilingue assyro-araméenne*. Paris: Éditions Recherche sur les Civilisations.

Baines, J. 1994. On the Status and Purposes of Ancient Egyptian Art. *CAJ* 4:67–94.

Beaulieu, P.-A. 1989. *The Reign of Nabonidus, King of Babylon, 556–539 B.C.* New Haven: Yale University Press.

Borger, R. 1956. *Die Inschriften Asarhaddons, Königs von Assyrien*. BAfO 9. Graz.

Charpin, D. 2004. Histoire politique du Proche-Orient Amorrite (2002–1595). In *Mesopotamien: Die altbabylonische Zeit* by D. Charpin, D.O. Edzard, and M. Stol, pp. 23–480. OBO 160/4. Fribourg: Academic Press; Göttingen: Vandenhoeck & Ruprecht.

Childe, V.G. 1994. Facsimile of a Letter Dated 16 December 1956 from Gordon Childe to Soviet Archaeologists. In *The Archaeology of V. Gordon Childe: Contemporary Perspectives*, ed. D.R. Harris, pp. 94–99. Chicago: University of Chicago Press.

de Vries, J. 1984. *European Urbanization 1500–1800*. Cambridge, MA: Harvard University Press.

Edzard, D.O. 1997. *Gudea and His Dynasty*. The Royal Inscriptions of Mesopotamia, Early Periods Vol. 3(1). Toronto: University of Toronto Press.

———. 2004. Palast. A.III. Altbabylonisch. In *Reallexikon der Assyriologie und Vorderasiatischen Archäologie* 10(3/4), pp. 205–8. Berlin: W. de Gruyter.

Ellis, R.S. 1968. *Foundation Deposits in Ancient Mesopotamia*. Yale Near Eastern Researches 2. New Haven, CT.

Frayne, D.R. 1990. *Old Babylonian Period (2003–1595 BC)*. Royal Inscriptions of Mesopotamia, Early Periods, vol. 4. Toronto: University of Toronto Press.

Fuchs, A. 1994. *Die Inschriften Sargons II. Aus Khorsabad*. Göttingen: Cuvillier.

Garelli, P., ed. 1974. *Le Palais et la Royauté*. Paris: Geuthner.

Gates, M.-H. 1984. The Palace of Zimri-Lim at Mari. *The Biblical Archaeologist* 47:70–87.

Glassner, J.-J. 1984. La division quinaire de la terre. *Akkadica* 40:17–34.

———. 2004. *Mesopotamian Chronicles*. Writings from the Ancient World Society of Biblical Literature 19. Atlanta, GA: Scholars Press.

Grayson, A.K. 1975. *Assyrian and Babylonian Chronicles*. Texts from Cuneiform Sources 5. Locust Valley, NY: J.J. Augustin.

———. 1987. *Assyrian Rulers of the Third and Second Millennia BC (to 1115 BC)*. Royal Inscriptions of Mesopotamia. Assyrian Periods, vol. 1. Toronto: University of Toronto Press.

———. 1991. *Assyrian Rulers of the Early First Millennium BC I (1114–859 BC)*. Royal Inscriptions of Mesopotamia. Assyrian Periods, vol. 2. Toronto: University of Toronto Press.

Horsnell, M.J.A. 2003. Why Year Names? *Orientalia* n.s. 72:196–203.

———. 2004. On the Use of Year-Names in Reconstructing the History of the First Dynasty of Babylon. In *From the Upper Sea to the Lower Sea: Studies on the History of Assyria and Babylonia in Honour of A.K. Grayson*, ed. G. Frame, pp. 165–86. Leiden: Nederlands Instituut voor het Nabije Oosten.

Jacobsen, T. 1936. Inscriptions. In *Khorsabad, Part I, Excavation in the Palace and at a City Gate*, by G. Loud, pp. 129–33. OIP 38. Chicago: University of Chicago Press.

———. 1939. *The Sumerian King List.* Assyriological Studies 11. Chicago: University of Chicago Press.

Jursa, M. 2004. Palast. A.IV. Mittel- und Neubabylonisch. In *Reallexikon der Assyriologie und Vorderasiatische Archäologie* 10(3/4), pp. 208–12. Berlin: W. de Gruyter.

Lackenbacher, S. 1982. *Le Roi bâtisseur: Les récits de construction assyriens des origines à Teglatphalasar III.* Paris: Éditions Recherche sur les civilisations.

———. 1990. *Le palais sans rival. Le récit de construction en Assyrie.* Paris: Découverte.

Luckenbill, D.D. 1926–1927. *Ancient Records of Assyria and Babylonia.* 2 vols. Chicago: University of Chicago Press.

Mann, M. 1986. *The Sources of Social Power.* Vol. 1, *A History of Power from the Beginning to AD 1760.* Cambridge: Cambridge University Press.

Matthiae, P., A. Enea, L. Peyronel, and F. Pinnock, eds. 2000. *Proceedings of the First International Congress on the Archaeology of the Ancient Near East: Rome, May 18th–23rd 1998.* Rome: Università degli studi di Roma "La Sapienza."

Miglus, P.A. 2004. Palast. B. Archäologisch. In *Reallexikon der Assyriologie und Vorderasiatische Archäologie* 10(3/4), pp. 233–73. Berlin: W. de Gruyter.

Parpola, S. 1993. *Letters from Assyrian and Babylonian Scholars.* State Archives of Assyria 10. Helsinki: Helsinki University Press.

———. 1995. The Construction of Dur-Šarrukin in the Assyrian Royal Correspondence. In *Khorsabad, le palais de Sargon II, roi d'Assyrie*, ed. A. Caubet, pp. 47–77. Paris: La Documentation française.

Pedersén, O. 1990. Review of Grayson 1987. *Bibliotheca Orientalis* 47:686–707.

Postgate, J.N. 2004a. Palast. Einleitung. In *Reallexikon der Assyriologie und Vorderasiatische Archäologie* 10(3/4), pp. 195–200. Berlin: W. de Gruyter.

———. 2004b. Palast. A.V. Mittel- und Neuassyrisch. In *Reallexikon der Assyriologie und Vorderasiatische Archäologie* 10(3/4), pp. 212–26. Berlin: W. de Gruyter.

Radner, K. 2005a. *Die Macht des Namens. Altorientalische Strategien zur Selbsterhaltung.* Santag 8. Wiesbaden: Harrassowitz.

———. 2005b. Pitru (Pitūru) = Ana-Aššur-utēr-aṣbat. In *Reallexikon der Assyrio-*

logie und Vorderasiatische Archäologie 10(7-8), pp. 585–86. Berlin: W. de Gruyter.

———. 2006. Provinz. C. Assyrien. *Reallexikon der Assyriologie und Vorderasiatische Archäologie* 11(1/ 2), pp. 42-68. Berlin: W. de Gruyter.

Roaf, M.D. 1990. *Cultural Atlas of Mesopotamia and the Ancient Near East.* New York: Facts on File.

———. 2000. Survivals and Revivals in the Art of Ancient Mesopotamia. In *Proceedings of the First International Congress on the Archaeology of the Ancient Near East: Rome, May 18th–23rd 1998,* ed. P. Matthiae, A. Enea, L. Peyronel, and F. Pinnock, pp. 1447–59. Rome: Università degli studi di Roma "La Sapienza."

———. 2001. Continuity and Change from the Middle to the Late Assyrian Period. In *Migration und Kulturtransfer: Der Wandel vorder- und zentralasiatischer Kulturen im Umbruch vom 2. zum. 1. vorchristlichen Jahrtausend,* ed. R. Eichmann and H. Parzinger, pp. 357–69. Bonn: Habelt.

———. 2007. Persepolis and the Kingship of the Persians. In *Le Capitali del Vicino Oriente Antico: Regalità e culto, monumentalità e amministrazione. Atti del Convegno internazionale, Milano, 28 gennaio 2006,* ed. M. Forlanini, pp. 93–109. Milan: Ares.

———. 2008. The Decor of the Throne Room of the Palace of Ashurnasirpal. *In New Light on Nimrud: Proceedings of the Nimrud Conference 11th–13th March 2002,* ed. J.E.L. Curtis et al., pp. 209–13. London: British Institute for the Study of Iraq.

Sallaberger, W. 2004. Palast. A.I. Mesopotamien im III. Jahrtausend. In *Reallexikon der Assyriologie und Vorderasiatische Archäologie* 10(3/4), pp. 200–204. Berlin: W. de Gruyter.

Schaudig, H. 2001. *Die Inschriften Nabonids von Babylon und Kyros' des Grossen: Textausgabe und Grammatik.* AOAT, vol. 256. Münster: Ugarit-Verlag.

Schmidt, E.F. 1970. *Persepolis III: The Royal Tombs and Other Monuments.* OIP 70. Chicago: University of Chicago Press.

Seux, M.-J. 1967. *Épithètes royales akkadiennes et sumériennes.* Paris: Letouzey et Ané.

Steinkeller, P. 1986. The Administrative and Economic Organization of the Ur III State: The Core and the Periphery. In *The Organization of Power. Aspects of Bureaucracy in the Ancient Near East,* ed. McG. Gibson and R.D. Biggs, pp. 19–41. SAOC 46. Chicago: Oriental Institute of the University of Chicago.

Suter, C.E. 2000. *Gudea's Temple Building. The Representation of an Early Mesopotamian Ruler in Text and Image.* Cuneiform Monographs 17. Groningen:

Styx.

Van De Mieroop, M. 1997. *The Ancient Mesopotamian City.* Oxford: Clarendon.

Winter, I. 1981. Royal Rhetoric and the Development of Historical Narrative in Neo-Assyrian Reliefs. *Studies in Visual Communication* 7:2–38.

———. 1983. The Program of the Throne Room of Assurnasirpal II. In *Essays on Near Eastern Art and Archaeology in Honor of Charles Kyle Wilkinson*, ed. P.O. Harper and H. Pittman, pp. 15–31. New York: Metropolitan Museum of Art.

———. 2000. Babylonian Archaeologists of The(ir) Mesopotamian Past. In *Proceedings of the First International Congress on the Archaeology of the Ancient Near East: Rome, May 18th–23rd 1998*, ed. P. Matthiae, A. Enea, L. Peyronel, and F. Pinnock, pp. 1785–98. Rome: Università degli studi di Roma "La Sapienza."

Zgoll, A., and M.D. Roaf. 2002. Sternenschrift auf schwarzem Stein: Entzifferung assyrischer Astroglyphen. *Antike Welt* 33:7–15.

Zimansky, P. 1995. An Urartian Ozymandias. *Biblical Archaeologist* 58(2): 94–100.

———. 2005. The Cities of Rusa II and the End of Urartu. In *Anatolian Iron Ages* 5, ed. A. Çilingiroğlu and G. Darbyshire, pp. 235–40. British Institute of Archaeology at Ankara Monograph 31. London.

12

Expeditions to the Wadi Hammamat: Context and Concept

ALAN B. LLOYD

The Wadi Hammamat lies in the desert area between the Nile Valley and the Red Sea (Fig. 12.1). It provided a major source of high-quality stone throughout Pharaonic history (Fig. 12.2), as well as yielding significant deposits of gold and providing a road facilitating Egyptian trade with the Red Sea area, above all the land of Punt (Eritrea, Somaliland, South Sudan).

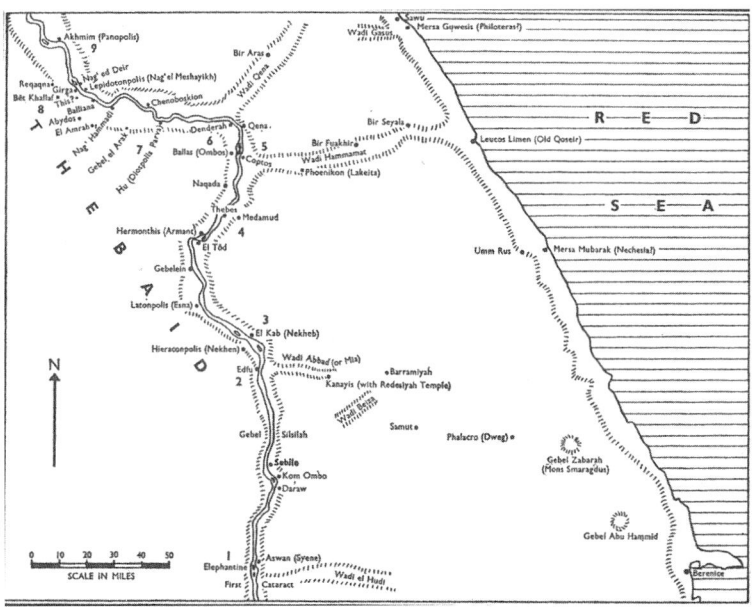

12.1. The Eastern Desert (after H. Kees, 1961).

12.2. The greywacke quarries in the Wadi Hammamat. Photo: courtesy of Mike Shepherd.

Expeditions reflecting these foci of interest took place throughout Egyptian history, but the intention in this chapter is to look mainly at evidence from the Middle Kingdom (ca. 2008–1756 BC), though data will also be invoked from a uniquely informative text of the reign of Ramesses IV (ca. 1151–1145 BC) to supplement and confirm the findings of the analysis of earlier data. The concern throughout is not preeminently with technology (on which see Klemm 1988, Harrell and Brown 1992, Klemm 1993) but with the conceptual world within which the Egyptians located these activities.

It would be very natural for the modern mind to regard quarrying and mining expeditions as economic activities of a purely secular character, but the Egyptian attitude to these events could hardly have been more different; for the inscriptional record reveals that these enterprises were regarded as highly charged with religious significance. We shall analyze five texts recorded on the quarry walls of the Wadi Hammamat to try to establish what that significance was.[1]

TEXT 1

Regnal Year 2, month 2 of Akhet, day 15 (under) the Horus Nebtawy, the Two Ladies Nebtawy, the Gods of Gold, the King of Upper and Lower Egypt Nebtawyre, son of Re, Montuhotpe, may he live for ever. His Majesty commanded to set up this stele for his father Min, lord of the desert lands, in this august and primeval mountain, pre-eminent of place in the land of the horizon-dwellers, the god's palace endowed with life, the divine bird-pool of Horus, in which this god is content, his pure place of enjoyment which is upon the desert lands, the god's land, in order that his *ka* might be happy and that the god might rejoice at his favorite, at that which the king who is on throne does, he who is pre-eminent of places, eternal of monuments, the efficient god, lord of joy, great of fear, mighty of love, the heir of Horus in his two lands, he whom Isis nursed, the divine one, the mother of Min, the great of magic in relation to the kingship of the two banks of Horus, the King of Upper and Lower Egypt Nebtawyre, may he live for ever: he says, "My Majesty caused that there should come forth the hereditary lord, overseer of the residence city, vizier, overseer of works, the confidant of the king, Amenemhet, together with an expeditionary force of 10,000 men from the southern nomes of Upper Egypt and from the *Peru-wabu* of the Theban nome so as to bring for me an august stone, a pure precious stone which is in this mountain, whose efficient power Min made so as to be an eternal memorial (consisting of) a lord of life, more than[2] the monuments in the temples of Upper Egypt, as one sent by the king who is lord of the two lands, so as to bring for him his heart's desire from the desert lands of his father Min. As his memorial for his father Min of Coptos, lord of the desert lands, master of the nomads, did he do it, that he might be given life in great plenty[3] like Re eternally.

"Day 27. There went down the lid of this lord of life consisting of a stone 4 cubits by 8 cubits by 2 cubits as one which comes forth from the works. There were slain cattle; there were sacrificed small cattle; and incense was placed on the flame as an expeditionary force of 3000 men from the crews of the nomes of Lower Egypt escorted it in safety to Ta-meri (i.e. Egypt)." (Trans. Lloyd; hieroglyphic text in Couyat and Montet 1912:100; Buck 1970:74)

The text begins with the full fivefold titulary of the king, though the standard "Horus of Gold" title is replaced by the much rarer "Gods of Gold" title which makes an even wider claim for the king's divinity. The presence of the titulary is normal in such royal inscriptions and serves both as a signature and, much more importantly, as an assertion of legitimacy. The inscription is stated to have been set up by royal command "for" the god Min who was the master of the area, a point which is emphasized elsewhere in the text, and its purpose is partly to give the god pleasure through the king's action, but there is also a *do-ut-des* dimension in that the king expects to be given life as a reward by the god.

The conceptualization of the mountain is most intriguing. In the first place, it is claimed to be *shepsy (špsy)*, "august," a term frequently used of gods and things divine.[4] Certainly the word can be applied in non-religious contexts, but the associations here place it firmly in the religious sphere of meaning in this passage. The claim that the mountain is *paty (p3ty)*, "primeval," connects the mountain with creative forces, and its association with the horizon-dwellers links it to the sun-god, himself a demiurgic force. It is described as the god's palace, i.e., as a place where he lives, and it is also a source of life. The mountain is stated to be the "divine birdpool of Horus," and, since Horus here is identical with Min (the divine guardian of the area: see Fig. 12.3), the claim means that the mountain is the birthplace of Min-Hor(us). As a place of purity it is in a state of maximum efficacy and, as such, it is aptly described as *ta netjer (t3 ntr)*, "God's Land," i.e., a place where divine presence is particularly in evidence (Saleh 1981:107ff.) and a term very commonly employed in Egyptian texts to define places generally to the

12.3. One of many representations in the Wadi of the resident deities. Pharaoh (far right) makes offerings to Min who is represented in his standard ithyphallic form. Photo: courtesy of Mike Shepherd.

east outside the Nile Valley from which they derived desirable materials or assets, e.g., it can refer to the deserts surrounding Egypt, the land of Punt, or Lebanon. It clearly does not mean that the Egyptians were denying the presence of the gods in Egypt but rather that these areas had something particularly numinous about them, i.e., divine power was in some sense particularly present and powerful there, and they were, therefore, particularly objects of wonder. It is this element of wonder which made it possible to use the term *bia* (*bi3*) to refer to such areas (see below).

These attitudes bring with them, in turn, the idea that the natural products or attributes of these lands belong to the gods and, if the Egyptians get their hands on them, they do so because the gods allow that to happen. That requires from the Egyptians the right attitude to the divine denizens of *Bia*-lands and a willingness to take the appropriate ritual means to win their approval and activate their generosity. Harwerre, another Middle Kingdom expedition leader, expresses this thinking extremely well in one of the Sinai inscriptions where he advises all comers to keep on the right side of Hathor, Mistress of the Turquoise, in the following terms: "Offer, offer to the Lady of Heaven. Make your peace with Hathor. If you do so, it will be well with you. If you do more than that, prosperity will be with you, and you will render more that is commanded of you. Excellently did I conduct my expedition, without a voice being raised against my work" (trans: Lloyd; hieroglyphic text in Sethe 1959:86; Gardiner and Peet 1952–1955, II:97–98).

The stone which is brought down in our Hammamat text is said to be *špsy*, "august," and *wab* (*wʿb*), "pure," and it is also claimed to possess *menkhu* (*mnḫw*), "efficient power,"[5] imparted to it by Min himself, who had intended the stone to be used for the sarcophagus and for temple monuments. The term *menkhu* is most interesting in that it is conceptually closely connected with the ideas expressed by the word *ma'at* (*mʿ3t*) which basically means "the moral and physical order of the universe"; something or someone can be described as *mnḫ* if it/he does its/his job according to *mʿ3t* so that, if a king is described as *mnḫ*, it is being claimed that he is doing exactly what kings are supposed to be doing according to that order, and if he is claimed to possess *mnḫw*, he is claimed to enjoy powers which enable him to achieve that. There can be no greater accolade than this. The assertion on the god's intention is particularly intriguing because it implies that the god's intentions mattered. The stone is his, and the Egyptians are only justified in taking it because they are fulfilling the god's intentions. His good will in assisting with the lid of the sarcophagus is, therefore, recognized appropriately with a series of offerings at the end of the text.[6]

TEXT 2

Nebtawyre, may he live eternally.
Regnal Year 2, month 2 of Akhet, day 15. The royal commission performed by the hereditary lord and count, overseer of the residence city, chief justice and vizier, the confidant of the king, overseer of work(s), the great one in his office, the mighty one in his dignity, the pre-eminent of place in the house of his lord, the inspector of councils, the head of the six great <houses>,[7] the judge of the aristocracy and commoners, he who hears the pleas of the Sun-folk,[8] he to whom the great ones come bowing down, the entire land being prostrate on its belly, he whose offices his lord advanced, his intimate in the gate of the south,[9] he having controlled millions of the lapwing-folk so as to do for him his heart's desire in relation to his monument which will abide eternally on earth, the great one of the King of Upper Egypt, the might one of the King of Lower Egypt, the controller of the mansions of the Red Crown, the servant of *Duau*[10] in stretching the cord, he who judges without partiality, the overseer of the south in its entirety, he to whom everything is reported, the controller of the business of the lord of the two lands, he who is discreet concerning a royal mission, the inspector of inspectors, the controller of overseers, the vizier of Horus in his manifestations Amenemhet, he says, "I was sent by my lord (life, prosperity, health),[11] the King of Upper and Lower Egypt Nebtawyre, may he live eternally, as a god sends a limb from himself, so as to establish his memorial in this land, he having advanced me before his city, I being honoured before his court. Furthermore, His Majesty commanded that I should come forth to this august desert land, an expeditionary force being with me (consisting of) men from the choice of the entire land, stone masons, craftsmen, quarrymen, sculptors, scribes of forms,[12] metal-workers, callers,[13] gold-workers, seal-bearers of the Great House, every seal office of the Treasury and every office of the royal house being united behind me. As a river did I make the desert land, and its upper wadis as a road of water. I brought for him an eternal memorial (consisting of) a lord of life which would endure for eternity. Never had its like gone down from

this desert since the time of the god. Without loss to it did the expeditionary force return. No man perished. No contingent turned back.[14] Not a donkey died. There was no deficiency to the craftsmen (i.e. no harm came to them). The reason why this happened to the majesty of my lord was because of the power made for him by his father Min in virtue of his love for him, that his *ka* might endure on the throne in the kingship of the two banks of Horus, he having made (it, i.e. the kingdom) greater than it was (?).[15] I am his servant, his favorite, he who does everything which he praises in the course of every day." (Trans. Lloyd; hieroglyphic text in Couyat and Montet 1912:79; Buck 1970:75).

This is a very different text from the preceding royal document in that it is the account of the official responsible for the operation, and, instead of concentrating on the conceptual context, it is much more concerned with singing the praises of the expedition leader and with the practicalities of the expedition. Nevertheless, the text does concede the commander's subordinate position as the emissary of the king and, although he leaves us in no doubt of his own prowess and the effectiveness of his leadership, he admits at the end the critical role of the king's divine support in ensuring success: it was only possible to achieve what was done because the god Min gave the Pharaoh the *bau* (*b3w*), "effective power," out of love for him, and the text then goes on to state that he would endure on the throne of Egypt because of his contribution to its greatness through this expedition (*ir.n.f m ꜥ3t r.s*, "having made (it) something greater than itself," i.e., "than it was before" [?]).

In tune with the tone of self-congratulation almost half the text is taken up with the titles or epithets of the vizier which cover every aspect of his all-embracing power, and later in the text this thread is developed further in Amenemhet's emphasis on the way in which he had been singled out by the king. This insistence on dependence on royal favor is a commonplace of the ideology of Egyptian official inscriptions, whatever the realities of the situation may have been. The text then proceeds to inform us that the purpose of the expedition was to establish the king's memorial in the desert, i.e., the quarrying and mining dimensions are a means to an end, not an end in themselves, and the presence of sculptors and scribes of forms fits perfectly with this aim. The issue of creating an eternal aspect to the work arises also in a rather different point of reference when we are informed that the sarcophagus itself is a *sḫȝ nḥḥ wȝḫ(w) n ḏt*, "an eternal memorial which will last for ever." As in the previous text, the word *špsy*, "august," is used, but this time of the desert.

One of the major problems of desert operations was spectacularly overcome in that an abundance of water was made available through the vizier's agency. This issue is understandably a recurrent theme in texts relating to expeditions into the Eastern Desert, but it probably passes beyond sheer practicalities to assert the cosmic aspects of the process, i.e., the desert is being brought to life, tamed, and reclaimed for the world of order. The staff is enumerated, and this list reveals that gold-mining is also an interest, but it is the quarrying work on the sarcophagus which features explicitly.

TEXT 3

The King of Upper and Lower Egypt Nebtawyre, may he live eternally. This marvel which happened to His Majesty. The wild game of the desert went down for him, and a pregnant gazelle came with much movement (?), its face towards the men straight before it. Its eye looked straight ahead without it turning behind it, until it reached this august mountain, this stone, as it lay in its place (destined) for this lid of this sarcophagus. She gave birth on it, and this expeditionary force of the king looked on. Then was its throat cut, it being sacrificed on it as a burnt offering. It (i.e. the stone) returned in safety; for, furthermore, it was the majesty of this august god, lord of the desert lands, who paid attention to his son Nebtawyre, may he live for ever, in order that his heart might rejoice and that he might continue living on his seats for ever and ever, and might perform millions of Sed-Festivals.

The hereditary lord and count, overseer of the pyramid city, vizier, overseer of all officials who deliver judgement, overseer of that which heaven gives, earth creates, and the Nile brings forth, the overseer of everything in this entire land, the vizier Amenemhet. (Trans: Lloyd; hieroglyphic text Couyat and Montet 1912:77; Buck 1970:76)

This text begins with the briefest of signatures and then concentrates on a *biayet* (*biȝyt*), "wonder," which was one of two which occurred during the expedition. It begins with a bald narrative of what happened, making the point right at the beginning that a *biȝyt* is at issue and relating it explicitly to the king. The account of the gazelle's behavior is marked by insistence on its uncannily focused nature, and it also refers to the mountain as *špsy* and implies that the stone had been destined to serve as the lid of the sarcophagus. The importance of the birth episode is brought out by the syntactical construction used to describe it.[16] The animal is then sacrificed as a holocaust, an unusual Egyptian cult practice, except in contexts where the sacrifice is made outside Egypt itself. The text then proceeds to the conceptualization, insisting that this has happened because Min has "paid attention" to the king who is stated to be his son, and it should be noted that our old friend the adjective *špsy* is used of the god himself. The reason attributed to the god for sending the *bi3yt* is that he wished the king to rejoice but also to enjoy millions of *Heb-Sed* festivals (festivals of royal rejuvenation). While the logic of the first is immediately clear, the same cannot be said for the second, but the thought process must be that the king will get the god's support (and, therefore, a long life) because the king is doing what a king ought to be doing according to the standard pattern of royal behavior. This interpretation would fit in perfectly with the standard concept of what a *bi3yt* was, i.e., an extraordinary event orchestrated by the gods in order to indicate that they approved of what the king was doing (Graefe 1971). In the case of Montuhotep IV this was particularly important because his claim to the throne seems to have been suspect.[17]

TEXT 4

The King of Upper and Lower Egypt Nebtawyre, may he live for ever, born of King's Mother Imi. Month 2 of Akhet, day 23. Beginning the works in this mountain on a lord of life (consisting of an) eternal stone. The second marvel. The issuing of a divine command. The seeing of the manifestations of this god. The displaying of his power to the lapwing-folk.[18] The making of the desert into a flood. The bringing forth of water from the rough surface of the rock. The finding of a well in the midst of the wadi 10 cubits by 10 cubits on its rim (lit. "its entire mouth"), filled with water to its brim, being pure and clean from gazelles, and hidden from the desert nomads. Expeditions of the ancestors and the kings who had existed before had come forth and returned on its sides. No eye saw it. No face of man fell on it. It was revealed to His Majesty himself; for, furthermore, he (i.e. Min) had concealed it, knowing this exact moment, having planned the issue of this moment in order that his power might be seen and that the efficient power of His Majesty might be known, he doing something new in his desert lands for his son Nebtawyre, may he live for ever, in order that it might be heard by those who are in *Ta-meri* (i.e. Egypt) and by the lapwing-folk who are in Egypt, Upper Egypt and Lower Egypt bowing their heads to the ground, worshipping the youthful vigour of His Majesty for ever and ever. (Trans: Lloyd; hieroglyphic text Couyat and Montet 1912:97ff.; Buck 1970:77ff.)

There has been much discussion of this text and some disagreement on the translation.[19] My analysis will be based on my own rendering and interpretation of what the text is trying to say. Like its predecessor it begins with a simple signature, but it then proceeds to name the king's mother, a most unusual feature which presumably means that she was crucial to his claim to the throne.[20] The text then proceeds to describe the process of extracting the stone for the sarcophagus, stating that the stone is *wakhu* (*w3ḫ(w)*, "enduring"). The tone then changes as we are informed that the events that followed were another *bi3yt* which unequivocally involved divine involvement, the terminology speaking of the god's *hu* (*ḥw*), "(divine) command" and his *b3w*, "(active) power" which is "given," i.e., made available, to the Egyptian people. The "marvel" consists of the revelation of a well in pristine condition which had never been seen before, and the novelty of the god's action in bringing this about is asserted later in the text and is clearly considered to be of considerable importance. The text then proceeds to emphasize strongly that it was revealed to the king by special dispensation of the god who had planned the event for several reasons, i.e., to show his own power and also to provide a means of demonstrating that the king was possessed of *menkhu* (*mnḫw*). The text concludes by asserting that this revelation of divine favor will lead to adoration of the king by all the Egyptians which will particularly focus on his *neferu* (*nfrw*). *Nfr* (and its affiliates) is another word which is quite impossible to translate but whose core of meaning lies in the area of "youthful vigour and creative force" (James 1953:12; Donohue 1978:143ff.).[21] Not surprisingly, therefore, it can be used of the sun-god himself when he appears as Nefertum over the eastern horizon in the morning to re-create, or guarantee, the continued existence of the ordered universe.

TEXT 5

The final text for consideration is the great Hammamat inscription of Regnal Year 3 of Ramesses IV (Christophe 1949, Kitchen 1969, Peden 1994). This lengthy document starts with eight lines of introductory material which begins by dating it and then establishes the king's validity, giving his full fivefold titulary and a long list of attributes which describe him in all respects as meeting the template of Egyptian kingship: military prowess at home and abroad, his association with *maat*, his longevity, divine origins, close bonds of affection with the gods (among whom the highly apposite Min, Horus, and Isis are *specifically* mentioned), his association with the qualities implied by *nfr* and *nfrw*, his wisdom, and his all-embracing power. The text then proceeds to describe the expedition.

> He (sc. the Pharaoh) opened up the way to God's Land which those who had existed previously had not known, a path far removed from the mind(s) of other people, their mind(s) being ignorant of (how) to enter it.
> Now His Majesty was quick in his mind like his father Horus, son of Isis, and he led the way to the place wherever he wished. He searched the august mountain in order to make monuments, marvels for the father of his fathers and all the gods and goddesses (of) Egypt. He set up a stela on this mountain which was engraved with the great name of: the King of Upper and Lower Egypt: Heqamare Setepenamun, the Son of Re, Ramesses IV Maaty Meriamun, given life like Re.
> Now His Majesty commanded,
> the Scribe of the House of Life, Ramesses-Ashahebsed,
> the Scribe of the Temples (1), Hori,
> and the Priest of the Temple of Min, Horus and Isis in Coptos, Usimare-nakht,
> to seek out the materials for the Place of Truth, in the mountain of *Bekhen-stone*, when it was discovered that they were of extremely good quality, being (truly) great monuments to marvel at. His Majesty commanded that orders be given to the High-Priest of Amun and Superintendent of Works, Ramessesnakht, justified, in order to bring them to Egypt. The butlers and senior officials who were with him were:
> The Royal Butler, Usimare-sekheper;

The Royal Butler, Nakhtamun;
The Deputy of the Army, Khaemtir;
The Overseer of the Treasury, Khaemtir;
The Chief Taxing-Master and Mayor of Thebes, Amenmose,
The Chief Taxing-Master and Superintendent of Cattle of the Estate of Usimarc Meriamun, Bakenkhons;
The Charioteer of the Residence, Nakhtamun;
The Marshalling Scribe of the Army, Sunero;
The Scribe of Distribution for the Army, Ramessesnakht;

Army-scribes,	20 men
Stablemasters of the Residence,	20 men
the Chief Administrator (1) of the Army, Khaemmale;	
Army-administrators (?),	20 men
Charioteers of the Chariotry,	50 men
an Overseer of Priests,	
and a Superintendent of Cattle;	
Priests, Scribes, and Agents,	50 men
Army-personnel,	5,000 men
Sailors of Units Fishermen of the Residence,	200 men
Apiru of the Troops of Anuit,	800 men
Personnel of the Temples of Pharaoh,	2,000 men
Deputy-Chief of M(edjay-Troops),	1 man
Medjay-(Troops),	50 men
the Overseer of Craftsmen, Nakhtamun;	
Chief of Works for the Quarrymen,	30 men
Quarrymen and Stonemasons,	130 men
Draughtsmen,	2 men
Sculptors,	4 men
and ... who are omitted from this list,[22]	900 men
Total:	8,368 men

There was transported for them the (essential) supplies from Egypt, in 10 wagons, with 6 spans of oxen per wagon, pulling (them) from Egypt as far as the mountain of Bekhen-stone. [There were] many [port]ers laden with loaves of bread, meat, and cakes beyond number. From the Southern City there were brought the offerings to satisfy the gods of heaven and earth, they having been purified in a great purification (ceremony), and they being shouldered [...4 *groups lost*...] they being placed upon asses so that they might be purified (?) as one (together).

Longhorn bulls were slaughtered, shorthorn bulls were butchered, incense was cast into its fire, (the smoke reaching up) to heaven; pomegranate wine and ordinary wine (flowed) like a floodwater and milk and beer were proffered in this place.

The lector-priest, his voice announced a pure oblation for Min, Horus, Isis [and ... 5.5 *groups lost* and] all the gods (of) this mountain so that their hearts might be joyful when they received their offerings and so act with hundreds of thousands of jubilees for their beloved son; the King of Upper and Lower Egypt and Lord of the Two Lands: Heqamare Setepenamun, the Son of Re and Lord of Diadems, Ramesses IV Maaty Meriamun, given life forever. (Trans: Peden 1994 [adapted])

There is much that is familiar here: the quarry area is described as being in *tȝ nṯr*, "God's Land"; the mountain is said to be *ḏw špsy*, "the august mountain"; the stone is said to be *nfr iḳr*, "superbly *nefer*," and the monuments are destined to be *biȝt*, "marvels." The prominence of the High Priest of Amun is best explained by his prominence in secular matters—and he is stated to be the Minister of Works—but the presence of priests leaves no doubt about the religious dimensions of the operation, and the inclusion of a lector-priest (a ritual expert) illustrates the importance of getting the rituals right. Not surprisingly, therefore, cult activity is very much to the fore. These rituals were directed in the first instance at Min, Horus, and Isis, but to ensure that no target is missed, they also applied to "all the gods of this mountain," and we are told that the purpose of the offerings is to give pleasure to the gods and also to get long life from them for the king. The king's proactive omniscience is stated to be critical, the unique nature of his achievement in getting to the area is strongly emphasized, and the working of his *sia* (*siȝ*), "(superhuman) perception," is obliquely adumbrated (Bonnet 1952:715). The object of the exercise is to produce marvellous monuments for the gods of Egypt, but it is also explicitly stated that another aim was to produce mortuary equipment for Western Thebes. The setting up of the stele was intended to preserve the name of the king, and the importance of leaving an epigraphic record is reflected in the presence of draughtsmen and sculptors, though the numbers are very small.

CONCLUSIONS

These texts, and those like them, fall into two categories: ostensibly royal texts and those left by officials. Both types leave us in doubt that the Wadi Hammamat quarry area was regarded as sacred, though this issue is much more prominent in the inscriptions set up on behalf of kings than those created to glorify the achievements of their servants. That is hardly surprising when we bear in mind that the most important function of the Egyptian king was his priestly role as guarantor of the entire cosmic order of which a central part was maintaining the good will of the gods. That said, we need to dig a little deeper.

The Egyptians conceptualized their world along two axes, the vertical and the horizontal (in general, see Loprieno 1988, Adams and Roy 2007). The vertical axis recognized three levels: heaven, earth, and the Underworld, each of which was regarded as containing its own divinities of varying degrees of importance. The horizontal axis was conceptualized in an essentially concentric format the center of which is the Pharaoh's residence (hence frequently called *khenu* [*ḥnw*], "the inside"); the next "ring" is the Nile Valley which was divided in two, either longitudinally, in which case the Egyptians refer to Egypt as "The Two Banks," or laterally, in which case they describe Egypt as "The Two Lands." Either way, Egypt also could be called *ḥnw*. Finally, the outer circle embraced everything else and belonged unequivocally to "the other." Whatever the context, however, the world was a plenum full of immanent divine powers which may be benign, destructive, or both, depending on circumstances. The East was particularly associated with beneficent powers since it was the context for the daily creative emergence of the sun-god, and its furthest reaches were the land of "The Horizon Dwellers" who were particularly associated with him. The East is, therefore, frequently described as "God's Land," the West, on the other hand, is an altogether more ambiguous context associated with the uncertainties of death and chaotic forces.[23] In order to maintain control, or, perhaps more accurately, create the illusion of control, of their conceptual world the Egyptians generated the idea that it was possible to enlist, placate, or repel these forces by ritual activity. This world was not something which was regarded as being governed by anything like our concept of natural law, so that the concepts of "the natural" and "the supernatural" are quite inappropriate in describing Egyptian concepts of the way the universe worked. Rather it was a place of infinite possibilities where the appropriate distinction lay in allocating an event to any point on a continuum stretching from events which are normal and frequent to events which are possible but may not even have happened as yet.

The Egyptians, like everyone else in antiquity and many much later, operated on the basis that there were some places where the numinous was present with particular potency, without in any way compromising their general notion of the ubiquity of divine power. Such places we are accustomed to describe as sacred space, but the very concept of sacred space raises the question as to why certain areas were singled out in this way (Alcock and Osborne 1994, Tilley 1994, Richards 2005, Dorman and Bryan 2007, Lupo 2007). The answer could lie in a number of possible factors: there may be some physical feature of the site which recalls or is identified with a divine force, perhaps a rock formation reminiscent of the iconography or an attribute of a deity, e.g., the Qurn looming over the Valley of the Kings like a pyramid or the *akhet* (concave-shaped) declivity in the horizon east of el-Amarna; alternatively, a certain type of site may be regarded as particularly apposite for communication with the deity or to carry out cult activity on its behalf, e.g., a mountain top (e.g., the Eleventh Dynasty mountain shrine in Western Thebes [Vörös 1998]) or a cave penetrating deeply into the earth (e.g., Speos Artemidos and Abu Simbel; see Klemm 1988); there might also be something more general about a location which creates a strong sense of "the other," the uncanny. Whatever the reason, once a site has acquired the status of sacred space, it will be consolidated by frequent usage and may even preserve its status through changes in religious tradition, a tendency which is particularly evident in Egypt, e.g., the necropolis areas of Kubbet el-Hawa at Aswan and Asyut in Middle Egypt. Why the Hammamat quarry should be regarded as such a place we can only guess, but explaining the postulation of the presence of savior deities in the Eastern Desert itself is easy enough: its uncanny stillness and inscrutability are enough to generate a sense of "the other" with which one must come to terms, and the desert is also an intrinsically dangerous place. However, quarrying work in the Wadi is difficult, perilous, and likely to lead to considerable casualties, and that situation in itself would generate the need for divine help and the concomitant conviction that this divine assistance could be accessed immediately on this site.[24] It is very much of a piece with this that expedition leaders insist on the uniqueness of their achievement since their alleged incomparable success in this difficult area would be a reflection of divine support. The same would hold true of a marked trait of the commander's record discussed above which presents the common ideal picture, almost certainly completely false, of a totally trouble-free and completely successful expedition: "Without any loss to it did the army return; not a man perished; not a troop turned back; not an ass perished; and no craftsmen were maimed."

Given this body of concepts, it comes as no surprise to find that the produce of the Hammamat area is itself imbued with the divine properties of the area exemplifying the firm conviction of the ancient Egyptians that substances are not inert but possessed of dynamic powers which can be harnessed to their advantage. In the Montuhotep IV text of day 3 the stone, like the mountain, is said to be "august." In the text of day 23 the stone is stated to be "eternal" and the sarcophagus is described as a "lord of life," and, as part of Min's domain, the quarry area is seen as "God's Land." The stone is also said to be pure, and it has *mnḥw* which Min himself has created. In the commander's record it is stated to be "a monument of eternity which endures for ever." Finally, the Ramesses IV inscription's description of the stone as "superbly *nefer*" again evokes notions of demiurgic power.

The religious conception of these expeditions also made it possible to use them for propagandist purposes. Two of the Nebtawyre inscriptions are concerned with *biꜣyt*, i.e., "marvels." In the inscription of day 3 we read of a gazelle which gave birth on the stone which was to be used for the lid of the sarcophagus. The text of day 23 describes another *biꜣyt*, this time the discovery of a well where none had ever been seen before. Since a *biꜣyt* is a divine signal that the king is doing what the gods approve, both narratives function as divine endorsement of the actions of a ruler whose claim to the throne was clearly open to question.

Even the setting up of the inscriptions is seen in a religious light and raises the question of their function. The Montuhotep IV text of day 15 states clearly that it is being erected for the god Min himself, the god who exercised oversight of the desert lands. The intention was to place the king's achievement before the god in the god's own domain and thereby gain eternal life for the king, and we have a similar set of statements in the Ramesses IV text. The centrality of establishing a memorial to the king in the desert area is also emphasized in the commander's record which bears exactly the same day-date. However, the god is not likely to have been the only target;

for, while it is true that the capacity to read hieroglyphs was probably very restricted, even among the elite, it is clear that inscriptions were read by those who could do it, and this would mean that the texts could serve a commemorative function to guarantee the preservation of the king's name and achievement for future generations. There is, however, a further point. Text in ancient Egypt was not an inert thing. Inscriptions were dynamic instruments and were thought to be capable in themselves of eternalizing and even guaranteeing the actualization of what they described.

We often think and speak of the Eastern "Desert," but to the Egyptians this space was anything but deserted. It was a place full of awesome demiurgic power which they recognized and were determined to access, but success in any such enterprise could only be achieved through the good will of the gods, whose dwelling the deserts so clearly were. In a sense—and an important sense—the desert, as a numinous area where gods reside, was equivalent to a temple, and the transactions which took place there were not dissimilar to the rituals which unfolded each day in the temples in Egypt itself. Such a concept also helps to explain the development of rock temples. An ancient Greek philosopher once wrote, "All things are full of gods." That was certainly true of the ancient Egyptian world view, but the deserts had more than their fair share of divine presence.

NOTES

12.1 On the physical context of Hammamat expeditions see, e.g., Kees 1961, Seyfried 1981, Sayed 1983, Fattovich and Bard 2006.

12.2 The preposition *r* here is a little perplexing. It is generally treated as the *r* of comparison and translated by "als" or "than" (e.g., Schenkel 1965:265; Lichtheim 1975:114) so that the king ends up claiming the superior power of his sarcophagus as compared with that of any Egyptian temple monument. However, it is worth noting that in the preceding phrase the preposition is used before the expression "lord of life" in the final sense "for, so as to be." It is just possible that it has this sense before the word for "monuments" and that the claim is being made that the sarcophagus is not the only use to which the stone will be put; the stone is also intended for other temple monuments.

12.3 It often assumed that the expression *"Heb-Sed* festivals" has been omitted in error before the phrase translated "great plenty" (e.g., Schenkel 1965 and Lichtheim 1975). This is intrinsically highly probable and is supported by the run of the Egyptian at this point.

12.4   Erman and Grapow 1926–1963, IV:445; Meeks 1980– :1, 368; 2, 373; 3, 287–88.

12.5   On the significance of this word see Lloyd 1975:57n18.

12.6   There are sometimes ambiguities, doubtless intentional, in the wording of this text which create uncertainty at times as to whether the divine name "Horus" refers to the king and/or to the god Horus.

12.7   The Six Great Houses were ancient institutions concerned with legal administration (Strudwick 1985:176ff.).

12.8   This term is frequently used to denote Mankind/Egyptians (Gardiner 1947, II:289).

12.9   I.e., Aswan, to the ancient Egyptians the southernmost point of Egypt proper.

12.10 *Duau* was the divinized royal placenta which featured in the *Heb-Sed* Festival and also, as here, in the ritual of the stretching of the cord which took place when a temple was founded (cf. Ward 1982:113, 942).

12.11 This phrase is an extremely common adjunct to references to the king and the palace.

12.12 In this case, the draughtsmen who would draw the representations and hieroglyphic inscriptions which would be left on the quarry walls (cf. Gardiner 1947, I:71*). The fact that they form part of the team is a clear indication that the intention to leave a record had been formulated before the expedition even began.

12.13 These members of the team were responsible for the chants and the hand-clapping which were designed to ensure that workmen engaged in pulling large objects all pulled at the same time. We can see one in action in the colossus representation in the tomb of Djehutyhotpe II at El-Bersheh (Newberry 1893: pl. XII, standing on the knee of the colossus).

12.14 Schenkel translates the verb which appears here as "fehlte" (1965:267). The meaning "turn back" is firmly established for this word (Erman and Grapow 1926–1963, II:353, 13–15) and seems more appropriate to the context.

12.15 The meaning of this clause is far from clear. Schenkel renders: "Möge für ihn noch grösseres als dies getan werden (?)." It seems preferable to interpret it as giving a reason why Min so favored the king: the expansion of the kingdom is deserving of reward.

12.16 The *sḏm ir(w).n.f* construction introduced a new and significant phase in a text; Allen aptly describes its use as follows: "Like the narrative infinitive, the *sḏm pw jr.n.f* construction and its passive counterpart *sḏm pw jry* (which is much rarer) seem to occur after breaks in the narration—mostly at places where the translation might begin a new paragraph" (2000:169).

12.17 He is omitted from all the extant kinglists (cf. Grajetzki 2006:25–6).

12.18 This term is frequently used generally of "mankind," i.e., the Egyptians as a whole,

12.19 Schenkel 1965:267 ff.; Lloyd 1975:54 ff.; Polotsky 1986:31ff. The major problem is the ambiguity of the pronouns which can only be resolved by grasping the underlying thought process.

12.20 It is also intriguing that in Hammamat 110 A (Schenkel 1965:263) the king's Regnal Year 2 is stated to be the date of his first *Heb-Sed* Festival. By later standards this is extremely early for the first of these festivals of royal rejuvenation, which also served as a means of reaffirming legitimacy, and its celebration at this point may well reflect a need to assert the justice of the king's claim to the throne at the beginning of his reign against serious opposition.

12.21 James 1953:12; Donohue 1978:143ff.

12.22 The area marked here by three dots contains signs which have been universally translated "the dead" in line with an old proposal by Spiegelberg (1899). There is no doubt what the hieroglyphic signs following this problematic area read, nor is there any dispute about their translation, but Spiegelberg's rendering amounts to nothing more than a highly speculative piece of guesswork. The group in question is meaningless and is best treated as a scribal or sculptor's error. It is extremely improbable, given the ethos of such texts, that any casualties would be admitted. Since the list overall is clearly tabulating the staff taken out to the quarries, the best guess for any exceptional addition to explain the 900 would be that they were already in the quarries engaged in other work or that they had finished another project and were simply waiting for this expedition, but no obvious restoration for what is obviously a corruption presents itself.

12.23 Cf. Pyramid Texts 2175: "Do not travel [on] those western waterways, for those who travel thereon do not return, but travel on those eastern waterways among the Followers of [Re . . .] an arm [is upraised] in the East ...."

12.24 The Gebel es-Silsileh quarries provide an obvious parallel.

REFERENCES

Adams, C., and J. Roy, eds. 2007. *Travel, Geography and Culture in Ancient Greece, Egypt and the Near East*. Leicester Nottingham Studies in Ancient Culture 10. Oxford: Oxbow Books.

Alcock, S., and R. Osborne, eds. 1994. *Placing the Gods: Sanctuaries and Sacred Space in Ancient Greece*. Oxford: Clarendon Press.

Allen, J. P. 2000. *Middle Egyptian: An Introduction to the Language and Culture of*

Hieroglyphs. Cambridge: Cambridge University Press.

Bonnet, H. 1952. *Reallexikon der ägyptischen Religionsgeschichte*. Berlin: W. de Gruyter.

Buck, A. de. 1970. *Egyptian Readingbook*. Vol. 1, *Exercises and Middle Egyptian Texts*. 3rd ed. Leiden: Nederlands Instituut voor het Nabije Oosten.

Christophe, L. 1949. La stèle de l'an III de Ramsès IV au Ouâdi Hammâmât (N°12). *Bulletin de l'Institut français d'archéologie orientale* 48:1–38.

Couyat, J., and P. Montet. 1912. *Les inscriptions hiéroglyphiques et hiératiques du Ouâdi Hammâmât*. Institut français d'archéologie orientale, mémoires 34. Cairo: l'Institut français d'archéologie orientale.

Donohue, V.A. 1978. *Pr-nfr. JEA* 64:143–48.

Dorman, P.F., and B.M. Bryan, eds. 2007. *Sacred Space and Sacred Function in Ancient Thebes*. Occasional Proceedings of the Theban Worshop. SAOC 61. Chicago: Oriental Institute of the University of Chicago.

Erman, A., and H. Grapow. 1926–1963. *Wörterbuch der Aegyptischen Sprache*. 7 vols. Leipzig: J.C. Hinrichs.

Fattovich, R. and K. Bard. 2006. À la recherche de Pount: Mersa Gaouasis et la navigation égyptienne dans la mer Rouge. *Égypte, Afrique & Orient* 41:7–30.

Gardiner, AH. 1947. *Ancient Egyptian Onomastica*. 2 vols. London: Oxford University Press.

Gardiner, A.H., and T.E. Peet. 1952–1955. *The Inscriptions of Sinai*. 2nd rev. ed. Memoirs of the Egypt Exploration Society 45. 2 vols. London: Egypt Exploration Society.

Graefe, E. 1971. *Untersuchungen zur Wortfamilie bi3*. Inaug. diss., Universitat Koln, 1969. Cologne.

Grajetzki, W. 2006. *The Middle Kingdom of Ancient Egypt. History, Archaeology and Society*. Duckworth Egyptology. London: Duckworth and Co.

Harrell, J., and V.M. Brown. 1992. The Oldest Surviving Topographical Map from Ancient Egypt (Turin Papyri 1879, 1899, 1969). *JARCE* 29:81–105.

James, T.G.H. 1953. *The Mastaba of Khentika Called Ikhekhi*. Archaeological Survey of Egypt 30. London: Egypt Exploration Society.

Kees, H. 1961. *Ancient Egypt: A Cultural Topography*. London: University of Chicago Press.

Kitchen, K.A. 1969. *Ramesside Inscriptions, Historical and Biographical*, Vol. VI, 1. Oxford: B.H. Blackwell.

Klemm, R. 1988. Vom Steinbruch zum Tempel. Beobachtungen zur Baustruktur einiger Felstempel der 18. und 19. Dynastie im ägyptischen Mutterland.

ZÄS 115:41–51.

———. 1993. *Steine und Steinbrüche in Alten Ägypten*. Berlin: Springer-Verlag.

Lichtheim, M. 1975. *Ancient Egyptian Literature*. Vol. I, *The Old and Middle Kingdoms*. Berkeley: University of California Press.

Lloyd, A.B. 1975. Once More Hammamat Inscription 191. *JEA* 61:54–66.

Loprieno, A. 1988. *Topos und Mimesis: Zum Ausländer im ägyptischen Literatur*. Wiesbaden: O. Harrassowitz Verlag.

Lupo, S. 2007. *Territorial Appropriation during the Old Kingdom (XXVIIIth–XXIIIrd Centuries BC). The Royal Necropolises and the Pyramid Towns in Egypt*. British Archaeological Reports International Series 1595. Oxford: Archaeopress.

Meeks, D. 1980– . *Année lexicographique*. Paris: Imprimerie de la Margeride.

Meyer, C. 1997. Bir Umm Fawakhir: Insights into Ancient Egyptian Mining. *Journal of the Minerals, Metals and Materials Society* 49(3): 64–68.

Newberry, P. 1893. *El Bersheh. Part 1 (The Tomb of Tehut-hetep)*. Archaeological Survey of Egypt 3. London: Egypt Exploration Fund.

Peden, A.J. 1994. *The Reign of Ramesses IV*. Warminster: Aris and Phillips.

Polotski, H.J. 1986. "His Majesty" in Hammamat 191. In *Essays on Egyptian Grammar*, ed. W.K. Simpson, pp. 31–33. Yale Egyptological Studies 1. New Haven, CT: Yale Egyptological Seminar, Yale University.

Richards, J. 2005. *Society and Death in Ancient Egypt: Mortuary Landscapes of the Middle Kingdom*. Cambridge: Cambridge University Press.

Saleh, A.-A. 1981. Notes on the Ancient Egyptian *t3 nṯr* "God's Land." *Bulletin de l'Institut Francois d'Archéologie Orientale*, 81, suppl.:107–17.

Sayed, A.M.A.H. 1983. New Light on the Recently Discovered Port on the Red Sea Shore. *Chronique d'Égypte* 58:23–37.

Schenkel, W. 1965. *Memphis, Herakleopolis, Theben: Die epigraphischen Zeugnisse der 7.–11. Dynastie Ägyptens*. Ägyptologische Abhandlungen, 12. Wiesbaden: Harrassowitz.

Sethe, K. 1959. *Ägyptische Lesestücke zum Gebrauch im akademischen Unterricht. Texte des Mittleren Reiches*. 3rd ed. Hildesheim: Georg Olms Verlagsbuchhandlung.

Seyfried, K.-J. 1981. *Beiträge zu den Expeditionen des Mittleren Reiches in die Ost-Wüste*. Hildesheimer Ägyptologische Beiträge 15. Hildesheim: Gerstenberg Verlag.

Spiegelberg, W. 1899. Varia XLII. *Recueil de travaux rélatifs à la philologie et à l'archéologie égyptiennes et assyriennes* 21:48–49.

Strudwick, N. 1985. *The Administration of Egypt in the Old Kingdom. The High-*

est Titles and Their Holders. Studies in Egyptology. London: Routledge and Kegan Paul.

Tilley, C. 1994. *Phenomenology of Landscape: Place, Paths, and Monuments*. Oxford: Berg Publishers.

Vörös, G. 1998. *Temple on the Pyramid of Thebes. Hungarian Excavations on Thoth Hill at the Temple of Pharaoh Montuhotep Sankhkare 1995–1998*. Budapest: Százszorszép Kiadó és Nyomda.

Ward, W.A. 1982. *Index of Egyptian Administrative and Religious Titles of the Middle Kingdom: With a Glossary of Words and Phrases Used*. Beirut: American University of Beirut.

13

"Imaginal" Landscapes in Assyrian Imperial Monuments

MEHMET-ALI ATAÇ

> La géographie ancienne ne restituait pas les données d'une science positive, même si, ici ou là, certains sites et paysages sont parfaitement réels. C'était une géographie imaginaire qui nous instruit de la manière dont la terre fut méditée et perçue, le fruit d'une pensée "schématico-cosmographique" selon le mot de B. Landsberger.
>
> — Glassner 1984:30

INTRODUCTION

That ideas of a timeless and philosophical nature could exist side by side with the contemporary and political in the art of the Neo-Assyrian Empire (883–612 BCE) is perhaps best apparent in the orthostat reliefs of the Northwest Palace of Ashurnasirpal II (883–859 BCE) at Nimrud (Kalhu). The reliefs, especially those in the throne room, feature what may have been the chief emblematic signifiers of the contemporary Assyrian intellectual tradition. These elements are the antediluvian sages and the so-called sacred tree, which are adjacent to, but not entirely blended with, the series of historical reliefs that depict scenes from the various military campaigns of Ashurnasirpal II (Fig. 13.1).[1] As if to counterbalance this separation, unlike the reliefs of the later Neo-Assyrian kings, the full identity of

13.1. Ashurnasirpal II flanked by bird-headed *apkallus*. Northwest Palace of Ashurnasirpal II at Nimrud. British Museum, ANE 124584-5. Photo: author.

the historical reliefs is not explicated by captions on the narrative scenes, such that the whole picture is somewhere between chronicle and epic.

The capital city of Ashurnasirpal II and its palace stand at the very beginning of the Neo-Assyrian period. Throughout the following three centuries, there is an increase in emphasis on the historical component in the palace reliefs, resulting in the panoramic depictions of a variety of military and other events against their native landscapes in the palaces of Sennacherib (704–681 BCE) and Ashurbanipal (668–627 BCE) in the last capital city of the empire, Nineveh. In the meantime, palace architecture displays a parallel elaboration too, with larger dimensions and an increase in the number of the "state apartments" that surround the two principal courtyards of the palace enclosures. Both the historical and the emblematic modes in the Assyrian visual representation of the 1st millennium BCE extend back to the Late Bronze Age in Mesopotamia, to the Middle Assyrian Period (ca. 1350–1000 BCE), as do Assyrian palace architecture and the royal annalistic tradition.

The co-existence of, and sometimes tension between, what is mythical on the one hand and what is political-propagandistic on the other in the historiography of the ancient Near East has received fresh scholarly attention in recent years (Liverani 2004, Porter 2005). If, for instance, Ramesses III (Twentieth Dynasty, 1184–1153 BCE) depicted the Battle of Kadesh, fought between Ramesses II (Nineteenth Dynasty, 1279–1213 BCE) and the Hittite king Muwatalli II (1295–72 BCE) around 1274 BCE, anachronistically in his monuments as if he had fought it and won a victory (Hornung 1992:155–56), are we talking about a ritual reenactment of a historical moment of military glory, or when such ideological elements enter representation and historiography, are we missing certain parameters for a thorough understanding of the ancient historical tradition?

I do not intend to resolve this long-standing issue here, but would nevertheless like to point out one particular avenue in the ancient world in which ritual or myth and "reality" are inseparable and blended, and that is geography and cosmology, and their visual representation. My objective in this chapter is to trace ideas of the inhabited earth, juxtaposed to its edges or limits, and what lies beyond in ancient Mesopotamian thought, and inquire if such ideas may have guided the representational and historical tradition of the Assyrian Empire, understood here as a continuum constituted by both the Middle and Neo-Assyrian periods. My goal is also to discuss the relevance of such a formulation of geography and landscape to kingship and notions of universal rule. Finally, I suggest that mythical and philosophical structures were the primary building blocks of the way "reality" per se was perceived and recorded in the ancient Near East.

THE "EDGES OF THE EARTH" IN ANCIENT MESOPOTAMIAN THOUGHT

Ancient Near Eastern geography made a distinction, as did certain other ancient traditions such as the Greek, between the inhabited or familiar earth—to which I henceforth refer, after James S. Romm (1992:37), as the *oikoumene*—and regions that were thought to lie beyond this zone. Chief among the sources from the 1st millennium BCE that reveal a Mesopotamian sense of the *oikoumene*, its limits, and what lies beyond are the so-called Babylonian *mappa mundi*, a Late Babylonian cuneiform tablet (BM 92687) (Fig. 13.2); the Standard Babylonian version of *The Epic of Gilgamesh*; and the so-called *Sargon Geography*, also written in Standard Babylonian. The latter text presents the territory of the historical figure of Sargon of

13.2. Babylonian *mappa mundi*, probably from Sippar, ca. 700–500 BCE. British Museum, ANE 92687. Photo: Erich Lessing/Art Resource, NY.

Akkad (2334–2279 BCE) as a world empire that stretched from the "Upper Sea" to the "Lower Sea," incorporating traditions about Sargon that "presumably date back to the Old Akkadian period" (Horowitz 1998:77).

The Babylonian map of the world is perhaps the most revealing of these documents in its combining the textual medium with the visual. It presents a depiction of the world in map form, showing what may be understood as the *oikoumene*, the main continent, with Babylon as its nucleus, surrounded by a band that represents the cosmic ocean, *marratu* in Akkadian. Beyond the ocean are the *nagû*, the "distant unspecified areas," shown in the form of triangular radials emanating from the circular *oikoumene*. "When complete, the map may have included as many as eight such *nagû*" (Horowitz 1998:30). The tablet identifies the regions and countries shown on the map by captions, in addition to bearing a rather poorly preserved text that provides further information about the zones depicted on the map.

The map and its text have been studied in detail by Wayne Horowitz, who describes one of their purposes as illustrating "where these distant areas were located in relation to familiar locales, such as Babylon, Assyria, and the Euphrates" (Horowitz 1998:40). Horowitz summarily contextualizes the tablet's contents as follows:

> The obverse related these distant places to familiar literary figures and exotic animals, and the reverse described conditions in the far-away regions. The ancient author's interest in distant places reflects a general interest in distant areas during the first half of the first millennium, when the Assyrian and Babylonian empires reached their greatest extents. Other manifestations of this interest include the construction of *kirimāḫu* "botanical gardens" filled with the flora of distant lands in Assyria during the reigns of Sargon II, Sennacherib, Esarhaddon, and Ashurbanipal; the . . . expedition of Shalmaneser III to the sources of the Tigris and Euphrates . . . ; and the writing of *The Sargon Geography*, a text purporting to describe the worldwide empire of Sargon of Akkad—all during this same period." (1998:40)

In the domain of literary texts, it is in the Standard Babylonian version of the *Epic of Gilgamesh* that we find the most explicit references to places beyond the *oikoumene*. These are clearly places that not only lie beyond familiar geography but also beyond ordinary human experience. In this regard, one can cite the Cedar Forest, where Gilgamesh is engaged in an expedition against the monster Humbaba with Enkidu, the setting of Tablet IV, and the journey of Gilgamesh alone, after Enkidu's death, that culminates in the "edenic" land where Utnapishtim lives eternally, the incidents of Tablets IX-XI. The latter journey entails Gilgamesh's following the path of the sun at night in the netherworld, his emergence out of darkness into a grove of gem-bearing trees, his arrival at the tavern of Siduri by the shore of the cosmic sea, the "waters of death," his crossing this body of water with the ferryman Urshanabi, and his final encounter with the Flood hero Utnapishtim beyond the "waters of death." According to Horowitz, thought of in terms of the Babylonian map, Gilgamesh's journey consists of traveling from Babylonia to the shores of the cosmic ocean *marratu*, "and a sea crossing to one of the *nagû* across the *marratu*" (1998:106).

The main text on the Babylonian map of the world, too, mentions certain unusual and mythical features in the geography of the earth, such as the northern *nagû* identified as "Great Wall ... where the Sun is not seen";[2] the names of some of the creatures of Tiamat known from the Babylonian poem of cosmogony, *Enuma Elish*; fauna of distant lands such as hyenas, panthers, red-deer, lions, monkeys, ostriches, and gazelle, the like of which were also brought home by Assyrian kings from their campaigns; and the Flood hero Utnapishtim himself (Horowitz 1998:32). In sum, it is plausible to think of the *nagû*, represented by the triangular radials on the Babylonian map, as lands beyond the *oikoumene*, which is bordered by the ocean.

It is noteworthy that some of the distant mythical lands encountered in *The Epic of Gilgamesh* are associated with known geographic locales. As such, the Cedar Forest, or the Cedar Mountain, "is the name for the mountains northwest of Assyria in modern Lebanon, Syria, and Turkey. From Old Akkadian times onward, this term is often identified with the Lebanon and Amanus ranges" (Horowitz 1998:79–80). As for the land of Utnapishtim, it is associated with Dilmun, identified today as the island of Bahrain in the Persian Gulf (Alster 1983:52). In the *Sumerian Flood Story* (ca. 1600 BCE), Ziusudra, the Sumerian name for Utnapishtim, "is settled in the direction of the rising sun (east) in the land of Dilmun . . . In the inscriptions of Sargon II, Dilmun also lies offshore, in the direction of sunrise from Mesopotamia" (Horowitz 1998:104). In fact, Samuel Noah Kramer went so far as concluding that the land of Ziusudra and the Cedar Mountain of the Sumerian poem *Bilgames and Huwawa* are coextensive in their capacity as the "Land of the Living," in that they both constitute the same antechamber that enables a transition from the human domain to a fully divine realm (Kramer 1944:23–26; Gresseth 1975:11; see also Thomason 2001:81).

It is likely that in Gilgamesh's journey to Utnapishtim, the enchanted lands the hero visits already belong to the *Jenseits*, as is also the case with Odysseus when he is among the Phaeacians (Cook 1992:241, idem 2004:43).[3] The implications of this situation may be twofold. First, their identification with known geographic places may not constitute an impediment to our understanding locales such as the Cedar Forest and the land of Utnapishtim as belonging to the Jenseits. Second, this identification may be thought to show how for ancient thinking the known physical geography was by no means divorced from an understanding of the suprasensory (Thomason 2001:65).

One particular example for how places that are distant and foreign to the center, and even the *oikoumene*, acquire on the one hand a tangible and concrete quality and on the other a rather formulaic and conceptual nature is the group of places known as Dilmun, Magan, and Meluhha, often mentioned together in 3rd millennium BCE Mesopotamian royal inscriptions as trade partners with Sumer and Akkad. In addition to the identification of Dilmun as the island of Bahrain, modern research has identified Magan with "the upper Persian Gulf Coast including modern Oman," and Meluhha with the Indus Valley culture (Horowitz 1998:328).[4] After the Ur III period (ca. 2112–2004 BCE), contact with these three lands diminished, but their "names continued to be remembered in geographic lists, literary texts, and historical omens, as well as through goods identified as being of the Dilmun, Magan, or Meluhha type" (Horowitz 1998:329).

Two of these places are almost hallowed on account of the precious materials that they supplied to Mesopotamia, Magan, and Meluhha. We can only remember how important it is for Gudea to mention persistently that his statues are fashioned out of diorite that comes from Magan (e.g., Gudea E 3/1.1.7.StB: vii 10-13 [Edzard 1997:35]). Carnelian, which came from the Indus Valley, was also much prized, as was lapis lazuli, which came from Afghanistan.

That such precious materials may have been associated with distant or magical lands is apparent in the episode of *The Epic of Gilgamesh* from Tablet IX, in which the hero finds himself in an orchard of gem-bearing trees after emerging out of the path of the sun at night. Even though the text is extremely fragmentary here, both carnelian and lapis are mentioned in association with the unusual trees of this orchard. Horowitz suggests that the idea of a fabulous distant grove of gemstones "reflects an ancient Mesopotamian belief that gemstones, which had to be imported into the Mesopotamian plain from afar, were plentiful in distant lands" (1998:102). Thus, in addition to their inherent value as rare materials, the value and prestige attached to these substances and the artifacts made of them may to a certain extent have been on account of their places of origin as distant lands of an unusual nature.

TOWARDS AN ANCIENT MESOPOTAMIAN CONCEPTION OF THE *OIKOUMENE*

An understanding of the inhabited or familiar world, the *oikoumene*, as opposed to distant or foreign lands, can be detected in the ancient Mesopotamian royal inscriptions as well. Even in a medium that we might deem more "historical" than poetry, the same conceptual understanding of geography and the cosmos guides the sense of place and the environment. Horowitz pinpoints the description of Mount Mashu in the Standard Babylonian version of the *Epic of Gilgamesh*, where Gilgamesh's journey to Utnapishtim begins, in comparison to "wondrous mountains that Mesopotamian kings encounter on their campaigns in foreign lands" (1998:98). Furthermore, Mario Liverani (1990:98) draws attention to the international royal rhetoric of reaching the farthest point, setting up a stele, or crossing peripheral regions, such as mountains, deserts, marshes, woodlands, that are difficult to cross:

> There is a logic in the geographic setup of the world (which is the work of god): the meaning of these obstacles is that nobody has to venture this far. Do they belong to the world that has been already physically arranged by the gods, and must now be politically and culturally arranged by the king, or are they instead part of chaos, of darkness, of death?
>
> In his activity as demiurge the king ventures through these zones (he is the first one to do so) and "opens" new roads, improving them through a technical and cultural activity so that they are henceforth inserted into the human/civilized world. The opening of a new road entails splitting rocks and cutting timber in the mountains, excavating wells in the desert, thus making the access easier for the less heroic followers.

Further clues to a conceptually codified geography in both Mesopotamia and Egypt include formulaic designations or classifications of foreign or outlandish areas such as "foreign lands" or "rebel lands" (kur.kur and ki.bala in Sumerian, respectively) in Mesopotamia, and also "foreign lands" and the "nine bows" in Egypt (Janssen 1951:215; Uphill 1967, Kinnier Wilson 1979:2; Cooper 1978:2). In both instances, the exact significance of such designations and their identification with actual geographic zones are still unclear and debated in scholarship. This situation may be taken as indicative of the fact that we miss certain parameters in a full understanding of ancient Near Eastern and Egyptian conceptions of the geographic environment, especially as expressed by the scribal culture of royal courts.

One final example we can mention in this regard would be the implications of the land of Punt for the ancient Egyptians. Modern research proposes a number of regions in northeastern and equatorial Africa as the location of Punt, ranging from eastern Sudan eastward, to the Red Sea, to the great lakes of eastern Africa (Kitchen 1971:184–88; Wicker 1998). The Egyptian designation *ta netjer*, "God's Land" or "No Man's Land," may have referred to Punt, among other places, such as the land of the Hittites (Janssen 1951:214; Dixon 1968:55; Wilkinson 1998:84). In addition to the aromatic substance par excellence known as *'ntyw* (Dixon 1968:55), frankincense or myrrh, with which this land supplied Egypt, it also must have had significance from the point of view of the understanding of an *oikoumene* that we are dealing with here. Punt was surely a far-away land of fascination for the ancient Egyptians, and its depiction in art, especially as evidenced by the reliefs of Hatshepsut (Eighteenth Dynasty, 1473–1458 BCE) at Deir el-Bahri, features unusual and exotic elements such as a rhinocerus, a giraffe, and monkeys, animals that are not part of the native fauna of Egypt (Smith 1962:60; Kitchen 1971:187). In this respect, Punt was surely located on one of the edges of the ancient Egyptian *oikoumene*, if not beyond it, and expeditions into this realm were probably not without the implications of leaving the limitations of familiar dimensions of space and time (Liverani 1990:240).

In sum, even though what defined the *oikoumene*, its edges, and the zones beyond in ancient Mesopotamia is not clearly spelled out in texts, certain basic elements pertaining to this geographic knowledge may still be gleaned from the available sources. According to the Babylonian *mappa mundi* and other reference points, we can certainly suggest that the Mesopotamian plain, with its age-old cultural capital Babylon, did constitute some kind of an *oikoumene*, especially in the 1st millennium BCE.[5] It was delimited by what is referred to as the Upper Sea, the Mediterranean in the North, and by the Lower Sea, the Persian Gulf in the South.[6]

The entire earth's surface consisted of three major components, "a central continent, a cosmic sea, and land(s) across the sea" (Horowitz 1998:105). In both ancient Mesopotamian and ancient Greek traditions of cosmology, an all-encircling Ocean represented the outer limits of both geographic space and the basic human comprehension of the world, with the borders sometimes blended or co-extensive with what may lie on the other shore of the Ocean (Liverani 1990:53; Romm 1992:12–20; Horowitz 1998:29–30, 305).[7] In other words, it is sometimes unclear if the edges or ends are those of the *oikoumene* proper, the central land mass of the Babylonian map in the ancient Mesopotamian case, or those of the entire surface of the earth, which then would include the lands beyond the Ocean, the *nagû* (Horowitz 1998:331).

One of the canonical borders of an ancient Mesopotamian conception of the *oikoumene* seems to be Cedar Mountain in the North. On the Babylonian map, the northern edge of the main land mass features an oval-shaped region marked "mountain," where the Euphrates originates. According to Horowitz, "this region must be the mountains of modern Turkey by the sources of the river. In the *Sargon Geography*, these mountains form part of the Cedar Mountain. Because there are no lands beyond the Cedar Mountain in the text, it is reasonable to assume that the author of the *Sargon Geography* believed that a northern arm of the cosmic sea lay beyond the mountains, just as the *marratu* flows along the northern rim of the continent on the World Map" (1998:93). Perhaps, the emphatic interest on the part of certain Middle and Neo-Assyrian rulers, especially Tiglath-Pileser I (1114–1076 BCE) and Shalmaneser III (858–824 BCE), in the so-called Source of the Tigris may also be explicable in terms of this locale's suggestiveness of one of the limits or edges, if not the northernmost one, of an Assyrian understanding of the *oikoumene* (Grayson 1991:39–45; Harmanşah 2007). The implications of such an understanding at the level of royal ideology would have been extending the imperial territory to the edges of the known world and hence universalizing an imperial administrative system (Liverani 1990:56; Romm 1992:161).

As for the other edges of an ancient Mesopotamian conception of the *oikoumene*, no doubt both the Zagros Mountain range and the Persian Gulf would have constituted natural limits to a geographic environment that was the most familiar. The Zagros Mountains were associated with the unknown, chaos, and nomadic foreign peoples as attested both by written sources from the 3rd millennium BCE onward, and monuments, especially the Stele of Naram-Sin from the Akkadian period (ca. 2334–2154 BCE) (Cooper 1978:2; Kinnier Wilson 1979:4–5; Black 1988:23; Wiggermann 1992:153). In ancient Mesopotamian cosmography, the Zagros Mountains, or the Mountain of Elam, also contained the Sumerian phenomenon of the *ganzir*, the entrance to the netherworld, one of the characteristics of the edges of the *oikoumene* in its capacity of leading out of the familiar environment into the suprasensory (Horowitz 1998: 270).[8] As already mentioned, in the South, the Persian Gulf must have constituted a natural border for the ancient Mesopotamian *oikoumene* with Dilmun, Magan, and Meluhha as the lands beyond it. In the *Sargon Geography*, all three of these lands, among others, are presented as lying outside the central continent, "just as the *nagû* are drawn across the *marratu* on the World Map" (Horowitz 1998:94).

THE KING OF THE "FOUR QUARTERS"

That such formulations of ancient Mesopotamian geography and cosmology are deeply tied with the idea of kingship is apparent in some of the royal titles, especially the title *šar kibrāt arba'im*, King of the Four Quarters, or the title *šar kiššatim*, usually rendered as King of the World in English, but literally meaning "king of the totality" (Glassner 1984:24). The Sumerian and Akkadian terms for the four quarters are in reference to the division of the earth's surface into quadrants corresponding to the four cardinal directions (Glassner 1984:18, Horowitz 1998:324–25). The Babylonian *mappa mundi* as well as other sources take the idea of the four quarters as "all the land areas on the earth's surface" (Horowitz 1998:299). This definition would encompass not only the *oikoumene*, but also the lands beyond the cosmic Ocean, the *nagû* of the Babylonian map (Horowitz 1998: 299, 325).

In fact, Glassner (1984:18, 25–26) understands the title king of the four quarters as emphatically referring to the eccentric, outlandish, or "fabulous" lands that lie beyond ordinary human reach, in contrast to the term *kiššatu*, which represents the totality of the center and the lands immediately around it that recognize the authority of the sovereign, again in a way the *oikoumene*. Glassner even sees a tension between the two conceptions of territorial rule, opposing the idea that the two terms were more or less equivalent (1984:30). In his view, *kiššatu* and *kibrāt arba'im* both had the vocation to stretch their zones against one another to occupy the entire surface of the earth all by themselves.

Whether or not the territories suggested by each title are as clearly defined as Glassner might think, the edges of the *oikoumene* and what lies beyond, the *nagû*, are clear players in the construction of royal ideology in ancient Mesopotamia. In this respect, if one is King of the Four Quarters, one is not simply a king who rules over the known world, but one who is emphatically claiming familiarity with and power over the "fabulous" lands and dimensions beyond the *oikoumene* as well.

HENRY CORBIN'S *MUNDUS IMAGINALIS* AS A PARADIGM FOR ANCIENT MESOPOTAMIAN THOUGHT

I hope to have highlighted in the foregoing how complex, and at times opaque, a body of lore the ancient Near Eastern understanding of the geographic environment is (Glassner 1984:19; Liverani 1990:46–47). What we might today deem the "fabulous" or "fantastic" was also clearly a fundamental component in this body of knowledge. In an attempt to probe further the role and nature of the "fabulous" in this picture, I should like to appeal to the scholarship of the Islamicist Henry Corbin, concentrating on the writings and philosophy of the 12th century CE Persian scholar Suhrawardi, who pursued "the aim of reviving in Islam the wisdom, the theosophia, of ancient Persia" (Corbin 1977:52). What Corbin emphasizes in Suhrawardi's cosmology and metaphysics is the presence of a concrete and "real" intermediate world that lies between ordinary sensory perception and pure intelligence, for which he coins the Latin phrase *mundus imaginalis*:

> Between the two is placed an intermediate world, which our authors designate as *'ālam al-mithāl*, the world of the Image, *mundus imaginalis*: a world as ontologically real as the world of the senses and the world of the intellect, a world that requires a faculty of perception belonging to it, a faculty that is a cognitive function, a *noetic* value, as fully real as the faculties of sensory perception or intellectual intuition. This faculty is the imaginative power, the one we must avoid confusing with the imagination that modern man identifies with "fantasy" and that, according to him, produces only the "imaginary." (Corbin 1995:9)

In his analyses, Corbin often underscores the substantial and corporeal nature of this intermediate, or "imaginal" world, which can be summarized through two direct quotations from his works:

> This eighth climate, this world in the subtle state, which includes many degrees, and which is impenetrable by the sensory organs, is the *real* place of all psycho-spiritual events (visions, charismas, thaumaturgical

actions breaching the physical laws of space and time), which are considered simply as imaginary—that is, as unreal—so long as one remains in the rational dilemma which is restricted to a choice between the two terms of banal dualism, "matter" or "spirit," corresponding to that other one: "history" or "myth." (1977:78–79)

Let us emphasize then, that this does not mean knowing things as abstract idea, as philosophical concept, but as the perfectly individuated features of their Image, meditated, or rather premeditated, by the soul, namely their archetypal Image. That is why in this intermediate world there are Heavens and Earths, animals, plants, and minerals, cities, towns, and forests. (1977:81)[9]

Furthermore, Corbin points out the thoroughly "imaginal" nature of the Mazdean scheme for the geography of the earth, gleaned from the much later Zoroastrian sources of the 9th–10th centuries CE, morphologically quite comparable to the Babylonian *mappa mundi*. According to this scheme, the entire surface of the earth comprises seven *keshvars*, "zones of the *Terra Firma*," with the central *keshvar* surrounded by the cosmic ocean, beyond which are located six other *keshvars*, which "actually correspond to *mythical* regions" (Corbin 1977:17–18; see also Boyce 1984:16–17). Corbin pinpoints the central *keshvar*, the Xvaniratha, as "the cradle or seed of the Aryans (= Iranians)" and of the Mazdean religion whence it spread into the other *keshvars*: "there will be born the last of the Saoshyants [saviors], who will reduce Ahriman to impotence and bring about the resurrection and the existence to come" (1977:19). One may certainly think in this vein of Babylon as the center of the *mappa mundi* and the heroic position of Marduk against the agents of chaos in his reorganization of the cosmos, the chief event commemorated and reenacted in the Babylonian New Year's festival as well. One should note, however, how much more organic and "realistic" the Babylonian map appears in contrast to the neatly symmetrical configuration of Corbin's map, and yet the same concentric visual statement is nevertheless very much in the Babylonian scheme as well.

In Corbin's view, this Iranian *Imago Terrae* is not a depiction of "positive geography," but rather "an instrument for meditation that makes it possible to reach the center, the *medium mundi*, or rather to take position there directly" (1977:16). Thus, Corbin actually emphasizes concentration on the center, rather than dispersion away from it to the edges, the *keshvars*, which he sees as originating from the center. It is hence the center that determines the location, direction, and orientation of the *keshvars*: "This was, for example, the meaning of the art and structure of gardens in Iran (it is known that our word *paradise* originated from a Medean word, *pairiadaeza*). That is why it can be said that the representation of the Earth with its seven *keshvars* as an archetype-Figure is an instrument for meditation. It is offered as a *mandala*" (1977:20–21).

After this basic overview of Corbin's premises of an "imaginal" world, I should like to suggest that we take them as a model in approaching the geographic lores of the ancient world as well. In other words, it is possible that the idea of a *mundus imaginalis,* explained by medieval Islamic scholars such as Suhrawardi and Ibn al-Arabi (13th century CE), was present in one form or the other in the ancient Near East as well. I have already pointed out the episodes in the *Epic of Gilgamesh* taking place in locales that belong to the Jenseits, and it might now be more suitable to think of this Jenseits more specifically as the equivalent of this intermediate domain, the *mundus imaginalis*.

We might think of the *nagû* of the Babylonian *mappa mundi* as regions of the ancient Mesopotamian counterpart of the *mundus imaginalis* as well. From this standpoint, what has been emphasized earlier as the central *oikoumene*, the inhabited familiar world, is, in accordance with Corbin's system, also the center governing the *nagû* of the Babylonian map. In ancient Near Eastern imperial ideologies, making the center itself encompassing the outlandish, the exotic, or even the "fabulous" may have been meaningful from this very philosophical perspective. In a typical ancient Mesopotamian idiom, the Babylonian *mappa mundi* may be thought of as managing simultaneously to be both a map with references to specific places and some sort of *mandala* for the contemplation of the supernatural knowledge embedded in it.

Even though there is no clearly delineated idea of a "paradise" in ancient Mesopotamian religion, clues exist as to the presence of certain "golden age" qualities attached to certain locales, such as the place where Utnapishtim is settled after the Flood, whether it is the so-called mouth of the rivers of the Standard Babylonian version of the *Epic of Gilgamesh* or the Dilmun of the *Sumerian Flood Story*, or domains associated with Enki described in other Sumerian texts such as *Enki and Ninhursag* and *Enmerkar and the Lord of Aratta* (Alster 1983:54–58). The relationship between Utnapishtim and Enki/Ea and his abode, the Apsu, clearly expressed in the Flood Story of the Standard Babylonian version of the *Epic of Gilgamesh* (George 2003, 1:523–24), can also be taken as a further clue as to the existence in ancient Mesopotamian thought of places analogous to the Greek Islands of the Blessed or Elysium.

In ancient Greece, as well, certain "fabulous" places display certain "golden age" elements, especially the lands of the Hyperboreans and Ethiopians, with climatic privileges and a superabundance of food, respectively (Romm 1992:64–65). Plato's Atlantis, too, as a land now lost and out of sight, is described as "paradisical and divinely blessed, as if to equate the geographic limits imposed by the Mediterranean with mankind's exclusion from the world of the golden age" (Romm 1992:127; on Atlantis, see also Griffiths 1991:8–11).

THE FLORA AND FAUNA OF DISTANT LANDS IN MIDDLE ASSYRIAN IMPERIALISM

The ancient Mesopotamian and Egyptian visual traditions could not have been devoid of this important "imaginal" component, as I tried to argue in the previous discussion, especially in visual representations of flora, fauna, landscape, and architecture. In dealing with examples from ancient Mesopotamia and Egypt side by side, we should keep in mind that a sense of the "imaginal" would have been a shared player in the cultural expressions of both civilizations, especially in the Late Bronze Age and Iron Age, as were certain other structures such as the center versus periphery and the native versus the foreign. I would submit that in the ancient Near East, the "imaginal" domain in the cosmos would have been expressed primarily through the medium of the exotic, the foreign, and the "paradisical."

In tracing elements of the "imaginal" in Assyria, one should start with the royal inscriptions and monuments of the Middle Assyrian Period. The royal inscriptions of Tiglath-Pileser I provide one of the earliest and richest bodies of texts that mention elements of the exotic in Assyria. In addition to mentioning his slaying bulls, lions, and elephants, this king boasts of having collected foreign plants and trees, and having gathered flocks and herds of wild beasts from different military campaigns (Tiglath-pileser I A.0.87.1: vi 105-vii 27 [Grayson 1991:26–27]).[10] Tiglath-Pileser I also mentions marching to Lebanon and obtaining certain trees and exotic animals:

> By the command of the gods Anu and Adad, the great gods, my lords, I marched to Mount Lebanon. I cut down (and) carried off cedar beams for the temple of the gods Anu [and Adad], the great gods, my lords. I continued to the land Amurru (and) conquered the entire land [Amur]ru. I received tribute from the city Arvad (and) the lands Byblos (and) Sidon (and) a crocodile (and) a large female monkey of the sea coast. Finally, upon my return I became lord of the entire land Hatti (and) imposed upon Ini-Tešub, king of the land Hatti, tax, tribute, and (impost consisting of) cedar beams. (Tiglath-pileser I A.087.4: 24-30 [Grayson 1991:42])

Monkeys and elephants are also among the animals depicted on the Black Obelisk of Shalmaneser III from the Neo-Assyrian period, in great likelihood in association with the idea of the distant lands, as discussed below.

Among the most interesting accounts of Tiglath-Pileser I is his fashioning of certain animal figurines and setting them up at his palace entrance at Assur:

> I made replicas in basalt of a *nāhiru*, which is called a sea-horse (and) which by the command of the gods Ninurta and Nergal, the great gods, my lords, I had killed with a *harpoon* of my own making in the [(Great)] Sea [of the land] Amurru, (and) of a live *burhiš* which was brought from the mountain/land Lumaš . . . on the other side of the land Habhu. I stationed (them) on the right and left at my [royal entrance]. (Tiglath-pileser I A.0.87.4: 67-71 [Grayson 1991:44, 57]; see also Harmanşah 2005:126–27)[11]

"Fragments of these figurines with traces of inscriptions were found by the German excavators at the palace entrance..." (Grayson 1991:39). There is also an interest in Neo-Assyrian palaces in fantastic creatures that incorporate fish scales, especially in the Northwest Palace of Ashurnasirpal II, in the form of *lamassu* at doorways (Paley and Sobolewski 1987: Pl. 3). In the Palace of Sargon II (721–705 BCE) at Khorsabad certain mythical creatures, a fish-man (*kulullû*), a winged bull, and a *lamassu* are shown floating in the water in a relief scene that depicts the transportation of timber, possibly cedar from Lebanon (Fig. 13.3). In fact, this scene is a perfect example of how the "fabulous" often permeates even what we might deem the most immediately mundane and documentary of the reliefs.

13.3. Detail of marine scene with transport of wood showing a winged human-headed bull (*lamassu*). Panel 2, Façade n, Palace of Sargon II in Khorsabad. Paris, Louvre. Photo: author.

13.4. Detail of marine scene with transport of wood showing a winged bull (Bull of Heaven?). Panel 2, Façade n, Palace of Sargon II in Khorsabad. Paris, Louvre. Photo: author.

The Middle Assyrian interest in the exotic and the foreign can also be encountered in the so-called Broken Obelisk, "which was found at Nineveh but originally must have been erected in Assur . . . The stela was almost certainly made during the reign of Ashur-bel-kala, as shown by close parallels between passages in its text and in the annals" (Grayson 1991:99). Following the lead of the annals of Tiglath-Pileser I, Ashur-bel-kala's (1073–1056 BCE) annalistic text on the Broken Obelisk, too, contains a lengthy and detailed description of the royal hunt. The lengthy hunt passage, which cites different geographic areas including Mount Lebanon, the land of Hatti, understood by the Assyrians as the Syro-Hittite realm, and mountains in the East, as well as wild animals, culminates in the following statement:

> He formed (herds) of dromedaries, bred (them), (and) displayed herds of them to the people of his land. The king of Egypt sent a large female monkey, a crocodile, (and) a "river-man," beasts of the Great Sea. The remainder of the numerous animals and the winged birds of the sky, wild game which he acquired, their names are not written with these animals, their numbers are not written with these numbers. (Aššur-bēl-kala A.0.89.7: iv 27-33 [Grayson 1991:103–4])

Again, the mention of a monkey and exotic aquatic creatures, including a "river man," may be taken as an indication of an Assyrian interest in lands beyond the *oikoumene*. Even though these aspects of the text do not find expression in the relief carved on the surviving portion of the monument, the obelisk form in Assyrian imperial art, with its quadrilateral morphology and ziggurat-shaped top, is hardly noted with regard to its cosmological significance. As is the case with the royal title King of the Four Quarters, with its four sides and annalistic component, the obelisk form, too, must have been in reference not only to the *oikoumene* but also to all the lands beyond it, over which the imperial administration claimed influence.

THE FLORA AND FAUNA OF DISTANT LANDS IN EGYPTIAN IMPERIALISM

Aspects of the outlandish, both in terms of flora and fauna, can also be encountered in ancient Egypt during the New Kingdom (ca. 1550–1070 BCE). Even though no archaeological evidence exists for the *'ntyw* trees, frankincense or myrrh, planted by Hatshepsut in the terraces of her temple at Deir el-Bahri, both textual and visual accounts speak to an interest on her part to incorporate the source of this prized exotic commodity into Thebes, the center, and she may not have been the first Egyptian king to have done so (Dixon 1968:56, 58; Hugonot 1989:69, 72; Wilkinson 1998:47–48). The whole effort of bringing aspects of Punt into Egypt, which also continued beyond Hatshepsut, plays into the idea of bringing out in the center of the *oikoumene* those prized traits and privileges of the edges of the earth, as Hatshepsut's own inscription states: "I made for him [Amun-Re] a Punt in his garden, just as he commanded me for Thebes" (Hugonot 1989:72; Wilkinson 1998:72).[12] In fact, beyond questions of disease and alterity, even the figure of the fat queen of Punt in Hatshepsut's Deir el-Bahri reliefs may be understood, in highly codified terms, as one of the visual signifiers of the "imaginal" world that Punt represents. This perception of Punt would certainly not have competed with this country's being a real trading partner with Egyptian administrations.

Romm mentions how among the ancient Greeks, in addition to the conventional ethnocentrism encountered in all ancient Near Eastern cultures, there also existed a reversal of this view (1992:46–48):

Ethnocentrism, in the most literal sense of the word, denotes a construct of space which sees the center of the world as the best or most advanced location, and therefore demotes distant peoples to the status of unworthy savages. An inversion of this scheme, by contrast, privileges the edges of the earth over the center ... [T]he inverse or negative ethnocentric scheme envisions foreigners growing not less but more virtuous in proportion to their distance from the Greek center ...

[W]hether these outermost tribes—among them the Ethiopians, Hyperboreans, Arimaspians, Scythians, and *Kunokephaloi*—were imagined in terms of "soft" or "hard" versions of primitive life, their extreme distance seemed to the Greeks to confer on them a unique ethical prerogative, licensing them to mock, preach to, or, simply ignore the peoples of the interior. In their eyes "normal" human values, as defined by those who imagine themselves at the privileged center, can appear arbitrary and even laughably absurd.

An inversion of ethnocentrism may well have been present in the ancient Egyptian attitudes to Punt, which could not have been as simple as seeing it as a source of bounty that could be exploited for its raw materials and exotic resources.

Another ancient Egyptian example, the so-called Botanical Room of Thutmose III (Eighteenth Dynasty, 1479–1425 BCE) at Karnak pertains to recording exotic flora and fauna in the New Kingdom. This room is located inside the Festival Hall, the Akhmenu, a temple "with the theme of regeneration" (Bell 1997:158), built by Thutmose III inside the great temple of Amun at Karnak in order to commemorate his and Amun-Re's universal rule, especially in association with Thutmose's western Asian campaigns. The room constitutes a vestibule to the cella of the Akhmenu, and bears on its walls representations in relief sculpture of the flora and fauna of the Egyptian *oikoumene* and those encountered by Thutmose III during his wide-ranging campaigns outside Egypt (Fig. 13.5). These depictions presented a virtual garden and zoo of plants and creatures that existed within and outside Egypt.

It is not clear if Thutmose brought specimens of all the foreign plants and animals to the center, or if he simply had them represented by his

13.5. Relief decorations in the Botanical Room of the Festival Hall (Akhmenu) of Thutmose III. Temple of Amun, Karnak, Thebes, Egypt. Photo: James Morris/Art Resource, NY.

artists (Hugonot 1989:40). The accuracy of the depictions is without question, however, as is an interest in geography, since the plants are grouped by geographic area—Egypt, Syria, the Mediterranean islands, and Arabia (Hugonot 1989:40). Rather than a catalogue of war booty, the whole configuration again betrays an interest in the *oikoumene* and its edges, and hence an interest in expressing the universality of Amun's divine and Thutmose's imperial rule (Hugonot 1989:42; Bell 1997:158). Furthermore, the fact that these representations are inside a temple may again be thought to bring to the fore an important contemplative element in representations that pertain to flora, fauna, and landscape.[13] Such royal catalogues of flora seem to have been an international phenomenon in the ancient Near East, as we find them in the Neo-Assyrian period as well. In describing the canal that he dug from the Upper Zab to the gardens of Nimrud, Ashurnasirpal II, too, lists on his so-called Banquet Stele the trees and plants that he encountered in the "lands through which [he] marched and the highlands which [he] traversed" (Ashurnasirpal II A.0.101.30: 36b-52 [Grayson 1991:290]).[14]

THE "IMAGINAL" IN THE ART OF ASHURNASIRPAL II AND SHALMANESER III

With such depictions of trees, plants, and animals, in addition to the exotic, both Egyptian and Assyrian cultures may have addressed the element of the "paradisical," again in this term's significance as an ordinarily inaccessible ideal domain on the *terra firma*. A visual example from the Middle Assyrian period is the ivory pyxis from Assur Tomb 45, an elite burial considered to date to the period shortly before or shortly after Tukulti-Ninurta I (1243–1207 BCE) (Moortgat 1969:113) (Fig. 13.5).[15] As far as the landscape scene on the pyxis is concerned, Paul Collins (2006:101–2) has aptly drawn attention to the alternation between coniferous trees, native to the lands around Assyria, and the fruit-bearing date palm, at home in Babylonia but not in Assyria, with hens perched on the female date palms and roosters on the conifers.

While Collins has approached this imagery from the perspective of gender and symbolism of abundance,[16] also valid in many such instances is the creation of an "imaginal" landscape, a landscape that suggests an extraordinary spatial dimension. This latter aspect would in fact not conflict with the idea of fertility and abundance, since understood on another plane, both fertility and abundance would have connotations of regeneration, especially noteworthy in a funerary context. While we certainly do not have explicit accounts of ideas of postmortem rebirth in another realm in ancient Mesopotamia, ideas of death and immortality are certainly at home in the *Epic of Gilgamesh*, some of whose settings, especially those that are most relevant to the questions of death and eternal life, are "imaginal," as already emphasized. Corbin, too, stresses how it is the *mundus imaginalis* that enables the resurrection in esoteric Islam (1977:96).

13.6. Drawing of the ivory pyxis found in Assur Tomb 45. Photo: after Haller 1954: Abb. 161.

It is at the very beginning of the Neo-Assyrian Period, with Ashurnasirpal II's moving the capital from Assur to Nimrud and building a new palace there, that we see the rhetoric of abundance and fertility attain a high point. The combination of the conceptual aspects of the date palm and the cone is almost ubiquitous in the state apartments of the palace, through the Assyrian "sacred tree" and the antediluvian sages holding fir cones, constantly signaling ideas of regeneration and the "paradisical." In this instance, the "paradisical" is very much tied to the idea of an antediluvian cosmos and with the Apsu as the seat of the antediluvian privileges ideologically in the possession of the Neo-Assyrian court scholars (Ataç 2006) (Figs. 13.1 and 13.6). In this respect, the fact that the Apsu is a blessed land that is on the one hand part of the earth but on the other ordinarily unreachable and inaccessible places it in the same status as the lands beyond the *oikoumene*.

If my understanding of the Assyrian "sacred tree" as an embodiment of the Apsu and the antediluvian cosmos (Ataç 2006) has validity, then in

"Imaginal" Landscapes in Assyrian Imperial Monuments   405

13.7. The Assyrian "sacred tree" flanked by two bird-headed *apkallus*, Room I, Northwest Palace of Ashurnasirpal II at Nimrud. British Museum, ANE 124583. Photo: author.

the Northwest Palace, we see a perfect example of how the center of an *oikoumene*, the capital city of an empire, ideologically takes on the characteristics of the lands beyond the *oikoumene* and becomes the veritable center of the latter. In other words, with its persistent emphasis on the Assyrian "sacred tree" and the antediluvian sages, the Northwest Palace is the setting for an "imaginal" landscape executed in carved orthostat reliefs (Fig. 13.7).

The narrative art of Shalmaneser III is perhaps the most emblematic of all the Neo-Assyrian kings, with battles absent from his fortress-palace (*ekal mašarti*) known as Fort Shalmaneser, even though such scenes abound in his bronze gates from Balawat. In relief sculpture, Shalmaneser's emphasis is rather on scenes of tributaries bringing gifts and exotica, as well as on scenes of submission and reconciliation. I would argue that the "imaginal" finds expression in the art of Shalmaneser III both in its "paradisical" manifestation, in the form of an elaborate "sacred tree" depicted on the glazed-brick panel in Fort Shalmaneser (Reade 1963), and in its manifestation of the exotic, in some of the registers of the so-called Black Obelisk, discovered by Layard at Nimrud (Fig. 13.8).

The geographic picture presented by the Black Obelisk has been analyzed by Michelle Marcus (1987:89), who concludes that by showing submission and tribute from a variety of different geographic areas, the obelisk presents "a statement of the expansion of Assyria's commercial network under Shalmaneser, and of the maintenance of economic prosperity through access to a wide range of foreign raw materials and goods."[17] Marcus emphasizes that the "organizing principle" of some of Shalmaneser's monuments is geographic rather than chronological (1987:81), even though she does not always lay out how each register of these compositions fits in a coherent geographic scheme.

Each individual register on the obelisk is identified by an epigraph, but there is no extant longer text that surveys the relevant campaigns associated with these scenes of tribute. As Marcus points out, not every toponym mentioned in the captions of the Black Obelisk has been identified for certain, and her own geographic reconstructions of Shalmaneser's monuments often leave certain matters unaccounted for. As such, in this monument, too, we lack some of the important parameters that would guide us in understanding the relevant design principles. Without attempting to propose a new reading

13.8. One side of the Black Obelisk of Shalmaneser III found at Nimrud. British Museum, ANE 118885. Photo: author.

"Imaginal" Landscapes in Assyrian Imperial Monuments 407

13.9. Detail of Figure 13.8. Photo: author.

of the Black Obelisk, I should like to build on the emphasis on geography provided by Marcus, and suggest that in addition to commercial and territorial implications, the monument may be an expression of the rule of Shalmaneser over lands bordering on, or beyond, the Assyrian *oikoumene*, as again enhanced by the obelisk form.

In addition to the two-humped Bactrian camels, not part of the native Mesopotamian fauna, depicted on the uppermost register, the third register from the top all around the obelisk seems to have been devoted exclusively to exotic animals. Two tributaries wearing headbands are shown in the act of leading apes that look more humanoid and somewhat disproportionate in comparison to the apes shown in the well-known composition on the façade of Ashurnasirpal's throne-room (D-5, Meuszynski 1981–1992: Tafel 5) (Fig.

13.9). Along the same register-level, but on the other faces of the obelisk, are represented further horned animals, and what look like humanoid quadrupeds (Fig. 13.10). In the epigraph that accompanies this register, Shalmaneser III declares: "I received tribute from Egypt: two-humped camels, a water buffalo (lit. "a river ox"), a *rhinoceros*, an antelope, female elephants, female monkeys, (and) apes" (Shalmaneser III A.0.102.89 [Grayson 1996:150]).

Even though the animals mentioned in the caption are all natural animals, and they match those shown on the register, an element of the fantastic may nevertheless have been incorporated into this representation, perhaps apparent in the unusually human-looking depictions of the apes. Catherine Breniquet (2002:167) suggests that "no artistic stereotype" existed in ancient Mesopotamia for such unusual animals, and that "artists caught sight of them at a specific event. The image they tried to reconstruct from memory is far from nature, as these animals appear as more monstrous than natural."[18]

Rather than artistic incompetence, however, it is perhaps the case that this register of the Black Obelisk was meant to make a deliberate allusion to the idea of the fauna of distant lands, and hence to a mythical domain, given how such animals are

13.10. Detail of one side of the Black Obelisk of Shalmaneser III found at Nimrud. British Museum, ANE 118885. Photo: author.

"Imaginal" Landscapes in Assyrian Imperial Monuments 409

13.11. Detail of Figure 10. Photo: author.

lacking in the rest of the registers (Figs. 13.12, 13.13). As already mentioned, Assyrian kings are known to have brought home hyenas, panthers, red deer, lions, monkeys, ostriches, and gazelles with them from their campaigns and placed these animals in royal zoological parks. As Horowitz (1998:36) also suggests, these creatures may have been considered as the fauna of distant lands. The rhetoric of the strange and wondrous plants and beasts brought back by Assyrian kings, such as Sennacherib, also "included trees that bore wool for making clothing instead of food to eat ... and *pagû* and *pagītu* 'male and female monkeys,' which are depicted in Neo-Assyrian reliefs with almost-human heads, hands, and feet, but animal bodies" (Horowitz 1998:330; see also Aynard 1972:51; Breniquet 2002:167; and Foster 2002:286).

Shalmaneser's interest in the edges of the *oikoumene* is further clear in his (re)visiting the so-called Source of the Tigris and leaving his image and inscription there next to those of Tiglath-Pileser I (Shalmaneser III A.0.102.6: ii 34-40 [Grayson 1996:37]). In addition to the sources of the rivers, both the land of Hatti and the Amanus range seem to have been reference points for the Neo-Assyrian kings in delineating their domain in the Northwest, as Shalmaneser III proclaims: "Conqueror from the upper and lower seas to the land Nairi and the great sea of the west as far as the Amanus range: I gained dominion over the entire land Hatti. I (lit. 'he') conquered from the source of the Tigris to the source of the Euphrates" (Shalmaneser III A.0.102.6: iv 26-30 [Grayson 1996:41]). Both the Amanus range and the land of Hatti are also sources of inspiration especially for the Sargonid kings in creating their royal gardens and the columned porticoes associated with them (Oppenheim 1965:331–32; Stronach 1989:477–78; Thomason 2001:80; Novák 2002:447). This foreign element in the creation of such pleasure gardens may again be thought

13.12. One side of the Black Obelisk of Shalmaneser III found at Nimrud. British Museum, ANE 118885. Photo: author.

13.13. Detail of Figure 12. Photo: author.

to stand for the "imaginal" in these enclosures of flora, fauna, and architecture.

THE "IMAGINAL" LANDSCAPES OF SENNACHERIB AND ASHURBANIPAL

The rhetoric of incorporating the flora and produce of "all the lands" into royal gardens, the *kirimāḫu*, is most pronounced in the inscriptions and art of the Sargonids, especially Sennacherib and Ashurbanipal. In addition to

Sennacherib's Bavian inscription, which includes an account of his botanical activities (Luckenbill 1989 [1926–1927]: no. 33), many other passages from the inscriptions of this king describe his public works at Nineveh with the leitmotifs of Mount Amanus and the "portico, patterned after a Hittite (Syrian) palace, which they call in the Amorite tongue a *bît-hilâni*":

> Beams of cedar, the product of Mount Amanus, which they dragged with difficulty out of (those) distant mountains, I stretched across their ceilings(?). Great door-leaves of cypress, whose odor is pleasant as they are opened and closed, I bound with a band of shining copper and set them up in their doors. A portico, patterned after a Hittite (Syrian) palace, which they call in the Amorite tongue a *bît-hilâni*, I constructed inside them (the doors), for my lordly pleasure. (Luckenbill 1989 [1926–1927]: no. 366)

13.14. One side of the Black Obelisk of Shalmaneser III found at Nimrud. British Museum, ANE 118885. Photo: author.

A great park, like unto Mount Amanus, wherein all kinds of herbs and fruit trees, trees, such as grow on the mountains and in Chaldea, as well as trees bearing wool, were set out, I planted by its (the palace's) side. (Luckenbill 1989 [1926–1927]: no. 368)

"Imaginal" Landscapes in Assyrian Imperial Monuments 413

The area of Nineveh, my royal city, I enlarged. I widened its squares and made it shine like the day. The outer wall I built and made it mountain high. Above the city and below the city I laid out parks. The wealth of mountains and all lands, all the herbs of the land of Hatti (Syria), myrrh plants, *among which fruitfulness was greater than their (natural) habitat,* all kinds of mountain vines, all the fruits of (all) lands (settlements), herbs and fruit-bearing trees I set out for my subjects. (emphasis added; Luckenbill 1989 [1926–1927]: no. 399)

I would once again posit that in addition to an imperial interest in foreign curiosities and matters of luxury, the persistent mention of Mount Amanus, the land of Hatti, and other outlandish elements in garden design and architecture in the inscriptions of the Sargonids would have contained specific and codified allusions to the edges of the *oikoumene*, what lies beyond them, and the "paradisical." The creation and representation of such pleasure gardens and their representation in the visual arts would hence have had a significant contemplative element, and cannot have been confined to an effort to depict the feats of an imperial ruler. Beyond hyperbole, the idea of these gardens' creating an even more fertile ground for foreign plants or trees than their original habitats can again be seen as an ideological effort to collect and bring out in the center all those elements inaccessible to ordinary space and time. The Assyrian imperial efforts to create a new center of the *oikoumene* in Assyria proper also find expression in Sennacherib's projects of making Nineveh the new Babylon and establishing a new ground for the Babylonian New Year's Festival in Assur, which also included a garden in association with the new *bīt-akitu* outside the city walls (Luckenbill 1989 [1926–1927]: nos. 434–451; Reade 1978:47; Dalley 1993:6; 1994:50; Thomason 2001:81–82; Frahm 2008:17).

As far as the visual record is concerned, I would like to submit that it is this particular ideological consciousness that should also guide our perception of the landscape scenes of the Sargonids, especially those that depict pleasure gardens in peaceful modes, such as the well-known slab of Ashurbanipal that not only shows a columned portico, which may be an example of the *bīt-ḫilāni* mentioned in the royal inscriptions, but also one of Sennacherib's aqueducts at a distance (Albenda 1976:49–53; Dalley 1993:9; 1994:51) (Fig. 13.10).

Other examples include the relief fragments of Ashurbanipal that show lions relaxing in the midst of flowers and vegetation[19] and the famous

13.15. Relief panel showing royal gardens. Panel 7, Room H, North Palace of Ashurbanipal at Nineveh. British Museum, ANE 124939. Photo: The Trustees of the British Museum / Art Resource, NY.

garden scene of Ashurbanipal, which was part of a larger relief composition depicting the aftermath of the battles with the Elamites (Albenda 1976). If the *bīt-ḫilāni* is indeed the kind of portico that appears in the reliefs of Ashurbanipal and those of Sargon II before him, the entrance portico of the North Palace of Ashurbanipal at Nineveh, too, should count as one. In fact, Pauline Albenda (1976:53) has suggested that the portico that appears on the relief slab that features the aqueduct on its background is the very entrance portico of the North Palace of Ashurbanipal (Fig. 13.15). Furthermore, even the orthostat slab tradition per se is one that belongs to the lands west and northwest of Assyria, namely Syria and the region of the Neo-Hittite states, in a continuum that reaches as far back as the Middle Bronze Age, the first half of the 2nd millennium BCE (Winter 1982, Harmanşah 2005). In this respect, even the physical building blocks of the Assyrian interior space, and not just decorative programs and representation, may have been loaded with certain allusions to the outlandish.

In light of the foregoing discussion, I find I am not satisfied with the interpretation of the well-known Garden Scene of Ashurbanipal (Fig. 13.16)

13.16. Detail of the "Garden Scene" of Ashurbanipal showing the king banqueting with his queen. Panel C, Room S1 ("fallen into S"), North Palace of Ashurbanipal at Nineveh. British Museum, ANE 124920. Photo: author.

as one in which it is the power of the king, especially in the aftermath of the war with the Elamites, that is conveyed as the primary message (Albenda 1977:44–45). The alternation between the fruit-bearing date palm and the coniferous trees on the background,[20] the grapevine, which must have had symbolic significance in ancient Egyptian art as well (Hugonot 1989:172–74),[21] and the decapitated head hanging from one of the trees, all resonate with death and decay on the one hand, and the "paradisical" on the other, presented within an overarching historical framework. The scene shows how much the idea of the emblematic landscape has changed over time within the Neo-Assyrian period. Long gone is the separation between the "sacred tree" and the historical reliefs of Ashurnasirpal II, and we now see the two domains of representation intertwined in a complex system of signification.

CONCLUSION

In the foregoing, I argued that Assyrian conceptions of geography, landscape, and the physical environment drew on a long-standing and international tradition of seeing the earth in its potential to give access to an "imaginal" domain above the ordinary senses, expressed primarily through landscapes, the exotic, and the foreign. Trees, plants, and animals that were not part of the native flora and fauna of Assyria not only referred to the expanse of the empire (Marcus 1995:193; Collins 2004:1), but also constituted an indication that rule was now extended to the edges of the *oikoumene* and even beyond, such that what used to be outside was now fully within, with the center now emerging as the veritable nucleus of the four quarters, the latter again understood in their capacity of including the "fabulous" lands. By stretching his rule to the edges of the *oikoumene* and beyond, and by coinciding the center of the four quarters with that of the *oikoumene*, the ideal ruler could also hope to bring about the transfiguration of the world, inaugurating a new "paradisical" dimension, or a golden age. The *pax assyriaca* expressed in monuments such as the Black Obelisk or the agrarian abundance signaled by the "sacred tree," as well as by the alternation of the date palm and the conifer in other Assyrian imperial monuments, would hence point toward the establishment of such an ideal imperial domain.

NOTES

13.1   For an analysis of the narrative scenes of the throne-room of Ashurnasirpal II, see Winter 1981 and 1983.

13.2   Horowitz (1998:32) suggests that "some Babylonians might have believed that the Sun never reached the northern skies because of the 'Great Wall.'"

13.3   I use the German word *Jenseits* following Cook, who suggests that "'world beyond' and 'otherworld' are in certain contexts too vague, and 'underworld,' and 'netherworld' are inaccurate as applied to Elysium."

13.4   See further Horowitz 1998:329, where it is stated that "[i]n the first millennium, all three lands occur in Neo-Assyrian inscriptions. Dilmun, which lies in the middle of the sea in the inscriptions of Assurbanipal, Sargon II, and Sennacherib, continues to be a name for Bahrain, but Magan and Meluhha are moved from the Persian Gulf to the borders of Egypt."

13.5   The identity of the center certainly changes from period to period, since in the inscriptions of Naram-Sin (2254–2218 BCE), the center was represented by the capital Agade (Glassner 1984:18).

13.6   The representatives of the "Upper Sea" were not fixed either. Liverani (1990:53) points out how each time a large lake was reached on the northern side of the Mesopotamian alluvium, "it was considered as a representative of the 'Upper Sea':

this is the case with Lake Van already in the middle Assyrian period, and will eventually be the case with Lake Urmia and with the Caspian Sea." See also Marcus 1987:88.

13.7 "The relationship between the Apsu and the sea on the earth's surface is not completely clear. Many passages in Akkadian texts suggest that the two were identical in some way, physically connected, or that the deep part of the ocean was called *apsû*" (Horowitz 1998:34).

13.8 According to Horowitz (1998:103–4), "[a] belief that the distant reaches of the ocean were connected with death may derive from the notion that one could pass directly into the underworld through the waters of the far reaches of the sea, just as the sun appears to rise and set directly from/into the ocean by the seashore." For the idea of a single mythical narrative's exhibiting features both of Elysium and Hades in ancient Greek literature, see Cook 1992:239-240.

13.9 The phrase "imaginal" is a well-established term in the study of the works of Suhrawardi and Ibn al-Arabi. In this respect, see also Chittick 1989, esp. pp. 112–24, and idem 1994.

13.10 On the horticultural activities of the Middle Assyrian kings, see also Oppenheim 1965:331; Stronach 1989:476; Dalley 1993:3–4.

13.11 Gelb et al. (1956–2006) defines *nāhiru* and *burhiš* as "whale" and "a wild foreign ox"; whereas Black, George, and Postgate 2000 define the same words as "dolphin" and "buffalo," respectively.

13.12 Wilkinson (1998:85–86) stresses that Hatshepsut's inscription does not clarify where exactly the trees were planted, her temple to Amun at Deir el-Bahri, her own funerary temple, and the temple of Amun at Karnak all being possibilities: "Her mention of creating a 'Punt' does not indicate what characteristic of Punt she had in mind: whether the terraces or the type of trees, or a combination of both."

13.13 Jean-Claude Hugonot (1989:45) indicates that the "botanical garden" of Thutmose III and the complex spatial access to it underscore the mysterious and "Amunian" aspect of the monument. The representations of the plants and animals enhance the directionality toward the main shrine of the temple.

13.14 Oppenheim (1965:331) argues that the efforts of Middle Assyrian kings such as Tiglath-Pileser I to collect exotic flora was for "utilitarian" purposes, as it was the Sargonids who turned this endeavor into one of display and prestige, replacing the ancient term for garden, *kirû*, with *kirimāḫu*. I would nevertheless maintain that even the Middle Assyrian kings' statements about the creation of the gardens that included foreign flora would have had ideological implications. See also Stronach 1989:476–77, which endorses Oppenheim's view.

13.15 For a recent study of the artifacts found in this tomb, see Feldman 2006.

13.16 On the symbolism of agrarian abundance in the Neo-Assyrian visual record, see Winter 2003.

13.17 The first register from the top on the Black Obelisk shows the tribute from Gilzanu, in northwestern Iran, and the second the submission of Jehu of Israel, the farthest east and west that Shalmaneser had advanced, according to Marcus. The third register from the top is Muṣri, with uncertain identification, and the fourth Suhi, "securely identified with modern Ana on the middle Euphrates." The last register is Patina or Unqi, "situated in the far west, also an important trade road—a land route leading south to the cities of the Phoenician seacoast and northwest to the principal metal sources in Asia Minor" (Marcus 1987:89).

13.18 In this regard, see also Lion 1992:360, where the discrepancy between the animals cited in the inscriptions and those shown on the monument is noted.

13.19 For an illustration, see Barnett 1976: pl. 15.

13.20 See Collins 2004:2–3, which also points out the fruiting date palm to the right of Ashurbanipal, indicating that "palms are prone to die from frost and do not bear fruit" in the climate of Assyria. Whereas Collins suggests that the setting for the scene is Elam or Babylonia, whose climates are more suitable for date palm cultivation, I would again draw attention to the ideological dimension of this representation in its reflecting the notion of the center's providing a new, and perhaps even better, habitat for foreign flora.

13.21 Hugonot, however, does not indicate what the symbolism of the vine in ancient Egypt would have been. The presence of a religious significance behind the vine in Ashurbanipal's garden scene is noted by both Albenda (1974:14) and Collins (2004:3–4).

REFERENCES

Albenda, P. 1974. Grapevines in Ashurbanipal's Garden. *Bulletin of the American Schools of Oriental Research* 215:5–17.

———. 1976. Landscape Bas-Reliefs in the *Bīt-Ḫilāni* of Ashurbanipal. *Bulletin of the American Schools of Oriental Research* 224:49–72.

———. 1977. Landscape Bas-Reliefs in the *Bīt-Ḫilāni* of Ashurbanipal. *Bulletin of the American Schools of Oriental Research* 225:29–48.

Alster, B. 1983. Dilmun, Bahrain, and the Alleged Paradise in Sumerian Myth and Literature. In *Dilmun: New Studies in the Archaeology and Early History of Bahrain*, ed. D.T. Potts, 39–75. Berlin: Dietrich Reimer Verlag.

Ataç, M.-A. 2006. Visual Formula and Meaning in Neo-Assyrian Relief Sculpture. *The Art Bulletin* 88:69–101.

Aynard, J.M. 1972. Animals in Mesopotamia. In *Animals in Archaeology*, ed. A.H. Brodrick, pp. 42–68. London: Barrie and Jenkins.

Barnett, R.D. 1976. *Sculptures from the North Palace of Ashurbanipal at Nineveh (668–627 B.C.)*. London: British Museum.

Bell, L. 1997. The New Kingdom "Divine" Temple: The Example of Luxor. In *Temples of Ancient Egypt*, ed. B.E. Shafer. Ithaca, NY: Cornell University Press.

Black, J. 1988. The Slain Heroes—Some Monsters of Ancient Mesopotamia. *The Bulletin of the Canadian Society for Mesopotamian Studies* 15:19–27.

Black, J., A. George, and N. Postgate, eds. 2000. *A Concise Dictionary of Akkadian*. Wiesbaden: Harrassowitz.

Boyce, M. 1984. *Textual Sources for the Study of Zoroastrianism*. Manchester: Manchester University Press.

Breniquet, C. 2002. Animals in Mesopotamian Art. In *A History of the Animal World in the Ancient Near East*, ed. B.J. Collins, pp. 145–68. Leiden: Brill.

Chittick, W.C. 1989. *The Sufi Path of Knowledge: Ibn al-Arabi's Metaphysics of Imagination*. Albany, NY: State University of NewYork Press.

———. 1994. *Imaginal Worlds: Ibn al-Arabi and the Problem of Religious Diversity*. Albany, NY: State University of New York Press.

Collins, P. 2004. The Symbolic Landscape of Ashurbanipal. *Source: Notes in the History of Art* 23(3): 1–6.

———. 2006. Trees and Gender in Assyrian Art. *Iraq* 68:99–108.

Cook, E. 1992. Ferrymen of Elysium and the Homeric Phaeacians. *The Journal of Indo-European Studies* 20:239–67.

———. 2004. Near Eastern Sources for the Palace of Alkinoos. *American Journal of Archaeology* 108:43–77.

Cooper, J.S. 1978. *The Return of Ninurta to Nippur. an-gim dím-ma*. AnOr 52. Roma: Pontificium Institutum Biblicum.

Corbin, H. 1977. *Spiritual Body and Celestial Earth: From Mazdean Iran to Shī'ite Iran*, trans. N. Pearson. Bollingen Series 91(2). Princeton, NJ: Princeton University Press.

———. 1995. *Swedenborg and Esoteric Islam,* trans. L. Fox. Swedenborg Studies 4. West Chester, PA: Swedenborg Foundation.

Dalley, S. 1993. Ancient Mesopotamian Gardens and the Identification of the Hanging Gardens of Babylon Resolved. *Garden History* 21:1–13.

———. 1994. Nineveh, Babylon and the Hanging Gardens: Cuneiform and Classical Sources Reconciled. *Iraq* 56:45–58.

Dixon, D.M. 1968. The Transplantation of Punt Incense Trees in Egypt. *JEA* 54:55–72.

Edzard, D.O. 1997. *Gudea and His Dynasty*. The Royal Inscriptions of Mesopotamia: Early Periods 3(1). Toronto: University of Toronto Press.

Feldman, M.H. 2006. Assur Tomb 45 and the Birth of the Assyrian Empire. *Bulletin of the American Schools of Oriental Research* 343:21–43.

Foster, B. 2002. Animals in Mesopotamian Literature. In *A History of the Animal World in the Ancient Near East*, ed. B.J. Collins, pp. 271–88. Leiden: Brill.

Frahm, E. 2008. The Great City: Nineveh in the Age of Sennacherib. *The Canadian Society for Mesopotamian Studies* 3:13–20.

Gelb, I.J., et al. 1956–2006. *The Assyrian Dictionary of the Oriental Institute of the University of Chicago*. Chicago: The Oriental Institute.

George, A.R. 2003. *The Babylonian Gilgamesh Epic: Introduction, Critical Edition and Cuneiform Texts*. 2 vols. Oxford: Oxford University Press.

Glassner, J.J. 1984. La division quinaire de la terre. *Akkadica* 40:17–34.

Grayson, A.K. 1991. *Assyrian Rulers of the Early First Millennium BC I (1114–859 BC)*. The Royal Inscriptions of Mesopotamia: Assyrian Periods 2. Toronto: University of Toronto Press.

———. 1996. *Assyrian Rulers of the Early First Millennium BC II (858–745 BC)*. The Royal Inscriptions of Mesopotamia: Assyrian Periods 3. Toronto: University of Toronto Press.

Gresseth, G.K. 1975. The Gilgamesh Epic and Homer. *The Classical Journal* 70:1–18.

Griffiths, J.G. 1991. Atlantis and Egypt. In *Atlantis and Egypt with Other Selected Essays* by J. G. Griffiths, pp. 3–30. Cardiff: University of Wales Press.

Haller, A. 1954. *Die Gräber und Grüfte von Assur*. Ausgrabungen der Deutschen Orient-Gesellschaft in Assur A. Baudenkmäler aus Assyrischer Zeit 7. Wissenschaftliche Veröffentlichung der Deutschen Orient-Gesellschaft 65. Berlin: Gebr. Mann.

Harmanşah, Ö. 2005. Eski Yakın Doğu'da Ortostatlı Yapıların Tektonik Estetiği ve Kültürel Bağlamı: Bölgeler-arası Paylaşılan Mimari bir Pratiğin Oluşumu. In *Eskiçağ'ın Mekanları / Zamanları / İnsanları: ODTÜ Mimarlık Tarihi Yüksek Lisans ve Doktora Programı Doktora Araştırmaları Sempozyumu III. 2-3 Haziran 2003, ODTÜ, Ankara*, ed. L. Özgenel, pp. 110–32. Istanbul: Homer.

———. 2007. Source of the Tigris: Event, Place and Performance in the Assyrian Landscapes of the Early Iron Age. *Archaeological Dialogues*. 14(2): 179–204.

Hornung, E. 1992. *Idea into Image: Essays on Ancient Egyptian Thought,* trans. E. Bredeck. New York: Timken Publishers.

Horowitz, W. 1998. *Mesopotamian Cosmic Geography*. Winona Lake, IN: Eisenbrauns.

Hugonot, J.-C. 1989. *Le jardin dans l'Egypte ancienne*. Europäische Hochschulschriften 27. Frankfurt am Main: Peter Land.

Janssen, J.M.A. 1951. Notes on the Geographical Horizon of the Ancient Egyptians. *Bibliotheca Orientalis* 8:213–17.

Kinnier Wilson, J.V., with H. Vanstiphout. 1979. *The Rebel Lands: An Investigation into the Origins of Early Mesopotamian Mythology*. Cambridge: Cambridge University Press.

Kitchen, K.A. 1971. Punt and How to Get There. *Orientalia* 40:184–203.

Kramer, S.N. 1944. Dilmun, the Land of the Living. *Bulletin of the American Schools of Oriental Research* 96:18–28.

Lion, B. 1992. La circulation des animaux exotiques au proche-orient antique. In *La circulation des biens, des personnes et des idées dans le proche-orient ancien: Actes de la XXXVIIIe Rencontre Assyriologique Internationale*, ed. D. Charpin and F. Joannès, pp. 357–65. Paris: Éditions Recherche sur les Civilisations.

Liverani, M. 1990. *Prestige and Interest: International Relations in the Near East ca. 1600–1100 B.C.* Padova: sargon srl.

_____. 2004. *Ritual and Politics in Ancient Mesopotamian History,* ed. and trans. Z. Bahrani and M. van de Mieroop. Ithaca: Cornell Univeristy Press.

Luckenbill, D.D. 1989 [1926–1927]. *Ancient Records of Assyria and Babylonia*. Vol. 2, *Historical Records of Assyria*. London: Histories and Mysteries of Man.

Marcus, M.I. 1987. Geography as an Organizing Principle in the Imperial Art of Shalmaneser III. *Iraq* 49:77–90.

_____. 1995. Geography as Visual Ideology: Landscape, Knowledge, and Power in Neo-Assyrian Art. In *Neo-Assyrian Geography*, ed. M. Liverani, pp. 193–202. Rome: Università di Roma, Dipartimento di scienze storiche, archeologiche e antropologiche dell'Antichità.

Meuszynski, J. 1981–1992. *Die Rekonstruktion der Reliefdarstellungen und ihrer Anordnung in Nordwespalast von Kalhu (Nimrud)*. Mainz am Rhein: P. von Zabern.

Moortgat, A. 1969. *The Art of Ancient Mesopotamia: The Classical Art of the Near East*. London: Phaidon.

Novák, M. 2002. The Artificial Paradise: Programme and Ideology of Royal Gardens. In *Sex and Gender in the Ancient Near East: Proceedings of the 47th Rencontre Assyriologique Internationale, Helsinki, July 2–6, 2001*, ed. S. Parpola and R.M. Whiting, pp. 443–60. Helsinki: The Neo-Assyrian Text Corpus Project.

Oppenheim, A.L. 1965. On Royal Gardens in Mesopotamia. *JNES* 24:328–33.

Paley, S., and R.P. Sobolewski. 1987. *The Reconstruction of the Relief Representations and Their Positions in the Northwest-Palace at Kalhu (Nimrud) II: (Rooms I. S. T. Z. West-Wing)*. Mainz am Rhein: P. von Zabern.

Pittman, H. 1996. The White Obelisk and the Problem of Historical Narrative in the Art of Assyria. *The Art Bulletin* 78:334–55.

Porter, B.N., ed. 2005. *Ritual and Politics in Ancient Mesopotamia*. New Haven, CT: American Oriental Society.

Reade, J.E. 1963. A Glazed-Brick Panel from Nimrud. *Iraq* 25:38–47.

Reade, J. 1978. Studies in Assyrian Geography. Part I: Sennacherib and the Waters of Nineveh. *Revue d'Assyriologie* 72:47–72.

Romm, J.S. 1992. *The Edges of the Earth in Ancient Thought: Geography, Exploration, and Fiction*. Princeton, NJ: Princeton University Press.

Smith, W.S. 1962. The Land of Punt. *JARCE* 1:59–60.

Stronach, D. 1989. The Royal Garden at Pasargadae: Evolution and Legacy. In *Archaeologia Iranica et Orientalis: Miscellanea in Honorem Louis vanden Berghe*, ed. L. de Meyer and E. Haernick, vol. 1, pp. 475–502. Gent: Peeters.

———. 1990. The Garden as a Political Statement: Some Case Studies from the Near East in the First Millennium B.C. *Bulletin of the Asia Institute* 4:171–80.

Thomason, A.K. 2001. Representations of the North Syrian Landscape in Neo-Assyrian Art. *Bulletin of the American Schools of Oriental Research* 323:63–96.

Uphill, E. 1967. The Nine Bows. *JEOL* 6:393–420.

Weidner, E.F. 1958. Die Feldzüge und Bauten Tiglatpilesers I. *AfO* 18:342–60.

Wicker, F.D.P. 1998. The Road to Punt. *The Geographical Journal* 164:155–67.

Wiggermann, F.A.M. 1992. *Mesopotamian Protective Spirits: The Ritual Texts*. Cuneiform Monographs 1. Groningen: Styx.

Wilkinson, A. 1998. *The Garden in Ancient Egypt*. London: The Rubicon Press.

Winter, I.J. 1981. Royal Rhetoric and the Development of Historical Narrative in Neo-Assyrian Reliefs. *Studies in Visual Communication* 7:2–39.

———. 1982. Art as Evidence for Interaction: Relations between the Assyrian Empire and North Syria. In *Mesopotamien und seine Nachbarn: politische und kulturelle Wechselbeziehungen im Alten Vorderasien vom 4. Bis 1. Jahrtausend v.*

Chr. XXV: Rencontre Assyriologique Internationale, Berlin, ed. H.-J. Nissen and J. Renger, pp. 355–82. Berlin: Dietrich Reimer Verlag.

———. 1983. The Program of the Throne-room of Assurnasirpal II. In *Essays on Near Eastern Art and Archaeology in Honor of Charles Kyrle Wilkinson*, ed. P.O. Harper and H. Pittman, pp. 15–31. New York: The Metropolitan Museum of Art.

———. 2003. Ornament and the "Rhetoric of Abundance" in Assyria. In *Archaeological, Historical and Geographical Studies in Honor of Hayim and Miriam Tadmor, Eretz-Israel 27*, pp. 252–64. Jerusalem: Israel Exploration Society.

Appendices

Appendix 1
Chronologies for Ancient Egypt and the Near East (ca. 5000 BC–AD 396)

CHRONOLOGY	EGYPT	MESOPOTAMIA	CHRONOLOGY
c. 5300–3000 BC	Predynastic Period	Ubaid Period	c. 5000–4000 BC
c. 3000–2690 BC	Early Dynastic Dynasties 1–2	Uruk Period	c. 4000–3100 BC
c. 2690–2180 BC	Old Kingdom Dynasties 3–6	Jemdet Nasr Period	c. 3100–2900 BC
c. 2180–2055 BC	First Intermediate Period Dynasties 7–11	Early Dynastic Period	c. 2900–2350 BC
c. 2055–1650 BC	Middle Kingdom Dynasties 11–13	Old Akkadian Period	c. 2350–2200 BC
c. 1650–1550 BC	Second Intermediate Period Dynasties 14–17	Gutian and Ur III Periods	c. 2200–2000 BC
c. 1550–1070 BC	New Kingdom Dynasties 18–20	Old Babylonian Period Old Assyrian Period	c. 2000–1500 BC
c. 1070–664 BC	Third Intermediate Period Dynasties 21–25	Middle Babylonian Period Middle Assyrian Period	c. 1500–1000 BC
c. 664–332 BC	Late Period Dynasties 26–30	Neo-Babylonian Period Neo-Assyrian Period	c. 1000–500 BC
c. 332–30 BC	Ptolemaic Period	Persian Period	c. 500–300 BC
c. 30 BC– AD 395	Roman Period	Seleucid Period	c. 300–150 BC

[NB: This chronology follows the approximate dates compiled for the Egyptian chronology in I. Shaw, ed., *The Oxford History of Ancient Egypt* (Oxford: Oxford University Press, 2000), pp. 479–83; the Mesopotamian chronology is adapted from M. Roaf, *Cultural Atlas of Mesopotamia and the Ancient Near East* (New York: Facts on File, 1996), pp. 8–9.]

Appendix 2
Map of Major Egyptian Sites

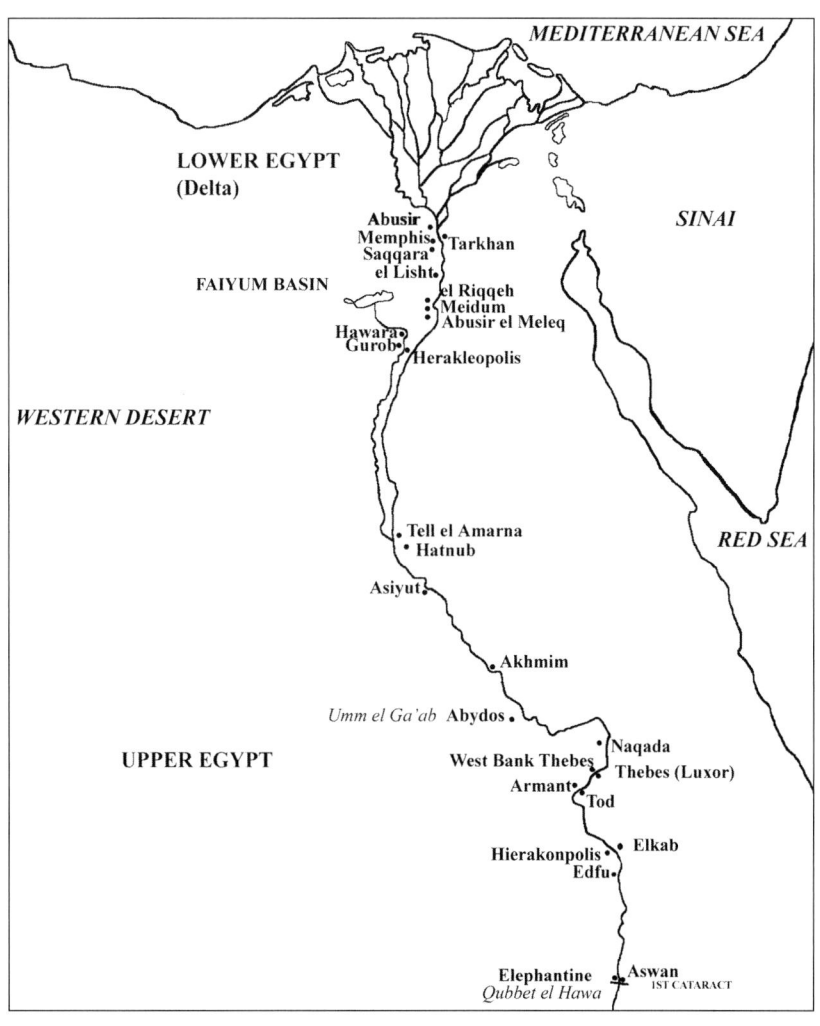

Appendix 3
Map of Major Mesopotamian Sites

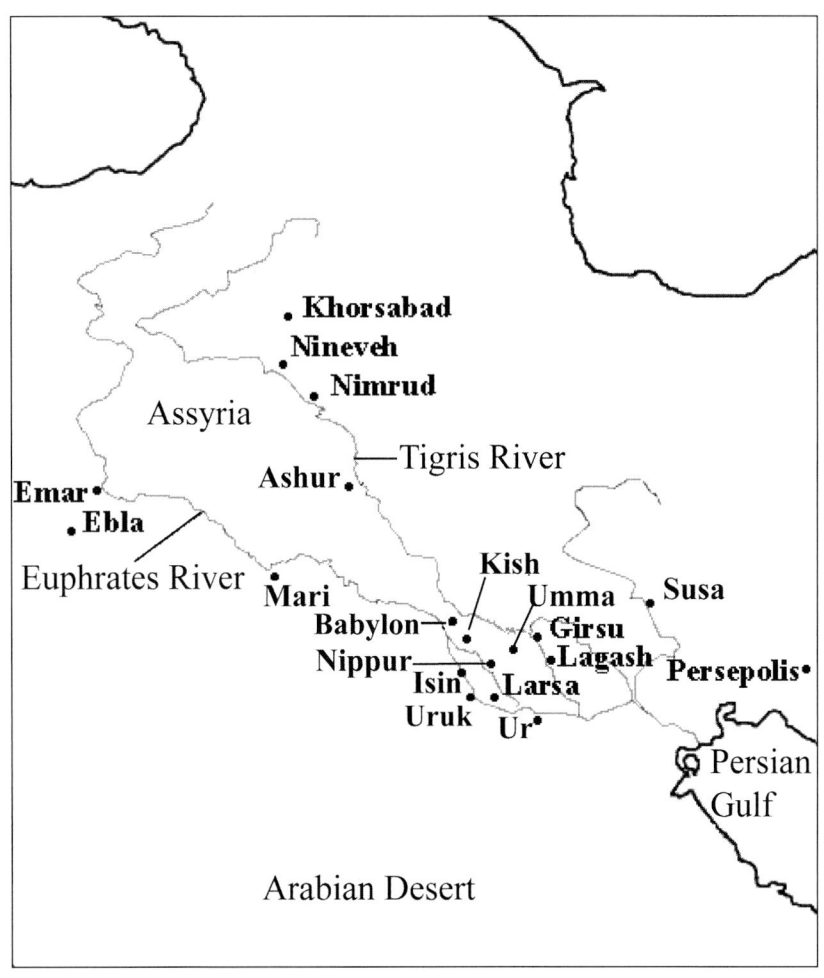

Index

A-bara-gi (king) 319
AbarSAL 78
Abi-eshuh 74, 75, 85
Abiešuh-kima-ilim 75
Abisko 211
Abu Rawash 262,
Abusir 201, 260, 262, 264, 265, 268, 275, 277
Abu Zeidan knife-handle 126–28
Abydos xx, 13, 36, 37, 38, 46, 49, 50, 52, 55, 57, 129, 145, 146, 187, 188, 189, 190, 191, 192, 193, 194, 196, 203, 206, 207, 273, 321, 322
Abzu 162. *See also* Apsu
Achaemenids 186
Adad 8, 66, 78, 79, 80, 81, 88, 89, 100, 102, 104, 105, 110, 112, 173, 237, 288, 303, 332, 336, 341, 343, 349, 355, 398
Adad/Addu 78, 79
Adad-nirari II 100, 173, 349
Adad-šumu-uṣur 102, 104, 105
Adapa 163
Addiya 65
Adonis 165, 166, 167, 168

Adoring-Horus-of-the-Sky Festival 47
Ahapuba of Mendes 194
Ahuna 162
Akatiya 87
Akhenaten 98
Akītu 107, 174
    festival 104, 109, 113, 165
Akītu-house garden 174
Akhethotep 207
Akhmim 204, 205, 206, 207, 272, 273
Akkad 65, 74, 83, 103, 155, 158, 159, 185, 297, 333, 343, 386, 387, 389
Alalakh 224
Aleppo 72, 73, 79, 82
Alexander the Great 153
Alexandria 33, 345
altarpiece 124
Amarna 66, 84, 98, 225, 375
Amaterasu 100
Amenhotep II 18, 34
Amenhotep III 34, 41, 56
Ammi-ditana 68, 75, 78, 87
Ammiditana-iluni 75
Ammi-saduqa 68, 72, 76, 77, 85

Ammisaduqa-iluni 75
Amon, temple at Karnak 29, 212
Amos 111, 114, 115
Andarig 70
Anedjib 42
Ankhmahor 269
Ankhnespepi (queens) 206
Ankhudjes 200
An Nasiriya 316
Anu 67, 71, 81, 106, 108, 109, 160, 163, 288, 336, 398
Anubis 46
Anum 74
Anunītum 162
Anzû Myth 295
Apis-bull 43
Apishal 228
Apsu 16, 107, 397, 404, 417. See also Abzu
Aramaic 299, 335
Archi, A. 220, 221, 222, 233, 236, 238, 239, 243
Armant 188, 190
Ashur (deity) xviii, 12, 21, 98, 107, 110, 112, 113, 152, 153, 154, 155, 157, 173, 174, 175, 238, 247, 287, 288, 289, 291, 292, 295, 296, 297, 298, 299, 300, 301, 302, 303, 305, 333, 336, 341, 343, 344, 345, 346, 349, 350, 351, 353, 354, 400
 letter to the king 295, 296, 297, 301, 303, 305
 royal report to 295, 296, 297, 300, 301, 303, 305
 temple of xviii, 107, 113, 247, 288, 289, 291, 292, 297, 298, 299, 300, 301, 302, 303

Ashur-bel-kala 349
 Broken Obelisk of 238, 400
Ashur-nadin-shumi 154
Ashurbanipal 88, 102, 104, 153, 154, 155, 158, 173, 175, 294, 297, 300, 301, 302, 305, 341, 344, 384, 387, 411, 413, 414, 415, 418
Ashurnasirpal I 349
Ashurnasirpal II 339, 345, 348, 349, 383, 384, 398, 403, 404, 405, 415, 416
Assur Charter 157, 302
Assur, city(-state) xiv, xix, 12, 25, 70, 98, 157, 226, 287, 288, 289, 290, 291, 292, 295, 298, 299, 300, 301, 302, 303, 304, 305, 350, 398, 400, 403, 404, 413
Assyria xv, 19, 23, 65, 98, 104, 155, 157, 166, 173, 238, 258, 285, 286, 287, 288, 289, 290, 291, 293, 300, 303, 334, 335, 336, 340, 341, 344, 346, 351, 387, 388, 397, 403, 406, 413, 414, 416, 418
Aswan 33, 190, 198, 201, 211, 375, 378
Asyut 46, 375
Aššur-ṣalam-ilāni 113
Aššur-šamshī 112
Atamrum (of Andarig) 70
Aten 98
Athena 145
Atrahasis 19, 159, 160
Atet, wife of Nermaat 267
Attis 166
Atum 44
Augustus 33, 153, 154, 332
aulos 129, 145

Baal 82, 160, 163
Baal Epic 163
Babel 110
Bābilim xix, 100
Babylon 65, 67, 68, 70, 71, 79, 82, 83, 84, 97, 99, 100, 101, 107, 109, 111, 153, 154, 155, 174, 224, 289, 292, 333, 334, 337, 339, 341, 344, 346, 386, 387, 391, 395, 413
Babylonia 65, 104, 153, 173, 291, 301, 302, 333, 334, 337, 339, 346, 388, 403, 418
Babylonian Chronicle 285
Baer, K. 41, 270
Baines, J. 3, 38, 41, 45, 46, 54, 58, 129, 231, 258, 259, 321
Baka (king) 264
battlefield palette 44, 146
'Bawu temple' archive 225
Bear, the (constellation) 115
'beer and bread texts' 220
Beit Khallaf 192
Bēl-agê 113
Belet-ili 172
Bēl-Marduk 109
Beni Hassan 193
Bersheh 192, 196, 209, 378
Biga, M.G. 220, 239, 243, 249
Bīt-rimki ("house-of-bathing" ritual) 103
Bīt-salā'-mê ritual 104, 112
Black Kings gang 315, 316
Borghesian 122
Bourgois, P. 323
boustrophedon 135, 142
British Museum xiv, 129, 316, 384, 386, 405, 406, 408, 410, 412, 414, 415

bronze (commodity) 104, 145, 156, 157, 226, 227, 230, 235, 241, 337, 405
Bull Palette 43, 146
Buto (*Dbʿwt*) xxii, 49, 54, 146
Buto Palette 146

calamus 84
Chalcolithic 130
Canaan 37, 50
Canaanite(s) 111
Cang Jie 122
catfish (sign) 42, 126, 127
CATFISH (king) 127
Caucasian silver vessel 144
ʿAṯtar 111
Cemetery U (Abydos) 57
Charles I 154
Chicago xiii, xv, 315
Childe, V.G. 261, 354
China 121, 122, 145
Christ (= Jesus Christ) 74, 161, 164, 166, 167, 168, 169, 170, 173, 175
Christian 102, 112, 124, 154, 163, 166, 168, 173, 175
Christianity 166, 168
Chthonia 167
Cities Palette 44, 45, 51
city-state 20, 122, 158, 230, 246, 247
Clayton rings 188
Cohen, A. 164, 305, 314, 316
Collins, R. 313, 323, 403, 416, 418
conflict theory 312, 313, 314, 315, 316, 324
copper (commodity) 41, 222, 227, 230, 239, 241, 249, 412
Coptos 200, 202, 204, 205, 206, 210, 211, 273, 363, 371. *See also* Koptos

corvée xvii, 78, 204
Court of the Date Palm 223
"cult of ancestors" 77
"cutting the ribbon" (= event/ritual) 56

Dahshur 262, 263, 266, 267
Dakhla Oasis 188, 189
Dara 209
Davis comb 126, 135, 136
decorum 45
decree of Samsuiluna
Deir el-Gebrawi 273
Delta xxi, 48, 50, 51, 53, 54, 57, 188, 190, 192, 193, 203, 204, 208, 209, 211
Demeter 167
Den (king) 50
Dendereh 273
Dēr (city) 111
Deserkheprure-setpenre. *See* Horemheb
Deshasha 273
Deuteronomy (Deut.) 111
Deutsches Archäologisches Institute 321
Diesing, P. 313
Dilmun 227, 249, 388, 389, 393, 396, 416
divination 8, 22, 68, 69, 71, 74, 78, 79, 80, 81, 84, 106, 111, 289, 291, 292, 304, 351
Djau 206
Djedkara (king) 272
Djer (king) 17, 50, 52, 322
Djet (king) 54
Djoser (king) 190

Double Treasury 199
Drehem treasure 238
Dreyer, G. 50, 51, 55, 135, 261, 321
Du'uzu 162, 165
Dumuzi 9, 19, 22, 24, 73, 152, 159, 160, 161, 162, 163, 164, 165, 166, 167, 168, 169, 170, 171, 172, 173, 175
D-ware pots 58

Esharra 107
Eshnunna 76
Ea 107, 113, 114, 397
Eanna, temple of 226, 342
Ea-ṣalam-ilī 113
Easterner 53
Ebabbar of Sippar 68, 226, 347
Ebla xiii, xiv, xvi, 78, 219, 220, 221, 222, 223, 224, 226, 231, 233, 234, 236, 237, 238, 239, 240, 241, 242, 243, 247, 248, 249, 250
ecstasis 129
Edfu 199, 204, 207, 273
Ehursaggalkurkurra 298
eidolon 156
Elali 81
Elam 70, 79, 141, 155, 392, 418
El-Amarna 66
Elamite(s) 68, 70, 111
El-Bersheh 192, 196, 378
elephants 126, 132, 188
Elephantine 50, 190, 192, 273, 277
elephant-vulture 126
Eleusinian mysteries 167
El-Hawawish 199, 200, 204, 205, 206
Elkab 192, 194, 195, 204, 205, 206, 211

El-Kab 192, 194, 195, 204, 205, 206, 211
El-Mahâsna 194
Emar 194
Enmeduranki Legend 287
Enki 287
Enlil (= Illil) 287
ensi 195, 332. *See also* ensi₂
ensi₂ xix, 227, 228. *See also* ensi
Enūma Anu Enlil 81, 106, 108, 109
Enūma eliš 89, 107, 108. *See also* Epic of Creation
Epic of Creation 98, 99. *See also Enūma eliš*
Epic of Tukulti-Ninurta 87
Ereshkigal 152, 153, 160, 163, 164, 170
Erishti-Aya (letter of) 87
Eridu Genesis 172
Erkalla 164
Erra Epic 164, 289
Esagil 67, 68, 83, 97, 107, 155
Esarhaddon xiv, 100, 101, 102, 105, 106, 107, 108, 110, 154, 285, 296, 301, 303, 339, 347, 353, 387
Euphrates River 316
Exorcist's Manual 289
extispicy rituals 78
eye-paint 137, 139
Ezbet Rushdi 209

Farmer, P. 312, 323
Fayum 204, 263
festival of Nisannu 113, 170
festival of Tashritu 104, 170
Fictive Dialogue between Ashurbanipal and Nabû 294

First Intermediate Period 12, 18, 46, 59, 201, 209, 277, 427
Flinders Petrie, Sir W.M. *See* Petrie, W.M.F.
flute 41, 321
Foster, B.R. 74, 89, 98, 108, 160, 161, 164, 173, 175, 230, 231, 299, 305, 410
"fragrance of Horus" (= incense) 41, 42
Frankfort, H. 3, 4, 5, 10, 13, 14, 16, 25, 41, 46, 54, 59, 98, 142, 155, 156, 157, 160, 161, 163, 165, 169, 172, 175, 258, 286
Frazer, J.G. 3, 4, 5, 10, 13, 14, 16, 25, 29, 41, 46, 54, 59, 98, 142, 155, 156, 157, 160, 161, 163, 165, 169, 172, 175, 258, 286

Gabbi-ilāni-Aššur 113
gala-mah 80
Gala el-Sheikh 189
Galileo 121
gamlum-weapons 80
Gardens of Adonis 167
Gardiner, A.H. 48, 58, 365, 378, 379
"Gate-of-the-path-of-the-(stars)-of-Enlil" 107
"Gate-of-the-wagon-star" 107
gazelle 133, 368, 369, 376, 388
Geshtinanna 162, 163
Gebelein papyri 194
Gebel el-Tarif knife-handle 135, 136
Gebel el-Teir 194
Gebel Ouenat 189
Gebel Sheikh Suleiman 50, 188
Gebel Tjauti 188

Geertz, C. 7, 138, 259
Gilf el-Kebir 189
Gilgamesh 16, 24, 152, 160, 171, 172, 331, 385, 387, 388, 389, 390, 396, 397, 404
Girsu; lady of 225, 226, 227, 229, 230, 231, 246, 249, 338, 340, 343
Girsu Sasa 227
Giza 34, 262, 264, 275
gnu-antelope 133
goat 133, 168, 169, 173
Goddess-Abides (shrine) 47
gold (commodity) xxi, 48, 72, 152, 169, 170, 222, 223, 225, 227, 230, 232, 233, 234, 235, 238, 239, 241, 243, 244, 245, 249, 318, 319, 361, 366, 368
gold rings 223, 230
Golden Horus name 43
Gombrich, E. 144
good shepherd 74, 171, 172, 173, 175
Great Seer 199
griffin 128, 131, 132, 133, 135, 138
Gudea 121, 227, 338, 340, 350, 353, 389
Guichard, M. 235
Gula 66
Gundlach, R. 276, 277
Guttmann Collection 104

Hades 167, 417
Haldi (deity) 296, 299
Halley (comet) 111
Ḫammurapi (= Hammurabi = Hammurabi) 24, 65, 67, 68, 69, 70, 71, 72, 75, 76, 77, 78, 79, 83, 84, 89, 100, 101, 299, 332, 337

Ḫammurapi, Code of 65, 67, 68, 69, 70, 71, 72, 75, 76, 78, 79, 83, 84, 89, 100, 101
Ḫammurapi-ili 75
Ḫammurapi Shamshi 76
Ḫammurapī-^{d}Šamšī 100
ḪAR-gud (lexical list) 115
Harkhuf of Aswan 198
Harran 163, 165, 302, 341
haruspex xvii, 289, 290
Hatnub 198
Hatti (land of) 174, 345, 398, 400, 410, 413
Hattusa 219, 224
Hattusili III 78
Hazip-Teshup (of Razamâ) 72
Heb-Sed 4, 21, 43, 48, 55, 369, 377, 378, 379
Hebat 73
heliacal rising 162
Henenu of Thebes 210
Heosphoros 112
Herakleopolis 209
Hermionians 167
"He-who-guides-aright" (= *muštēširu*) 74
Hierakonpolis xxi, 11, 21, 35, 38, 42, 43, 45, 50, 53, 54, 55, 58, 60, 122, 128, 139, 140, 146, 187, 188, 189, 190, 201
high priest of Ptah 40
High-is-Khasekhemwy (statue) 41
Hilâlu (*hll*) 111
Hireling, The (constellation) 162, 163
Hittite(s) 66, 99, 219, 290, 346, 385, 400, 412, 414
Hodgson, D. 320, 321

Hor-Aha (= Horus-the-fighter)
    (king) 37, 42, 44, 50
Horemheb 48, 435
Horizon A 50
Hornung, E. 41, 56, 262, 385
Horus xxi, xxii, 7, 8, 21, 22, 35, 37,
    40, 41, 42, 43, 44, 45, 46, 47, 48, 49,
    55, 56, 57, 58, 190, 362, 363, 364,
    366, 367, 371, 373, 378
Horus name 42, 43
Horus-first-of-the-corporation-of-
    gods xxi, 43
Horus-star-of-the-corporation-of-
    gods xxi, 43
"House of True Decisions" (Ur) 80
human rights 82
ḫupšu-soldiers 157
hyena(s) 133, 134, 145

Ishi-Addu (Qatna) 84
Ishtar 89, 107, 155, 158, 160, 162,
    164, 168, 169, 170, 171, 172, 173,
    296, 341
Ištar-šamšī 112
Ibbi-Suen of Ur 224, 229, 230
ibex-tilapia 126, 128
Ibi of Der el-Gebrawi, biography
    of 198
IBIS (king) 139
Iddin-Dagan 80, 88
Igigi gods 159
Ikû (constellation) 107, 108
Illil. See Enlil.
Imeny of Beni Hassan 193
ina saparri oath 83
Inanna 81, 158, 160, 162, 164, 166,
    170, 171, 172, 175

Inbatum (letter of) 87
Inibshina (letter of) 87
integration theory 313, 314, 324
Iput (queen) 205
Irunetjeru 201
Isaiah 110, 111
Isesi, statue of 196
Isin 80, 99, 103, 158, 161, 165, 171,
    224, 230, 334, 339, 343
Isin hymns 171
Isin-Larsa 103
Isis 48, 363, 371, 373
Ishbi-Erra 224
Itur-Mer 79

jackal xx, 129, 131, 137, 138
jackal-human hybrid 129, 137, 138
Jesus Christ 74, 435
Julius Caesar 153, 154
Jupiter (planet = Nēbiru) 9, 97, 106,
    108

Kai-Khent of El-Hammamiya 194
Kaiwan 114
Kalḫu 152
Kantorowicz, E. 5, 6, 102, 105
Karnak 196, 211, 212, 402, 417
Kassite(s) 70, 339
Kashtiliash 70
Kayyamānu (= Kiyyûn) 109, 111,
    115
Khamerernebty, wife of Ptahshepses
    268
Khafra (king) 264, 266. See also
    Rakhef
Kharga Oasis 188
Khasekhemwy (king) 18, 41, 53, 187,

190, 204
Khentikaupepi of Dakhla 207
Khor el-Aqiba, inscriptions 193
Khorsabad 288, 398, 399
Khosr (waters of) 174
Khufu (king) 264, 265, 266, 267
Khui of Abydos, husband of Nebet 273
Kibsatum 76
Kiru (letter of) 87
Kisir-Ashur, son of Nabû-bessunu 289
Kislimmu 162
kispum ritual 77
Kisri 174
Kiyyûn (= Kayyamānu) 111, 114
kleptocracy 315
Kokopelli 130
Kom el-Ahmar/Sawaris 273
Kom el-Hisn 204
Koptos 38, 44, 45. See also Coptos
Koptos colossi 38, 47
Kumaya 153, 154, 174
Kurigalzu 65, 339, 345
Kurunta (of Tarhundasha) 78
Kussulu 81

Lagash 122, 226, 338
Lalgar 107, 114
Lamb of God 167, 173
Landgráfová 260
Lanfranchi, G. 172, 285, 286, 293, 294, 296, 303, 304, 305
language game (= "Sprachspiel") 138
lapis lazuli 69, 163, 169, 170, 173, 225, 230, 240, 241, 318, 319, 389
Larsa 81, 103, 250

Late Bronze Age 224, 384, 397
lead (commodity) 241
leopard 133, 138
Levant 188
Levine, L.D. 302, 305
Libyan(s) 53
lion 44, 133, 135, 138, 145, 146
Lion Hunt Palette 146
Lipit-Ishtar 99, 158
Liverani, M. 294, 385, 390, 391, 392, 394, 416
Louis XIV 66
Louvre Museum xiii, xv, 67, 68, 82, 83, 139, 140, 146, 399
Louvre palette 139, 140
Lucifer (= Satan) 112
Ludlul I 75, 102
Lugalanda (king) 227, 249
Lugal-e 99, 108, 289
Luke 112

Macedonians 186
Machiavelli, N. 311
mastabas 59, 192, 194, 264
Mashkan-shapir 70
Mafdet 46
Maikop culture 144
Main Deposit (Hierakonpolis) 35, 36, 38, 53, 55
Malkata 59
Mann, M. 6, 60, 314, 353
maṣhatum-meal 70
Marcus Terentius Varro 97
Marduk 67, 68, 70, 77, 79, 87, 89, 97, 98, 99, 102, 106, 108, 109, 112, 155, 163, 164, 165, 171, 174, 290, 346, 353, 395

Marduk Prophecy 155, 290
Mari xiii, xiv, 70, 72, 73, 76, 79, 82, 84, 85, 110, 162, 165, 219, 221, 223, 224, 233, 234, 235, 237, 238, 241, 243, 247, 248, 250, 342, 343, 351
Mari letter(s) 162
Mars (star) (= Fox star, Wolf star) 9, 108, 109
Marsyas 9, 108, 109
Marx, K. 245, 353
Matthiae, P. 220, 248
Maya civilization, kingship 258, 276
"Mazzaroth" (< Akk. *mazzaltu*) 115
Medamud 211
Megalake Chad 188
Meidum 262, 263, 266, 267
Meidum ware pottery 266
Meir 206, 273
Mehu of Mendes 201, 203, 207
Memphis 25, 39, 43, 47, 56, 188, 190, 192, 200, 203, 205, 208, 209, 211, 263, 264, 271, 273, 275
Memphite Theology 47
Mendes 193, 194, 201, 203, 204, 207
Menes (king) 37
Menkauhor (king) 272
Menkaura (king) 194, 264
Mentuhotep (vizier) 15, 40, 53
Merenra (king) 206, 273
Mereruka (vizier) 269
Mesoamerica 122
Mesolithic 121
Mesopotamia xv, xxvii, xxix, 3, 4, 5, 6, 7, 9, 10, 11, 13, 14, 16, 17, 19, 21, 22, 24, 25, 52, 57, 65, 66, 84, 97, 99, 100, 103, 121, 122, 125, 126, 141, 143, 144, 151, 153, 161, 162, 164, 172, 223, 231, 233, 241, 242, 245, 248, 286, 311, 316, 322, 324, 331, 332, 336, 337, 338, 339, 340, 342, 345, 346, 352, 384, 388, 389, 390, 391, 393, 397, 404, 408, 427
mes-tree 166
"messenger texts" 220
Metjen 192, 198, 203
Middle Bronze Age 223, 414
mîšarum xviii, 68, 71, 72, 73, 74, 78, 84, 85, 86
Min 38, 44, 46, 47, 200, 205, 362, 363, 364, 365, 367, 369, 371, 373, 376, 378
minas 229, 230, 233, 238, 239, 240, 241, 243, 249
Molleson, T. 320, 321
moon-god 8, 78, 80, 81
Morenz, L. xxiv, 7, 9, 11, 17, 22, 25, 122, 123, 125, 126, 127, 129, 132, 133, 139, 140, 144, 145, 235, 249
Mot 163
Mount Lebanon 153, 398, 400
Mouth-of-Horus (shrine) 47
MU.DU texts of Ebla 238
Mukama 59
Mukannishum 224, 237
Müller-Wollermann, R. 276, 277
Musasir 19, 296, 299, 335

Nabada 226. *See also* Tell Beydar
Nabû 109, 114, 171, 294, 300, 301
Nabû-aḫḫē-erība 109, 114
Nabu-shallim-shunu, chief scribe of Sargon II 300
Nader, L. 323, 324
Naga ed-Der 194

Nagar 226, 233, 248, *See also* Tell Brak
namburbi-rituals 74
Nanna 78, 80, 81, 86, 88, 170, 230, 343
    temple at Ur 78, 80, 81, 86, 88, 170, 230, 343
Naqada (culture) 188
Naqada (site), South Town 187
Naqada II 38, 43, 50, 187, 188
Naqada III 37, 50
Nar (I) 127, 128, 133, 134, 139, 141, 145, 146
Naramtum (letter of) 87
Nar-meher (= Narmer) (king) 133, 134, 139, 141, 145, 146
Narmer (king) 7, 18, 21, 35, 36, 37, 38, 39, 41, 42, 43, 44, 49, 50, 51, 53, 55, 57, 59, 60, 204. *See also* Nar-meher
Narmer macehead 36, 39, 44, 49, 55, 59
Narmer palette 36, 39, 44, 49, 55, 59
Naurouz 167
Nay 145
Nebet of Abydos, wife of Khui 206, 273
Nebhepetra Mentuhotep II (king) 53
Nebuchadnezzar I, palace of 224, 347
Nebuchadnezzar I 66, 155
Nebuchadnezzar II 66, 155
Neferirkara (king) 194, 195, 196, 266
    papyri of 195
Nefermaat (vizier, husband of Atet) 267, 440
Nefershemem of Elkab 195
Nefershutba of Mendes 194

Neith 46
Nekhbet 53, 54
Nemti-hetep of Qau 195
Neo-Assyrian archives 11, 219, 224
Neolithic 121, 130, 144
Nergal 160, 162, 163, 169
nesu-bity name 56
net xvii, 18, 66, 67, 81, 83, 89, 134, 315
Netjerikhet (= The-Divine-One-of-the-Corporation-of-Gods) (king) 55
New Kingdom 10, 15, 33, 41, 185, 212, 262, 400, 402, 427
New Year's Festival 163, 413
Nikaankh of Tehne 196
Nimrud xiv, 173, 219, 288, 344, 383, 384, 403, 404, 405, 406, 408, 410, 412
nine bows 19, 51, 390
Nineveh 25, 88, 107, 108, 174, 224, 246, 289, 339, 345, 349, 384, 400, 412, 413, 414, 415
Ningirsu 159, 338
Ninsianna 8, 78, 80, 81
Ninurta 66, 70, 87, 100, 103, 110, 155, 161, 171, 288, 336, 341, 345, 349, 350, 351, 355, 398, 403
Nippur 87, 223, 248, 333, 338, 339, 343
Nisannu 113, 170
Nofret, wife of Rahotep 267
nomarchs 209, 273
nomes, 16th of Upper Egypt 194, 197, 273
Nubia xxii, 18, 48, 50, 51, 145, 187, 188, 189, 190, 193, 201

Nubians 53, 189
Nyoro king 58
Nyuserra (king) 267, 268, 269, 271, 272, 274, 276

oath xvii, 70, 71, 75, 79, 83, 88, 170, 291
Octavianus 154
oikos 220
On (= Heliopolis) 48
Oppenheim, A.L. 98, 295, 298, 299, 305, 410, 417
oracle xix, 78, 79, 80, 84, 88, 89, 294, 295, 301
ordeal 71
Origen 112
Orion 110, 115, 162
oryx-antelope 133
OSTRICH (king) 139, 140, 141, 146
Ostrich ceremonial palette 139, 140, 141, 146
Osiris (deity) 4, 23, 268
    concept of resurrection 162, 163, 167, 404

Palace G at Ebla 220, 221
Palamedes 122
Palestine (southern) 187, 188, 190
Panaetius 97
Paoletti, P. 223, 229, 238, 239, 240, 249
Parpola, S. xiv, 102, 105, 109, 112, 113, 114, 155, 161, 162, 169, 285, 288, 289, 294, 300, 302, 304, 344, 353
Pegasus (constellation) 107
penis-sheath 129, 130, 131, 145

Pepy I (king) 207, 269, 273, 276
Pepy II (king) 34, 198, 206, 273, 278
Per-neser 54, 56
Persephone 167, 168
Persia 167, 334, 339, 394
Per-wer 54, 56
Petrie, Sir W.M.F. 41, 321
PG 789 318, 319
PG 800 318, 319, 320
Phaeton 111
phonograms 122
Piankh (king) 34
Pitt-Rivers knife-handle 127, 129
Pleiades 115
Polanyi, K. 245
Pollock, S. 232, 320, 321, 324
psuche 156
Ptah 40, 47, 275
    temple of in Memphis 47, 275
Ptahhotep 207, 269
Ptahshepses (vizier), husband of Khamerernebty 40, 268
Pu-abi (queen) 319, 320
Puzrish-Dagan 219, 221, 223, 224, 227, 228, 230, 234, 238, 247
Pyramid Texts xv, 55, 268, 379

Qar of Edfu 199, 204, 207
Qasr el-Sayed 201, 273
Qustul 50, 189, 190

Ra 48, 259
Radjedef (king) 264
Rahotep, husband of Nofret 267
Rakhef (king) 264. *See also* Khafra
Rameses II 34, 41, 78
Ram in the Thicket, artifact 318

Raneferef (king) 260, 266, 275
  papyrus archives of 266, 275
Red Crown 56, 366
Redikhnum of Dendera 210
Red Sea 188, 361, 391
rekhyt-birds 52, 53, 441
Renan, E. 312, 322
Renger, J. 160, 175, 230, 2453
Reniqer 201
Reqaqnah 192, 194
Rim-Sin 80, 88
ring xvii, xviii, 84, 155, 163, 173, 175, 374
rite de passage 104, 441
Robert Taylor Homes 315
rod xvii, 84, 155, 173
Rome xiii, xv, xxix, 175
ruah 156

Sabean(s) 163
Sabni of Aswan 201
Sahura (king) 265, 266
Sacred Marriage 158, 164, 165, 166, 170, 175
St. Augustine 97
St. Barbara 167
Saite (kings) 186
Sakkuth 114
Samarkand 257
Shamash 10, 66, 67, 68, 69, 70, 71, 72, 73, 74, 78, 79, 80, 81, 83, 84, 86, 88, 89, 100, 153, 154, 155, 156, 171, 173, 175, 297, 301, 344, 347, 355
Shamash-shum-ukin 153, 154, 155, 175, 297, 301, 344
Samsu-iluna 71, 72, 85
Samsuiluna-nūr-mātim 71

šangû-priest 292
Saqqara 13, 52, 57, 59, 199, 262, 264, 267, 268
Sargon of Akkade 220
Sargon Geography 385, 387, 392, 393
Sargon II 12, 19, 23, 24, 25, 108, 111, 157, 287, 288, 295, 296, 297, 298, 299, 300, 301, 302, 303, 304, 305, 336, 339, 344, 345, 348, 351, 387, 388, 398, 399, 414, 416
Sargon II's Report to Ashur on His Eighth Campaign 287, 296
Sargonid Period 285
saskûm-meal 70
Saturn (= black star) xvii, 8, 22, 109, 110, 111, 114, 115
Saumaise, Cl. 154
Sayala 201
scent 7, 33, 41, 42
Scheper-Hughes, N. 323
scion 83
SCORPION (II) 139, 141, 145, 146
Scorpion (king) 21, 35, 41, 43, 50, 55, 60
Scorpion macehead 36, 51, 52, 53, 55, 56, 57, 59
seals 57, 141, 142, 319, 354
  cylinder 36, 42, 51, 57, 141, 142, 319, 339, 354
  stamp 354
Second Intermediate Period 211, 427
Sed (god) 4, 21, 29, 43, 46, 55, 56, 59, 368, 369, 377, 378, 379
Sed Festival 43
sedja-beast 132
sekhemty (= the Two-powers) 54

Semerkhet (king) 41
semiophore 129, 138
semiotic 102, 123, 128, 137
Sennacherib 15, 23, 24, 107, 108,
    153, 154, 173, 174, 246, 294, 304,
    339, 344, 345, 351, 353, 384, 387,
    409, 411, 412, 413, 416
  murder of 23, 153, 154, 173, 294
Senusret I (king) 40
Senusret III (king) 34
Septuagint 112
serekh(s) 10, 42, 49, 50, 188
serpents 126, 145
serpopard 133
Service, E. 313, 314
Seth 38, 42, 45
Shalmaneser (Nimrud's fort) 100,
    157, 173, 297, 303, 305, 341, 344,
    345, 349, 387, 392, 398, 403, 405,
    406, 407, 408, 410, 412, 418
Shalmaneser III 100, 345, 387, 392,
    398, 403, 405, 406, 408, 410, 412
Shalmaneser IV 297, 303, 305
Shalmaneser V
ṣalmu 102, 103, 104, 105, 113, 115,
    155
Shamash hymn 66, 100
ᵈŠamšī 100
Shamshi-Adad, treasure of 237
Šamši-libur 87
Šamši-lu-dari 87
Shamshi Adad V
Shara-isa archive 227
Šarru-kên 157
Sheikh Said 273
shekel xix, 159, 233, 249
Shemai of Coptos 206

Shepsipuptah 202
Shewrum-parat 73
"[She]-who-sees-Horus-and-Seth" 45
Shil, E. 277
Shimdatum (letter of) 87
Shubat-Enlil (modern Tell Lailan) 223
Shubria 296, 301
Shu-ilishu of Isin 65, 224
Shukaletuda 162
Šulgi 99
Shulgi Prophecy 290
Šulgi-šamšī 87, 99
Shusharra (modern Shemshara) 223
Sikkût/Sakkut 111, 114
silver (commodity) 48, 85, 144, 152,
    157, 169, 170, 219, 221, 222, 223,
    224, 225, 227, 228, 229, 230, 232,
    233, 234, 235, 237, 238, 239, 240,
    241, 242, 243, 244, 245, 246, 248,
    249
  rings 223, 234
Sin of Sargon 285, 304
Sin-shar-ishkun 290
Sîn 70, 73, 81, 101
Sin-kashid, palace of 223
Sîn-mushallim 70, 73, 81, 101
Sin 72, 78, 79, 80, 81, 83, 86, 88, 89,
    223, 285, 290, 304, 332, 338, 341,
    343, 344, 347, 392, 416
Sin-muballit 72
Sinni 87
Sinuhe 40
Sippar 67, 68, 72, 75, 80, 86, 226,
    250, 341, 347, 386
Sippar-Amnanum 80
Siut 209
slaves (commodity) 234, 236, 237,

240, 241
snake(s) 126, 128, 131, 133, 139
Senedjemib 207
Sneferu (king) 194, 262, 263, 264, 265, 266, 267
Sokar Festival 47
"Son of Dawn" 110, 111, 112
Sopdu Festival 47
South Wind 163
sr-giraffe xxii, 126, 133
Stalin, J. 323
stelae, slab of the Old Kingdom 264, 267
stele of Ugarit (Louvre Museum) 82
Storm-god 78, 79, 81, 82, 89
structural violence, concept of 323, 324, 325
Strudwick, N. 40, 270, 272, 378
subsidiary burials 322
Sudan 188, 361, 391
Suffering Servant 167, 169, 175
Sukkukum 77
Sumer 29, 65, 74, 83, 158, 159, 171, 172, 333, 389
Sumerian lamentation series 171
Sumu-la-El 83
Sun-god 8, 65, 71, 72, 73, 74, 78, 82
"Sun of all the human beings" 66
"Sun of his land" 65, 66
"Sun of Sumer" 65
Susa 68, 83, 141, 339, 343, 345, 346
Synchronistic King List 290
Syria 173, 290, 335, 388, 403, 413, 414

taboo 45
Tab-shar-Ashur 300
Tab-sil-Esharra, governor of Sargon II 302
Tadmor, H. 285, 286, 287, 294, 299, 302, 304, 305
Tainter, J.A. 277
talents (currency) 238
Talhayum 77
Tell ar-Rimah 224, 443
taklimtu, ritual of 291
Tammuz 151, 160, 161, 163, 165, 166, 168, 169
Ta-Seti (region) 50
Tashritu 104
taxes 10, 58, 155, 159, 228, 231, 237
Sebetu 300
Tell Basta 204
Tell Beydar 226, 248
Tell Brak 226, 233, 338, 342
temple HK29 (Hierakonpolis) 54
Tehna 194, 195
Tehna, temple of Hathor at 194
Tenno 100
textiles (commodity) 11, 219, 221, 222, 223, 224, 225, 227, 228, 233, 234, 235, 237, 238, 240, 241, 242, 244, 245, 246, 248, 249
theaters of cruelty (concept) 323
Thebes 18, 25, 192, 194, 209, 210, 211, 273, 274, 372, 373, 375, 401, 402
The-Water-Mountain-of-Redjedef 189
Thinite period 190
Third Intermediate Period 212, 427
Thoth 41
Throne-of-Horus-the-Harpooner (shrine) 47

Thrones-of-the-Gods (shrine) 47
Thutmose III 59, 402, 417
Tiberius Cannutius 154
Tiglath-pileser III 298, 304, 336, 349, 392, 397, 398, 400, 410, 417
Tilly, C. 314, 315, 316
Timur 257
tin (commodity) 222, 239, 241, 249
titles 16, 47, 73, 108, 190, 192, 193, 194, 195, 196, 199, 203, 204, 205, 260, 262, 270, 271, 272, 273, 274, 275, 332, 333, 336, 337, 348, 367, 393
  "hereditary prince" 274
  "keeper of the secrets" 271
  "overseer of priests" 273
  "overseer of the granaries" 273
  "overseer of Upper Egypt" 204, 206, 207, 211, 271, 272, 273
Tjehenu 51
Tjeti-Kaihep 199, 200, 205, 207
Tomb 100 (= "Painted Tomb," Hierakonpolis) 50, 58
tomb, "family"; mastaba 194, 267, 268
Tomb U-547 (Abydos) 55
Tomb U-j (Abydos) 49, 55, 57
torch 72, 85, 88
transubstantiation 103
Tree of Life 173
Tudhaliya IV 78
Tukulti-Ninurta I 66, 100, 155, 288, 336, 341, 345, 355, 403
Tukulti-Ninurta II 100, 349
Turin Canon 46
Turin Linen 58
Tutankhamun (king) 41, 42

Ty; tomb at Saqqara 268

'Ubaid period 316
Uffata 145
Uganda 58
Ugarit xvi, 82, 290, 351
Umma 164, 165, 227, 228, 229, 230, 237, 241, 244, 246, 249, 250, 343
Umm el-Qa'ab 321, 322
Unas (king) 272
University of Pennsylvania Museum of Archaeology and Anthropology xxvii, xxix, 316
Ur xv, xvi, 9, 13, 17, 24, 80, 81, 87, 88, 99, 161, 164, 165, 169, 170, 171, 185, 219, 220, 221, 223, 224, 227, 228, 229, 230, 234, 240, 241, 245, 246, 247, 248, 249, 311, 312, 316, 317, 319, 320, 321, 322, 323, 324, 325, 332, 333, 335, 336, 339, 341, 343, 344, 389, 427. *See also* An Nasiriya
  death pits 311, 316, 317, 320, 324
  Royal Tombs 311, 316, 317, 320, 324, 325
Ur III xv, 24, 87, 99, 161, 164, 165, 170, 171, 185, 219, 220, 221, 224, 227, 228, 229, 240, 241, 248, 249, 336, 389, 427
Uruinimgina 159
Uruk 141, 142, 143, 172, 223, 226, 291, 336, 339, 342, 343, 427
Ur-Utu 80
Userkaf (king), pillar of 196, 265, 276
Ūta-mīšaram 249
Ut-Napishtim 160

Utu 80, 81, 88, 100

Van De Mieroop, M. 69, 248, 288, 342, 346
Veblen, Th. 243
Venkatesh, S. 315, 316
Venus (star) 78, 80, 81, 89, 107, 162
vizier, office of xxii, 40, 57, 199, 201, 203, 206, 207, 236, 243, 267, 270, 271, 272, 273, 363, 366, 367, 368
von Reden, S. 248

Wadi Howar 189
Wadi Mineh 188
Wadi Qash 188
Wadi Um Balad 188
Wadjet 54
Wagner-Hasel, B. 242, 2554
Warad-Sîn (of Andarig) 70
Washptah 40
Weber, M. 175, 259, 286, 353
Weidner Chronicle 290
Weltbild 138
Weni of Abydos 193, 203, 207
Wepwawet (= the Opener-of-the-Ways) 46
West Nubian Palaeolake 189
White Crown 56
white walls of Memphis 56
wine (commodity) 168, 174, 223, 224, 233, 241, 373
Wines, M. 315
Winter, I. 18, 102, 105, 113, 153, 155, 156, 173, 340, 347, 348, 414, 416, 418
Wittgenstein, L.J.J. 123
wool (commodity) 156, 223, 227, 228, 234, 235, 237, 241, 248, 249, 409, 412
Woolley, Sir Leonard 311, 316, 317, 318, 319, 320, 322, 324
writing xviii, 54, 57, 107, 108, 113, 121, 122, 123, 125, 126, 135, 137, 138, 139, 141, 144, 145, 261, 291, 355, 387

Yam (= the Sea) 82
Yankh 200
Yasmah-Addu 73
Yoffee, N. 3, 231, 232, 258, 259, 321

Zaire 58
Zapotec civilization, kingship 258
Zawyiet el-Aryan 262, 264
Zawiyet el-Mayetin 273
Zibānītu (= constellation; Libra) 109
Zimbabwe 314, 315
Zimri-Lim (of Mari) 70, 72, 73, 76, 77, 79, 82, 85, 237, 343, 351
Zodiac 162